Middleware'98

Springer
London
Berlin
Heidelberg
New York
Barcelona
Budapest
Hong Kong
Milan
Paris
Santa Clara
Singapore
Tokyo

Nigel Davies, Kerry Raymond, Jochen Seitz (Eds)

Middleware'98

IFIP International Conference on Distributed Systems Platforms and Open Distributed Processing

Springer

Nigel Davies
Seitz Jochen
Distributed Multimedia Research Group, Lancaster University, Lancaster, LA1 4YR
Raymond Kerry
DSTC, Australia

ISBN-13:978-1-4471-1285-3 e-ISBN-13:978-1-4471-1283-9
DOI: 10.1007/978-1-4471-1283-9

British Library Cataloguing in Publication Data
A catalogue record for this book is available from the British Library

Softcover reprint of the hardcover 1st edition 1998

Typesetting: camera-ready by contributors

34/3830-543210 Printed on acid-free paper

CONTENTS

Session 5: ORB Architecture

Session 6: Components

Session 7: Type Safety and Security

Session 8: Mobile Objects

Session 9: Web Series

PREFACE

Welcome to Middleware'98 and to one of England's most beautiful regions.

In recent years the distributed systems community has witnessed a growth in the number of conferences, leading to difficulties in tracking the literature and a consequent loss of awareness of work done by others in this important field. The aim of Middleware'98 is to synthesise many of the smaller workshops and conferences in this area, bringing together research communities which were becoming fragmented.

The conference has been designed to maximise the experience for attendees. This is reflected in the choice of a resort venue (rather than a big city) to ensure a strong focus on interaction with other distributed systems researchers. The programme format incorporates a question-and-answer panel in each session, enabling significant issues to be discussed in the context of related papers and presentations. The invited speakers and tutorials are intended to not only inform the attendees, but also to stimulate discussion and debate.

The key to a good conference is a strong technical programme and this can only be achieved by having a significant number of submissions and a diligent programme committee. Since the composition of the programme committee also influences the submission rate, the role of these individuals is doubly important. In assembling the programme committee, we brought together researchers well-known for their expertise, experience, and leadership in distributed systems research. Our dedicated committee was vital to the creation of a successful programme for Middleware'98, as the conference attracted over 150 technical submissions including 135 full paper submissions. Each was reviewed at least 3 times, resulting in over 500 reviews. The final acceptance ratio for Middleware technical papers was a little over 1 in 5.

The programme presented here reflects the state of the art in middleware research, addressing issues such as ORB architectures, engineering of large-scale systems, and multimedia. The traditional role of middleware as a point of integration and service provision has remained intact, but there is a clear emphasis on emerging "must-have" features such as extensibility, mobility, and quality of service.

Finally, we would like to take this opportunity to thank the numerous people who have made this conference possible and, in particular, the General Chair, Gordon Blair, for offering us the opportunity to serve as Programme Co-chairs for the conference, the Local Arrangements Chair, Geoff Coulson, the Tutorials Chair, Richard Sinnott and the Publicity Chair, John Bates. Special thanks are also due to Steve Wade for his help with the conference web site and Jochen Seitz for his tremendous contribution to the editing of these proceedings.

Nigel Davies
Kerry Raymond

Programme Co-chairs.

PREFACE

Welcome to Middleware '98 and to one of ... [illegible]

In recent years the distributed systems community has witnessed a growth in the ... [illegible]

COMMITTEES

General Chair
Gordon Blair, Lancaster University, UK.

Programme Chairs
Nigel Davies, Lancaster University, UK.
Kerry Raymond, DSTC, Australia.

Tutorials Chair
Richard Sinnott, GMD-Fokus, Germany.

Publicity Chair
John Bates, Cambridge University, UK.

Local Arrangements Chair
Geoff Coulson, Lancaster University, UK.

Steering Committee
Jan De Meer (Chair), GMD-Fokus, Germany.
Partha Dasgupta, Arizona State University, USA.
Kerry Raymond, DSTC, Australia.
Alex Schill, TU Dresden, Germany.
Jacob Sloman, Dalhousie University, Canada.

Programme Committee
Jean Bacon, Cambridge University, UK.
Gregor von Bochmann, University of Ottawa, Canada.
Robert Cole, Hewlett-Packard Laboratories, UK.
Frank Eliassen, University of Tromso, Norway.
Andrew Herbert, APM, UK.
Teruo Higashino, Osaka University, Japan.
Peter Honeyman, CITI, University of Michigen, USA.
Rodger Lea, Sony Labs, Japan.
Peter Leydekkers, KPN, The Netherlands.
Peter Linington, University of Kent, UK.
Claudia Linnhoff-Popien, RWTH Aachen, Germany.
Luigi Logrippo, University of Ottawa, Canada.
Derek McAuley, Microsoft Research, UK.
Elie Najm, ENST, France.
Gerald Neufeld, University of British Columbia, Canada.
Stephen Pink, Lulea University/SICS, Sweden.
Robert van Renesse, Cornell University, USA.
Harry Rudin, IBM Zurich, Switzerland.
Doug Schmidt, Washington University, USA.
Morris Sloman, Imperial College, UK.
Richard Soley, OMG, USA.
Jean-Bernard Stefani, CNET, France.
Doug Terry, Xerox PARC, USA.
Chris Vissers, TRC, The Netherlands.

Additional Readers

Jan Aagedahl, SINTEF, Norway
Daniel Amyot, University of Ottawa, Canada
Charles Antonell, University of Michigan, USA
Elarbi Badidi, University of Montreal, Canada
Bela Ban, Cornell University, USA
John Bates, Cambridge University, UK
Andy Bond, DSTC, Australia
Brenton Camac, DSTC, Australia
Haijun Chen, University of Twente, the Netherlands
Fábio Costa, Lancaster University, UK
Ciro de Barros Barbosa, University of Twente, the Netherlands
Cliver Ricardo Guareis de Farias, University of Twente, the Netherlands
Pascal Dechamboux, France Telecom – CNET, France
Nikolay Kirilov Diakov, University of Twente, the Netherlands
Keith Duddy, DSTC, Australia
Naranker Dulay, Imperial College, UK
Bruno Dumant, France Telecom – CNET, France
Kazi Farooqui, University of Ottawa, Canada
Leonard Franken, KPN Research, the Netherlands
Adrian Friday, Lancaster University, UK
Valerie Gay, Université de Picardie – Jules Verne (UPJV), France
Hubert Le Van Gong, Sony Distributed Systems Lab, USA
Voicu Groza, University of Ottawa, Canada
Øyvind Hansen, University of Tromsø, Norway
Hiroaki Higaki, Tokyo Denki University, Japan
Yigal Hoffner, IBM Research, Switzerland
Hiroki Horiuchi, KDD, Japan
Francois Horn, France Telecom – CNET, France
David Ingram, Cambridge University, UK
Val Jones, University of Twente, the Netherlands
Georgios Karagianis, University of Twente, the Netherlands
Brigitte Kerhervé, University of Montreal, Canada
Douglas Kosovic, DSTC, Australia
Kazuhiro Kusunoki, Mitsubishi Electronics Co. Ltd., Japan
Laurent Leboucher, France Telecom – CNET, France
Ulf Leonhardt, Imperial College, UK
Heiko Ludwig, IBM Research, Switzerland
Emil Lupu, Imperial College, UK
Chaoying Ma, Cambridge University, UK
Simon McBride, DSTC, Australia
Patrick McDaniel, University of Michigan, USA
Zoran Milosevic, DSTC, Australia
Mohamed-Vall O. Mohamed-Salem, University of Montreal, Canada
Greg Morrisett, Cornell University, USA
Jun Munemori, Osaka University, Japan
Keng Ng, Imperial College, UK
Abdelkrim Nimour, ENST, France
Sadao Obana, KDD, Japan
Frank Olsen, ENST/CNET, France
Nikos Parlavantzas, Lancaster University, UK
Lums Ferreira Pires, University of Twente, the Netherlands
Aiko Pras, University of Twente, the Netherlands
Nat Pryce, Imperial College, UK
Dick Quartel, University of Twente, the Netherlands
Andry Rakotonirainy, DSTC, Australia
Pierre Guillaume Raverdy, Sony Distributed Systems Lab, USA
Nicolas Rivierre, France Telecom – CNET, France
Wayne Robbins, University of Montreal, Canada
Philippe Robin, Lancaster University, UK
Fumiaki Sato, Shizuoka University, Japan
Andreas Schade, IBM Research, Switzerland
Ruud Schoonderwoerd, Hewlett-Packard Laboratories, UK
Oliver Seidel, Cambridge University, UK
Jochen Seitz, Lancaster University, UK
Mark Spiteri, Cambridge University, UK
Ron Sprenkels, University of Twente, the Netherlands
Keizo Sugiyama, KDD, Japan
Yoshiaki Terashima, Mitsubishi Electronics Co. Ltd., Japan
Steffen van Bakel, Imperial College, UK
Bram van der Waaij, University of Twente, the Netherlands
Marten van Sinderen, University of Twente, the Netherlands
Alexey Vaysburd, Cornell University, USA

Session 1

Workflow

A CORBA Compliant Transactional Workflow System for Internet Applications

S.M. Wheater, S.K. Shrivastava and F. Ranno
Department of Computing Science, The University, Newcastle upon Tyne, NE1 7RU, England.
Tel: +44 (0) 191 222 8066 Fax: +44 (0) 191 222 8232
{Stuart.Wheater, Santosh.Shrivastava, Frederic.Ranno}@newcastle.ac.uk

Abstract

The paper describes an application composition and execution environment implemented as a transactional workflow system that enables sets of inter-related tasks to be carried out and supervised in a dependable manner. The paper describes how the system meets the requirements of interoperability, scalability, flexible task composition, dependability and dynamic reconfiguration. The system is general purpose and open: it has been designed and implemented as a set of CORBA services, running on top of a given ORB. The system serves as an example of the use of middleware technologies to provide a fault-tolerant execution environment for long running distributed applications.

Keywords

Distributed systems, fault-tolerance, CORBA, middleware, transactions, workflow systems.

1 INTRODUCTION

The Internet frequently suffers from failures which can affect both the performance and consistency of applications run over it. We are particularly interested in the domain of electronic commerce that covers divergent application areas such as electronic retailing, home banking, home entertainment, information and service brokerage etc. A number of factors need to be taken into account in order to make these applications fault-tolerant.

First, most such applications are rarely built from scratch; rather they are constructed by composing them out of existing applications. It should therefore be possible to compose an application out of component applications in a uniform manner, irrespective of the languages in which the component applications have been written and the operating systems of the host platforms. Second, the resulting applications can be very complex in structure, containing many temporal and data-flow dependencies between their constituent applications. However, constituent applications must be scheduled to run respecting these dependencies, despite the possibility of intervening processor and network failures. Third, the execution of such an application may take a long time to complete, and may contain long periods of inactivity (minutes, hours, days, weeks etc.), often due to the constituent applications requiring user interactions. It should be possible therefore to reconfigure an application dynamically because, for example, machines may fail, services may be moved or withdrawn and user requirements may change.

Bearing the above observations in mind, we present a generic solution to the construction of fault-tolerant distributed applications. We have implemented an application composition and execution environment as a *transactional workflow system* that enables sets of inter-related tasks to be carried out and supervised in a dependable manner. Our system meets the requirements of *interoperability, scalability, flexible task composition, dependability* and *dynamic reconfiguration* implied by the above discussion.

Workflow systems are widely used by organizations that need to automate their business processes, and there are many products available in the market. However, currently available workflow systems are not scaleable, as their structure tends to be monolithic. Further, they offer little support for building fault-tolerant applications, nor can they inter-operate, as they make use of proprietary platforms and protocols. Our system represents a significant departure from these; our system architecture is decentralized and open: it has been designed and implemented as a set of CORBA services, running on top of a given ORB. An overview of our system appears in (Ranno 1997). This paper expands on distributed fault tolerant aspects of our system. Our system architecture is the basis of Nortel's submission to the OMG for a workflow standard (Nortel 1998).

2 WORKFLOW MANAGEMENT SYSTEMS

Workflows are rule based management software that direct, coordinate and monitor execution of tasks representing business processes. Tasks (activities) are application specific units of work. A Workflow schema (workflow script) is used explicitly to represent the structure of an application in terms of tasks and temporal dependencies between tasks. An application is executed by instantiating the corresponding workflow schema.

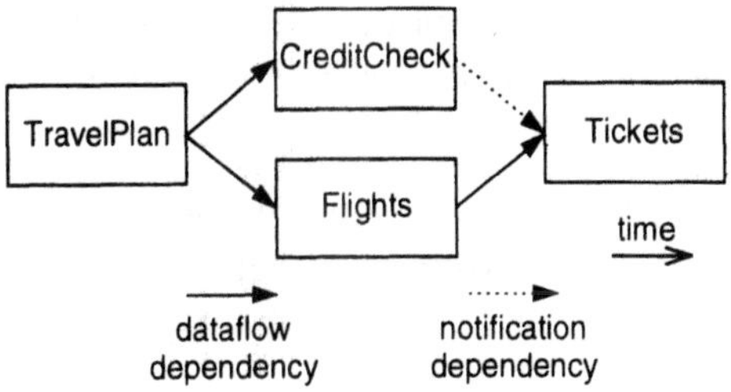

Figure 1 Inter-task dependencies

Imagine an electronic travel booking workflow application. Fig. 1 shows its 'activity diagram' depicting the *temporal dependencies* between its four constituent applications (or tasks), *TravelPlan*, *CreditCheck*, *Flights* and *Tickets*. Tasks *CreditCheck* and *Flights* execute concurrently, but can only be started after the *TravelPlan* task has terminated and supplied the necessary data, so these two tasks have *dataflow dependencies* on the *TravelPlan* task. Task *Tickets* can only be started after *Flights* task has terminated and supplied the necessary data and task *CreditCheck* has terminated in an 'ok' state. In this case, task *Tickets* has a dataflow dependency on *Flights*, and a restricted form of dataflow dependency (called *notification dependency*) on *CreditCheck*.

There are several organizations involved in the above application (customer organization, travel agency, credit card agency, etc.). Each organization may well possess its own workflow system for carrying out its activities. A specific way of executing this application could be: the travel agency has the application description (workflow script) and is responsible for coordinating the overall execution and it itself executes tasks *TravelPlan* and *Tickets*; its workflow system will invoke *CreditCheck* task and *Flights* task at other organizations.

Clearly, there is a need for a standard way of representing application structure and sending and receiving 'work items', if organizations are to cooperate. Standardization efforts are therefore underway. The Workflow Management Coalition (WfMC), an industry-wide consortium of workflow system venders, has proposed a reference model that defines interfaces with the aim of enabling different workflow systems to inter-operate (Lawrence 1997). Unfortunately, it is a rather centralized model, not suitable for wide-area distribution (Paul 1997). Currently, the Object Management Group (OMG), the consortium of IT vendors and users, is evaluating new proposals for a workflow facility standard.

Our system serves as an example of the use of middleware services to construct a workflow system that provides a fault-tolerant application composition and execution environment for long running distributed applications.

3 SYSTEM OVERVIEW

3.1 Meeting the application requirements

We discuss how our system has been designed to meet the requirements stated earlier, namely: interoperability, scalability, flexible task composition, dependability and dynamic reconfiguration.

- *Interoperability*: The system has been structured as a set of CORBA services to run on top of a CORBA-compliant ORB thereby supporting interoperability including the incorporation of existing applications and services.
- *Scalability*: There is no reliance on any centralized service that could limit the scalability of workflow applications.
- *Flexible Task Composition*: The system provides a uniform way of composing a complex task out of transactional and non-transactional tasks. This is possible because the system supports a simple yet powerful *task model* permitting a task to perform application specific input selection (e.g., obtain a given input from one of several sources) and terminate in one of several outcomes, producing distinct outputs.
- *Dependability*: The system has been structured to provide dependability at *application level* and *system level*. Support for application level dependability has been provided through flexible task composition mentioned above that enables an application builder to incorporate alternative tasks, compensating tasks, replacement tasks etc., within an application to deal with a variety of exceptional situations. The system provides support for system level dependability by recording inter-task dependencies in transactional shared objects and by using transactions to implement the delivery of task outputs such that destination tasks receive their inputs despite finite number of intervening machine crashes and temporary network related failures.
- *Dynamic Reconfiguration*: The task model referred to earlier is expressive enough to represent temporal (dataflow and notification) dependencies between constituent tasks. Our application execution environment is *reflective*, as it maintains this structure and makes it available through transactional operations for performing changes to it (such as addition and removal of tasks as well as addition and removal of dependencies between tasks). Thus the system directly provides support for dynamic modification of workflows (*ad hoc workflows*) (Shrivastava 1998). The use of transactions ensures that changes to schemas and instances are carried out atomically with respect to normal processing.

3.2. System Architecture

The workflow management system structure is shown in fig. 2. Here the big box represents the structure of the entire distributed workflow system (and not the software layers of a single node); the small box represents any node with a Java capable browser. The most important components of the system are the two transactional services, the workflow *repository* service and the workflow *execution* service.

Workflow Repository Service: The repository service stores workflow schemas and provides operations for initializing, modifying and inspecting schemas. A schema is represented according to the model described in the next section, in terms of tasks and dependencies. We have designed a scripting language that provides high-level notations (textual as well as graphical) for the specification of schemas. The scripting language has been specifically designed to express task composition and inter-task dependencies of fault-tolerant distributed applications whose executions could span arbitrarily large durations (Ranno 1998).

Workflow Execution Service: The workflow execution service coordinates the execution of a workflow instance: it records inter-task dependencies of a schema in persistent atomic objects and uses atomic transactions for propagating coordination information to ensure that tasks are scheduled to run respecting their dependencies. Its design is discussed in section 5.

These two facilities make use of CORBA Object Transaction Service (OTS). The implementation for OTS used for the workflow management facility is OTSArjuna, which is an OTS compliant version of Arjuna distributed transaction system built by us (Parrington 1995). In our system, application control and management tools required for functions such as instantiating workflow applications, monitoring and dynamic reconfiguration etc., (collectively referred to as *administrative* applications) themselves can be implemented as workflow applications. Thus the administrative applications can be made fault-tolerant without any extra effort. A graphical user interface to the these administrative applications has been provided by making use of Java applets which can be loaded and run by any Java capable Web browser.

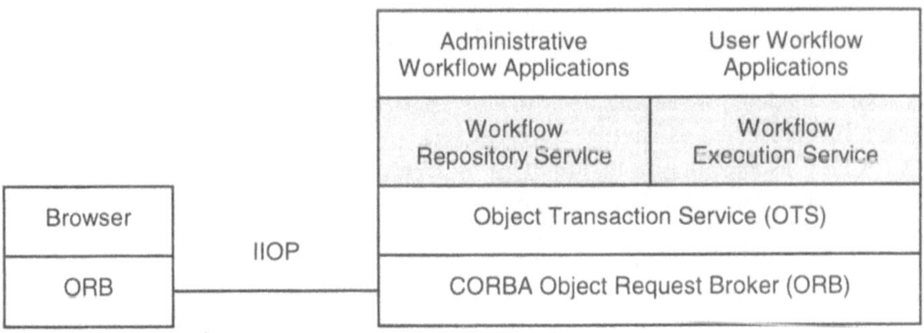

Figure 2 Workflow management system structure.

4 REPOSITORY SERVICE

A workflow schema must be expressive enough to be able to represent temporal dependencies of applications. The schema represents a workflow application as a collection of tasks and their dependencies. A task is an application specific unit of activity that requires specified input objects and produces specified output objects. As indicated earlier, dependency could be just a *notification* dependency (indicating that the 'down-stream' task can start only after the 'up-stream' task has terminated) or a *dataflow* dependency (indicating that the 'down-stream' task requires in addition to notification, input data from the 'up stream' task). We next present the *task model*, highlighting first some of its features that enable flexible ways of composing an application:

- *Alternative inputs*: A task can start in one of several initial states, representing distinct ways in which the task can be started, each associated with a distinct set of input objects. This is useful to introduce time related processing (e.g., a set of 'normal' inputs and a set for an exceptional input such as a timer enabling a task to wait for normal inputs with a timeout).
- *Alternative input sources*: A task can acquire a given input from more than one source. This is the principal way of introducing redundant data sources for a task and for a task to control input selection.
- *Alternative outputs*: A task can terminate in one of several output states, producing distinct outcomes. Assume that a task is an atomic transaction that transfers a sum of money from customer account *A* to customer account *B* by debiting *A* and crediting *B*. Then one outcome could be the result of the task committing and the other outcome could be an indication that the task has aborted.
- *Compound tasks*: A task can be composed from other tasks. This is the principal way of composing an application out of other applications. Individual tasks that make up an application can be *atomic* ('all or nothing' ACID transactions, possibly containing nested transactions within, with properties of: Atomicity, Consistency, Isolation and Durability) or *non-atomic*.
- *Genesis tasks*: A genesis task represents a place holder for a task structure, and is used for on demand instantiation. For a complex application (modeled as a set of compound tasks) this enables instantiation of only those components which are strictly necessary. This also allows the execution of repetitive tasks.

A task is modeled as having a set of *input sets* and a set of *output sets*. In fig. 3, task t_i is represented as having two input sets I_1 and I_2, and two output sets O_1 and O_2. A task instance begins its life in a *wait* state, awaiting the availability of one of its input sets. The execution of a task is triggered (the state changes to *active*) by the availability of an input set, only the first available input set will trigger the task, the subsequent availability of other input sets will not trigger the task (if multiple input sets became available simultaneously, then the input set with the highest priority is chosen for processing). For an input set to be available it must have received all of its constituent input objects (i.e., indicating that all dataflow and notification dependencies have been satisfied). For example, in fig. 3, input set I_1 requires three dependencies to be satisfied: objects i_1 and i_2 must become available (dataflow dependencies) and one notification must be signaled (notifications are modeled as data-less input objects). A given input can be obtained from more than one source (e.g., three for i_3 in set I_2). If multiple sources of an input become available simultaneously, then the source with the highest priority is selected.

A task terminates (the state changes to *complete*) producing output objects belonging to exactly one of a set of output sets (O_1 or O_2 for task t_i). An output set consists of a (possibly empty) set of output objects (o_2 and o_3 for output set O_2).

Task instances, which represent applications, manipulate references to input and output objects. Such tasks are associated with one or more implementations (application code); at run time, a task instance is bound to a specific implementation.

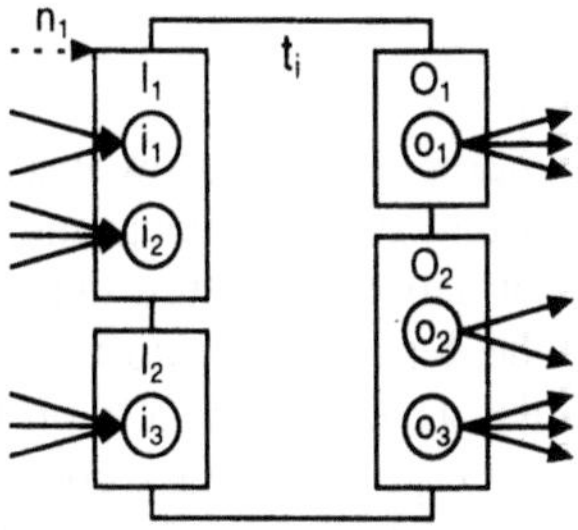

Figure 3 A task

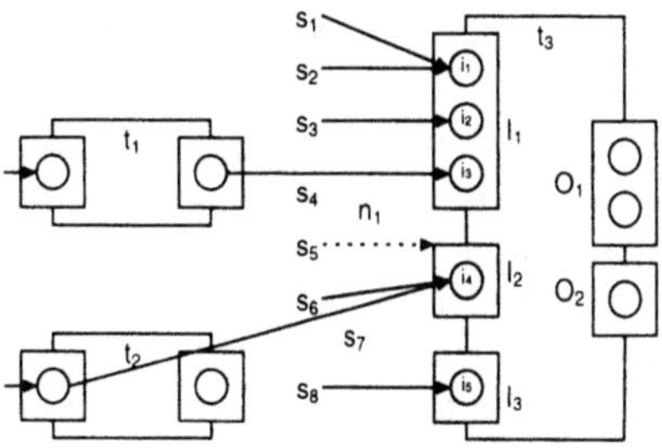

Figure 4 A Workflow schema indicating inter-task dependencies.

A schema indicates how the constituent tasks are 'connected'. We term a source of an input an *input alternative.* In fig. 4 all the input alternatives of a task t_3 are labeled s_1, s_2, ..., s_8. An example of an input having multiple input alternatives is i_1, this has two input alternatives s_1 and s_2. Note that the source of an input alternative could be from an output set (e.g., s_4) or from an input set (e.g., s_7); the latter represents the case when an input is consumed by more than one task.

The notification dependencies are represented by dotted lines, for example, s_5 is a notification alternative for notification dependency n_1.

To allow applications to be recursively structured, the task model allows a task to be realized as a collection of tasks, this task is called a *compound task.* A task can either be a *simple task* (primitive task), a genesis task or a compound task composed from simple, genesis and compound tasks. A compound task undergoes the same state transitions as a simple task. The figure below illustrates a compound task, t_1, composed of tasks t_2 and t_3. A given output of a compound task can come from one or more internal sources (*output alternatives*). If multiple sources of an output become available simultaneously, then the source with the highest priority is selected.

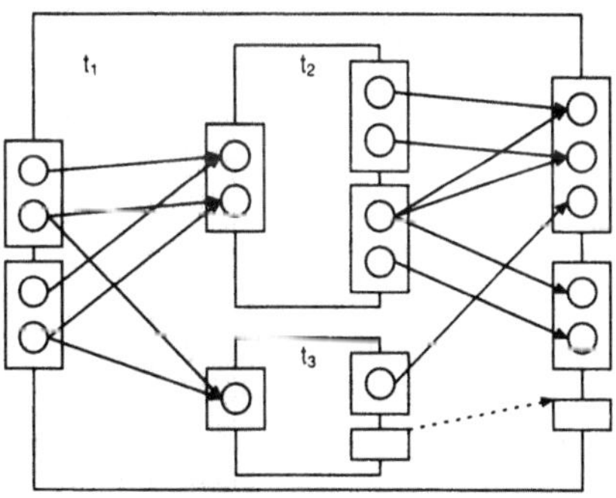

Figure 5 A compound task.

The workflow system stores workflow schemas in a repository and it is possible to modify the structure of a stored schema using transactions. For a complete specification of the repository service interfaces see (Nortel 1998).

5 EXECUTION SERVICE

The workflow execution service coordinates the execution of a workflow instance: it records inter-task dependencies of a schema in persistent atomic objects and uses atomic transactions for propagating coordination information to ensure that tasks are scheduled to run respecting their dependencies. The dependency information is maintained and managed by *task controllers*. Each task within a workflow application has a single dedicated task controller. The purpose of a task controller is to receive notifications of outputs (and inputs) from other task controllers and use this information to determine when its associated task can be started. The task controller is also responsible for propagating notifications of outputs of its task to other interested task controllers. Each task controller maintains a persistent, atomic object, *TaskControl* that is used for recording task dependencies. A task controller is an active entity, a process, that contains an instance of a *TaskControl* object (however, to simplify subsequent descriptions, no distinction between the two will be made). The structure is shown in fig. 6. For example, task controller tc_3 will co-ordinate with tc_1 and tc_2 to determine when t_3 can be started and propagate to tc_4 and tc_5 the results of t_3.

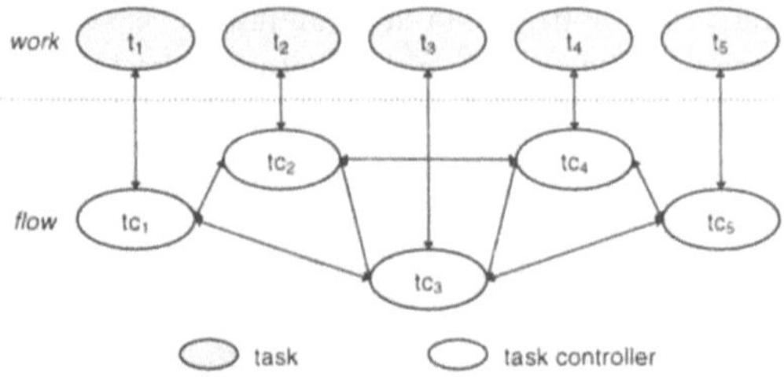

Figure 6 Tasks and task controllers.

In addition to *TaskControl*, the workflow execution service maintains two other key objects: instances of *Resource*, and instances of transactional objects *Task*. Objects whose references are to be passed between workflow tasks are derived from *Resource*. *Task* objects represent the workflow tasks which make up a workflow application (*Tasks* are 'wrapper' objects to real application tasks). The most important operation contained within the *Task* interface is *start*, which takes as parameters: a reference to a *TaskControl* and a sequence of *Resource* references. The *TaskControl* reference is that of the controller of the task, and the sequence of *Resource* objects are the input parameters to the workflow task.

The *TaskControl* object provides a *get_status* operation that returns its current state. During the initial setup phase, operations can be performed on the task controller to set inter-task dependency information. If task controller (tc_i) depends on an input from the input or output set of some task controller (tc_j) it must 'register' with tc_j by invoking *request_notification* operation of tc_j (a complementary, 'unregister' operation is available for deregistering). When the relevant input/output object of tc_j becomes available, tc_j invokes the *notification* operation of tc_i to inform input availability.

Once a task controller has been setup, it enters the waiting state. The waiting, active and completed states correspond respectively to the waiting, active and completed states of a task. The task controller uses the *start* operation to start its task. Upon termination, a task invokes the *notification* operation of its controller to pass the results.

A novel feature of our system is that task controllers of an application can be grouped in an arbitrary manner. Fig. 7 show a possible configurations.

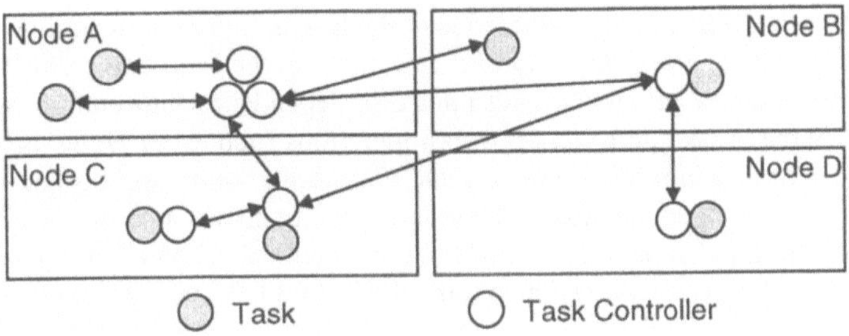

Figure 7 Task coordination

Nodes *B*, *C* and *D* are depicted, in fig. 7, as using a distributed coordination scheme, where a controller is co-located with the corresponding *Task* object, whereas a centralized scheme is being used by node *A*, where all the controllers have been grouped together at a given machine. A suitable configuration can be selected using the workflow administration application that is responsible for instantiating a schema (see below). The choice of a given schema could depend on various factors (e.g., dependability, performance, monitoring, administrative convenience etc.), and is left to the users and administrators. If dependability is crucial to the workflow application, then the task controllers can be placed on multiple machines so that the failure of a single machine will have a minimal effect on the progress on the workflow application. If the monitoring of the progress of the workflow application is more important than its dependability, then the task controllers can be grouped on the monitoring machine so reducing communications overhead. In most cases the placement policy for the task controllers within the workflow application will be a compromise between these two extremes.

Instantiating a workflow schema

A workflow schema stored in the repository contains almost all the information required to create an instance for execution by the execution service; the only additional information required is its initial inputs. The creation of a workflow instance involves six steps:

- *creating task controller objects*: for each simple, genesis and compound task within the schema, a task controller will be created. The placement of task controllers will depend on the various factors indicated earlier and is a user level choice.
- *creating task objects*: for each simple task within the schema, a *Task* object will be created and bound to appropriate implementation (application code of the task). If there are several conformant implementations, then the choice is left to the user.
- *assigning tasks to their task controllers*: tasks need to be assigned to task controllers so that the initiation and termination of the tasks can be controlled. A

task is assigned to a task controller by invoking the *set_task* operation of the task controller with an object reference to the task as a parameter.

- *assigning task controllers of genesis tasks with task definitions*: task controllers of genesis tasks need to be assigned a task definition, this task definition being instantiated by the task controller, when the task is started. A task controller is assigned a task definition by invoking the *set_task_definitions* operation of the task controller with an object reference to the task definition as a parameter.
- *linking task controllers to form the structure of the workflow schema*: Task controllers must be initialized with inter-task dependency information contained in the schema. Task controllers possess operations such as *set_input_alternative* and *set_output_alternative* (*set_output_alternative* only appropriate to task controllers of compound tasks); these are performed on a 'down-stream' task controller to initialize it with the information about the "source" of a dependency ('up-stream' task controller). Once this information has been provided, a 'down-stream' task controller will invoke the *request_notification* operations on all the source 'up-stream' task controllers to register itself as a sink of dependencies.
- *providing the initial input*: the execution of a workflow instance will not start until the input conditions of the "root" task controller have been satisfied. This will be an application specific activity.

Workflow execution

The execution of a workflow application is controlled by the exchange of notifications between task controllers and tasks. Notifications are generated when a controller of a task, either simple, genesis or compound, selects an input set or produces an output set. As stated earlier, these notifications are sent from an 'up-stream' task controller to a 'down-stream' task controller by the former invoking the *notification* operation on the latter. The parameters of the *notification* invocation contains information indicating: the source of the notification, the identity of the input/output set which caused the notification, and the objects which constitutes the input/output set contents. Referring to fig. 4, assume that the input set maintained by the task controller for task t_2 becomes ready; in this case, the task controller will invoke the *notification* operation on the controller of t_3.

A novel dependability feature of our system is that for an atomic task (i.e., the task is performed as transaction), its task controller can provide the guarantee that the task as well as some or all of its notifications are performed atomically. Fig. 8(a) shows a schema. Assume that task *t1* is not transactional; then dependencies *A* and *B* will generate two notification transactions (*A* and *B*, fig. 8(b)) as we have discussed already. If however, task *t1* is transactional, then if desired, the execution of this transaction as well as the two notification transactions can be enclosed within an outermost transaction *T* (fig. 8(c)). Thus it can be arranged that the effects of the task's execution will only be committed if all of the notifications are completed successfully. This allows the successful completion of an atomic task to be predicated on the completion of a set of "required notifications". Such a facility may well be attractive in electronic commerce applications.

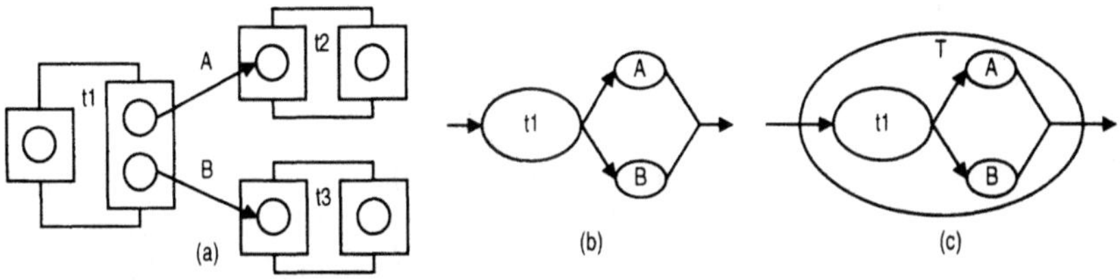

Figure 8 Atomic notifications

The actual algorithm used by a task controller to control its task (either simple, genesis or compound) is very simple; an important feature of this algorithm is that it can be restarted after failure. The following pseudo code describes the algorithm.

The following variables represent the state required to control a task, all variable being persistent and manipulated by transactions:

```
Boolean                                isSimpleTask;
sequence Alternative<>                 inputAlternatives;
Boolean                                inputSetSelected;
ObjectSet                              inputSet;
sequence NotificationRequester<>       inputSetNotificationRequesters;
TaskDefinition                         taskDefinition;
Boolean                                instantiateDefinition;
sequence Alternative<>                 outputAlternatives;
Boolean                                outputSetProduced;
ObjectSet                              outputSet;
sequence NotificationRequester<>       outputSetNotificationRequesters;
```

The first part of the algorithm involves collecting notifications to form an input set. This corresponds to the activity of a task controller in its ‘waiting’ state; the controller is repeatedly checking if any of its input sets is complete. Note that error handling in not included in the pseudo code.

```
// Collect notifications to form input set
if not inputSetSelected then
    loop
        transaction
            inputSetSelected := CheckForInputSet(inputAlternatives);
            if inputSetSelected then
                inputSet := BuildInputSet(inputAlternatives)
            endif
        endtransaction
    when inputSetSelected exit
        ProcessNotification(inputAlternatives)
    endloop
endif;
```

The second part of the algorithm involves sending notifications to all task controllers which are interested in the contents of the input set (this would be the case for shared inputs, e.g., input set of task *t2*, fig. 4 or if the input set belongs to a compound task, fig. 5).

```
// Send notifications to requesters of input set
loop
    when not ExistUnsentNotification(inputSetNotificationRequesters) exit
    transaction
        NotificationRequester notificationRequester;
        notificationRequester := GetUnsentNotification(inputSetNotificationRequesters);
```

```
        SendNotification(notificationRequester, inputSet);
        MarkAsSent(notificationRequester)
    endtransaction
endloop;
```

The third part of the algorithm involves obtaining the output set (the controller is in state 'active'). This is done in one of three ways depending on whether the task is a simple task, a genesis task or a compound task. For a simple task this involves: beginning a transaction, starting the task with the input set, collecting the results some time later, then committing the transaction (assuming all has gone correctly). For a genesis task, this involves instantiating the task structure in its associated task definition, starting their executions and obtaining the results. For a compound task, this simply involves collecting notifications to form an output set.

```
// Obtain output set
if not outputSetProduced then
    if isSimpleTask then
        // Invoke task and obtain output
        transaction
            StartTask(inputSet);
            CollectResults(outputSet);
            outputSetProduced := true
        endtransaction
    else if isGenesisTask then
        // Instantiate task defintions and obtain output
        if not instantiateDefinition then
            transaction
                InstantiateDefinition(taskDefinition);
                instantiateDefinition := TRUE
            endtransaction
        endif;
        transaction
            StartSubTaskController(inputSet);
            CollectResults(outputSet);
            outputSetProduced := true
        endtransaction
    else // isCompoundTask
        // Collect notifications to form output set
        loop
            transaction
                outputSetProduced:= CheckForOutputSet(outputAlternatives);
                if outputSetProduced then
                    outputSet := BuildOutputSet(outputAlternatives)
                endif
            endtransaction
        when outputSetProduced exit
            ProcessNotification(outputAlternatives)
        endloop
    endif
endif;
```

The fourth and final part of the algorithm involves sending notifications to all task controllers which are interested in the contents of the output set (the task controller switches to state 'complete').

```
// Send notifications to requesters of output set
loop
    when not ExistUnsentNotification(outputSetNotificationRequesters) exit
```

```
    transaction
        NotificationRequester notificationRequester;
        notificationRequester:= GetUnsentNotification(outputSetNotificationRequesters);
        SendNotification(notificationRequester, outputSet);
        MarkAsSent(notificationRequester)
    endtransaction
endloop;
```

In summary, our system provides a very flexible and dependable task coordination facility that need not have any centralized control. Because the system is built using the underlying transactional layer, no additional recovery facilities are required for reliable task scheduling: provided failed nodes eventually recover and network partitions eventually heal, task notifications will be eventually completed. For a complete specification of the execution service interfaces, see (Nortel 1998).

6 ADMINISTRATIVE APPLICATIONS

As stated earlier, in our system, application control and management tools required for functions such as instantiating workflow applications, monitoring and dynamic reconfiguration etc., (collectively referred to as administrative applications) themselves can be implemented as workflow applications. This is made possible because the repository and execution services provide operations to examine and modify the structure of schemas and instances respectively. A graphical user interface (GUI) has been provided for these applications.

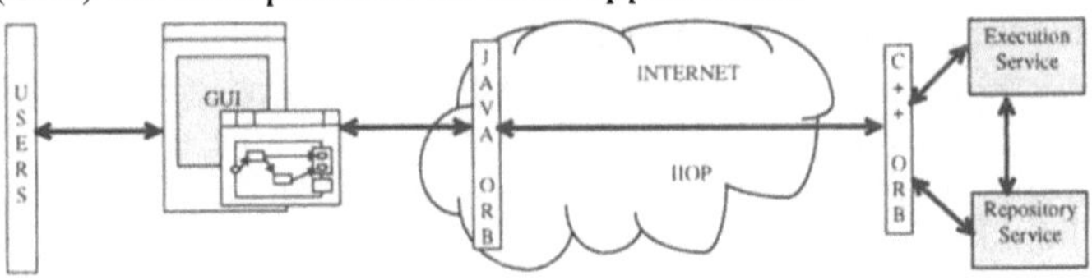

Figure 9 Graphical User Interface.

The GUI has been implemented as a Java applet and as a result it is platform independent, and can be loaded and run by any Java capable Web browser. This component of the toolkit is important as it makes it easier to use the workflow system, enabling a user to specify, execute and control workflow applications with minimal effort.

One of the purposes of the GUI is to help the designer compose the specification of a workflow application. The specification of a workflow application can be performed either from scratch by specifying all of the application components (in our script notation (Ranno 1998), these are object classes, task classes, tasks and compound tasks) and the relationships between them or by composing the application out of existing components which have been already specified. Existing component specifications can be obtained from the workflow repository.

The GUI can be used to view graphical representations of tasks and their instances, which can then be modified, using a forms style interface to input the required modifications. Fig. 10 shows a screen dump from the Java applet showing the graphical representation of a task. Here compound tasks are represented by double line rectangles.

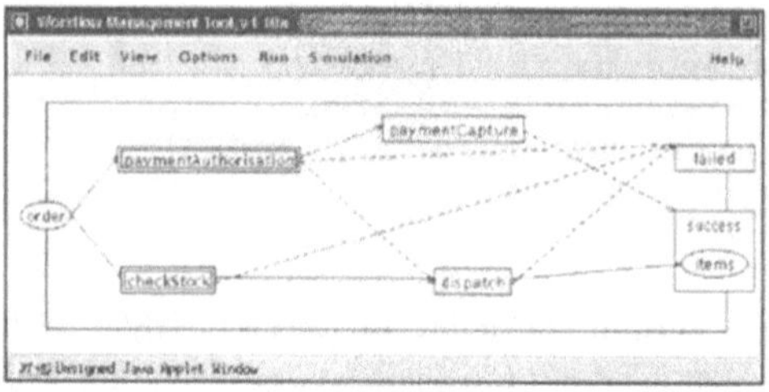

Figure 10 Graphical representation of a task.

A navigation system is also available that lets users zoom in and out of a specification. Zooming in on a compound task lets users see its component tasks, while zooming in on a simple task displays its task class as well as all the dependencies it is involved in. The zoom-out is the reverse action: zooming out lets users see the embedding workflow.

Consistency checking and simulation tools are also available. The script semantics can be expressed as Petri nets. So Petri net tools can be used to check the specification. We have done this using $B(PN)^2$ Petri net tool kit (Best 1995) available to us. This tool kit can be used for checking for safeness, reachability, deadlocks and liveness. The simulator allows animating of the script in a variety of ways.

The GUI can be used for observing the execution of an application. This is possible because the GUI can access the *TaskControl* objects of the workflow execution service and hence can display the starting and completion states of tasks (recall that *TaskControl* objects store information on dependencies and task states). In addition to this simple monitoring, the GUI can also be used for driving the workflow administrative applications for dynamically modifying the execution of an application by forcing certain tasks to abort (when possible) or even by adding/removing tasks and dependencies (Shrivastava 1998).

7 RELATED WORK

The workflow approach to coordinating task executions provides a natural way of exploiting distributed object and middleware technologies (Georgakopoulos 1995) (Warne 1995). However, currently available workflow systems are not scaleable, as their structure tends to be monolithic. There is therefore much research activity on the construction of decentralized workflow architectures. Systems such as ours, RainMan (Paul 1997) and ORBWork from the METEOR research group (Das 1997) represent a new generation of (research) systems that can work in arbitrarily distributed environments. We briefly compare and contrast these two systems with ours.

RainMan is a distributed workflow system based on a generic workflow framework called RainMaker. The RainMaker framework defines a model in which *sources* generate service requests and *performers* manage the execution of service requests. The RainMan workflow system implementation, in Java, uses the interfaces specified by the RainMaker framework. There is a *builder* application that acts as both an interactive graphical environment for specifying workflows (as directed acyclic graphs) and as a *source* from which service requests are generated (directed acyclic graphs interpreter). The *builder* application represents a central point of co-ordination of the workflow, but is also a single point of failure.

The sources and performers of RainMan/RainMaker represent respectively, task controllers and tasks of our system. The centralized coordination configuration of our system corresponds to the 'builder' approach. As we have indicated, our system can support arbitrary placement of task controllers, so can be made immune from a central point of failure. There is no support for fault tolerance in RainMan.

ORBWork is a CORBA based workflow enactment system for the $METEOR_2$ workflow model. In the $METEOR_2$ model the workflow system's runtime is divided into two types of components: *task managers* and *tasks*. The purpose of a *task manager* is to control/schedule the execution of a *task* within a workflow application. The specification of the control/schedule is stored in Workflow Intermediate Language (WIL). The WIL is used to automatically generate code fragments (C++) which are combined with ORBWork task manager code to create programs which can be used to control the workflow application. $METEOR_2$ model distinguishes different types of *tasks* components depending on their behaviour, for example, transactional, non transactions or user tasks. For each behavioural set an appropriate *task manager* is specified, with an appropriate IDL interface.

The task managers and tasks of ORBWork correspond to task controllers and tasks respectively of our system. However, unlike our system, ORBWork does not implement a transactional task coordination facility: task managers and tasks are not transactional CORBA objects. Therefore, as we have stated earlier, our system does not need special recovery facilities to deal with failures. Naturally, recovery facilities need to be implemented in ORBWork; the cited paper describes its design.

There are two features of our system that distinguishes it from the rest: i) The use of a transactional task coordination facility means that the system naturally provides a fault-tolerant 'job scheduling' environment. ii) Our system is reflective: computation structure is maintained by the system at run time and exposed in a careful manner for dynamic control. The execution service directly maintains the structure of an application within task controllers making it available through transactional operations. This makes the provision of system monitoring and dynamic workflows relatively easy.

8 CONCLUDING REMARKS

We have described the design and implementation of an application composition and execution environment that enables sets of inter-related tasks to be carried out and supervised in a dependable manner. The system meets the requirements of interoperability, scalability, flexible task composition, dependability and dynamic reconfiguration. Our system architecture is decentralized and open: it has been designed and implemented as a set of CORBA services to run on top of a given ORB. Wide-spread acceptance of CORBA and Java middleware technologies make our system ideally suited to building Internet applications.

Acknowledgements
This work has been supported in part by grants from Nortel Technology, Engineering and Physical Sciences Research Council, ESPRIT CaberNet and ESPRIT LTR Project C3DS (project no. 24962). Mark Little has played a key role in making the OTS compliant version of Arjuna. Support from colleagues Samantha Merrion, Dave Stringer, Harold Toze and John Warne at Nortel Technology, Harlow is gratefully acknowledged.

REFERENCES

Best E., and Grahlmann G. (1995) "PEP: Programming Environment based on Petri nets", Documentation and User Guide, Version 1.4, Universitat Hildersheim.

Das S., Kochut K., Miller J., Seth A. and Worah, D., (1997) "ORBWork: A reliable distributed CORBA-based workflow enactment system for METEOR2", Tech. Report No. UGA-CS-TR 97-001, Dept. of Computer Science, University of Georgia.

Georgakopoulos D., Hornick, M. and Sheth A. (1995) "An overview of workflow management: from process modeling to workflow automation infrastructure", Intl. Journal on distributed and parallel databases, 3(2), pp. 119-153.

Lawrence P., (ed.) (1997) "WfMC Workflow Handbook", John Wiley & Sons Ltd.

Nortel and University of Newcastle upon Tyne, (1998) "Workflow Management Facility Specification", Revised submission, OMG document bom/98-03-01.

Parrington G.D., Shrivastava S.K., Wheater S.M., and Little M.C. (1995) "The design and implementation of Arjuna", USENIX Computing Systems Journal, vol. 8 (3), pp. 255-308.

Paul S., Park E., and Chaar J. (1997) "RainMan: a Workflow System for the Internet", Proc. of USENIX Symp. on Internet Technologies and Systems.

Ranno F., Wheater S.M., and Shrivastava S.K. (1997) "A System for Specifying and Co-ordinating the Execution of Reliable Distributed Applications", IFIP Conference on Distributed Applications and Interoperable Systems (DAIS'97), Cottbus, Germany.

Ranno F., Shrivastava S.K., and Wheater S.M. (1998) "A Language for Specifying the Composition of Reliable Distributed Applications", The 18th International Conference on Distributed Computing Systems (ICDCS '98), Amsterdam, The Netherlands.

Shrivastava S.K., and Wheater S.M. (1998) "Architectural Support for Dynamic Reconfiguration of Large Scale Distributed Applications", The 4th International Conference on Configurable Distributed Systems (CDS'98), Annapolis, Maryland, USA.

Warne J.P. (1995) "Flexible transaction framework for dependable workflows", ANSA Report No. 1217.

BIOGRAPHY

The authors are researchers at the University of Newcastle. S.M. Wheater is a Research Fellow, S.K. Shrivastava is a Professor and F. Ranno is a PhD student.

A Generic Workflow Environment based on CORBA Business Objects

Alexander Schill[a] and Christian Mittasch[b]
[a]Fakultät Informatik, TU Dresden D-01062 Dresden, Germany
[b]Institut für Informatik, TU Bergakademie Freiberg D-09596 Freiberg, Germany
schill@ibdr.inf.tu-dresden.de / chris@informatik.tu-freiberg.de

Abstract

This paper describes a generic approach for building object-oriented workflow management systems in a distributed environment. It is based on business objects that encapsulate resources and basic business processes. They are accessible via CORBA interfaces. As opposed to more conventional work-flow approaches, control is fully decentralised, arbitrary workflow control structures can be modelled, and involved resources maintain autonomy. Moreover, the approach is not limited to one specific implementation of a workflow management system but can be applied on a more generic basis.

The concepts are validated by an implementation on top of Orbix and are illustrated by concrete examples of workflows. All distributed interactions are based on CORBA object communication. Selected CORBA services such as naming, events, persistence and externalisation are utilised, and experiences with their integration into our environment are reported, too.

Keywords:

Workflow management, distributed systems, business objects, middleware, CORBA

1 INTRODUCTION

According to the Workflow Management Coalition's (WfMC) definition (WfMC 1994), a workflow consists of a set of linked activities that collectively realise a business objective within an organisation. In general, different activities are executed within a highly distributed environment, typically interconnected by an Intranet, potentially also involving Internet-based interactions.

Due to the importance of workflows to most companies, a large number of workflow management systems have been developed in the recent past; examples are FlowMark (Leymann & Roller 1997), WorkParty (Siemens-Nixdorf 1995), Exotica (Mohan *et al.* 1995) and Meteor (Sheth 1997). Moreover, standardisation efforts have been initiated by the WfMC (WfMC 1994, 1995, 1996a) and currently by the OMG (OMG 1997a, 1997b, 1997c) in order to achieve interoperability, portability of workflow applications and integration into existing standards.

Most of the existing approaches, however, are based on a rather centralised view and are implemented on top of a particular database system (Alonso *et al.*). This leads to a lack of scalability and adaptability in the context of widely distributed environments. In addition, the interfaces of existing systems are mostly proprietary; therefore, it is often difficult to interface between such an overall workflow management system and arbitrary local resources involved in workflow processing. Finally, it is difficult to customise the implementation of workflow management systems for specific application areas ranging from insurance companies via electronic commerce to medical systems and many other fields.

Advances in software technology support the development of generic solutions: software components (especially frameworks) and business objects. Both concepts are quite similar: Their basic idea is the development of coarse-grained objects (expressing essential pieces of business semantics, i.e. resources and behaviour), see for instance (Taylor 1995, Jacobson *et al.* 1997). Developers and users expect two main advantages of business-object-based WfMS: (1) better reuse in other business information systems, and (2) better scalability and adaptability. These factors depend hardly on the underlying middleware. Therefore, the business object based architecture needs an appropriate distribution platform and an adaptable configuration management.

In this paper, we present a generic and open workflow environment based on CORBA middleware. It uses business objects that encapsulate basic processing facilities and resources and uses CORBA-based open communication. Workflow objects and associated workflow types can be defined on top of business objects. Different to more conventional workflow approaches, control is fully decentralised, arbitrary workflow control structures can be modelled, and involved resources maintain autonomy. Finally, the system is generic. It offers different levels of re-use to be easily applied to specific application scenarios.

The paper is organised as follows. Section 2 introduces the general characteristics and architecture of our environment and compares it with existing approaches in more detail. Section 3 explains the major concepts with respect to distributed system aspects, to the use of CORBA middleware, and to implementation issues based on Orbix. Section 4 reports about specific experiences and validation results. Section 5 concludes with an outlook to current and future work.

2 FOUNDATIONS AND ARCHITECTURAL OVERVIEW

In this section, we introduce the foundations of our approach using a typical application example. We also give a more detailed comparison with existing systems.

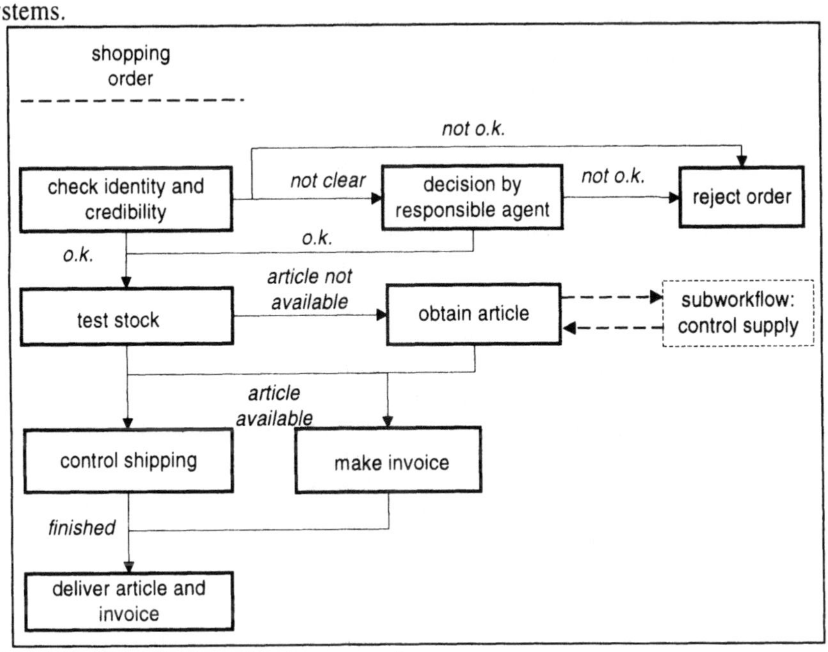

Figure 1: Workflow application example

Figure 1 shows a typical workflow application example of the electronic commerce area. A registered customer issues an order via the Internet, for example using HTML forms or a Java applet. The order is received by a retailer, leading to the initiation of a workflow. The identity and credibility of the customer are checked within an initial task. If a standard test of customer credentials against a customer database fails due to former credit problems, the workflow is aborted and the order is rejected. If the test results are unclear, the customer request is forwarded to an authorised agent who does a manual check. Once the order is approved automatically or manually, the stock management is contacted within a subsequent task. If the desired article is not available, a wholesale ordering task is issued; this might even lead to the initiation of another subworkflow handling the order. Eventually, the order can be processed further: The requested article is packed, and the associated invoice is prepared in parallel. Finally, goods and invoice are shipped to the customer. Other workflows are started in succession of the order processing, for example payment supervising.

This example includes the typical execution elements of workflows and can be used to illustrate basic requirements for workflow management support:

- *Workflow execution structures:* Sequential, conditional, and parallel processing of tasks, and subworkflows are to be supported. Task execution is intrinsically distributed among different, potentially heterogeneous computer systems; this has to be supported by a distributed runtime system. Autonomy of organisational units can be modelled with subworkflows.
- *Resource management:* The workflow accesses very different resources for task execution, ranging from automated servers via databases to human interaction facilities. A uniform way of encapsulating these entities is desirable. Moreover, resources should be easily reusable within the context of different workflows.
- *Task mapping:* Typically, a 1:n-relationship between tasks and resources exists; for example, several servers might be available for order checking. Therefore, a flexible, role-based task mapping as supported by ODP trading services (ISO 1997, Mittasch *et al.* 1996a) is desirable.
- *Workflow control and monitoring:* In order to handle inquiries, it should always be possible to track down the current status of a workflow. Nevertheless, control should mainly be decentralised in order to improve scalability and in order to be able to tolerate partial system failures. A monitor should be able to supervise workflows and resources as well.

As already discussed in the introduction, various conventional workflow management systems to support such scenarios have been developed in the past and are available as products now. While typically supporting the major execution structures required, these systems fall short in addressing the other requirements, especially encapsulation and reuse of resources and workflows, flexible task mapping, and decentralised control. Additionally, they have difficulties with demands for quick changes in business tasks of an enterprise.

Earlier research approaches addressed these problems - especially the distributed systems aspects - to some larger degree; examples are Action Paths (Artsy 90), EuroCoop (Hennessy *et al.* 1992), Mentor (Wodtke *et al.* 1996), Meteor (Das 1997, Sheth 1997), WASA (Weske *et al.* 1996), Exotica (Mohan *et al.* 1995), Mobile (Bussler & Jablonski 1995) and Income/Star (Oberweis 1994). Some approaches also address specific aspects such as mobile systems and user mobility (Bußler 1995), workflow evolution (Casati *et al.* 1996), web integration (Miller *et al.* 1997), or virtual enterprises (Ott & Nastansky 1997). However, although the mentioned systems resulted in basic prototypes, they hardly provided language and tool support. In addition, they were not using standardised middleware but relied on either proprietary or rather low-level protocols. Based on the standardisation efforts of the WfMC (WfMC 1994), some additional progress has been made with respect to a common system model. However, these definitions still remain at a very abstract level and do not incorporate middleware or implementation aspects. Unfortunately, their workflow description language (WfMC 1995) standard has been retired and the interoperability specification has not been finished yet (WfMC 1996b).

More recently, the notion of business objects (Taylor 1995, Jacobson *et el.* 1997, OMG 1997d) has been recognised by standardisation bodies such as the OMG. Business objects encapsulate application-specific functionality and provide standard interfaces. They are typically imbedded into an inheritance hierarchy and can be reused this way. Moreover, such objects can flexibly be imbedded into a workflow processing environment for performing selected tasks within a workflow. Essential additional characteristics are:

- *Autonomy:* Each business object is responsible for its own instantiation, atomicity, durability and access control.
- *Composition:* Business objects can consist of hierarchical components; for example a business process may include other business processes or sub-processes. They may be fractale.
- *Non-redundancy:* The modelling of business objects should be carried out with a minimum of redundancy, i.e. functionality should be defined at optimal locations in the class-hierarchy.

The OMG also works towards the integration of business objects into so-called frameworks (Cotter & Potel 1995, Mittasch *et al.* 1996b). A framework is a set of co-operating classes representing a reusable design solution for a specific application area. In addition to this definition we would like to stress further characteristics of frameworks: A framework for workflow management should control workflows autonomously. It only should offer interfaces to assign tasks to the framework (so called „hot spots"). On top of CORBA and CORBA services, a business object framework has been defined by the OMG in the context of CORBA facilities. Specific application frameworks for application areas such as finance, transportation, or medicine are being derived. One dedicated example is a workflow framework (Mittasch *et al.* 1996a) that deals with repository and execution tasks of workflows. In addition, common business objects are base types of business behaviour, such as address, partner, currency, task. They can be specialised by domain specific tasks.

We consider these concepts a starting point for the development of a generic work-flow environment. The major challenge, however, is to detail these rather abstract concepts significantly in order to provide an implementable systems solution.

Considering the discussion above, we designed a CORBA-based environment for the generic support of workflow management systems. It is called BPAFrame (Framework for Business Process Automation) and has evolved from subsequent predecessors (Mittasch *et al.* 1996b).

An implementation-oriented view of the system architecture is given in figure 2. The main constituents are a visualisation services framework with administration and user services for workflows, and the CORBA-based distributed runtime environment. All administration and user tools inherit from our visualisation services framework. Within the user services, a so-called workspace realises the front-end application for authenticated users of BPAFrame. It contains a task list for users involved in workflows, the list of started workflows and the list of workflow types that may be started by the user. A monitor component is also being developed that enables the inspection of active workflows and of resources as well. Finally, the user services negotiate data to existing applications via so-called interaction servers.

Our prototype does not contain special design tools at the moment. Organisational structure, resources and workflow types must be implemented with simple text editors, compare also figure 5.

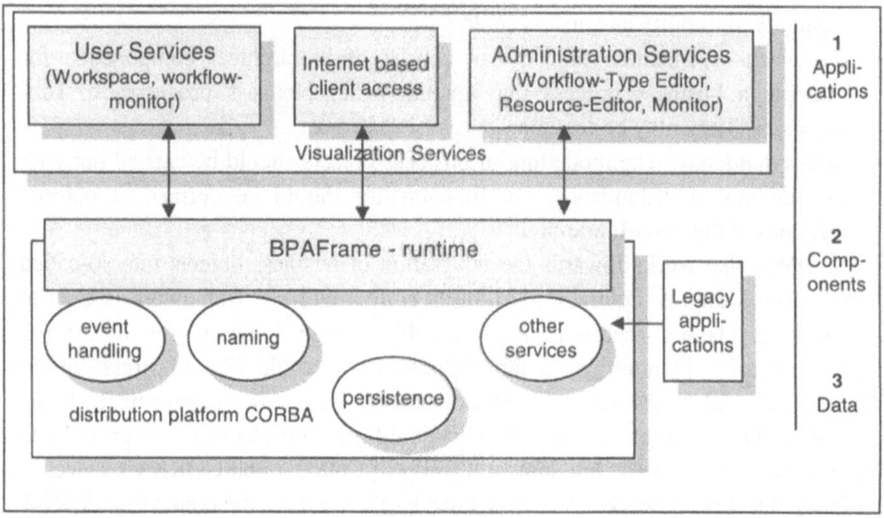

Figure 2: System architecture

Workflows are always associated with predefined workflow types. Their control structure is specified by an execution graph as outlined by the example application. Workflow instances are able to switch between different states with different behaviour during their life cycle (working, suspended, successfully terminated, aborted). Workflow instances contain an interpreter object that is able to interpret the textual description of the execution graph at runtime by accessing adequate resources for task processing. Resources can also be reserved in advance to starting a workflow in order to promise their availability. The runtime environment makes use of ORB communication, event handling, naming, persistence and several other services. Encapsulated legacy applications can also be accessed based on business object encapsulation. Specific implementation aspects are reported below.

3 IMPLEMENTATION ASPECTS

This section discusses specific implementation aspects, namely the class structure, the notation to specify execution graphs, and the distributed workflow execution protocols. The system implementation is based on Windows NT 4.0 with Microsoft Visual C++ and the CORBA implementation Orbix of IONA.

3.1 Class Structure

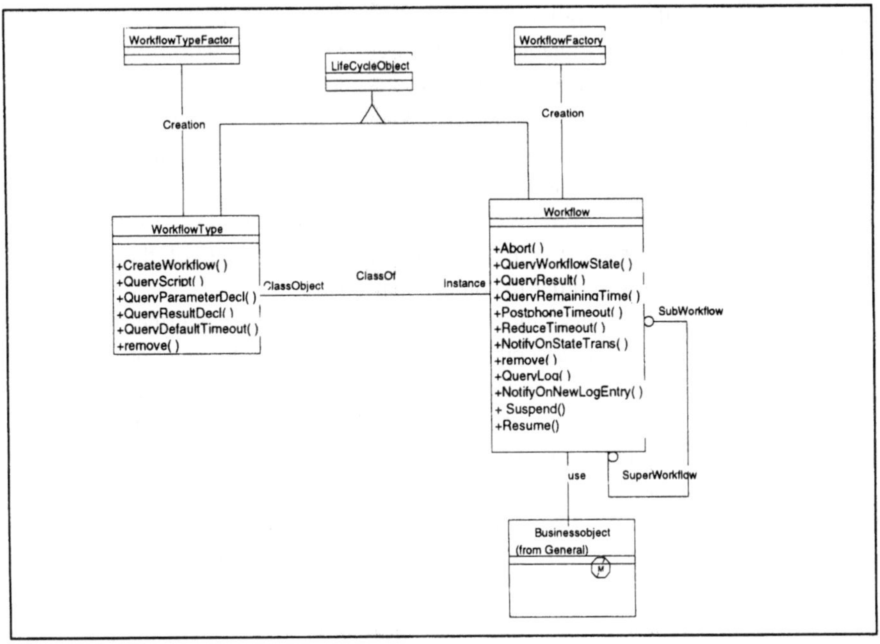

Figure 3: Class structure

```
interface Workflow : LifeCycleObject
{
  ...
  void Abort() raises(InternalError);
  void Suspend(in boolean hardSuspend) raises(InternalError);
  void Resume() raises(InternalError); // ongoing work of a suspended
workflow
  void PostphoneTimeout(in Ttime additionalTime)
raises(InternalError);
  void ReduceTimeout(in Ttime Difference) raises(InternalError);

  WorkflowType   QueryClassObject();
  TParameterList QueryParameter() raises(InternalError);
  TResultList    QueryResult() raises(InternalError);

  void  QueryState(out TWorkflowState State);
  void  QueryStateDesc(out string Description);
  Ttime QueryRemainingTime() raises(InternalError);

  TParameterList QueryParameter() raises(InternalError );
  TResultList QueryResult() raises(InternalError);
  TLogEntryList QueryLog();
  TWorkflowList QuerySubWorkflows();
  WorkflowType QueryClassObject();

  CosEventChannelAdmin::ConsumerAdmin NotifyOnStateTrans();
  CosEventChannelAdmin::ConsumerAdmin NotifyOnChangeStateDesc();
...
};
```

Figure 4: Interfaces of the class Workflow

Figures 3 and 4 show the class structure and some essential interfaces of classes of the workflow control module. An interpreter controls the processing of the workflow graph and the invocation of resources. It is discussed in section 3.3.

The workflow type factory enables the creation of individual workflow types via tools of the user services. Each workflow type is represented by a business object and offers methods for creating dedicated instances and for querying instantiated workflows. The workflow interface allows its clients to change the workflow's state and to manipulate or query its parameters. This way, workflows can be inspected interactively via different tools. WorkflowType factories are very similar. Both are responsible for the distributed life-cycle management of their objects. They are key components in order to control their distribution.

Based on a workflow factory object, workflow instances of predefined types can be generated at runtime. The associated workflow objects offer methods to query their status and their subsequent results. They control time-out management, notify interested instances (for example the initiator) about state changes, and manage execution logs according to progress of task execution. Workflow objects also enable aggregation via the communication facilities of event channel objects. Subworkflows are running autonomously.

During their execution, workflows access various business objects according to their execution graph and the mapping of tasks. Additional auxiliary classes exist for handling input parameters and results of workflows.

3.2 Specification of Execution Graphs

With each workflow type, an execution graph is associated and has to be specified via interactive tools. Then, it is mapped into an internal linguistic representation (in textual format) and is interpreted by the runtime system during workflow execution. Figure 5 shows an extract of the workflow specification according to our order processing example of section 2.

```
// Extract of the workflow example Online-Shopping, see figure 1:
call and first step

extern Any shoppingorder; // input data for the workflow

// declaration of required interpreter functions,
extern getObject(String name, Object obj);  // resolve name
extern suspend(); // possibility to suspend the workflow
...
Object CustomerCheck,AbortBehavior, DetailedCustomerCheck, Stock,
SupplierOfFunds,
       Controlling, Shipping;
String rc; // returncode

void main() {

initGlobalObjects();
  try {
  CustomerCheck.checkOrder(in shoppingorder, out rc);
  }
  catch(...) {
    printErrorMsg(„The customer check failed...");
```

```
    return;
  }

  if(rc == „not clear") { // condition comlied: branch to „decide by
responsible"
    try {
      getObject(„manager", DetailedCustomerCheck);
      DetailedCustomerCheck.checkOrder(in shoppingorder, out rc);
    }
    catch(...) {
      printErrorMsg"The customer check by the manager failed...");
      return;
    } // catch
  } // if(rc == „not clear")
```

Figure 5: Example of a workflow specification

After the definition of auxiliary data types and external operations, the execution graph is specified within the main body. Each task specification also comprises an exception handling clause. Parallel execution (for example, of packing and invoice processing) is implemented by subworkflows that are managed independently by another group of workflow type object and workflow object. Execution is resynchronised by using a CORBA event channel. That means, the successful termination of a subworkflow leads to an appropriate event notification at its event channel. This allows the interpreter of the superworkflow to synchronise the processing. In addition to the constructs shown in the example, repetitive task execution is also possible.

A workflow definition is checked for syntactic and semantic correctness by a parser as part of our architecture. It transforms the definition into an internal representation and passes this to the interpreter component. Standard compiler tools (Lex and Yacc) were used for the parser. The interpreter consists of a set of implementation classes based on object-oriented design.

3.3 Communication System of the Distributed Workflow Execution

The communication subsystem of BPAFrame2 defines interfaces of the internal event communication. The supplier delivers information of all kinds of events (e.g. user accepts job, object is created, etc.). There exist four modes of event channel communication: push or pull supplier and push or pull consumer. Supplier and consumer may be interconnected indirectly via event channel objects in different manners in order to fulfil different communication protocols.

Clients can act as event consumers (push or pull) to monitor workflows, to collect all information of their current workflows or to collect history information in a workflow data recorder. Additionally, the subsystem uses factories as discussed in section 3.1 for the remote creation of objects (object life cycle). Workflow objects contain additional characteristics (e.g. time-out-value, owner, priority) and operations necessary for interactions with active workflows (abort, reduce time-out, etc.). The job control subsystem works like the workflow control, but for single tasks. The main difference is the necessity to reserve resources and to interact with them. Roles only organise the notification of resources. Thus, role-servers and jobs are essential for the performance of the BPAFrame system.

For all remote interactions, the dynamic invocation interface (DII) of CORBA is used. This way, all calls can be implemented within the basic platform independent from the actual type of the invoked resources. The specific type information is then accessed at runtime, enabling a type-conforming call structure.

The distribution platform is able to manage all distribution aspects. That liberates the workflow control from tasks, like invocation, start of objects (if required), or distribution-error detection. Moreover, the runtime system must not be aware of the persistent state of objects. Orbix activation services (IONA 1997) together with our own implementation of the CORBA persistence service manage the reload of passive objects, if necessary. Abstractions from security details can be provided in a similar way.

The module of the event channel objects follows the specification of (OMG 1995). We have some restrictions in the use of data types and in the exceptions for implementation reasons. Thus, it may be exchanged by commercially available implementations in the future. The figure illustrates the administration of communication-connections via event channels objects. It is possible to realise push or pull communication protocols between suppliers and consumers.

Persistence of Business Objects has been achieved using an own implementation of the CORBA services persistence (POS) and externalisation. This way, workflows can also be suspended and can be stored persistently for later reactivation. For example, after notifying a workflow object of a suspension request, the interpreter is informed and synchronises the request with the ongoing execution. At a possible synchronisation point (e.g. after finishing a particular task), the state of the workflow is changing to "suspended". Then, a confirmation is sent to the workflow object. It calls methods to save its state itself: Here, it is converted into an output stream and saved persistently. Reactivation operates reversed.

POS consists of a layered structure (OMG 1995). That allows a very flexible use of available data storages. We implemented two versions of POS-connections to data storage: POSIX-files for workflow types and resources and ODBC for workflows. It is necessary to add at least two more CORBA services to the Business Objects of BPAFrame: Time and Security. Two problems can be solved with the help of the Time Service. Firstly, processing times of workflows and jobs become more reliable (now time-correctness depends on the exclusive use of trusted server machines). Secondly, the Time Service works as a required basic service for security and transaction services.

The CORBA Security Service as well as the Transaction Service is now commercially available as implementation. Their integration into BPAFrame is prepared in form of policies and rules. The integration only depends on requirements of practical use.

Another important facility of the runtime system is the environment object. We decided to have one environment object in every organisational unit. It is responsible for the use of its resources. It manages references of all current services of BPAFrame in its organisational unit. Furthermore, it is capable to hide for instance allocation policies like "random" or "round robin" for resources.

4 VALIDATION AND EXPERIENCES

The described runtime environment has been implemented completely under Windows NT with Orbix and C++, and its functionality has been validated by concrete applications. All components have been shown to co-operate successfully. The use of CORBA has significantly facilitated the implementation and has contributed to a relatively rapid completion of the system.

By using event channels, the protocols for distributed workflow management could be significantly simplified as opposed to using purely synchronous, RPC-style invocations. Moreover, all interactions between clients and workflows as well as with monitoring components were reduced to one single type of interaction mechanism. Message transmission between suppliers (workflows, resources) and consumers are separated by EventChannel-Objects. This allows to handle message transmission orthogonal to workflow processing and independent from the behaviour of event consumers (users, monitor front-end, etc.). On the other hand, it costs additional system resources, see fig. 6.

In order to get a first idea of performance aspects and implications, we did a performance study of CORBA inter-object invocations at the basic CORBA API level. Considering these results we can conclude that an acceptable performance at higher system layers with response times of less than a few hundred milliseconds can be achieved. The results are also within the same order of magnitude as observed with typical remote procedure call facilities such as DCE RPC. A detailed investigation of performance behaviour of CORBA implementations (including Orbix) is set out in (Gokhale & Schmidt 1996). It illustrates the potentials of improvement of the throughput of the middleware of more than 50% comparing to our standard solution (Orbix on NT). But, the application area of WfMS does not require such optimisations because of the lack of transmission of multimedia data. Additionally, delay time of BPAFrame (200 ms - 2 s) does not influence the processing of workflows with processing times between minutes and days.

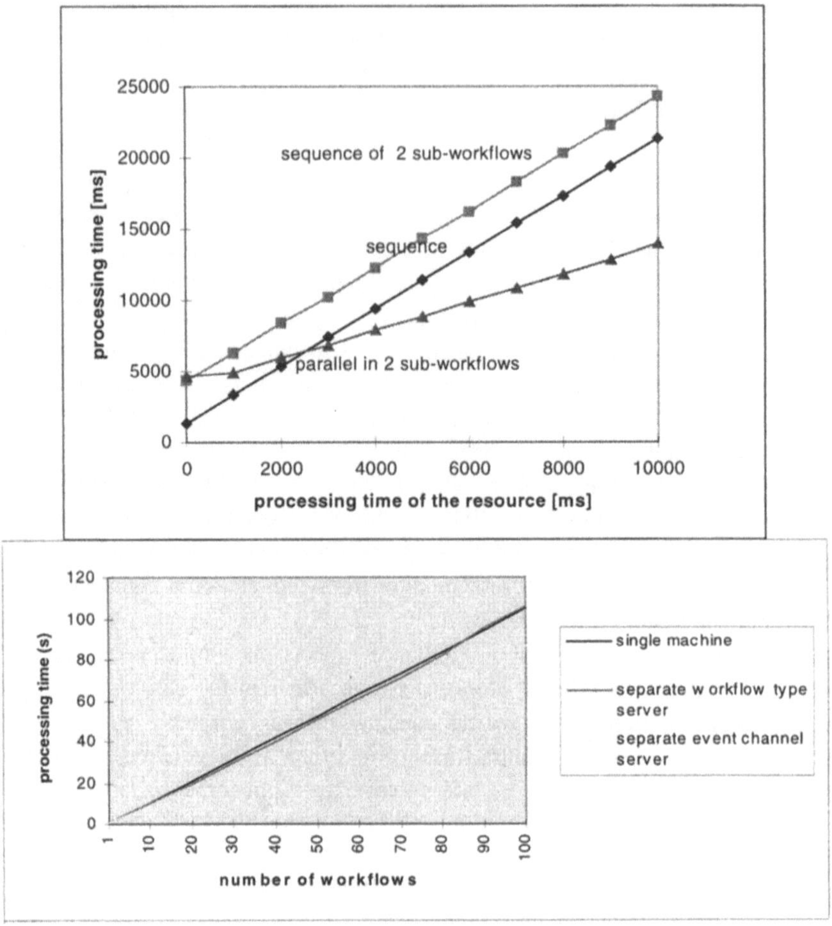

Figure 6: Processing time of workflows and additional delay caused by event channel servers in BPAFrame

Nevertheless, there are still potential bottlenecks within the current prototype, although these problems are not a design but only an implementation issue. For example, there is only a single factory for all workflow type objects and just one factory per type for workflow instances. Further investigations concerning scalability have to be done in the near future. Possible ideas are to adaptively select the number of factories by defining events and performance conditions which might initiate the start or termination of factories.

Further optimisations are possible by using non-exclusive resources. Such objects have to be able to handle a table of active tasks in order to allow for the parallel processing of jobs and in order to manage job priorities.

The organisational model also has to be extended in order to reflect the real-world co-operation of organisations and organisational units more appropriately. The mechanism of substitutes in conjunction with the load of resources has to be enhanced. Another future extension deals with the integration of a start-up service based on the corresponding CORBA service. Moreover, selected interactions within a workflow should also be embedded into transactions, making use of the CORBA transaction service.

As already mentioned in the previous section, BPAFrame uses the advantages of a naming service in conjunction with our environment objects. The latter are responsible for the caching of naming information in smaller domains (in organisational units). The naming service takes control of the general names: Start-up servers, the organisational structure, names of related organisations and so on. With other words, naming is responsible for general (and open usable) information, that does not remain under control of domains. Additionally, this way of sharing reduces the security problem in conjunction with names of essential parts of an organisation: Only freely available names are stored in the naming service. Other identified possibilities allow to improve the performance of the system based on improved implementation details:

Role servers could play a more active role for the scalability of resources, if they would actively take part in the workflow-resource protocol. We intend to compare the current protocol with alternative role servers, that are responsible for resource invocation and substitute management.

There is a lot of redundant work in software development as well as in maintenance processes of current business information systems. Information systems are using the same resources of an enterprise as WfMS or reengineering tools. The control flows of business processes of WfMS and of production control systems or of transport control of a haulage business are very similar. Therefore, concrete business objects and also principle solutions (e.g. patterns of control flows) can both be reused. In order to support this, BPAFrame supports different levels of reuse:

The software architecture was designed with the Unified Modelling Language (UML). The application of UML-based software-engineering tools supports the development of new versions of the framework as well as the development of additional tools. The use of event channel implementation in other projects and the application of a simplified workflow control for the task control (jobs) in BPAFrame are examples.

The abstraction provided by business objects enables their reuse within different workflows and even within different heterogeneous systems other than workflows. This is especially supported by the strict distinction between the workflow processing logic and the encapsulated internal business object implementations.
Models of business processes may also be reused or be further refined to special needs of other information systems. Similar processing paths can be found, for instance, in geographical information systems.

In summary, reuse of both kinds of business objects (workflows and resources) is enabled by our approach.

5 CONCLUSIONS AND FUTURE WORK

This paper has presented a CORBA-based environment for building workflow management systems. We have outlined that workflows require generic support with special emphasis on decentralisation, reuse of components, encapsulation of resources, and the use of standards. CORBA and CORBA services have been proven to present a viable middleware platform for such an environment. Based on the abstraction of business objects, a flexible and reusable modelling of resources and of workflows has been enabled. The resulting system implementation has been validated by several examples. First experiences are quite positive with respect to ease of modelling, reuse and scalability.

Current implementation work focuses on the integration of additional tools for workflow specification and management. Moreover, additional CORBA services, namely security, are being exploited. The front-end will be augmented with Internet access facilities based on HTML and CORBA-Java-Applet communication. The performance aspects of the runtime system will be investigated in detail in order to analyse possibilities for optimisation. Future work will also address design and implementation of other, possibly application-dependent workflow management schemes. This might lead to the design of a hierarchy of workflow type and business process models and a library of workflow components. This way, we expect to achieve improved user acceptance in practice. Finally, the integration of distributed multimedia components like video-conferencing, and the support of mobile environments are additional mid-term issues.

References

Alonso, G., Agrawal, D., El Abbadi, A., Mohan, C. (1997): *Functionalities and Limitations of Current Workflow Management Systems*, 1997, http://www.almaden.ibm.com/cs/exotica/exotica

Artsy, Y. (1990): Routing Objects on Action Paths; *IEEE Int. Conf. on Distributed Computing Systems*, Paris, 1990, pp. 572-579

Bussler, C.; Jablonski, S. (1995): Scalability and Extensibility through Modularity : Architecture of the MOBILE Workflow Management System. In. *Proc. Of the 5th Ws. on Inf. Techn. And Systems*, p.98-107, Amsterdam, Dec. 1995

Bußler, C. (1995): User Mobility in Workflow-Management-Systems. In: *Proc. Of the Telecommunication Inf. Networking Architecture Conf. (TINA'95)*, Melbourne, Feb. 1995

Casati, F.; Ceri, S.; Pernici, B.; Pozzi, G. (1996): Workflow Evolution. Presentation at *ER'96*, Cottbus, Germany,Oct. 1996

Cotter, S.; Potel, M. (1995): *Inside Taligent Technology*. Reading (Mass.): Addison-Wesley, 1995

Das, S. (1997): *"A Reliable Distributed CORBA-based Workflow Enactment System for METEOR_2"*, Technical Report UGA-CS-TR-97-001, Department of Computer Science, University of Georgia, Feb. 1997

Gokhale, A.; Schmidt, D.C. (1996): Measuring the Performance of Communication Middleware on High-Speed Networks. In: *SIGCOMM Conference*, Stanford, 1996

Hennessy, P., Kreifelts, T., Ehrlich, U. (1992): Distributed Work Management: Activity Coordination within the EuroCoOp Project; *Computer Communications*, Vol. 15, No. 8, Oct. 1992, pp. 477-488

IONA (1997): *Orbix - Distributed Object Technology, Programmer's Guide*. - Dublin, IONA Techn.Ltd.1997

ISO (1997): *ODP Trading Function, Part 1; Specification* ISO/IEC IS 13235-1, ITU/T Draft Rec X950 - 1, (1997).

Jacobson, I., Griss, M., Jonson, P. (1997): *Software Reuse*. New York: ACM Press, 1997

Leymann, F.; Roller, D. (1997): Workflow-based applications; *IBM Systems Journal*. Vol. 36 (1997), No. 1 - Application Development, 1997

Mittasch, Ch.; König, W.; Funke, R. (1996a): Trader supported Distributed Office Applications. - *International Conference on Distributed Platforms*, Dresden, 1996, In: Schill, et. al. (Eds.): *Distributed Plattforms Conf. Proceedings*, pp. 230-244, 1996

Mittasch, Irmscher, Ziegert, Müller, Sommerfeld (1996b): Design and Use of BPAFrame - a Decentralized CORBA-based WfMS. *IFIP World Computer Congress*, Canberra, Sept. 1996, In: Terashima, N.; Altman, E. (Eds.): Advanced IT Tools, Chapman & Hall, S. 303-310, 1996

Mohan, C.; Alonso, G.; Günthör, R.; Karnath, M.; Reinwald, B. (1995): An Overview of the Exotica Research Project on Workflow Management Systems. *Proc. 6th Int'l. Workshop on High Transaction Systems*, Asilomar, Sept. 1995

Mohan, C. (1997): Recent Trends in Workflow Management Products, Standards and Research, To appear in *Proc. NATO Advanced Study Institute (ASI) on Workflow Management Systems and Interoperability*, Istanbul, August 1997, Springer Verlag, 1998.

Miller, J.A. et al. (1996): CORBA-Based Runtime Architectures for Workflow Management Systems. *Journal of Database Management*, Special Issue on Multidatabases, vol. 7 (1996), No. 1, pp.16-27

Miller, J., Sheth, A., Kochut, K. and Palaniswami D. (1997), „The Future of Web-Based Workflows," Proc. of the *Int. Workshop on Research Directions in Process Technology*, Nancy, France, July 1997.

Oberweis, A. (1994): Workflow Management in Software Engineering Projects. In: *Proc. of the 2nd Int. Conf. On Concurrent Eng. And Elt. Design Automation*, Bownemouth, UK, 1994.

OMG (1995): *CORBAservices*: Common Object Services Spec. 1995

OMG (1997a): *Workflow Management Facility*, RfP, May, 1997

OMG (1997b) Business Object Domain Task Force: *Workflow Management Facility Submission jFlow*, Nov, 97

OMG (1997c) Business Object Domain Task Force: *Workflow Management Facility Submission Nortel*, Aug. 97

OMG (1997d) Business Object Domain Task Force: *Common Business Objects*. Version 1.3, Nov., 97

Ott, M.; Nastansky, L. (1997): Modelling Organizational Forms of Virtual Enterprises. In: Griese, J.; Sieber, P. (Eds.): *VoNet, The Newsletter Department of Information Management University of Berne*, Vol. 1, No. 4, September 1, 1997, pp. 20-39.

Sheth, A. (1997): From Contemporary Workflow Process Automation to Adaptive and Dynamic Work Activity Coordination and Collaboration. *Ws. on Workflows in Scientific and Eng. Appl.* Toulouse, Sept. 1997

Taylor, D.A (1995): *Business Engineering with Object Technology*. 1995

Workflow Management Coalition (1996a): *WfMC Spec. Terminology and Glossary*. Docu. No WFMC-TC-1011, Issue 2.0, June 1996

Workflow Management Coalition (1994): *The Workflow Reference Model*. TC00-1003, issue 1.1, Nov. 94

Workflow Management Coalition (1995): *Interface 1, Workflow Process Definition Read/Write Interface*: RfC,. WFMC-WG01-1000, Feb 1995

Workflow Management Coalition (1996b): *Interface 4 - Interoperability - Abstract Specification*, WFMC-TC-1012, issue 1.0, Oct. 96

Siemens-Nixdorf (1995): *WorkParty Documentation*, 1995

Weske, M. et al. (1996): Scientific Workflow Management: WASA Architecture and Applications. *Fachbericht Angewandte Mathematik und Informatik* 03/96-I, Universität Münster, 1996

Wodtke, D. et al. (1996): The Mentor Project: Steps Towards Enterprise-Wide Workflow Management. - *ICDE'96*, New Orleans 1996

BIOGRAPHY

Alexander Schill has been a professor for computer networks at Dresden University of Technology since 1993. His major research interests are distributed systems, industry standards for client/server environments, high performance communication and quality of service, and mobile computing. After completing his diploma in Computer Science, he was a research staff member at the University of Karlsruhe, Germany and holds a PhD from this university. Dr. Schill also spent a postdoc research year at the IBM T.J. Watson Research Center, Yorktown Heights, New York. He is the author or co-author of more than 100 publications on computer networking. Currently, he participates in several research cooperations with industry.

Christian Mittasch is currently working as a senior researcher at the computer science department of Freiberg University of Technology and Mining. His major research interests are distributed systems, especially distributed applications development and validation and middleware services. He received the Dr.-Ing. degree in computer science from Dresden University of Technology in 1990.

Session 2

Scalability

A Scalable Middleware Solution for Advanced Wide-Area Web Services

Maarten van Steen, Andrew S. Tanenbaum
Vrije Universiteit, Fac. Math. & Comp. Sc.
De Boelelaan 1081a, 1081 HV Amsterdam
{steen,ast}@cs.vu.nl

Ihor Kuz, Henk J. Sips
Delft University of Technology, Dept. Comp. Sc.
Zuiderplantsoen 4, 2628 BZ Delft
{i.t.kuz,h.j.sips}@cs.tudelft.nl

Abstract

To alleviate scalability problems in the Web, many researchers concentrate on how to incorporate advanced caching and replication techniques. Many solutions incorporate object-based techniques. In particular, Web resources are considered as distributed objects offering a well-defined interface.

We argue that most proposals ignore two important aspects. First, there is little discussion on what kind of coherence should be provided. Proposing specific caching or replication solutions makes sense only if we know what coherence model they should implement. Second, most proposals treat all Web resources alike. Such a one-size-fits-all approach will never work in a wide-area system. We propose a solution in which Web resources are encapsulated in physically distributed shared objects. Each object should not only encapsulate state and operations, but also the policy by which its state is distributed, cached, replicated, migrated, etc.

Keywords

Worldwide scalable middleware, distributed systems, World-Wide Web, distributed Web services

1 INTRODUCTION

As the Web continues to gain popularity, we are increasingly confronted with its limited scalability. Web servers are often unreachable due to an overload of requests for pages. Likewise, we are faced with long downloading times caused by bandwidth limitations and unreliable links. Many of these problems are caused by the growing number of users and the steadily increasing size of resources such as images, audio, and video.

Traditional scaling techniques, such as caching and replication (Neuman, 1994), have been applied as solutions. Unfortunately, inherent to these techniques are *consistency problems*: modifications to one copy of a cached or replicated Web page makes that copy different from the other replicas. Also, most proposals assume that a single consistency model is required and appropriate for all resources. With the large variety of Web pages already existing, and the increasing alternative applications of Web technology, it is clear that such a one-size-fits-all approach will eventually fail. Instead, different consistency models based on the content and semantics of Web resources will need to coexist if we are to solve scalability problems.

Consider, for example, a seldom-accessed personal home page. Caching such a page is hardly effective and doing so simply wastes storage capacity. On the other hand, it could make sense to actively push updates of popular home pages to areas with many clients in order to reduce bandwidth and latency problems. Other examples easily come to mind.

Another problem faced by the Web is its limited flexibility with regards to the introduction of new resources and services. Although nonstandard resources, such as Java applets, have been integrated into the Web, the means by which this is done usually requires a unique solution for each new type of resource. Creating such solutions is not always an easy task, and they are rarely elegant.

It is clear that a different approach is needed to overcome the limited scalability of the current Web. Our starting point is that caching and replication are crucial to scalability, but that effective solutions can be constructed only if we take application-level requirements into account. In this light, we are currently developing an object-based middleware solution called Globe. Key to our approach are physically distributed objects that encapsulate not only state and methods, but also complete distribution policies. In other words, each object in our approach carries its own solution to the distribution of its state, including how that state is partitioned, replicated, migrated, etc. Consequently, all implementation aspects are hidden from clients, who see only the interfaces offered by the object.

By offering a framework that allows us to apply scaling techniques on a per-object basis, we will be able to develop worldwide scalable components from which the next generation of networked applications can be built. To demonstrate the feasibility of our approach, we are currently developing a large-scale, wide-area distributed Web service. The service is transparently distributed across a (potentially large) number of servers in a global network. In this paper we describe Globe and its application to the Web service.

This paper makes two main contributions. First, we show how scalability problems in wide-area systems can be alleviated by a middleware solution in which objects are physically distributed and fully encapsulate their own distribution policy. Second, we describe an alternative organization of Web-based applications that allows us to deal with distributed Web resources in an elegant and scalable way. We also show how our service can be fully integrated into the current Web.

The paper is organized as follows. In Section 2 we describe the basic approach followed in Globe. How Globe can be used to build a wide-area distributed Web service is described in Section 3, which is partly based on our experience with a Java prototype. Related work is described in Section 4; we conclude in Section 5.

2 SCALABLE DISTRIBUTED OBJECTS

2.1 Distributed-Object Technology

An important goal of distributed systems is *distribution transparency*: providing a single-system view despite the distribution of data, processes, and control across multiple machines. Examples include transparency of access, locaton, migration, replication, and persistence. Object technology came into vogue some years ago as the means for realizing transparency in distributed systems. For example, access transparency can be achieved by following an interface-based approach as is in CORBA (OMG, 1997) and ILU (Janssen and Spreitzer, 1996). Likewise, location and migration transparency can be supported by means of forwarding pointers as in the Emerald system (Jul et al., 1988) and more recently in the Voyager toolkit (ObjectSpace, 1997). Finally, seamless integration of object persistence has been investigated for distributed systems such as Spring (Radia et al., 1993).

However, when we take a closer look at the way distribution is actually supported in object-based systems, it appears that objects are used only in a restricted way to address transparency problems. For example, all well-known systems today adopt the remote object model. In this model, an object is located at a single location only, whereas the client is offered access transparency through a proxy interface. At best, the object is allowed to move to other locations without having to explicitly inform the client.

There are a number of serious drawbacks to the remote object model, most notably its lack of scalability. To alleviate scalability problems it is necessary to apply techniques such as caching and replication. This means that multiple copies of the object reside at different locations. Having only a remote invocation mechanism available, we now have to solve the problem how an invocation is to be propagated between the object replicas. Unfortunately, there is no standard solution. For *active replication*, an invocation or the results could be shipped to every replica. In addition, we generally have to implement a total ordering on concurrent invocations. In the case of *passive replication*, update invocations are to be propagated to a master copy only, whereas read invocations can often be performed at backup copies. There are numerous variations on this theme.

The remote object model itself provides no mechanisms that support a developer in designing and implementing different invocation schemes, which is necessary if we are to apply scaling techniques such as caching, replication, and distribution.

2.2 Globe: An Alternative Approach

As an alternative to the remote object model, we have developed a model in which processes interact and communicate through **distributed shared objects**. Like distributed objects in other models, an object offers one or more **interfaces**, each consisting of a set of methods. Objects are passive, but multiple processes may simultaneously access the same object. Changes to the object's state made by one process are visible to the others. However, unlike any other model, a distributed object in Globe is *physically distributed*, meaning that its state may be partitioned and replicated across multiple machines at the same time. Clients of an object are unaware of such a distribution: they see only the interface(s) made available to them by the object.

Besides being physically distributed, each object fully encapsulates its own **distribution policy**. In other words, there is no system-wide policy imposing how an object's state should be distributed and kept consistent. For example, we may have a distributed object whose state is replicated at each client, and where method invocations are forwarded to all clients. Another object may have adopted an approach in which state updates always occur at a master copy and are subsequently shipped to the replicas. Likewise, there may be objects that move their state between locations, have their state highly secured against malicious clients, or keep state at highly fault tolerant servers only. The important thing is that clients need not be aware of such details as they are hidden behind an object's interface.

In order for a process to invoke an object's method, it must first **bind** to that object by contacting it at one of the object's contact points. A **contact address** describes such a contact point, specifying a network address and a protocol through which the binding can take place. Binding results in an interface belonging to the object being placed in the client's address space, along with an implementation of that interface. Such an implementation is called a **local object**. This model is illustrated in Figure 1.

2.2.1 Architecture of a Distributed Shared Object

A local object resides in a single address space and communicates with local objects in other address spaces. Each local object is composed of several subobjects, and is itself again fully self-contained as also shown in Figure 1. Ignoring security issues, a minimal composition consists of the following four subobjects.

Semantics subobject. This is a local subobject that implements (part of) the actual semantics of the distributed object. As such, it encapsulate the functionality of the distributed object. The semantics subobject consists of user-defined primitive ob-

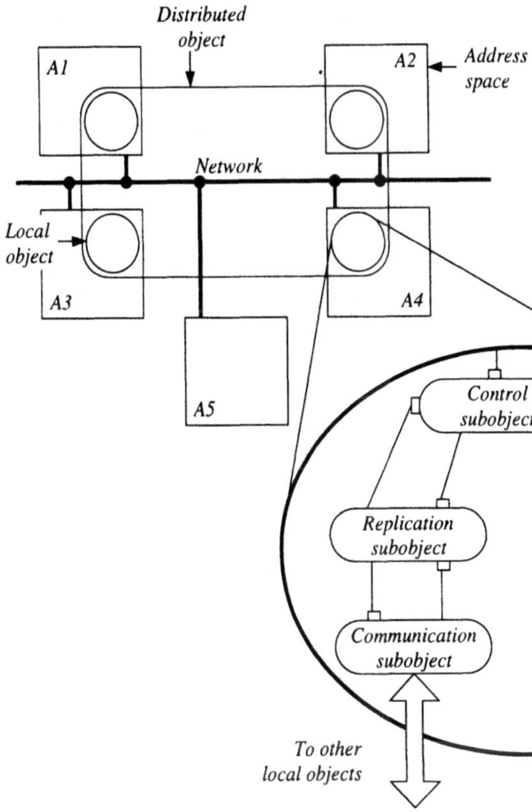

Figure 1 Example of an object distributed across four address spaces.

jects written in programming languages such as Java, C, or C++. These primitive objects can be developed independent of any distribution or scalability issues.

Communication subobject. This is generally a system-provided subobject. It is responsible for handling communication between parts of the distributed object that reside in different address spaces. Depending on what is needed from the other components, a communication subobject may offer primitives for point–to–point communication, multicast facilities, or both.

Replication subobject. The global state of the distributed object is made up of the state of its various semantics subobjects. Semantics subobjects may be replicated for reasons of fault tolerance or performance. In particular, the replication subobject is responsible for keeping these replicas consistent according to some (per-object) coherence strategy. Different distributed objects may have different replication subobjects, using different replication algorithms.

An important observation is that the replication subobject has a standard interface. However, implementations of that interface will generally differ between replication subobjects. In a sense, this subobject behaves as a meta-level object comparable to techniques applied in reflective object-oriented programming.

Control subobject. The control subobject takes care of invocations from client processes, and controls the interaction between the semantics subobject and the replication subobject. This subobject is needed to bridge the gap between the user-defined interfaces of the semantics subobject, and the standard interfaces of the replication subobject.

A key role, of course, is reserved for the replication subobject. An important observation is that communication and replication subobjects are unaware of the methods and state of the semantics subobject. Instead, both the communication subobject and the replication subobject operate only on invocation messages in which method identifiers and parameters have been encoded. This independence allows us to define standard interfaces for all replication subobjects and communication subobjects.

2.2.2 *Client-to-Object Binding*

To communicate with a distributed object, it is necessary for a process to first **bind** to that object. Binding consists roughly of two phases: finding the object, and installing the interface. This process is illustrated in Figure 2.

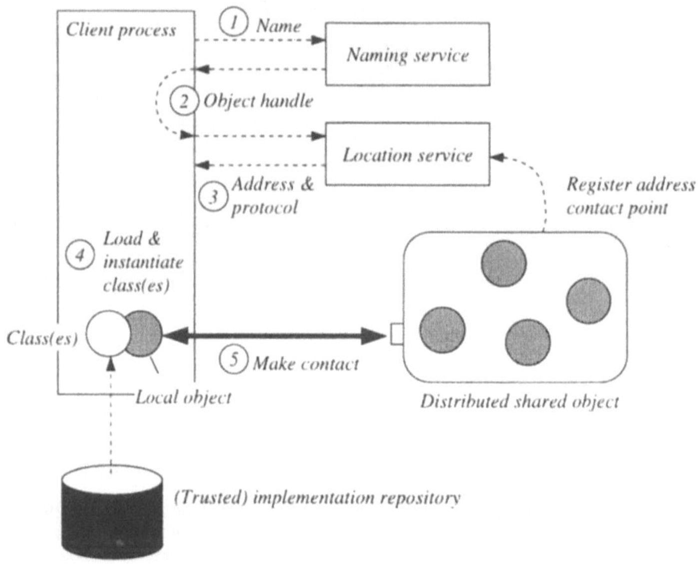

Figure 2 Binding a process to a distributed shared object.

To find an object, a process must pass a name of that object to a naming service that can resolve that name (step ① in Figure 2). The naming service returns an **object handle** (step ②), which is a location-independent and universally unique object identifier, such as a 128-bit number, which is used to locate objects. It can be passed freely between processes as an object reference. The object handle is given to a location service, which returns one or several contact addresses (step ③).

This organization of a naming and a location service allows us to separate issues related to naming objects from those related to contacting objects. In particular, it is now easy to support multiple and independent (human-readable) names for an object, analogous to multiple links to a file name in UNIX. Because an object handle does not change once it has been assigned to an object, a user can easily bind a private, or locally shared name to an object without ever having to worry that the name–to–object binding changes without notice. On the other hand, an object can update its contact addresses at the location service without having to consider under which name it can be reached by its clients. However, we do require a scalable location service that can handle frequent updates of contact addresses in an efficient manner. We have designed such a service (van Steen et al., 1998) and are currently implementing a prototype version that is being tested on the Internet.

Once a process knows where it can contact the distributed object, it needs to select a suitable address from the ones returned by the location service. A contact address may be selected for its locality, but there may also be other criteria for preferring one address over another.

A contact address describes *where* and *how* the requested object can be reached. The latter is contained as protocol information in the contact address. The protocol information is used to load classes from a (trusted) implementation repository, and to subsequently instantiate those classes (step ④ in Figure 2). Finally, the client needs to contact the distributed shared object (step ⑤). The local object implements the interface(s) offered by the distributed shared object.

3 SCALABLE DISTRIBUTED WEB SERVICES

To illustrate how our approach can be applied to solve scalability problems of the World-Wide Web, we are currently developing a Globe-based distributed Web service. In this section we explain how such a service can be designed and implemented using the Globe middleware solution.

3.1 Overview of the Globe Web Service

3.1.1 Globe Web Documents

The essence of a Globe-based Web service is that it allows clients access to Globe Web documents, referred to as GlobeDocs. Conceptually, a **GlobeDoc** is a distributed shared object containing a collection of logically related Web pages. Each page may consist of text, icons, images, sounds, animations, etc., as well as applets, scripts, and other forms of executable code. We refer to these parts as **page elements**. The hyperlinked structure as normally provided by Web pages is maintained in a GlobeDoc. An **internal hyperlink** that is part of some page, refers to a page element on that same page or on another page contained in the same GlobeDoc. An **external hyperlink** refers to a page element of another GlobeDoc.

For simplicity, all pages, page elements, and hyperlinks of a GlobeDoc are col-

Table 1 Interfaces offered by the semantics object of GlobeDocs

Interface	Contains methods for . . .
Document interface	Listing, adding, and removing pages to a GlobeDoc
Page interface	Listing, adding, and removing elements to a page
Content interface	Reading and writing the content of a page
Attribute interface	Attributes of page elements, such as type, last modification date, etc.

lected into a single archive, which is subsequently wrapped into a (nondistributed) semantics subobject. This semantics subobject offers several interfaces as shown in Table 1. In principle, these interfaces are available to each client that is bound to the GlobeDoc. Details on how these interfaces are implemented are described in Section 3.2.

3.1.2 Document Coherence

What makes our approach unique compared to existing Web services, is that each GlobeDoc has its own associated distribution policy. For example, a document containing personal information as in the case of ordinary personal home pages, may support a policy by which updates are always done at a master copy and clients are offered only remote access to that copy. On the other hand, a document consisting of a shared whiteboard may adopt a policy by which each client has local access to a full replica of the whiteboard, and by which updates are immediately propagated to all other clients. Other distribution policies can easily be associated with a document and will generally depend on what, how, and where the document offers functionality to its clients.

For our distributed Web service, we are currently concentrating primarily on scalability. Security issues are subject to present research, of which the results will be incorporated in due time.

Instead of tackling scalability problems by focusing directly on caching and replication, we advocate that it is necessary to concentrate first on coherence issues. Coherence deals with the effect of read and write operations by different clients on a possibly replicated distributed object, as viewed by clients of that object. Caching and replication are part of *coherence protocols*, which implement a specific *coherence model.* In Globe, we distinguish two types of coherence models:

Object-centric coherence models describe the coherence a distributed shared object offers to concurrently operating clients. The models are based on those developed for distributed shared memory systems, and include sequential, PRAM, causal, and eventual consistency (Tanenbaum, 1995).

Client-centric coherence models allow a client to express its own coherence requirements. Our approach here is similar to work done in the Bayou project (Terry et al., 1994). Bayou provides mobile users weak consistency support in a replicated database. We have basically retained their models, which include scenarios for monotonic writes, monotonic reads, writes follow reads, and read your writes.

Details on our support for coherence models are described elsewhere (Kermarrec et al., 1998). Important for our present discussion, is that each GlobeDoc has an associated object-centric coherence model, which is implemented by means of the replication and communication objects described in Section 2.2.1. In addition, implementations are provided to support client-centric coherence models as well.

3.1.3 System Architecture

It is necessary to offer storage facilities for the various components that comprise a document. In particular, being a distributed shared object, a GlobeDoc will generally consist of a number of replicas, each replica located at a different machine. In our model, each replica is kept at a **store**. In principle, clients may perform read and write operations at any store where the document resides, that is where a replica is located. We distinguish three different types of stores:

Permanent stores implement persistence of a GlobeDoc. This means that if there is currently no client bound to the document, the document will be kept only at its associated permanent stores. The permanent stores keep replicas consistent according to the object-centric coherence model that the document offers to its clients. A Web server is an example of a permanent store.

Object-initiated stores are installed as the result of the document's global replication policy. Replicas are kept consistent independent of clients although these stores may, for performance reasons, support a weaker coherence model than the one guaranteed by the permanent stores. A typical example of an object-initiated store is a mirrored Web site.

Client-initiated stores are comparable to caches. They are installed independent of the replication policy of the document and fall under the regime of the client processes that read and update the document. A site-wide cache at a Web proxy is an example of a client-initiated store.

Stores are organized in a layered fashion as shown in Figure 3. This architecture allows us to separate replicas managed by servers (permanent and object-initiated stores) from those managed by clients (client-initiated stores). Whereas permanent stores must implement a document's coherence model, object-initiated and client-initiated stores may offer weaker coherence, but perhaps offering the benefit of higher performance. Effectively, for some applications, some delay in propagating a change is often acceptable. It is generally up to the client to decide to which replica it will bind.

3.1.4 Integration with the Current Web

It is important that GlobeDocs are integrated into the current Web infrastructure such that they can be accessed and manipulated by existing tools such as browsers. Our approach is to use a filtering gateway that communicates with standard Web clients (e.g. browsers). The main purpose of the gateway is to allow standard Web clients

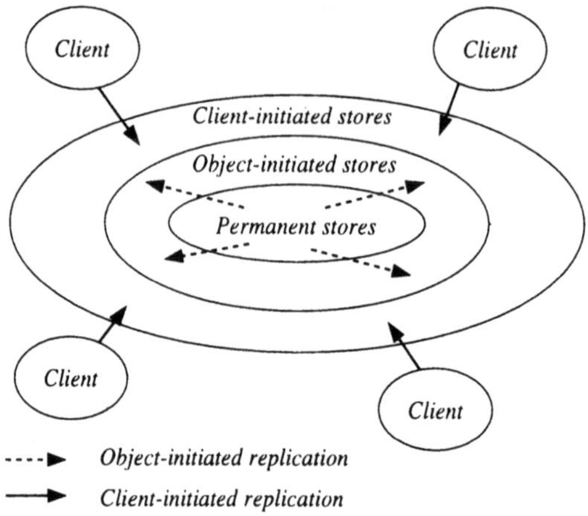

Figure 3 A system model for replicated Globe Web documents (GlobeDocs).

that communicate through HTTP, to access GlobeDocs. The gateway is a process that runs on a local server machine and accepts regular HTTP requests for a document. In our model, GlobeDocs are distinguished from other Web resources through naming. A Globe name is written as a **Globe URL**, that is a URL with globe as scheme identifier. So, for example, globe://cs.vu.nl/~steen/globe/ could be the name of our project's home document, constructed as a distributed shared object.

The gateway accepts all URLs. Normal URLs are simply passed to existing (proxy) servers, whereas Globe URLs are used to actually bind to the named distributed shared object. Because most browsers cannot handle extensions to the URL name space, we are forced to build a front end that translates Globe URLs to a form that is embedded in an HTTP URL. For example, globe://cs.vu.nl/~steen/globe/ is embedded into the HTTP URL http://globe.cs.vu.nl/~steen/globe/. When a Globe URL is passed to the gateway, the gateway binds to the GlobeDoc named by that URL, and passes the document's state in HTML form to the browser. In this way clients are unaware of the fact that they have actually accessed a distributed shared object.

The drawback of this approach is that we are constrained to the functionality of Web clients. In particular, this means that it may be hard to support GlobeDocs containing interactive parts. Ideally, we can make use of extensible browsers that can dynamically download the necessary support code for actually binding to distributed shared objects and subsequently presenting the object's interfaces to the user. Unfortunately, such browsers are not commonly available.

However, it is realistic to assume that Web clients support Java. In that case, a GlobeDoc having interactive content should provide a Java applet that can be downloaded into the client's browser, and which subsequently presents the object's interfaces in any way that is felt appropriate by the developer of the document. Effectively, we are extending the distributed shared object to the Web client by means of a simple Java applet instead of using a Globe local object. This situation is shown in Figure 4, and is the approach followed in our prototype.

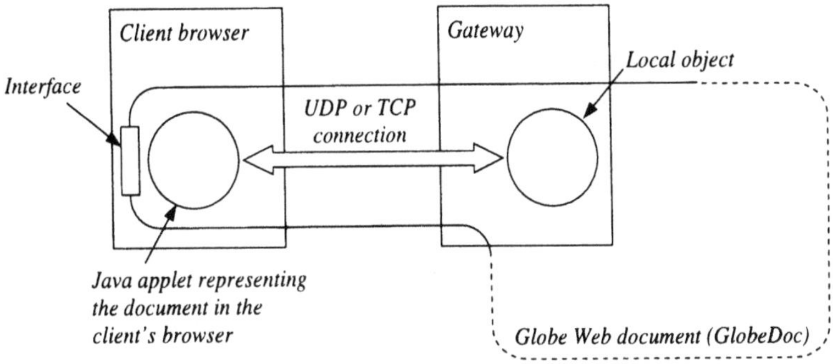

Figure 4 Using Java-enabled browsers to interface to interactive GlobeDocs.

3.2 Constructing a GlobeDoc

There are many ways to actually construct a GlobeDoc and make it available as a distributed shared object. In the following, we outline a solution which we are currently deploying.

3.2.1 Constructing the First Replica

Completely analogous to the construction of Web pages, a GlobeDoc is constructed by first providing all the necessary content. This includes HTML files containing hyperlinks, files containing executable code, files for images, audio, etc. All these content files are then collected into a **state archive**. Effectively, a state archive is a structured representation of the information offered by a document. In our initial set-up, a state archive is transferred as a whole to clients, although it will also be possible to transfer only those parts that a client needs.

Besides providing the state archive, a developer will also construct definitions of the interfaces containing the methods that give access to a document's content. In the case that the GlobeDoc consists of only noninteractive data, such as HTML text, animations, etc., we envisage that all interfaces and their implementations can be generated automatically from the archive. For interactive parts, such as editors, spreadsheets, whiteboards, and calculators, a developer explicitly specifies interfaces in the Globe Interface Definition Language (Globe IDL). Note that a developer may provide several implementations of the same interface. For example, clients of a document containing a calculator, may be offered a choice between an interpreted and a compiled version.

A state archive combined with the appropriate interfaces and their implementations, is in fact a semantics object. We separate the interfaces and implementations from the actual state, by collecting the former in a **class archive**. A class archive not only contains implementations, but also identifies how those implementations are to be (down)loaded by a client.

Taking the interface definitions of the semantics subobject, we then generate one or more implementations for the control subobject, and add those to the class archive.

The next important step is to select an object-centric coherence model for the

GlobeDoc, and add implementations for the replication and communication subobject of that model to the class archive. In addition, implementations of the client-centric coherence models that will be supported also are added to the class archive. We envisage that a developer will generally choose default implementations provided as part of the development kit for documents, and possibly fine-tune those to specific requirements. However, there is nothing that prevents a developer from providing his own implementation of a coherence model.

As we have described so far, a Web document consists of a separate state and class archive. Of course, it is also possible to construct more than one state or class archive, or alternatively to combine them into a single archive. For our present discussion we ignore such alternatives.

3.2.2 Making a GlobeDoc Worldwide Available

Having state and class archives allows us to actually construct a distributed shared object to which clients can bind. First, we make the class archive available by storing it in one or more **implementation repositories**. Such a repository can be as simple as an ftp-able file system, or as sophisticated as a worldwide distributed database. We assume that when a class archive is stored, the repository returns an **implementation handle** that can be uniquely resolved to the archive. We return to this aspect below.

The state and class archives are initially combined at one permanent store, where the first replica is subsequently instantiated. The store returns a network address that can be used to contact the replica. If the store is willing to make the class archive available as well, that is it willing to act also as an implementation repository, it will additionally return an implementation handle. At this point, we have actually created a distributed shared object. More replicas can be registered at other permanent stores, provided those stores cooperate in keeping the replicas consistent. In principle, this requires the stores to run the implementation of the coherence model as contained in the class archive forming part of the replica.

The distributed shared object is registered at the Globe location service, which subsequently returns an object handle. A network address that has been returned by a permanent store, is taken together with one or more implementation handles as returned by the repositories, to form a contact address. Note that the implementation handles implicitly describe the protocol by which the object can be contacted. These contact addresses are subsequently inserted into the location service so that they can be looked up by clients. The final step consists of registering the object handle at one or more (worldwide) naming services.

3.3 Client-to-Document Binding

Binding a client to a GlobeDoc is now fairly straightforward. We first describe the simple binding process in which a client contacts a document at one of its permanent stores. We then proceed by explaining how client-initiated stores, such as caches, can be used.

3.3.1 Simple Binding through Permanent Stores

After looking up a contact address for a document through the naming and location service, a client passes the implementation handles contained in that contact address to a local **implementation service**. This service is responsible for selecting and downloading an appropriate implementation. An implementation may not be appropriate for several reasons. For example, the client or the local implementation service may require that an implementation has been certified by a specific authority. Another possible reason is that an implementation does not match the architecture of the client machine, or that specific libraries are not available.

An implementation handle implicitly refers to the repository where the class archive is stored. In the case of simple repositories, such as an ftp-able file system, the implementation handle may consist of an IP address and a pathname identifying the class archive. More sophisticated solutions exist as well. For example, an object-oriented database may offer a front end to its clients in the form of a distributed shared object. In that case, an implementation handle may contain an object handle that is to be resolved to a contact address for that front end. The local implementation service must then first bind to the front end following the complete binding procedure as described in Section 2.2.2.

After an implementation has been selected and the client has loaded the class archive into its address space, the implementations (i.e., classes and objects) are instantiated, followed by a preliminary initialization by means of the network address that was part of the contact address. The client has now set up a connection to the replica through the permanent store. The store, in turn, activates the replica, after which the necessary state as contained in the state archive is shipped to the client.

3.3.2 Advanced Binding: Selecting a Store

A client should also be allowed to cache GlobeDocs independently of the object-centric coherence model offered by that document. In case caching is to be done at the client only, we can basically follow the approach for binding through a permanent store. The client need only provide an implementation for locally storing its copy of the docment's semantics object.

Making use of a proxy cache, as is common for many client Web sites, is somewhat more intricate. We have adopted the following model. A process, called a **cache manager** that is prepared to offer caching facilities registers itself as a **cache manager object** at the Globe location service. A cache manager object is just a distributed shared object whose contact address is made only locally available by the location service. A client process wishing to bind to a GlobeDoc using local caching facilities, simply passes the document's object handle to the location service, indicating that it is also prepared to accept contact addresses of local, site-wide cache manager objects.

When a contact address is returned, the client binds to the object associated with the contact address, as usual. The contact address indicates whether the client is binding to a cache manager object, or to the GlobeDoc. In the former case, the client passes the document's object handle to the cache manager object. The cache manager, in turn, will bind to the GlobeDoc at one of the document's contact addresses.

When the cache manager is bound to the GlobeDoc, it inserts one or more local contact addresses for the document at the location service. The client that originally initiated the binding process is now instructed to bind to the document at an address offered by the cache manager, and to unbind from the cache manager object.

Note that after the cache manager is bound to the GlobeDoc, subsequent clients can bind directly to the document through its local contact address(es) as inserted into the location service by the cache manager. There is no need to bind to the cache manager object as before.

4 RELATED WORK

To alleviate scalability problems in the Web, research has mainly concentrated on traditional caching techniques. Replication has been applied in the form of mirroring popular Web sites. Recently, it has been recognized that more advanced forms of caching and replication are needed. Wessels (1995) proposes to allow servers to grant or deny a client permission to cache a resource. Push-caching (Gwertzman and Seltzer, 1996) allows popular resources to be optimally distributed to other servers based on knowledge of the resource's access patterns. In a similar fashion, Baentsch et al. (1997) propose a replication scheme in which replicas are pushed to a collection of replication servers, and in which clients locate the nearest server for downloading a Web page. Harvest caches (Chankhunthod et al., 1995) provide a hierarchically organized solution, and are currently gaining popularity in the Web. Yet another approach is to use the facilities of large-scale distributed file systems, such as in the case of AFS (Spasojevic et al., 1994).

Research has also concentrated on replication schemes for specific classes of Web resources. For example, the distribution point model (Donnelley, 1995) is tailored to active replication of relatively static sets of bulk, non real-time data. It is mainly applicable to magazine-like Web documents such as those that appear as electronic periodical publications.

Hardly any proposals exist that allow each resource to have its own replication scheme. In the Bayou system a mobile client can specify coherence requirements for data that is replicated and distributed across multiple servers (Terry et al., 1994; Petersen et al., 1996). We have adopted some of the results of the Bayou project in our own work. In the W3Objects system, Web resources are encapsulated into distributed objects that can have their own replication scheme (Ingham et al., 1995). Their model is strongly based on the notion of remote objects, which we argue is less flexible than a model in which objects can be truly physically distributed. Also, where we strive for distribution transparency, the developers of the W3Objects system aim at a highly visible caching mechanism.

In general, much work is currently being done to incorporate CORBA and similar distributed object technologies into the Web. It is especially the combination of

Java and CORBA that is receiving much attention. These approaches hardly tackle the problem of scalability, and do not provide solutions for caching, replication and consistency. In this respect, a perhaps more interesting development is the proposed HTTP-ng protocol, the goal of which is to present a new object-based protocol for the Web. In particular, HTTP-ng will allow clients and servers to specify options for caching individual Web pages.

A solution that comes close to ours is the work based on fragmented objects (Makpangou et al., 1994). Fragmented objects, like Globe's distributed shared objects, are physically distributed across multiple machines, encapsulating their own distribution policy. However, fragmented objects have not been designed for worldwide scalability and do not address caching and replication as we do.

5 FUTURE RESEARCH

We have presented Globe's distributed shared objects, in the form of GlobeDocs, as a solution to a number of the Web's scalability problems. A GlobeDoc is a physically distributed object encapsulating one or more Web resources. Each document takes care of its own distribution issues such as caching, replication, consistency, and communication. In addition, our approach provides a flexible and extensible approach for implementing future Web resources.

To assess our research, we have developed a simple prototype implementation of a Globe distributed Web service in Java. The main purpose of this prototype was to obtain feedback on the feasibility of our approach, and also to gain insight in possible implementations. Currently, we are developing a toolkit in Java that will allow us to more easily construct the GlobeDocs as described in this paper.

There are still a number of open issues that we need to address. We are investigating how we can incorporate security into our framework such that security policies can be attached to individual GlobeDocs in a similar fashion as distribution policies. Also, more research is needed with respect to different caching and replication policies, and how policies can be implemented efficiently in a worldwide system. With respect to Globe-based distributed Web services, we also need support for partitioning and distributing state archives, as well as user-oriented tools that replace much of the manual construction of GlobeDocs.

REFERENCES

Baentsch, M., Baum, L., Molter, G., Rothkugel, S., and Sturm, P. "Enhancing the Web's Infrastructure: From Caching to Replication". *IEEE Internet Comput.*, 1(2):18–27, Mar. 1997.

Chankhunthod, A., Danzig, P., Neerdaels, C., Schwartz, M., and Worrell, K. "A Hierarchical Internet Object Cache". Technical Report CU-CS-766-95, Department of Computer Science, University of Colorado – Boulder, Mar. 1995.

Donnelley, J. "WWW Media Distribution via Hopwise Reliable Multicast". *Comp. Netw. ISDN Syst.*, 27(6):781–788, 1995.

Gwertzman, J. and Seltzer, M. "The Case for Geographical Push-Caching". In *Proc. Fifth HOTOS*, Orcas Island, WA, May 1996. IEEE.

Ingham, D., Little, M., Caughey, S., and Shrivastava, S. "W3Objects: Bringing Object-Oriented Technology To The Web". *The Web Journal*, (1):89–105, 1995.

Janssen, B. and Spreitzer, M. *ILU Reference Manual.* Xerox Corporation, May 1996.

Jul, E., Levy, H., Hutchinson, N., and Black, A. "Fine-Grained Mobility in the Emerald System". *ACM Trans. Comp. Syst.*, 6(1):109–133, Feb. 1988.

Kermarrec, A., Kuz, I., van Steen, M., and Tanenbaum, A. "A Framework for Consistent, Replicated Web Objects". In *Proc. 18th Int'l Conf. on Distributed Computing Systems*, pp. 276–284, Amsterdam, The Netherlands, May 1998. IEEE.

Makpangou, M., Gourhant, Y., Le Narzul, J.-P., and Shapiro, M. "Fragmented Objects for Distributed Abstractions". In Casavant, T. and Singhal, M. (eds.), *Readings in Distributed Computing Systems*, pp. 170–186. IEEE Computer Society Press, Los Alamitos, CA., 1994.

Neuman, B. "Scale in Distributed Systems". In Casavant, T. and Singhal, M. (eds.), *Readings in Distributed Computing Systems*, pp. 463–489. IEEE Computer Society Press, Los Alamitos, CA., 1994.

ObjectSpace Inc. *Voyager User Guide*, July 1997. http://www.objectspace.com/.

OMG. "The Common Object Request Broker: Architecture and Specification, revision 2.1". OMG Document 97.09.01, Object Management Group, Aug. 1997.

Petersen, K., Spreitzer, M., Terry, D., and Theimer, M. "Bayou: Replicated Database Services for World-wide Applications". In *Proc. Seventh SIGOPS European Workshop*, pp. 275–280, Connemara, Ireland, Sept. 1996. ACM.

Radia, S., Madnay, P., and Powell, M. "Persistence in the Spring System". In *Proc. Third Int'l Workshop on Object Orientation in Operating Systems*, Asheville, North Carolina, Dec. 1993. IEEE.

Spasojevic, M., Bowman, M., and Spector, A. "Using a Wide-Area File System Within the World-Wide Web". *Comp. Netw. ISDN Syst.*, 26, 1994.

Tanenbaum, A. *Distributed Operating Systems.* Prentice Hall, Englewood Cliffs, N.J., 1995.

Terry, D. B., Demers, A. J., Petersen, K., Spreitzer, M. J., Theimer, M. M., and Welsh, B. B. "Session Guarantees for Weakly Consistent Replicated Data". In *Proc. Third Int'l Conf. on Parallel and Distributed Information Systems*, pp. 140–149, Austin, TX, Sept. 1994. IEEE.

van Steen, M., Hauck, F., Homburg, P., and Tanenbaum, A. "Locating Objects in Wide-Area Systems". *IEEE Commun. Mag.*, 36(1):104–109, Jan. 1998.

Wessels, D. "Intelligent Caching for World-Wide Web Objects". In *Proc. INET '95*, Honolulu, Hawaii, June 1995. Internet Society.

BIOGRAPHY

Maarten van Steen is assistant professor at the Vrije Universiteit in Amsterdam since 1994. He received an M.Sc. in Applied Mathematics from Twente University (1983) and a Ph.D. in Computer Science from Leiden University (1988). He has worked at an industrial research laboratory for several years in the field of parallel programming environments. His research interests include distributed-software engineering, operating systems, computer networks, and distributed systems. Van Steen is a member of IEEE Computer Society and ACM.

Andrew S. Tanenbaum has an S.B. from M.I.T. and a Ph.D. from the University of California at Berkeley. He is currently a Professor of Computer Science at the Vrije Universiteit in Amsterdam and Dean of the interuniversity computer science graduate school, ASCI. Prof. Tanenbaum is the principal designer of three operating systems: TSS-11, Amoeba, and MINIX. He was also the chief designer of the Amsterdam Compiler Kit. In addition, Tanenbaum is the author of five books and over 80 refereed papers. He is a Fellow of ACM, a Fellow of IEEE, and a member of the Royal Dutch Academy of Sciences. In 1994 he was the recipient of the ACM Karl V. Karlstrom Outstanding Educator Award and in 1997 he won the SIGCSE award for contributions to computer science.

Ihor Kuz has an M.Sc. in Computer Science (1996) from the Vrije Universiteit in Amsterdam. He is currently a Ph.D. student at the Delft University of Technology, doing research in the field of worldwide scalable distributed Web services. His research interests include operating systems, scalable distributed systems, and Web-based technologies.

Henk J. Sips received his M.Sc. degree in 1976 in electrical engineering and his Ph.D. in 1984 from Delft University of Technology. Currently, he is Professor in Parallel and Distributed Systems at Delft University. His research interest include computer architecture, parallel programming, parallel algorithms, and distributed systems. He is member of IEEE and ACM.

A Gossip-Style Failure Detection Service

*Robbert van Renesse, Yaron Minsky, and Mark Hayden**
Dept. of Computer Science, Cornell University
4118 Upson Hall, Ithaca, NY 14853

Abstract

Failure Detection is valuable for system management, replication, load balancing, and other distributed services. To date, Failure Detection Services scale badly in the number of members that are being monitored. This paper describes a new protocol based on gossiping that does scale well and provides timely detection. We analyze the protocol, and then extend it to discover and leverage the underlying network topology for much improved resource utilization. We then combine it with another protocol, based on broadcast, that is used to handle partition failures.

1 INTRODUCTION

Accurate failure detection in asynchronous (non-realtime) distributed systems is notoriously difficult. In such a system, a process may appear failed because it is slow, or because the network connection to it is slow or even partitioned. Because of this, several impossibility results have been found (Chandra, Hadzilacos, Toueg & Charron-Bost 1996, Fischer, Lynch & Patterson 1985).

---

*This work is supported in part by ARPA/ONR grant N00014-92-J-1866, ARPA/RADC grant F30602-96-1-0317 and AFOSR grant F49620-94-1-0198. The views and conclusions contained herein are those of the authors and should not be interpreted as necessarily representing the official policies or endorsements, either expressed or implied, of these organizations or the U.S. Government.
The current address of Mark Hayden is DEC SRC, 130 Lytton Ave., Palo Alto, CA.

In systems that have to make minimal progress even in the face of process failures, it is still important to try to determine if a process is reachable or not. False detections are allowable as long as they are reasonable with respect to performance. That is, it is acceptable to report an exceedingly slow process, or a badly connected one, as failed. Unfortunately, when scaled up to more than several dozens of members, many failure detectors are either unreasonably slow, or make too many false detections. Although we are not aware of any publications about this, we know this from experiences with our own Isis, Horus, and Ensemble systems (van Renesse, Birman, Hayden, Vaysburd & Karr 1998, van Renesse, Birman & Maffeis 1996, Vogels 1996), as well as from experiences with Transis (Amir, Dolev, Kramer & Malkhi 1992).

In this paper, we present a failure detector based on random gossiping that has, informally, the following properties:

1. the probability that a member is falsely reported as having failed is independent of the number of processes.
2. the algorithm is resilient against both message loss (or rather, message delivery timing failures) and process failures, in that a small percentage of lost (or late) messages or small percentage of failed members does not lead to false detections.
3. if local clock drift is negligible, the algorithm detects all failures or unreachabilities accurately with known probability of mistake.
4. the algorithm scales in detection time, in that the detection time increases $O(n \log n)$ with the number of processes.
5. the algorithm scales in network load, in that the required bandwidth goes up at most linearly with the number of processes. For large networks, the bandwidth used in the subnets is approximately constant.

The protocol makes minimal assumptions about the network. There is no bound on message delivery time, and indeed messages may be lost altogether. We *do* assume that most message are delivered within some predetermined, reasonable time. Processes may crash or become unreachable. We assume a fail-stop rather than a Byzantine failure model, which basically means that processes do not lie about what they know. (The actual implementation uses checksums and other sanity checks on messages to approximate the fail-stop model as closely as possible.) We also assume that the clock rate on each host is close to accurate (low drift), but do not assume that they are synchronized. The basic version of the failure detector will place a limit on how many hosts may become unreachable. The final version will drop this limitation, and will tolerate arbitrary crashes and network partitions.

In our protocol, each host in the network runs a failure detector process that executes the protocol and offers continuous process failure and recovery reports to interested clients..Output from one of the failure detector processes in our department is used to generate and automatically update the web page*, which gives an overview of our department's network status, and a log of recent activity on it. We

* http://www.cs.cornell.edu/home/rvr/mbrship.html

view the failure detector as a middleware service. Other middleware services, such as system management, replication, load balancing, group communication services, and various consensus algorithms that rely on reasonably accurate failure detection (Chandra, Hadzilacos & Toueg 1992), can use the failure detection service to optimize their performance in the face of failures.

Approaches based on hierarchical, tree-based protocols have the potential to be more efficient than the ones described in this paper. However, we are not aware of publications describing any such protocols. Having tried to build one, we believe this is because tree-based failure detector protocols require complex agreement protocols to construct the tree and repair it as failures occur. Gossip protocols do not have this problem, and in fact one of their important advantages is their simplicity.

In this paper, we first present a simple protocol that assumes a uniform network topology, as well as a bounded number of host crashes. We analyze this protocol in Section 3. In Section 4, we extend the protocol to discover some information about the actual network topology and to use this information to optimize network resources. Section 5 presents another protocol that, when combined with gossiping, deals with arbitrary host failures and partitions.

2 BASIC PROTOCOL

The basic protocol is simple. It is based on gossiping as pioneered in the Clearinghouse project (Demers, Greene, Hauser, Irish, Larson, Shenker, Sturgis, Swinehart & Terry 1987). Long before that, Baker and Shostak (Baker & Shostak 1972) describe a gossip protocol, using *ladies* and *telephones* in the absence of the widespread availability of computers and networks. In gossip protocols, a member forwards new information to randomly chosen members. Gossip combines much of the efficiency of hierarchical dissemination with much of the robustness of flooding protocols (in which a member sends new information to all of its neighbors). In the case of Clearinghouse directories, it was used to resolve inconsistencies. Our protocol gossips to figure out whom else is still gossiping.

Each member maintains a list with for each known member its address and an integer which is going to be used for failure detection. We call the integer the *heartbeat counter*. Every T_{gossip} seconds, each member increments its own heartbeat counter, and selects one other member at random to send its list to. Upon receipt of such a *gossip* message, a member merges the list in the message with its own list, and adopts the maximum heartbeat counter for each member.

Each member occasionally broadcasts its list in order to be located initially and also to recover from network partitions (see Section 5). In the absence of a broadcast capability, the network could be equiped with a few *gossip servers*, that differ from other members only in that they are hosted at well known addresses, and placed so that they are unlikely to be unavailable due to network partitioning.

Each member also maintains, for each other member in the list, the last time that its corresponding heartbeat counter has increased.* If the heartbeat counter has not increased for more than T_{fail} seconds, then the member is considered failed. T_{fail} is selected so that the probability that anybody makes an erroneous failure detection is less than some small threshold $P_{mistake}$.

After a member is considered faulty, it cannot immediately be forgotten about. The problem is that not all members will detect failures at the same time, and thus a member A may receive a gossip about another member B that A has previously detected as faulty. If A had forgotten about B, it would reinstall B in its membership list, since A would think that it was seeing B's heartbeat for the first time. A would continue to gossip this information on to other members, and, in effect, the faulty member B never quite disappears from the membership.

Therefore, the failure detector does not remove a member from its membership list until after $T_{cleanup}$ seconds ($T_{cleanup} \geq T_{fail}$). $T_{cleanup}$ is chosen so that the probability that a gossip is received about this member, after it has been detected as faulty, is less than some small threshold $P_{cleanup}$. We can make $P_{cleanup}$ equal to P_{fail} by setting $T_{cleanup}$ to $2 \times T_{fail}$.

To see why, let B be some failed member, and consider another member A that heard B's last heartbeat at time t. With probability P_{fail}, every other member will have heard B's last heartbeat by $t + T_{fail}$, and so every process will fail B by time $t + 2 \times T_{fail}$. Thus, if we set $T_{cleanup}$ to $2 \times T_{fail}$, then with probability P_{fail}, no failed member will ever reappear on A's list of members once that member has been removed.

Note that this protocol only detects hosts that become entirely unreachable. It does not detect link failures between hosts. In particular, if hosts A and B cannot talk to each other, but they can both communicate with some other host C, A will not suspect B nor the other way around. When these kinds of partial connectivity occur commonly throughout the systems, the protocol may cycle through adding and removing hosts. However, the dynamic Internet routing protocols should eventually take care of the problem.

In Section 4 we will extend this protocol to scale well in the Internet. This requires that part of the network topology is discovered, which we accomplish through gossiping as well. First, we will analyze the basic protocol to come up with a reasonable value for T_{fail}.

3 ANALYSIS

In order to find suitable parameters for the basic protocol, in particular the rate of gossiping and T_{fail}, it is necessary to understand how these parameters affect the probability of a false detection. In this section, we analyze the protocol for a system in which the population of processes is static (that is, no new processes are added),

*It is possible that the heartbeat counter overflows, so it is necessary to use a *window* such as used in sliding window protocols.

and known to all members. The discovery of new members only poses a problem when a large number of new members join at once, since that would lengthen the time it takes for the dissemination of information, and would potentially cause processes that have not yet learned of the enlarged membership to suspect other processes falsely. Section 5 discusses the behavior of the system in situations with sharp changes in membership.

The probabilities involved in gossiping can be calculated using epidemic theory (Bailey 1975, Demers et al. 1987, Golding & Taylor 1992, Birman, Hayden, Ozkasap, Budiu & Minsky 1998). A typical way of doing this is using stochastic analysis based on the assumption that the execution is broken up into synchronous rounds, during which every process gossips once. A member that has new information is called *infected.* For analysis, initially only one member is infected, and this is the only source of infection in the system, even though in reality new information may be introduced at multiple processes at once. At each round the probability that a certain number of members is infected given the number of already infected members is calculated. This is done for each number of infected members. Allowing all members to gossip in each round makes this analysis stochastically very complex, and usually approximations and/or upper bounds are used instead.

This section suggests a simplified analysis that we believe may be more accurate to boot. In practice, the protocols are not run in rounds. Each member gossips at regular intervals, but the intervals are not synchronized. The time for propagation of a gossip message is typically much shorter than the length of these intervals. We therefore define a different concept of round, in which only one (not necessarily infected) member is gossiping. The member is chosen at random and chooses one other member to gossip to at random. Thus, in a round, the number of infected members can grow by at most one, which is what simplifies the analysis.

Let n be the total number of members, k_i be the number of infected members in round i, and $P_{arrival}$ be the probability that a gossip successfully arrives at a chosen member before the start of the next round. (Actually, the probability can be chosen less conservatively, since all that is required is that the gossip arrives at the member before it itself gossips next.) The probability $P_{arrival}$ is independent for each message. Note that if the system behaves better than $P_{arrival}$ (for instance if no messages are dropped), then the protocol becomes more efficient. Initially, only one member p is infected. We assume that no more than f members fail.

For simplicity, we assume, conservatively, that all f members have failed at the beginning of the protocol. They are gossiped to, but they cannot pass gossips on. This way the number of infected members cannot shrink. We also assume that the initially infected member does not fail.* If k out of n members are infected already,

*We believe this assumption will not affect the outcome by more than one round. For it to be more than one, the initially infected member would have to gossip, then crash, and the next infected member would have to do the same thing again.

then the probability that the number of infected members is incremented in a round is

$$P_{inc}(k) = (k/n) \times \frac{n-f-k}{n-1} \times P_{arrival} \quad (1)$$

Therefore, the probability that the number of infected members in round $i+1$ is k $(0 < k \leq n-f)$ is

$$P(k_{i+1} = k) = P_{inc}(k-1) \times P(k_i = k-1) + (1 - P_{inc}(k)) \times P(k_i = k) \quad (2)$$

(with $P(k_i = 0) = 0$, $P(k_0 = 1) = 1$ and $P(k_0 = k) = 0$ for $k \neq 1$).

Then, the probability that any process does not get infected by p after r rounds is $P_{mistake}(p,r) = 1 - P(k_r = n - f)$. To find $P_{mistake}(r)$, which is the probability that any process is not infected by any other process, we need to range over all members. For any two processes p and q, $P_{mistake}(p,r)$ and $P_{mistake}(q,r)$ are not independent. We will bound $P_{mistake}(r)$ using the Inclusion-Exclusion Principle (Kozen 1991): $Pr(\cup_i A_i) \leq \sum_i Pr(A_i)$. Using this principle, we can bound $P_{mistake}(r)$ as follows:

$$P_{mistake}(r) \leq (n-f)P_{mistake}(p,r) = (n-f)(1 - P(k_r = n-f)) \quad (3)$$

From this we can calculate how many rounds are needed to achieve a certain quality of detection. (The calculation is best done not recursively, such as suggested here, but iteratively starting at the first round. Even then, it is costly. In (van Renesse, Minsky & Hayden 1998) we present an alternative analysis that works well if the number of members is at least about 50, and that can be calculated more easily.)

Next, we calculate how often members should gossip so that worst-case bandwidth use is linear in the number of members. Say that each member is allowed to send B bytes/second, and that 8 bytes per member are necessary in each gossip message (6 bytes for the address, and 2 bytes for the heartbeat counter). From this, the interval between gossips, T_{gossip} has to be $8n/B$ seconds. If n is small and B is large, then we may wish to place a minimum on T_{gossip}, since we assume that the common communication delay is less than T_{gossip}. (In the case of a pure switched network, as opposed to a broadcast-based network such as an Ethernet, the bandwidth per link will only be 2B bytes per second, independent of the number of members. Still, the total load on the switches increases with the number of members.) Note that members will receive, on average, B bytes/second worth of gossip information as a result, limiting the incurred overhead of the protocol.

We are interested in the time that it takes to reach a certain low probability p of a false failure detection being made. By iterating $P_{mistake}$, we can find how many rounds this takes, and multiply this by T_{gossip}. We have plotted this for different values of n, $P_{mistake}$, and $f = 1$, in Figure 1. The near-linearity in n can be confirmed visually. In actuality, the growth of the curve is $O(n \log n)$, because the number of

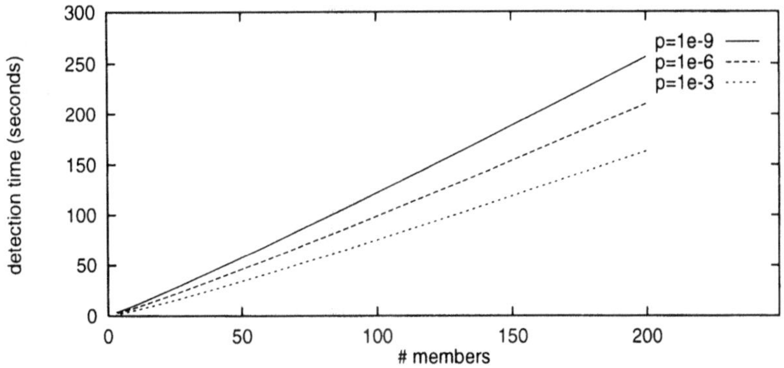

Figure 1 This graph depicts the failure detection time for three different mistake probabilities ($p = P_{mistake}$). The bandwidth per member is 250 bytes per second, and one member has failed. The protocol has $O(n \log n)$ behavior, which appears as being approximately linear in the graph.

rounds increases logarithmically with the number of members and the spacing between rounds linearly.

Readers familiar with other presentations on gossip protocols may be disappointed, and expected to see much better than linear degradation in detection time. The reason for this is that much other gossip work either disseminated information that did not grow linearly with the number of members, or were only interested in message complexity, not in the bandwidth taken up by the messages. In our work, we decided to slow gossiping down linearly with the number of members because of the growing message size, which introduces a linear factor into our detection time.

There is a trade-off between minimizing the probability of making a false detection, and the failure detection time. In Figure 2 we show that this trade-off is satisfactory, in that little extra time is necessary for better quality.

Next, we look into the resilience of the protocol against process failures. Obviously, if many members fail, many gossips will be wasted, and it will take longer to distribute new heartbeat counters. We show this effect in Figure 3. Notice that even if we assume that half of the members can fail, it takes less than twice as long to detect a failure than if we had assumed that no members would fail. This is because if half of the processes fail, then half of the gossips will be wasted, which is roughly equivalent to gossiping half as often. In general, it is easy to show that allowing for the failure of a fraction p of the members will increase the detection time by approximately $1/(1-p)$. Thus, the detection time begins to rise rapidly as p becomes larger than one half (note that the y-axes in this graph is logarithmic).

Therefore, in case of a network partition in which a small subgroup of members can get partitioned from a large group, the basic gossip algorithm does not perform satisfactorily (from the viewpoint of the small subgroup). For any reasonable detection time, the members of the subgroup will presume each other faulty because they are unlikely to gossip to each other. Section 5 presents a solution for this.

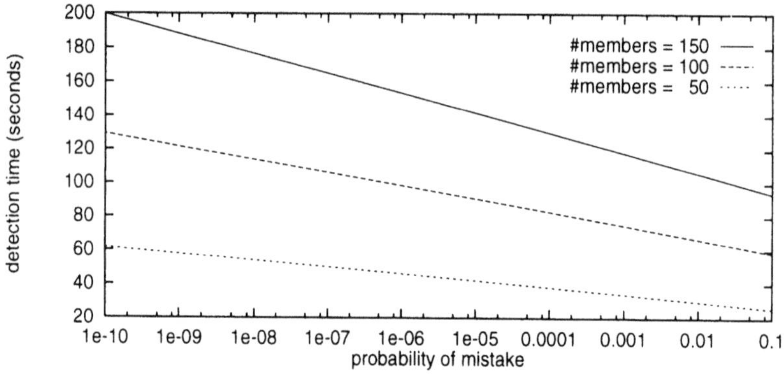

Figure 2 This graph shows the cost of quality of detection. Note that the x scale is logarithmic, thus the cost for better quality is excellent.

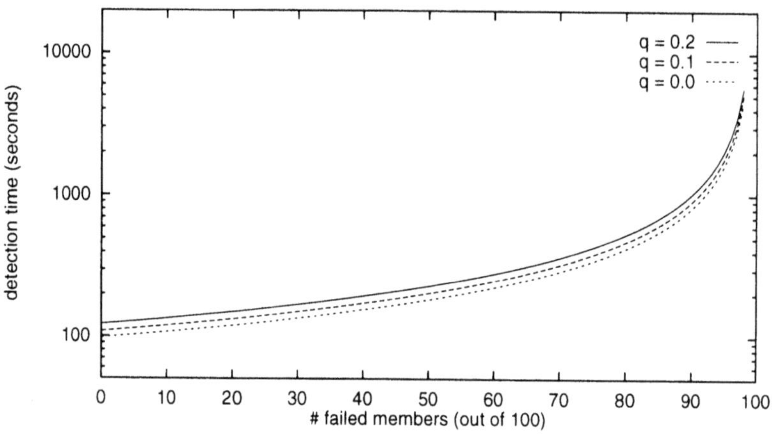

Figure 3 This graph shows, for three different probabilities of message loss q, the effect of failed members on detection time. It can be observed that the algorithm is quite resilient to process failures up until about half of the members have failed.

Finally, we investigate the impact of message loss. In Figure 4 we show for three different group sizes the effect of message loss on failure detection time. Again, we see satisfactory resilience. Even if we assume that 10% of the gossips get lost, we pay only a small price in detection time.

4 MULTI-LEVEL GOSSIPING

In a large system, the basic protocol has an inefficiency that can be corrected fairly easily, with an important improvement in scalability. The problem is that members choose other members at random, without concern to the topology of the network

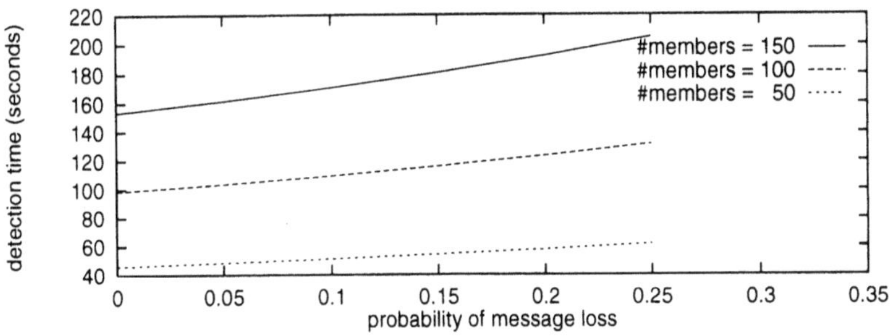

Figure 4 This graph shows the effect of message loss on detection time ($P_{mistake} = 10^{-6}$). It can be observed that the algorithm is quite resilient to message loss.

through which they are connected. As a result, the bridges between the physical networks are overloaded with much redundant information. In this section, we will show how members can correct this by automatically detecting the bounds of Internet domains and subnets, and reducing gossips that cross these bounds.

Before we present our modified gossiping protocol, we will review the structure of Internet domains and subnets. Internet addresses are 32-bit numbers subdivided into three fields. We call these fields the *Domain number*, *Subnet number*, and *Host* number. For example, here at the Cornell University campus the Domain number for all hosts is the same, and, roughly, each Ethernet (or other LAN) has its own Subnet number. The Host number identifies individual hosts on a subnet. The three fields form a hierarchy that reflects fairly accurately the underlying physical topology of networks.

The fields are variable length. The length of the Domain number can be determined by looking at the first few bits of it. The length of the Subnet and Host numbers cannot be determined that way, and can be different for any particular domain. * In case of Cornell, it happens that both the Subnet and Host numbers are 8 bits, but this is not visible externally. In fact, Cornell may decide to change this overnight without notifying anybody outside of Cornell, and this need not have any effects on routers outside of Cornell.

We will now present our modified protocol. There are two aspects to this protocol. First, the lengths of Subnet and Host numbers for each domain are gossiped along with the heartbeat counters of each host. Secondly, gossips are mostly done within subnets, with few gossips going between subnets, and even fewer between domains.

As for the first aspect, hosts now maintain two lists. One is the same as in the basic protocol, and contains the hosts and their heartbeat counters. The second list contains the Domain numbers and their so-called *Subnet Masks* that determine the length of the Subnet and Host numbers. An invariant of our protocol is that for every host in the first list, there has to be an entry in the second that corresponds to that

* Subnets may be *subsubnetted* further to add another level to the hierarchy. We do not currently take this into account, which is not optimal, but does not affect the correctness of our protocol.

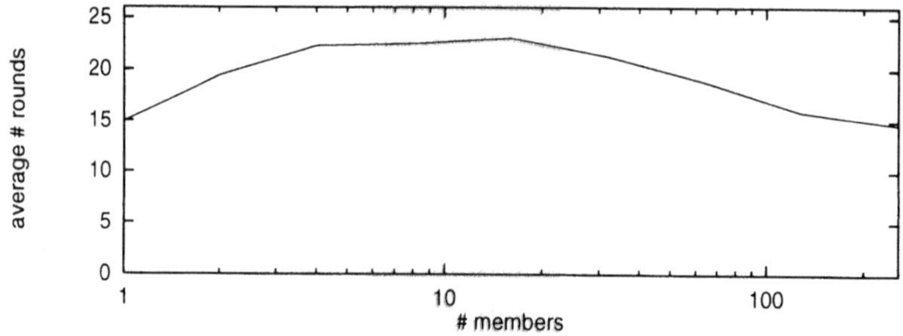

Figure 5 This graph shows the result of simulating the protocol for 256 members evenly distributed over a number of subnets.

host's domain and subnet. (Since typically many hosts are in the same subnet, the second list will be much shorter.) The second list is gossiped along with the first, and merged on arrival, which maintains this invariant.

Within subnets, we run the basic protocol as described in Section 2. For gossips that cross subnets and domains we run a modified version of the protocol. This modified protocol tunes the probability of gossiping so that every round, on average one member per subnet will gossip to another subnet in its domain, and one member per domain will gossip to another domain. Thus, the bandwidth use at each level will be proportional to the number of entities contained at the next level down. So, for example, the cross-subnet bandwidth in a given domain will depend only on the number of subnets in that domain.*

To achieve this average behavior, every member tosses a weighted coin every time it gossips. One out of n times, where n is the size of the subnet, it picks a random (other) subnet in its domain, and within that subnet, a random host to gossip to. The member then tosses another weighted coin, but this time with probability $1/(n \times m)$, where m is the number of subnets in its domain, it picks a random (other) domain, then a random subnet within that domain, and then a random host within that subnet to gossip to.

This protocol significantly reduces the amount of bandwidth that flows through the Internet routers, since the gossiping is concentrated on the lower levels of the hierarchy. The protocol also allows for accelerated failure detection times within subnets, and is more resilient against network partitions. On the down side, it has a negative influence on the number of rounds needed for information to be disseminated through the system, and hence on failure detection times across subnets and domains.

To show this negative effect, we simulated the protocol, and have plotted the average of the number of rounds it takes to gossip a new heartbeat counter to all members in a group of 256 members in Figure 5. We have spread the members evenly across a

*We have chosen here to keep the bandwidth use per subnet and per domain equal to the bandwidth use per member at the subnet level. The protocol can trivially be generalized.

number of subnets, ranging from one subnet of 256 members to 256 subnets of one member each (all within a single domain). As we can see, we may pay as much as approximately 50% for certain subdivisions. We appear to pay most when the number of subnets and the sizes of the subnets are equal (16 in this case). But at this point we also are most efficient in bandwidth use, and use 16 times less bandwidth than we would have on a flat broadcast based network.

In fact, we may conclude that bandwidth use is approximately constant for large networks. To see this, let's see what happens when we double the number of members in a large network. We would not do this by doubling the number of members on each subnet, but by doubling the number of subnets, or, if there are many of those already, doubling the number of domains. When we double the number of members, the size of gossip messages doubles, but at the same time gossiping slows down by a factor of two. Therefore, within subnets and within domains, the bandwidth used remains the same. The only increase in bandwidth use would be at the highest level of the hierarchy, consisting of messages between domains. Fortunately, the Internet is designed to accommodate a constant amount of traffic per domain.

We can make calculations much like in (van Renesse, Minsky & Hayden 1998) (generalizing those of Section 3 becomes too complex) for any particular division of members into subnets and domains to figure failure detection times for members in particular subnets. The failure detection times for members in the same subnet will improve, while the other times will be longer than before, but generally not more than 50% longer. If this is a problem, we may choose to use some of the gain in bandwidth to increase the gossip frequency and hence reduce failure detection times.

In previous work, Agarwal et al. (Agarwal, Moser, Melliar-Smith & Budhia 1995) have shown that it is possible to exploit the network topology in membership and total ordering protocols. In their work, called Totem, it is necessary to run special software on the gateway machines between networks, while our protocol automatically discovers the boundaries of subnets and does not require special software other than on end-host machines. The intention of Totem is not providing rigorous guarantees about failure detections, but efficient membership and totally-ordered multicast in a local area network consisting of multiple physical networks.

Vogels (Vogels 1996) suggests multiple confidence levels of failure reports, and node failure monitors on each subnet in order to enhance scalability of failure detection. Our work implicitly follows the latter suggestion. (Vogels 1996) does not provide an analysis of scalability nor of quality of detection.

5 CATASTROPHE RECOVERY

Gossip algorithms do not work well if a large percentage of members crash or become partitioned away (see Figure 3). The problem is that too many gossips get wasted by sending them to unreachable processes. In order to deal with this, the failure detector does not immediately report members whom it has not heard from for time T_{fail}. Instead, it waits longer, but it does stop gossiping to these members.

In the meantime, we use a broadcast protocol to attempt to restore the connections to remaining members.* Since we know the *Subnet Masks* of each subnet (these were found using the protocol of Section 4), we can determine the broadcast addresses of each subnet (using either all zeroes or all ones for the Host Number).

The protocol below will guarantee, with high probability, that a broadcast is generated at least once every 20 seconds. In a failure-free environment, however, it will generate on average one broadcast every 10 seconds, imposing only a low load on the hosts in the network. (We have chosen exact parameters here for ease of explanation, but these parameters can be chosen more-or-less arbitrarily.)

Each member decides every second, probabilistically, on whether it should send a broadcast or not, based on how recently it has received a broadcast. If it was recent, then the member broadcasts with very low probability. If the member received the last broadcast almost 20 seconds ago, then it will broadcast with very high probability. The probability is also chosen so that the expected time that somebody first sends a broadcast is after 10 seconds. A function that appears to work well for this is $p(t) = (t/20)^a$. $p(t)$ is the probability that a member sends t seconds after receiving the last broadcast, and a is a constant chosen so that the expected first broadcast sent by any member is after $\mu = 10$ seconds. To find a, we first have to calculate the probability q(t) that anybody sends a broadcast after t seconds. This is $q(t) = 1 - (1 - p(t))^n$. Thus the probability $f(t)$ that the first broadcast is sent at time t is

$$f(t) = q(t) \times \prod_{i=0}^{t-1} (1 - q(i)) \tag{4}$$

Finally, the expected time μ at which the first broadcast is sent is

$$\mu = \sum_{t=0}^{20} t \cdot f(t) \tag{5}$$

For example, for $n = 1000$, we find that a has to be approximately 10.43 to make $\mu \approx 10$. We have plotted these functions for this example in Figure 6, and it can be seen that with high probability the next broadcast is around 10 seconds after the last one. The expected number of senders around 10 seconds is $1000 \times p(10)$, which is only 0.7, making it very unlikely that more than one member broadcasts at a time.

But what if a large fraction of members becomes unreachable? Clearly, with high probability, the next broadcast is before 20 seconds. The more members are unavailable, the closer the expected time gets to 20 seconds. The concern is that, as the expected time gets closer to 20 seconds, the probability that any member sends a broadcast, $q(t)$, goes up rapidly. Therefore, too many members may broadcast at the

---

*In the absence of a broadcast capability, a small set of hosts at well known addresses may be used to gossip through. The gossip servers should be placed strategically so they remain available in the case of partitions. We have not yet analyzed this approach.

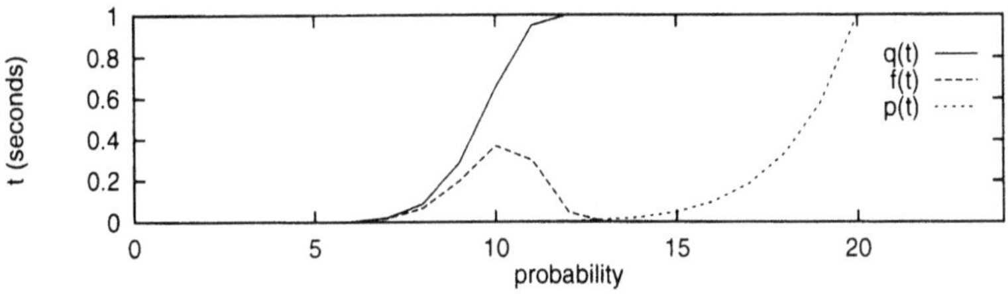

Figure 6 This graph shows $p(t)$, the probability that a particular member sends a broadcast after t seconds, $q(t)$, the probability that any member does, and $f(t)$, the probability that the first broadcast is sent after t seconds. The number of members is 1000 here.

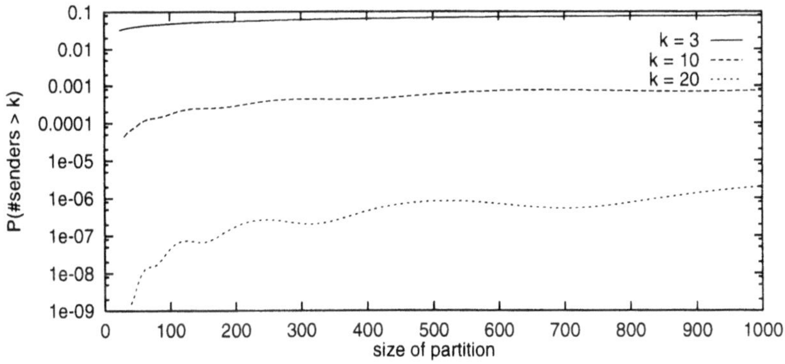

Figure 7 This graph shows, for every size of a partition of a group of 1000 members, the probability that more than k members broadcast at the same time for $k = 3, 10, 20$. Note that the y-axes is logarithmic.

same time, leading to a storm of broadcasts. It turns out that the probability that more than 20 members broadcast at a time, in a group of 1000 members, is less than 10^{-5} (see Figure 7 and (van Renesse, Minsky & Hayden 1998)). The reason is that the smaller the partition becomes, the smaller the number of prospective senders, which offsets the growing probability with which the members do send.

This broadcast protocol may be made to scale better by using the hierarchy determined by the gossip protocol. Each subnet would run an instance of the broadcast protocol among the hosts, as well as each domain among the subnets, and the domains among each other. This is an improvement, because most partitions are not arbitrary, but occur along the boundaries of subnets and domains. Each host would determine three values for a to decide whether to broadcast in only its subnet, in the entire domain, or everywhere. (With three levels in the hierarchy, this would increase the total number of broadcasts by a factor of three, which may be corrected by adjusting the protocol's parameters.)

Now that the time to the next broadcast is bound, we can calculate how quickly the members within a new partition can find each other. (It should be taken into account that broadcast messages may get lost and that therefore the bound is probabilistic and may be somewhat larger than 20 seconds, but we are ignoring this issue here.) After the first broadcast in the new partition, all its members know just the originator of that broadcast, and will gossip to only it. Within $8/B$ seconds (where B is the bandwidth assigned to each member), the originator will know the entire membership, and gossip this information on (again, ignoring the probability of message loss). We can calculate the amount of time that is necessary to gossip the entire membership using the same analysis of Section 3. The maximum size of such a partition is $n - f$ members (f chosen as in Section 3). The maximum time to the next broadcast should be chosen so that the members within a partition have enough time to locate each other before they report each other as failed.

A particular instance of a catastrophic situation is at a cold start of one or more hosts, which do not know any other members to gossip to. A problem in this situation is that the domains and subnets are not initially known. Without this information, we can only determine the broadcast address of our own subnet. Currently, we extract a list of subnets in our own domain (for which we know the Subnet Mask) by scanning the *Hosts* data base that most computer networks maintain. Knowledge about subnets in other domains has to be manually configured.

6 CONCLUSION

In this paper we have presented a failure detection service based on a gossip protocol. The service provides accurate failure detection with known probability of a false detection, and is resilient against both transient message loss and permanent network partitions, as well as host failures. The service uses two separate protocols that automatically take advantage of the underlying network topology, and scale well in the number of members.

We have implemented a system based on these ideas and have run it within the `cs.cornell.edu` domain for the last three weeks. Over that period, it has measured over 100 failures and recoveries, without missing any failures and without making a single false failure detection. The output of the failure detector can be observed at http://www.cs.cornell.edu/home/rvr/mbrship.html. We have also implemented the basic protocol in the Ensemble system (van Renesse, Birman, Hayden, Vaysburd & Karr 1998).

The failure detection service can be used by distributed applications directly, or support other middleware services such as system management, replication, load balancing, and group communication and membership services. As such, failure detection is a valuable extension to current O.S. services.

Acknowledgments

The authors wish to thank Ken Birman, Nancy Lynch, Dexter Kozen, and the anonymous referees for helpful comments.

REFERENCES

Agarwal, D. A., Moser, L. E., Melliar-Smith, P. M. & Budhia, R. K. (1995), A Reliable Ordered Delivery Protocol for Interconnected Local-Area Networks, *in* 'Proc. of the International Conference on Network Protocols', Tokyo, Japan, pp. 365–374.

Amir, Y., Dolev, D., Kramer, S. & Malkhi, D. (1992), Transis: A communication subsystem for high availability, *in* 'Proc. of the Twenty-Second Int. Symp. on Fault-Tolerant Computing', IEEE, Boston, MA, pp. 76–84.

Bailey, N. T. J. (1975), *The Mathematical Theory of Infectious Diseases and its Applications (second edition)*, Hafner Press.

Baker, B. & Shostak, R. (1972), 'Gossips and telephones', *Discrete Mathematics* **2**(3), 191–193.

Birman, K. P., Hayden, M., Ozkasap, O., Budiu, M. & Minsky, Y. (1998), Bimodal multicast, Technical Report 98-1665, Cornell University, Dept. of Computer Science.

Chandra, T. D., Hadzilacos, V. & Toueg, S. (1992), The weakest failure detector for solving consensus, *in* 'Proc. of the 11th Annual ACM Symposium on Principles of Distributed Computing'.

Chandra, T. D., Hadzilacos, V., Toueg, S. & Charron-Bost, B. (1996), On the impossibility of group membership in asynchronous systems, *in* 'Proc. of the 15th Annual ACM Symposium on Principles of Distributed Computing', Philadelphia, PA.

Demers, A., Greene, D., Hauser, C., Irish, W., Larson, J., Shenker, S., Sturgis, H., Swinehart, D. & Terry, D. (1987), Epidemic algorithms for replicated database maintenance, *in* 'Proc. of the Sixth ACM Symp. on Principles of Distributed Computing', ACM SIGOPS-SIGACT, Vancouver, British Columbia, pp. 1–12.

Fischer, M. J., Lynch, N. A. & Patterson, M. S. (1985), 'Impossibility of distributed consensus with one faulty process', *Journal of the ACM* **32**(2), 374–382.

Golding, R. & Taylor, K. (1992), Group membership in the epidemic style, Technical Report UCSC-CRL-92-13, UC Santa Cruz, Dept. of Computer Science.

Kozen, D. (1991), *The Design and Analysis of Algorithms*, Springer Verlag.

van Renesse, R., Birman, K. P., Hayden, M., Vaysburd, A. & Karr, D. (1998), 'Building adaptive systems using Ensemble', *Software—Practice and Experience*.

van Renesse, R., Birman, K. P. & Maffeis, S. (1996), 'Horus: A flexible group communication system', *Comm. of the ACM* **39**(4), 76–83.

van Renesse, R., Minsky, Y. & Hayden, M. (1998), A gossip-style failure detection service, Technical Report 98-1687, Cornell University, Dept. of Computer Science.

Vogels, W. (1996), World wide failures, *in* 'Proc. of the 7th ACM SIGOPS Workshop', Connemara, Ireland.

7 BIOGRAPHY

Robbert van Renesse is a Senior Research Associate at Cornell University, vice-president of Reliable Network Solutions, Inc., and editor for IEEE Transactions on Parallel and Distributed Systems. His research interests include fault tolerance and security. Currently he works on the Ensemble group communication project, and on the Tacoma mobile code project.

Yaron Minsky is a graduate student at Cornell University. His research interests include fault tolerance and security in distributed systems and cryptography. Currently he works on the Tacoma project.

Mark Hayden is a research staff member at the Digital Systems Research Center. He recently completed his PhD at Cornell University, where he took part in the Ensemble project. His research interests include distributed systems and the application of formal methods and programming languages in distributed systems.

System Support for Scalable and Fault Tolerant Internet Services

Yatin Chawathe and Eric A. Brewer
Computer Science Division, University of California at Berkeley
{yatin, brewer}@cs.berkeley.edu

Abstract

Over the past few years, we have seen the proliferation of Internet-based services ranging from search engines and map services to video-on-demand servers. All of these kinds of services need to be able to provide guarantees of availability and scalability to their users. With millions of users on the Internet today, these services must have the capacity to handle a large number of clients and remain available even in the face of extremely high load.

In this paper, we present a generic architecture for supporting such Internet applications. We provide a substrate for Scalable Network Services (SNS), on top of which application developers can design their services without worrying about the details of service management. We back our design with three real-world services: a web distillation proxy, a proxy-based web-browser for PDAs, and an MBone archive server.

Keywords

Scalable Network Services, fault tolerance, scalability, availability, load balancing

1 INTRODUCTION

The explosive growth of the World-Wide Web has spawned a number of network-based services such as map servers (MapQuest 1996), search engines (Inktomi Corp. 1996, Digital Corporation 1996), anonymizing web-proxies (Anonymizer Inc. 1996), and directory services (Yahoo! Inc 1995, CitySearch Inc. 1997). Similarly, the expansion of the Internet multicast backbone (MBone) (Deering, Estrin, Farinacci, Jacobson, Liu & Wei 1996, Deering 1991) has created a demand for services such as video-on-demand servers (Bolosky, Fitzgerald & Douceur 1997, Almeroth & Ammar 1998) and real-time audio/video gateways (Amir, McCanne & Zhang 1995).

As these types of services get more popular, they will be required to provide certain guarantees with respect to their level of service. With millions of users on the Internet, these services must have the capacity to handle a large number of clients and remain available even in the face of extremely high load. We identify two critical issues that any Internet service must address in its design:

System Scalability: The service must be able to scale incrementally with offered load. To ensure linear scalability, the service must distribute the load across all of its resources. Further, the service must be capable of absorbing any peaks in load.

Availability and Fault Tolerance: As much as possible, the service must remain available in the face of network failure, system crashes, and hardware upgrades. A key component of service availability is the ability to maintain a well-known and reliable name that clients can use to locate the service. In addition, a service must also ensure that faults in its internal operation do not take down the entire service.

In (Fox, Gribble, Chawathe, Brewer & Gauthier 1997), we argued that clusters of workstations (Anderson, Culler, Patterson & the NOW team 1994) are ideal for most Internet service requirements. Internet services tend to be highly parallel with many simultaneous independent tasks that can easily be distributed across a cluster of commodity PCs. Clusters have the advantage of the ability to grow incrementally by simply adding more PCs as the workload grows. Not only do PCs have cost/performance benefits, but also the natural redundancy in a cluster of PCs is excellent for masking failures in the service and ensuring high availability.

However, designing and managing a system that is distributed across a cluster poses a number of challenges. In this paper, we describe an architecture substrate for building cluster-based systems that can satisfy the above requirements. We isolate the key functions of scalability, load balancing, and fault tolerance into a reusable substrate, called the "Scalable Network Services" (SNS) architecture. Service developers build their systems on top of the SNS, and interact with the SNS through a narrow and well-defined interface. The SNS substrate allows application writers to concentrate on the semantics of their application rather than worrying about the details of service management. We demonstrate the effectiveness of our architecture through examples of three different kinds of services.

2 A REUSABLE "SCALABLE NETWORK SERVICES" ARCHITECTURE

To make best use of a cluster of workstations, we have defined an architecture based on independent composable modules. We have carefully designed the service ar-

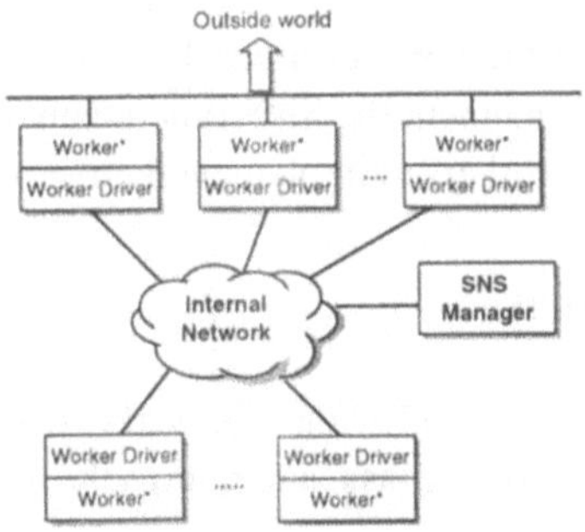

Figure 1 The SNS Architecture. (*—Service developers customize these components; all other components are part of the SNS)

chitecture to separate the service support layer from the rest of the system, thereby isolating the rest of the system from having to deal with the SNS issues described in Section 1.

The SNS subsystem assumes that the application is distributed across a number of service-specific modules, called *workers*. Workers implement the actual semantics of the service. They can be of two types:

- A back end engine that simply receives tasks from the rest of the system, operates on those tasks, and returns a result.
- A more active component that possibly interfaces with the outside world. Such a worker receives requests or commands from clients, and either handles them directly, or "shepherds" them to other workers.

For example, a web-based map service can implement a "front end" worker that actively listens for HTTP requests from end-clients, and acts as a control center for the service. The front end may rely on a back end map worker that generates appropriate map images based on the HTTP request and returns them to the front end for eventual delivery to the client. Some other workers may communicate directly with their clients; for example, a worker in a video archive server can stream video data directly to its clients, instead of shuttling it through a front end.

The simplest form of worker has no dependencies, and can be executed on any node in the system. Some workers, however, may rely on specific aspects of the system that are available only on one or a subset of the nodes in the cluster. For example, a front end worker for an HTTP service has an affinity for the IP address (or DNS name) associated with the service. Similarly, a video archive worker has affinity for the disk on which the archived session has been stored. Worker affinity introduces additional factors in the SNS subsystem's decision to place workers on nodes.

In addition to worker modules, the SNS architecture relies on a central management entity, the *SNS Manager*, to coordinate all the workers in the system by balancing load across workers, spawning new workers on demand, and ensuring that the system can recover from faults. Figure 1 shows a block diagram of the SNS. The SNS Manager is the core of the SNS substrate. *Worker Drivers* are libraries that are attached to workers, and implement the SNS functionality at the workers. Applications customize individual workers to implement their service.

2.1 Service Assumptions

Workers communicate with each other through *tasks*. A worker sends a task to another worker, which operates on the task, and returns the result back to the originator. The SNS subsystem makes certain assumptions about the semantics of workers and their tasks:

- Workers are grouped into classes. Within a given class, workers are identical and interchangeable, i.e. a task destined for the class may be handled by any worker in that class.
- Although workers may be tied to specific nodes in the cluster, tasks themselves have no dependencies.
- Workers have a simple serial interface for accepting tasks. A worker (the *originator*) sends a task to another worker (the *consumer*) by specifying the class and inputs for the task, and expects a result back from the consumer.
- The time required to handle a task and return a response is small relative to the acceptable latency from the system.
- Tasks are assumed to be atomic and restartable. The easiest way of implementing this assumption is to make workers completely stateless. Workers can build stronger semantics on top of these basic requirements.
- The SNS subsystem can detect task failure and take appropriate action to overcome the failure. Fault detection is either in the form of timeouts, or a preemptive signal that notifies the SNS subsystem of failure.

These assumptions simplify the design of the SNS layer and enable us to effectively provide the availability and fault tolerance guarantees promised by the service.

2.2 Centralized Resource Management

The SNS Manager has been intentionally designed to be a centralized entity rather than distributing its functionality across the entire cluster. If we can ensure the fault tolerance of the Manager, and make sure that it is not a performance bottleneck, a centralized design makes it easier to reason about and implement the various policies for load balancing and resource location/creation. We classify the functions of the SNS Manager into resource location, load balancing and scaling, and fault tolerance.

2.2.1 Resource Location

The main task of the SNS Manager is to act as a name service for the rest of the system. Workers contact the SNS Manager to locate other resources. The SNS Manager maintains a table of all available resources in the system. If it finds an appropriate resource, it returns the location of the resource to the worker. Workers cache this information, so they do not have to contact the manager for each request.

2.2.2 Load Balancing and Scalability

Although the final load balancing decision is distributed across all workers, the load gathering and reporting mechanisms are centralized in the manager. Based on load reports from each worker, the manager generates load balancing hints, which are used by workers to make local decisions regarding their choice of consumers for tasks.

As the load on the system grows, the SNS Manager pulls in idle nodes, and starts new workers. In addition, the system must be able to deal with sudden bursts in load (Leland, Taqqu, Willinger & Wilson 1994, Crovella & Bestavros 1995, Gribble, Manku, Roselli, Brewer, Gibson & Miller 1998). We deal with short traffic bursts by replicating workers and directing tasks across all replicated workers for greater throughput.

To handle more prolonged bursts, our design supports the notion of a pool of overflow nodes that are not dedicated to the system, and are recruited by the system only in the event of extreme bursts. For example, after the landing of the Pathfinder on Mars, NASA's web site experienced over 220 million hits in a four day period (National Aeronautics and Space Administration 1997) which excessively overloaded their web server. Overflow nodes can be machines that are usually used for other purposes (such as people's desktop machines), or machines that the service can "rent" on a pay-per-use basis from another service provider. When the SNS Manager runs out of dedicated machines to handle the system load, it may launch workers on idle machines from the overflow pool for the duration of the burst.

2.2.3 Fault Tolerance and Availability

An SNS must guarantee its ability to withstand failures and faults in the system. We rely on two basic design principles for achieving reliance against system failures: soft state and timeouts. By explicitly designing our system to rely entirely on soft state, we have managed to simplify our crash recovery process. No explicit crash recovery is required—recovery is built into the normal functioning of the protocol machinery. The system also uses *timeouts and retries*; if a task cannot be completed because of some failure in the system, the SNS subsystem will retry the task.

We use a fault tolerance strategy that we call *starfish fault tolerance* to detect and recover from faults in the system. The components in the SNS system monitor each other; when a component fails, one of its peers restarts it, possibly on a different node. Cached stale state carries the rest of the components through the fault while the failed component is being restarted; the new component gradually rebuilds its state and the system returns to a normal mode of operation. We describe our fault tolerance strategies in greater detail in Section 3.4.

3 SNS IMPLEMENTATION

This section focuses on the details of the design of the SNS components and describes the implementation of the system. The SNS functionality is encompassed in the SNS Manager and in the Worker Driver, which permits the actual worker implementations to be largely independent and ignorant of the SNS subsystem.

Task originators locate an appropriate consumer for their task with the help of the SNS Manager. The worker driver at the consumer maintains a queue of pending tasks; tasks are taken off the queue serially and handed to the worker for processing. The queue at the worker driver may be a simple first-in-first-out queue, or may use a more sophisticated queuing policy such as priority queues.

We now look at the three functions of the SNS Manager—resource location, load balancing, and fault tolerance—in detail.

3.1 Resource location

The resource location problem for the SNS encompasses three issues: how clients locate the service, how workers locate the centralized SNS Manager, and how workers locate each other.

3.1.1 Locating the Service

A service must present to the world a well-known and reliable name that clients can use to contact it. The mechanism used to locate the service depends largely on the service itself. Web-based services use Uniform Resource Locators (URLs) as the primary service location mechanism. Although this has fault-tolerance implications, techniques such as DNS round-robin (Brisco 1995) and specialized routers (Cisco Systems 1996, Anderson 1995) can be used to hide a number of replicated and/or distributed servers behind a single logical name. Smart clients (Yoshikawa, Chun, Eastham, Anderson & Culler 1997) can assist the service in transparent service location in the presence of faults by relying on browser support through Java and JavaScript. Similarly, services that rely on the IP multicast delivery model can use multicast as a level of indirection to locate the service (Amir, McCanne & Katz 1998). Service front ends actively listen on a well-known multicast channel; all clients that need to access the service broadcast their requests on the multicast channel.

3.1.2 Locating the SNS Manager

The SNS Manager is the centralized resource manager of the system. To avoid expensive fault recovery when the SNS Manager crashes, we use multicast as a level of indirection for locating the manager. The SNS Manager periodically beacons its existence on a well-known multicast address. All other components in the system subscribe to this multicast group and listen for beacons from the manager. This mechanism relieves the components from having to perform explicit fault recovery when the SNS Manager crashes and comes back up on a different location. The workers simply hear a new beacon from the manager, and redirect their communication to the new location.

3.1.3 Locating Workers

As described in Section 2.1, all workers are grouped into classes based on their semantics and the operations that they perform. Each class of workers is assigned a unique name that is loosely based on MIME types (Borenstein & Freed 1993). For example, all transformation workers that compress GIF images may be called *compress/image/gif*. Applications must pick names for their workers in a manner that makes sense for the service being implemented.

When a worker locates the SNS Manager, it registers itself with the manager. This registration message contains the name of the worker's class and the worker's location, which the SNS Manager uses to build a table of all active components in the system. When an originator of a task needs to locate a consumer, it sends a *Find* message to the manager. The manager performs a lookup in its *active components table* and returns a list of all workers that match the specification. The originator caches this list in a *local active components cache* to avoid contacting the SNS Manager on every request.

3.2 On-demand Launching of Workers

The SNS Manager may not be able to locate an appropriate worker in response to a *Find* message. The manager must then either start a new worker, or respond with a *NotFound* message.

The manager maintains a *launch table* of all workers that can be part of the service and the executables associated with each worker. The manager consults this table and attempts to start a new worker on a lightly loaded node in the cluster. We use a simple scheme where the manager relies on the load balancing information that it gathers from other workers (see Section 3.3) and selects the least loaded node. We believe that this simple policy is sufficient; more fine-grained load balancing is performed at the task level by the SNS Manager. In addition to load, the spawning policy also takes into account any affinities that a worker might have for specific nodes in the cluster.

If the manager is unable to locate or spawn a new worker, this information is cached in a *negative cache* at the originator. This ensures that the originator does not bother the manager again for that class of workers. The negative cache is flushed whenever the launch table is updated by the manager, so no stale information causes denial of service.

3.3 Load Balancing and Scalability

A good service implementation must smooth out the load on the service across all its components. We divide the load balancing policy into three tasks: load measurement, communication, and resource allocation. The SNS Manager gathers load samples from all workers, and uses this information to make intelligent load balancing decisions.

3.3.1 Load measurement

CPU usage is the most common and often the most dynamic load metric. However, each application may have its own notion of load. Hence, we avoid building load semantics into the SNS layer and instead provide hooks for service developers to tailor the load metrics to each worker's needs. All tasks destined for a worker arrive at the worker driver, which invokes a method in the worker to perform a cursory analysis of the task and estimate the approximate "load" that would be generated by the task. For a number of Internet service applications, tasks are very short and the fine granularity of estimating the actual load per task is unimportant; for such tasks we use a default estimate of 1 unit of load per task, thus making the load equivalent to the number of pending tasks at the worker.

The worker driver maintains a running statistic of the current load. Periodically, it reports this information to the SNS Manager. The reporting interval itself is configurable on a per-worker basis and represents a tradeoff between system response time to load fluctuations versus the amount of network bandwidth consumed by the load reports.

3.3.2 Balancing the load

The SNS Manager centralizes all load information. It maintains a history of load reports from workers thereby allowing it to smooth out any small transient bursts of load. As mentioned in Section 3.1.2, the SNS Manager periodically beacons its existence to the rest of the system on a well-known multicast channel. The manager distributes the aggregate load information to all other components by piggy-backing it on these existence beacons. Workers cache this load information in their *local active components cache*, thus allowing them to perform the final load balancing decision locally. We use a scheme based on lottery scheduling (Waldspurger & Weihl 1994) for the load balancing algorithm. Each worker is assigned tickets that are inversely proportional to the load on the worker.

If tasks are generated at a much faster rate than the beaconing interval for load reports, stale load balancing information at the workers can result in incorrect decisions. We add feedback to the system by having each worker maintain a correction factor that corresponds to the tasks that it has already dispatched to a consumer. The worker adds this correction factor to the cached load balancing hints when it tries to pick a consumer. Section 5.1 discusses the effectiveness of the policy.

3.3.3 Auto-launch for scalability

A good load balancing protocol must include the ability to gradually scale the system as the load increases. The SNS Manager periodically checks the aggregate load statistics for workers in a particular class, and launches a new worker if the load gets too high.

Even after a new worker has started, it may take time before the load stabilizes across the new and old workers. To avoid further false triggers of the auto-launch mechanism, we disable the feature for workers of that class for a short duration after the new worker is created. The threshold for launching workers maps to the greatest delay the client is willing to tolerate when the system is under heavy load, while the time for which the spawning mechanism is disabled once a new worker is launched represents a tradeoff between stability (rate of spawning and reaping workers) and client-perceptible delay.

3.3.4 The overflow pool

As described in Section 2.2.2, the SNS subsystem supports the notion of an overflow pool to handle prolonged bursts in traffic that cannot be dealt with by the dedicated nodes. When the SNS Manager runs out of dedicated nodes to handle a burst, it tries to harness an unloaded node from the overflow pool. When the burst dies down, the overflow workers may be reaped and the machine can be returned to its original task. We use a priority scheme to implement the overflow pool. Dedicated nodes are assigned the highest priority level, while overflow nodes have lower priorities.

3.4 Availability and Fault Tolerance

We leverage the natural redundancy of clusters to achieve availability and mask transient failures in the system: each node in the cluster is independent of the others. We rely on two main principles in our handling of failures: component restart and timeouts used by a mode of fault tolerance that we call *starfish fault tolerance*.

3.4.1 Starfish Fault Tolerance

Most traditional systems have relied on *primary/secondary fault tolerance* (Anderson 1995, Bartlett 1981) to ensure availability of the system. This involves replicating each component: one of the clones acts as the primary process and participates in the system, while the other is the secondary and simply monitors the primary to mirror its state. If the primary crashes or fails in any other way, the secondary takes over the job of the primary and creates its own secondary.

Instead of a primary/secondary configuration, all components in the SNS architecture are fault tolerance "peers" and each monitors the others to ensure that all necessary components are always available. The SNS Manager is the centralized fault tolerance agent; it acts as a peer for all other components, monitoring and restarting them in the event of a crash. Similarly, workers monitor the SNS Manager and restart it upon failure. As long as there is at least one component active in the system, it can eventually regenerate all other components.

3.4.2 Worker Failure

To detect worker failure, the SNS Manager relies on the (loss of) periodic load reports from the workers. A crash may result in loss of tasks pending in the worker driver queue. Since tasks are restartable, the system can simply retry the task upon failure.

For passive workers that only respond to requests from other workers, the SNS Manager simply relies on the on-demand launch mechanism to restart the worker if and when it is needed. Workers that actively operate even in the absence of tasks may need to be restarted immediately after failure (for example, an ongoing video session, or an HTTP front end whose job is to wait for connections from clients). When the SNS Manager detects the death of such a worker, instead of the usual on-demand recovery, it immediately launches a new one.

For workers that have affinity to specific nodes, the SNS Manager must restrict the respawning to those nodes. In the extreme case of affinity for a single node, the manager may simply be unable to restart the worker if the node itself has crashed. In many situations, we may be able to hide the affinity through other means. Affinity to IP addresses can be hidden via DNS round-robin (Brisco 1995) or specialized routers (Cisco Systems 1996, Anderson 1995). Disk affinity may be reduced by using a shared disk across multiple nodes.

3.4.3 SNS Manager Failure

In Section 2.2, we emphasized the use of a centralized SNS Manager to simplify the design of the system. We now show how our strategies ensure that the centralized manager does not end up becoming a fault tolerance nightmare.

All workers in the system collaborate to monitor the SNS Manager. When beacons from the manager are lost, a distributed restart algorithm is triggered. Each worker starts a random timer; the worker whose timer expires first wins the arbitration process and restarts the manager. It multicasts an *AmRestarting* message to the rest of the system, allowing other components to back off their timers. In spite of this arbitration algorithm, multiple managers may get spawned. When the managers detect each other's beacons, all but one commit suicide.

Even while the manager is dead, the system can continue to function, albeit at some loss of functionality, using cached information on the workers. The use of soft state updates ensures that crash recovery itself is relatively simple. When the manager restarts and begins beaconing again, all workers detect the new beacons and re-register with the new manager. With time, all workers report their load and the manager can regain its lost load information.

If a network partition splits the system into two, each half of the system will grow into a full-fledged SNS with its own manager and workers. Once the partition is removed, the two systems coalesce together, and one of the managers kills itself, returning the system to a stable state.

3.4.4 Timeouts and Retries

The final mechanism to deal with faults is the use of timeouts throughout the system. Workers use timeouts to bound the time they must wait for a consumer to return the result of a task, before retrying the task on a different worker. Other uses of timeouts and retries include launching of new workers, handling software faults in a worker application that cause it to spin in an endless loop while handling a task, etc.

To ensure that a systematic failure does not cause repeated retries, we limit the number of retries to a small finite number. In the event that a systematic failure does occur (possibly due to bad input), the SNS subsystem returns an error that may be trapped by the service in an application-specific manner.

The heavy use of timers all over the SNS subsystem for fault recovery, beaconing, and load reporting can result in synchronization effects, as have been observed in a number of systems, both naturally occurring phenomena and computer-based systems (Floyd & Jacobson 1994). To counter these effects, we introduce a randomized element to the timeout values. We use a uniformly distributed random value centered around the required absolute value for all timers in the system. For randomized timers that are used to suppress duplicate events (e.g. SNS Manager restart), exponential timers have been shown to provide better results (Nonnenmacher & Biersack 1998). However, in practice, we have found uniform timers to be sufficient.

3.4.5 Soft State for Fault Tolerance

Our use of soft state all over the system in preference to a hard state design has greatly simplified our implementation. Traditional crash recovery systems such as ACID databases (Gray 1981) use write-ahead logging (Mohan et al. 1992) to ensure that no data is lost. This piece of code is extremely difficult to understand and debug: it is rarely invoked, yet it has to work without any errors. By ensuring that the SNS subsystem has no hard state, we have precluded the need for any explicit data recovery protocols upon a crash. Moreover, with this use of soft-state, no mirror processes are required for fault tolerance. Each "watcher" process need only detect that its peer is alive, and be able to restart the peer.

4 EXAMPLE APPLICATIONS

The SNS architecture provides an abstract layer for building various kinds of network services. We describe a few of the applications that we and other researchers have built using this architecture.

4.1 *TranSend*: A Web Distillation Proxy

TranSend (Fox et al. 1997) is an HTTP proxy whose goal is to provide fast access to the web for clients connected via low-bandwidth links by performing lossy compression of images and other rich data on the fly (Fox, Gribble, Brewer & Amir 1996, Fox, Gribble, Chawathe & Brewer 1998). TranSend uses four types of workers:

- front end workers that listen for HTTP requests, forward them through the system, and return the result to the client;
- web cache workers that fetch the actual content from the web, and cache it for optimization;
- image distillation engines for compressing GIF and JPEG images;

- an HTML engine that marks up inline image references with distillation preferences and adds links next to distilled images, so users can retrieve the originals.

Most of these workers took 5-6 hours to implement, and although program bugs may sometimes cause the worker to crash, the fault tolerance mechanisms built into the SNS reduce the need to eliminate all such possible bugs from the worker code.

4.2 *Wingman*: A Web Browser for the PalmPilot

Wingman (Fox, Goldberg, Gribble, Polito, Lee & Brewer 1998) represents a class of applications that use an infrastructural proxy to build a split application for "thin clients" such as PDAs. Most of the application functionality is moved to a powerful proxy, while the client application is a stripped-down program. Wingman is a proxy-based web browser for the 3COM PalmPilot (3COM Corporation 1996); it uses the SNS architecture to convert web content into much simpler representations.

- Front end workers listen for requests from the Wingman client, much like the front end in TranSend, while web cache workers fetch content from the web.
- A specialized HTML layout engine converts HTML documents into simple draw operations that are shipped to the client.
- Specialized image converters transform web images into the PalmPilot's native 2 bits/pixel bitmap representation.

Both TranSend and Wingman have been released to the general public for use, and we currently have a user population of approximately 12,000.

4.3 *MARS*: A Multimedia Archive Server

MARS is a server for distributing archived MBone content which was developed by researchers at Berkeley using the SNS system as the underlying platform (Schuett & Raman 1997). This system uses two types of workers: a *server manager* that clients contact to initiate new sessions, and an audio/video worker that performs the actual playback onto the MBone using the Real-time Transport (RTP) (Schulzrinne, Casner, Frederick & Jacobson 1996) protocol. Once a session has begun, clients can directly communicate with the A/V worker to control the session parameters. This worker is different from workers in the previous examples, because it has state: the session it is playing, the current playback point in the stream, etc. The application relies on smart clients to regenerate this state for the worker, in case it dies and must be restarted.

The SNS architecture has been used for other services, including a proxy-based electronic shared whiteboard for PDAs (Chawathe, Fink, McCanne & Brewer 1998), and Cha-Cha, a system for contextualizing web-search results by augmenting them with semantics such as document location, content, etc. (Chen & Hong 1997).

5 SYSTEM EVALUATION

We used the TranSend proxy as a test-bed for measuring our implementation . We present some of our results for the load balancing strategies employed, the ability of the system to tune itself to the offered load, and its scalability. Load was generated using a simple tool to play out HTTP requests based on trace data that was gathered from the UC Berkeley dialup IP users (Gribble & Brewer 1997).

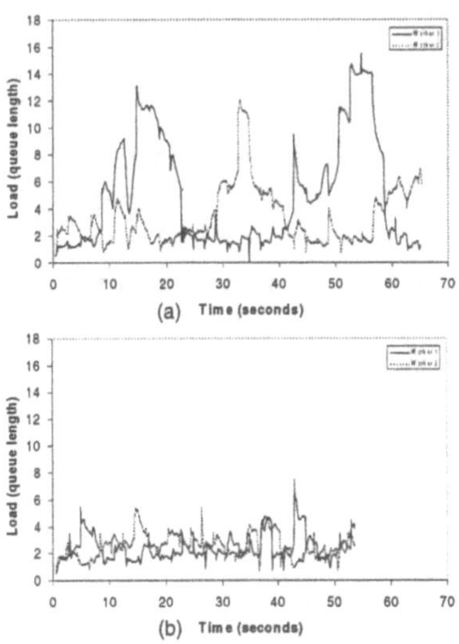

Figure 2 Load balancing algorithm: (a) Without feedback: load oscillates between two workers, (b) With feedback.

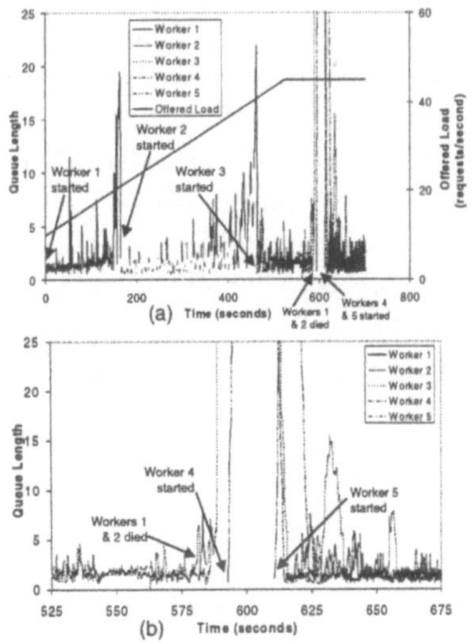

Figure 3 Worker queue length observed over time as the load presented to the system fluctuates and as workers are brought down manually. Figure (b) is an enlargement of a section of (a).

5.1 Load Balancing

The TranSend proxy uses queue lengths in the worker drivers as the default load metric. Figure 2 shows the effects of the load balancing strategy (a) without, and (b) with the correction feedback included in the selection algorithm. The absence of any feedback manifests itself in oscillations in the load experienced by workers. During a single beaconing interval, one worker is lightly loaded and most tasks are directed to it; when load information is updated in the front end's cache, the front end immediately stops directing further tasks to this worker and redirects them to a less loaded worker.

Figure 2 (b) shows the results of running the same experiment with the improved feedback-based algorithm. As expected, the oscillations are reduced and queue levels generally stay below five requests at any time.

5.2 Self Tuning

Figure 3 (a) shows the variations in worker queue lengths over time. The system was bootstrapped with one front end and the SNS Manager. We observe on-demand spawning of the first worker as soon as load is offered to the system. With increasing load, the worker queue gradually increases until the SNS Manager decides to spawn a second worker, which reduces the queue length of the first worker and balances the load across the two workers within five seconds. Continued increase in load causes a third worker to start up.

Figure 3 (b) shows an enlarged view of a section of the graph in Figure 3 (a). During the experiment, we manually killed the first two workers, causing the load on the remaining worker to rapidly increase. (To show greater detail in the graphs, this peak has been cut off in Figure 3.) The manager immediately reacted and started a new worker. The second worker was not sufficient to bring the system back to a stable state, and the manager had to start yet another worker.

5.3 Scalability

Requests/ second	# of front ends	# of workers	Element that saturated
0-24	1	1	workers
25-47	1	2	workers
48-72	1	3	workers
73-87	1	4	FE Ethernet*
88-91	2	4	workers
92-112	2	5	workers
113-135	2	6	workers and FE Ethernet
136-159	3	7	workers

Table 1 Results of the scalability experiment (*—Ethernet leading into the front end)

The data in Table 1 demonstrates the system's incremental scalability. We started with a minimal instance of the system (one front end and one worker), and gradually increased the request rate. As the load increased,the manager spawned more workers as needed. At 87 requests per second, the Ethernet segment leading into the front end saturated, requiring a new front end. We were unable to test the system at rates higher than 159 requests per second, since all the nodes in our cluster were used up at that point. Our prototype worker could handle approximately 23 requests per second, and a 100 Mb/s Ethernet segment into a front end can handle approximately 70 requests per second.

A possible concern is that the centralized SNS Manager might prove to be a bottleneck in the system. Our experience, and a simple experiment shows that this has not been a problem—the SNS Manager was easily able to manage at least 900 workers in the system. A potential concern for scalability is the amount of network bandwidth consumed by control traffic (load reports, existence beacons, etc.). However, most of these packets are relatively small. We can impose a strict limit on the amount of control traffic by adjusting the rate, by either intelligently selecting dynamic data over data that changes less rapidly, or using a scheme similar to the MBone Session Announcement Protocol (Handley 1996) which limits its traffic to a maximum bandwidth by requiring clients to adjust their rate of generating messages as the size of the multicast group increases.

6 RELATED WORK

The SNS architecture has been used as the basis for a programming model, *TACC* (Fox 1997): Transformation (filtering, compressing, or format conversion of data), Aggregation (combining data from multiple sources), Caching (both of original and transformed data), and Customization (a persistent data store of per-user preferences to control the behavior of the service). In fact, both the TranSend and Wingman examples build upon this model.

The active service framework (Amir et al. 1998) is another approach at a substrate for network service applications that is designed for the MBone. This framework uses many concepts similar to ours: the use of clusters for availability and scalability, and soft state. It has been used as a building block for deploying media gateways for real-time audio/video transformation (Amir et al. 1995).

Our style of starfish fault tolerance is related to the peer-mode fault tolerance exhibited by early "Worm" programs (Shoch & Hupp 1982) and to "Robin Hood/Friar Tuck" fault tolerance (Raymond, E. S., ed. 1991). In (Mitzenmacher 1997), the authors analyze various load balancing policies for distributed systems that use periodic load reporting. As a rule of thumb, they found that selecting the less loaded of two randomly chosen workers worked well.

A number of other systems have used the notion of soft state to achieve better performance and robustness. Networking systems for routing protocols (McQuillan, Richer & Rosen 1980, Deering et al. 1996) and performance optimization (Balakrishnan, Seshan, Amir & Katz 1995) rely on soft state to update their tables; this allows them to continue operating in the event of partial failures and ensures that no special recovery protocols are needed to regenerate state that might have been lost in a crash. Various soft state systems such as Bayou (Demers, Peterson, Spreitzer, Terry, Theimer & Welch n.d.) have explicitly traded consistency for availability in application-specific ways.

7 CONCLUSIONS

We have presented an architecture substrate for building Internet service applications. We rely on clusters of workstations to provide guarantees of scalability and availability to the service application. Application developers program their services to a well-defined narrow interface that is used to communicate with the rest of the system. The SNS takes care of resource location, spawning, and fault detection and tolerance for the application.

Our architecture reflects principles that we believe are fundamental to the design of a scalable, available Internet service. Trading off consistency for availability via the use of soft state and periodic beaconing greatly simplifies the design and makes fault tolerance and recovery much simpler. We rely on a mode of fault tolerance that we call starfish fault tolerance. This has many advantages over traditional primary/secondary fault tolerance in terms of resource usage and recovery algorithms.

We have used this architecture for building a number of applications: a web proxy (TranSend), a proxy-based graphical web browser for PDAs (Wingman), and an MBone archive server (MARS). These applications demonstrate the versatility of the architecture, and the ability of individual applications to customize it to their requirements. Our evaluation of the system demonstrates that the load balancing strategies work in practice, and that the system is able to scale incrementally with increasing load. Two of the above services have been deployed on a permanent basis on the UC Berkeley campus, and have approximately 12,000 regular users.

As Internet services become ubiquitous, we expect to see many more systems based on our (or a similar) architecture. The exponential growth of the web will only increase the demand for application platforms for building services quickly and easily. The SNS architecture is a step in that direction.

REFERENCES

3COM Corporation (1996), '3COM PalmPilot'. http://www.palmpilot.com/.

Almeroth, K. & Ammar, M. (1998), The Interactive Multimedia Jukebox (IMJ): A new paradigm for the on-demand delivery of audio/video, *in* 'Proceedings of the Seventh International World Wide Web Conference'.

Amir, E., McCanne, S. & Katz, R. (1998), An Active Service Framework and its Application to Real-time Multimedia Transcoding, *in* 'Proceedings of ACM SIGCOMM '98'.

Amir, E., McCanne, S. & Zhang, H. (1995), An Application-level Video Gateway, *in* 'Proceedings of ACM Multimedia '95', San Francisco, CA, pp. 255–265.

Anderson, E. (1995), The Magicrouter: An Application of Fast Packet Interposing. Class report, UC Berkeley.

Anderson, T. E., Culler, D. E., Patterson, D. A. & the NOW team (1994), A Case for Networks of Workstations: NOW, *in* 'Principles of Distributed Computing'.

Anonymizer Inc. (1996), 'The Web Anonymizer'. http://www.anonymizer.com/.

Balakrishnan, H., Seshan, S., Amir, E. & Katz, R. (1995), Improving TCP/IP Performance Over Wireless Networks, *in* 'Proceedings of the first ACM Conference on Mobile

Computing and Networking', Berkeley, CA.

Bartlett, J. F. (1981), A NonStop Kernel, *in* 'Proceedings of the 8th SOSP'.

Bolosky, W. J., Fitzgerald, R. P. & Douceur, J. R. (1997), Distributed schedule management in the Tiger video fileserver, *in* 'Proceedings of the Sixteenth ACM Symposium on Operating Systems Principles'.

Borenstein, N. & Freed, N. (1993), *MIME (Multipurpose Internet Mail Extensions): Mechanisms for Specifying and Describing the Format of Internet Message Bodies*. RFC-1521.

Brisco, T. (1995), *DNS Support for Load Balancing*. RFC-1764.

Chawathe, Y., Fink, S., McCanne, S. & Brewer, E. (1998), 'A Proxy Architecture for Reliable Multicast in Heterogeneous Environments'.

Chen, M. & Hong, J. (1997), Cha-Cha: Contextualizing Hypertext Searches. Class report, UC Berkeley.

Cisco Systems (1996), 'Local Director'. http://www.cisco.com/warp/public/751/lodir/.

CitySearch Inc. (1997). http://www.citysearch.com/.

Crovella, M. E. & Bestavros, A. (1995), Explaining world wide web traffic self-similarity, Technical Report TR-95-015, Computer Science Department, Boston University.

Deering, S. E. (1991), Multicast Routing in a Datagram Internetwork, PhD thesis, Stanford University.

Deering, S., Estrin, D., Farinacci, D., Jacobson, V., Liu, C.-G. & Wei, L. (1996), 'An Architecture for Wide-area Multicast Routing', *IEEE/ACM Transactions on Networking* **4**(2).

Demers, A., Peterson, K., Spreitzer, M., Terry, D., Theimer, M. & Welch, B. (n.d.), 'The Bayou Architecture: Support for Data Sharing Among Mobile Users'.

Digital Corporation (1996), 'The AltaVista Search Engine'. http://altavista.digital.com/.

Floyd, S. & Jacobson, V. (1994), 'The Synchronization of Periodic Routing Messages', *IEEE/ACM Transactions on Networking* **2**(2), 122–136.

Fox, A. (1997), The Case For TACC: Scalable Servers for Transformation, Aggregation, Caching and Customization. *Qualifying Exam Proposal, UC Berkeley Computer Science Division.*

Fox, A., Goldberg, I., Gribble, S. D., Polito, A., Lee, D. C. & Brewer, E. A. (1998), Experience with Top Gun Wingman, A Proxy-Based Graphical Web Browser for the 3COM PalmPilot, *in* 'Proceedings of Middleware '98'.

Fox, A., Gribble, S., Brewer, E. & Amir, E. (1996), Adapting to Network and Client Variability via On-demand Dynamic Distillation, *in* 'Proceedings of ASPLOS-VII', Cambridge, MA.

Fox, A., Gribble, S., Chawathe, Y., Brewer, E. & Gauthier, P. (1997), Cluster-based Scalable Network Services, *in* 'Proceedings of SOSP '97', St. Malo, France, pp. 78–91.

Fox, A., Gribble, S. D., Chawathe, Y. & Brewer, E. A. (1998), Adapting to Network and Client Variation Using Active Proxies: Lessons and Perspectives, *in* 'A special issue of IEEE Personal Communications on Adapation'.

Gray, J. (1981), The Transaction Concept: Virtues and Limitations, *in* 'Proceedings of VLDB '81', Cannes, France, pp. 144–154.

Gribble, S. D. & Brewer, E. A. (1997), System Design Issues for Internet Middleware Services: Deductions from a Large Client Trace, *in* 'Proceedings of the 1997 Usenix Symposium on Internet Technologies and Systems', Monterey, CA.

Gribble, S. D., Manku, G. S., Roselli, D., Brewer, E. A., Gibson, T. J. & Miller, E. L. (1998), Self-Similarity in File Systems, *in* 'Proceedings of ACM SIGMETRICS '98'.

Handley, M. (1996), *SAP: Session Announcement Protocol*. Internet Draft.

Inktomi Corp. (1996), 'The HotBot Search Engine'. http://www.hotbot.com/.

Leland, W. E., Taqqu, M. S., Willinger, W. & Wilson, D. V. (1994), 'On the Self-Similar Nature of Ethernet Traffic (extended version)', *IEEE/ACM Transactions on Networking* **2**.

MapQuest (1996). http://www.mapquest.com/.

McQuillan, J., Richer, I. & Rosen, E. (1980), 'The New Routing Algorithm for the ARPANET', *IEEE Transactions on Communications* **28**(5), 711–719.

Mitzenmacher, M. (1997), How useful is old information? Extended abstract: Using stale information for load balancing in distributed systems.

Mohan et al. (1992), 'ARIES: A Transaction Recovery Method Supporting Fine-Granularity Locking and Partial Rollbacks Using Write-Ahead Logging', *TODS* **17**(1), 94–162.

National Aeronautics and Space Administration (1997), 'The Mars Pathfinder Mission Home Page'. http://mpfwww.jpl.nasa.gov/default1.html.

Nonnenmacher, J. & Biersack, E. W. (1998), Optimal Multicast Feedback, *in* 'Proceedings of IEEE INFOCOM '98', San Francisco, CA.

Raymond, E. S., ed. (1991), 'The new hackers dictionary', MIT Press. Also http://www.ccil.org/jargon/jargon.html.

Schuett, A. & Raman, S. (1997), MARS: A Media Archive Server for On-demand Remote Playback. Class report, UC Berkeley.

Schulzrinne, H., Casner, S., Frederick, R. & Jacobson, V. (1996), 'RTP: A Transport Protocol for Real-Time Applications', Internet Engineering Task Force, Audio-Video Transport Working Group. RFC-1889.

Shoch, J. F. & Hupp, J. A. (1982), 'The "Worm" programs: Early Experiences with Distributed Systems', *Communications of the Association for Computing Machinery* **25**(3), 172–180.

Waldspurger, C. & Weihl, W. (1994), Lottery Scheduling: Flexible Proportional Share Resource Management, *in* 'Proceedings of the First OSDI'.

Yahoo! Inc (1995). http://www.yahoo.com/.

Yoshikawa, C., Chun, B., Eastham, P., Anderson, T. & Culler, D. (1997), Using Smart Clients to Build Scalable Services, *in* 'Proceedings of USENIX '97'.

8 BIOGRAPHY

Yatin Chawathe is a doctoral student at the University of California, Berkeley. He received a Bachelor of Engineering (Computer Engineering) degree from the University of Bombay, India, and a Master of Science (Computer Science) from the University of California, Berkeley. His primary interests are Internet services and application support for reliable multicast in heterogeneous environments.

Eric A. Brewer is an Assistant Professor of Computer Science at the University of California, Berkeley, and received his PhD in Computer Science from MIT in 1994. Interests include mobile and wireless computing (the InfoPad and Daedalus projects); scalable servers (the NOW, Inktomi, and TranSend projects); and application- and system-level security (the ISAAC project). Previous work includes multiprocessor-network software and topologies, and high-performance multiprocessor simulation.

Session 3

Availability and Integrity

Highly Available Trading System: Experiments with CORBA

Xavier Défago, Karim R. Mazouni, André Schiper
Département d'Informatique, École Polytechnique Fédérale
CH-1015 Lausanne, Switzerland.
Tel +41 21 693 4240. Fax: +41 21 693 6770
email: {Xavier.Defago,Karim.Mazouni,Andre.Schiper}@epfl.ch

Abstract

The Swiss Exchange system (SWX system) was the first stock exchange system in service to be fully computerised. For high availability, the trading system is built as a replicated service based on Isis. For portability reasons, the SWX team has considered basing the next version of the trading system on CORBA. Despite the numerous advantages of a CORBA based solution, it was necessary not only to meet the functionality requirements of the system, but also to evaluate the performance of the chosen middleware.

This paper describes a model that simulates the communication behavior of the trading system on Iona's Orbix and OrbixTalk. We have evaluated this model in order to illustrate some of the performance limitations of this communication infrastructure. We have also studied the fault-tolerance of the system and found that a key aspect in such a system is the state transfer. We have extended our model to support different schemes for state transfer. Measurements have shown us the conditions under which a state transfer could be performed in the background, concurrently with the normal operations.

Keywords

CORBA, event service, IP-multicast, performance prediction, state transfer, high availability

1 INTRODUCTION

Back in 1996, the Swiss Exchange system (SWX system) was the first stock exchange system in service to be fully computerised (Piantoni *et al.* 1997). The architecture of the system is based on two main components, the *exchange system* (ES) and the *trading system* (TS) (see Figure 1). The exchange system is unique and runs at the SWX headquarters in Zurich. The TS is run by SWX clients, and acts like a cache, extended with local information. For higher availability, the TS is built as a replicated service based on Isis (Birman *et al.* 1993). After one year of activity, the proprietary aspect of Isis, as well as some scalability problems, have led SWX to consider basing the next version of the TS on CORBA (OMG 1995). In addition, it was observed that the current system makes no use of the virtual synchrony provided by Isis.

In a collaboration with SWX, we have developed a model of the TS based on Iona's Orbix (IONA 1996*a*), and evaluated the performance of the communications. Our role was twofold: 1) to investigate the performance of Orbix, and 2) to improve the fault-tolerance of the system by working on the state transfer mechanism.

Concerning 1), one of the most critical part of the TS regarding the performance and scalability of communication is the broadcasting of quotes to the traders. For scalability reasons, we have built this mechanism on top of OrbixTalk (IONA 1996*b*), an implementation of the event service (OMG 1996) based on IP-multicast and a negative acknowledgement protocol.

Concerning 2), since the TS is a replicated service, an important problem is the recovery of a replica after a crash. When a crashed replica recovers, it needs to update its state according to the current state of the system. This is done by transferring the state of an up-to-date replica to the recovering replica. The mechanism that Isis provides for implementing the state transfer was found to be much too costly. Furthermore, the Isis mechanism for state transfer blocks the whole replicated service until the state has been transferred. As a result, in the current implementation the state transfer has to be done off-line, during the night. In the new TS, one of the requirements is to be able to perform an on-line state transfer. We designed an adequate mechanism that is compatible with this requirement, and evaluated its performance.

The rest of the paper is structured as follows. In Section 2, we give an quick overview of the Swiss Exchange System, with a clear emphasis on the TS. In Section 3, we present the environment in which our measures have been performed. We also show the architecture of the TS in this environment. In Section 4, we answer some important questions about the performance limits of the system. In Section 5, we illustrate the problems that we encountered when designing the on-line state transfer mechanism. Finally, Section 6 concludes the paper.

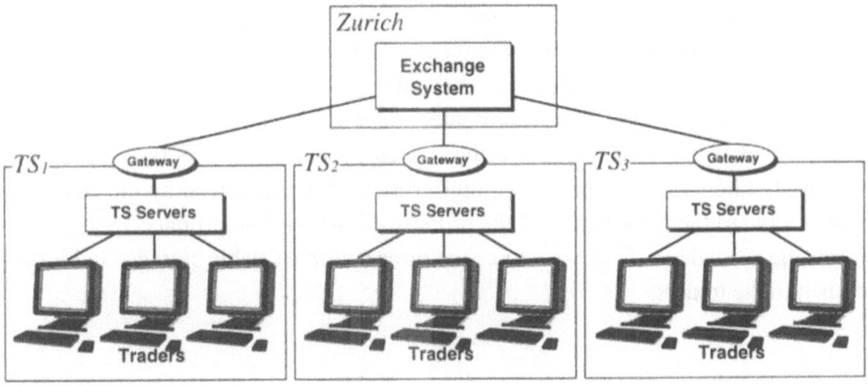

Figure 1 Architecture of the Swiss Stock Exchange.

2 THE SWISS STOCK EXCHANGE

The architecture of the SWX system is described in (Piantoni *et al.* 1997). We give here a brief overview of this architecture (see Figure 1). The Exchange System (ES) is the core of the SWX system, and is based in Zurich. It allows trading against a central order book. Market changes are interactively forwarded to all members.

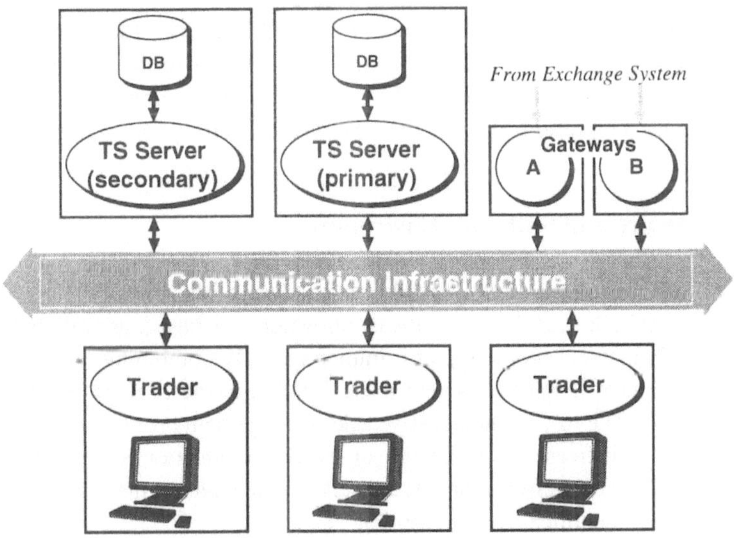

Figure 2 Architecture of the Trading System.

The SWX clients receive information issued by the ES, through a (possibly replicated) gateway. Each SWX client runs a TS which caches the information coming from the gateways. The TS is an intermediary between the traders and the ES, and allows as well traders to interact with each other.

The architecture of the TS is represented in Figure 2. The communication infrastructure makes it possible for the different components of the TS to communicate with each other. The information coming from the ES is received by the gateways, which forward the information to the primary TS server. The primary TS server informs the secondary TS server, stores the information on stable storage, and broadcasts it to the traders.

3 CONTEXT OF OUR EXPERIMENTS

3.1 Trading System Model

We have modelled the different entities of the TS as objects, represented in Figure 3. The *traders* represent the different objects that receive information from the TS server and issue information to the TS server. The TS server is replicated. The *primary server* is the active part of the TS. First, it receives messages from the Exchange System: information coming from the ES is generated in our model by the *source* (see Figure 3, arrow 1). Second, it broadcasts the relevant information changes to the traders (see Figure 3, arrow 2), and it keeps information on stable storage. The *secondary server* has a passive role. Similar to the primary, it keeps persistent information, but it does not broadcast any information to the traders. Arrow 3 in Figure 3 represents the state transfer and is discussed in Section 5.

3.2 Hardware and Software Environment

We have implemented our model using Orbix and OrbixTalk. One of the main reason to choose OrbixTalk, was the IP-multicast on which it is based, as well as the negative acknowledgement protocol that it implements. By combining these two characteristics, we have found the system to be scalable in the context of a local area network (LAN). The role of the negative acknowledgement protocol that OrbixTalk implements is to increase the reliability of the communication. OrbixTalk retransmits messages in a best-effort manner; a receiver which detects that a message could not be delivered is notified by an exception.

The environment in which the measures have been performed is a cluster of workstations. The cluster consists of Sun's SPARC stations (Sparc-20 50 MHz and Ultra Sparc-1 167 MHz) running Solaris 2.5.1, and interconnected with a 10 Mbits Ethernet.

The measures that we present in Section 4 and Section 5 were performed with OrbixTalk 1.04, and Orbix 2.1MT. Earlier versions of OrbixTalk had very limited

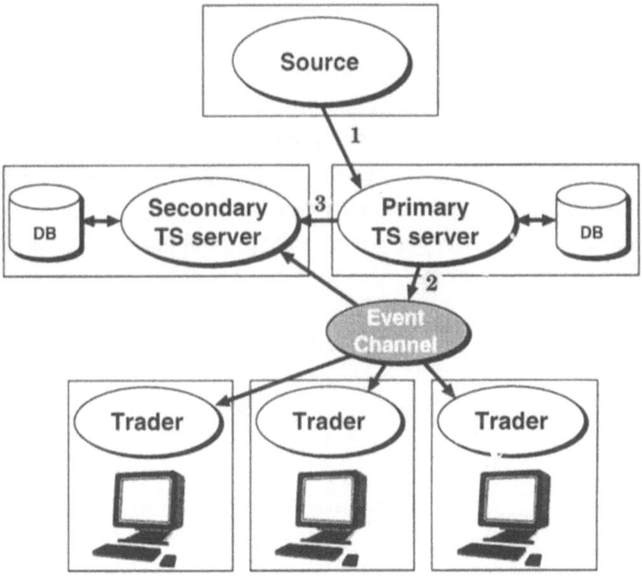

Figure 3 Model of the Trading System.

performance with respect to our needs. With Orbix 1.04, the performance is satisfactory.

4 INFORMATION FLOW BETWEEN THE PRIMARY SERVER AND THE TRADERS

One of the most critical performance aspect of the TS is the flow of information between the primary server and the traders. Since the expected throughput of messages emitted by the primary server is more than 200 Kb/s and the number of traders can be over a hundred, the scalability of the communication is of great importance: these figures are expected to increase in the future.

The main reason for building our prototype was to answer questions related to the design of the TS.

- *Is OrbixTalk scalable with respect to the number of traders?*
- *What is the effect of a slow trader on the overall system?*
- *What throughput can be reached using an OrbixTalk event channel?*
- *What about using two OrbixTalk event channels in parallel?*

4.1 Measures

We have considered a source (Figure 3) that emits messages at a given *target throughput*. These messages are received by the primary TS server, which emits them to the traders through an OrbixTalk event channel. A dozen of traders where receiving those messages. We measured the rate at which messages where actually emitted by the primary, and the rate at which they were received by the traders. Our results show the *instantaneous throughput*, which is the throughput achieved at every single instant in time.

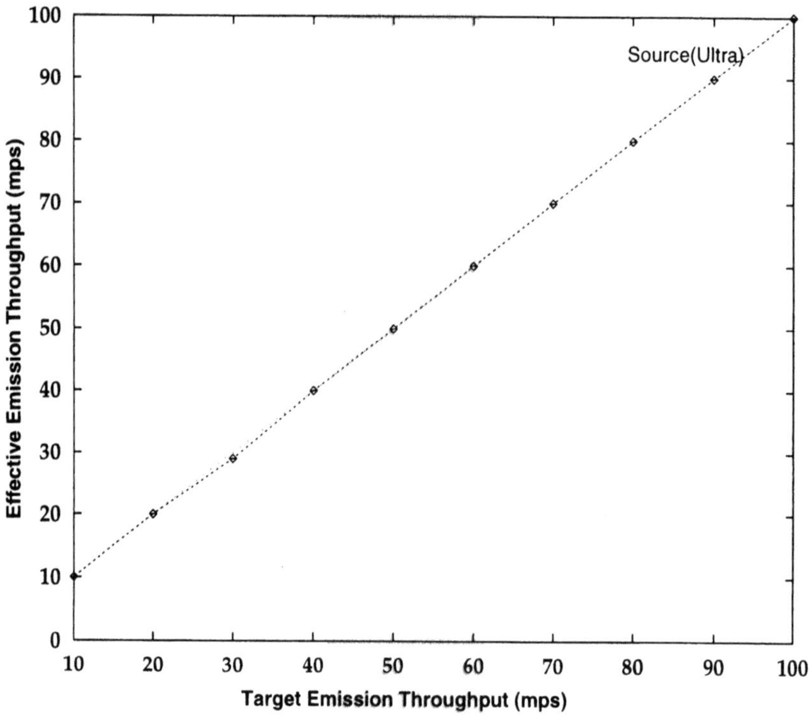

Figure 4 Effective emission throughput.

The size of the messages is 8 Kb. Associated with each incoming message, the traders perform a 5 ms processing. The primary TS server was run on an UltraSparc workstation. The traders run on a group of Sparc-20, and UltraSparc workstations. There is exactly one trader on each workstation and a total of 12 traders.

We measured the effective emission throughput with increasing emission rates. These measures are illustrated in Figure 4. We see that the source can emit messages at any required rate between 10 and 100 messages per second. Measures performed under the same conditions, with earlier versions of OrbixTalk could not go beyond 70 messages per second.

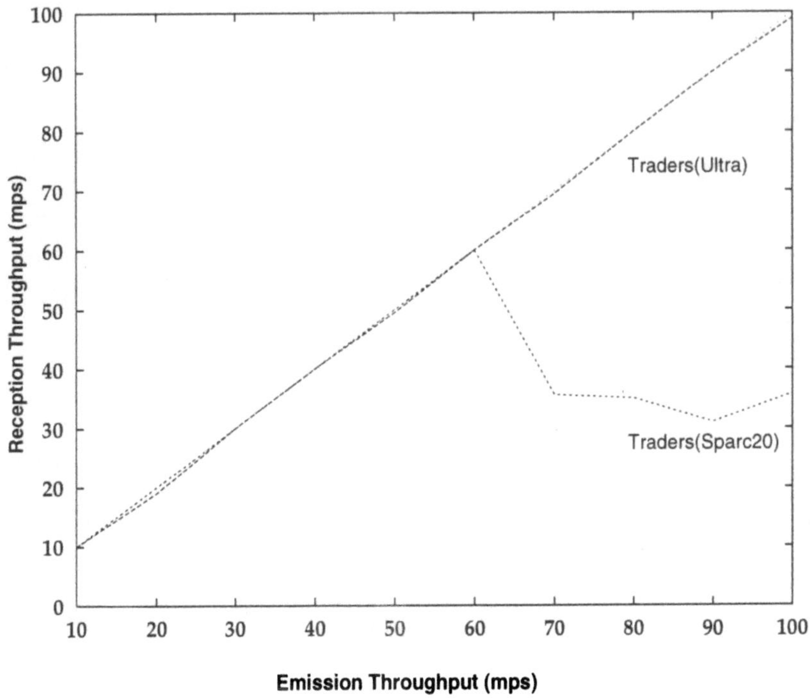

Figure 5 Emission vs. reception throughput.

Figure 5 represents the evolution of the reception throughput, as the emission throughput increases. When the traders are not overloaded, the reception throughput is equal to the emission throughput. Nevertheless, Figure 5 shows that some traders cannot cope with a rate higher than 60 messages per second (the traders that run on a Sparc-20 workstation). In that case, the reception throughput is lower than the emission throughput. As a result, an increasing number of messages get stored into buffers, and eventually, messages have to be dropped. Figure 5 shows different reception throughput for the two types of workstations. This shows that the actual bottleneck is not the network, but rather the software layers that handle the reception of messages.

Figure 6 represents the temporal evolution of the instantaneous throughput at a target emission rate of 70 messages per second. Figure 6 shows a strong disparity between platforms. A superposition of the curves of both the source and the fast traders (Ultra-1) in Figure 5, shows that the fast traders can cope with a rate of 70 messages per second. However, the traders that run on the Sparc-20 workstations can clearly not cope with a rate of 70 messages per second. The temporal behavior of the reception throughput gives a good indication of what may happen here. The traders receive messages at a rate they cannot handle, i.e. the reception buffers overflow. When this

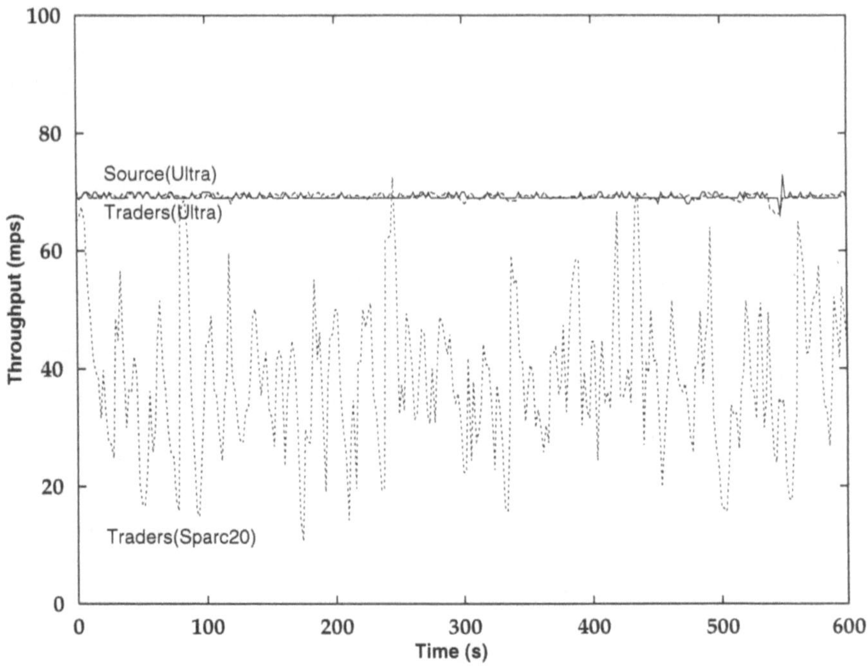

Figure 6 Emission throughput of 70 msg/s.

situation arises, OrbixTalk drops a bunch of messages to have a chance to catch up with the reception rate. This behavior confers a 'saw-like' aspect to the curve.

Initially, we thought that the emission of messages would be a bottleneck in the TS. We were surprised to see that the actual bottleneck lies in the reception of messages. This is probably due to the higher cost of *unmarshaling* of parameters compared to the cost of *marshaling* of parameters.

To sum up, the performance of the system is limited by the performance of the traders (the bottleneck is located at the reception). We observe a great disparity between traders, depending on the computational performance of the machine on which they are running.

4.2 Discussion

The analysis of the measures that we have gathered from our experiments allows us to answer our questions. These questions about performance are quite fundamental when it comes to consider building a demanding application on a new platform. Knowing the limits of such a platform is almost as important as the capabilities since it determines whether the non-functional requirements of the application can be reached.

- *Is OrbixTalk scalable with respect to the number of traders?*
  Among the measures that we have performed on OrbixTalk (these measures are not presented here), we have observed that the number of traders does not slow down the emission of messages.
- *What is the effect of a slow trader on the overall system?*
  One of the most interesting aspect of the measures presented in Figure 6 is the fact that slow traders (Sparc-20) do not affect the whole system; the fast traders (Ultra-1) and the source can still sustain the desired rate, although the slow traders cannot. This is confirmed by Figure 5.
- *What throughput can be reached using an OrbixTalk event channel?*
  We have found this question to greatly depend on the CPU power of the workstations. For traders running on Sparc-20, the limit is clearly lower than for traders running on Ultra-1. Indeed, Figure 5 show that slow traders (Sparc-20) stall when the system throughput exceeds 60 messages per second. On the other hand, fast traders (Ultra-1) can still cope with a throughput of 100 messages per second.
- *What about using two OrbixTalk event channels in parallel?*
  In other measures that are not presented here, we have tested other communication architectures, among which two event channels in parallel to see if this could increase the maximum throughput from the primary server to the traders. We have found the maximum throughput not to depend on the number of event channels. In other words, two event channels do not allow for a higher emission throughput than a single one since they compete for the same resources (network, CPU).

5 ON-LINE RECOVERY

In the current TS based on Isis, the state transfer is performed off-line. In other words, when a server crashes, it can only be restarted during the night, when the stock exchange is closed. This leads to two major problems. 1) the reliability is reduced since a second failure in the same day cannot be masked, and 2) it makes it impossible to guarantee 24 hours a day availability as may be required in the future (Piantoni *et al.* 1997).

The reason that led to such a limitation on the Isis based TS has to do with the mechanism that Isis provides for state transfer. During a state transfer Isis requires the whole group to block until the state transfer is finished. Although such a limitation is acceptable for systems with small states, the TS cannot allow it. The state to transfer is quite large (30 Mb or more, depending on the down-time). We have performed further measurements to answer the following question.

- *Is it possible to implement a non-blocking on-line state transfer?*
  A non-blocking state transfer means that, during the state transfer, the primary is not blocked and can still provide its normal service.

To answer this question, we have tried to find the conditions under which a non-blocking state transfer is possible.

5.1 Measures

We have implemented a mechanism that allows us to measure the impact of the state transfer on the normal execution of the TS. Messages are sent to the primary at a constant rate by the source, using CORBA method invocations (Figure 3, arrow 1). The messages are relayed to the traders by the primary, through an event channel (Figure 3, arrow 2 to the traders). In our experiment, the secondary starts after 5 minutes and requests a state transfer from the primary, with a CORBA method invocation (Figure 3, arrow 3). At the same time, the secondary begins to receive messages from the primary, through the event channel (Figure 3, arrow 2 to the secondary).

The tests have been made with the following parameters: the messages are emitted by the source at a rate of 50 messages per second. The state to transfer from the primary to the secondary has a size of 20 Mb. The source, the primary, and the secondary run on UltraSparc workstations. The traders run on Sparc-20, and UltraSparc workstations. There is exactly one trader on each workstation in the cluster, and a total of 10 traders.

In Figure 7, the state is transferred in one block of 20 Mb, with a single Orbix invocation. This transfer starts after about 300 s and is responsible of the black-out period shown in Figure 7. Figure 7 clearly shows that this solution leads to instabilities once the transfer is finished (the 'saw-like' aspect of the curves). With a larger state, the resulting instabilities become even stronger. This behavior poses at least two major problems, 1) the unavailability of the system during the state transfer breaks some of the requirements of the TS (Piantoni *et al.* 1997), and 2) if the network is slightly more loaded, the traders may stall and never be able to catch up.

In order to circumvent this problem, we have modified the mechanism for state transfer, to allow the transfer of the state in smaller messages. Further measures where taken, where the 20 Mb state was transferred in 640 chunks of 32 Kb each (i.e., 640 Orbix invocations). Surprisingly, the resulting measures showed exactly the same behavior than a state transfer in one block (see Figure 7).

In Figure 8, the state is also cut into 640 chunks of 32 Kb (for a total of 20 Mb). But, unlike the previous measures, the chunks are sent one after another, with a pause interval of 50 ms between the emission of two chunks. As shown in Figure 8, this solution does not hinder the normal execution, and the flow of messages to the traders is not influenced by the state transfer.

To summarise, our measures show that it is not enough to implement state transfer in a separate thread, but it is also important to split the state into smaller chunks and add a pause between the emission of two chunks.

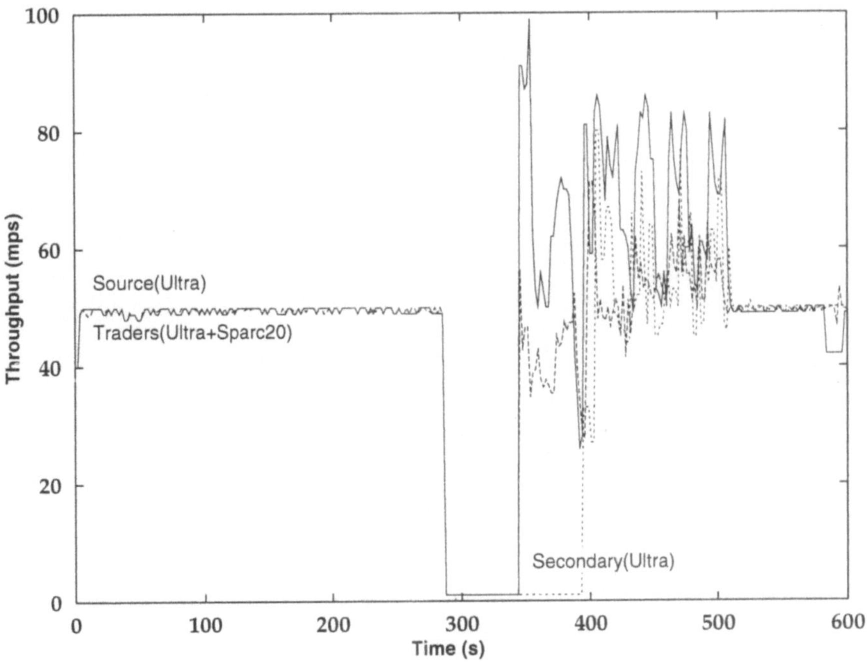

Figure 7 State transfer (1 × 20 Mb).

5.2 Discussion

This simulation of a state transfer gives us invaluable information on the behavior that we can expect from Orbix and OrbixTalk. The problem of a state transfer (or the transfer of a large amount of information) is a common problem in practice, but often neglected. In highly-available distributed applications, a state transfer is needed whenever a secondary server recovers from a crash.

In the context of the TS, the only way to allow an online recovery of the secondary server is to implement a non-blocking state transfer. In other words, if the primary server is blocked for the whole duration of the state transfer, the state transfer has to be made off-line. Among other things, such a restriction makes it impossible to consider running the service 24 hours a day. It also reduces the number of failures tolerated by the system during a single day.

- *Is it possible to implement a non blocking on-line state transfer?*
  Considering the measures made in Section 5.1, the answer is yes. However, this is only possible under the following conditions.

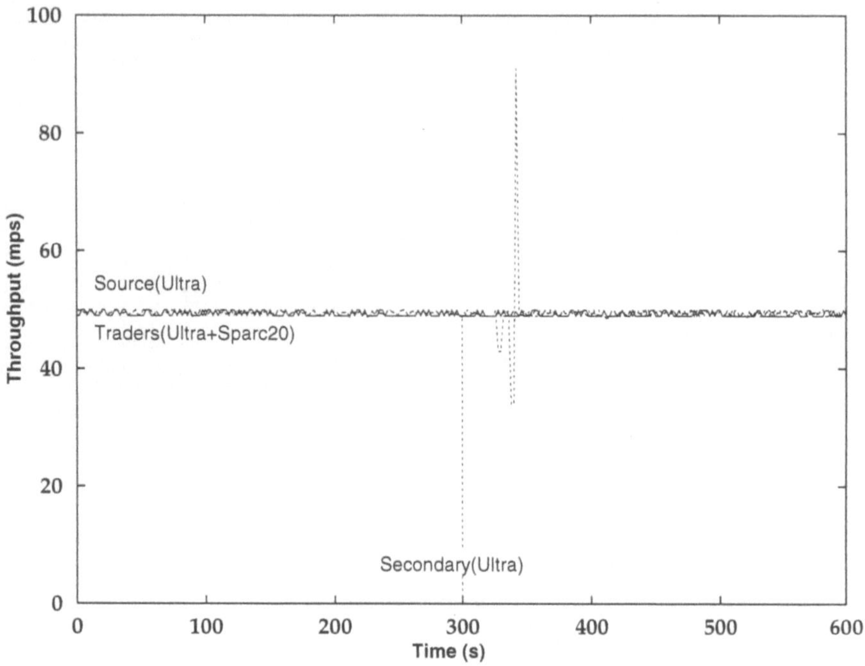

Figure 8 State transfer (640 × 32 Kb).

- The state transfer mechanism is decoupled from the servers; i.e., the state transfer is performed by another thread.
- The state is cut into smaller chunks, with a pause between the emission of each chunk.

6 CONCLUSION

The experiments described in the paper have enabled us to answer some important questions with respect to using a CORBA based communication infrastructure for the TS.

In Section 4, we have investigated the performance aspect of OrbixTalk with respect to the emission of information to the traders. We have seen this performance to greatly depend on the CPU power of the involved machines, rather than the network capabilities. The development of our model has shown us that i) most of the overhead comes from the unmarshaling of parameters, ii) the performance of OrbixTalk has improved between versions, iii) decent performance could only be reached by modifying undocumented parameters, iv) slow receivers do not slow down the whole system.

In Section 5, we have investigated the state transfer aspect of the TS. We have shown that, with an adequate mechanism, a non-blocking state transfer is possible, even if the state to transfer is large. This not only requires to decouple the state transfer from the normal service, but also to split the state into smaller chunks and introduce a pause between the emission of two consecutive chunks. To sum up, the experiments have shown us the problems raised by requirements such as responsiveness, throughput, or scalability, in particular in the context of state transfer. A system with a blocking state transfer such as Isis, is not realistic for applications with a large state. This is not only a practical problem, but it also comes in contradiction with the high availability that such a system is supposed to provide.

ACKNOWLEDGEMENTS

We would like to thank the SWX laboratory and more specifically Rico Piantoni, Constantin Stancescu, and Benoît Jardin.

REFERENCES

Birman, K. and van Renesse, R. (1993), *Reliable Distributed Computing with the Isis Toolkit*, IEEE Computer Society Press.

IONA (1996*a*), *Orbix Programming Guide*, IONA Technologies Ltd.

IONA (1996*b*), *OrbixTalk Programming Guide*, IONA Technologies Ltd.

Object Management Group (1995), *The Common Object Request Broker: Architecture and Specification*, OMG. Revision 2.0.

Object Management Group (1996), *CORBAservices: Common Object Services Specification*, OMG.

Piantoni, R. and Stancescu, C. (1997), Implementing the Swiss Exchange trading system, *in* 'Proceedings of the 27th International Symposium on Fault-Tolerant Computing', IEEE Computer Society Press, Seattle, Washington, USA, pp. 309–313.

BIOGRAPHIES

Xavier Défago graduated from the EPFL (Federal Institute of Technology in Lausanne) in 1995. After working for a year on parallel operating systems at NEC C&C Central Research Labs. in Kawazaki (Japan), he joins Prof. André Schiper's Operating Systems laboratory as a research assistant and a PhD student. His research interests are in the areas of fault-tolerant distributed systems, distributed algorithms, operating systems principles, and real-time systems.

Karim Riad Mazouni received a PhD (EPFL, 1996), an MSc. (Univ. of Paris, 1990) and an engineer's degree (Univ. of Algiers, 1988) in Computer Science. He spends several years at the EPFL, teaching operating systems, and doing research on fault-tolerant and object-oriented distributed systems. At that time, his research focused on support for replicated objects invocation. In January 1998, he joins the Union Bank of Switzerland (UBS) as a system architect. His current activities at UBS focus on the design of object-oriented distributed services (such as a corporate-wide directory service) that will implement the core functionality of the company's distributed computing platform.

André Schiper has been professor of Computer Science at the EPFL (Federal Institute of Technology in Lausanne) since 1985, leading the Operating Systems laboratory. He has worked on the implementation of communication primitives for the Isis system, developed at Cornell University. His research interests are in the areas of fault-tolerant distributed systems and group communication. In the context of CORBA, his group is currently working on the specification and the implementation of a replication service.

André Schiper is a member of the ESPRIT Basic Research Network of Excellence in Distributed Computing Systems Architectures (CaberNet).

Integrity management in GUARDS

E. Totel[♠], *Lj. Beus-Dukic*[♣], *J.-P. Blanquart*[♦], *Y. Deswarte*[♠], *D. Powell*[♠], *A. Wellings*[♣]

♠*LAAS-CNRS, 7 avenue du Colonel Roche, 31077 Toulouse 4, France, phone: 33 561 33 64 06, fax: 33 561 33 64 11, e-mail: {totel, blanquart, deswarte, dpowell}@laas.fr*

♣ *Department of Computer Science, University of York, York, YO1 5DD, United Kingdom, phone: 44 1904 432735, fax:44 1904 432767, e-mail: {ljerka,andy}@cs.york.ac.uk*

♦ *Matra Marconi Space, 31 avenue des cosmonautes, 31042 Toulouse Cedex 4, France, phone: 33 562 19 69 56, fax: 33 5 62 19 57 78, e-mail: {jean-paul.blanquart}@tls.mms.fr*

Abstract

We present an approach for the management of highly critical tasks coexisting with non-critical tasks in a single processor or multiprocessor architecture. To prevent error propagation from non-critical to critical tasks, an integrity level is assigned to groups of tasks according to their trustworthiness. Multiple levels of integrity are implemented using spatial and temporal isolation, and mediation via an integrity policy. The integrity policy defines the rules for data flow between integrity levels and resource utilisation by the tasks at different levels. Since the GUARDS project aims to provide generic solutions for a variety of application domains, the described integrity management can be implemented either in a middleware, the operating system or both. In this paper, we show a CORBA-compliant implementation of the integrity policy.

Keywords

integrity level, integrity policy, integrity firewalls, middleware, CORBA

1 INTRODUCTION

A consortium of European companies and academic partners is currently developing a Generic Upgradable Architecture for Real-time Dependable Systems (GUARDS[1]), together with an associated development and validation environment. The end-user companies in the consortium have very different requirements and constraints resulting from the diversity of their application domains: nuclear submarine, railway and space systems. Hence, one of the fundamental goals of the project is to support reusability of hardware and software components and architectures in multiple applications and domains. In addition to genericity, GUARDS pledges to minimise the impact of hardware faults and the presence of software design faults.

The GUARDS consortium decided to use commercial off-the-shelf (COTS) hardware and software components as building blocks for any specific instance of GUARDS generic architecture. This decision is in line with the effort to produce cost-effective and open architectures that will replace costly proprietary architectures traditionally used for real-time dependable systems. However, some of the components have to be purpose-designed and built. These specific GUARDS components implement the dependability mechanisms and effectively form a middleware layer that lies between a COTS operating system layer and an application layer. Among these dependability mechanisms, we focus here on the GUARDS multiple level integrity mechanisms.

The GUARDS architecture (Powell, 1997) includes multiple levels of integrity whose purpose is to protect critical components from the propagation of errors due to residual design faults in less-critical components. The notions of multiple integrity levels and multiple criticality levels are very tightly linked, but there is an important distinction. Integrity levels are associated with an integrity policy that defines what is allowed in terms of data flow between levels and resource utilisation by the components at different levels. Criticality levels are defined in terms of the potential consequences of failures of components at each level.

The aim of integrity level management is to ensure that low-integrity information does not contaminate high-integrity information. This requires the enforcement of an integrity policy to mediate the communication between software components of different levels. It must also be ensured that it is not possible to by-pass the controls put into place to enforce the policy, i.e., illicit communication between application components of different levels of integrity must be prohibited. This is achieved by spatial and temporal isolation.

The most effective spatial and temporal isolation is to have software components of different levels of integrity supported by totally separate machines. In this case,

---

[1] GUARDS is partially financed by the European Commission as ESPRIT project n° 20716. The consortium consists of three end-user companies: Technicatome (France), Ansaldo Segnalemento Ferrovario (Italy) and Matra Marconi Space France; two technology-provider companies: Intecs Sistemi (Italy), Siemens AG Österreich PSA (Austria); and three academic partners: LAAS-CNRS (France), Pisa Dependable Computing Centre (Italy) and the University of York (United Kingdom).

the only means for communication between them is through the network. The controls for integrity policy enforcement are then concerned only with network messages. However, this approach is expensive since it requires the use of several machines, even when a single machine is sufficiently powerful to support all the applications.

When several levels of integrity must be supported by a single machine, isolation is more problematic. Spatial isolation requires that each application resides in a different section of memory and is protected by memory management hardware. Temporal isolation must ensure that low-integrity processes do not prevent high integrity processes from accessing essential system resources (such as CPUs or communication paths).

The integrity policy defined in this paper is based on this notion of integrity levels (similar to the safety integrity levels of IEC 1508 (IEC, 1995)), and focuses on the problem of the interactions between software components at different integrity levels. The interactions may occur through sharing of hardware or software resources or by explicit co-operation between entities. Interactions can thus occur either at the system level (the system being composed of the operating system software and the hardware it is running on) or at the application level. Interactions can be divided into two groups: spatial interactions (i.e., modification of code or data) and temporal interactions (e.g., hogging of a resource that becomes unavailable for other application entities). More precisely, each interaction can be either the consequence of normal operation or the result of a residual fault in a software component. Our model aims to contain such faults. Thus, we apply a mediation on information exchange to verify that all information flows during an execution are legal. To prevent contamination of a high integrity component by lower integrity component containing residual design faults, our integrity policy defines rules on data flows.

The rest of the paper is organised as follows. Section 2 shows how the integrity policy fits into an object-oriented model, and Section 3 gives details of the actual integrity mechanisms. In Section 4, the feasibility of the integrity mechanism implementation is demonstrated in CORBA. Section 5 presents some of the related work, and Section 6 concludes with a summary and discussion of the implementation phase.

2 THE GUARDS APPROACH

The integrity management model proposed in the GUARDS architecture is based on an object-oriented approach. Our purpose is to define a generic way to characterise and check the information flows between the different objects running in the system. We are then able to prevent the contamination of high integrity objects by lower integrity ones.

2.1 Object-model paradigm

Our model considers that an object is an entity that provides services that can be requested by clients (OMG, 1995). It is the instance of a class, and is composed of both its internal state (known as its attributes), and its methods (i.e., the services it provides).

The model of invocation is based on message exchange. Each time an object requests a service from another object, it must send it a message which carries both the name of the invoked method and the data items necessary to complete its execution (the parameters). Each message received by an object results in the execution of the requested service. The execution of a given method can, of course, provoke new invocations, and so the creation of new messages.

Each object is classified within a particular integrity level according to how much it can be trusted (the more trustworthy an object is, the higher its integrity level). The degree to which an object can be trusted depends on the evidence that is available supporting its correctness, and the consequences of its failure (i.e., its criticality). We consider that a message has the same integrity level as the object which created it (we can trust the message contents as much as its creator), and that an integrity label carried by the message itself defines this level. The integrity label enables the integrity rules to be checked at message reception.

2.2 Information flows

Our aim is to avoid error propagation from low integrity level objects to higher level objects. No upward information flow should be allowed, because a low integrity object could provide faulty or corrupted information to a high integrity object. This is the main goal of our policy and is the basis of others (Biba, 1977). However, in an object model, all invocations of an object do not necessarily produce a flow of information that can corrupt the invoked entity. Consequently, we will apply constraints on information flows, and not on invocations (Jajodia and Kogan, 1990).

Generally speaking, no information flow should be allowed from low integrity objects to high integrity objects. However, this approach is inflexible. An object can get a data item of higher integrity than itself, but the data item will then inherit the level of integrity of this object. This results in a degradation of the information, without any possibility to restore it. We deal with this drawback by providing a special kind of objects (*Validation Objects*) whose role is to apply fault tolerance mechanisms on information flows. The purpose of these objects is to output reliable information by using possibly corrupted data items as input (i.e., with a low integrity level). Such objects upgrade the trustworthiness of data items and allow thereby information flows from low to high integrity levels.

3 INTEGRITY MECHANISMS

In the following sections, we define the integrity mechanisms used to ensure that no low integrity object can corrupt high integrity objects.

3.1 Definitions and notations

Our intent is to define a flexible integrity policy, which can be easily applicable and usable in a variety of systems and applications. For this reason, we define three kinds of objects:

- **Single Level Objects (SLOs)** are assigned a single constant integrity level, which represents the level of confidence we can have in their execution. Like any object, they can contain information and so create flows using their internal data. Basically, they should not read data items of lower integrity level than themselves, and should not provide information to higher integrity levels. However, these rules are very restrictive when building an application: if a service must be made available to many objects with various integrity levels, an instance of the object must be created at every level where it is needed.
- **Multi Level Objects (MLOs)** provide a solution to this problem. They allow more flexibility by being able to provide service to several integrity levels. They are validated to a given integrity level (in the same way as SLOs) and can dynamically modify their current integrity level to be able either to provide a service or use data at the needed level. However, they must be designed so that they cannot produce illegal information flows from low to high levels, even between different invocations. To guarantee this property, we choose to ensure that these objects have no memory, i.e., they do not store any state from one invocation to another. This can be done by creating a new object (and so a new context) at each invocation. Such an object does not keep any memory of previous invocations (e.g., a stateless file server such as NFS) and can be used to implement services needed at every level.
- **Validation Objects** are particular instances of SLOs that fulfil the requirements to allow flows from low to high integrity levels. Such upward flows are essential in many applications. Consider, for example, an airplane guidance control function that needs pressure information coming from unreliable pitot tubes. Sensor data (and the drivers whose role it is to make their values available) are given a low integrity level since they are unreliable. However, the guidance task is given a high integrity level because it is highly critical. As it is currently defined, the information flow policy would prevent the guidance task from reading sensor values. In such systems with unreliable sources, it is common to use several redundant sensors to be able to tolerate the failure of some of them. For instance, the computation of the median of a vector of sensor values will produce a more trustworthy information than any single sensor. In that case, the median computation result can be given a high integrity level, even if each of its inputs is low integrity data. That is the purpose of validation objects: they take low integrity inputs and apply fault

tolerance mechanisms to produce high integrity outputs. Consequently, they can be authorised to produce what should be otherwise considered as illegal information flows from a low integrity level to a high integrity level.

Formally, we define O the set of objects of the system, which are either single-level objects or multilevel objects, defining thus a partition of O: $\{SLO, MLO\}$. I is the set of the integrity levels and il: $O \rightarrow I$ associates to each object o its *current* integrity level $il(o)$. We also define a partial order relation ($\leq$) between the elements of I.

3.2 GUARDS integrity policy

We will now describe our integrity policy and how we apply it to control information flows. The integrity architecture we propose is described in Figure 1.

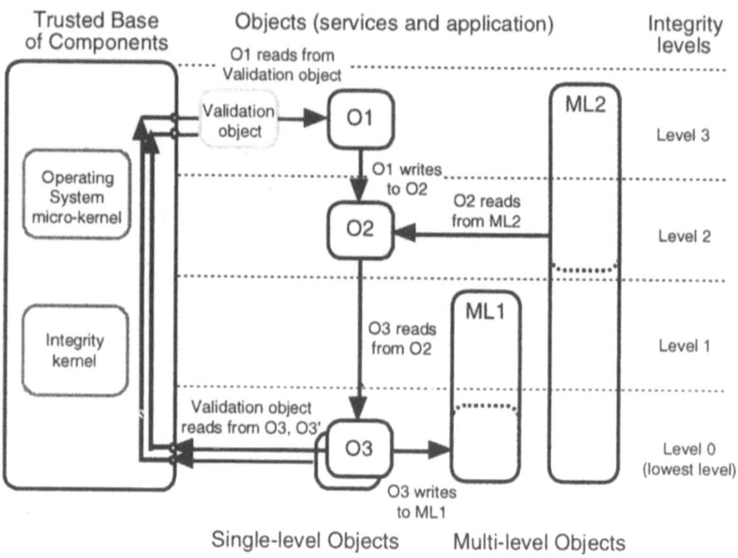

Figure 1: GUARDS Integrity Architecture.

Method classification

Two sorts of information flow can occur: *explicit* data flow, i.e., attributes passing as parameters of an object method invocation, and *implicit* data flow, i.e., when the execution of the called method can potentially have a consequence on the object state, even if no parameters are passed (e.g., when an object is requested to increment one of its internal attributes). In both cases, a flow of information sent to a method can corrupt it. To control the data flows, we must be able to determine whether a call to a method is carrying information or not. We thus distinguish three types of methods:

- **Read invocation**: the invocation provokes no state modification of the called object. Typically, this corresponds to a request to obtain information from an object. There is an information flow from the invoked object to the caller.
- **Write invocation**: the invocation provokes a modification of the state of the called object. The method either modifies the internal state of the object, or uses parameters as entries. There is an *explicit* or *implicit* information flow from the caller to the called object.
- **Read-Write invocation**: this type of method generates a bi-directional flow between the calling and the called object.

This classification is the basis of the rules we define in the next section. According to the type of a given method, we can evaluate if an invocation could corrupt an object, and decide if an invocation is permitted or not, depending on the integrity levels of the calling and called objects.

SLO to SLO access rules

Each SLO is assigned a single integrity level according to the evidence gathered in support of its trustworthiness. The only rules it must follow are that it cannot access data with a lower integrity level than itself, or accept information from a lower integrity object. Consequently, SLOs may be read by lower or equal integrity level objects and may write to lower or equal integrity level objects. An SLO is described using a singleton $\{il(O)\}$. The rules we define on SLO to SLO accesses can be described as follows:

- To invoke Read methods:
  $\forall (O_1, O_2) \in SLO \times SLO,\ O_1\ read\ O_2 \Rightarrow il(O_1) \leq il(O_2)$
- To invoke Write methods:
  $\forall (O_1, O_2) \in SLO \times SLO,\ O_1\ write\ O_2 \Rightarrow il(O_2) \leq il(O_1)$
- To invoke Read-Write methods:
  $\forall (O_1, O_2) \in SLO \times SLO,\ O_1\ readwrite\ O_2 \Rightarrow il(O_2) = il(O_1)$

The three rules can be explained as follows: an object O_1 can read an information from an object O_2 only if O_1 has at most the same integrity level as O_2, i.e., if O_1 can provide information with a sufficient level of integrity, so that O_2 cannot be corrupted. Moreover, an object O_1 can provide information to an object O_2 (write rule) only if it has at least the same integrity level as O_2, i.e., it can provide data which are reliable enough to be used by this object. Finally, read-write operations (i.e., information exchange) can, of course, be completed only if both objects can have mutual confidence. The read-write rule is in fact defined as a logical **and** between the read and write rules.

MLO access rules

Like a single level object, an MLO is also assigned an integrity level, according to the evidence gathered in support of its trustworthiness. This level is called its *intrinsic* level. But unlike a single level object, an MLO is able to run at any level less than or equal to its intrinsic level. Since it is necessary to isolate different invocations which execute concurrently within an MLO, we require that the MLO have no memory (i.e., no persistent state used from one invocation to another). Due to our basic requirements for no upward information flow, an MLO can downgrade its integrity level during a method execution to reflect the level of information it uses, but is not able to upgrade it until the full completion of this method execution.

The MLO rules are generally the same as the SLO rules, but take into account the particular properties of these objects. MLO to MLO access rules are not described in detail here, but can be built using the SLO to SLO access rules and can be found in (Totel *et al.*, 1998).

Validation objects

Validation Objects must be designed in the application at the needed level of integrity (cf. Figure 2) with the development and validation methods appropriate to that level. Generally speaking, the validation objects should be as simple as possible, and should implement only the fault tolerance mechanisms needed to successfully validate the data. Keeping such objects as simple as possible should facilitate their validation. The information flow produced by a validation object must be considered as an exception to the integrity policy rules. The exceptions are identified and defined by the application programmer, and then authorised by the integrity kernel.

3.3 Firewalls

To ensure that application processes of different criticality do not interfere with one another, processes are restricted not only by different integrity levels but also through spatial and temporal protection mechanisms. Spatial firewalls are necessary to protect the application's address space while temporal firewalls are needed to police the execution time of each process or thread.

Spatial firewalls

Spatial protection of a process is usually achieved with memory management hardware and software. A minimum set of features must be provided at the hardware level to support the implementation of a policy at the software level. Some policies implemented in memory management units (MMUs) can be quite complex: for example, the Intel 80x86/Pentium processors can handle four levels of memory protection and apply a ring level protection policy on memory segment accesses (the rules it applies are very different to those of our integrity policy).

The memory protection must provide a strict isolation between process memory segments to ensure that information flow control between processes cannot be by-passed. This basic functionality is part of every protection mechanism provided by the memory management units of the different processors chosen for the current GUARDS prototypes (Motorola 68xxx, Intel x86/Pentium, Sparc V7).

Temporal firewalls

Even with spatial firewalls and the integrity policy mediating inter-object communication, it is still possible for a low criticality process to affect high criticality processes by consuming more resources (e.g., CPU) than anticipated. This is particularly a problem where the low and high criticality processes share the same infrastructure. In order to facilitate a predictable temporal behaviour of a GUARDS application, both computational and scheduling models have to be defined. An application conforming to the GUARDS computational model consists of periodic and sporadic processes and the mechanisms for their communication. Three computational models are defined (Wellings and Beus-Dukic, 1996): a) time-triggered, b) event-triggered, c) mixed (time and event-triggered). The time-triggered computational model consists of a fixed set of periodic processes which are released by a timer event. In the event-triggered model, sporadic processes are released by an event originating from either another process or an interrupt. The computational model chosen for the GUARDS prototype is a mixed computational model consisting of periodic and sporadic processes which communicate asynchronously through shared memory.

A scheduling model dictates the way in which the processes of an application conforming to a particular computational model are executed at run-time. The runnable processes are executed in the order determined by their priority. In the GUARDS pre-emptive priority scheduling model, if a higher priority process becomes runnable (e.g., it is released by a timing event) then the current lower priority process is stopped from executing and the high priority process is executed. The lower priority process executes again when it is the highest priority runnable process. Pre-emptive priority scheduling automatically provides a limited form of temporal firewalling between processes with different priorities. However, the assignment of a priority to a process is not solely a result of the process's criticality. Rather, deadline monotonic priority ordering (for example) assigns priorities according to the deadlines. Hence, it is possible for a low criticality process to have a short deadline and therefore potentially a high priority. To solve this problem, either the priority range needs to be divided and/or CPU budget timers need to be supported (Burns and Wellings, 1995). In the time-triggered computational model, temporal firewalls between different processes require the use of budget timers. A CPU budget timer is set to the amount of CPU time required by a process for each invocation. Whenever the process is pre-empted, the timer is stopped, and is restarted next time it executes. In the event-triggered computational model, the kernel must maintain a sporadic process's invocation rate and budget timer to ensure the temporal firewalls between the processes.

4 IMPLEMENTATIONS

The GUARDS integrity policy aims to define how the interactions between the different software components in a system must be checked to ensure that no highly critical component can be corrupted by a possibly faulty low integrity component. As stated above, these interactions can appear at many different system levels. The policy we defined in Section 3 can thus have an impact at many different system layers. This is described in Section 4.1. But to be reusable and portable on many different systems, it is necessary to apply these rules at a middleware layer. This approach is the subject of Section 4.2.

4.1 Influence of the policy on the different system layers

There are many hardware or software loopholes at various levels in an execution environment that can allow a faulty object to corrupt another object. To be able to apply our policy to all possible information channels at the different layers, we need to interpret our policy to fit the current existing system architectures.

Basically, the object model encapsulates both the data items and the functions necessary to execute the service. An object can modify the internal state of another object by calling an execution entry point called a method. In our model, the contexts of the different objects are private to each object and can be modified only by the methods encapsulated inside the object itself.

Hardware layer

We could consider implementing our policy at the hardware level. In this case, only the process which allocates a data segment should access it, and each entry point in the code segment (called a Call Gate in the Pentium MMU) should be defined, and integrity rules applied to any call through these gates. Some refinements could be envisaged so that a code segment could read data segments with an integrity level greater than or equal to its level, and write into segments of equal or lower integrity. Although valuable and of interest, this is not realistically feasible in a COTS-oriented approach. Instead, the GUARDS approach is to verify that the MMU can provide a full spatial isolation of the different processes (see Section 4).

System layer

In addition to memory management, an operating system provides the application layer with different communication channels. Once sufficient isolation between the processes (defined by their code and data segments) is ensured, the communication primitives provided by the operating system kernel are the only way for the processes to exchange information. These communication functions can have proprietary or standardised interfaces (particularly POSIX communication interfaces) that we must adapt to be able to apply integrity rules on the information flows. An integrity kernel integrated in the operating kernel is then in charge of verifying which information flows are permitted or not. This approach requires access to the kernel source code (which is not the case in most situations) but has the advantage of ensuring that the integrity checks cannot be bypassed by the applications. We have completed an implementation of this approach in the Chorus micro-kernel (Rozier, 1991), but it can be implemented on any operating system (such as QNX and VxWorks, which are used in the GUARDS project).

Middleware layer

In a COTS-oriented approach, modifying the operating system kernel is not appropriate. The only way to have reusable components on many platforms is to implement the integrity checks in a layer of software that lies above the operating system kernel. The idea is that all communication between application processes goes through this middleware layer so that it is controlled by the integrity mechanisms. There are two ways in which this can be achieved:

1) A GUARDS component is called *explicitly* by the application every time it wishes to communicate.
2) A GUARDS component is called *implicitly* (in a transparent manner) by linking to an alternative library (e.g., Integrity Metaobject described in section 4.3) to that which would normally be used to call the kernel. This technique was used in the Newcastle Connection (Brownbridge and Marshall, 1982): all system calls are intercepted, code is executed to check that the integrity rules have been adhered to, and the appropriate trap to the kernel is then performed.

The latter approach is adopted in GUARDS as it enables integrity level checks to be transparent to the GUARDS application.

4.2 Firewalls

The requirements for a GUARDS operating system include: a standard off-the-shelf operating system, POSIX compliance (IEEE, 1996), facilities to support the GUARDS computational and scheduling model (e.g., clock access, support for different process priority levels, scheduling algorithms, interrupt handling, pre-emption), and facilities to support spatial and temporal firewalling (e.g., memory management, CPU timers).

The requirement for POSIX compliance initially included compliance with POSIX 1003.1 (the basic operating system interface), 1003.1b (the real-time extensions) and 1003.1c (the threads extensions). A typical GUARDS application needs:

1. basic operating system services (process creation and deletion, signals, basic I/O, and terminal handling),
2. real-time services (clocks and timers, process scheduling control, real-time signals, semaphores, shared memory, message queues, asynchronous I/O),
3. thread services providing the ability to run multiple, concurrent threads within a single address space, since processes in POSIX execute in separate address spaces (pthreads, mutexes and condition variables).

The facilities provided by POSIX support the GUARDS computational and scheduling model as they provide the functionality needed for periodic and sporadic processes, communication and synchronisation between processes, and pre-emptive priority based scheduling. The two operating systems chosen for GUARDS applications are VxWorks and QNX. As both operating systems are compliant only to POSIX 1003.1 and 1003.1b, we decided to use the POSIX service if it is implemented, otherwise to use the equivalent proprietary service. Here we describe how the operating systems chosen for GUARDS support spatial and temporal firewalls, and integrity level management.

Spatial firewalls

Spatial firewalls exist to prevent a low criticality process from accessing the virtual memory space of a high criticality process. POSIX provides suitable mechanisms for spatial firewalls in the form of process abstractions. Different processes need to be mapped to separate address spaces so that the memory management facilities provided by the host processor ensure spatial firewalling. However, VxWorks does not support processes. Furthermore, MMU hardware and software are optional in VxWorks. Hence, the trust of the spatial firewalls implementation in VxWorks lies on its architecture-independent interface to the CPU's memory management unit in the form of the virtual memory support option VxVMI. In QNX, the operating system kernel fully utilises the MMU to deliver the POSIX multi-process model.

Temporal firewalls

Temporal firewalls should prevent a process from using the processor or a system resource for longer than has been allocated. To ensure that a process does not exceed the processor usage that it reserved, the processor usage of each process must be tracked. Watchdog timers can be created from the POSIX timer mechanisms, and therefore deadline overrun can be detected. However, CPU budget timers are currently not defined by the POSIX standards (although they are under consideration). Consequently, it is not possible to confine an error resulting from one process consuming more CPU time than has been allocated to it. The inevitable result of this poor error confinement is that damage assessment is difficult when a deadline overrun occurs.

4.3 CORBA implementation

The choice of CORBA (OMG, 1995) to demonstrate the feasibility of the mechanisms defined by our policy was dictated by several parameters. First, our model is based on an object model that is very close to that of CORBA. The natural notion of distribution in such an environment facilitates the implementation of a distributed integrity kernel. Moreover, each object in such an environment owns a context that is isolated from the other objects (spatial isolation); temporal isolation cannot be implemented on top of a CORBA layer, but we assumed this is achieved at operating system layer. Finally, due to the recent evolutions in object technology, the reflexivity notion (Kiczales et al., 1991) was fully applicable and usable to ensure that the integrity checks are transparent and cannot be bypassed.

This implementation can also have a real significance in wide area networks, where heterogeneous systems are interconnected via an Object Request Broker (ORB). It could be used to prevent the contamination of local critical applications by external unknown software entities. Particularly, we could easily imagine applications on Internet where Java applets can use the CORBA communication interface.

Global architecture

The distributed architecture we assume is described in Figure 2. Objects are executed on several distributed hosts and can communicate via the ORB. Each machine hosts a local integrity kernel whose role is to check the method invocations.

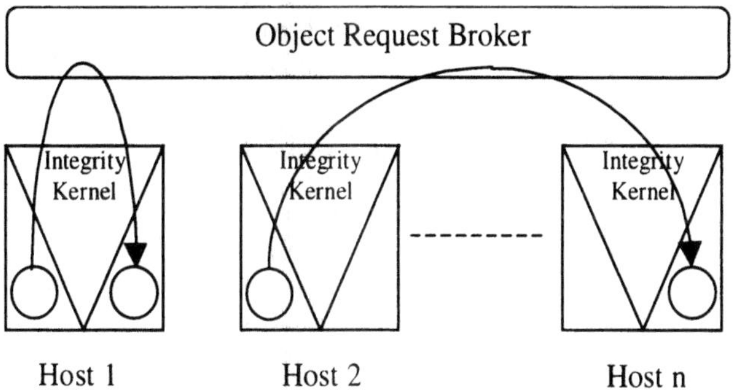

Figure 2: CORBA Integrity Architecture.

Integrity kernel

The distributed integrity notion we use stems from the security kernel approach defined by the National Computer Security Center (NCSC) in the red book (NCSC, 1987). Each integrity kernel has the responsibility of checking accesses to local objects (local to local as well as distant to local accesses). An important point to note is that in this approach, each integrity kernel trusts the other kernels hosted on other sites. If an object O_1 requests access to an object O_2, the kernel at the first site sends the request to the second site. It also builds an integrity label containing the information items necessary to check the access. This label will be carried by the message sent to the distant site.

Each integrity kernel has the knowledge of the integrity properties of every object that will run on its site. It will thus be able to initialise the integrity levels of the different objects at their creation. The definitions produced during the development of the application are stored in a local configuration file (Table 1) and used by the kernel each time an object is created. Once the object is created, the kernel dynamically manages its levels during its execution.

The information available in the configuration file describes:

- The type of the class and its name (all objects instantiated from this class will be registered with the information declared in this file).
- The level of the class (the intrinsic level for MLOs).
- The different public methods which can be invoked by other objects, and their mode.

- The access exceptions induced by the use of validation objects. In the example presented in Table 1, the validation object *Vsensor* devoted to the validation of data items provided by the low integrity *Sensors*, has the right to access their method *GetSensor* by the way of its own *GetVSensor* method.

Table 1: Configuration File

```
SLO Sensor
{
    LEVEL 0;
    METHOD GetSensor <READ>;
}

VO Vsensor
{
    LEVEL 2;
    METHOD GetVSensor <READ>
    EXCEPTION Sensor METHOD GetSensor;
}

SLO Monitor
{
    LEVEL 1;
    METHOD Run <WRITE>;
}

MLO FileServer
{
    LEVEL 2;
    METHOD Write <WRITE>;
}
```

Use of metaobjects

In a standard middleware approach, all functions necessary for communication must be enclosed in a library. These functions will then call appropriately the integrity kernel object. One of the main problems with this approach is that the programmer must explicitly call the integrity-related communication primitives; otherwise, his/her application will bypass the integrity checks.

In object-oriented development, the use of metaobjects has been shown to be a valuable concept for implementing fault-tolerance, providing transparency and reusability (Fabre and Pérennou, 1998). We followed this approach by encapsulating the integrity functions in a metaobject whose role is to trap all method invocations. This metaobject then calls the integrity kernel, which permits or refuses the execution (Figure 3). Depending on the result, the metaobject will continue or abort the method execution. At the end of method execution, the same procedure is applied on return from the invocation.

On the client side, we need to add a label to the message sent to the called object. This is implemented using another metaobject whose role is to trap every method call to CORBA objects and to request from its local integrity kernel to add integrity information to the message, so that the integrity kernel of the destination host can apply the checks on invocation.

We used Open-C++ V2 (Chiba, 1995) for this implementation. It generates a pre-compiler that encapsulates all metaobject definitions. The programmer has just to use this pre-compiler and to declare that every object must be supervised by the integrity metaobject.

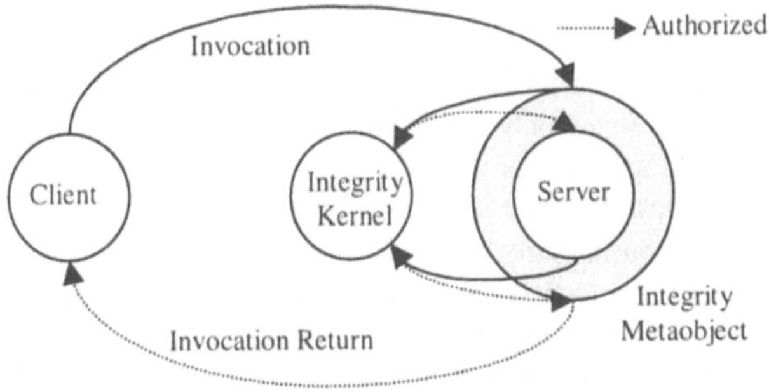

Figure 3: Integrity Kernel Invocation checks.

Results

Measuring the efficiency of the checks was one of the main reasons for this implementation. We measured several time parameters on a sample of 50000 invocations. The average measures obtained on a SUN Sparc station 20 are summarised in Table 2. The time overhead is composed of both additional communication time due to the messages which invoke the kernel services, and the time necessary to check the client inside the kernel. The comparison between a checked invocation (Integrity Kernel active) and a normal one (Integrity Kernel inactive) was based on the delay from call to return as seen from the client. The result was that an invocation checked by the integrity kernel is about 4 times slower than a normal one. However, the time needed to perform all checks inside the kernel (invocation plus return of invocation checks) is not significant compared to a normal invocation time (0.02 ms compared to 0.62 ms). The bulk of the overhead is thus due to the metaobject trapping mechanisms and the communication delays they induce. So, if the checks were directly inserted into the Object Request Broker (this would be the correct implementation in a CORBA middleware layer), the integrity policy check times could be considered as negligible.

Table 2: Invocation time

With Integrity kernel		**Without Integrity kernel**
Total invocation time	Total checking time	Total invocation time
2.44 ms	0.02 ms	0.62 ms

5 RELATED WORK

Biba defined a multilevel integrity policy based on the definition of a one-way information flow in a lattice of security labels (Biba, 1977). The goal of this policy is to prevent access by subjects (active entities including users, processes) to data items (passive entities called objects) and component services that would be illegal from an integrity point of view. The checks defined by Biba are concerned with all kinds of data flow (observation, modification and invocation of components). The rules used can be summarised as follows: an object can be read by a subject only if the integrity level of the subject is lower than the object integrity level; an object can be modified by an object only if the object integrity level is less than or equal to the subject level; a subject can invoke another subject only if the latter has an integrity level that is less than or equal to the former.

The Clark and Wilson integrity policy (Clark and Wilson, 1987) was built for commercial purposes and focuses on the preservation of data integrity. Each data item can be modified only through the use of a certified procedure whose role is to process the data. This certifies that the data will keep its integrity. Moreover, the data items can be verified by dedicated procedures whose role is to certify their integrity. Unlike Biba's policy, the integrity rules focus on the correctness of data modification instead of information flow control.

Kopetz presents an interesting but very different notion of temporal firewall that aims to avoid temporal locks between tasks that co-operate (Kopetz, 1997). It is defined as a data-sharing interface: the data items it provides are the results of the subsystem execution behind the firewall and are certified to be temporally accurate at their time of use. A producer can make information available to the consumer by way of the firewall. The consumer can then access the data items when needed in the time interval defined for this purpose. This temporal firewall can be considered as an error containment interface since data errors can only propagate from the producer to the consumer through a one-way communication channel. It could be used in GUARDS to prevent temporal interactions between objects.

Part of the Boeing 777 avionics relies on an architecture called Integrated Modular Avionics (IMA), that provides spatial and temporal isolation as well as error confinement properties. The isolation is based on the notion of a partition. Such a partition supports the execution of a collection of software processes. The partitions defined in the system have separate memory spaces which may be shared with other partitions, but cannot be written to prevent data or code contamination. Moreover, an error that occurs in a partition cannot affect other partitions (complete mechanisms are implemented to separate executions in a partition from other partition executions, such as saving all processor registers used by a given partition). The spatial isolation is implemented using a memory management unit, and time-partitioned access to shared resources through SAFEbus (Hoyme and Driscoll, 1992). The temporal isolation is based on deterministic scheduling (each partition has the guaranteed access to a needed hardware resource in a given time slot) and is implemented through SAFEbus partition synchronisation. The execution isolation of processes is more complete than in GUARDS but is not based on a COTS approach. However the access rules defined in our approach are more complete than in the IMA access policy.

6 CONCLUSION

As stated above, integrity management can influence the different architecture layers. In some approaches (such as in IMA), the checks rely mainly on the lowest layer, i.e., hardware. In GUARDS, the use of COTS hardware involves implementing the checks in the operating system or in a middleware layer. But this requires that strong hardware properties are verified (e.g., a full spatial isolation). A more general approach would be to use the complementarity of both hardware and software layers to provide a homogeneous control of the interactions at every level of the architecture. In particular, temporal aspects of integrity management can be integrated in middleware at the cost of a performance decrease (e.g., the use of timers to prevent tasks from hogging CPU is not very effective). However, the current implementation of integrity checks inside the Chorus operating system should prove that the complementarity of an operating system and middleware approach is sufficient to fulfil our requirements (as long as a sufficient isolation is performed in hardware). On the other hand, a complete implementation in a middleware layer, on top of a COTS operating system, would not prevent the existence of covert channels inside the operating system itself.

7 REFERENCES

Biba, K. (1977) Integrity Considerations for Secure Computer Systems, MITRE Co, Bedford, MA, USA.

Brownbridge, D. and Marshall, L. (1982) The Newcastle connection or UNIXes of the world unite! *Software Practice and Experience,* **12,** 1147-1162.

Burns, A. and Wellings, A. J. (1995) Safety Kernels: Specification and Implementation. *High Integrity Systems,* **3,** 287-300.

Chiba, S. (1995) A Metaobject Protocol for C++, in *ACM conference on Object-Oriented Programming, Systems, Languages and Applications,* Austin, TX, pp. 285-299.

Clark, D. D. and Wilson, D. R. (1987) A Comparison of Commercial and Military Computer Security Policies, in *IEEE Symposium on Security and Privacy* (Ed, Press, I. S.) Oakland, CA, pp. 184-194.

Fabre, J.-C. and Pérennou, T. (1998) A Metaobject Architecture for Fault-Tolerant Distributed Systems: The FRIENDS Approach. *IEEE Transactions on Computers,* **47**.

Hoyme, K. and Driscoll, K. (1992) SAFEbus, in *11th Digital Avionics Systems Conference* (Ed, Press, I. S.) Seattle, WA USA, pp. 68-73.

IEC (1995) Functional Safety: Safety-Related Systems, International Electrotechnical Commission SC 65 A.

IEEE (1996) Information technology - Portable Operating System Interface (POSIX) - Part 1: System Application Program Interface (API) [C Language], IEEE.

Jajodia, S. and Kogan, B. (1990) Integrating an Object-Oriented Data Model with Multilevel Security, in *International Symposium on Security and Privacy*, IEEE Society Press, Oakland, CA, pp. 76-85.

Kiczales, G., des Rivières, J. and D.G., B. (1991) *The Art of the Metaobject Protocol*, MIT Press.

Kopetz, H. (1997) Component-Based Design of Large Distributed Real-Time Systems, in *the IFAC Workshop on Distributed Computer Control Systems, DCCS 97*, Seoul, Korea.

NCSC (1987) Trusted Network Interpretation of Trusted Computer Security Evaluation Criteria, National Computer Security Center (USA), pp. 278.

OMG (1995) The Common Object Request Broker: Architecture and Specification, OMG.

Powell, D. (1997) Preliminary Definition of the GUARDS Architecture, LAAS, Toulouse.

Rozier, M. (1991) Chorus Overview, Chorus systemes.

Totel, E., Blanquart, J.-P., Deswarte, Y. and Powell, D. (1998) Supporting Multiple Levels of Criticality, in *IEEE Symposium on Fault Tolerant Computing Systems (FTCS-28)*, Munich, pp. 10.

Wellings, A. and Beus-Dukic, L. (1996) Computational Models and Time-Related Dependability Mechanisms for GUARDS, Department of Computer Science, University of York, UK.

8 BIOGRAPHIES

Eric Totel is currently completing his Ph.D. at LAAS-CNRS in the framework of LIS joint laboratory on Dependability Engineering.

Ljerka Beus-Dukic is a Research Fellow in the Department of Computer Science at the University of York. Her research interests include real-time operating systems, communication protocols and COTS software procurement.

Jean-Paul Blanquart is an engineer at Matra Marconi Space France, which is one of the five industrial partners of the LIS joint laboratory on Dependability Engineering at LAAS-CNRS.

Yves Deswarte is an INRIA Research Director, and member of the Fault Tolerance and Dependable Computing research group at LAAS-CNRS. His research interests are centred on fault-tolerance and security.

David Powell is a CNRS Research Director and leads the Fault Tolerance and Dependable Computing group at LAAS-CNRS. His research interests include distributed fault tolerance and fault injection.

Andy Wellings is Professor of Real-Time Systems in the Department of Computer Science at the University of York. He is interested in all aspects of real-time systems, particularly operating systems and programming languages.

The Realize middleware for replication and resource management *

P. M. Melliar-Smith, L. E. Moser, V. Kalogeraki, P. Narasimhan
Department of Electrical and Computer Engineering
University of California, Santa Barbara, CA 93106, USA
Tel:(805) 893-8438,-4897,-7788,-7788, Fax:(805) 893-3262
E-mail: pmms,moser,vana,priya@alpha.ece.ucsb.edu

Abstract

The Realize middleware manages the resources of CORBA distributed systems for soft real-time applications, and replicates CORBA objects to provide high availability and fault tolerance. By measuring the usage of the resources and by monitoring the behavior of the application, Realize allocates the objects to the processors and schedules the tasks in order to balance the load and to meet soft real-time deadlines. By using totally ordered multicast messages, Realize maintains the consistency of the replicas of the objects. The difficult issues of distribution, real-time scheduling, replication, consistency, and fault detection and recovery are handled by Realize and are hidden from the application programmer.

Keywords

CORBA, fault tolerance, replication, resource management, real time

*This research has been supported by DARPA and AFOSR, Contracts N00174-95-K-0083 and F30602-97-1-0284, and by Rockwell Science Center through the State of California MICRO Program, Grant 97-12.

1 INTRODUCTION

The Realize middleware extends the Common Object Request Broker Architecture (CORBA) (Object Management Group, 1997; Soley, 1992) with replication for high availability and fault tolerance and with resource management for soft real-time applications. Realize operates on top of standard operating systems and works with any commercial implementation of CORBA, exploiting the portability, location transparency and interoperability that CORBA provides. Using Realize, the application programmer programs a fault-tolerant, soft real-time distributed application, without having to address the difficult issues of distribution, real-time scheduling, replication, consistency, fault detection and recovery.

To manage the resources of the system, Realize monitors the system during operation, measuring the utilization of the resources and the durations and numbers of method invocations. It uses this information to balance the loads on the resources by moving objects, and to drive a least-laxity, soft real-time scheduler.

Realize replicates the application objects to provide high availability and fault tolerance without requiring the modification of those objects. Both client and server objects can be replicated, and objects can act as both clients and servers. Realize maintains the consistency of the replicas of the objects, even in the presence of faults.

Thus, the Realize system provides

- support for simple programming of fault-tolerant, soft real-time distributed applications;
- replication of objects across the distributed system and maintenance of the consistency of the object replicas for high availability and fault tolerance; and
- resource management to balance the load on the resources and to meet soft real-time objectives.

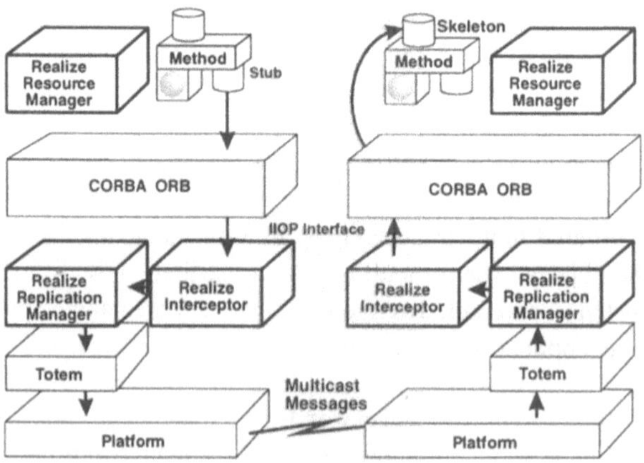

Figure 1 The structure of the Realize system, consisting of the Replication Manager, the Resource Manager and the Interceptor.

The structure of the Realize system is shown in Figure 1. The application objects operate over any standard commercial implementation of CORBA. The Object Request Broker (ORB) of CORBA packages the operations into messages, formatted according to the Internet Inter-ORB Protocol (IIOP), and subsequently passes those messages to TCP/IP for communication to other CORBA objects over the same ORB or over different ORBs. The Interceptor (Narasimhan, Moser and Melliar-Smith, 1997), however, intercepts the IIOP messages before they reach TCP/IP, and diverts them instead to the Replication Manager and subsequently to the Totem multicast group communication system (Moser, Melliar-Smith, Agarwal, Budhia and Lingley-Papadopoulos, 1996), which multicasts the messages to the object replicas.

The Replication Manager maintains consistency of the states of the object replicas, and provides fault detection and recovery. It transparently translates invocations of operations on an object group into invocations of operations on the individual object replicas. Using the Quality of Service Definition Language (QDL) definitions (Zinky, Bakken and Schantz, 1997) in the Interface Repository, the Resource Manager determines the number of replicas of an object to be created, and subsequently distributes those replicas across the system. The Resource Manager is itself implemented as a collection of CORBA objects and, thus, benefits from CORBA's interoperability and Realize's fault tolerance.

Realize imposes some additional overhead on each method invocation. Using Orbix, the round-trip time required for a remote invocation without replication and without Realize is increased by approximately 20% with Realize and with triplicated active replication of both client and server objects. More than 700 remote invocations per second can be sustained, using Realize with a commercial CORBA ORB such as Orbix.

2 REPLICATION IN REALIZE

In Realize, object replication, multicasting of invocations and responses, maintenance of replica consistency and recovery from faults are transparent to the application objects and to the ORB. The type of replication and the reliability requirement, which implies the degree of replication, are determined by the QDL definitions for each object. Realize operates under the following assumptions:

- independence of faults in the replicas of an object; and
- deterministic behavior of the objects.

2.1 Types of replication

The Replication Manager supports both active and passive replication, as shown in Figure 2. The application and the types of faults that must be tolerated dictate the type of replication that is employed.

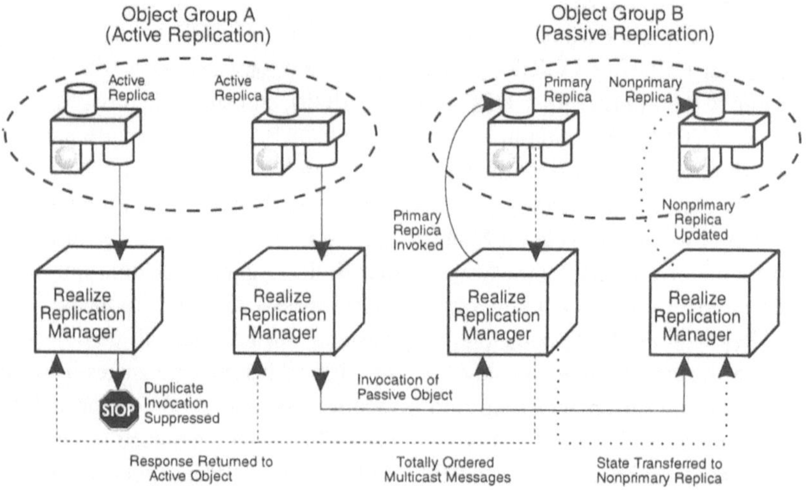

Figure 2 The mechanisms within Realize to ensure replica consistency for active and passive replication.

2.1.1 Active replication

In active replication, when a client object invokes an operation on a server object, Realize multicasts the operation to the server object group via Totem and each server replica then performs the operation. The underlying reliable totally ordered multicast protocol ensures that all of the replicas of an object receive the same messages in the same order and, thus, that they perform the operations in the same order. This ordering of operations ensures that the states of the replicas are consistent at the end of the operation.

2.1.2 Passive replication

In passive replication, when a client object invokes an operation on a server object, Realize multicasts the operation to that group via Totem and only one of the server replicas, the *primary replica*, performs the operation, as shown in Figure 2. The Replication Manager at each of the other replicas logs the message containing the invocation so that one of those replicas can reinvoke the operation, should the primary replica fail. At the end of the operation, Realize multicasts the updated state of the primary replica to the nonprimary replicas and multicasts the results to the client object via Totem. During the operation, the states of the nonprimary replicas may differ from that of the primary replica; however, the state transfer achieves replica consistency at the end of the operation.

2.2 Fault detection and recovery

In an asynchronous distributed system that is subject to faults, it is impossible to distinguish between an object or processor that has failed and one that is merely slow. Thus, Realize and Totem detect faults by using unreliable fault detectors based on timeouts. The failure of a processor or of the Replication Manager on a processor results in the failure of all object replicas on that processor.

For active replication, if any one of the replicas fails, service is uninterrupted (because the other replicas perform the operation) and the results are returned to the invoking object. The replicas must also preserve the state of the object for subsequent transfer to a new or recovered replica.

For passive replication, the effect of a fault depends on whether the failed replica is a primary or nonprimary replica. The failure of a nonprimary replica during an operation is transparent to a client, because the object group membership mechanisms of Realize remove that replica from the group, while the primary replica continues to perform the operation.

If the primary replica fails, the object group membership mechanisms of Realize detect the fault and determine a new primary replica. The new primary replica must perform the operations that it has logged and for which it has not received a response and state transfer from the prior primary replica. Invocations on other objects, and even responses, can be generated by both the original and the new primary replicas. The Replication Manager suppresses such duplicate invocations and responses.

2.3 Replica consistency

To ensure that the replicas of an object are updated consistently, Realize exploits the reliable totally ordered message delivery service of an underlying group communication system, in our case Totem. The invocations of operations on the replicas, and the corresponding responses, are contained in multicast messages. Because the messages are delivered in the same total order at each object replica, the operations are performed by each replica in the same order, thereby maintaining consistency of the states of the replicas.

For active replication, this ensures that the invocation of an operation, and the corresponding response, is received by all of the replicas of an object or by none of them. Consequently, the operation is performed by all of the replicas or by none of them. For passive replication, this ensures that either all of the nonprimary replicas have the updated state of the object or, alternatively, all of the nonprimary replicas know that none of them has the updated state.

A reliable totally ordered message delivery service alone does not suffice to maintain the consistency of the states of the replicas. To maintain replica consistency, Realize also detects and suppresses duplicate operations and transfers state between replicas. It also ensures that, at any time, only one invocation is being processed within each process, reordering messages as necessary to ensure this. More details of the replica consistency mechanisms used by Realize can be found in (Melliar-Smith and Moser, 1995; Moser, Melliar-Smith and Narasimhan, 1998; Narasimhan, Moser and Melliar-Smith, 1997).

2.4 Degree of replication

The Resource Manager, described below, determines the number of replicas of each object needed to satisfy fault-tolerance requirements. If a processor or other resource is lost because of a fault, the Resource Manager may need to reallocate replicas to maintain the appropriate degree of replication for critical objects, provided that the system's resources do not become overloaded.

The value of a replica of an object is assessed by considering incidents in which faults occur so rapidly that all replicas are exhausted before new replicas can be created. Let V be the value of the object to the application as defined by the designer of the application, k be the number of replicas of the object and q be the probability of a fault affecting a replica during the period required to generate a new replica after a fault. With k replicas, one of which has failed and assuming independence of faults, there is a probability q^{k-1} that all of the other replicas will fail before an additional replica can be created. The value of the kth replica, assessed from the value of averted failures, is

$$V \times \left((k-1)q^{k-2} - kq^{k-1}\right)$$

In civilian applications, the value of q can be small, typically less than 10^{-6}, and it is unlikely that it will be appropriate to remove the only replica of an object in order to create another replica of a more important object. If, however, ample resources are available, it may be appropriate to create additional replicas because even the small value of an additional replica is greater than the value of an idle resource.

In military applications, there is a high risk of loss of objects to hostile actions during short periods of the mission. In such circumstances, the value of q can be quite high, 10^{-2} or even 10^{-1}, and it may be appropriate to remove some objects entirely to accommodate additional replicas of other objects.

3 RESOURCE MANAGEMENT IN REALIZE

Figure 3 shows the structure of resource management in Realize, implemented as a Resource Manager for the system and a Profiler for each processor. The Resource Manager is implemented as a set of CORBA objects and operates like other CORBA objects to meet soft real-time and fault-tolerance objectives. The Resource Manager may itself be replicated but, as with other replicated objects, logically there is only a single copy of the Resource Manager.

The Resource Manager is responsible for assigning objects to processors and for moving objects from one processor to another. As new applications are introduced into the system, the Resource Manager determines, using the Profilers' information, whether it can satisfy their requests and then allocates resources to them accordingly. During operation, the Resource Manager might determine that a resource is overloaded or that a task is not meeting its deadlines, necessitating reallocation of the replicas or reduction of the degree of replication. The Resource Manager also determines the number of replicas that are needed to satisfy reliability requirements. If

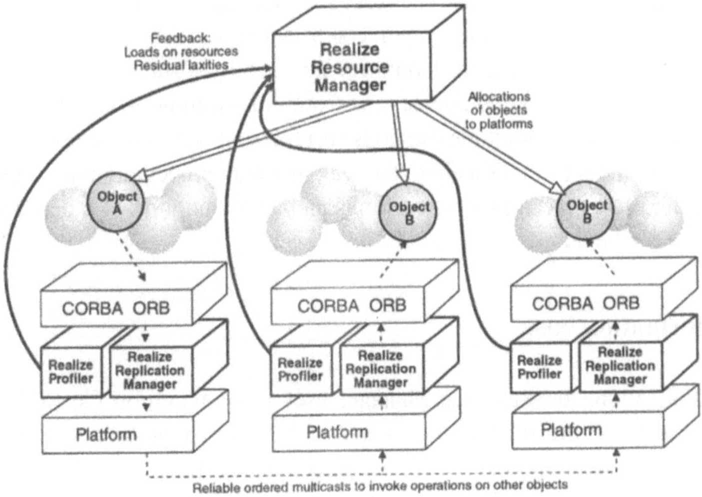

Figure 3 Resource management in Realize.

a processor or other resource is lost because of a fault, the Resource Manager might need to reallocate the replicas to maintain a sufficient degree of replication to meet those requirements.

Thus, the soft real-time performance objectives of the Resource Manager are

- to increase the probability of satisfying soft real-time response time requirements for each application task (sequence of operations between an input and an output);
- to balance the load (utilization) of the resources (processors, memory, communication network) by allocating the application objects to the processors and reallocating them as necessary; and
- to satisfy reliability requirements by determining the degree and type of replication of the objects, as well as the placement of the object replicas.

The Resource Manager operates under the following assumptions:

- The behavior of each method invocation is independent of the context. Thus, the processing time of each method and of methods invoked by a method, and the communication costs to invoke those methods, do not depend on when or why the method is invoked.
- Each resource is used for multiple activities, performed independently and asynchronously, and each such activity individually contributes only a small proportion of the total load on the resource.
- All resources are lightly loaded, with processor utilizations that are typically less than 0.5 and laxities that are typically at least half the time until the deadline. These margins are assumed to be sufficient to accommodate statistical … load with acceptable probability.

The first assumption may make the Resource Manager unsuitable for systems in which nominally equivalent tasks involve substantially different numbers of operations; nevertheless, the Resource Manager might still be suitable for components of the system. Well-understood deviations from this assumption can be handled, if necessary, by providing multiple methods to represent different behaviors. In the absence of specific information about the way in which processing times depend on task data, the use of mean processing times and an assumption of independence is the best that can be done.

3.1 Information base

Upon initialization, the Resource Manager uses a configuration file to define the physical configuration available to it, including the different processors and communication media along with their specific characteristics (processing speed, memory size, network bandwidth). For each such resource, the Resource Manager periodically receives current load information (processing load, available memory, communication load) from the Profilers on the individual processors. The Resource Manager uses this information to adapt to changing system conditions.

For each application task, the Resource Manager maintains a list of the method invocations required for that task, a deadline for completion of the task, and an importance metric that is used to decide which tasks should be abandoned in the event of system overload.

For each method of each object, the Resource Manager maintains estimates of the computation time and the communication time for invocations of that method. These estimates are used to determine the initial laxity when an application task starts.

3.2 The Profilers

For complex distributed applications, it is difficult to obtain accurate projections of resource requirements and other behavioral characteristics. Consequently, Realize adopts an approach based on monitoring the resource utilization and the behavior of the application objects using the Profilers to supply feedback information that can be used to adjust the scheduling of tasks and the allocation of objects to processors. The Resource Manager allocates objects to processors, the objects execute and use resources, and the Profilers report resource usage to the Resource Manager, enabling it to adjust the allocations accordingly.

Each processor has its own Profiler which, like the Replication Manager, is implemented between the CORBA ORB and the operating system. Each Profiler reports

- the current utilization of resources for its processor;
- the mean time required for the invocation of each remote method, determined by exponentially weighted averaging;
- the mean time and memory required for the invocation of each local method, determined by exponentially weighted averaging;

- for each local method, the mean number of invocations of each other method during one invocation of that local method, determined by exponentially weighted averaging; and
- the mean residual laxity for each task on completion of the task, determined by exponentially weighted averaging.

Exponentially weighted averaging defines the expectation $E[a]$ for a measurement a, given a constant c, as follows:

$$E_1[a] = a_1$$

$$E_{i+1}[a] = E_i[a] * (1 - c) + a_{i+1} * c$$

where $a_1, a_2, a_2, \ldots$ is the sequence of measurements of a, the most recent measurement is weighted by c, and the prior expectation is weighted by $1 - c$.

3.3 Feedback loops

The Resource Manager uses a three-level feedback loop structure (Kalogeraki, Melliar-Smith and Moser, 1997):

- The first level (milliseconds) uses measurements of elapsed time to refine the estimated residual laxity of executing tasks, which are used by the least laxity scheduler.
- The second level (seconds) uses measurements of elapsed time and measurements of resource loads to refine the initial estimates of the laxity for the tasks as they start.
- The third level (several seconds) uses measured resource loads and measured residual laxities to revise the allocation of objects to processors.

3.4 Least laxity scheduling

Realize uses least laxity scheduling, as shown in Figure 4, which is an effective strategy for scheduling tasks across multiple processors provided that the system is not overloaded. In least laxity scheduling, the laxity L_t of a task t represents a measure of urgency of the task, defined as

$$L_t = D_t - C_t$$

where D_t is the deadline by which task t must be completed and C_t is the estimated remaining computation time for task t.

As shown in Figure 4, when a task starts, triggered by some external or internal event, the scheduler calculates a target deadline for it, and then subtracts the projected task latency, provided by the Resource Manager, to yield the initial laxity. The strategy that the Resource Manager uses to estimate the projected task latency

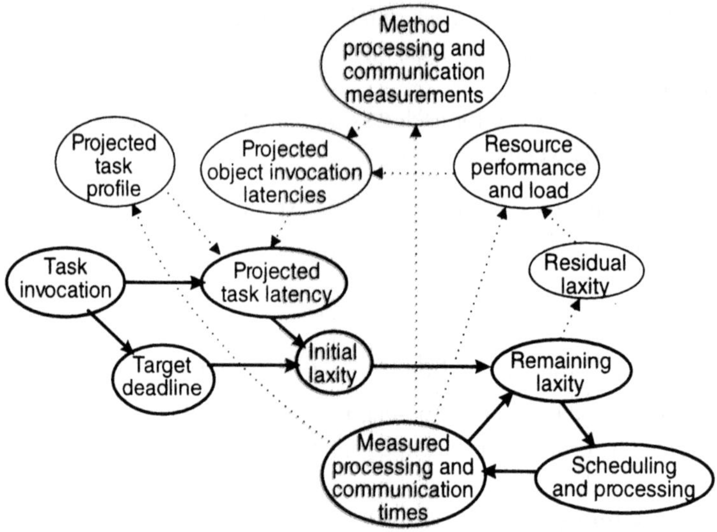

Figure 4 Least laxity scheduling. The first level feedback loop is shown with solid lines, and the second level feedback loop is shown with dotted lines.

is described below. As the application executes, the least laxity scheduler schedules the task according to the remaining laxity for that task.

The execution of the task involves the invocation of methods of objects. Each such invocation requires communication to invoke the method, processing for the method, and communication to return the results. The time required for this communication and processing is measured by the Profilers, using exponentially weighted averaging, and is reported to the Resource Manager where it is used to estimate the projected task latency. The actual time to perform the operation may be variable, and increases with the load on the processor and on the communication medium.

When a method is invoked, the time of the invocation is recorded using the operating system's high resolution timer. When the response is received, the time is again noted, and the difference between these two times is the actual time required for the method. This actual time is subtracted from the projected time, and the difference is added to the remaining laxity of the task. If another method is invoked multiple times and the number of invocations exceeds the number estimated by the Profiler, the projected time of the excess invocations is zero.

The remaining laxity of the task is included in the message that communicates a remote method invocation. This allows the method to be scheduled appropriately on the remote processor hosting the object. There is no need to include a remaining laxity in a response message. As described above, the remaining laxity is adjusted using the measured time at which the response is received. When the task completes, the remaining laxity is recorded as a residual laxity, which is reported back to the Resource Manager as a measure of the current timing margins in the system.

The adjustment of the remaining laxity provides a feedback loop. If a task is delayed, its laxity will diminish and its scheduling priority will increase. All of the computations required to calculate the deadlines and laxities are local to the individual processors. Consequently, overheads are low and priority adjustments can be made on a microsecond-by-microsecond basis. In contrast, the feedback loops used to estimate the projected task latency, from which the initial task laxity is derived, operate more slowly on a timescale of seconds.

3.5 Allocation of objects to processors

The Resource Manager tries to accommodate all tasks of the application, meeting their task requirements, but this cannot always be achieved. Moreover, the addition of a new task can result in degradation of the performance of existing tasks. Thus, satisfying the requirements of a new task can trigger the movement of objects to different processors or the reduction of the degree of replication of an object. Reallocation of objects may also be required after failure of a processor or when the current load on a processor is too high. In general, it is difficult to determine in advance which processors are most appropriate for the allocation of objects.

The Resource Manager maintains a global view of the applications in the system and allocates objects to specific processors; all other scheduling decisions are made locally. From the reports of the Profilers, the Resource Manager constructs estimates for the time to invoke a method remotely and for the time to invoke it locally. The difference provides an estimate of the communication cost for invoking the method. From the reports for each method of the mean numbers of invocations of other methods and of the mean times to invoke those methods, coupled with the local mean time for each method, the Resource Manager determines a mean computation time for each method. These mean communication times and mean computation times represent not only actual processing transmission times but also queueing delays. Assuming an M/M/1 queueing model, the mean time for execution of method m on processor p is

$$\frac{\tau_{mp}}{1-\rho_p}$$

where τ_{mp} represents the mean processing time for method m on processor p and ρ_p represents the load on processor p. Similarly, the mean transmission time for method m on communication medium c is

$$\frac{\sigma_{mc}}{1-\rho_c}$$

where σ_{mc} represents the mean transmission time on communication medium c for invoking a method m excluding queueing delay, and ρ_c represents the load on communication medium c.

From the reports of the mean number of invocations of other methods, the Resource Manager constructs an estimate for each task of the number of invocations of each method required to execute that task. From this, the Resource Manager estimates the projected latency for a task as

$$\sum_{m} \min_{p:m\in p} \left\{ \frac{r_m \tau_{mp}}{1-\rho_p} \right\} + \frac{r_m \sigma_{mc}}{1-\rho_c}$$

where the min is taken over all processors p that host replicas of objects of which m is a method and r_m represents the mean number of invocations of method m required for one execution of the task. Both r_m and $\frac{\tau_{mp}}{1-\rho_p}$ are reported by the Profilers and constitute the profile of the task. Thus, the Resource Manager estimates the projected task latency and checks its estimates against the residual laxities reported by the Profilers.

To move an object because a processor is overloaded, the Resource Manager uses a *cooling algorithm*. It selects the overloaded processor and the processor with the lowest load. It then selects the object imposing the highest load on the overloaded processor whose movement to the other processor would allow the load on that processor to remain lower than the load on the overloaded processor. Before moving the object, the Resource Manager checks that the effect of this movement on the latencies of tasks is acceptable, as described below. Moving an object is not free of cost, but that cost can be justified by amortization over many invocations. The cost of object movement is thus a constraint on the rate at which objects are moved, rather than on their movement.

To move an object because a task latency is too high, the Resource Manager uses a *hot spot algorithm*. It selects the object i for which

$$\sum_{m\epsilon i} \frac{r_m \tau_{mp}}{(1-\rho_p)} - r_m \tau_{mp} = \sum_{m\epsilon i} \rho_p \frac{r_m \tau_{mp}}{(1-\rho_p)}$$

is largest. This is the object i executing on processor p, whose methods m cause, in aggregate, the largest delay for the task. The Resource Manager then attempts to move the object to the processor with the lowest load, as described above. If this object would cause the load on the other processors to exceed the load on processor p, or the maximum load limit, the Resource Manager then attempts to move the object with the next largest delay on processor p.

To estimate the effect of moving an object on the projected task latencies, the Resource Manager considers the effects of increased or decreased processor load on the times required to invoke the methods. It assumes an M/M/1 queueing model for each processor. The estimated time required for invocations of method n on processor p before moving object i containing method m to processor p is

$$\frac{r_n \tau_{np}}{1-\rho_p}$$

After moving the object i containing method m to processor p, the estimated time is

$$\frac{r_n \tau_{np}}{1-\rho_p - r_m \tau_{mp}} = \frac{r_n \tau_{np}}{1-\rho_p} * \frac{1-\rho_p}{1-\rho_p - r_m \tau_{mp}}$$

$$= \frac{r_n \tau_{np}}{1-\rho_p} * \left(1 + \frac{r_m \tau_{mp}}{1-\rho_p} + \left(\frac{r_m \tau_{mp}}{1-\rho_p}\right)^2 + \ldots\right)$$

$$\approx \frac{r_n \tau_{np}}{1-\rho_p} * \left(1 + \frac{r_m \tau_{mp}}{1-\rho_p}\right)$$

where the approximation is justified by the assumption that method m contributes a small proportion of the total load on processor p, and is useful because it is expressed in terms of quantities measured by the Profilers. A similar estimate is made for the reduced time required for method invocations on the processor from which the object is moved.

Figure 5 shows how the projected latencies of Figure 4 are exploited for object allocation and reallocation. Objects are allocated or reallocated when a new application task is introduced into the system, when a processor has been lost due to a fault, when the load on some resource is too high, or when the latency for some task is too high. As the new application task runs, a profile of the method invocations for that task is constructed and is added to the Resource Manager's information base. A tentative allocation is then made of new objects to processors, using a greedy algorithm that allocates objects to the most lightly loaded processors. This increases the load on the processor's resources and requires new projections of the task latencies. If it is acceptable, the allocation is actually performed. However, if a resource load is too high or a latency is too long, then objects are reallocated, or the degree of replication of an object is reduced, or the least important task is suspended. This process is repeated until an acceptable allocation is found, as shown by the solid lines in Figure 5.

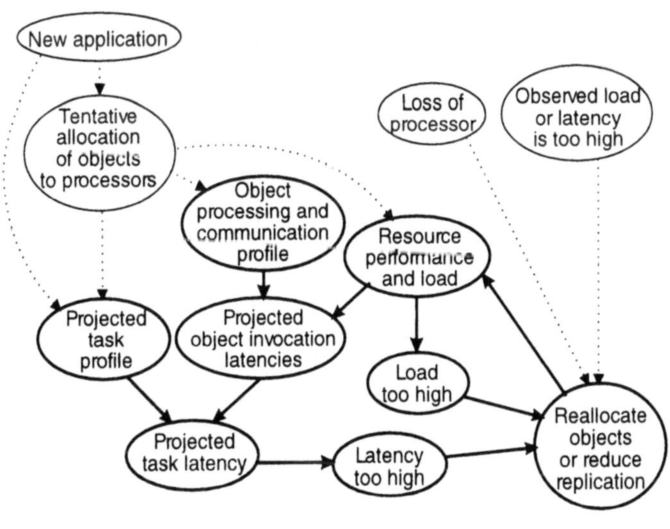

Figure 5 Object allocation and reallocation. The third level feedback loop is shown with solid lines.

4 RELATED WORK

Several efforts are underway to extend CORBA with real-time and fault-tolerance capabilities, including work by the OMG (Object Management Group Realtime Platform Special Interest Group, 1996).

Zinky et al (Zinky, Bakken and Schantz, 1997) have developed an architecture, called Quality of Service for CORBA Objects (QuO), for constructing adaptable applications with QoS guarantees. QuO extends the Interface Definition Language (IDL) of CORBA with a Quality of Service Description Language (QDL). QDL defines three sublanguages: a Contract Description Language (CDL) that describes object usage and performance, a Structure Description Language (SDL) that describes object resource utilization, and a Resource Description Language (RDL) that describes available resources. QuO provides mechanisms for measuring and enforcing QoS contracts and taking appropriate actions when those contracts are violated.

Wolfe et al (Wolfe, DiPippo, Ginis, Squadrito, Wohlever, Zykh and Johnston, 1997) have provided support for real-time extensions to CORBA applications, called timed distributed method invocations. They have defined server- and client-based timing constraints and attach a separate object with timing characteristics to each method invocation. They do not address other QoS issues, such as CPU loading and memory use.

Schmidt et al (Schmidt, Levine and Mungee, 1998) have developed a custom high-performance real-time ORB, called TAO. TAO supports real-time properties designed to provide QoS guarantees for distributed real-time applications. Their focus is mainly on hard real-time systems using rate monotonic scheduling. Currently, we are investigating the integration of TAO with Realize.

Other researchers have developed middleware that extends CORBA with fault tolerance. The Electra toolkit (Landis and Maffeis, 1997; Maffeis 1993) built by Maffeis on top of Horus (van Renesse, Birman and Maffeis, 1996) provides support for replicated CORBA objects, as does Orbix+Isis (Landis and Maffeis, 1997) on top of Isis (Birman and van Renesse, 1994). Unlike Realize, Electra and Orbix+Isis are nonhierarchical object systems and support only active replication. Both Electra and Orbix+Isis use an integration approach in that the replication and group communication mechanisms are integrated into the ORB and require modification of the ORB. In contrast, Realize uses the interception approach, which requires no modification to the ORB.

Another approach to fault tolerance and high availability, adopted by the OpenDREAMS toolkit (Felber, Garbinato and Guerraoui, 1996), adds replication and group communication as services (implemented as CORBA objects) on top of the ORB, and requires no modification of the ORB. The service approach exposes the replication of objects to the application programmer and allows the programmer to modify the class library to construct customized replication and group communication services. In contrast, Realize is transparent to the application and the application programmer.

Unlike Realize, none of the above systems has addressed both soft real time and fault tolerance for CORBA applications.

5 CONCLUSION

The Realize system extends the services of CORBA with object replication and resource management to support fault-tolerant, soft real-time applications. The Replication Manager replicates objects and maintains the consistency of replicated objects using reliable totally ordered multicast messages. The Resource Manager employs a three-level feedback loop structure, based on the profiling of the application objects, to provide soft real-time scheduling and to balance the load across the system by moving objects. Realize simplifies the programming of fault-tolerant distributed applications by hiding the difficult issues of distribution, real-time scheduling, replication, consistency, fault detection and recovery from the application programmer, while taking advantage of the portability, location transparency and interoperability that CORBA provides.

REFERENCES

Birman, K.P. and van Renesse, R. (1994) *Reliable Distributed Computing with the Isis Toolkit*. IEEE Computer Society Press, Los Alamitos, CA.

Felber, P., Garbinato, B. and Guerraoui, R. (1996) Designing a CORBA group communication service. *Proceedings of the IEEE 15th Symposium on Reliable Distributed Systems*, Niagara on the Lake, Canada, 150–9.

Kalogeraki, V., Melliar-Smith, P.M. and Moser, L.E. (1997) Soft real-time resource management in CORBA distributed systems. *Proceedings of the IEEE Workshop on Middleware for Distributed Real-Time Systems and Services*, San Francisco, CA, 46–51.

Landis, S. and Maffeis, S. (1997) Building reliable distributed systems with CORBA. *Theory & Practice of Object Systems*, **3**, 31–43.

Maffeis, S. (1993) Electra — Making distributed programs object-oriented. *Proceedings of the USENIX Symposium on Experiences with Distributed and Multiprocessor Systems*, **IV**, San Diego, CA, 143–156.

Melliar-Smith, P.M. and Moser, L.E. (1995) Simplifying the development of fault-tolerant distributed applications. *Proceedings of the Workshop on Parallel/Distributed Platforms in Industrial Products, 7th IEEE Symposium on Parallel and Distributed Processing*, San Antonio, TX.

Moser, L.E., Melliar-Smith, P.M., Agarwal, D.A., Budhia, R.K. and Lingley-Papadopoulos, C.A. (1996) Totem: A fault-tolerant multicast group communication system. *Communications of the ACM*, **39**, 54–63.

Moser, L.E., Melliar-Smith, P.M. and Narasimhan, P. (1998) Consistent object replication in the Eternal system. *Theory & Practice of Object Systems*, **4**, 81–92.

Narasimhan, P., Moser, L.E. and Melliar-Smith, P.M. (1997) Exploiting the Internet Inter-ORB protocol interface to provide CORBA with fault tolerance. *Proceedings of the Third USENIX Conference on Object-Oriented Technologies and Systems*, Portland, OR, 81–90.

Narasimhan, P., Moser, L.E. and Melliar-Smith, P.M. (1997) Replica consistency of CORBA objects in partitionable distributed systems. *Distributed Systems Engineering*, **4**, 139–50.

Object Management Group. (1997) *The Common Object Request Broker: Architecture and Specification*, Rev. 2.1, OMG Technical Document PTC/97-09-01.

Object Management Group Realtime Platform Special Interest Group. (1996) *Real-time CORBA*, White Paper.

Schmidt, D., Levine, D. and Mungee, S. (1998) The design of the TAO real-time object request broker. *Computer Communications*, **21**, 294–324.

Soley, R.M. (1992) *Object Management Architecture Guide*, Object Management Group, OMG Document 92-11-1.

van Renesse, R., Birman, K. and Maffeis, S. (1996) Horus: A flexible group communication system. *Communications of the ACM*, **39**, 76–83.

Wolfe, V.F., DiPippo, L.C., Ginis, R., Squadrito, M., Wohlever, S., Zykh, I. and Johnston, R. (1997) Expressing and enforcing timing constraints in a dynamic real-time CORBA system. Technical Report, Department of Computer Science and Statistics, University of Rhode Island.

Zinky, J., Bakken, D. and Schantz, R. (1997) Architectural support for quality of service for CORBA objects. *Theory & Practice of Object Systems*, **3**, 55–73.

BIOGRAPHIES

P. Michael Melliar-Smith is a professor in the Department of Electrical and Computer Engineering at the University of California, Santa Barbara. His research interests include fault-tolerant distributed systems and high-speed communication networks and protocols. He received a Ph.D. in Computer Science from the University of Cambridge, England.

Louise E. Moser is a professor in the Department of Electrical and Computer Engineering at the University of California, Santa Barbara. Her research interests include distributed systems, computer networks and software engineering. She is currently an area editor for *Computer* magazine in the area of networks and an associate editor for *IEEE Transactions on Computers*. She received a Ph.D. in Mathematics from the University of Wisconsin, Madison.

Vana Kalogeraki is a Ph.D. student in the Department of Electrical and Computer Engineering at the University of California, Santa Barbara. Her research interests include real-time systems, distributed systems, computer networks and CORBA. She received a B.S. in Computer Science from the University of Crete, Greece in 1994 and an M.S. in Computer Science from the University of Crete, Greece in 1996.

Priya Narasimhan is a Ph.D. candidate in the Department of Electrical and Computer Engineering at the University of California, Santa Barbara. Her research interests include distributed object systems, frameworks, CORBA, fault tolerance and evolution. She received an M.S. in Electrical and Computer Engineering from the University of California, Santa Barbara in 1995.

Session 4

ORB Engineering

DIMMA – A Multi-Media ORB

D. I. Donaldson, M. C. Faupel, R. J. Hayton, A. J. Herbert, N. J. Howarth, A. Kramer, I. A. MacMillan, D. J. Otway, S. W. Waterhouse
APM Limited
Poseidon House, Castle Park,
Cambridge, UK. CB3 0RD
Tel: +44 (0) 1223 515010 Fax: +44 (0) 1223 359779
Email: apm@ansa.co.uk

Abstract

DIMMA – A Distributed Interactive Multi-Media Architecture – is an open distributed processing (ODP) platform that facilitates the production of distributed applications. It has particular support for those applications that have soft real-time constraints, and those that make use of multi-media.

DIMMA consists of a portable layer of distribution engineering (middleware), together with tools to interface applications to this engineering. The most popular commercial ODP platform is the Common Object Request Broker Architecture (CORBA) whose definition is managed by the Object Management Group (OMG). In recognition of this popularity, DIMMA supports a CORBA compliant API so that CORBA applications may be easily ported to or from the DIMMA platform.

This paper describes the example implementation of DIMMA. It gives an overview of the motivations behind the design of DIMMA and then highlights some key features of the DIMMA implementation. It concludes with a brief analysis of DIMMA's performance

Keywords

ORB, Multi-media, CORBA, QoS, flow

1 INTRODUCTION

1.1 The goal of the DIMMA project

Object Request Brokers (ORBs) have been developed to provide support for distributed object-oriented applications, hiding much of the complex engineering needed to implement distribution. These can now be regarded as stable technology; the most wide-spread ORB architecture, OMG's CORBA (OMG, 1998), was first introduced in 1987, and many commercial and public-domain implementations of their CORBA ORB specification are now available.

However, combining this provision of distributed object-orientation with support for multi-media is not straight-forward, as it imposes a number of requirements on the ORB:

- Support for specifying flow interfaces
  Most ORBs only support RPC type interfaces, i.e., call an object and (possibly) receive a return value. Multi-media applications often require handling of continuous flows of data being transmitted and received.
- Control over resources used
  Many types of multi-media service are particularly sensitive to quality of service. For instance, a video stream must deliver its frames at a regular and timely rate in order to avoid the picture being jerky or corrupted. This requires the system to guarantee that the resources are available to deliver this quality of service, which in turn requires the system to provide the programmer with control over those resources, possibly including those provided by an underlying real-time OS.
- Support for new protocols to be easily added
  CORBA ORBs can work correctly while only supporting one RPC protocol (IIOP). Due to the diverse nature of multi-media though, there are a much larger number of protocols that a multi-media ORB may have to support, and more are being developed all the time. This requires a multi-media ORB to provide an easy method for adding new protocols.
- Minimum necessary footprint
  Multi-media services make heavy use of system resources (buffers, CPU time, network bandwidth). For this reason, the ORB itself should have the minimum necessary use of such resources so as to avoid impacting the quality of the services that it is supporting. Furthermore it should be scaleable to allow its use in a range of environments from small devices to large switches.

DIMMA was designed in the context of verifying the ISO Reference Model for Open Distributed Processing computational model (ISO, 1995). The ability to support CORBA APIs and the IIOP protocol were important subgoals.

The goal of the DIMMA project was to produce an architecture for a multi-media ORB that met these requirements, and a practical implementation of that architecture, making as few assumptions as possible about the host OS. It aimed to create a small, efficient, modular ORB, with support for flows and resource control, and the flexibility to add new protocols and new styles of application interface.

1.2 The application of DIMMA

DIMMA is intended primarily as an experimental vehicle. The focus is on using DIMMA to identify the needs of multi-media and real-time distributed applications in terms of proposed core ORB facilities and to prototype the resultant ideas.

Although DIMMA will run "out of the box", it is of greatest value to those who wish to customise the core ORB. The internal structure is very flexible and the components are built according to a set of well defined frameworks. For example, new protocols may be easily added using the DIMMA protocol framework which facilitates the reuse of layered modules.

The explicit binding model, together with the flexible resource reservation mechanisms allow a considerable range of applications to be built: applications that are not possible on most standard commercial ORBs. This should be of interest to those involved in telecommunications applications such as video on demand.

1.3 Paper structure

The remainder of this paper highlights particular features of the design of DIMMA and how it has been extended to support the achievement of the goals outlined above. It concludes with a summary of the performance of the final version of DIMMA, demonstrating the results possible when explicit control of quality of service is given to the application programmer.

2 DIMMA STRUCTURE

2.1 Overview

DIMMA is constructed as a set of small components that may be combined in many different ways to suit the diverse needs of applications. This also acknowledges the fact that the real world needs ORBs that are high performance, down-sizeable and scaleable. In this sense, DIMMA may be regarded as an ORB core.

The components of DIMMA are considered to be subdivided into groups and arranged in layers; this is also reflected in the source structure. This layering is depicted in Figure 1.

DIMMA provides two interfaces for the application programmer: a proprietary one based on a mapping of the ODP-RM computational language into C++ – the

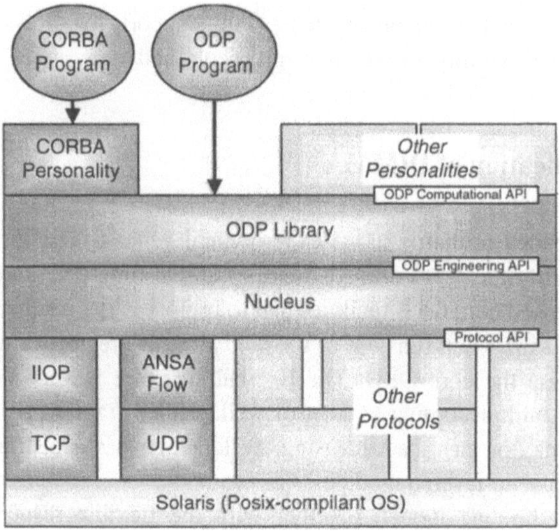

Figure 1 Structure of DIMMA

ODP Computational API – and a CORBA extended subset called "Jet". This is implemented as a personality built on top of the ODP facilities and hence shares a number of features with the former. Further personalities could be added if required.

Both APIs are mapped onto a common ODP Engineering API by the ODP Library in order to facilitate hosting on different ORB cores (or Nuclei in ODP terminology). The DIMMA nucleus supports the ODP Engineering API directly, whilst adapters can be provided for other ORBs. To date only one experimental adapter has been produced, which was to allow applications written using Jet or ODP to communicate over APM's ANSAware (Li, 1995).

The DIMMA nucleus provides the distribution engineering apparatus such as binders and communications protocols. Currently two protocols are provided: the CORBA Internet Interoperability Protocol 1.0 (IIOP) for interoperability with other vendors' ORBs and a proprietary protocol (ANSA Flow), optimised for transporting multi-media flows. New protocols can be added within a well-defined framework; furthermore existing protocol components (e.g., the TCP part of the IIOP stack) can be reused by these new protocols as required.

2.2 Target platform

To exploit the full range of QoS controls offered by DIMMA, the DIMMA nucleus must be hosted on an operating system able to provide the necessary soft real-time facilities. DIMMA makes use of Posix interfaces (IEEE, 1992) to access OS resources; in particular the Posix threads interface is relied upon to support control of multi-tasking. DIMMA has been tested and released on Solaris 2.5.

3 COMMUNICATIONS FRAMEWORK

The purpose of the communications framework is to simplify the production of new protocols by encouraging and facilitating reuse, through providing general components and standard interfaces, and through providing a uniform approach to resourcing for quality of service.

The communications framework comprises a set of generic interfaces and components, and informal guidelines pertaining to their use.

Due to the requirement to support many diverse protocols, e.g., connection oriented, connectionless, RPC, flow, etc., the protocol framework cannot be too prescriptive and aims instead to provide a minimal number of generally useful "building blocks". Likewise, many of the compositional constructs are too informal to express in a strongly typed language like C++ and instead are presented as a "cook book" of guidelines.

The framework considers a protocol to comprise a set of modules, each supporting a layer of protocol. The definition of what constitutes a protocol layer is not a formal one: it may be anything that is reasonably self-contained in terms of the framework interfaces. That said, a protocol layer typically has at least one of the following characteristics:

- performs message multiplexing
- dispatches messages to stubs
- interfaces with OS network facilities.

To this end, a module (providing a layer of protocol) will normally be associated with specific message header information, i.e., it will typically add a header on message transmission and remove it on receipt. This header is used to hold addressing information for message multiplexing.

Modules create channels in response to requests from their associated protocol and these act as conduits for message transmission and reception. Like the modules of a protocol, channels are also layered, forming a channel "stack". In other words, modules are the static representation of available protocol layers, while channels are the objects created dynamically when a binding is set up using that protocol, which manage the resources associated with the binding.

Client call and server reply messages are presented to the top channel and go down the channel stack until they reach the lowest level channel (called an anchor channel) which passes them to the operating system network interface.

The processing of incoming messages is not necessarily symmetric with that of transmission. Messages arriving from the network are processed by low level channels but cannot necessarily be passed directly to the next higher level channel, e.g., when there is channel multiplexing. In this case, the message is passed by the channel to the next higher level module, which interprets the associated header information to identify the next higher level channel to which the message is then passed. In this way, the message makes it way up through the protocol, alternating between channel and module, until it reaches the highest channel where it is dispatched to the stub or server object.

The framework allows for optional message concurrency on a channel through the concept of a session layer. This may be regarded as a layer of multiplexing between the highest level channel and the stub. Session objects are assigned for each concurrent flow or invocation on a stub. They act as state machines, preserving any information required by each caller and linking the calling threads to the messages that are passing through the channel to carry out their operations.

4 FLOW SUPPORT

There is a class of applications for which the operational RPC mechanism is inappropriate. These applications deal naturally in continuous flows of information rather than discrete request/reply exchanges. Examples include the flow of audio or video information in a multimedia application, or the continuous flow of periodic sensor readings in a process control application.

A flow has a distinct type and an associated direction with respect to the binding, e.g., video information might flow out of a producer binding associated with a camera and into a consumer binding associated with a TV monitor on which the output of the camera is to be displayed. It follows that flow interface types exist in pairs that are related by the reversal of the flow.

The type of flow is characterised by the set of possible frames that it can support. For example, a video flow might be able to carry both MPEG and JPEG frames.

DIMMA extends the functionality of a basic ORB in three ways in order to support flows:

1. The ODP library provides a means to represent and manipulate flows
2. The CORBA IDL compiler understands a new type of flow interface, mapping them on to the appropriate ODP library facilities
3. An example flow protocol is provided to demonstrate the use of flows.

Additionally, the use of flow interfaces generally requires the ability to specify QoS parameters; the support for this is dealt with in more detail in subsequent sections.

4.1 Flow Interfaces in IDL

The IDL extension to support flows proved very simple from the user's point of view: all that is changed is that the keyword "flow" is used instead of "interface" in CORBA IDL. It actually required more changes behind the scenes though to support this, such as checks in the IDL compiler to ensure that the operations within the flow were legal (e.g., no inout parameters).

A flow interface is modelled in Jet IDL in terms of one-way operations and will result in the generation of both producer and consumer components, in an analogous way to client and server components generated from an operational interface. The main difference is that the operations are one-way and data is unidirectional with respect to the binding. The operations within a flow interface correspond to frame types and these are further described by the parameters of the operation.

For example, a simple video flow consisting of a single frame type (Frame1) consisting of a frame number and the video image data (image), could be described in IDL as follows:

```
flow Video
{
    void Frame1( in long frame_no, in string image );
};
```

Note that both parameters are described as input (in) and that the operation returns no result (void type).

The ODP standard defines an additional concept called stream which is described as a set of unidirectional flows, e.g., a TV stream might be considered a logical entity consisting of an audio and video flow. DIMMA does not implement the stream concept directly, although in principal, a stream binding could be constructed by an application from a set of flow bindings.

Although flows appear to be similar to operational interfaces in IDL, they are distinct entities and a flow cannot inherit from an interface, nor can an interface inherit from a flow.

The protocol that was added to demonstrate flows within DIMMA is called ANSA Flow. It is a lightweight but fully functional multicast protocol based on RTP (Schultzrinne, 1996) over UDP. Note though that it is not a full implementation of all possible RTP packet types; just the parts of it needed to support ANSA Flow's proprietary packets.

5 RESOURCE MANAGEMENT

5.1 Overview

DIMMA provides for application control and management of resources through the use of QoS parameters. All resources needed by an application affect QoS, but many are managed by the OS and/or the network, and the application has only limited influence over them. This constrains what can be achieved in terms of guaranteeing QoS.

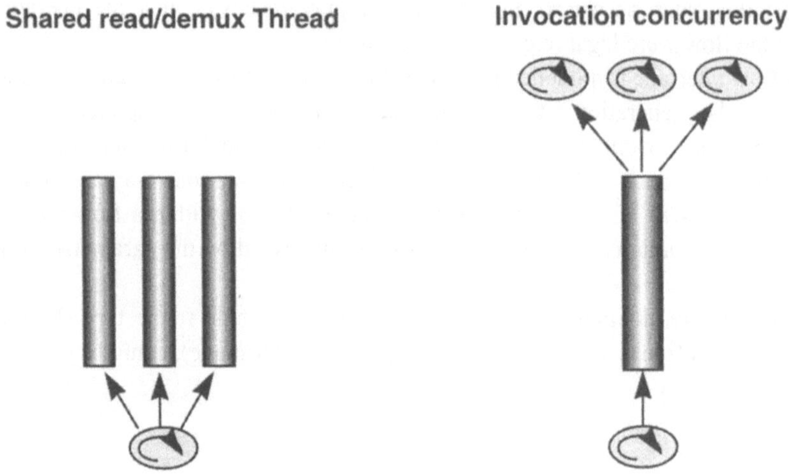

Figure 2 Possible thread sharing policies

In practice, with current OSs, an ORB may control sharing within a capsule (process), e.g., the number of tasks, or how channels are multiplexed. It may exert some influence over inter-capsule behaviour, e.g., via task priorities. To do any better than that requires a specialist resource-aware OS and a resource-aware network protocol.

DIMMA QoS parameters are specified in terms of attributes such as buffers, threads, communication endpoints and so on. Mapping between application specific QoS parameters (e.g., jitter, frame rate, etc.) and these "engineering" parameters remains the responsibility of the application.

The DIMMA QoS infrastructure allows the application explicit control over the resource allocation policy to be used within a given channel. For example, buffer allocation may be defined to be "on demand", or a set of buffers may be preallocated for the channel's exclusive use.

Channels may share a read/demultiplex thread. This is shown on the left-hand side of Figure 2. The channel itself may be shared between multiple application-level threads as shown on the right-hand side. One extreme (not shown) is one thread per capsule, i.e., the single threaded case.

Figure 3 gives an example of two possible resourcing policies for a complete end-to-end channel. The left-hand diagram gives a typical policy for "default" quality of service. The calling threads share a common channel, and at the server side, there is only a single listener thread which, on receipt of an incoming call, causes a new thread to be created to handle the call and then passes control to that thread (which is destroyed on call completion). All resources are allocated on demand through factories and deleted when finished with.

The right-hand diagram shows a policy for high-performance quality of service. The client has a dedicated channel so there is no need to maintain session

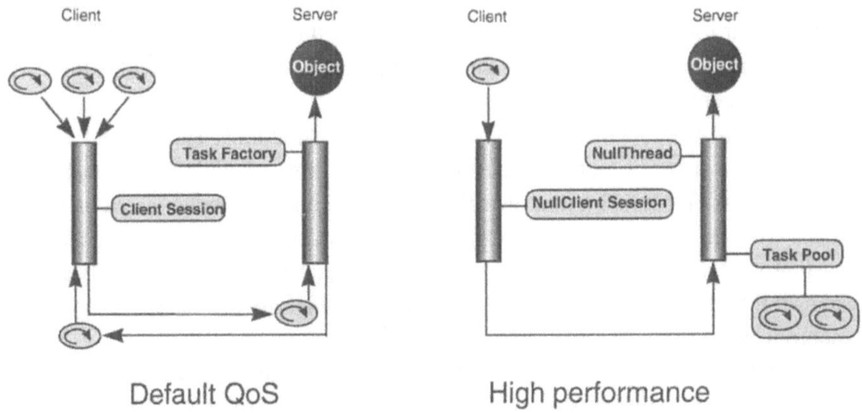

Figure 3 Two channel resourcing strategies

information, and there is no context switch on calling; the thread waits for the response. At the server side, when a call is received, the receiving thread calls the server object and returns the result, so again there is no context switch. While the call is being executed, a new thread is drawn from a pool ready for the next receive. When the call has been completed, that thread is returned to the pool. All resources used by the configuration are drawn from pre-allocated pools and returned when finished with.

5.2 Generic resource framework

The aim of the components of the DIMMA resource framework is to provide a generic way of controlling all resources while allowing different specific resource control policies to be implemented. To achieve this, all resources are allocated through a generic Allocator interface behind which different policies can be implemented, e.g., "create a new resource each time it is needed" (factories), or "take a pre-allocated resource from a pool" (pools). The resources themselves implement a generic Resource interface to allow them to be freed once finished with.

Buffers, sessions and threads can all be controlled via this framework, and different policies can be put together for different parts of a protocol to form a wide range of overall resourcing policies. Buffer and session allocation is straightforward; threading requires a little more explanation.

5.3 Threading

DIMMA offers both single-threaded or multi-threaded operation, switchable at compile time through a configuration flag. The latter is implemented internally using Posix threads; the former is made available to produce a high-performance executable, or for platforms that don't support multi-threading. Since CORBA does not define any standards for multi-threaded operation, DIMMA provides its own interfaces to control threading.

The DIMMA model of threading provides two abstractions: Threads and Tasks. Threads are a unit of potential concurrency and are scheduled over tasks by DIMMA. Tasks represent a unit of real concurrency and are implemented as Posix threads (bound to a lightweight process on Solaris). Tasks are scheduled pre-emptively by the underlying operating system and it is the applications responsibility to ensure that access to data shared between tasks is properly synchronised.

Three threading policies are provided with DIMMA; these control what is done when there is a possibility of a context-switch within the protocol. The "null task" policy means that the calling task carries on executing, thus avoiding a context switch. The "normal task" policy means that control is handed over to another task and the calling task returns. The "scheduled thread" policy allows a specified number of prioritised threads to be scheduled over a number of tasks. The threads are added to a prioritised queue and the first on the queue is executed as and when a task becomes available.

5.4 Specifying resource requirements

In order to provide any kind of bounded QoS, it must be possible for an application to communicate its requirement to the underlying infrastructure, both distribution layer and host operating system.

DIMMA supports a resource reservation model and allocates resources according to the specified QoS when an application establishes a binding, e.g., when a client binds to a server. Resources are reserved for all parts of the underlying channel, e.g., communications resources, buffers, tasks, etc. The binding model used by DIMMA to support the specification of QoS is dealt with in the next section.

6 BINDING

6.1 Overview

With standard RPC systems, binding is done implicitly, i.e., when a remote reference is first used, a binder sets up an appropriate communications channel to it. This is the model adopted by the majority of ORBs and provides maximum transparency to the application in terms of hiding irrelevant engineering details. However, there is a trade-off: transparency implies little or no control over the QoS of the binding that is established.

When quality of service can be specified, binding must be done explicitly (because the binder will not know which of a range of possible quality levels is wanted); this requires extra support from the binding apparatus. Although explicit specification of Quality of Service parameters can be provided for RPC protocols as well, it is essential for flow protocols. QoS is specified on a per-connection basis so as to allow the same service to be accessed with different levels of quality, e.g., a video source could be provided at different levels of quality over different bandwidth connections.

DIMMA supports both implicit and explicit binding models.

6.2 Implicit binding

Implicit binding in DIMMA is provided by Binder objects which implement a predefined binding policy, and make use of default QoS parameters. In keeping with the DIMMA component philosophy, the implicit binders may be replaced by application specific implicit binders which implement a different binding policy appropriate to the application.

6.3 Explicit binding

To meet the needs of multi-media and real-time applications, DIMMA provides a model of explicit binding. Explicit binding allows both the QoS and the time of binding to be controlled and hence allows resource reservation. The downside is the increased complexity of the mechanism required to establish the binding.

An explicit binding is accomplished in several stages and is bootstrapped using the implicit binding mechanism. An application wishing to offer a service must do so via a binding manager which offers its own interface as a proxy for the real service. The binding manager is responsible for placing each party's local explicit binder in communication with the other. These in turn will set up the local bindings with the specified QoS and establish the network connection. This procedure is illustrated in Figure 4.

1. The service interface is exported via the server's binding manager.
2. When the service interface reference is exported (e.g., as a call parameter or via a trader), a reference to the server's binding manager interface is passed instead.
3. The client, on binding to the service, calls the binding manager passing it the parameters for the binding (e.g., QoS requirements).
4. The binding manager hands off the binding request to the server's local endpoint binder, which creates a service endpoint and…
5. …returns the details to the binding manager, which in turn…
6. …returns the details to the client.

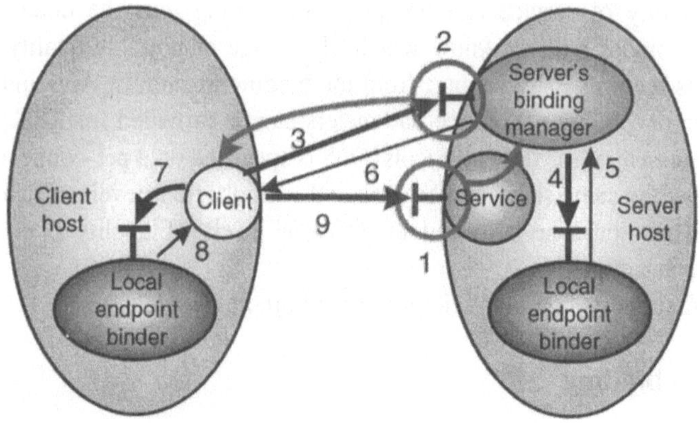

Figure 4 Explicit binding

7. The client then passes the remote endpoint details plus other binding parameters to its local endpoint binder, which sets up the binding and...
8. ...returns an invocation reference to the client...
9. ...which the client then uses to call the service.

All these machinations though are transparent to the client application, which simply imports what it believes to be the interface reference for the service and binds to it.

6.4 Binding and resource control

The protocol-specific QoS specification provided during explicit binding is passed to the top level protocol binder at each end of the binding. In the usual case where the protocol is made up of a number of layers, the QoS specification for the top level layer will contain a pointer to the QoS for the next layer down, and so on. When creating the channel for the binding, each layer extracts the QoS for the next layer down and then passes that to a create channel request on the lower layer recursively until the bottom layer is reached. The bottom layer extracts the resourcing information from the QoS parameters it is given to create its channel and then returns that to the next layer up, which repeats the process until the top layer is reached again. Thus each layer resources its part of the channel appropriately.

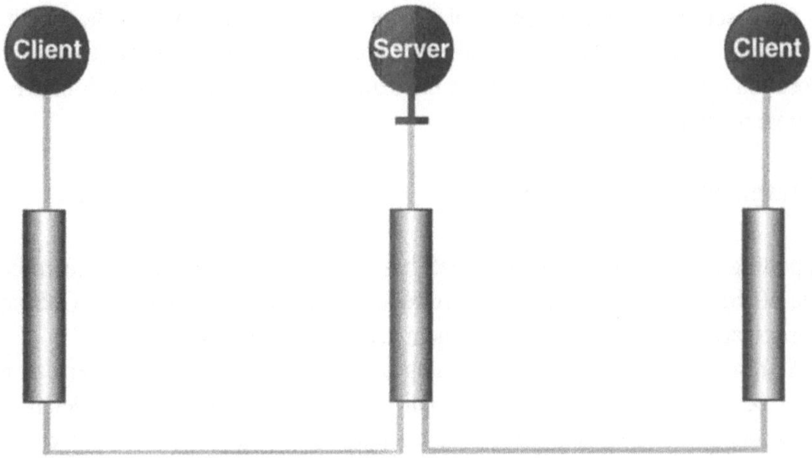

Figure 5 Standard ORB sharing a single network endpoint

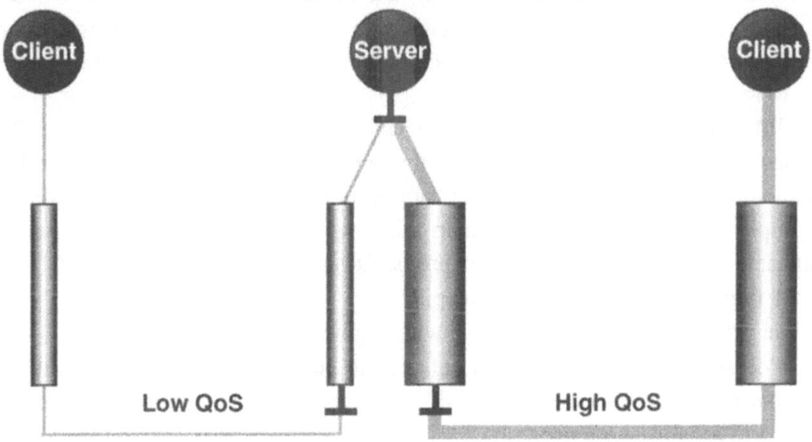

Figure 6 Multiple endpoints for varying QoS

6.5 Implications for network endpoints

Supporting Quality of Service affects how network endpoints are used. For a standard RPC system with implicit binding, all connections to a service can be multiplexed through the same network endpoint because they all have the same (default) quality of service. See Figure 5.

With an ORB such as DIMMA, which supports access to the same service with different levels of quality of service, a server must be able to offer multiple network endpoints in order to support the different QoS (Figure 6).

Although supporting QoS requires support for multiple network endpoints for the same service, this extra level of complexity is masked within the binding mechanism outlined above, and all the application ever sees is a standard invocation reference that encapsulates the details necessary to distinguish between multiple possible endpoints.

6.6 Implications for binders

Supporting explicit specification of QoS has a number of implications – there is a trade-off between the amount of control allowed to the application over QoS and the transparency to the application of the mechanisms being used.

As resource usage and thus QoS is specific to each protocol, a binder can no longer be generic. This requires the application to understand the QoS details of each protocol it uses, i.e., it too can no longer be generic. It also affects the dynamic loading of protocols – if QoS is protocol specific, how do we determine and select from the possibilities offered by a dynamically loaded protocol?

This problem of lack of transparency can be mitigated by defining a more generic sort of QoS and then having each protocol be able to map from the generic QoS to its own specific QoS.

DIMMA has support for this concept of generic QoS, which is called engineering QoS. It is at a higher level than protocol specific QoS, though it does not attempt to provide very high level "application" QoS. It is the responsibility of the implementer of a protocol to map this engineering QoS into terms that are applicable to the protocol. The two protocols supplied with DIMMA, IIOP and ANSA Flow, both implement this mapping.

The options currently configurable with engineering QoS are:

- Processing concurrency, which defines the maximum number of tasks to run concurrently. A special "null task" value indicates that the message reading task is to process the operation.
- Message concurrency, which defines the maximum number of messages that can be simultaneously processed (and hence the size of the buffer pool). If this is greater than processing concurrency, message processing is scheduled over the available tasks as described earlier in section 5.3.
- Buffer size, which defines the size of the buffers in the pool and hence the maximum size of a message.
- Channel policy, which defines whether or not channels are multiplexed on transport connections.

By having this engineering QoS it allows application programmers to write applications that control QoS without having to hard-code decisions about protocol use throughout the program. It also means that the choice of which protocol to use can be deferred until runtime, allowing dynamically loaded protocols (that were not necessarily known about at design time) to be used.

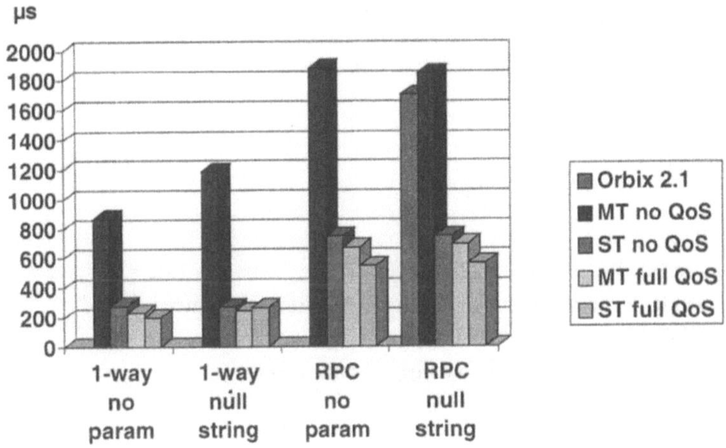

- Orbix 2.1 - a popular commercial CORBA ORB from Iona
- MT no QoS - multi-threaded build, default QoS configuration
- ST no QoS - single-threaded build, default QoS configuration
- MT full QoS - multi-threaded build, high-performance QoS
- ST full QoS - single-threaded build, high-performance QoS

Figure 7 Performance results

7 PERFORMANCE

The default QoS configuration in DIMMA is comparable with commercial ORBs. The high-performance QoS configuration is 2-3 times faster than commercial ORBs. Descriptions of the default and high-performance QoS configurations are given earlier in Figure 7.

The tests were carried out using 5,000 iterations of a remote call using IIOP on a 167MHz Sparc Ultra 1 with 128Mb of memory. The first two tests used CORBA oneway operations; the second two used standard operations. The "no param" tests used an operation with no parameters, the "null string" tests used an operation with a single string parameter, which was passed a zero length string.

8 SUMMARY

DIMMA was designed to explore how the needs of multimedia applications may be met in the context of an ODP platform. To this end it provides applications with control over their allocation and use of resources through quality of service (QoS) parameters, and supports multi-media flows through flow interfaces.

We have shown how application control of QoS can have a significant impact on performance. However for true *end-to-end* quality of service, QoS control of the network and operating system are also required.

REFERENCES

IEEE (1992) POSIX.
IEEE POSIX Standard 10003.4a.

ISO (1995) Reference Model of Open Distributed Computing.
ISO/IEC 10746-3.

Li, G. (1995) An overview of real-time ANSAware 1.0.
Distributed Systems Engineering Vol 2. No. 1

Schulzrinne, H., Casner, S., Frederick, R., and Jacobson, V. (1996) RTP: A Transport Protocol for Real-Time Applications.
RFC 1889. Audio-Video Transport Working Group, January 1996.

The Object Management Group (1998) The Common Object Request Broker: Architecture and Specification, revision 2.2.
OMG 98-02-33. OMG Headquarters, Framingham MA, U.S.A.

9 BIOGRAPHIES

APM is a recognised world leader in distributed system technology, offering research and consulting services to customers world-wide. It specialises in the application, management and security of mobile objects and innovative technologies in networked and distributed systems. APM Research manages and operates the ANSA open, collaborative research programme (Advanced Networked Systems Architecture).

Douglas Donaldson is currently on the FollowMe research project, investigating the impact of mobility on information systems, and designing a persistent object store. Matthew Faupel has contributed an implementation of IIOP and a protocol negotiator to the FlexiNet project, and has now moved to APM's consultancy branch. Richard Hayton is managing the FlexiNet project, and is currently developing a Java network class loader for enhancing object mobility. Andrew Herbert is Technical Director of APM Limited. Nicola Howarth, Andre Kramer and Ian MacMillan have joined Digitivity Inc., APM's product arm, which develops products to support the secure deployment and management of mobile code. Dave Otway and Simon Waterhouse are working for APM's consultancy branch with specific involvement in security and distributed architectures.

The Implementation of a High Performance ORB over Multiple Network Transports

Sai-Lai Lo, Steve Pope
Olivetti & Oracle Research Laboratory
24a Trumpington Street
Cambridge CB2 1QA, England
+44-1223-343000, +44-1223-313542
s.lo@orl.co.uk, slp@orl.co.uk

Abstract

This paper describes the implementation of a high performance Object Request Broker (ORB)– omniORB2. The discussion focuses on the experience in achieving high performance by exploiting the protocol and other characteristics of the CORBA 2.0 specification. The design is also highly adaptable to a variety of network transports. The results of running the ORB over TCP/IP, shared memory, Scalable Coherent Interface (SCI) and ATM Adaptation Layer 5 (AAL5) are presented. In both null calls and bulk data transfers, the performance of omniORB2 is significantly better than other commercial ORBs.

Keywords

CORBA, omniORB2, SCI, AAL5, performance,transport

1 INTRODUCTION

In this paper, we describe the implementation of a high performance Object Request Broker (ORB)- omniORB2. OmniORB2 is the second generation ORB developed at ORL (hence the name "omniORB two"). The initial goal was to produce a standard conforming ORB that can deliver the performance required by the applications developed in-house.

In the past, we have used different RPC-style communication systems in various projects. For instance, the Active Badge system (Want *et al.* 1992) was built on top of the Ansaware. Our experience have shown that while a good programming paradigm for building distributed system is important, it is of little practical use if the implementation cannot deliver adequate performance. For instance, the Medusa system (Wray *et al.* 1994) was developed with its own message-passing system partly because the RPC systems at the time were found not to be able to deliver the performance required.

The ability to reuse a distributed system infra-structure over a new network transport is also an important consideration. Medusa was designed to run directly on top of ATM transports. Existing RPC systems at the time were usually designed to run on top of UDP or TCP. The effort required to add the ATM support is almost the same as writing a message-passing system from scratch. The need to support a new transport is not an one-off requirement. The laboratory has always been interested in new networking technologies. ATM is extended into the wireless domain by Radio ATM (RATM 1988); a low-power and short range radio networking system (Piconet) (Piconet 1988) is being developed; and the potential of high performance interconnects is being explored. Clearly, it is important to design the ORB so that a new network transport can be added without changing the majority of the code base.

It is becoming technically and economically feasible to connect a cluster of (inexpensive) computers by very fast interconnects to create a high performance distributed computing platform. These interconnect technologies, such as SCI and fiber channel, offer very high bandwidth and, more importantly, very low latency user-space to user-space data transfer. This has the effect of removing the dominant part of a RPC round-trip time, i.e. the delay introduced by the kernel and the network protocol stack. In this environment, the overhead incurred by the so called "middleware" will become the dominant factor in deciding the performance of remote invocations. Although omniORB2 is primarily used with conventional networking, we try to minimise the call overhead as much as possible and at the same time stay compliant with the CORBA (OMG 1996) specification. We hope that in future the design will prove to be useful in low-latency computer clusters. The initial results of running omniORB2 over SCI are encouraging.

In this paper, we present the considerations and choices made in the design of omniORB2*. The discussion will focus on the experience in achieving high perfor-

---

*OmniORB2 is publicly available under the GNU public licences. More information is available at *http://www.orl.co.uk/omniORB2/omniORB2.html*

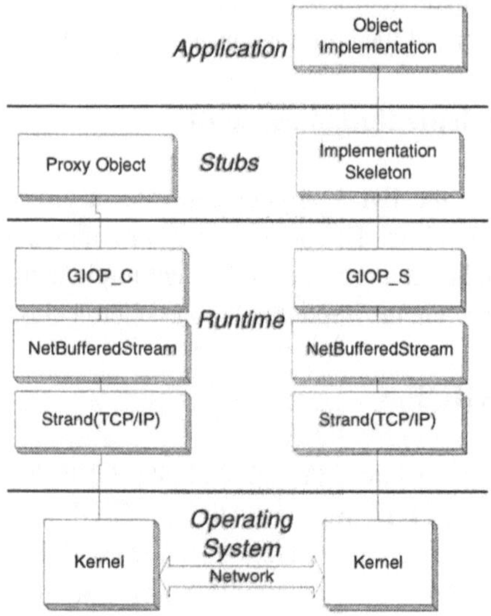

Figure 1 Internal Architecture

mance by exploiting the protocol and other characteristics of the CORBA specification. The results of several performance tests are included. The data show that in both null calls and bulk data transfers, the performance of omniORB2 is significantly better than other commercial ORBs. The results of running omniORB2 over several transports: ATM/AAL5, shared memory and SCI, are presented. The data show that omniORB2 is highly adaptable to the characteristics of these transports and can achieve a significant improvement in performance over the TCP/IP.

2 INTERNAL ARCHITECTURE

CORBA provides a standard framework for building distributed applications. The ORB is the "middleware" that allows a client to invoke an operation on an object without regard to its implementation or location.

In order to invoke an operation on an object, a client must first acquire a reference to the object. If the object is remote (i.e. in a different address space), the ORB has to create a local representation of the object- a "proxy" in the client's address space. When the client invokes an operation on the proxy object, the ORB delivers the invocation to the remote object. Exactly how the ORB arranges to deliver the invocation is not specified by CORBA. Nevertheless, in order to permit interoperability, CORBA mandates that IIOP (Internet Inter-ORB Protocol), a RPC protocol layered over TCP/IP, be supported by all ORBs. However, the standard does not preclude the use of other transport mechanisms when available.

Figure 1 outlines the main components that are involved in the delivery of remote invocations. The functions of the components are as follows:

2.1 Proxy and Implementation Skeleton

For each IDL interface, the IDL compiler generates a proxy object class and an implementation skeleton class. The proxy object provides a local represent of the remote object. The application provides the object implementation and connects to the ORB upcall structure via the implementation skeleton class.

2.2 GIOP_C and GIOP_S

GIOP_C and GIOP_S together drive the General Inter-ORB Protocol (GIOP). IIOP is a mapping of GIOP over TCP/IP. We choose to layer GIOP, not just on top of TCP/IP, but on all the network transports available to the ORB. Of course it is possible to use an entirely different protocol for a non-TCP/IP transport. While we think GIOP is hardly the most optimised protocol and a more efficient Environment Specific Inter-ORB Protocol (ESIOP) (a term used in CORBA to refer to other non-GIOP protocol) could be designed, the overhead incurred by the increased complexity to accommodate two protocols may outweigh any performance benefit. For instance, the overhead in multiplexing incoming requests via different protocol paths to the same upcall structure on the server side could be substantial.

Using GIOP-only allows us to tightly integrate the run time and the IDL interface specific stubs. One benefit of the tight integration is that some of the more complex and less performance critical functions in driving the GIOP protocol can be delegated to the stubs. One example is in handling location forwarding. In response to an invocation, the server could response with a location-forward message to point the client to the new location of the object. The client is expected to retry the invocation, without any application intervention, at the new location. If the runtime is to retry the invocation, it must keep the complete request in its own buffer until a reply comes back from the server. For calls with very large arguments, this will result in excessive buffer allocation. In omniORB2, GIOP_C does not perform the retry, control is passed back to the stub code and the call arguments are re-marshalled. There is no need for the runtime to buffer the whole request message.

2.3 NetBufferedStream

NetBufferedStream performs data marshalling from call arguments to a bidirection data connection. Marshalling functions for all IDL primitive types and for a vector of bytes are provided. Ideally, we would like to generate optimal marshalling code from an IDL interface. In practice, we found that the scope to speed up data marshalling is somewhat limited by the coding rules of GIOP.

GIOP specifies that all primitive data types must be aligned on its native boundaries. Alignment is defined as being relative to the beginning of a GIOP message.

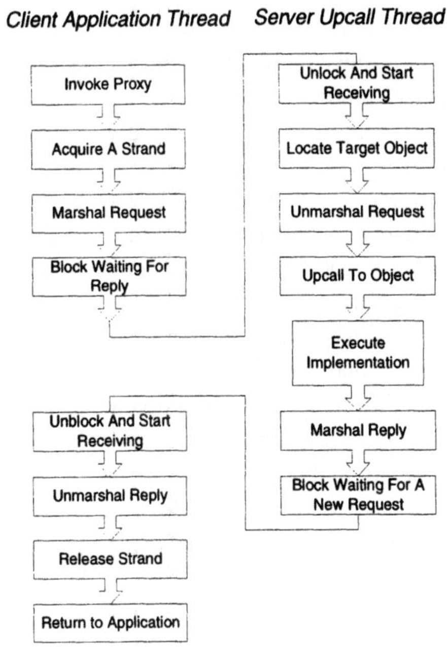

Figure 2 Call-chain of a Remote Invocation

Unfortunately, a GIOP request or reply message starts with a variable size header. The size of the header is only known during the invocation because it contains fields that are variable length and context dependent. It is therefore not possible to pre-compute at compile time whether padding bytes have to be inserted to make a call argument correctly aligned.*

Despite of these limitations imposed by the GIOP specification, there is still scope for further optimisation in the marshalling code. Future omniORB2 releases will further improve the stub code to speed up data marshalling. Techniques used in previous work such as Flick (Flick 1988) may be useful.

3 THREADING MODEL

OmniORB2 uses the thread-per-connection model. The model is selected to achieve two objectives. Firstly, the degree of concurrency is to be maximised while any thread overhead is kept to a minimum. Secondly, the interference by the activities of other threads on the progress of a remote invocation is to be minimised. In other

---

* Also, fixed size *struct* and *union* constructor types cannot be marshalled in bulk and has to be done for each field member individually. This is because the memory layout of constructor types is both compiler and processor dependent. Even if the memory layout agrees with the GIOP alignment rules, the internal alignment between field members will be affected by what precedes the structure in the GIOP message.

words, thread "cross-talk" should be minimised within the ORB. The thread-per-connection model helps to achieve these objectives because the degree of multiplexing at every level is kept to a minimum.

Figure 2 shows the call-chain of a remote invocation. On the client side of a connection, the thread that invokes on a proxy object drives the GIOP protocol directly and blocks on the connection to receive the reply. On the server side, a dedicated thread is spawned per connection (this is why the threading model is called thread-per-connection). The server thread blocks on the connection until a request arrives. On receiving a request, it performs the upcall to the object implementation and sends the reply when the upcall returns. There is no thread switching along the call chain.

Note that there is at most one call "in-flight" at any time in a connection. The GIOP specification allows the client to have multiple outstanding requests down the same connection at the same time; the replies can be returned in any order. To use this call multiplexing scheme, both ends must implement two levels of thread dispatch. In the lower level, each end must have a dedicated thread to (de)multiplex the call. Once demultiplexed, the call has to be dispatched to the upper level: the application threads on the client side and the upcall threads on the server side. To process a call, this involves four thread switchings (two on each side). The overhead is simply too high and there is little/no advantage over the "one-call-per-connection" scheme used in omniORB2. Worst, the two-level thread dispatch structure introduces undesirable "cross-talk" among different threads because all the remote invocations are multiplexed down to a single thread at both ends.

If there is only one connection, concurrent invocations to the same remote address space would have to be serialized (because at most one call is "in-flight" per connection). This severely limits the degree of concurrency. Also, a deadlock can occur*. To eliminate this limitation, omniORB2 creates multiple connections to the same remote address space on-demand. In other words, if two concurrent calls are made to the same remote address space, the ORB would establish two connections to handle the call.

4 DYNAMIC CONNECTION MANAGEMENT

In CORBA, as in most distributed systems, remote bindings are established implicitly without application intervention. CORBA does not specify when such bindings should result in a connection being established between the two address spaces. Instead, the ORBs are free to implement implicit binding in a variety of ways. In om-

*Consider the case where object A is in address space 1 and object B and C are in address space 2. In address space 1, a thread invokes on object B; B then performs a nested invocation on A; A in turn performs a nested invocation on C. At this point, there are two calls originating from address space 1. The first call can only be completed after the second call returns. If the second call is serialised, a deadlock situation occurs.

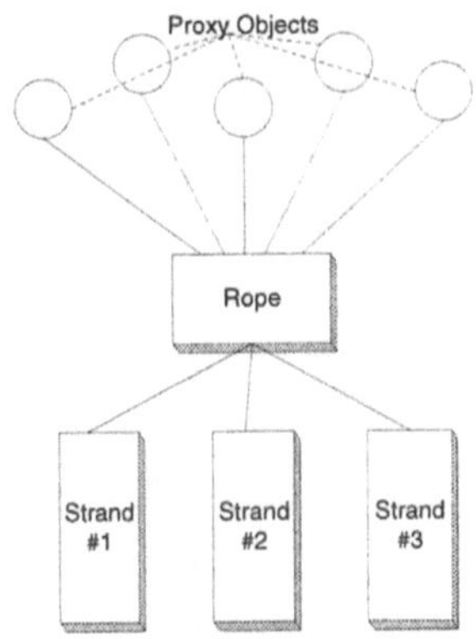

Figure 3 Dynamic Connection Management

niORB2, connections are established only when invocations have to be passed on to other address spaces.*.

Connections are managed collectively by a "Rope". The Rope abstraction provides an association between two address spaces. The connection point of each address space is identified by an Endpoint. On demand, a Rope creates a "Strand" to connect the two Endpoints. The Strand abstraction is a bidirectional data connection. Each Strand is mapped directly onto a network connection.

Just as a real rope often consists of multiple strands, a Rope may be composed of one or more Strands. The relationship between the entities are further illustrated in figure 3. As indicated in the figure, every pair of address space is always associated by one Rope. This association is shared by multiple proxy objects that bind to the implementation objects in the other address space. When the client invokes an operation via a proxy object, exclusive access to a Strand is acquired from the Rope. At this point, the Rope may have to create a new Strand in order to satisfy the demand. When the invocation is completed, the Strand is returned to the Rope.

Once created, a Strand is left opened in case it might be reused again by other invocations shortly afterwards. However, it is wasteful to leave a Strand opened when it has been left unused for a considerable time. It is particularly bad on the server side because too many idle network connections could block out new connections when the server process runs out of spare channels. Within the ORB, two threads are dedicated to close down idle connections.

To support a large number of clients, it is important for the server to be able to shutdown idle connections unilaterally. However, this function is only useful when the client is able to distinguish such an orderly shutdown from those caused by abnormal

*It is obviously a better approach than, for instance, to always open a connection to the remote object whenever the ORB is building a proxy object in the client's address space. Consider a server, such as a naming service, which acts only as a repository of object references for other clients; the server would not invoke on these objects. The naive approach of connecting to all the remote objects would quickly overwhelm the server with unnecessary connections.

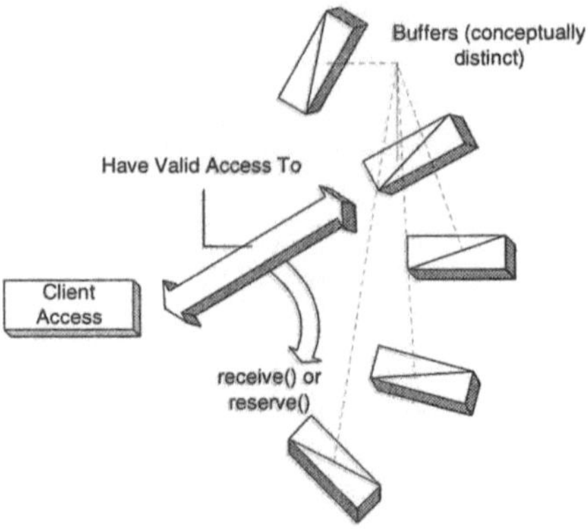

Figure 4 Buffer Management Scheme

conditions such as server crashes. When omniORB2 is about to close a connection on the server side, it uses the *GIOP closeConnection* message to inform the client this is an orderly shutdown. The client should recognise this condition and retry an invocation transparently if necessary. This is in fact the compliant behaviour. What it should not do is to treat this as a hard failure and raise a *COMM_FAILURE* system exception. Unfortunately, very few of the ORBs we have tested for interoperability are able to response correctly.

As illustrated in figure 3, the default behaviour of omniORB2 is to multiplex proxy objects to the same remote address space onto a common pool of connections. Some applications may prefer a dedicated connection per proxy object. For instance, a proxy object may be used to push live video to the other address space. The problem with implicit binding, i.e. the default behaviour of omniORB2, is that it provides no opportunity for the application to influence the ORB's binding policy on a per-binding basis. This makes it impossible for applications with specific performance requirements to control, for instance, the timing of binding establishment; the multiplexing of bindings over network connections; and the selection of the type of network connection itself. This is an issue that has not been addressed by existing CORBA standards. We believe one solution is to augment the binding model with explicit binding. In other words, the application is given direct control on setting up bindings via proxy objects. This is work in progress and the details are beyond the scope of this paper.

5 THE STRAND

The Strand abstraction provides a bidirectional data connection. This abstraction has been implemented over several network transports. This section describes the distinct features of its interface. The term "client" is used in this section to refer to the entity that invokes on the interface.

5.1 Receive and Send

To receive data, the client invokes the `receive` method.*

To send data, the client first requests for a buffer with the `reserve` method. Roughly speaking, `reserve` is the converse of `receive`.

The buffer management scheme is special. The buffers are allocated and deallocated inside the Strand. Furthermore, the buffer returned by `receive` is only guaranteed to contain valid data until the next `receive` call. In other words, the next `receive` call automatically invalidates the data pointer returned by this call. Figure 4 provides an illustration of how buffers are managed. Similarly, the client can write to the buffer returned by `reserve` until the next `reserve` call. In other words, the next `reserve` call automatically invalidates the data pointer returned by this call (figure 4). Moreover, the strand is free to transmit the implicitly relinquished buffers any time hereafter.

There are two reasons for adopting this scheme.

Firstly, because buffer allocation is hidden behind the interface, a Strand implementation could be optimised for a network interface that provides memory-mapped network buffers and zero-copy receive semantics. The clients could unmarshal data directly from the network buffers returned by the Strand.

Secondly, the interface inherently puts a limit on the buffer space that the Strand has to commit to the clients. At any time, there is only one buffer the client can access. Any buffers that have previously been given out to the client are released implicitly and can be recycled immediately. Furthermore, the size of each buffer is limited to a maximum fixed by the Strand. To unmarshal large call arguments, the client will have to call `receive` repeatedly to fetch all the data. There is no need for the Strand to allocate extra buffers to handle the call. Instead the unmarshalling of data by the client can be pipelined with the fetching of more data from the network by the strand.

We believe the buffer management scheme has a direct impact on performance. It is possible to take advantage of zero-copy network buffers to improve data marshalling efficiency. Because there is no need to cater for special cases, such as calls with very large data arguments, the program logic is simple and can be implemented efficiently. It also helps to avoid the contention for buffer resources among different strands. For instance, in all the strand implementations we have done so far, we are able to avoid dynamic buffer allocation completely. Each connection is allocated one or two fixed size buffer statically*. From the point of view of minimising the interference among different thread of executions, the absence of dynamic buffer allocation helps by eliminating an obvious point of resource contention.

---

*Apart from the buffer management scheme, the semantics of the method is quite straightforward. The client specifies how many bytes it expects to receive, whether the strand should return when it has less in its buffer and whether the returned buffer should be 8, 16, 32 or 64 bits aligned. The method returns a structure which contains a pointer to the data area and the number of bytes in that area.

*To avoid unnecessary fragmentation in the operating system, the size of each buffer is set to accommodate the maximum PDU size of the network interface.

Notice that we have to walk through the marshalling arguments twice when sending data! This is necessary because GIOP version 1.0 does not permit data fragmentation and the total message size must be written to the header. To avoid the need to buffer the whole message, the message size is calculated in the first pass. The performance penalty due to the size calculation varies with the type of arguments. It can be substantial in cases such as a long sequence of strings. Having said that, this performance penalty will soon be history with GIOP version 1.1. There is no need to pre-compute the total message size as a request or a reply can be sent in multiple and consecutive GIOP messages.

5.2 Bulk Data Send/Receive

Two methods are provided for bulk data transfer. `receive_and_copy` is equivalent to a `receive` and a memory copy to the buffer provided by the client. Similarly, `reserve_and_copy` is equivalent to a `reserve` and a memory copy from the buffer provided by the client. A naive implementation may have to copy the client data to/from its internal buffer. Depending on the network interface, this copy action may be optimised away. For instance, with a BSD-style TCP socket interface, the `reserve_and_copy` can be collapsed into a single `send` system call directly from the client's buffer; the `receive_and_copy` can be collapsed into a single `recv` system call. Using this optimisation, the ORB is able to handle bulk data, such as sequence of octets, with very little overhead (zero copy within the ORB).

5.3 Exactly-Once and At-Most-Once Semantics

The strand abstraction is not intended to be a general purpose bidirectional data connection. Instead, the goal is to specialise the interface and encapsulate sufficient functionalities to support request-reply and oneway interactions efficiently.

When implemented on top of a reliable stream transport (such as TCP/IP), both request-reply and oneway calls are exactly-once by default. On the otherhand, invocations implemented on top of an unreliable transport (such as ATM/AAL 5) are by nature at-most-once because data packets could be dropped in transit. Exactly-once semantics can be obtained if the sender is able to retransmit lost-packets and the receiver is able to remove duplicates. We believe that while exactly-once semantics is desirable for request-reply interactions, at-most-once semantics is more suitable for oneway calls. This is particularly true when oneway calls are used to transmit isochronous data. With this data type, retransmission should be avoided because undesirable jitters will be introduced otherwise.

For this reason, the strand allows the client to specify whether a call should be invoked as exactly-once or at-most-once. Using this information*, the strand decides whether lost-packets are retransmitted internally.

*The method: `reserve_and_startMTU` is provided. This method is the same as `reserve` except that the former takes an extra boolean argument to indicate if the call semantics should be exactly-once. Also, the `startMTU` and `endMTU` boolean arguments in the `receive` and `reserve` methods are used to indicate the

Platform	Transport	Time per call(μsec)
Linux Pentium Pro 200MHz (gcc-2.7.2 no compiler optimisation)	TCP/intra-machine	340
	TCP/ethernet(ISA card)	1000
	TCP/ATM	440
Windows NT 4.0 Pentinum Pro (MS Visual C++ -O2)	TCP/intra-machine	360
	TCP/ethernet(ISA card)	1000
Digital Unix 3.2 DEC 3000/600 (DEC C++ -O2)	TCP/intra-machine	750
	TCP/ethernet	1050
Solaris 2.5.1 Ultra 1 167MHz (Sunpro C++ -fast)	TCP/intra-machine	540
	TCP/ethernet	710

Table 1 The Null Echo Round Trip Time of omniORB2 on Various Platforms

6 TCP TRANSPORT

The implementation of the tcp transport is quite straightforward. The noteworthy features are as follows:

Each connection is allocated a fixed size buffer (8Kbytes). Once the buffer is filled up, the data are transmitted. The transfer of sequence and array of primitive types are optimised. The stub code marshals these data types with `receive_and_copy` and `reserve_and_copy`. If the data size is bigger that the buffer space available, the data in the buffer are flushed to the network and the sequence/array is then sent directly from the application buffer.

6.1 Performance

6.1.1 Null Echo

The time to echo a zero length (null) string is measured . This is a measure of the overhead incurred by the ORB and the operating system.* The measurements taken from a number of platforms are shown in table 1. The data are the average of 5000 invocations.

To put the measurements into context, the same test is used to measure the performance of several commercially available ORBs. All the tests were conducted on a pair of Sun Ultra 1 running Solaris 2.5.1. The results are shown in figure 5. OmniORB2 takes 540μsec intra-machine and 710μsec inter-machine. Compare to om-

beginning and the end of an invocation. This is necessary because exactly-once calls may be interleaved with at-most-once calls, the strand must be able to distinguish the packets that can be dropped, i.e. those from at-most-once calls, from those that have to be retransmitted. Of course, none of these arguments have any effect when the strand is implemented on top of a reliable stream transport.

*The IDL interface consists of a single operation: `string echoString(string mesg);`

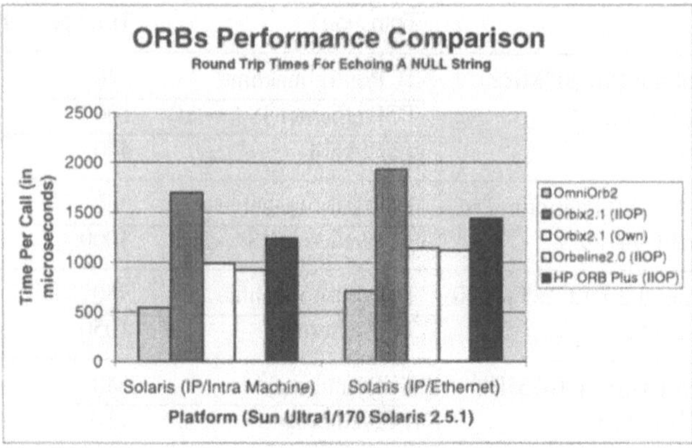

Figure 5

niORB2, other ORBs take 70% to 214% longer for intra-machine and 58% to 172% longer for inter-machine calls.

6.2 Bulk Data Transfer

The performance in bulk data transfer is measured by sending multiple sequence of octets using oneway operations.* The test is conducted using two Ultra 1 that are connected via 155Mbits ATM.* The time to send 100Mbytes of data in multiple sequences of octets was measured. Different sequence sizes were used. Figure 6 plots the throughput against the send data size in each test run. The throughput from using direct socket programming is also shown. This curve represents the performance envelope obtainable from the test platform.

At small send data size, the throughput is CPU-bound. As the send data size increases, the throughput changes from CPU-bound to link-bandwidth-bound. The yield point where the throughput changes from CPU-bound to link-bandwidth-bound is directly proportional to the ORB's overhead, i.e. the higher the yield point, the higher the ORB's overhead.

With 64 bytes data size, the throughput of omniORB2 is 39% of the direct socket throughput. The figure rises to 63% at 2048 bytes where the throughput is still CPU-bound. This is an indication that the ORB overhead does not increase linearly with the size of the call arguments. In other words, the ORB's overhead has quickly become insignificant at moderate data size, the operating system overhead is the dominant factor.

*The IDL interface consists of a single operation oneway void receive(in Buffer data); where Buffer is a sequence<char>.

*The machines are connected via three ATM switches in this order: ATML Virata VM1000⟷Fore ASX-200WG⟷ATML Virata VM1000. Classical IP over ATM is used to provide TCP/IP connectivity. The MTU size of the ATM interfaces is 9180 bytes. The default socket send and receive buffer size is used. The socket option TCP_NODELAY is not set.

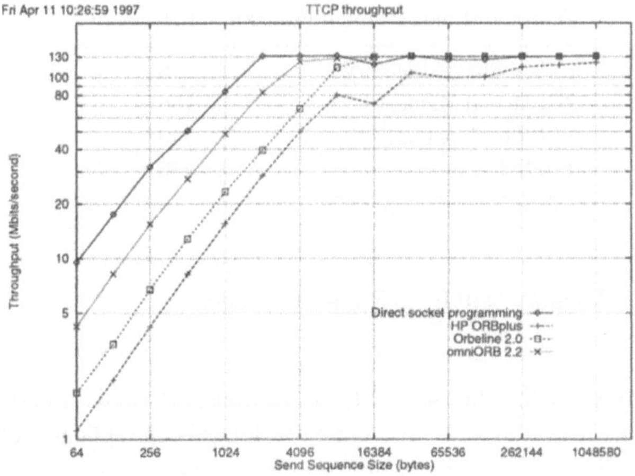

Figure 6 ORBs Bulk Data Throughput Comparison

The throughput of other ORBs are also shown in figure 6*. All the ORBs remain CPU-bound well beyond the point when omniORB2 is already able to saturate the link. Before the yield point, the CPU-bound throughput of other ORBs are 52% to 67% less than that of omniORB2.

7 SHARED MEMORY TRANSPORT

A shared memory transport was designed as a complementary transport, useful where two address spaces may communicate through a segment of shared memory. While this usually corresponds to the client and server being located on the same machine, we have also used the transport over a high performance interconnect which presents an abstraction of shared memory for inter-machine communication.

A server instance of the transport creates a large shared memory segment which is carved up into a number of communication channels, each channel with a semaphore set to allow for synchronisation. One channel is reserved for new clients to rendezvous with the server. During the rendezvous, the server allocates a channel for the client and passes a key to the allocated channel back to the client through the rendezvous channel. All subsequent communication between the client and server takes place through the allocated channel.

7.1 Performance

The shared memory transport is implemented using the standard System V primitives for shared memory and semaphores. The same transport was also ported over the SCI interconnect from Dolphin Interconnect Solutions. The round trip times of *null echo* using the two transports are shown in table 2.

*The test cannot be performed using Orbix 2.1MT because of a memory leakage problem in its runtime.

Transport (Linux Pentium Pro 200)	Latency(us)
SYS V Shared Memory	270
SCI Shared Memory	156
TCP/Local loopback	340
TCP/ATM	440

Table 2 Shared Memory Null Echo Round Trip Time

These results show that the shared memory transport yields a performance improvement in the region of 20%. The same result has been replicated on other Unix platforms. The results illustrate a significant improvement in latency when using the SCI transport. It has been estimated that for the Linux platform, 110us is spent in the ORB with protocol and marshalling overhead, the remainder being spent in performing transmission and synchronisation through the shared buffer. It is interesting to note that the inter-machine time using SCI is significantly faster than intra-machine using standard shared memory primitives. This is due to the parallelisation of the GIOP and the avoidance of a context switch between the client and server. A more in depth discussion of the SCI transport and more performance analysis can be found in (Hodges *et al.* 1998).

8 ATM AAL5 TRANSPORT

The ATM AAL5 transport is intended to run directly on top of the native ATM API of the host platform.* Unlike the transports described so far, the underlying transport– AAL5– is unreliable although the packets are guaranteed to arrive in-order. As discussed in section 5.3, we would like to provide exactly-once semantics for request-reply and at-most-once semantics for oneway calls. As the size of each packet is limited to 9180 bytes*, a GIOP request or reply message that exceeds this limit would have to be transmitted as multiple packets. To support exactly-once semantics, the transport must be able to retransmit any packets that are lost in transit. The retransmission is only done for the request-reply calls and not for the oneway calls. In general, request-reply calls may be interleaved with oneway calls, the transport must be able to adapt and alter the retransmission policy on the fly.

To satisfy these requirements, a very light-weight protocol– omniTransport– is designed to layer on top of the ATM API. A detail discussion of omniTransport and its implementation can be found in (Pope *et al.* 1998). Unlike other transport protocols designed to run in the user address space, omniTransport is not a general purpose design but is targeted to support asymmetric interactions where one end

*For the moment, the transport has been implemented over the Linux ATM API. It should be straight forward to port the implementation to another platform API.

*This is the MTU size of the Linux ATM network interface.

Transport	Time per call (μsec)
TCP/ATM	440
omniTransport/ATM	380
raw ATM	360

Table 3 omniTransport/ATM Null Echo Round Trip Time Comparison

always plays the role of the client and the other the server. This greatly simplify the design because the number of possible protocol states is much smaller than a more general purpose protocol.

Although omniTransport is first implemented on top of an ATM API, the design is well suited for use over any network which offers in-order packet delivery semantics. By inference, one should be able to port omniORB2 to run on top of these networks.

8.1 Performance

The performance of omniTransport is discussed in detail in (Pope *et al.* 1998). For completeness, the round trip times of null Echo are shown in table 3.*

The timing of *raw/ATM* is the round trip time for running the test without the exactly-once guarantee. This represents the performance upper bound achievable on this platform. The timing of *TCP/ATM* is the round trip time using Classic IP (CIP) over ATM. The timing of *omniTransport/ATM* is the round trip time with exactly-once semantics. The protocol adds an extra 20 μsec overhead which is well below the overhead of the kernel-based CIP.

9 CONCLUSION

Our experience with omniORB2 has confirmed that it is possible to design a high performance and compliant Object Request Broker. Good performance is achievable by tailoring the design to the protocol and other characteristics of CORBA. At ORL, omniORB2 has been in use for over a year. It is the software backbone for controlling the Virtual Network Computer (VNC) via the Active Badge and for building the distributed infrastructure of a fine-grain 3D location system– Active Bat. It is also an integral component of Ouija– a CORBA-database integration toolkit that provides seamless integration of an object-oriented frontend, developed in CORBA, with the Oracle 7 relational database server. Given the experience we have with its deployment, we are confident in the robustness and scalability of omniORB2.

We are interested in enhancing omniORB2 to include some notion of "quality of

*The measurements were taken from two Pentium Pro 200Mhz Linux machines interconnected using the Efficient Networks 155Mbps adaptor and an ATML Virata VM1000 switch.

service". This would allow applications with specific performance requirements to influence the way the ORB performs some actions that are necessarily transparent to the applications. For instance, the applications may specify the performance requirements for streaming real-time audio and the ORB should select the suitable network transport and binding model with the appropriate performance guarantee.

We have demonstrated that omniORB2 is adaptable to a variety of transport mechanisms. There is currently an interest at ORL in high bandwidth and low latency interconnect technologies. OmniORB2 has been ported to run on top of one of these technologies– SCI. We believe a software backbone based on CORBA has a lot of potential in passing on the performance improvement provided by the underlying interconnect technology to many distributed applications. We'll continue to explore new improvements to omniORB2 for running on top of fast interconnects.

REFERENCES

Flick, Flick idl compiler *http://www.cs.utah.edu/projects/flux.*

Piconet, The piconet project, 1998 *http://www.orl.co.uk/piconet/.*

RATM, The radio atm project, 1998 *http://www.orl.co.uk/radio/.*

OMG. Common Object Request Broker Architecture and Specification, July 1996. *Revision 2.0, Available electronically via http://www.omg.org.*

Pope, S. and Lo, S. The Implementation of a Native ATM Transport for a High Performance ORB. In ORL Technical Report 98.5, 1998.

Pope, S. Hodges, S. J. Mapp, G. E. Roberts, D. E. and Hopper, A. Enhancing Distributed Systems with Low-Latency Networking In ORL Technical Report 98.6, 1998.

Want, R. and Hopper, A. (1992) Active badges and personal interactive computing objects. IEEE Transactions on Consumer Electronics, February 1992.

Wray, S. Glauert, T. and Hopper, A. (1994) The medusa applications environment. in International Conference on Multimedia Computing and Systems, May 1994.

10 BIOGRAPHY

Sai-Lai Lo received his Ph.D degree from the Computer Laboratory at the University of Cambridge U.K, in 1994. He is currently at the Olivetti and Oracle Research Laboratory in Cambridge. He is the architect and the main developer of omniORB2. His current research interests include distributed object technologies and high performance communication systems.

Steve Pope received the B.A and Ph.D degrees from the Computer Laboratory at the University of Cambridge U.K, in 1993 and 1997. He is currently at the Olivetti and Oracle Research Laboratory in Cambridge, interested in distributed systems, networks and operating systems.

Session 5

ORB Architecture

Jonathan: an Open Distributed Processing Environment in Java

B. Dumant, F. Horn, F. Dang Tran, J.-B. Stefani
France Télécom-CNET, DTL/ASR
38–40 rue du général Leclerc,
92794 Issy Moulineaux Cedex 9, FRANCE
tel: +33 1 45 29 62 93. fax: +33 1 45 29 66 04
email: `bruno.dumant@cnet.francetelecom.fr`

Work partially supported by ACTS project ReTINA AC048.

Abstract

This article describes a minimal and modular ORB framework from which highly flexible ORBs supporting the introduction of arbitrary binding mechanisms between interacting objects can be built. This framework essentially extends the Java notion of object reference to make it distributed. Jonathan is a Java implementation of this framework, featuring a CORBA 2.0 "personality" and several different binding factories. It could be easily extended with new binding factories and personalities (e.g. a RMI personality) or scaled down to fit particular needs.

Keywords

ORB, ODP, CORBA, telecommunications, realtime, multimedia

1 INTRODUCTION

The success of Object Request Brokers –namely distributed object-oriented systems (not necessarily CORBA compliant platforms)– in telecommunications essentially depends on the possibility to adapt them to the specifics of telecommunication systems, and in particular to the support of interactive multimedia services.

This implies that ORBs should be uniformly available across traditionally separate systems, ranging from low-end network equipments such as routers and cross-connects to high-end information processing intensive nodes such as those supporting network operation and management functions and operators' information systems.

Another strong requirement on telecommunication ORBs is their support of various binding and interaction models. The term *binding* should be understood as both the process of associating or interconnecting different objects of a computing system according to a specific communication semantics, and as the end result of this process. Binding implies setting up an access path between objects, which in turn typically comprises locating objects, checking access rights and setting up appropriate data structures to enable communication between objects. Even in the standard client-server case, there is a wide variety of communication semantics that reflect different application requirements. For instance, servers may be persistent, replicated, or may use caches with various consistency policies to improve performance, availability, etc. Other forms of bindings include e.g. multimedia stream bindings with various communications topologies (one-to-many, many-to-many...), group bindings, with various communication semantics and dependability properties, and QoS-constrained bindings whose lifecycle and resource multiplexing policy are controlled by the application.

Lastly, telecommunication systems are typically open, realtime systems, and it is crucial that ORBs achieve realtime behaviour and performance.

By realtime systems, we understand in this paper systems whose users are allowed to specify timeliness and throughput quality of service (QoS) requirements and to obtain guarantees about the fulfillment of these requirements. The nature of guarantees provided may vary from best-effort (where the system provides no quantitative guarantee of how well or how often it will meet application QoS requirements) to deterministic (where the system guarantees that application requirements will be strictly met throughout the lifetime of the application).

An open realtime system is a system whose set of supported applications is not known before-hand and which may vary over time. It seems unlikely that a single scheduling policy or even task model will be applicable in all cases and all application domains. Consequently, a telecommunications ORB should refrain from embodying any particular resource management policy, but instead be flexible enough to accommodate different such policies and provide direct control of system resources such as processors, memory and communication to applications.

Architectures like CORBA or JAVA-RMI still do not meet these requirements (cf. the current OMG RFPs on minimal and realtime CORBA). These architectures remain largely monolithic and disallow adapting or extending the internal machinery short of resorting to proprietary extensions. In terms of computing and network resources, they offer very little control on how resources are allocated and multiplexed. As a result, it is not clear how to provide adaptations required to support multimedia and realtime applications or to scale down these architectures to fit resource-constrained devices such as portable phones or interactive TV set-top boxes.

The work pursued in the context of the ACTS ReTINA project is to specify and implement a flexible ORB architecture whose machinery is exposed to the systems or application programmer. The prime characteristic of this architecture is the ability to plug arbitrary forms of binding policies between objects beyond the implicit binding model for client-server interactions assumed by standard architectures like CORBA or RMI. This goal has been achieved by designing a minimal ORB kernel whose role is to provide a generic environment that arbitrary binding factories can use to create and manage specific bindings. In this approach, a CORBA compliant ORB can be built as a particular "personality" (i.e. a set of APIs and language mappings), thus decoupling the specifics of the CORBA API from the personality-independent kernel interface. This is also true for a non-CORBA personality like Java-RMI.

The aim of this paper is to provide a clear description of the ORB kernel architecture, and to show how a CORBA ORB can be built on top of it. To illustrate this, we shall use the Jonathan Distributed Processing Environment (DPE), developed in Java at CNET, that implements the specifications of the ORB kernel and a CORBA personality.

The ReTINA architecture also features a communication framework and a resource framework. The communication framework allows the modular construction of protocols (suited for RPC or stream styles of interactions), and the reuse of protocol components between binding implementations. This framework, implemented in Jonathan, is very similar to the *x*-kernel framework (Peterson *et al.* 1989), and the reader is referred to Dang Tran *et al.* (1997) for a more detailed description. Lastly, the resource framework features a number of abstractions to manage realtime resources, that provide direct control of system resources to applications. The resource framework has not been implemented in Jonathan since it requires an access to the underlying system-level resources, that current implementations of the Java virtual machine do not provide.

This paper is structured as follows: Section 2 describes the ORB kernel architecture, and how it is implemented in Jonathan; Section 3 describes in more details how a CORBA ORB may be built on top of the Jonathan kernel, and in particular how a binding factory able to create RTP multicast channels can be built in this context; Finally, Section 4 concludes by providing more information about the current status of the Jonathan DPE, comparing with related works, and sketch future research.

2 A FLEXIBLE ORB FRAMEWORK

2.1 Architectural Model

At least three problems must be addressed in an object method invocation: Referencing the target, checking its type, and finally accessing it and interacting with it. The role of an ORB is to provide solutions to these problems in a distributed setting. Since ORBs may operate over heterogeneous platforms and programming languages, there is a need for an abstract object model that can be mapped on specific platforms and languages: Jonathan (like CORBA) is based on the Reference Model of Open Distributed Processing (RM-ODP (ODP 1995)):

- An **object** is an entity containing (encapsulated) information and offering services; RM-ODP objects may be of arbitrary granularity (from one byte to a telephone network...).
- RM-ODP objects can only interact at **interfaces**: Informally, the interfaces of an object are its access points, which means that all the interactions of an object with its environment must occur at one (and only one) of its interfaces.

2.1.1 Binding objects and binding factories

To address the interaction problem, RM-ODP introduces the notion of **binding object**. Two objects –say O_1 and O_2– may interact in two different ways: If they belong to the same capsule (addressing space), O_1 may directly invoke an operation on O_2, otherwise it invokes the same operation on a binding object whose role is to transmit the invocation to O_2 and to return a result if necessary (cf. Figure 1).

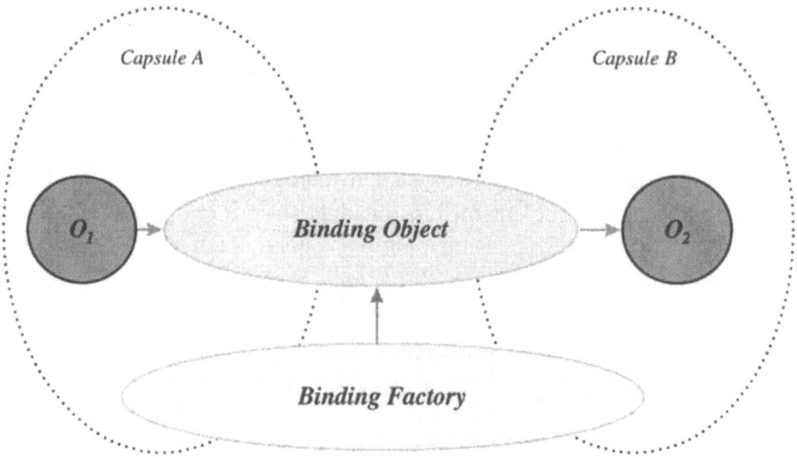

Figure 1 A point-to-point binding.

Binding objects are usually composite objects, distributed over several capsules. Binding objects encapsulate the full end-to-end computational binding between interacting objects, including communication resources, protocols, stubs, etc. In our model, bindings have a type, the type of a binding representing the protocols used, possible quality of service constraints, or any other kind of binding property. Note that binding objects can represent not only client-server bindings, but any kind of binding including e.g. those described in the introduction.

Bindings are constructed by special entities named **binding factories**. Binding factories have two main roles: First they create and manage interface identifiers; Identifiers are introduced in the next section, and this role of binding factories is further discussed in Section 2.2.3; Second, they establish and manage bindings of a specific type (we identify the type of the bindings created by a binding factory and the type of the binding factory itself); This role is further explained in Section 2.4.

2.1.2 Types and references

To address the typing and referencing problem, RM-ODP introduces the notion of **interface reference**. An interface reference may be seen as a generalized Java object reference. Interface references are characterized by two elements: A **type**, and a set of **identifiers**.

Like Java references, interface references have a type, whose role is to allow the creation of safe bindings.

There is no universal type system, and different type systems (and type conformance rules) may be used for different bindings. In our model, type systems are related to **personalities**: A personality defines the type system used by binding factories belonging to it (plus a set of APIs and language mappings). For instance, CORBA is a personality: It defines types by the means of IDL declarations. It is then possible to build various CORBA binding factories, using different protocols, that will use this type system: For instance, all the binding factories provided with Jonathan use the CORBA type system.

However, an interface reference may have to be manipulated in different personality contexts. To make this possible, the interface reference associated type must be defined in a reference, personality-independent, type system defined by the **ORB kernel**. Each personality present in the capsule must provide ways to translate types from its own type system to the reference type system, and conversely (cf. Section 2.3).

An **identifier** is created by a binding factory before the interface reference is sent out of its originating capsule, and may be used by another binding factory of the same type in a different capsule to unambiguously designate the referred interface. An identifier is thus always associated to a given binding type. An interface reference may have identifiers of different types, corresponding to different ways to designate the target interface. An identifier is the distributed counterpart of the memory address contained in a Java object reference.

Thus, the three problems stated above (distributed referencing, typing and access) are represented by different abstractions: Interface references for the referencing problem, personalities for the typing problem, and binding factories for the access problem. The next subsections illustrate these points in the case of Jonathan.

2.2 Distributed references

The first thing an RM-ODP compliant ORB has to define is its own way to map the notion of interface in a specific implementation language.

When an object oriented language is used, an RM-ODP object is usually implemented by a collection of language level objects. Some of these language level objects correspond to access points to the corresponding (abstract) RM-ODP object and as such constitute implementations of its interfaces. In Jonathan, an interface is represented by a Java object of type `Interface`:

```
public interface Interface {}
```

A reference (in the Java sense) to an object of type `Interface` represents an interface reference.

2.2.1 Surrogates

According to the ODP and CORBA computational models (ODP 1995, OMG 1995), interfaces are passed by reference in invocations. As long as the interface reference remains in its original capsule, there is no need for extra information: Its type is defined by the actual Java type of the interface, and there is no need for specific identifiers. But as soon as an interface reference is sent out of its capsule, we need a way to associate more explicitly type information and identifiers with it. Since an interface reference may be associated with identifiers created by various binding factories, this way must be normalized to allow interoperability. To achieve this, we introduce the `Surrogate` type:

```
public interface Surrogate extends Interface {
  Type _type();
  IfRef _ifRef();
}
```

A surrogate is an interface reference, containing the information needed to manage distribution. It is characterized by two elements: A **type** and an **IfRef**.

The type information corresponds to the local type of the surrogate*.

The IfRef is the container for the identifiers of the designated interface and its type. IfRefs in Jonathan are structured as follows:

```
public class IfRef {
  Type type()...
  Key key()...
  BindingDataSet bindingDataSet()...
}
```

* In Java (or C++), the type of an object reference is not necessarily the most refined type of the designated object, but must be a supertype of that object. Likewise, the type of a surrogate is not necessarily the most refined type of the interface it represents, but must be one of its supertypes.

An IfRef contains type information about the designated interface, a **key**, and a set of **binding data**. Identifiers are not represented directly in an IfRef, but by all the possible ⟨key, binding data⟩ combinations.

The key identifies an interface in the context of its originating capsule. A key is thus a context-dependent name that need not be directly interpretable in the context of the capsule where the caller of operation `key()` resides: It is an identifier whose domain of validity is restricted to the interface's originating capsule. The key can typically be used by any binding factory in conjunction with a hash table to access interfaces in a capsule.

Binding data are added to an IfRef by binding factories, and contain binding factory specific information. Typically, for remote invocation protocols based on TCP/IP (like Java RMI or CORBA IIOP), binding data consist of a host name and a port number, in which case the binding data directly designate a specific address space; But it is possible to imagine very different kinds of binding data.

Structuring identifiers as ⟨key, binding data⟩ pairs allows a factorization across different binding factories of the same key for identifying a given interface. In the Jonathan DPE, the kernel maintains a hashtable associating keys and interfaces, that any binding factory can use. Note that this does not prevent different binding factories to use their own (equivalent of) keys (which should then be hidden in the binding data).

Both IfRefs and surrogates represent interface references, and it would have been possible (though not necessarily convenient) to have only one type for both. In fact, they are not used at the same level:

- Surrogates are used at the application level to support distribution transparency. In particular, a user expects a surrogate to be of the same type as the interface it represents: If an interface is of type `A`, the surrogate type of interest should be described as the generic type `Surrogate<A>`, and be a subtype of `A`. The surrogate interface is in particular implemented by stubs.
- IfRefs are lower level constructs. Each interface reference appearing in an invocation must be marshalled in some concrete on-the-wire representation: IfRefs constitute abstractions of such representations, allowing access to the different elements of an exportable interface reference.

2.2.2 *Creating surrogates*

Each binding factory must be able to create a surrogate –i.e. a distribution-ready interface reference– for a given interface. The simplest* form of this operation is the following:

```
LocalSurrogate export(Interface itf);
```

*More sophisticated `export` methods could manage e.g. offered quality of service descriptions, or more simply type information (it is the case of all binding factories in Jonathan 1.2). Java RMI only provides the simplest `export` form as the `exportObject` method of `java.rmi.server.UnicastRemoteObject`.

The `export` operation takes an interface as parameter and returns a surrogate for this interface. The IfRef of this surrogate contains binding data added by the invoked binding factory*.

The returned surrogate is of type `LocalSurrogate`: The specificity of local surrogates is to be equipped with a **continuation** pointing to the designated interface. This continuation signifies the relation between the IfRef held by the local surrogate and the represented interface.

```
public interface LocalSurrogate extends Surrogate {
  Interface _continuation();
  void _continuation(Interface itf);
}
```

2.2.3 *Maintaining reference chains*

One essential role of binding factories is to make sure that when an interface reference is sent as a parameter in a remote invocation, the invoked object will receive an interface reference that references the right interface. The above condition may be decomposed into two simpler invariants that binding objects must maintain:

1. A binding object must marshal an interface reference i into an appropriate IfRef when that interface reference is passed as an argument to an outgoing invocation. This means that either i is a surrogate –and its IfRef is used–, or it is not (it is simply of type `Interface`), and it must be exported to a binding factory, so that an IfRef representing it is created.
2. A binding object must unmarshal an IfRef into an appropriate interface reference on receiving an incoming invocation bearing that IfRef.
   This interface reference is either a surrogate bearing the received IfRef, or the interface reference represented by the IfRef (if it can be proved that it is local).

If these invariants are maintained, every (non local) surrogate s can be associated with a local surrogate l (possibly located in another capsule) bearing the same IfRef, and the interface represented by s is the continuation of l, or the interface designated by that continuation. Since nothing prevents surrogates from being explicitly exported to binding factories, the continuation of a local surrogate is indeed not necessarily the effective implementation of the designated interface, but may be one of its surrogates.

2.3 Distributed typing

Several type systems may have to cohabit in the same capsule, and the ORB kernel has to define a reference representation of types (and binding types) that different

*It may also contain other binding data, if the same interface has been previously exported by other binding factories.

personalities will have to translate into their own type system. This reference type system is represented in Jonathan by the `Type` type. As Jonathan is written in Java, it is natural that the `Type` objects represent Java types. That's why a `Type` object may be constructed from the string representation of a Java type, i.e. a Java scoped name (like `"jonathan.kernel.Interface"`). The main operation on types is the `is_a` operation that takes one argument, and tests whether the target type is a subtype of the argument.

2.4 Distributed access

Binding factories are responsible for the creation and management of bindings of a given type. To create bindings (i.e. instantiate binding objects), they use the identifiers of the interfaces to bind, and in particular the binding data of the appropriate type: Binding factories implement binding functions, that can resolve such identifiers into effective access chains to the remote interfaces, thus enabling interaction.

2.4.1 Implicit binding

When an IfRef is received in a capsule, and if it cannot be proved that the IfRef corresponds to an interface residing in the capsule, a surrogate bearing it must be created. This surrogate may be directly invocable, like in the classical **implicit** binding case in ORBs or distributed object systems: In this case, a communication channel is set up either at the creation of the surrogate, or at the first invocation.

This surrogate must know which binding factory to invoke to set up the communication channel, but there is no reason to impose that the binding factory used to create the current binding (used to perform the invocation) should also be able to bind the new surrogate: The received IfRef may not contain an appropriate identifier.

To deal with this problem, the kernel maintains a table of the binding factories in the capsule that can be used to implicitly bind surrogates. As each of these binding factories is associated with a binding type, the kernel simply needs to know the types of the binding data present in an IfRef to find –if possible– a binding factory able to create and implicitly bind a surrogate bearing it.

- If a suitable binding factory can be found, it instantiates a surrogate (usually a stub) that is returned to the invoking binding object.
- Otherwise, the binding object must create a surrogate that is not a stub, but simply an holder for the IfRef: This surrogate cannot be used directly in interactions, but still refers to the right interface, and may be used to **explicitly** establish a binding involving it.

This discussion shows that our framework makes a clear distinction between stubs and surrogates:

- The only role of surrogates is to reference remote interfaces, not to give access to them.
- Stubs belong to binding objects, and their principal role is to allow an access to a remote interface. Since accessing an interface implies that it is designated, stubs are surrogates, but the converse is not true.

2.5 Explicit binding

If the kernel can't find any suitable binding factory to implicitly bind the surrogate, explicit binding must be used. Binding factories may define a `bind` operation that is used to explicitly create bindings. The form of this operation may be very different from one binding factory to another. In its general form, it takes as parameters a set of interfaces to bind and quality of service constraints that need to be guaranteed, and returns a control interface on the created binding object. Note that our framework does not constraint the possible binding scenarios, and that any one can thus be implemented (including third-party binding, cf. Dang Tran *et al.* (1996)).

Explicit binding is used by the `Stream` binding factory provided with the Jonathan DPE, to create multicast RTP channels (cf. Section 3.3).

3 BUILDING A CORBA ORB ON TOP OF THE JONATHAN KERNEL

Building a CORBA 2.0 ORB on top of the Jonathan kernel means providing:

- A CORBA personality, namely the standard set of CORBA APIs (ORB, Object, etc) and an IDL to Java mapping (defining in particular the mapping between the CORBA type system and the Jonathan reference type system);
- CORBA binding factories, and in particular an IIOP binding factory.

3.1 The CORBA personality

The CORBA* personality is implemented as a set of four packages containing the standard CORBA definitions. The only extensions of the CORBA standard can be found in the definitions of `org.omg.CORBA.Object` and `org.omg.CORBA.ORB`.

- `org.omg.CORBA.Object` extends the `jonathan.kernel.Surrogate` interface. It is natural in Jonathan, since the CORBA ORB class must be able to implement the `object_to_string` method, that turns an object into a stringified IOR. IORs are in fact a mere encoding of IfRefs, and consequently the existence of the `object_to_string` method implies that it must be possible to associate an

*Jonathan only implements a subset of CORBA 2.0. It is not complete since CORBA features like the `Any` type or the Interface Repository are not implemented. However, the implemented subset is rich enough to implement non-trivial applications.

IfRef to any `org.omg.CORBA.Object`, which means that CORBA objects are surrogates.

- As stated above, the role of a personality is also to provide a bridge between the personality type system and the reference type system to binding factories. This is expressed in Jonathan by the addition to the `org.omg.CORBA.ORB` class of two methods to turn CORBA types, described by their interface repository representation, to the corresponding Java type string representations, and conversely.

The Jonathan implementation provides a **stub factory**. In the ReTINA architecture, a stub factory is simply an object whose role is to instantiate stubs and skeletons. As it is a CORBA stub factory, it comes with an IDL compiler that generates code for stubs. An interesting property of the current Jonathan stub factory is that it is independent of the underlying protocols, and of the binding factories that may use it.

Like in standard CORBA implementations, the generated stubs are CORBA Objects, and thus surrogates. The generated skeletons are also CORBA objects, and implement the `LocalSurrogate` interface. This way, the local surrogate abstraction may be introduced at no cost in the system: When an invocation is received from a remote capsule, there is no unnecessary indirection due to the existence of a local surrogate. The resulting interface types hierarchy is depicted on Figure 2.

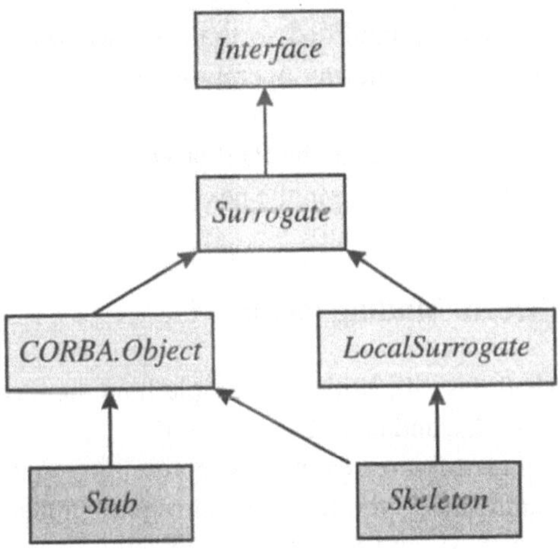

Figure 2 Interface types hierarchy.

3.2 Binding factories

CORBA Object Adapters can be understood as server-side interfaces to binding factories. In particular, the `create` operation on the `BOA` is a specific form of `export`.

In its present version, Jonathan doesn't provide a standard `BOA` interface, but three binding factories. As we have seen, binding factories are responsible for the creation and management of bindings, and rest on specific libraries (protocols, stub factories, personalities) to achieve this.

Jonathan provides five independent protocol packages built following the communication framework sketched in the introduction: The `protocols.tcpip` package represents the TCP/IP protocol (it is built on top of the `java.net` package), the `protocols.multicastip` package lets the user open multicast channels, the `protocols.rtp` package is a limited implementation of the Real Time Protocol, `protocols.giop` provides an implementation of CORBA's GIOP protocol, and `protocols.miop` provides an implementation of a simpler invocation protocol.

In Jonathan 1.2, all three binding factories use the same personality and stub factory, but use different protocols.

- The IIOP binding factory implements the IIOP protocol, by stacking the GIOP protocol on top of TCP/IP. It allows implicit binding.
  The binding data used by the IIOP binding factory contain a host name, a port number, and a key (represented as an array of bytes encoding the IfRef key): They are represented by instances of the `org.omg.IIOP.ProfileBody` class.
- The JIOP binding factory stacks the MIOP protocol on top of TCP/IP. It is more experimental, and could be modified so that, for instance, twoways operations use TCP connections while oneway operations on the same interface use UDP connections.
- The Stream binding factory stacks the RTP protocol on top of Multicast IP. It is further explained with an example in the next section.

3.3 A CORBA Stream binding factory

In this section, we shall describe with an example how the Stream binding factory provided in Jonathan works, and how it can be used.

The Stream binding factory creates objects representing multicast RTP channels. These objects are manifested to the users by surrogates containing a specific multicast address (cf. Figure 3), and may be dynamically extended to bind different interfaces.

The type of the channel is defined by the user thanks to an IDL declaration. For instance, the following declaration can be used:

```
// IDL
typedef sequence<octet> frame;
interface DataChannel {
  oneway void send(in frame data);
}
```

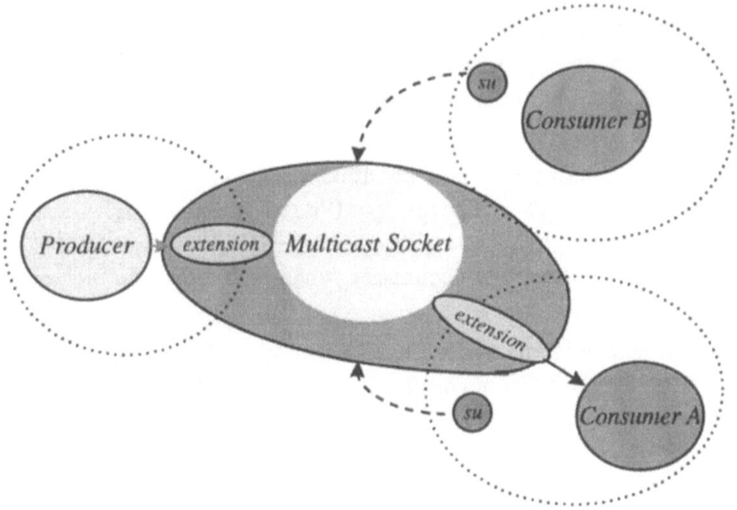

Figure 3 A stream channel.

This declaration defines a `DataChannel` type. Only oneway operations are considered, and trying to use twoways operations results in a runtime exception.

The binding factory can create multicast channels of a given type, simply by providing the type, a class D IP address, and a standard UDP port number: The following invocation on `StreamBF` (the Stream binding factory), returns a surrogate of the multicast channel specified in the invocation:

```
// Java
DataChannel channel = (DataChannel)
  StreamBF.getInvocable("DataChannel","224.10.0.0",9000);
```

The IP address and the port number are stored as binding data in the returned surrogate's IfRef. This surrogate is implicitly bound: A producer can immediately emit data in the channel by invoking a method on the returned object:

```
channel.send(new byte[1024]);
```

At the first invocation on the surrogate, the stream channel is extended. The extension is represented on Figure 3 by an object in the capsule of the producer. The role of this object is to compose RTP packets with the data sent, and write them to the multicast channel.

Since the object representing the stream channel is a surrogate, it can be passed as argument in any CORBA invocation (even if another binding factory is used). For instance, it can be registered in a trader under the name `"data_channel"`.

A consumer must be an implementation of the `DataChannel` interface. To receive data, a consumer must first retrieve a reference on a channel (e.g. by invoking the trader where the channel is registered), and then explicitly get bound to the channel. This is achieved by the `bindConsumer` method of `StreamBF`:

```
DataChannel consumer = new DataConsumer();
DataChannel channel = Trader.get("data_channel");
StreamBindingCtl ctl =
  StreamBF.bindConsumer(consumer,channel);
```

The `get` invocation on the trader returns a surrogate of the multicast channel. At this point, the situation is that of consumer B in Figure 3: There is a surrogate of the stream channel in the capsule. The `bindConsumer` invocation extends the stream channel with an object (see the situation of consumer A) that reads RTP packets from the multicast socket, and recomposes the original message before forwarding it to the consumer.

`ctl` is a control interface of the binding between the channel and the consumer. It comprises a `release()` method that can be used to stop forwarding data from the channel to the consumer: The `release` method destroys the extension created by `bindConsumer`.

4 CONCLUSION

We have described in this paper a highly flexible and modular DPE architecture organized around a very small binding-independent core. This architecture essentially introduces a distributed reference abstraction properly interfaced with that of binding. This separation enables the encapsulation of reference management and binding management in different objects: The ORB kernel for references, and various binding factories for bindings. It is thus possible to introduce in a modular fashion new bindings within an ORB based on this framework, while retaining interoperability. In the case of Java, the ORB kernel could in fact be completely integrated in the virtual machine: Surrogates are simply an extension of the notion of object reference; They could be implemented in a reflective Java virtual machine by modifying the implementation of object references, thus enabling a seamless integration of distribution in the language.

The current Java implementation of this DPE architecture –Jonathan*– has confirmed that it is stable and generic enough to accommodate arbitrary types of binding and communications mechanisms, while remaining efficient:

- We have been able to build a CORBA personality on top of the DPE kernel,

*Jonathan is available freely for non-commercial use. Interested readers can contact the authors to obtain a copy of the software (Java sources are included).

featuring a Stream binding factory that shows that, for instance, non client-server bindings can be developed easily. We could in the same way develop an RMI-like personality.

- Jonathan has not been developed with performance in mind. However, the few performance tests we made show that this implementation compares well with commercial CORBA implementations in Java like Visibroker or OrbixWeb: It is never more than 40% slower than these implementations, and may be just as fast for arrays of basic types for instance (using IIOP). It should be noted that according to our tests, ORBs in Java run with a JIT compiler are still between 2 and 3 times slower than C++ ORBs. Comparison with RMI is harder to analyze: RMI is slightly faster on very simple cases, but may become much slower (up to 10 times) if serialization is used. Moreover, Jonathan is able to detect if the client and server are in the same capsule, and invocations are direct calls in this case. RMI does not detect this case, and calls systematically go through all the marshalling and demarshalling process. This issue may become very important if objects are mobile.

  Jonathan also scales very well, since we have been able to test a capsule running 100,000 server objects, the effect of the number of servers on an invocation duration being only related to swap overhead.

  The last point on performance is that the modular organization of Jonathan makes it very easy to add specific protocols for realtime, or change the stub factory for a more specialized one. Our experience with Jonathan shows that the modular and flexible architecture we propose can be implemented at no cost in terms of performance.

This work has been inspired in part by the Spring distributed system (Hamilton *et al.* 1993) and the SOR system (Shapiro 1994). Spring provides the notion of subcontract that allows application programmers to define new client-server communication mechanisms. SOR provides a flexible binding protocol which can be used to establish arbitrary client-server bindings. The framework proposed here generalizes these approaches to arbitrary types of interactions and in particular to multiparty multimedia communication schemas. It also generalizes more language-dependent ORB designs such as Network Objects (Birrell *et al.* 1995) and Java-RMI (Sun Microsystems 1996). Our architecture can also be seen as a weak form of the SSP chains framework (Plainfosse 1994): In particular, the two reference chains invariants described in Section 2.2.3 are the first two invariants required for the proper integration of the garbage collection algorithm of (Plainfosse 1994). SSP chains could be developed as a specific binding factory maintaining the remaining necessary invariants, thus enabling acyclic garbage collection.

Future work on Jonathan will focus on the areas of resource management and admission control in order to provide full support for end-to-end QoS. Reflexivity will be used as the major architectural principle to achieve this goal, in particular to implement the ReTINA resource control framework in a highly flexible and modular way.

REFERENCES

Birrell, A., Nelson, G., Owicki, S. and Wobber, E.: 1995, Network objects, *SRC Research Report 115*, Digital Systems Research Center.

Dang Tran, F., Dumant, B., Horn, F. and Stefani, J.-B.: 1997, Towards an extensible and modular ORB framework, *Workshop on CORBA use and evaluation, ECOOP'97*, Jyväskylä, Finland. submitted for publication.

Dang Tran, F., Perebaskine, V., Stefani, J.-B., Crawford, B., Kramer, A. and Otway, D.: 1996, Binding and streams: the ReTINA approach, *Proceedings TINA'96 International Conference*, Heidelberg, Germany.

Hamilton, G., Powell, M. and Mitchell, J.: 1993, Subcontract: a flexible base for distributed programming, *Proceedings of the 14th Symposium on Operating Systems Principles*, Asheville NC.

ODP: 1995, ODP Reference Model: Overview, Foundations, Architecture and Architectural Semantics, ITU-T | ISO/IEC Recommendations X.901–X.904 | International Standard 10746-1–10746-4.

OMG: 1995, The Common Object request Broker: Architecture and Specification, CORBA V2.0, Object Management Group.

Peterson, L. L., Hutchinson, N., O'Malley, S. and Abbott, M.: 1989, RPC in the *x*-kernel: Evaluating new design techniques, *Proc. of the 12th ACM Symp. on Operating Systems Principles*, Litchfield Park, AZ, USA, pp. 91–101.

Plainfosse, D.: 1994, *Distributed garbage collection and referencing management in the Soul object support system*, PhD thesis, University of Paris VI, Paris, France.

Shapiro, M.: 1994, A binding protocol for distributed shared objects, *14th International Conference on Distributed Computer Systems (ICDCS)*, Poznan, Poland.

Sun Microsystems: 1996, Java Remote Method Invocation Specification, *Technical report*, Sun Microsystems, Moutain View, CA, USA.

5 BIOGRAPHY

All authors are research engineers in the Distributed Systems Architecture department at France-Télécom-CNET, lead by **Jean-Bernard Stefani**, and work on different aspects of telecommunications distributed systems: Systems architecture, real-time operating systems, multimedia applications, formal methods and calculi... During the past years, they have participated to several international projects in this area, and in particular to the ACTS project ReTINA since september 1995.

An Architecture for Next Generation Middleware

G.S. Blair, G. Coulson, P. Robin, M. Papathomas
Distributed Multimedia Research Group
Computing Department, Lancaster University, Bailrigg, Lancaster LA1 4YR, UK
Tel: +44 1524 65201, Fax: +44 1524 593608
E-mail: {gordon, geoff, pr, michael}@comp.lancs.ac.uk

Abstract

This paper proposes an approach to the design of configurable and open middleware platforms based on the concept of reflection. More specifically, the paper introduces a language-independent reflective architecture featuring a per-object meta-space, the use of meta-models to structure meta-space, and a consistent use of object graphs for composite components. This is complemented by a component framework supporting the construction of meta-spaces. The paper also reports on experiences of implementing the architecture (with emphasis on experiments with open bindings).

Keywords

Middleware, (re-)configuration, reflection, open implementation, open bindings.

1 INTRODUCTION

Middleware has emerged as an important architectural component in supporting distributed applications. The role of middleware is to present a unified programming model to application writers and to mask out problems of heterogeneity and distribution. The importance of the topic is reflected in the increasing visibility of standardisation activities such as the ISO/ITU-T Reference Model for Open Distributed Processing (RM-ODP), OMG's CORBA, the Java RMI, Microsoft's DCOM and the Open Group's DCE.

Although middleware is now well established, it is crucial that the standards remain responsive to new challenges such as groupware, multimedia, real-time, and increasingly mobility. In our opinion, such challenges require new approaches to the engineering of middleware platforms in terms of being able to *configure* the underlying support offered by the middleware platform. For example, multimedia applications require very specific support in terms of specialised communications protocols and resource management. Similarly, real-time applications may require lightweight, small footprint Object Request Brokers (ORBs). Although essential, configurability is not enough. It is also important to adopt an *open engineering* approach allowing *inspection* and *adaptation* of underlying components at run-time. For example, mobile systems need to detect and adapt to drastic changes in connectivity; this may involve changes at a number of different levels in the system (e.g. introducing header compression, altering the protocol stack, inserting filtering components, etc).

Support for configurability and open engineering is not available in the current generation of middleware platforms, which typically adopt a *black box* philosophy to their design (thereby hiding implementation details from the applications). Although there are good reasons for this approach, there are already signs that the black box philosophy is becoming untenable. For example, the OMG have recently added internal interfaces to CORBA to support services such as transactions and security. The recently defined Portable Object Adapter is another attempt to introduce more openness in their design. Nevertheless, their overall approach can be criticised for being rather ad hoc. Similarly, a number of ORB vendors have felt obliged to expose selected aspects of the underlying system (e.g. filters in Orbix or interceptors in COOL). These are however non-standard and hence compromise the portability of CORBA applications and services. The RM-ODP architecture does address this issue by distinguishing between computational and engineering concerns. However, we believe this approach is still not sufficient to meet the demands of the next generation of distributed applications (see section 3.3 below).

This paper proposes an approach to the design of configurable and open middleware platforms based on the concept of *reflection*. More specifically, the paper presents a reflective architecture for next generation middleware platforms, supplemented by an open and extensible component framework. We view reflection as a principled (as opposed to ad hoc) means of achieving our desired characteristics.

2. BACKGROUND ON REFLECTION

The concept of reflection was first introduced by Smith (1982). In this work, he introduced the reflection hypothesis which states:

> "In as much as a computational process can be constructed to reason about an external world in virtue of comprising an ingredient process (interpreter) formally manipulating representations of that world, so too a computational process could be made to reason about itself in virtue of comprising an ingredient process (interpreter) formally manipulating representations of its own operations and structures".

The importance of this statement is that a program can access, reason about and alter its own interpretation. Access to the interpreter is provided through a *meta-object protocol (MOP)* which defines the services available at the *meta-level.* Examples of operations available at the meta-level include altering the semantics of message passing and inserting before or after actions around method invocations. Access to the meta-level is provided through a process of *reification.* Reification effectively makes some aspect of the internal representation explicit and hence accessible from the program. The opposite process is then *absorption* where some aspect of meta-system is altered or overridden.

Smith's insight has catalysed a large body of research in the application of reflection. Initially, this work was restricted to the field of programming language design (Kiczaleset al, 1991) (Watanabe and Yonezawa, 1988) (Agha, 1991). More recently, the work has diversified with reflection being applied in operating systems (Yokote, 1992) and, more recently, distributed systems (see section 5).

The primary motivation of a reflective language or system is to provide a principled (as opposed to ad hoc) means of achieving open engineering. For example, reflection can be used to *inspect* the internal behaviour of a language or system. By exposing the underlying implementation, it becomes straightforward to insert additional behaviour to monitor the implementation, e.g. performance monitors, quality of service monitors, or accounting systems. Reflection can also be used to *adapt* the internal behaviour of a language or system. Examples include replacing the implementation of message passing to operate more optimally over a wireless link, introducing an additional level of distribution transparency in a running computation (such as migration transparency), or inserting a filter object to reduce the bandwidth requirements of a communications stream.

Although reflection is a promising technique, there are a number of potential drawbacks of this approach, in particular issues of *performance* and *integrity* must be carefully addressed (we return to these issues in section 3.3).

3. AN ARCHITECTURE FOR REFLECTIVE MIDDLEWARE

3.1. General principles

In common with most of the research on reflective languages and systems, we adopt an *object-oriented model of computation*. As pointed out by Kiczales et al (Kiczales et al, 1991), there is an important synergy between reflection and object-oriented computing:

> "Reflective techniques make it possible to open up a language's implementation without revealing unnecessary implementation details or compromising portability; and object-oriented techniques allow the resulting model of the language's implementation and behaviour to be locally and incrementally adjusted".

The choice of object-orientation is also important given the predominance of such models in open distributed processing (Blair and Stefani, 1997a). Crucially, we propose the use of the RM-ODP Computational Model, using CORBA IDL to describe computational interfaces. The main features of this object model are: i) objects can have multiple interfaces, ii) operational, stream and signal interfaces are supported, and iii) explicit bindings can be created between compatible interfaces (the result being the creation of a binding object). The object model also has a sophisticated model of quality of service including QoS annotation on interfaces. Further details of this object model can be found in (Blair and Stefani, 1997a). In contrast, with RM-ODP, however, we adopt a consistent object model throughout the design (see section 3.3).

The second principle behind our design is to have *per object* (or *per interface*) meta-spaces. This is necessary in a heterogeneous environment, where objects will have varying capacities for reflection. Such a solution also provides a fine level of control over the support provided by the middleware platform; a corollary of this is that problems of maintaining integrity are minimised due to the limited scope of change (see discussion in section 3.3). We do recognise however that there are situations where it is useful to be able to access the meta-spaces of sets of objects in one single action; to support this, we also allow the use of (meta-object) groups. This aspect of the design is discussed in more depth in section 3.2.2.

As our third principle, we adopt a *procedural approach* to reflection, i.e. the meta-level (selectively) exposes the actual program that implements the system (Maes, 1987). This approach has a number of inherent advantages over a more declarative approach. For example, a procedural approach is more primitive in the sense that it is possible to support declarative interfaces on top of procedural reflection but not vice versa. In addition, the required property of *causal connection* is automatically maintained (as the implementation itself is directly manipulated) (Maes, 1987). Procedural reflection also opens the possibility of an infinite tower of reflection (i.e. the base level has a meta-level, the meta-level is implemented using objects and hence has a meta-meta-level, and so on). This is important in our design and is revisited in section 3.2.1 below.

The final principle is to structure meta-space as a number of closely related but distinct *meta-space models*. This approach was first advocated by the designers of AL-1/D, a reflective programming language for distributed applications (Okamura et al, 1992). The benefit of this approach is to simplify the interface offered by meta-space by maintaining a separation of concerns between different system aspects. The three aspects currently employed are: *composition*, *encapsulation* and *environment*. This is however not a closed list and the range of models may be expanded later. Further details of each of the models can be found below.

3.2. Design

3.2.1. The structure of meta-space

The overall design of meta-space is illustrated in figure 1. The meta-space is structured as three distinct meta-space models, covering encapsulation, composition and environment. To support this, reflective objects must support a set of operations to reify each of the meta-space models. These operations are `encapsulation()`, `composition()` and `environment()` respectively. Crucially, these operations provide language *independent* access to the meta-space, although the level of access to each model may be language *dependent* (we return to this issue below when we look at the details of each individual model).

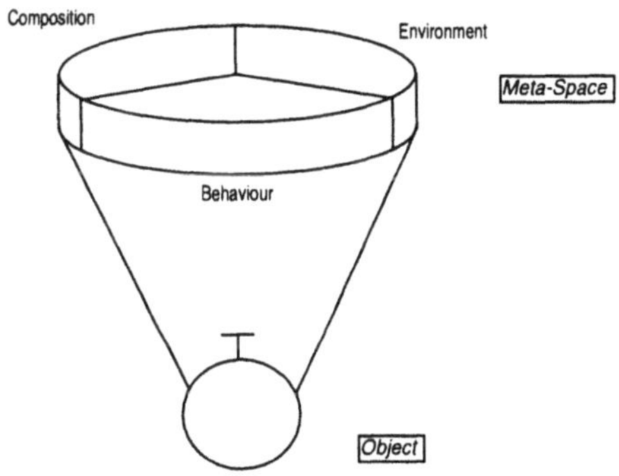

Figure 1 Overall structure of meta-space.

It is important to realise that, in our approach, objects can have multiple interfaces. Given this, meta-spaces are actually associated with *each interface* (as opposed to with each object). More precisely, each interface has an associated encapsulation and environment meta-model. The compositional model is however treated differently. In this case, the meta-model is associated with the object itself and is thus *common* to all interfaces. The compositional meta-model is accessed by calling the `composition()` operation on any of the interfaces associated with the object. This distinction should become clearer when the precise details of the different meta-models are considered below.

The *compositional meta-model* provides access to the *object* in terms of its constituent objects. The composition of an object is represented as an *object graph*, in which the constituent objects are connected together by *local bindings*. Local bindings are crucial in our design; they provide a language-independent means of implementing the interaction point between interfaces. Importantly, some objects in this graph can be (distributed) binding objects, allowing distributed configurations to be created (we return to this aspect in section 4.1 below). In practice, the `composition()` operation returns a graph object with operations to inspect and adapt the composite object, i.e. to view the structure of the graph, to access individual objects in the graph, and to adapt the graph structure and content. For objects that are not composite, the `composition()` operation returns null.

The *encapsulation meta-model* provides access to the representation of a particular *interface* in terms of its set of methods and associated attributes, together with key properties of the interface including its inheritance structure. The level of access provided by the encapsulation model is clearly language dependent. For example, with compiled languages such as C access may be limited to inspection of the associated IDL interface. With more open (interpreted) languages, such as Java or Python (see section 4.2), more complete access is possible, such as being able to add or delete methods and attributes. This level of heterogeneity is supported by having a type hierarchy of meta-interfaces ranging from minimal access to full reflective access to interfaces. Note however that it is important that this type hierarchy is open and extensible to accommodate unanticipated levels of access.

Finally, the *environment meta-model* represents the execution environment for each *interface* as traditionally provided by the middleware platform. In a distributed environment, this corresponds to functions such as message arrival, enqueing, selection, dispatching, unmarshalling, thread creation and scheduling (plus the equivalent on the sending side) (Watanabe and Yonezawa, 1988) (McAffer, 1996). Again, different levels of access are supported. For example, a simple meta-model may only deal with the arrival and dispatching of messages at the particular interface. More complex meta-models will allow the insertion of additional levels of transparency or control over thread creation and scheduling. As with the encapsulation meta-model, this level of heterogeneity is accommodated within an open and extensible type hierarchy. Crucially, the environment meta-model is represented as a composite object. Hence, this aspect of the meta-space is inspected and adapted at the meta-meta-level using the graph manipulation objects, i.e. by calling operations on `composition(environment(object))`. Such operations, can be used, for example, to insert a QoS monitor at the required point in the graph.

Note that there is a high level of recursion in the above definition. In particular, the meta-level is realised using object-oriented techniques. Hence, objects/interfaces at the meta-level are also open to reflection and have an associated meta-meta-space. As above, this meta-meta-space is represented by three (meta-meta-) models. Similarly, objects/interfaces at the meta-meta-level have an associated meta-meta-meta-space. This process continues providing an *infinite tower of reflection*. This is realised in our design by allowing such an infinite structure to exist in theory but only to instantiate a given level on demand, i.e. when it is reified. This provides a finite representation of an infinite structure (a similar approach is taken in ABCL/R (Watanabe and Yonezawa, 1988)). Access to different meta-levels is important in our design although most access will be restricted to the meta- and meta-meta-levels.

An initial implementation of the three meta-models is described in (Costa et al, 1998).

3.2.2. Reflective groups

As stated earlier, there are situations where it is useful to be able to access the meta-spaces of sets of interfaces in one action. Indeed, a number of reflective languages provide such a facility as core functionality (e.g. ABCL/R2 (Matsuoka et al, 1991)). We propose to accommodate this requirement through the general mechanism of group bindings (or simply groups). Groups provide a uniform mechanism for invoking a set of interfaces whether they are at the base-level, meta-level, meta-meta-level, etc. For example, groups can be used, at the base level, to multicast new share price information to a set of interested parties or, at the meta-level, to insert a new QoS monitoring method in a group of objects.

Importantly, groups are themselves reflective, in that it is possible to access each of the meta-models associated with the group. More specifically, groups are composite objects, where the compositional meta-model provides access to the individual interfaces comprising the group. Through access to the object graph, it is possible to tailor and adapt the semantics of group message distribution, e.g. by introducing a new ordering protocol. It is also possible to manipulate management aspects of the group, e.g. membership policies or collation policies.

3.2.3. Component framework

To complement our open architecture, we provide an open and extensible library of *components* which can be configured to build middleware platforms (i.e. meta-spaces) for a range of applications. The component framework is essential to populate the abstract architecture described above. Note that components can be used at all levels of the reflective architecture.

The component framework consists of both primitive components and composite components, each supported by associated *factory* objects (extending the component framework simply involves introducing a new factory object). Primitive components include:

- a range of low-level (indivisible) communications protocols, such as IP and IP-multicast, and, where appropriate, micro-protocol components to support the construction of protocol stacks, e.g. header compression, flow control, rate control, etc;
- a range of end-system components, such as filters, buffers, dispatchers, demultiplexers, threads, etc;
- a range of management components such as scheduling policies, dispatching policies, buffer allocation policies, and QoS management components;

- one or more implementations of the local binding operation, e.g. same address space or cross address space, same language or cross language, etc.

Composite components then represent off-the-shelf configurations of components (which may in turn include other composite components). The associated factories therefore embody a policy with respect to the selection and configuration of components. Examples of composite components include:

- a range of transport bindings supporting stream and operational interaction;
- end-to-end stream bindings featuring different filtering components (e.g. MPEG compression and decompression);
- pre-configured environment meta-spaces offering access to buffering, dispatching and scheduling components.

Crucially, *groups* are simply (composite) components in the component framework. A range of group bindings, with different group semantics, can be provided. This implies that groups can be exploited without the need for explicit architectural extension.

An initial set of primitive and compound components is currently being created in the GOPI project (Coulson, 1998).

3.3. Discussion

In our opinion, the reflective architecture described above provides a strong basis for the design of future middleware platforms and overcomes the inherent limitations of technologies such as CORBA (as discussed in section 1). In particular, the architecture offers principled and comprehensive access to the engineering of a middleware platform. This compares favourably with CORBA which, as stated above, generally follows a black box philosophy with minimal, ad hoc access to internal details.

More generally, we are proposing a concept of middleware as a customisable set of components which can be tailored to the needs of an application. Furthermore, the configuration can be adapted at run-time, should the initial environmental assumptions change. This approach is complemented by an open and extensible component framework, containing a range of re-usable services such as dispatching policies, filters and communication protocol or micro-protocols. The fine-grained nature of the component framework further enhances the flexibility of the approach.

We also believe that the reflective approach generalises the viewpoints approach to structuring advocated by RM-ODP. As stated above, RM-ODP distinguishes between the Computational Viewpoint (focusing on application-level objects and their interaction) and the Engineering Viewpoint (which considers their implementation in a distributed environment). Crucially, each viewpoint also has its own set of object modelling concepts (for example, the Computational Viewpoint features objects, interfaces and bindings, whereas the Engineering Viewpoint has basic engineering objects, capsules and protocol objects).

Consequently, as the models are different, the mapping between the two viewpoints is not always clear. In addition, this approach enforces a two-level structure, i.e. it is not possible to analyse engineering objects in terms of their internal structure or behaviour. Our approach overcomes these limitations by offering a consistent object model throughout, supporting arbitrary levels of openness.

Another benefit of our approach is that it minimises problems of maintaining integrity. This is due to our approach to scoping whereby every object/interface has its own meta-space. Thus changes to a meta-space can only affect a single object. Furthermore, the meta-space is highly structured, again minimising the scope of changes. An additional level of safety is provided by the strongly typed object model.

In contrast, the issue of performance remains a matter for further research. Nevertheless, our initial experiences with open bindings (see section 4.1 below) has convinced us that there is not necessarily an unfavourable trade-off between flexibility and performance.

4. EXPERIMENTS IN REFLECTIVE MIDDLEWARE

4.1. Open bindings

4.1.1. Introducing open bindings

As an initial experiment, we focused our attention on the open engineering of binding objects (*open bindings*). This work was carried out as part of the Adapt Project, a collaboration between Lancaster University and BT Labs, with the aim of exploiting open bindings to support mobile multimedia applications. In terms of our architecture, an open binding is an object which provides access to its compositional meta-model. As explained above, this meta-model is represented by a graph of objects, connected together by *local bindings*. For open bindings, objects in the graph may themselves be binding objects. The use of binding objects in graphs allows open bindings to span multiple address spaces or multiple nodes, i.e. bindings are distributed objects.

Note that binding objects in the graph can themselves be open bindings and hence also be composed in terms of object graphs. The nesting bottoms out by offering a set of *primitive bindings* whose implementation is closed. For example, a particular platform might offer RTP or IP services as primitive bindings (depending on the level of openness in the platform). This nested structure provides access to lower levels of the implementation (if required). At a finer granularity, each object in the graph can offer a meta-interface to control its individual behaviour.

The concept of (nested) open binding is illustrated in figure 2 below.

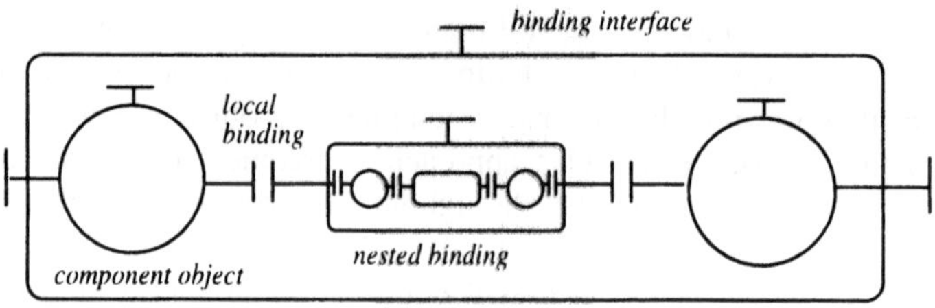

Figure 2 A nested open binding.

4.1.2. Implementation of open bindings

We have implemented an experimental middleware platform featuring the concept of explicit open bindings. This platform is based on a CORBA implementation from Chorus Systems (now Sun Microsystems), called COOL-ORB (Habertet al, 1990). This runs over a variety of computers and operating systems; our experimental testbed consists of laptop PCs running Window-NT. These are interconnected by a variety of networks, including Switched Ethernet, WaveLAN and GSM.

In order to support open bindings, the COOL platform has been extended as shown in figure 3.

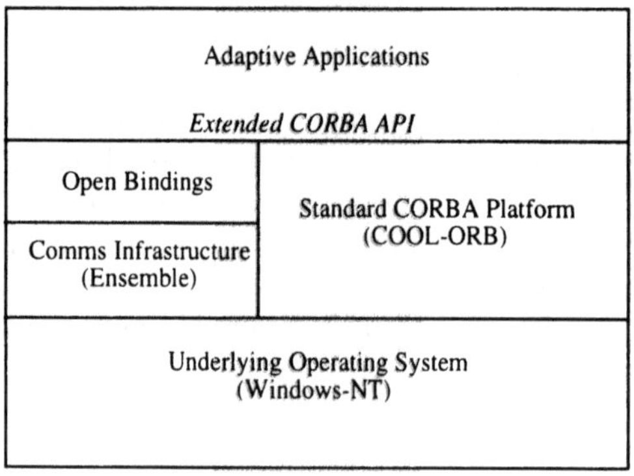

Figure 3 The extended CORBA platform.

Currently CHORUS/COOL-ORB support two communications infrastructures: TCP/IP and CHORUS IPC. In order to support higher degree of configurability, we have extended COOL with a third communications infrastructure based on Ensemble (Hayden, 1997) (the successor to Horus (van Renesse et al, 1996)). Ensemble enables the programmer to select a particular protocol profile at *bind time* by providing a list of the component modules. In addition, the software supports *run-time* adaptation, in terms of both modification of modules and dynamic reconfiguration. For example, the parameters for flow control can be modified at run-time. Similarly, Ensemble allows the programmer to *switch* to an alternative protocol stack at any point during an interaction. We are currently extending this capability to allow new modules to be introduced dynamically (via the compositional meta-model); such modules could either be an additional layer in the protocol stack or could implement a management function.

For operational bindings, the standard CORBA `bind()` call has been extended i) to enable the specification of the initial protocol graph, and ii) to return an interface providing access to the meta-space (i.e. the object graph representing the configuration of Ensemble modules). Crucially, Ensemble-based operational bindings provide a direct realisation of our concept of reflective groups (as discussed in section 3.2.2). In particular, they support the multicasting of messages to groups of objects (whether at the base-level, the meta-level, etc) and also allow the user to inspect or adapt the underlying protocol stack at run-time (thus altering the semantics of group message passing).

For stream bindings, we provide a set of binding factories offering pre-configured Ensemble stacks for continuous media interaction. Note that it is relatively straightforward to extend the range of bindings by constructing new binding factories from existing components. Prominent among the components are a range of filter objects for common media formats.

Further details of the Adapt Project can be found in the literature (Blair et al, 1997b) (Fitzpatrick et al, 1998).

4.2. Other aspects

In Adapt, the scope of the work is limited to open bindings and to the compositional meta-model. Nevertheless, the project has provided some invaluable experience in constructing open middleware platforms and has also demonstrated the potential of reflection in achieving much greater degrees of openness and adaptivity in such systems. We are now expanding the scope of our work to consider all aspects of middleware design and to develop a complete implementation of our reflective architecture. This work is being carried out using some reflective facilities developed in Python (Watters et al, 1996).

In a related development, we are investigating the potential of formal languages for the expression of scripts for management objects. More specifically, we are considering the role of timed automata in providing a direct representation of scripts for key QoS management functions such as QoS monitoring and adaptation. This work is part of the V-QoS project (a collaboration between Lancaster University and the University of Kent at Canterbury). Finally, we are also investigating the potential of object graphs to support the construction of open and extensible operating systems (Clarke and Coulson, 1998).

The longer term objective of this research is to develop a complete implementation of a reflective middleware platform, based on CORBA. The expected outcome from this research is the definition of a meta-object protocol for CORBA (i.e. a CORBA MOP).

5. RELATED WORK

There is growing interest in the use of reflection in distributed systems. Pioneering work in this area was carried out by McAffer (McAffer, 1996). With respect to middleware, researchers at Illinois have carried out initial experiments on reflection in Object Request Brokers (ORBs) (Singhai et al, 1997). The level of reflection however is coarse-grained and restricted to invocation, marshalling and dispatching. In addition, the work does not consider key areas such as support for groups or, more generally, bindings. Researchers at APM have developed an experimental middleware platform called FlexiNet (Hayton, 1997). This platform allows the programmer to tailor the underlying communications infrastructure by inserting/ removing layers. Their solution is, however, language-specific, i.e. applications must be written in Java. Manola has carried out work in the design of a "RISC" object model for distributed computing (Manola, 1993), i.e. a minimal object model which can be specialised through reflection. Researchers at the Ecole des Mines de Nante are also investigating the use of reflection in proxy mechanisms for ORBs (Ledoux, 1997).

Our design has been influenced by a number of specific reflective languages. As stated above, the concept of multi-models was derived from AL/1-D. The underlying models of AL/1-D are however quite different; the language supports six models, namely operation, resource, statistics, migration, distributed environment and system (Okamura et al, 1992). Our ongoing research on the environment and encapsulation meta-models is also heavily influenced by the designs of ABCL/R (Watanabe and Yonezawa, 1988) and CodA (McAffer, 1996). Both these systems feature decompositions of meta-space in terms of the acceptance of messages, placing the message in a queue, their selection, and the subsequent dispatching. Finally, the design of ABCL/R2 includes the concept of groups (Matsuoka et al, 1991). However, groups in ABCL/R2 are more prescriptive in that they enforce a particular construction and interpretation on an object. The groups themselves are also primitive, and are not susceptible to reflective access.

Our use of object graphs is inspired by researchers at JAIST in Japan (Hokimoto and Nakajima, 1996). In their system, adaptation is handled through the use of control scripts written in TCL. Although similar to our proposals, the JAIST work does not provide access to the internal details of communication objects. Furthermore, the work is not integrated into a middleware platform. Similar approaches are advocated by the designers of the VuSystem (Lindblad and Tennenhouse, 1996) and Mash (McCanne et al, 1997). The same criticisms however also apply to these designs. Microsoft's ActiveX software also uses object graphs. This software, however, does not address distribution of object graphs. In addition, the graph is not re-configurable during the presentation of a media stream.

6. CONCLUDING REMARKS

This paper has presented our design for a next generation middleware platform. This design exploits the concept of reflection to provide the desired level of configurability and openness. We believe that this approach addresses the needs of emerging application areas such as multimedia, real-time systems and mobile computing. Equally importantly, by adopting a principled approach, we believe that the design is sufficiently extensible to meet future demands.

The most important features of our design are i) the ability to associate a meta-space with every object/interface, ii) the sub-division of meta-spaces into three orthogonal models, and iii) the consistent use of object graphs to represent composite components in the architecture. Crucially, the architecture also provides a language-independent model of reflection (as required by the field of open distributed processing). The architecture is complemented by a component framework featuring an open and extensible set of primitive and composite components. Such components support the construction of meta-spaces.

We already have considerable experience from the Adapt Project in constructing configurable and open middleware platforms based on our architecture (focusing on open bindings). We are now extending this work to look at other aspects of our design (including groups and management). As stated above, the longer term aim of this research is to define a meta-object protocol for future middleware platforms such as CORBA.

7. ACKNOWLEDGEMENTS

The research described in this paper is partly funded by the CNET, France Telecom (CNET Grant 96-1B-239) and by the EPSRC together with BT Labs (Research Grant GR/K72575). We would like to thank our collaborators for their support. Particular thanks are due to Jean-Bernard Stefani and his group at CNET, and also Andrew Grace, Alan Smith and Steve Rudkin at BT Labs. Finally, we would like to acknowledge the contributions a number of researchers at Lancaster to the ideas described in this paper, namely Anders Andersen (also of the University of Tromsø, Norway), Lynne Blair, Mike Clarke, Fabio Costa, Hector Duran, Nikos Parlavantzas and Katia Saikoski.

8. REFERENCES

Agha, G., (1991) The Structure and Semantics of Actor Languages. *Lecture Notes in Computer Science*, **489**, 1-59, Springer-Verlag.

Blair, G.S. and Stefani, J.B. (1997a) Open Distributed Processing and Multimedia. Addison-Wesley.

Blair, G.S., Coulson, G., Davies, N., Robin, P. and Fitzpatrick, T. (1997b) Adaptive Middleware for Mobile Multimedia Applications. *Proc. 7th International Conference on Network and Operating System Support for Digital Audio and Video (Nossdav'97)*, St Louis, Missouri, USA., 259-273.

Clarke, M. and Coulson, G. (1998) An Architecture for Dynamically Extensible Operating Systems. *Proceedings of the 4th International Conference on Configurable Distributed Systems*, Annapolis, Maryland, USA.

Costa, F.M., Blair, G.S. and Coulson, G. (1998) Experiments with Reflective Middleware, Internal Report MPG-98-11, Lancaster University Computing Dept., Lancaster LA1 4YR, England. Submitted to Workshop on Reflective Object-Oriented Programming and Systems (in ECOOP'98), Brussels, Belgium, 20-24 July, 1998.

Coulson, G. (1998) A Distributed Object Platform Infrastructure for Multimedia Applications", To appear in *Computer Communications*.

Fitzpatrick, T., Blair, G.S., Coulson, G., Davies, N. and Robin, P. (1998) Supporting Adaptive Multimedia Applications Through Open Bindings. *Proceedings of the 4th International Conference on Configurable Distributed Systems*, IEEE.

Habert, S., Mosseri, L. and Abrossimov, V. (1990) COOL: Kernel Support for Object-Oriented Environments. Proceedings of ECOOP/ OOPSLA Conference, Ottawa, Canada, *ACM SIGPLAN Notices*, **25**, 269-277, ACM Press.

Hayden, M. (1997) The Ensemble System. *PhD Dissertation*, Dept. of Computer Science, Cornell University, USA.

Hayton, R. (1997) FlexiNet Open ORB Framework. *APM Technical Report 2047.01.00*, APM Ltd, Poseidon House, Castle Park, Cambridge, UK.

Hokimoto, A. and Nakajima, T. (1996) An Approach for Constructing Mobile Applications using Service Proxies. *Proceedings of the 16th International Conference on Distributed Computing Systems (ICDCS'96)*, IEEE.

Kiczales, G., des Rivières, J. and Bobrow, D.G. (1991) The Art of the Metaobject Protocol. MIT Press.

Ledoux, T. (1997) Implementing Proxy Objects in a Reflective ORB. *Proc. ECOOP'97 Workshop on CORBA: Implementation, Use and Evaluation*, Jyväskylä, Finland.

Lindblad, C.J. and Tennenhouse, D.L. (1996) The VuSystem: A Programming System for Computer-Intensive Multimedia. *Journal of Selected Areas in Communications*, **14** (7), 1298-1313, IEEE.

Maes, P. (1987) Concepts and Experiments in Computational Reflection. Proceedings of OOPSLA'87, *ACM SIGPLAN Notices*, **22**, 147-155, ACM Press.

Manola, F. (1993) MetaObject Protocol Concepts for a "RISC" Object Model. *Technical Report TR-0244-12-93-165*, GTE Laboratories, 40 Sylvan Road, Waltham, MA 02254, USA.

Matsuoka, S., Watanabe, T. and Yonezawa, A. (1991) Hybrid Group Reflective Architecture for Object-Oriented Concurrent Reflective Programming. Proceedings of the European Conference on Object-Oriented Programming (ECOOP'91), Geneva, Switzerland, *LNCS*, **512**, 231-250, Springer-Verlag.

McAffer, J. (1996) Meta-Level Architecture Support for Distributed Objects. *Proceedings of Reflection 96*, G. Kiczales (ed), 39-62.

McCanne, S., Brewer, E., Katz, R., Rowe, L., Amir, E., Chawathe, Y., Coopersmith, A., Mayer-Patel, K., Raman, S., Schuett, A., Simpson, D., Swan, A., Tung, T-K. and Wu, D. (1997) Towards a Common Infrastructure for Multimedia-Networking Middleware. *Proc. 7th International Conference on Network and Operating System Support for Digital Audio and Video (Nossdav'97),* St Louis, Missouri, USA.

Okamura, H., Ishikawa, Y. and Tokoro, M. (1992) AL-1/d: A Distributed Programming System with Multi-Model Reflection Framework. *Proceedings of the Workshop on New Models for Software Architecture*, November 1992.

Singhai, A., Sane, A. and Campbell, R. (1997) Reflective ORBs: Supporting Robust, Time-critical Distribution. *Proc. ECOOP'97 Workshop on Reflective Real-Time Object-Oriented Programming and Systems*, Jyväskylä, Finland.

Smith, B.C. (1982) Procedural Reflection in Programming Languages. *PhD Thesis*, MIT, Available as MIT Laboratory of Computer Science Technical Report 272, Cambridge, Mass.

van Renesse, R., Birman, K.P. and Maffeis, S. (1996) Horus: A Flexible Group Communications Service. *Communications of the ACM*, **39** (4).

Watanabe, T. and Yonezawa, A. (1988) Reflection in an Object-Oriented Concurrent Language. Proceedings of OOPSLA'88, *ACM SIGPLAN Notices*, **23**, 306-315, ACM Press.

Watters, A., van Rossum, G., and Ahlstrom, J. (1996) Internet Programming with Python. Henry Holt (MIS/M&T Books).

Yokote, Y. (1992) The Apertos Reflective Operating System: The Concept and Its Implementation. Proceedings of OOPSLA'92, *ACM SIGPLAN Notices*, **28**, 414-434, ACM Press.

9. BIOGRAPHY

Gordon Blair is a Professor of Distributed Systems in the Computing Department at Lancaster University. He has been responsible for a number of research projects at Lancaster in the areas of distributed systems and multimedia support and has published over a hundred papers in his field. He also recently completed a book with Jean-Bernard Stefani (CNET) on "Open Distributed Processing and Multimedia". His current research interests include distributed multimedia computing, open distributed processing, the impact of mobility on distributed systems, and the use of formal methods in distributed systems.

Geoff Coulson is a lecturer in the Computing Department at Lancaster University. Dr. Coulson has published many papers in his field and has contributed to a number of books in the area. He is a member of the ACM and the BCS and has served on program committees and been involved in the organisation of a number of workshops on systems support for multimedia. His current research interests are operating system support for continuous media, distributed systems architectures and high speed networking.

Philippe Robin is a research assistant at Lancaster University. He previously worked at Chorus Systèmes in the development of the CHORUS/MiX operating system and subsequently for a company developing fault-tolerant platforms based on Chorus technology. His areas of research include support of Quality of Service by distributed operating systems, real-time systems and multimedia systems. He is currently working on the design of protocol adaptation mechanisms for mobile platforms.

Michael Papathomas received his MSc and PhD in Computer Science from the University of Geneva, Switzerland in 1985 and 1992 respectively. Following a period as a postdoctoral researcher at Geneva, he joined Lancaster University in 1994 as a Visiting Research Fellow supported by a grant from the Swiss FNRS. On completion of this research, Michael worked as a CaberNet funded Visiting Research Fellow at IMAG, Grenoble, before returning to Lancaster in early 1997. His research interests include pragmatic and formal aspects of concurrent and distributed systems, reflection and object-oriented programming language design, and multimedia.

QuO's Runtime Support for Quality of Service in Distributed Objects

Rodrigo Vanegas, John A. Zinky, Joseph P. Loyall,
David Karr, Richard E. Schantz, David E. Bakken
BBN Technologies
10 Moulton St., Cambridge, Massachusetts 02138
{vanegas,jzinky,jloyall,dkarr,schantz,dbakken}@bbn.com
http://www.dist-systems.bbn.com/tech/QuO/

Abstract

Most distributed applications are brittle; they work in a limited environment and cannot adapt to changes in this environment. Making these applications less brittle is a complex engineering task that is hard for specific application areas and even harder to generalize. The Quality Objects (QuO) project offers a framework for creating applications that adapt to different Quality of Services (QoS) offered by the underlying resources. QuO offers several layers of tools for creating adaptive distributed applications using the familiar CORBA development process of code generators and runtime support libraries. In this paper we describe the QuO Runtime and the components it uses to maintain and adapt to QoS. The QuO Runtime is the base functionality on which QuO code generators specialize for a specific adaptive application. The QuO Runtime handles much of the complexity of collecting, organizing, and acting on changing QoS, thus reducing the burden for application developers.

Keywords

QoS, quality of service, distributed object computing, adaptive programming, CORBA

1 INTRODUCTION

Currently, distributed object applications are written with only an unwilling attention to quality of service (QoS) concerns (Zinky, 1997). Server hosts regularly fail or stall or otherwise impede what would otherwise appear to be simple interactions with local objects. The CORBA (OMG, 1996) interface itself seems to recommend ignoring quality of service issues by relegating all such possible failures to awkward exception handling and offering only the most meager methods for automatic recovery. In practice, application developers have found themselves constructing interface layers in addition to those provided by CORBA stubs below which various stock solutions to QoS problems are inserted ad hoc, such as automatic server selecting from a pool of variably available hosts. We have developed an extension to today's client-server based CORBA ORBs by augmenting the functional interfaces to distributed objects with formalized system interfaces dedicated to the management of QoS. We call such QoS-aware distributed objects *quality objects (QuO).*

The QuO system is a framework for making distributed applications that can adapt to changing quality of service. The goals of QuO are threefold: create more robust distributed applications, enhanced control over how applications adapt, and to support reuse of adaptive mechanisms. Let's examine each of these goals and how QuO achieves them.

The first goal is to create applications that run effectively over a wider range of operating conditions. Finding a single adaptive mechanism that works over a wide range of operating conditions is hard, but several specific mechanisms usually exist which work over limited operating regions. The QuO architecture supports the notion that wide range adaptation can be achieved by identifying the current operating region and dynamically selecting the most appropriate specialized mechanism.

The second goal is to give more control over the application's adaptive behavior during its entire life-cycle. Many different sources of information are available to help decide how a system should adapt. Unfortunately this information is spread out over multiple places, times and people, hence it is hard to gather and usually ignored. The QuO architecture helps organize and the move this information between the parties to enhance the effectiveness of adaptive decisions. For example at runtime, a remote method call conceptually just moves the methods parameters and results between the client and the object, but how this is done involves many subsystems (Figure 1). As we will see in later sections, the QuO Runtime adds many components help make this operation more adaptive, such as *System Conditions* to gather runtime information, *Contracts* to summarize operating regions and trigger adaptive behavior, and *Delegates* to execute alternative behaviors. QuO also partitions the task of creating adaptive application into many roles which create and use these components.

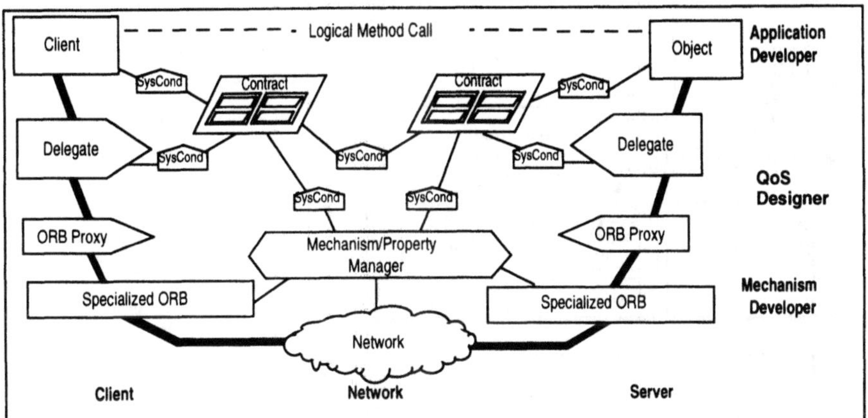

Figure 1: A remote method invocation in a QuO application

The third goal to support reuse of adaptive mechanisms across applications with different functional interfaces. QuO *opens up* distributed object implementations (Kiczales, 1996a), providing control of both the functional aspects of a program, already provided by IDL, and its implementation strategies, which are often hidden by IDL interfaces.

This paper is one in a series of papers about the QuO system and concentrates on the first runtime implementation of QuO and our design tradeoffs. The QuO architecture is described in (Zinky, 1997) and the QuO description languages and code generators are described in (Loyall, 1998a). We are also using QuO to integrate QoS adaptive mechanisms into CORBA applications, such as fault tolerance (Cukier, 1998) and resource reservation, and survivability. In this paper, we describe the implementation of the QuO runtime system in detail. Section 2 introduces the QuO runtime components and their interaction by tracing the execution of a QuO application. Section 3 describes the QuO runtime system and its components. Section 4 describes how to design and develop a QuO application in the QuO environment. Section 5 describes work related to our QuO research. Finally, Section 6 provides the current status of QuO and future directions.

2 RUNTIME EXECUTION MODEL OF A QUO APPLICATION

In a traditional CORBA application, a client makes a method call on a remote object through its functional interface. The call is processed by an ORB on the client's host, delivered to an ORB on the object's host, and processed by the remote object. The client sees it strictly as a functional method call. As indicated in Figure 1 and 2, a QuO application adds additional steps to this process. The QuO runtime measure the state of QoS before each remote method call, recognizes when system conditions change, triggers behavior and callbacks when the state of QoS changes, and choose behavior for the remote method call based upon the current state of QoS. The QoS designer role uses the QuO description languages (QDL) to specify how the application will

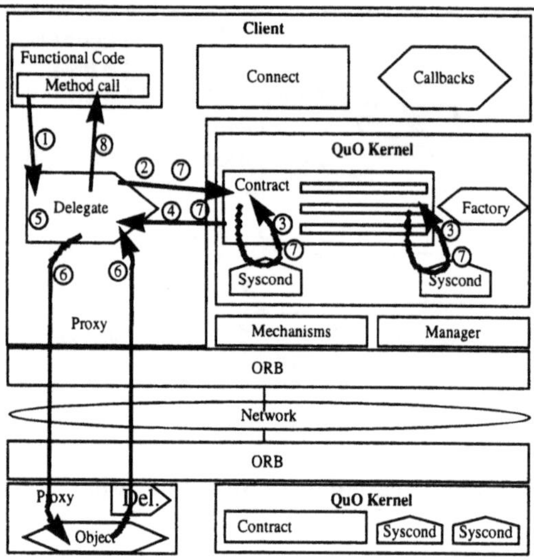

1) Client makes a remote method call, which is delivered to delegate
2) Delegate evaluates contract
3) Contract gets the current values of system conditions to determine current region (if a region transition occurs, callback behavior is triggered)
4) Contract returns current regions
5) Delegate chooses behavior based on the current regions; default is to pass the method call through to the remote object
6) Remote object is invoked, performs its method, and returns a value
7) Delegate re-evaluates contract, contract gets current values of system conditions, and returns current regions
8) Delegate chooses behavior based on the current regions; default is to pass the return value back to the client

Figure 2: Example remote method call in a QuO application

adapt. They define possible states of QoS, adaptive behavior, and system conditions that need to be measured and controlled. Code generators parse these description languages and IDL in the application's code and generate code that is linked in with the client code, the QuO kernel, and CORBA stubs and skeletons. The resulting generated code implementing the following components:

Contract objects that record the state of QoS in the system and trigger adaptive behavior when it changes. Each contract consists of a number of nested regions, each defined by a predicate on the values of system condition objects, and sets of transition behavior. The regions represent the possible states the system can be in with regard to QoS, including QoS desired by the client, expected by the remote object, and observed in the system. A transition from one active region to another can trigger *transition behavior*, which consists of client callbacks or method calls on system condition objects.

Delegates which provide identical interfaces to a client as the remote object, but contain code to check the current contract regions and choose local behavior based upon it. When a client calls a remote method, the call is passed to the object's local delegate which checks the current regions of relevant contracts. The delegate chooses how to process the method call based upon the current regions. For example, the delegate might choose between alternate methods, might block or buffer when QoS has degraded, or might simply pass the call through to the remote object. The delegate performs similar processing upon a method return, i.e., it evaluates the contract to obtain the current QoS regions and selects a behavior based upon the current regions

System condition objects interface between the contract and resources, mechanisms, objects, and ORBs in the system. These are used to measure and control QoS. Some system condition objects trigger contract evaluation when the values of the system elements they are monitoring change. Others, especially those whose values change frequently, do not trigger contract evaluation, but provide their values upon demand by the contract objects.

Figure 2 illustrates the steps that can occur during a remote method call in a QuO application. QuO replaces the CORBA binding of a client to a remote object with a connection through a series of delegates to the object. This is transparent to the client, because the remote object and the delegate have the same IDL interface.

When the client calls a method on the remote object, it is actually calling that method on the local delegate. The delegate optionally triggers contract evaluation, which grabs the current value of all system condition objects measuring aspects of the system's state relevant to the contract. The system condition objects return their values immediately with their current estimate of some system property. The work needed to determine the values is done continuously in anticipation of its need. That is, the updating of system condition object values is performed asynchronously with respect to contract evaluation, delegate execution, and client execution.

The contract consists of a set of nested regions which describe the relevant possible states of QoS in the system. Each of these regions is defined by a predicate on the values of system condition objects. The contract evaluates the predicates to determine which regions are active (i.e., their predicates are true) and passes the list to the delegate. This list of active regions represents the current state of QoS in the system with respect to this contract. If contract evaluation caused a region transition, i.e., caused a change in the list of active regions from the last time the contract was evaluated, it might trigger transition behavior. Transitions are behaviors associated with moves from regions, into regions, or between regions, and consist of callbacks for notifying the client or calls to methods on system condition objects for controlling QoS.

The delegate code includes a dispatch statement, i.e., **switch** in Java and C++. The active regions cause branches of the dispatch statement to be chosen, each of which specifies local delegate behavior alternative for the method call. The delegate's alternatives are specified by the QoS developer using QuO's description languages. In many cases, especially those in which the contract indicates that the QoS desired by the client is being satisfied by the system, the delegate will pass the method call through to the remote object. In others, especially when QoS requirements are not being met, the delegate can choose an alternate method on the remote object, might block or buffer the method call, or might throw an exception.

The delegate performs similar processing upon a method return, i.e., it evaluates the contract to obtain the current QoS regions and selects a behavior based upon the current regions. The default is usually to pass the return value to the calling client. Note in Figure 2, we show the connection consisting of only one client-side and object-side delegate, but the connection consist of an arbitrary call graph that can change dynamically at runtime.

Contract evaluation can also be triggered by changes in some system condition objects, i.e., those that are *observed* by the contract. Other system condition objects, especially those whose values change frequently, are *non-*

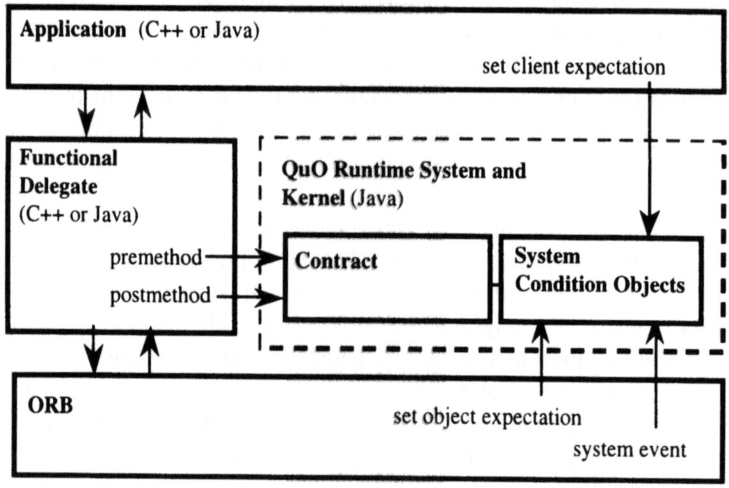

Figure 3: Components of QuO application

observed and do not trigger contract evaluation. Regardless of how contract evaluation is triggered (by a method call/return or change in a system condition), a transition from one active region to another can trigger *transition behavior*, which consists of client callbacks or method calls on system condition objects.

3 IMPLEMENTATION INTERNALS OF QUO COMPONENTS

In this section, we describe the implementation of the components of the QuO runtime system, illustrated in Figure 3. The QuO runtime can be implemented in several ways each satisfying different design criteria, e.g., the first release of QuO will be our fourth prototype. Ultimately, the QuO delegates, system conditions and contracts will be part of the ORB's proxies, much like the "smart proxies" available in the Visigenic or Orbix ORBs, but with all generated code. We are currently experimenting with these ORBs to discover how the proxies can be used. Consequently, we need a *flexible* runtime that can support several target applications that are written in different languages. Also, it is our belief that proxy performance is not a major issue, because the inherent cost of marshalling is so high, hence QuO runtime can afford a few levels of indirection to enhance flexibility. Our delegate performance goal is to be at the same order of magnitude as marshalling, which we have already met with the prerelease version of QuO runtime with "an integrated kernel". Also, QuO will mostly be used in situations where CPU is not the bottleneck and if CPU is the bottleneck, then QuO's adaptive behavior could be to "get out of the way."

The first release of QuO splits the runtime into a delegate that runs in the application and contracts and system conditions that run in an independent QuO Kernel. The delegate communicates with the kernel through a CORBA interface. This split helps flexibility is several ways. First, the code generators only have to support multiple target languages for the delegate generator, the contracts can all be output in the kernel's implementation language. Second, the asynchronous behavior of system condition, contracts and transitions, implies separate threads. By grouping these components into an independent subsystem, the concurrency constraints are vastly simplified. An alternative implementation of including the contract evaluation as inlined code in the delegate was prototyped and rejected for now, because of its inflexibility, but does offer the possibility of higher delegate performance in the future.

3.1 The QuO Kernel

The QuO kernel is a library of services, implemented in Java, providing the basis for the QuO runtime system, contracts, and system condition objects. The kernel library provides two essential services: an object *factory* and a *contract evaluator.*

The object factory creates and initializes contract and system condition objects. Currently all of these objects are created at the startup of a QuO application, although future QuO applications might require dynamically created contracts or system condition objects. The factory is implemented using reflection in Java, since it is difficult to anticipate at compile time the classes of contract or system condition objects that will be used by the runtime system and how many instances will be instantiated by the delegates. A delegate makes a CORBA call to the QuO kernel factory to instantiate an object, i.e., either a contract instance or a system condition object, passing the class of the object as a string. The factory locates the corresponding class file and loads it dynamically if it has not already been loaded. The factory then creates and initializes an instance of the class and returns the object reference to the delegate. The kernel maintains a record of the objects used by each delegate, so that it can clean up when applications quit or delegates disappear.

The contract evaluator schedules the evaluation of contract objects in the QuO runtime for a given application. A QuO application might involve any number of contract objects, whose evaluation can be triggered in the two following ways:

- A delegate's *premethod* or *postmethod* QoS check – When a client makes a remote method call, the call goes to the appropriate delegate. As described in Section 2, the delegate will often check the current state of QoS (as represented by the current regions of a contract) to decide what adaptive behavior to select (premethod). Likewise, the delegate will often check the state of the contract upon a method's return, to decide what to do with the return value. Each of these can trigger contract evaluation.
- A change in an observed system condition – Some of the system condition objects that a contract uses to collect data about QoS in the system are *observed* by the contract (as specified in QDL). When the value of any observed system condition objects changes, it triggers contract evaluation.

Even though there might be many contracts concurrently ready for evaluation, we expect the QuO kernel to consume a small overhead of CPU cycles relative to the application, therefore QuO does not concurrently evaluate contracts. Instead, triggering simply marks a contract object as ready for evaluation. The contract evaluator is a single high-priority thread that performs a round-robin check of all contract objects in the runtime. If a given contract object is marked, the evaluator evaluates it before proceeding to the next contract. If evaluation of a particular contract is triggered more than once before the evaluator gets to it, the contract is only evaluated once. Contract evaluation is described in more detail below.

The QuO kernel is flexible about its environment. It can run in its own process or in the same process as the application. It can run on the same or a different host as that of the application. Finally, any number of applications can share it whether or not they are on the same host. The kernel also includes a built in GUI for displaying the current state of contracts and system condition objects.

3.2 QuO Delegates

The function of the QuO delegate is to wrap a remote object with local behavior that can adapt to dynamic changes in QoS. The delegate code is generated from IDL and QDL. The IDL specifies the delegate's external interface to the client and internally specifies, at the least, how many distinct methods can be mediated to implement adaptive behavior. The contract description further constrains the implementation of adaptability by specifying how many and which distinct QoS regions the system can be in. Each region represents a possible state of QoS to which the delegate can adapt. Finally, the structural description specifies the selection mechanism and the alternative behaviors, such as selecting between methods, selecting between remote object references, or executing local code. QDL and the code generation process is described in more detail in (Loyall 1998a, 1998b). The generated delegate is implemented in the language of the client. Currently C++ and Java are supported.

One would hope that the mixing of such disparate sources (notwithstanding their variable languages) could be implemented with some kind of multiple implementation inheritance. But even if all sources could be expressed as classes in some common language, it doesn't seem that inheritance of any kind could satisfactorily produce the delegate we want. Our solution is to provide description languages for different aspects of QoS, e.g., QoS contracts and adaptation, and code generators that compile all the description languages and produce as output a single source program with each contributing element in the desired place. We see a basis for this solution in the ideas of aspect-oriented programming (Kiczales 1996a, 1996b) and adaptive programming (Lieberherr, 1995).

3.3 Bind-Time Configuration

Although the delegate provides an interface identical to the CORBA object it wraps, the application's client code requires a slight change to establish a binding to the delegate through QuO. We provide a facility similar to the *bind()* call provided by some commercial ORBs, such as Visibroker and Orbix. A QuO delegate's *connect()* call performs the functionality of the bind(), i.e., it instantiates a CORBA proxy to a remote object. In addition, it establishes the delegate's interface to the client and instantiates and establishes connections to the necessary QuO runtime objects. First, it either locates an existing QuO kernel thread or creates one. It then calls the kernel's factory object to locate or create the necessary contract and system condition objects. Finally, connect() initializes and links all of the runtime objects as necessary. In addition to initializing all necessary support within the QuO kernel, the configuration procedure may also make initializing calls to external quality of service brokers such as traders, or other control mechanisms as intended by the QoS designer.

One important feature of the QuO design is that delegates can be stacked, nested, or arranged in any rooted configuration, each with an association to its own or a shared contract object and each with its own local adaptation. The client establishes a connection only to the root delegate, whose connect() method recursively invokes those of the delegates below it. In other words, instantiating a delegate and calling connect() may in turn cause other delegates (of potentially different types) to be instantiated and have their connect()'s be called. Each will establish connections to a contract object and the necessary system condition objects. References to kernel objects can be passed to connect(), so that contract objects can be shared by different delegates, and system condition objects can be shared by different contract objects.

3.4 Contract Objects

Contract objects collect data from the system condition objects and analyze it to determine the current state of QoS in the system, as captured by a set of current regions. Contract evaluation is triggered as described in Section 3.1. The evaluation of a specific contract begins with the collection of all the most current system condition object values relevant to this contract. We call this a *snapshot* to emphasize that it should appear instantaneous to the application, though of course the values are read serially. The values are read quickly, with minimal blocking, and all values are cached for subsequent use during the evaluation. Each region of the contract is defined by a predicate over the values of some system condition objects. If a region's predicate is true, that region is active. The QuO runtime evaluates the regions of a contract in one large conditional statement of the form

```
if (pred1) then {region1} else if (pred2) then {region2}
```

The first predicate to evaluate as true determines the contract's current region, even if subsequent predicates also would evaluate to true. The kernel also includes a built in GUI for displaying the current state of contracts and system condition objects.

If the current region is different from the previous one, there is a region transition. If transition behavior has been specified for the particular transition, it is called at this time. Typically transition code includes either calls to methods of system condition objects or external mechanisms (to try to affect QoS), asynchronous calls to application callback objects (for notifying the client of changes in QoS), or both. Transition code can run synchronously or asynchronously. If it is specified to run synchronously then it is ensured that it will have finished before returning the current region to the delegate. This is useful if, for example, the delegate which triggered the evaluation should not act until certain external mechanisms are available. Asynchronous execution of transition is sometimes preferred since it reduces the overhead introduced by the QuO runtime in a remote method invocation.

Regions within contracts can be nested. In addition to helping organize the space of QoS regions, this adds flexibility in coding region transition behavior. For example, assume that there are two contract regions A, with nested region C, and B, with nested region E. If there were a region transition from E to C, the contract evaluator would run transition code associated with *exiting* region B, *entering* region A, going from B to A, *exiting* E, and *entering* C. Transition code can be associated with any or all of these in the QDL contract (Loyall, 1998a).

3.5 System Condition Objects

Every system condition object represents a single system property value, such as time elapsed since the last invocation or number of active jobs on a remote host. Contract objects use these values to determine the current region. In addition, arbitrary functionality can be inserted into the implementation of system condition objects such as control of mechanisms external to the QuO kernel or perhaps just internal logic required to compute the value which the system condition object represents. This functionality can execute asynchronously to the QuO runtime and contracts or it can be triggered by contract transitions.

Each system condition object is implemented as a Java class which *implements* a simple Java *interface* common to all system condition objects. This interface must provide a *getValue()* method used by contract objects to query system condition objects for their values. Some simple system condition objects, e.g., those which are internal to a contract, are completely specified if they implement the getValue() method. All other system condition objects must be CORBA objects and as such must inherit from an existing hierarchy of system condition CORBA objects. This requirement makes it possible for the delegate to instatiate the system condition objects (using the QuO kernel's factory).

Since system condition objects can publish their IDL interface, they can provide control and access to their values outside the QuO runtime, effectively allowing system condition objects to function as interfaces between QuO and system resources, mechanisms, managers, etc. external to QuO. Each system condition object may also run any number of threads exclusive to either each instance or to a class. The freedom to implement system condition values with asynchronous control does not interfere with the general control flow within the kernel and facilitates the implementation of certain kinds of objects such as timers or polling resources. A growing library of system condition classes that we provide and that can be composed or inherited from also facilitates the implementation of new system condition objects.

The following examples give a sense of the expected granularity of system condition objects. Of the five system condition classes that follow, the first four are part of the standard system condition library and the fifth can be trivially implemented in terms of the first.

- **ValueSysCond** is a simple system condition object representing a value holder. Its getValue() implementation simply returns its state, and its state is set (and read) externally by the methods writeVal() and readVal() defined in the class' IDL interface and implemented as one would implement the methods of any CORBA object.
- **MethodInvocationTimerSysCond** is a more complicated version implemented in terms of ProbeSysCond and TimerSysCond. The former provides the object with signals that indicate when a method invocation has begun and when it is about to end and the latter provides a generic implementation of a timer.
- **RemoteSystemLoadSysCond** isn't a CORBA object and so doesn't need an IDL interface, but it gets its value by periodically polling a remote host for its load statistics.
- **RSVP_SysCond** has a getValue() method that reports simply the current status of a particular RSVP connection. However, embedded in the implementation of this system condition object are the control mechanisms required to build up and tear down the RSVP connection whose status it is reporting.
- **RemoteObjectStateNoticeSysCond** reports when the state of a remote object last changed. Rather than implement this by polling, the remote object can signal this system condition object when its state changes.

4 PROGRAMMER'S VIEW OF QUO RUNTIME

We believe that you cannot automatically create an application which adapts to all shortcomings of a wide area distributed environment and make it look like the application is running on a dedicated local host, i.e., it is impossible to create some hidden services that mask all lower layer problems. Some of the burden must fall on programmers, system administrators, and even the users of the system. These players know valuable information that must somehow be injected into the system in order to make the right tradeoffs. A goal of the QuO architecture is to give a wide spectrum of support for these different players and their willingness to be bothered with system issues.

In this section we will address the degree of effort needed by programmers to write adaptive applications. The goal is that the large number of inexperienced programmers can reuse adaptive functionality created by fewer experts. We expect more users of adaptive than creators of adaptive objects and even fewer creators of underlying QoS mechanisms. We break the task of creating an adaptive application into several loosely defined roles:

The **client developer** uses a set of predefined adaptive objects, some of which may require no customization. Others may need hints about the expected usage patterns and QoS requirements for the client.
The **object developer** uses existing QuO connection types to create adaptive objects. They bind the regions in the contract with alternative behaviors. Object designers may also modify contracts and use new instances of system condition objects.
The **QoS developer** creates new QuO connection types, contracts, and system conditions. They are experts in creating adaptive code from existing adaptive techniques.
The mechanism developers are researchers who create new adaptive mechanisms. They can use the QuO runtime as interface to their mechanism at the object layer. The hooks in the QuO runtime for adding new mechanisms is beyond the scope of this paper.

4.1 Programming Without QuO

The normal development process for a CORBA object is for the object developer to compile the IDL for their object into client stubs and object stubs. The client stubs are used by the client developer and implement proxy objects that effectively look like a local version of the remote object. The server skeletons are modified by the object designer to add functional behavior. Basic CORBA works fine in cases where the underlying resources are stable and plentiful.

4.2 Programming Using Existing Quality Objects

Suppose the object developer has extended a CORBA object into a quality object by combining the implementation of a function interface (IDL) with a QuO connection type (QDL) . A client developer can use this quality object in much the same way they used the original CORBA object. The main difference is that the CORBA bind() operation to create a local reference to a remote object must be replaced with a QuO connection operation. The QuO connect() method may have additional parameters that give the connection hints about the expected QoS requirements and usage patterns at connect time. The quality object may have an extend interface to allow these hints to be change dynamically at invocation time. The client developer may have to set expectations by calling additional methods on the local object reference which really points to the QuO delegate. In addition the quality object may inform the client code asynchronously during a transition between regions. The client developer needs to create callback objects and their adaptive behavior. To the client developer the quality object looks similar to tradition library, but with a formal interface described in IDL and QDL.

4.3 Creating a Quality Object from an Existing QuO Connection

The object designer can add adaptive behavior to specialize a QuO connection type to handle a specific functional interface. The QuO connection type defines a contract and its regions. The object designer needs to bind adaptive code to these regions based on the functional interface. The object designer runs the QuO delegate generator which takes the IDL for the remote object and QDL describing QoS contracts and behavior alternatives. The delegate generator creates delegate stubs which can be compiled into the application in the same way as CORBA stubs. The resulting delegate supports the same interface as the original CORBA object, but has additional QuO interfaces and behavior added by the object designer.

The object designer may choose to modify an existing QoS contract, e.g., to add new QoS regions, new system condition objects, or different adaptation strategies. The edited QDL code is compiled to create Java classes for the contract object and a new delegate. Note that the object designer can easily change the external interface to the contract, by editing references to new system conditions and callback objects. Currently, there is no feature such as contract inheritance for managing contract modification and reuse.

4.4 Creating New System Conditions.

The QoS designer may need to create new system conditions to manage a system property needed by an object designer. New system conditions are implemented in Java and inherit from two distinct type hierarchies. The interface hierarchy defines the interfaces that the QuO contract will see including the type of the value, initialization methods, and methods that can be called during transitions. The interface can be defined in CORBA IDL. The implementation hierarchy is the base functionality for implementing these interfaces. Both definitions must be entered into the QuO interface repository before object designers can use them.

5 BACKGROUND AND RELATED WORK

There are other projects investigating ways of adding QoS to distributed object systems, although many of them are concentrating on specific applications, such as ReTINA (telecommunications), or look at QoS in the limited sense of bandwidth and throughput, such as TAO (Schmidt, 1997) and (Monteiro, 1995).

The ReTINA project is developing a distributed processing environment for telecommunication applications (Bosco, 1996) that complies with the Telecommunications Information Networking Architecture (TINA) standard. ReTINA provides real-time audio and video and network QoS guarantees.

TAO is a real-time CORBA ORB that provides end-to-end QoS by vertically integrating CORBA middleware with OS I/O subsystems, communication protocols, and network interfaces. TAO is the first real-time ORB supporting end-to-end QoS over COTS platforms and ATM networks (Schmidt, 1997).

Monteiro, et al describe a technique for specifying QoS for congestion in networks. The technique involves selecting a set of quantifiable parameters that comprise the QoS (Monteiro, 1995). Then the upper and lower bounds for a correct operating interval are selected, followed by the upper and lower values of an interval in which service is degraded, but acceptable. These values are combined into a matrix that defines a *service contract* between a client and a server.

In contrast, QuO is a general-purpose framework for incorporating QoS in new and existing distributed applications, where QoS is defined as any non-functional property of an application. This definition of QoS is often called "ilities" because it includes properties such as availability, dependability, reliability, and so on.

BeeHive shares QuO's goals of providing QoS in the broad sense, although its approach is different. BeeHive provides a set of service-specific application programming interfaces (APIs), through which objects can request QoS from a resource manager (Stankovic, 1997). They are currently developing APIs for real-time, fault-tolerance, and security requirements. Each API allows an object to request a requirement in application terms, e.g., Mean Time to Failure for fault-tolerance. The resource manager translates each request into low-level resource requests.

The QuO framework borrows and builds upon the concepts of open implementation, aspect-oriented programming, and adaptive programming. *Open implementation* (Kiczales, 1996a) allows programmers to access and control non-algorithmic parts of an application's implementation, such as access to system resources, alternate implementations of an algorithm, insight or control over choice of data structures, or control of scheduling or other operating system functions. QuO allows programmers to access implementation details that are normally hidden behind IDL interfaces in distributed object applications, but are necessary to satisfy the QoS requirements of many applications.

QuO also provides support for *Aspect-Oriented Programming* (AOP) (Kiczales, 1996b) using its specification languages, as described in detail in (Loyall, 1998b). In AOP, a program is divided into aspects of concern, each of which is programmed separately in a language suitable for expressing the particular aspect. The application is constructed by weaving (using code generators) the aspects together into a single, executable application. QuO allows an application developer to design and develop functional behavior using IDL and QoS contracts, alternate implementation, and adaptation strategies using QDL. QuO's code generators weave these together into a single application. All of these aspects would ordinarily have to be interleaved throughout an application, making design, development, maintenance, and portability more difficult.

The QuO work also parallels research in adaptive programming (Lieberherr, 1995) and its offshoots, such as variation-oriented programming (Mezini, 1997). Adaptive programming is the creation of software that adapts itself automatically to the contexts in which it is used, including changes in behaviors, structures, etc.

6 CONCLUSIONS

Distributed object applications need to be able to specify and control the QoS provided them, monitor it, and adapt as QoS changes. This is difficult to do in most of today's middleware, such as CORBA, because they hide implementation and environment specific details behind functional interfaces. QuO provides a framework for describing, controlling, monitoring, and adapting to changes in QoS. A key component of the QuO framework is the QuO runtime kernel, which creates, connects, and schedules key components of QuO applications, i.e., contract objects and system condition objects.

6.1 Present State of QuO System and Future Work

The QuO runtime kernel is implemented as a set of library services and works in conjunction with other QuO framework components, currently the QDL code generators, to create QuO applications. We currently have an internal alpha version 0.5 of the QuO development system, including the runtime kernel and code generators. We have developed two prototype applications using QuO: AquA (Cukier, 1998), which provides availability through object replication, and DIRM, which provides managed communication through resource reservation. During the coming months, we will be enhancing, extending, and stressing this runtime kernel to support additional QuO applications, and larger libraries of reusable contracts and system condition objects. We expect that our first external release will be made available in the fall.

7 REFERENCES

Bosco, P.G., Dahle, E., Gien, M., Grace, A., Mercouroff , N., Perdigues, N., and Stefani, J.B. (1996) The ReTINA project: an overview, *ReTINA Technical Report.*

Cukier, M., Ren, J., Sabnis, C., Henke, D., Pistole, J, Sanders, W., Bakken, D., Berman, M., Karr, D., and Schantz, R. (1998) AQuA: an adaptive architecture that provides dependable distributed objects. *Seventeenth Symposium on Reliable Distributed Systems (SRDS-17), IEEE,* October 1998.

Kiczales, G. (1996a) Beyond the black box: Open Implementation. *IEEE Software* January 1996.

Kiczales, G., Irwin, J., Lamping, J., Loingtier, J., Videria, C., Lopes, Maeda, C., and Mendhekar, A. (1996b) Aspect-Oriented Programming *ACM Computing Surveys*, **28(4es)**.

Lieberherr, K. (1995) *Adaptive object-oriented software: the Demeter Method with propagation patterns*, PWS Publishing Company, Boston.

Loyall, J., Schantz, R., Zinky, J., Bakken, D., (1998a) Specifying and measuring quality of service in distributed object systems, *Proceedings of the First International Symposium on Object-oriented Real-time distributed Computing (ISORC '98)*, April 20-22, Kyoto, Japan.

Loyall, J., Bakken, D., Schantz, R., Zinky, J., Karr, D., and Vanegas, R. (1998b) QoS aspect languages and their runtime interactions, (to appear in) *Lecture Notes in Computer Science*, Springer-Verlag.

Mezini, M. (1997) *Variation-oriented programming beyond classes and inheritance*, Ph.D. thesis, University of Siegen, Germany.

Monteiro, E., Boavida, F., Quadros, G., and Freitas, V. (1995) Specification, quantification and provision of quality of Service and congestion control for new communication services. *Proceedings of the 16th AFCEA Europe Symposium*, AFCEA (Association for Communications, Electronics, Intelligence & Information Systems Professionals)/IEEE COMSOC/IEE, October 18-20, Brussels, Belgium, 58-68.

Object Management Group (1996), *CORBA 2.0, July 96 revision,* OMG Document 96-08-04.

Schmidt, D.C., Bector, R., Levine, D., Mungee, S., and Parulkar, G. (1997) An ORB end system architecture for statically scheduled real-time applications. *Proceedings of the Workshop on Middleware for Real-Time Systems and Services*, IEEE, San Francisco.

Stankovic, J., Son, S., Liebeherr, J. (1997) BeeHive: global multimedia database support for dependable, real-time applications *Computer Science Report* **CS-97-08**, University of Virginia, April 21, 1997.

Zinky, J., Bakken, D., and Schantz, R. (1997) Architectural support for quality of service for CORBA objects. *Theory and Practice of Object Systems*, **3(1)**.

8 BIOGRAPHY

Rodrigo Vanegas has been at BBN for 3 years and implemented the QuO Kernel. **Dr. John Zinky** has been at BBN for 15 years, he is the architect for the QuO system and PI for the DIRM project. **Dr. Joseph Loyall** has been at BBN for 2 years. He designed and implemented the QDL code generators and is PI for the Open Implementation Toolkit project. **Dr. David Karr** has been a BBN for 2 years and he designed and implemented the fault tolerant mechanisms for the AQuA project. **Dr. Richard Schantz** has be at BBN for 25 years where he developed the Cronus system a precursor to modern CORBA systems. **Dr. David Bakken** has been at BBN for 4 years. He is the architect and PI for the Aqua Project.

Session 6

Components

Component Coordination in Middleware Systems

Matthias Radestock and Susan Eisenbach
Department of Computing
Imperial College of Science, Technology and Medicine
180 Queen's Gate, London SW7 2BZ, United Kingdom
Phone: +44 171 594 8264, Fax: +44 171 581 8024
Email: {M.Radestock,S.Eisenbach}@doc.ic.ac.uk

Abstract

Configuration and *coordination* are central issues in the design and implementation of middleware systems and are one of the reasons why building such systems is more difficult and complex than constructing stand-alone sequential programs. Through configuration, the structure of the system is established — which elements it contains, where they are located and how they are interconnected. Coordination is concerned with the interaction of the various components — when an interaction takes place, which parties are involved, what protocols are followed. Its purpose is to coordinate the behaviour of the various components in a way that meets the overall system specification. The open and adaptive nature of middleware systems makes the task of configuration and coordination particularly challenging. We propose a model that can operate in such an environment and enables the dynamic integration and coordination of components through observation of their behaviour.

Keywords

Coordination, Adaptive Open Distributed Systems, Novel Paradigms

1 INTRODUCTION

We can view a distributed system as a collection of distributed components that interact with each other. The concerns of any distributed system, including middleware systems, can be separated into four parts:

- The *communication part* defines *how* components communicate with each other.
- The *computation part* defines the implementation of the *behaviour* of individual components. It thus determines *what* is being communicated.
- The *configuration part* defines the *interaction structure*, or *configuration*. It states which components exist in the system and which components can communicate with each other, as well as the method of communication. Basically it is a description of *where* information comes from and *where* it is sent to.
- The *coordination part* defines patterns of interaction, ie. it determines *when* certain communications take place.

The interaction structure in middleware systems often changes dynamically: new components are created, existing components are destroyed, connections between components are established and broken up. Such dynamic configuration activities are derived from the functional specification of the system which may state, for instance, that a new member can join a video conference after receiving an invitation. These activities thus need to be triggered by the components in the system themselves, and so the configuration layer needs to be supported by the distributed system platform during the entire life-time of the system in order to enable dynamic access to its functionality.

Coordination specifies patterns of interaction. Such a pattern may, for instance, be that component A can only send message X to component B after component C has sent message Y to component D. Coordination requires configuration — the patterns of interaction need to be specified *before* the parties of interaction; which is precisely the task performed by configuration. We can make a distinction between static and dynamic coordination. In the former case, the interaction patterns are fixed throughout the life-time of a system. In the latter case, interaction patterns are altered dynamically as part of satisfying the application requirements, ie. the changes to the interaction structure and patterns are ultimately triggered by computational components. The coordination layer must exist during the entire life-time of the system. A mechanism is required that enables the interaction with the computation layer.

1.1 Adaptive Open Systems

A dynamic coordination model allows us to specify systems where all possible dynamic changes to the interaction structure and patterns are known at compile time and are triggered by application components. However, this is insufficient in many large distributed systems, especially middleware systems(Rock-Evans 1997) tasked with enterprise application integration(Black, Fournier and Kastner 1998). Such systems are typically long-lived, and require interactive management; both human and automated agents need to be able to reconfigure the system while it is running and even need to be able to alter the specification of the coordination, configuration and computation layers in order to make permanent changes to the overall system behaviour. An example would be a video-conferencing system where some new hardware, say a projection screen, is added to the system during a conference. The components representing the screen need to be added to the system's computation layer and the configuration layer needs to be modified to forward all data of the conferencing communication to that component. Finally we need to alter the coordination layer to ensure that the new component interacts with the rest of the system in the desired manner.

These so-called *adaptive systems* or *evolving systems* are capable of accommodating changes that were not anticipated during the original system development. This is in contrast to static and dynamic systems. Both of these can contain interactive user interfaces or can interact with external components, but such interaction and the resulting changes need to be implemented as *part* of the system functionality; the system functionality itself cannot be altered. Adaptive systems create considerable demands on the capabilities of a middleware architectures and the use of *reflection* (Matsuoka, Wanatabe and Yonezawa 1991, G. Kiczales 1991) as a means of supporting these advanced requirements has been advocated in recent research (Radestock and Eisenbach 1996a, Blair and Papathomas 1997).

A universal model for configuration and coordination has to be suitable for operating within the context of open systems; it has to be easy to integrate it into existing distributed system platforms and it needs to enable configuration and coordination of existing components without requiring any alterations to them. The model needs to function across heterogeneous systems that may be based on a variety of programming paradigms, languages and platforms. Not only should it be possible to control the configuration and coordination of components in a heterogeneous system, but it must also be possible to control it from the *inside* of the various platforms that make up the system — if configuration and coordination are part of application requirements, then they need to be controllable from potentially any part of the application.

In an open system little is known of the components' implementations and it may even be impossible to alter them. Thus for configuration and coordination to operate in a truly open setting and enable the dynamic integration of components, they must not depend on any knowledge of component behaviour. They certainly should not *rely* on any behaviour specifications, because in general it is impossible to ascertain whether components actually meet them, and hence system safety and security could be compromised. Coordinating components without relying on any explicit behaviour specification is crucial when it comes to middleware systems, where it is important to perform integration with a minimum impact on existing components. Typically, integration is achieved by embedding calls to some special communications API that enable interaction with other system components via the middleware infrastructure. The impact on the existing application in terms of code changes is usually minimal and introducing coordination should not increase this.

1.2 Related Research

The issues of configuration and coordination have received growing attention from the research community, and, as a result, several models, languages and implementations have been proposed and executed. Distributed System standards such as CORBA (Mowbray and Zahavi 1995, Pope 1997), DCE (Schill 1993) and RM-ODP (Blair and Stefani 1997), and their implementations, address the issue of configuration by introducing a *brokering* mechanism which matches requests by components for particular services with components providing these services. With this basic building block in place, most configuration issues can be addressed. However, coordination is not addressed at all and left entirely to the programmer of the components.

Formalisms, such as Gamma (Banatre and Metayer 1990) and languages such as Linda (Gelernter 1985, Banville 1996) have emerged. However, they are not aimed at integration with existing systems or operation in an open environment. Furthermore, only limited facilities exist for re-using coordination patterns, and coordination is typically embedded in application code rather than being separated. Research in software architecture (Garlan and Shaw 1993, Perry and Wolf 1992, Garlan and Perry 1994, Radestock and Eisenbach 1996b), by contrast, has placed considerable emphasis on layer separation. However, the distinct role of coordination has only been recognised recently. Consequently several systems have emerged that address coordination issues, usually as extensions to existing systems. Examples of this are *ToolBus* (Bergstra and Klint 1996) (an extension to the *PolyLith* software bus (Purtilo 1994)), ConCoord (Holzbacher 1996) and Midas (Pryce 1998) are extension of Darwin (Magee, Eisenbach and Kramer 1995). ActorSpace (Callsen and Agha 1994) is an extension of an actor language and *Manifold* (Arbab 1996) is based on a model where processes communicate anonymously via streams. Common to all approaches is the lack of openness — coordination in these systems relies on particular features that are unique to the specific system. Dynamic integration of existing components is usually possible, but only for components that have been designed, implemented and compiled for the particular system used. Dynamic change is supported, but systems cannot adapt to changes in the requirements that go beyond the scope of the original specification. Furthermore, the above coordination mechanisms only provide limited means of abstraction, ie. the construction of patterns of coordination and their reuse. This is mainly due to the use of separate coordination languages that lack expressiveness.

1.3 Outline of Our Approach

Our aim is to enable coordination in adaptive and open distributed systems, such as middleware systems. Further to that, we want to be able to integrate components on the level of source code, object code and running code, including existing and running legacy applications. The key element in our solution is a mechanism that enables the observation and coercion of dynamic component behaviour through the interception of messages. The first part of this paper is devoted to the description of this so-called *traps* model. Traps employ a sophisticated type system for specifying message patterns and rules for defining actions to be taken when messages have been intercepted. The patterns and rules can be altered dynamically and thus traps represent a dynamic configuration and coordination layer. Since traps operate without having any knowledge of the behaviour of the components, they do not depend on any component interface/behaviour specification. Traps integrate the configuration and coordination layers into the computation layer without jeopardising the benefits of clear separation. Thus coordination can be designed and implemented using the same techniques deployed in the design and implementation of the application components. As a result, coordination code can be reused in the same way as application code. The approach also enables *meta coordination*; the coordination of coordination itself. In the final part of this paper we use the well-known example of the Dining Philosophers to illustrate how our model can deal with various, increasingly complex, coordination tasks.

2 TRAPS — A NEW MODEL FOR COORDINATION

In order to facilitate configuration and coordination in an evolving heterogeneous distributed environment, we need to devise a suitable model that has very few demands on the system architecture and is thus easily incorporated into both existing and new systems. The first step in devising our coordination model is to take a slightly different view of the message-based communication model.

2.1 Message Spaces

A message between two components consists of

- the *originator*, ie. the component that sent the message,
- the *recipient*, ie. the component that is the intended recipient of the message,
- the *content*, ie. the data elements, and
- the *context*, ie. additional information required by the communication and coordination layers, such as time stamps and request ids.

The *type* of a message encompasses those elements that are visible to the programmer, ie. everything apart from the context information. Some examples of message types (in pseudo-code) are:

`device=>handler()`	an empty message from *device* to *handler*
`device=>handler(handle,data,12)`	a message from *device* to *handler* with three components as content: *handle, data* and *12*.

Note that we do not attach any special significance to the first element of the message content. In many object-oriented systems this will be the name of a method to be invoked, however, our model operates on a more abstract level and can therefore be oblivious to this special semantics.* It is important that message types are defined in terms of components and not component types, because coordination operates on the level of individual components rather than their types. Consequently the domain of message types can be very large (even infinite) and thus, plainly, locations in a message space cannot be real entities requiring system resources. They, along with the notion of message spaces, are just concepts.

In order to identify interesting messages, ie. messages requiring special treatment by the coordination layer, programmers use *message patterns*. A message pattern defines a subset of the domain of message types. They typically use the type system of the underlying programming language. However, it should be noted that the type system ought to be sophisticated, with the ability to dynamically construct types from instances and not just other types. If these capabilities are not present then a separate type system must be introduced to complement the existing one. Examples of some more sophisticated message patterns are:

```
device=>handler(handle,data,12)
Device=>Handler,'special(handle,Any)+^String
Device=>handler()+Any,Device=>Device(transfer)
Any=>Any()+Any
```

The first pattern covers exactly one message. The second pattern covers all messages from components of type *Device* to components of type *Handler* or the symbolic component *special*, with at least two arguments, the first of which must be the component *handle*, the second of which can be of any type, and the remaining arguments being of a type other than *String*.* The third pattern covers all messages from components of type *Device* to the component *handler* with any number of arguments of any type, and messages between components of type *Device* with *transfer* as an argument. The fourth pattern covers all messages. As can be seen from these examples, a sophisticated type system enables the concise specification of very complex patterns. Traps do not inherently depend on such type systems though, as there are other places in the trap system where such complex decisions can be made. However, the more expressive the type system is, the less computationally expensive the introduction of traps becomes.

Having introduced the notion message types, we now view communication between two components in the following way: Messages, instead of being sent directly to their intended recipients, are stored in locations of the so-called *message space*. Locations in a message space correspond to message types, hence messages sharing the same originator, recipient and content are stored in the same location. From that

*The => in our notation should not be confused with the -> method invocation construct found in languages like *C++*. In our notation the element to the left of the arrow is the *sender*, the element to the right is the *recipient* and the arguments follow.

*Upper case identifiers in our pseudo-code denote *types*, lower case identifiers denote *variables* holding component references and identifiers prefixed with a single quote denote symbols.

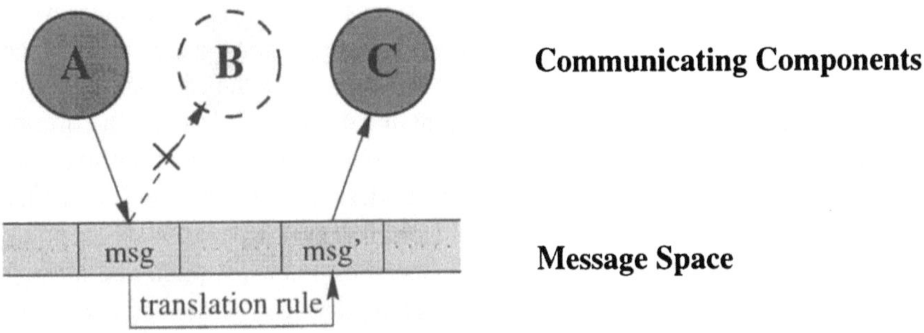

Figure 1 Message Relocation by Translation Rules

location they are then forwarded to the receiving component. It should be noted that this transformation of our view of the communication model happens on the *conceptual* level, unlike, for instance, in Linda where the tuple-space model is exposed to the programmer. The new view is transparent to the components involved; as far as the sending components are concerned they are still sending messages in the usual way and as far as the receiving components are concerned they are still receiving messages in the usual way. Conceptually though we can view things differently; the receiving components are *notified* of an 'interesting' activity.: a message that some component is trying to send to it.

2.2 Defining Traps

The new way of viewing the message-based communication model is obviously of not much use if all that happens is essentially the same as before; locations in the message space just serve as 'trampolines' that bounce messages to their target components. What we require for coordination is some means of altering the flow of messages. We achieve this by installing *translation rules* at locations in the message space. These translate the messages at the location into other messages, thus relocating them to different places in the message space and effectively intercepting the message.

The translation rule in Figure 1 translates the original message (from component A to component B) into a message that has component C as the target. The new message could be seen as having precisely the meaning presented earlier as an alternative perspective, ie. component C is notified of the attempt by component A to send a particular message to component B. Component C thus conceptually resides in the coordination layer. It could coordinate all the activities between component A and B if translation rules were specified that relocate any messages exchanged between the two components. Thereby C could act as a simple forwarder, or could accomplish arbitrarily complex coordination tasks, such as protocol translation and enforcement, interaction with other coordinators etc.

In our model, translation rules always translate messages into new messages where the content of the new message consists of a *message prefix* and the message wrapper of the original message, ie. an encapsulating component for the original message.* The recipient of the new message is a constant and does not depend on the original message. The originator of the new message is determined by a function that takes the original message as an argument. In our model there are only two such functions; one that extracts the originator from the original message and one that extracts the recipient. A translation rule thus simply specifies a new recipient and message prefix and the function to determine the originator. They can be defined completely independently of the underlying programming language since they do not perform any computation whatsoever. This keeps the semantics simple, offers opportunities for easy and efficient implementation, and enables deployment in a heterogeneous language/platform setting.

Messages resulting from the application of translation rules get stored at their appropriate locations in the message space. Hence they can be subject to further translation. Eventually the messages cannot be translated any further and are sent to their intended recipient. Since translation rules always generate messages containing an encapsulation of the original message as part of the content, the elements of the original message, such as the original recipient, can all be used in the further decision process by coordination components.

Placing a translation rule on a location in the message space is the equivalent of 'setting a trap', hence the name of this model. Instead of being bounced back and delivered to the intended recipient, a trapped message undergoes translation. The same translation rule often applies to many locations in the message space. As we noted before, the number of locations in the message space can be very large or even infinite. It is therefore impossible to install translation rules individually at every location in the message space. Hence a trap definition consists of two components:

- a *message pattern*— using the described type system for messages, this defines a subset of the domain for messages, ie. locations in the message space. Messages in the subset are caught by the trap.
- a *translation rule*— using a new recipient and message prefix, this translates it into a new message.

In our pseudo-code we define traps using a >> operator. For instance, the trap

```
Device=>Handler(handle)+Any >> logger('io-event)
```

will trap all messages sent from devices to handlers with *handle* as the first argument plus any number of further arguments of any type. It will translate these messages to messages to the component *logger*, with the symbolic component *'io-event* as

*The purpose of message wrappers is to expose messages as components in the programming language, even though messages themselves may not be components.

the first argument and the encapsulated original message as the originator. Note that message patterns are part of the type system and message wrappers can be matched against them. This enables the specification of traps that further translate a message that has already undergone some translation. For instance, messages generated by the above trap matches the pattern

```
Device=>logger('io-event,[Device=>Handler(handle)+Any]).
```

2.3 Coordination Protocol

When integrating a component into a system, the system needs to be configured in a way that translates messages sent from the component to other components into messages the other components understand and visa versa. This is accomplished by enclosing the component in a container that performs the required translation, and by defining traps that intercept messages sent from the component. Traps are applied recursively in order to translate a messages, resulting in a set of messages that logically replaces the original message. Every message in the message set is delivered to its new recipient. If the original message was a request requiring a reply then the first reply to any of the messages in the message set is sent back to the originator of the original message as the reply to the request. All further replies to messages in the message set are ignored, thus ensuring that at most one reply is returned. Typically all intercepted messages are translated into messages to the container component which in that case contains logic to perform the actual message translation. Thus the container component becomes a true wrapper around the integrated component, dealing with both the incoming and outgoing messages.

Configuration with traps is thus a function that is performed just after a message has been *sent*. By contrast, coordination is performed just before a message is *delivered*. It is concerned with ensuring that the processing of messages of an integrated component is synchronised, depending on the application logic, with the processing of messages by other components in the system. In our model, coordination is accomplished by encoding the required logic in components that receive intercepted messages. The principal decision to be made by the components is when the message should be submitted for processing to the original recipient. In order to make that decision, the coordination components need to interact with each other. This causes a software engineering problem because the coordination logic is often a composite entity whose elements are unaware of each other and hence cannot engage in any explicit interaction. This composite nature of the coordination logic is a result of the composite nature of applications — they are built out of components which each have their own coordination logic and are 'glued together' by yet more coordination logic. To overcome this problem we add a *coordination protocol* to our model that manages the interaction between coordinators transparently, ie. in a way that doesn't require coordinators to know about each other. As a result, coordinators can be implemented as state machines that perform state transition whenever an interesting event occurs and whose states corresponds to sets of constraints on occurrences of events.

2.4 Performance

Our model introduces overheads that affects performance in two different areas: message delivery and message processing. Message delivery is affected because messages need to be matched against message patterns and message translation needs to be performed. The impact of this can be reduced by use of efficient pattern matching algorithms and distribution/replication of traps between nodes. Restricting pattern definitions to allow only specification of patterns with a specific originator or recipient eliminates any performance overhead for communication between components that are not being coordinated. Since coordination usually applies to a small number of components (compared to the total number of components in the system) this significantly reduces the overall overhead.

The second area affected by our coordination model is message processing. The coordination protocol results in the delay of messages due to the overhead involved in synchronising multiple distributed coordinators. This overhead is minimised by tuning the coordination protocol in a way that minimises the number of messages required for synchronisation. Further improvements can be made by co-locating coordinators with coordinated components and by replicating coordinators. The message processing is also affected by the protocol itself since it may defer the processing of messages for longer than required by the application's coordination logic. As a result the inherent parallelism of component-based systems may not be fully exploited. The probability of a component being idle unnecessarily can be reduced at the expense of increasing the number of messages required for synchronisation and hence there is a performance trade-off between these two aspects.

3 AN EXAMPLE

We shall now demonstrate how configuration and coordination in applications can be accomplished with traps, using the well-known example of the 'Dining Philosophers'. Philosophers sit around a table with food. There is a chopstick between every two philosophers. Philosophers require both their left and right chopstick in order to eat. A chopstick can only be held by one philosopher at a time. It needs to be ensured that philosophers don't starve — we need to prevent situations of deadlock and livelock and ensure fairness. Philosophers and chopsticks are to be treated as 'given' types of components, ie. we do not have access to their source code and hence cannot modify it. Neither do we have any detailed knowledge of the components' behaviour. Thus coordinating philosophers and chopsticks in the context of Dining Philosophers is very similar to the integration/reuse of 'legacy' components in a heterogeneous distributed system, such as a middleware system. We investigate two variations of the example, with increasing degree of complexity and show how the additional complexity is primarily accommodated in an incremental fashion without the need for rewriting existing code.

3.1 Static Setting

Initially, we deal with static configuration only, ie. we create a certain number of philosophers and chopsticks and establish a configuration where philosophers are assigned chopsticks in the manner specified. We are assuming that coordination is performed by the philosophers and chopsticks themselves, which therefore have to be aware of the context they are being used in. When philosophers and chopsticks are created, the required coordinators are set up as well. After all coordination logic is in place, the philosophers are told to start eating. A philosopher attempts to pick up a chopstick by sending a `pick` message to the symbolic components `'left` or `'right`. It drops a chopstick by sending a `drop` message. We assign a coordinator to each philosopher, which installs traps that intercept the `pick` and `drop` messages of a philosopher and translate them into messages to the coordinator. Upon receipt of one of these messages the coordinator replaces the original `pick` or `drop` message with a `get` or `put` message to the actual left or right chopstick.

To facilitate reuse, philosophers and chopsticks should be completely unaware of the context in which they are being used, specifically philosophers should not require knowledge that picking up a chopstick requires coordination with other philosophers. Philosophers should be able to attempt picking up a chopstick at any time and dropping a previously picked up chopstick at any time. They can attempt to pick up both chopsticks at the same time or one after the other or pick one up and then drop it again. The only assumptions we make, for simplicity's sake, is that philosophers will not pick up a chopstick they currently hold, and will not drop a chopstick they do not currently hold. The result of this liberal approach is that a great variety of component implementations can fulfil the roles of philosophers or chopsticks. Thus there is a wide scope for reusing existing components in that role without the need for modification.

We coordinate the dining philosophers by ensuring that when a philosopher attempts to pick up the first chopstick, the request is delayed until *both* chopsticks are available. When the first chopstick is being picked up by a philosopher all requests by other philosophers to pick up the complementary chopstick are delayed. This policy ensures both freedom of deadlock and livelock as well as guaranteeing that chopsticks are only picked up by one philosopher at a time. In order to implement the coordination policy, coordinators create an auxiliary component. Traps are installed that intercept messages to the philosopher's chopsticks (cf. Figure 2). One set of traps intercepts the messages sent by the philosopher's coordinator, another set has a message pattern which matches messages to the chopsticks from *any* component. Since the latter pattern is less specific than the one of the first set of traps, these traps will intercept all messages sent to the chopsticks by other coordinators. The intercepted messages are submitted for synchronisation to the auxiliary components. The auxiliary components implement a state machine encapsulating the coordination policy by delaying `get` messages.

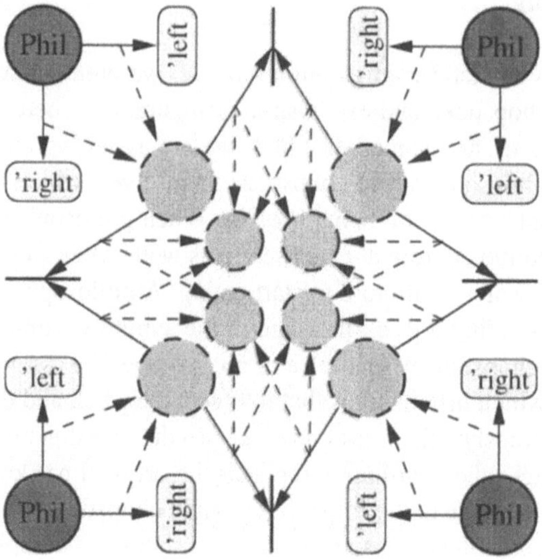

Figure 2 Coordinating the Dining Philosophers

3.2 Dynamic Change

In the previous two variations of the Dining Philosophers, the configuration of the system remained unchanged once it had been set up. However, coordination is often required in settings where components are created dynamically. We shall now demonstrate how this can be accomplished in a variation of the Dining Philosophers example in which we allow new philosophers to join the existing ones.

New philosophers are placed at the 'end' of the table, ie. next to the last philosopher. A new chopstick is created that will be shared between the new philosopher and the last philosopher. The coordinator of the last philosopher needs to be notified of the changed configuration so that it can amend its existing traps. We do this by sending it a `changeL` or `changeR` message, depending on whether the new philosopher is seated to the left or right of the last philosopher. The message contains a reference to the new chopstick and causes all existing traps of the coordinator to be removed and new traps to be installed. The resulting changes in the system configuration are illustrated in Figure 3.

Replacing a chopstick is not always safe. We cannot replace it while it is held by the philosopher in question. We therefore amend the coordinator state machine to defer the `changeL` and `changeR` message in certain states. Furthermore, it is important to initialise the coordinator of the philosopher in a way that reflects the current state, ie. which of its two chopsticks are currently held by other philosophers. We accomplish this by getting the initialisation code of the coordinator to ask the chopsticks whether they are currently being held by anyone. The traps for the coordinator are

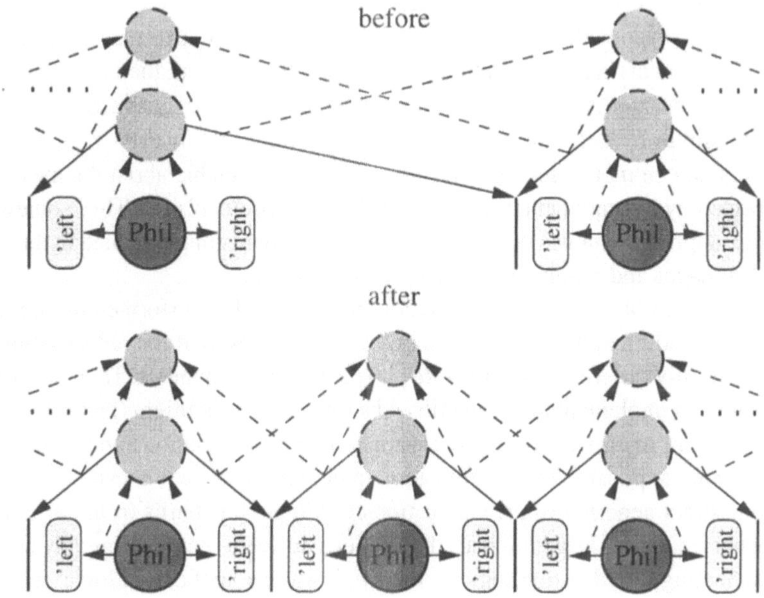

Figure 3 Introducing a new Philosopher

installed *prior* to submitting these requests, thus ensuring that the results obtained are current and won't change without involvement of the coordinator.

4 CONCLUSIONS

The model of coordination presented in this paper enables the coordination of components in open adaptive systems, independently from the underlying distributed system platforms. Some recent advances in this direction can be found in the notions of synchronisers (Frolund and Agha 1993, Frolund 1996), regulated coordination (Minsky and Ungureanu 1997) and programmable coordination media (Denti, Natali and Omicini 1997). Our approach shares many of the initial motivations and there are also some similarities between the concepts. For instance, the notion of a programmable coordination media is based on intercepting messages in a very similar way to our traps, and underlying synchronisers is a coordination protocol that is in many ways similar to ours. However, in our opinion these models are still not sufficiently open and only have very limited support for system evolution and the abstraction and reuse of coordination patterns in a truly open setting.

We can make several important observations on the model presented in this paper. Firstly, the presence of coordinating components is transparent to the components in the computation layer that are being coordinated. Coordination can be imposed without changes to these components by observing and coercing their visible behaviour. All that is required is the ability to observe (and intercept) the messages emitted from components. Secondly, coordination will only take place where it is needed. Components are free to interact with each other without the involvement of the coordination layer if the coordination layer hasn't specified that such an involvement is required, by defining suitable traps. The safety and liveness requirements of a system can be met using whatever information is available about the messages sent/expected by a component, it's internal behaviour, protocols etc. This, somewhat pragmatic, approach enables the integration of components implemented in a multitude of languages and running on a multitude of systems.

Finally, we can observe that coordination in our model is performed by ordinary components residing in the computation layer. This is a result of the reflective nature of traps. The only difference is in the *role* played by the components. Their specification, design and implementation can utilise the same tools, paradigms and languages. Hence the means of abstraction and reuse apply to our coordination logic in the same way as they are applicable to the application logic. For instance it doesn't take much effort to abstract generic resource allocation coordination patterns from our Dining Philosopher example. In addition to the obvious software engineering advantages of implementing coordination logic in the same way as application logic, we gain the ability to perform meta coordination, ie. coordinator components themselves can be subject to coordination by other components. Thus, instead of statically categorising components into those dealing with configuration/coordination and those dealing with computation, we have a dynamic relationship between components that is a result of the role they play with respect to each other at a particular point in time. This dynamic categorisation provides the means for implementing systems where coordination is an integral part of the functionality, and hence complex interactions take place between the coordination and computation layers.

Traps can easily be integrated into existing systems by modifying the communication layer. Thus all existing application code remains unaffected and the model functions in a heterogeneous setting, enabling the coordination of existing components across system boundaries. We have successfully implemented trap-based coordination in a heterogeneous setting consisting of a distributed actor-based system and a CORBA system. The model has been successfully used commercially by TECC Ltd in the design and implementation of several middleware applications (Taylor and Radestock 1998). Our current research concentrates on establishing a formal semantics for traps and their application in the definition of reusable coordination patterns.

5 ACKNOWLEDGEMENTS

We gratefully acknowledge the advice and help provided by the Distributed Software Engineering Research Section at the Imperial College Dept. of Computing and the members of the Middleware Systems Group at TECC Ltd, as well as the financial support from the EPSRC under grant ref: GR/K73282.

REFERENCES

Arbab, F.: 1996, The IWIM model for coordination of concurrent activities, *in* P. Ciancarini and C. Hankin (eds), *Coordination Languages and Models, 1st Int. Conference*, Vol. 1061 of *LNCS*, Springer Verlag.

Banatre, J.-P. and Metayer, D. L.: 1990, The Gamma model and its discipline of programming, *Science of Computer Programming* **15**, 55–77.

Banville, M.: 1996, Sonia: an adaption of Linda for coordination of activities in organizations, *in* P. Ciancarini and C. Hankin (eds), *Coordination Languages and Models, 1st Int. Conference*, Vol. 1061 of *LNCS*, Springer Verlag.

Bergstra, J. and Klint. P.: 1996, The ToolBus coordination architecture, *in* P. Ciancarini and C. Hankin (eds), *Coordination Languages and Models, 1st Int. Conference*, Vol. 1061 of *LNCS*, Springer Verlag.

Black, E., Fournier, J. and Kastner, P.: 1998, *Enterprise Application Integration: Advanced Technologies and A Sense of Process*, Aberdeen Group. `http://www.aberdeen.com`.

Blair, G. and Papathomas, M.: 1997, The case for reflective middleware, Proc. of the 3rd Cabernet Plenary Workshop `http://www.newcastle.research.ec.org/cabernet/workshops/3rd-plenary.html` .

Blair, G. and Stefani, J.: 1997, *Open Distributed Processing and Multimedia*, Addison Wesley Longman.

Callsen, C. and Agha, G.: 1994, Open heterogeneous computing in ActorSpace, *Journal of Parallel and Distributed Computing* pp. 289–300.

Denti, E., Natali, A. and Omicini, A.: 1997, Programmable coordination media, *in* D. Garlan and D. LeMetayer (eds), *Coordination Languages and Models, 2nd Int. Conference*, Springer Verlag.

Frolund, S.: 1996, *Coordinating Distributed Objects: An Actor-Based Approach to Synchronization*, MIT Press.

Frolund, S. and Agha, G.: 1993, A language framework for multi-object coordination, *ECOOP'93 Proceedings*, Vol. 707 of *LNCS*, Springer Verlag.

G. Kiczales, D. Gureasko, J. D. R.: 1991, *The Art of the Metaobject Protocol*, MIT Press.

Garlan, D. and Perry, D.: 1994, Software architecture: Practice, potential and pitfalls, *Proc. of the 16th Int. Conf. on Software Engineering*.

Garlan, D. and Shaw, M.: 1993, An introduction to software architecture, *Advances in Software Engineering and Knowledge Engineering*, Vol. 1, World Scientific Publishing Co.

Gelernter, D.: 1985, Generative communication in Linda, *ACM Transactions on Programing Languages and Systems* **7**(1), 80–112.

Holzbacher, A.: 1996, A software environment for concurrent coordinated programming, *in* P. Ciancarini and C. Hankin (eds), *Coordination Languages and Models, 1st Int. Conference*, Vol. 1061 of *LNCS*, Springer Verlag.

Magee, J., Eisenbach, S. and Kramer, J.: 1995, System structuring: A convergence of theory and practice?, *in* K. Birman, F. Mattern and A. Schiper (eds), *Theory and Practice in Distributed Systems, Proc. of the Dagstuhl Workshop*, Vol. 938 of *LNCS*, Springer Verlag.

Matsuoka, S., Wanatabe, T. and Yonezawa, A.: 1991, Hybrid group reflective architecture for object-oriented concurrent reflective programming, *in* O. Nierstrasz (ed.), *ECOOP'91 Proceedings*, LNCS, Springer-Verlag.

Minsky, N. and Ungureanu, V.: 1997, Regulated coordination in open distributed systems, *in* D. Garlan and D. LeMetayer (eds), *Coordination Languages and Models, 2nd Int. Conference*, Springer Verlag.

Mowbray, T. and Zahavi, R.: 1995, *The Essential CORBA: Using Systems Integration, Using Distributed Objects*, John Wiley & Sons.

Perry, D. and Wolf, A.: 1992, Foundations for the study of software architectures, *ACM SIGSOFT Software Engineering Notes* **17**(4), 40–52.

Pope, A.: 1997, *The CORBA Reference Guide: Understanding the Common Object Request Broker Architecture*, Addison-Wesley.

Pryce, N.: 1998, A model of interaction in concurrent and distributed systems, *Second International Workshop on Development and Evolution of Software Architectures for Product Families*.

Purtilo, J.: 1994, The POLYLITH software bus, *ACM Transactions on Programming Languages* **16**(1), 151–174.

Radestock, M. and Eisenbach, S.: 1996a, Agent-based configuration management, *Proc. of the 7th IFIP/IEEE Int. Workshop on Distributed Systems: Operation and Management*.

Radestock, M. and Eisenbach, S.: 1996b, Formalizing system structure, *Proc. of the 8th Int. Workshop on Software Specification and Design*, IEEE Computer Society Press, pp. 95–104.

Rock-Evans, R.: 1997, *Ovum Evaluates: Middleware*, Ovum. `http://www.ovum.com`.

Schill, A. (ed.): 1993, *DCE — The OSF Distributed Computing Environment*, Springer-Verlag.

Taylor, F. and Radestock, M.: 1998, TECCware product definition, *Technical report*, Trans Enterprise Computer Communications Ltd. `http://www.tecc.co.uk`.

6 BIOGRAPHY

Matthias Radestock is chief systems architect at TECC Ltd, a software company specialising in internet and middleware technology. He is a part-time Ph.D. student at Imperial College.

Susan Eisenbach is a senior lecturer at Imperial College. She is currently principal investigator on the EPSRC Multi-media Network Application BECALM project, where she works on language design for large-scale distributed languages suitable for multi-media applications and co-investigator on the EPSRC Systems Engineering project SLURP where she works on the semantics of the Java programming language.

Architecturing and Configuring Distributed Application with Olan

R.Balter[1], L.Bellissard[2], F.Boyer[1], M.Riveill[3], J.-Y.Vion-Dury[4]
SIRAC project, INRIA Rhône Alpes
655, Avenue de l'Europe F-38330 Montbonnot, France
e-mail: Luc.Bellissard@inrialpes.fr,
Tel: +33 4 76 61 52 78 Fax: +33 4 76 61 52 52

Abstract

Middleware platforms are today solutions to the problem of designing and implementing distributed applications. They provide facilities for heterogeneous software components to communicate remotely, according to various interaction model, for example client server communication or asynchronous message passing. However, middleware platforms, like message busses or object request brokers, hardly provide tools for the design, configuration and installation of complex software architectures. This paper presents the Olan environment which primary objective is the description of complex architecture, their configuration according to application requirements and the deployment on heterogeneous distributed environments. The Olan environment is based on an Architecture Description Language where the application is considered as a hierarchy of interconnected software components. A set of software engineering tools assist the application designer in his task of wrapping existing software modules into components which are in turned interconnected through various communication models and finally assembled together according to specific configuration criteria. At run time, a set of system services in charge of automating the installation of the components and their communication channels on a given middleware platform, thus facilitating the overall deployment process of the global application.

Keywords

Distributed software architecture, component programming, connectors

---

[1] Université Joseph Fourier
[2] Institut National Polytechnique de Grenoble
[3] Université de Savoie
[4] Rank Xerox Research Center – 6, Chemin de Maupertuis 38260 Meylan - France

1 INTRODUCTION

Middleware technologies are adopted increasingly in software development projects whenever some kind of mechanisms are required to enable remote communication between heterogeneous software components. Among the numerous available middleware, Object Request Brokers such as OMG's CORBA (OMG, 1995) or Microsoft's DCOM (Rogerson, 1997), are the leading references in the context of industrial development, but other mechanisms such as software busses (Reiss, 1990) or message queuing systems are also worth to be considered.

Basically, an ORB-like system provides features for the remote access to heterogeneous software. Integration of existing applications is realized with the separation of the core implementation and the interface. Interfaces are described in an homogeneous way with an IDL (Interface Description Language) independently of the programming language or the runtime system implementation. At runtime, each middleware platform provide a specific communication pattern; client server synchronous interactions in case of ORBs or anonymous communications based on asynchronous message passing in case of message queues or message busses.

In both cases, such middleware approach suffer from the lack of tools for describing the overall application architecture and to configure the set of software components according to the operational environment. In addition, interoperability between components supported by different middleware is difficult to achieve as it requires for the programmer the implementation of specific gateways.

The goal of the Olan environment is to provide a coherent basis for the construction, configuration and deployment of distributed applications. This environment relies on an Architecture Definition Language (ADL) (Allen, 1994) (Kramer, 1989) (Magee, 1994) (Shaw, 1995) which describes an application as a set of software components connected through communication objects called connectors. A key idea behind connectors is to separate the description of the components from that of their communication channels with other components. This should allow more flexibility as communications between components can be (re)configured independently from the components, according to functional dependencies or underlying middleware constraints. Compare to other ADL (Purtilo, 1994) (Magee, 1994) (Shaw, 1995) the Olan environment tries to provide an architectural view as close as possible to the executable image, in particular concerning the use of the communication services.

The Olan environment addresses four issues:

- The integration of legacy software within an application by wrapping them into components,
- The encapsulation of the middleware communication mechanisms in specific objects called connectors,
- The architecture definition, in terms of a hierarchy of interconnected components,
- The deployment of the application (i.e. components and connectors) on a distributed system. Deployment refers to the placement of application components, their installation on nodes and the set up of communication

channels between components according to the interconnections properties contained in the architecture description.

Section 2 outlines the main features of the Olan Configuration Language (OCL), the architecture definition language of the Olan environment. Section 3 describes the main functions of the Olan Configuration Machine (OCM), the system service that enables the deployment and installation of applications. Finally, section 4 presents the implementation of the OCM.

2 THE OLAN CONFIGURATION LANGUAGE

The Olan Configuration Language is an Architecture Definition Language specially designed for distributed applications. The targeted applications are in particular those involving multiple users in a distributed environment that cooperate together while using their favorite software, not necessarily designed to work remotely (Bellissard, 1996) Those applications require from the configuration language the ability to:

- integrate in an homogeneous way heterogeneous software components,
- have them distributed in various way across the networked computers according to users connections, and
- adapt the communication between components according to the designers' preferences, the components distribution and the middleware characteristics.

The design of OCL was initially inspired from Darwin(Magee, 1994) and its notion of hierarchically interconnected components. However, the dynamic behavior specification included in Darwin, as well as the limitation to specify communication properties, have lead us to incorporate new abstractions that will be detailed in this section. OCL defines the abstraction of connectors, representing the objects that rule the communication between components. The following sections will present the various features of OCL through an outlook of the required properties inherent to the targeted applications: the facilities to integrate legacy software, to define evolving architectures, and to distribute software components in a flexible way.

2.1 Integration of software

Primitive components are the unit of software integration. They are defined with an interface that describes the requirements and the provisions of the component. Thus the functional dependencies of the component with the outside world are shown at the interface level. The implementation part specifies what kind of software is encapsulated and where to get the information to have access to it. Primitive components are the basic bricks of an application because they integrate the legacy software modules. The other abstractions of OCL are mainly purposed for architectural issues.

Component Interface

The interface part describes the services that a component provides to other components, along with the services it requires for its execution. Services are described in terms of their signatures in the Olan Interface Language (OIL) which is a syntactic extension of IDL. As interfaces are expected to reflect as much as possible the behavior of the encapsulated software, OIL provides a specific type system which allows to express both the data flow and control flow constraints associated to services.

A specific OIL data type mapping is defined for several programming languages (actually C, C++, Java and Python). This mapping allows translating the data into a pivot format used to perform dynamic conversions between connected services which types can potentially mismatch.

From the point of view of the control flows, the types of provided services defined by OIL are divided in two parts: the classical services, intended to be called synchronously, and the event-based services which can be executed asynchronously in reply to a notification. Respectively, OIL defines two kinds of request that can be made by a component: synchronous service requests, and event submissions. This is summarized in **Table 1**.

Table 1 Types of Services

Services	*Data flow*	*Control flow*
Provide ●	in/out parameters	No specific constraints (usually executed synchronously, like procedure calls)
React ■	in parameters	The encapsulated implementation contains an execution flow that handles the service processing in an asynchronous way.
Require ○	in/out parameters	The encapsulated implementation is designed for synchronous external calls (e.g. procedure call)
Notify □	in parameters	The encapsulated implementation is designed for asynchronous external calls (e.g. event notification)

Exhibiting this information at the interface level is very useful since it characterizes the behavior of components outputs and entry points. In addition, such distinction has led us to define an operational semantics of the language as well as tools to check the validity of component compositions (Viondury, 1997)

```
typedef sequence <*, char> seq;
Interface listBoxItf {
     provide init();
     // services to add, remove or reverse the video of an entry
     provide addEntry(in seq entryContent);
     ...
     // notifications raised when the user manipulates an entry
     notify userAddEntry(in seq entryContent);
     ...};
```

A simplified example of a component interface, inspired from one of our experiment, is presented above. The interface reflects the notifications and the services provided by a Python module which manages a `listbox` widget. This module has been integrated in a distributed application from which are taken the different examples given in this paper.

Component Implementation

The component's implementation directly maps the interface specification to the integrated pieces of code. Primitive implementations are made of modules or classes, each of them referencing an integrated pieces of software, either a program source, a library, or an executable. Each module or class is typed according to the kind of software. Modules directly make references to a list of functions whereas classes enable the instantiation of an object when the primitive component is part of the application. For example, modules can be of type « C » or « Python » : a « C » module integrates either C source files or a library, a « Python » module integrates Python source code. If the available classes are written in « C++ » or « Java », the primitive components are built from their respective source files. A primitive implementation may contain several modules or classes of the same type. The definition of modules or classes is also described from an interface and it contains information about the location of the files representing the program, the library or the executable, as well as options for their inclusion in the application.

```
module "Python" listBoxMod : listBoxItf {
         path: "${OLAN-SRC}"+"/examples/URL";
         sourceFile : "listboxMod.py";
};
```

The integration of software is greatly helped by the OCL compiler as we will see later. The idea is to capture all incoming and outgoing function calls and use the previously mentioned pivot format. Then, calls from the modules gets out to a component object included in the runtime structures of the application. On the opposite, calls to the software modules gets first to the component object, that knows how to adapt the desired function call to the encapsulated module.

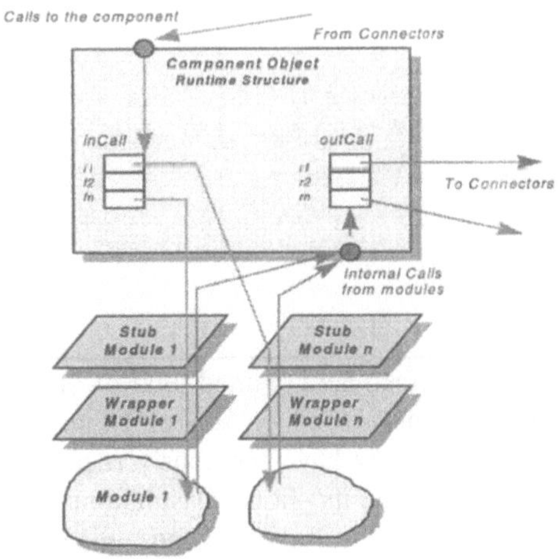

Figure 1. Software Integration at Runtime.

Figure 1 shows how things are working at runtime. In between the component object and the various modules, is the *stub*, that homogenize parameters format, and the *wrapper* that knows how to have access to the modules (if the call comes from the component) or the component object (if the call comes from the module). Stub and wrappers are automatically generated by the compiler. According to the kind of modules (or classes), the work to be done by the programmer to have his code integrated, ranges from almost nothing to the explicit redirection of the outgoing calls to the wrapper. The runtime architecture of components and modules will be detailed later in section 3.2.

2.2 Architecture Definition

The definition of an application architecture is basically made of the specification of the instantiation of components and the specification of their interconnection, i.e. the dependencies between required and provided services of their interfaces. The specification of components interconnection can be realized within the implementation of a particular kind of components, the composite.

Application Structure

Composite components are intended to describe the application's structure. They own an interface and an implementation like the primitive ones. The differences between both kind of components lies in the implementation part. A composite implementation contains the specification of a group of components of both kind, that realize the interface of the composite. In addition, the communication requirements between those sub-components is also specified at this level. The interesting facts about composite components is that the application designer can group components that may have some common properties, like the machine which is intended to host them.

```
Implementation URLNotifier
          uses ListBoxItf, URLMgrItf, URLEditorItf
{
   URLMgr = instance URLMgrItf;// mgt of the URLs of interest
   ListBox = instance ListBoxItf;// mgt of the user itf
   URLEditor = instance URLEditorItf;// edition of URLs

// expression of interactions between components (see 2.2.2)
  startURLNotifier() => URLMgrItf.init()
  URLMgr.initGUI() => ListBoxItf.init()
  ListBox.userAddEntry(URL) => URLMgr.addURL(URL)
  URLMgr.editURL(URL) => URLEditor.edit(URL)
...
}
```

As an example, the composite component described here (named `URLNotifier`) was used in a distributed application that we developed on top of Olan. This application warns users when some of the URL they have previously registered, points to a document that has changed since its last consultation. The `URLNotifier` component is composed of three sub-components, managing respectively the graphical user interface, the list of URLs of current interest, and the edition of a document associated with an URL (this last component encapsulates a Netscape browser). Let us notice that both the declaration of components instances as well as their interconnections or the interconnections between the composite interface and the components' instance are part of the implementation of the composite component.

The application itself is also a composite component which main feature is to be the root of the component hierarchy.

Interconnections

Interconnections specify how components communicate with each other. By the term « how », we refer to the functional dependencies between interface services, but also to the specification of the data flows, the execution flows, the communication protocol and the runtime mechanism intended to perform the communication. One particular object is dedicated to interactions : the connector.

Connectors are the abstractions in the architecture that specify the interconnections between a set of components. A set of predefined connectors are offered to the application architect (c.f. **Table 2**). Connectors are named in a unique way, each of which corresponding to a communication pattern and an implementation on top of a middleware platform.

From **Table 2**, one can notice that synchronous and asynchronous connectors both use ILU; an ORB, for remote communication between objects. However, creating another connector, with the same communication pattern but a different implementation (e.g. sunRpc or TCP/IP sockets), is possible. From the application architecture point of view, there is no difference, as long as the new connector provides a remote synchronous call.

Table 2. Some predefined Connectors.

OCL Name	*Caller*	*Callee*	*Protocol*	*Implementation*
SyncCall	1 require	1 provide	Synchronous communication Compatible signature or data flow transformation	Local: method call IPC: ILU method call Remote: ILU method call
AsyncCall	1 notify	1 react	Asynchronous Communication Compatible signature or data flow transformation	Local: method call from separate threads IPC : ILU asynch. method call Remote : ILU asynch. method call
RandSync Call	1 require	1 to n provide	Like syncCall, single randomly chosen callee	like syncCall

One important property of connectors, in addition to the above roles, is to manage component heterogeneity and to adapt the control and data flows traversing a set of components. For example, control flow adaptation may be required when one component, requiring a service asynchronously, is bound to another component, providing this service through a synchronous call. The OCL compiler handles such properties and specializes the connector for execution. Data flow adaptation is also an integration problem that often arises when the designer interconnects services with different signatures, notably containing different parameter types. In some cases, the adaptation can be derived by the compiler automatically (e.g. from type string to sequence of char) but it is good practice to specify it within the OCL description.

2.3 Distribution

In most architecture definition languages, the distribution of components is restricted to the placement on a named computer node (Magee, 1994) (Purtilo, 1994) (Shaw, 1995). However, when dealing with the application architecture, an important issue is the distribution of components in terms of processes. Darwin overpasses this issue by considering that every primitive component is associated to one activity (a thread). UniCon goes one step forward, allowing to explicit the association between a component and a process. However, only components affected to processes may be distributed, resulting in a per process basis for the distribution

The ideas developed in OCL are slightly different. The targeted applications mainly imply the cooperation of several users. Placing components in a distributed environment not only deals with the node of execution but also with the user for which the component can execute. In addition, since industrial distributed environments evolve, we have tried to allow the application designers or administrators specifying the placement policies themselves, avoiding the explicit naming of nodes.

The underlying abstraction for placing components is the *context*. A context corresponds to one (or several) execution space that belongs to a single user, on a single machine for a single application. Then, the distribution specification indicates in which context the component should be executed.

Management attributes

At the OCL level, the distribution and placement policies are described in a special section attached to a component. A policy is a predicate involving the *management attributes* of the component. A management attribute, associated to some component, corresponds to a physical resource that may be used at runtime. The predicate expression is evaluated when the installation of components takes place in order to find a hosting node.

Management attributes are made of several fields, each of which enables to characterize the resource. So far, the existing attributes are `Node` and `Owner`, which respectively enable to choose the execution host and the owner of the component execution.

```
management attribute Node {
   string name ;        // DNS name
   string IPAdr ;       // IP address
   string os;           // OS type
            (posix, nt, ..)
   ... }
```

```
management attribute Owner {
   string name;              // user name
   long uid;                 // user id
   ... };
```

Distribution policies

Policies to express the placement of components are combination of predicates on the management attributes. Such predicates can use various operators (boolean operations, operations on strings, integers, etc.) in order to denote a matching expression for the management attribute which has to be evaluated to true when installing the application.

```
Management URLNotifierMgt: URLNotifierImpl
{
  // All components on the domain .inrialpes.fr
  Host.name == "*.inrialpes.fr";
  // Co-locate the URLMgr and ListBox components
  URLMgr.Host.name == ListBox.Host.name  ;
};

Management URLMgrMgt: URLMgrImpl {
  // Locate the component which accesses the WWW servers on the local WWW server host
  URLPoller.Host.name == "pukapuka.inrialpes.fr";
}
```

The above example illustrates the use of distribution policies in the *URLNotifier* application. The component in charge of managing the list of the desired URL (*URLMgr*) should be collocated with the component of the user interface (*ListBox*), because these two components heavily communicate with each other. However, the *URLMgr* component uses a specialized sub-component (named *URLPoller*) for polling URL changes through communications with the WWW servers. We have decided to place the *URLPoller* sub-component on the node which hosts the WWW server of the local environment, in order to reduce significantly the network traffic.

3 ARCHITECTURE OF THE CONFIGURATION MACHINE

Once an OCL application is correctly described, the compiler generates the appropriate classes of components, collections and connectors needed by the application. These are placed in a distributed repository. The compiler also generates a script (called the *Configuration Machine script*) that contains orders and guidelines for the initial deployment of the application on a given distributed environment.

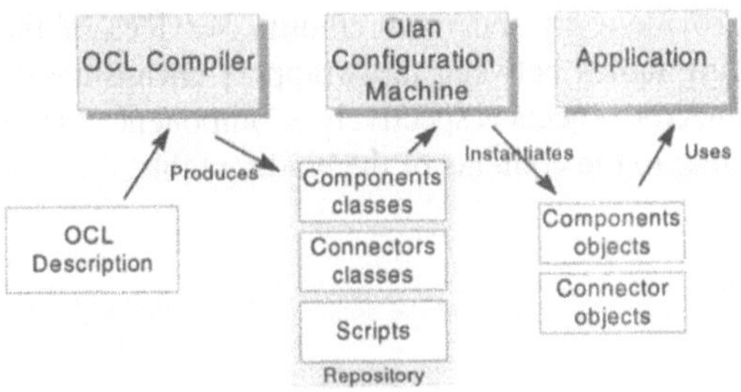

Figure 2. The Olan Development Cycle.

The Olan Configuration Machine is in charge of instantiating the appropriate execution structures (components and collections, connectors) in compliance with a given Configuration Machine Script. It relies on two main abstract machines (libraries) : the *Component library* providing features for managing component and collection structures and the *Connector library*, in charge of the connectors. The Configuration Machine itself is implemented on top of a CORBA-compliant ORB (Xerox ILU (Xerox, 1996)) for its internal management of the distribution.

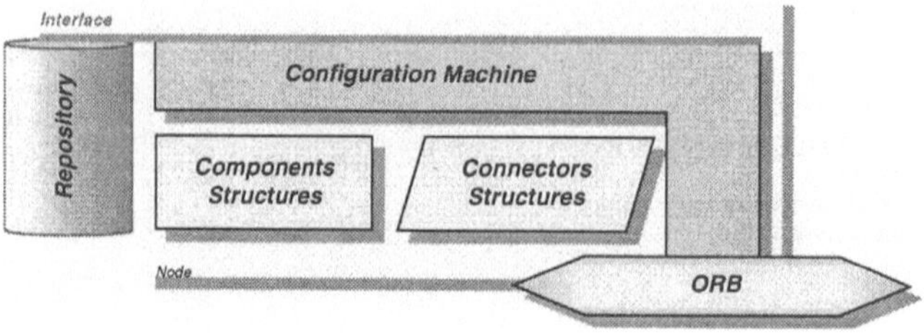

Figure 3. Olan Runtime Architecture.

This section presents the basic execution model of components interconnected with connectors. Then we will briefly introduce the role and functions of the configuration Machine, which is in charge of deploying and installing the components and connectors structures on a distributed environment.

3.1 Instantiation of Component Structures

We have already introduced the fact that components correspond to execution structures at runtime. They are composed of integrated software modules and a specific object that enables the communication of the encapsulated code with other components (cf. **Figure 1**). Since the Olan runtime is implemented in Python, these objects derive from Python classes. The main characteristic of such an object is to be configurable and its purpose is to allow dynamic positioning of the interconnections with other components as well as dynamic loading of integrated software.

Figure 4 illustrates the structure of such objects as well as the interconnection principles with the connector objects.

Component object includes two tables, `inCall` and `outCall`, indexed respectively by the name of the provide/react and require/notify services of the interface. Those tables act as binding tables between the wrappers encapsulating the integrated software and the connector objects respectively. Component objects trap every call and redirect it according to the contents of the binding table.

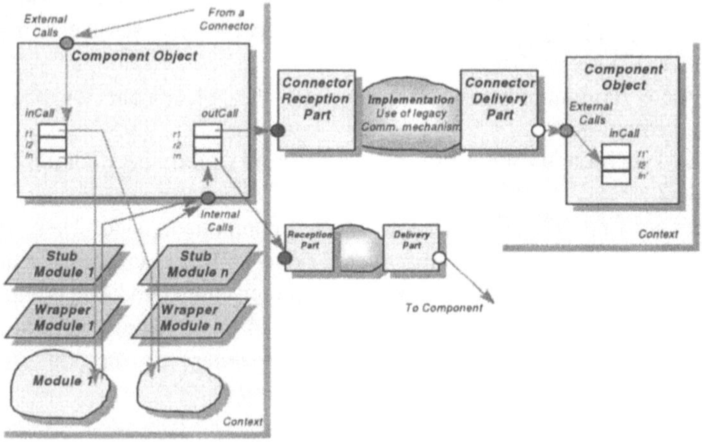

Figure 4. Runtime Interconnection Implementation.

Let us notice that a primitive component, as illustrated, is contained in a single context. A context may be a single process if the encapsulated software can be mapped in one component object context (i.e. can be directly accessed by the Python component object), otherwise it may be needed to have another process that contains the mechanisms to have the component object in Python dialog with its software modules. For example, when trying to have Java classes integrated in a components, we have to launch a Java interpreter from the Python object and have both processes communicate (in our case, UNIX domain sockets are used). A context, in this case, may comprise several processes. When trying to integrate executable software (like a UNIX command), the same principle applies.

3.2 Instantiation of Connector Structures

The main role of connectors is to bind a set of potential senders to a set of potential receivers for communication schemes based on service request or event notification broadcast. A connector is represented by two main kinds of Python objects: the *service adapters* (resp. notification) and the *sender/receivers* objects (c.f.
Figure 5).

The *adapters* represent both the entry and exit points for the connector structure. On a sender side, they provide a function that allows a given component to initiate a communication as described in OCL. On a receiver side, they have the ability to call a given function (representing either a provided service or a notification handler), provided by the component. The adapters are also in charge of executing the user-level code which may have been added to the connector description (e.g. code for data flow adaptation).

The *sender/receiver objects* are in charge of :

- encapsulating the use of the communication system,

- handling the possible control flow translations (e.g. when a sender asks for an asynchronous service request while the receivers provide the service in a synchronous way), and
- handling remote communication according to the placement of the interconnected components.

Let us detail the synchronous procedure call connector, which specification is described in **Table 2**.

Service adapters are first created on each connected components side. Then, if those adapters are on the same context no *sender/receiver object* is created ; both adapters communicate through a method call. In any other case, two objects, the `SCConnSender` and the `SCConnReceiver` are created. In this example, both are ILU objects and they exchange an ILU reference in order to communicate remotely. Then they are linked with their respective *service adapter*.
Information flowing through those objects is already marshaled data (done by the stub at the primitive component level). However, if data transformation code is specified at the OCL level, this code generated by the OCL compiler is inserted in between the sender's *service adapter* and the *sender object*. This code unmarshals parameters, applies data transformation and marshals the new result.

This example is rather simple because the `syncCall` connector handles a 1 to 1 connection. In case of a 1-N connection schema, the *sender/receiver object* structure is somehow more complicated because there must be some treatment for the delivery of the various results to the component that initiated the communication.

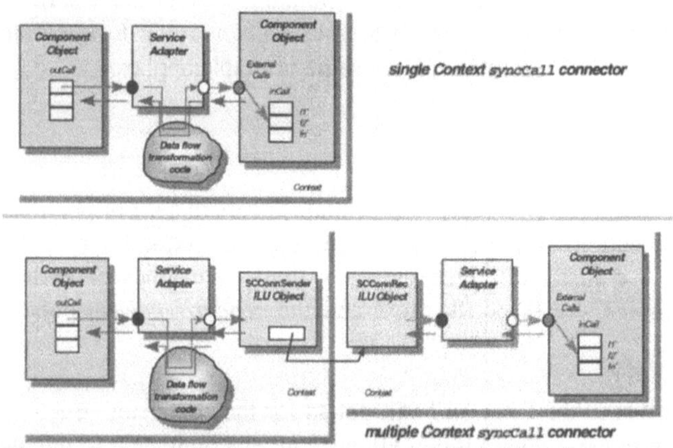

Figure 5. syncCall Connector execution Structures.

3.3 Deployment of an Application

The deployment and installation of an application is performed by the configuration machine. The initial deployment is performed through the execution of the *Configuration Machine Script* produced by the compiler. This script contains calls to primitives of the configuration machine which main functions are :

- the creation of components and collections,
- the creation of connector instances, and
- the binding between connector and component instances as described in the previous section.

Any application that should be installed is a hierarchy of components whose leaves are primitive components. This hierarchy is derived from the OCL description, and is encoded as a tree. The deployment algorithm is based on a depth first traversal of the tree. For each component, the configuration machine seeks for a node where the component can be installed according to the distribution constraints expressed in OCL. If no assignment is possible, the configuration machine reports the unfeasibility of the deployment to the administrator. Once primitive components are installed, their enclosing components are created. Interconnections require the instantiation of connector objects that are replicated or not according to the placement of sub-components as described in the previous section.

The execution of the application may then be started through an execution script generated by the compiler. This script allows launching of new applications or the connection to a running application, thus enabling the cooperation of multiple users using the same application.

4 IMPLEMENTATION AND EXPERIMENTS

The implementation of the OCL compiler and the Configuration Machine has been made in Python. Such a language is of a particular interest for rapid prototyping due to the lack of compilation phase, the dynamic typing, reflexivity features, easy manipulation of complex structures such as lists, dictionaries, etc. However, the price to be paid is related to the poor performance of such mechanism. The configuration machine is also implemented in Python and uses ILU, a CORBA compliant Object Request Broker. ILU's purpose is for the internal communication of the configuration between remote nodes. For example, when the machine tries to find a node where a component can be installed, communication between potential hosts are triggered through the use of the ORB. However, ILU is not used for the execution of the application, except if the architecture contains explicit use of a connector that communicate remotely with ILU. The component and connector structures are also implemented in Python, only stubs or wrappers may be partially in Python and in the language of the integrated software modules. Finally, the implementation of the communication inside connectors depends on the kind of connector which is used. For instance, there can be multiple implementations of a remote synchronous call: one using sockets, another one sun RPC, a third one using ILU.

As one can notice, good performances of the runtime system were not aimed at all. The choice of the various implementation languages and tools were motivated by the will to prototype rapidly a complex system, where a compiler and a runtime system are needed. The experience drawn from our experiments mainly concerns the ease of application configuration, the flexibility of the deployment and the transparent utilization of a distributed environment with no particular competence from the programmer.

Besides the examples used throughout the paper and some other applications (Bellissard, 1995), we have also experimented the Olan environment on an electronic mail application which goal is to help inexperienced users to easily configure some automatic treatments on their incoming messages with ready-to-use components.

The main feedback of the experiments confirms the difficulty to reengineer existing application. First, an application implementation is not always clearly separated in modules, and second, the components are not often designed to work in a distributed environment. The Olan environment is not supposed to answer directly to this problem, however the work of redesigning the application into a set of interconnected components is greatly assisted by the compiler. The communication and the distribution become completely separated from the core implementation, thus allowing non-specialists to build rather complex distributed applications from their own set of components and to produce various distributed configurations of the same application. As a promising consequence, reengineered applications have gained in reliability by using the efficiency of the automatically generated communication and distribution mechanisms.

The second feedback is the necessity of having graphical tools to assist non specialists in using a configuration language. We have always been designing the OCL language with graphical conventions in mind (Bellissard, 1996).

5 CONCLUSION

This paper has described the Olan Configuration Language (OCL), an architecture definition language for distributed applications design and construction. The idea behind the design of this language relies on the notion of "programming in the large", where the architecture definition of an application is separated from the core implementation of individual software components. By providing a clear separation between communication requirements and components implementation, such an approach brings flexibility in the configuration process of inter-components communication.

Compared to the related works, the main contributions of our proposal are the following.

- The integration of heterogeneous pieces of software through a uniform component-based model.
- The coordination of components through a generic connector model, which allows the application's designer to separate the communication aspects from the components, as well as to specialize some predefined schemes of communications.
- The integration of middleware platform specific features within the abstraction of the connector.

In addition, an application described with OCL can be derived into an executable image with the help of the OCL compiler. This executable image relies on the Configuration Machine which primary goal is to deploy components on a distributed execution environment, configure the interconnection between components and transparently handle remote communications with the connector objects.

Compared to « traditional » ADLs, the emphasis is placed on three aspects: the integration of existing code, the provision of configurable connectors and the expression of the software components distribution. Code integration is greatly eased by : (1) the use of a type system that brings flexibility when adapting components which are not necessarily designed to work together, (2) the use of complementary information that exports at the interface definition level the encapsulated execution model of components, and (3) by the automated generations of stubs and wrappers that enable the access to the core implementations of components written in different programming languages.

The distribution of components is achieved at the language level with the specification of placement constraints of the application components, which is more flexible than simple static node assignment. At runtime, a deployment algorithm ensures a correct installation of the application according to these constraints.

Acknowledgments

The authors would like to thank discussions with their colleagues of the SIRAC Project. We gratefully acknowledge the CNET for their financial support.

6 REFERENCES

Allen, R. and Garlan, D., (1994) Formal Connectors, Technical Report CMU-CS-94-115, School of Computer Science, Carnegie Mellon University, Pittsburgh, PA 15213.

Bellissard, L, Ben Atallah, S., Kerbrat, A. and Riveill, M., (1995) Component-based Programming and Application Management with Olan, *Object Based Distributed and Parallel Computation Franco-Japan Workshop (OBDPC'95)*, Eds. Briot J.P., Geib J.M., Yonezawa A., LNCS 1107, Springer Verlag.

Bellissard, L., Ben Atallah, S., Boyer, F. and Riveill, M., (1996) Distributed Application Configuration, *in Proc. of the 16th IEEE Intn'l Conference on Distributed Computing Systems (ICDCS'96),* Hong Kong, 579-85.

Garlan, D., and Shaw, M., (1993) An Introduction to Software Engineering, *in Advances in Software Engineering and Knowledge Engineering*, Vol. I, Eds. Ambriola and Tortora, World Scientific Publishing Co.

Kramer, J., Magee, J. and Sloman, M., (1989) Constructing Distributed Systems in Conic, *IEEE Transactions on Software Engineering*, Vol.15 (No.6), 663-75.

Magee, J., Dulay, N. and Kramer, J., (1994) A Constructive Development Environment for Parallel and Distributed Programs, *Proc. of the Intn'l Workshop on Configurable Distributed Systems*, Pittsburgh.

Luckham, D. C. and Vera, J., (1995) An Event-Based Architecture Definition Language, *IEEE Trans. Software Engineering*, vol.SE-21(N.9), 717-34.

Object Management Group, (1995) The Common Object Request Broker: Architecture and Specification, Revision 2.0.

Purtilo, J. M., (1994) The POLYLITH Software Bus, *ACM TOPLAS*, Vol.16 (No.1), 151-74.

Reiss, S., (1990) Connecting Tools Using Message Passing in the FIELD Environment, *IEEE Software*, 57-66.

Rogerson, D., (1997) Inside COM", Microsoft Press, Redmond WA.

Shaw, M., DeLine, R., Klein, D. V., Ross, T. L., Toung, D. M. and Zelesnik, G., (1995) Abstractions for Software Architecture and Tools to Support Them, *IEEE Trans. Software Engineering*, vol.SE-21(N.4), 314-35.

Vion-Dury, J.-Y., Bellissard, L. and Marangozov, V., (1997) A Component Calculus for Modeling the Olan Configuration Language, *in Proc. Of COORDINATION'97*, Berlin, Germany.

Xerox Co., (1996) ILU 2.0 Reference Manual, Xerox Parc, Palo Alto, CA.

7 BIOGRAPHY

Roland Balter is a Professor in Computer Science at the University Joseph Fourier (Grenoble). Roland is currently head of Sirac, a joined laboratory between the University and INRIA. His research activity is concerned with distributed systems and applications

Luc Bellissard is currently a teaching assistant at the Ecole National Polytechnique de Grenoble. Luc graduated from ENSIMAG in 1993 and has defended its PhD thesis in 1997. He is the main contributor of the OLAN environment.

Fabienne Boyer is a lecturer at Université Joseph Fourier (Grenoble). She graduated from the ENSIMAG in 1990 and defended her PhD thesis in 1994. She is a full time contributor of the Olan project.

Michel Riveill is a Professor at Université de Savoie, Chambéry since 1993. Michel has published several papers in the area of distributed systems, languages and programming environments for distributed systems, systems support for CSCW.

Jean-Yves Vion-Dury, holds an engineering degree in CS from Le Conservatoire National des Arts et Métiers, Paris,1993. He will defend soon a PhD in CS, and works as a Research Engineer at the Xerox Research Center Europe, Grenoble.

A Framework for Systematic Synthesis of Transactional Middleware

Apostolos Zarras, Valérie Issarny
INRIA/IRISA
Campus de Beaulieu, 35042 Rennes Cédex, FRANCE
email: {zarras, issarny}@irisa.fr

Abstract

Transactions are contracts that guarantee a consistent, transparent, individual system state transition and their use is widespread in many different kinds of computing systems. Some well known standards (e.g. CORBA) include the specification of services that provide transactional properties. In this paper, we present a formal method for the systematic synthesis of transactional middleware based on the combination of the aforementioned services. The synthesis of transactional middleware is based on (*i*) the formal specification of transactional properties and (*ii*) stub code generation.

Keywords

Atomicity, Consistency, Durability, Isolation, Middleware, Transaction

1 INTRODUCTION

The construction of a large-scale distributed software system is a complex task that involves design decisions relating to different aspects of the system's behavior. In particular, the developer has to address the provision of the system's functional (i.e. algorithmic aspect) and non-functional (i.e. quality of service with which the system's functions are performed) properties. While the provision of functional properties is system-specific, the one of non-functional properties appertains to the underlying Distributed Processing Environment (DPE) and is common to a variety of systems. The concern of improving software quality and reducing the duration of system development has led to a number of standardization efforts that propose specification of middleware services that are common to various systems.

In the framework of the ASTER project * at IRISA/INRIA, we are investigating design and development methods that aid the developer to select the appropriate services and integrate them within the system implementation (Issarny *et al.* 1998). In this paper, we focus on the treatment of non-functional properties relating to transactional processing, as they are among the primary concerns in building large-scale software systems. Transactions provide the warranty for a consistent transparent, individual system state transition (Gray 1981), properties which are indispensable in both centralized and distributed computing systems (e.g. databases, telecommunications, CAD/CAM, operating systems). However, the characteristics of those systems vary a lot and the transaction concept had to adapt with respect to them. As a result, a variety of transaction models (Moss 1982, Pu *et al.* 1988) were developed in order to deal with the newly imposed requirements (e.g. performance, cooperation). Moreover, some well known processing standards (e.g. CORBA (OMG 1995), ODP (ISO/IEC 1994)) include the specification of services that provide transactional properties (e.g. locking, persistence, recovery). However, to ascertain whether or not some required transactional properties are supported by existing standard services is a tedious task. For instance, let us consider the CORBA *Object Transaction Service* (OTS) which provides atomicity but whose support for the nested transaction model is optional in the standard service specification. Then, the developer must be aware of both the variety of standard services installed in the environment and of the particular features provided by their implementations. Furthermore, it is often the case that the property provided by a standard service should be extended in order to meet the current system's requirements. For example, the CORBA *Concurrency Control Service* (CCS) provides locking. In order to obtain the well known two-phase locking protocol, the developer must use the service in a certain way. Finally, there are cases where the non-functional properties provided by standard services should be refined. For instance, the ODP Transaction Function does not define the exact correctness criterion that guarantees a (conflict-)serializable execution. Discharging the developer from the arduous responsibility to manage such details at the low level of implementation is our motive. Towards that goal, we are proposing a systematic procedure that takes as input the transactional requirements for a given system and that takes in charge the selection of corresponding middleware services and their combination to build a middleware platform, customized to the system's needs.

This paper introduces our method for synthesizing transactional middleware from a system description including the specification of transactional non-functional properties. Section 2 gives the core elements of the method. Our method is exemplified

*See URL: http://www.irisa.fr/solidor/work/aster.html.

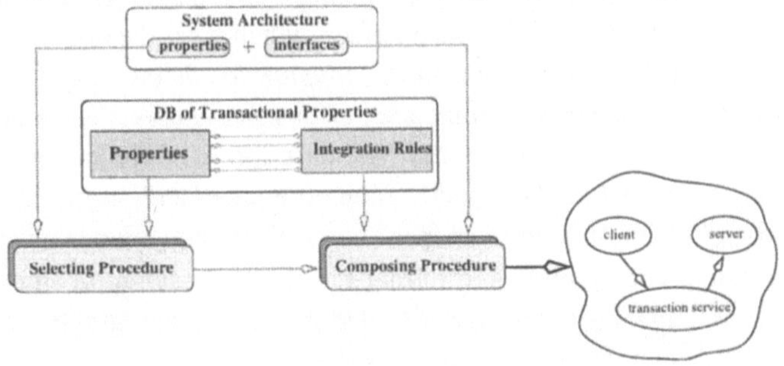

Figure 1 Synthesizing transactional middleware.

in Section 3 in the CORBA framework. Finally, conclusions are given in Section 4, summarizing our contribution and presenting a comparison with related work.

2 SYNTHESIS METHODOLOGY

The basic constituents of our method for synthesizing transactional middleware are (see Figure 1):

- A declarative language, known as *Architecture Description Language* or ADL for short (Shaw *et al.* 1995), for the description of systems software architectures. The ADL allows the developer to describe the gross organization of his software system in terms of the interconnection of functional components (i.e. computation unit or data store) defined by their interface. The ADL further supports the specification of transactional properties either provided or required by software components.
- A *selecting procedure* that takes as input a set of transactional requirements, reflecting the demand for a particular transactional model, and that verifies whether the requirements are supported by existing middleware services.
- A *composing procedure* that combines the middleware services meeting the system's transactional requirements with the system's functional components.

2.1 Specifying Transactional Requirements

The specification of transactional requirements relies on: (*i*) the description of software architectures and (*ii*) the formal specification of transactional properties used for systematic selection of middleware services. We examine these two issues in turn.

Describing system architectures

Using our ADL, the software architecture of a system is described in terms of the *component* and *configuration* abstractions. A *component* abstractly defines a unit of computation or data store in terms of its interface, which gives the operations that are imported and exported by the component. A *configuration* defines a system architecture by stating interconnections among a set of of components, i.e. by binding the imported operations to the exported ones. The description of components and configurations may further embed the specification of required and/or provided transactional properties. To simplify the developer's task, this specification is given in terms of properties names corresponding to formal specifications stored in an expandable database of transactional properties, as detailed in the next paragraph. An example of software architecture description is given below:

```
COMPONENT client {
  IMPORTS: VOID op();
  DEFINES TRANSACTIONAL Trans:
    MODEL = Tmodel;
    BEGIN = t_begin(); COMMIT = t_commit(); ABORT =  t_abort();
  REQUIRES: op: Trans
}
COMPONENT server {
  EXPORTS: VOID op(); REQUIRES: NOTHING;
}
CONFIGURATION system {
  USES: client, server;
  BINDS: client::op: server::op;
}
TRANSACTION_MODEL Tmodel {
  PROPERTIES: atomic AND isolated;
}
```

It is a simple client/server system where the client component requires the invocation of the operation op of the server to be executed within a transaction under the `Tmodel` model. Furthermore, the operations used within the client's source code to perform significant transactional events are `t_begin`, `t_commit`, and `t_abort`. The `Tmodel` transactional model is the conjunction of the `atomic` and `isolated` properties. These two properties may be refined into a number of more specialized ones (e.g. rollback recovery for atomicity and serializability for isolation), and hence a large number of middleware services are *a priori* eligible to meet these requirements.

Components of a configuration declare in their interface, their requirements for transactional processing. Two components involved in a nested control flow at runtime (e.g. a client component instance invokes the operation *op* of a server which invokes another server during the execution of *op*) may require distinct transactional models. In a first step, we address this issue by enforcing the requirement for a single transactional model at the level of a configuration. Given a configuration of components that require distinct transactional models, the developer should specify the model that applies for all the components (although they may not be involved in a nested control flow). By default, the transactional model that is enforced for a configuration is the conjunction of the strongest transactional properties among the specified ones. However, for the sake of flexibility, components that do not specify any transactional requirement are handled in a different way. The selected transactional model will be enforced for the operations they invoke only if the invocations happen within a transaction whose model is specified to be distributed.

Let us notice that our synthesis method applies to static configurations and hence is not directly suited for configurations based on dynamic bindings (e.g. using a trading service). The treatment of dynamic configurations is an open issue for future work.

Specifying transactional properties

For the specification of transactional properties, we use a refinement approach where each of the ACID (Atomicity, Consistency, Isolation, Durability) properties can be gradually refined into more specialized properties. The properties of a given transactional model correspond to the conjunction of one refinement of each of the ACID properties that are enforced by this model. Additionally, the transactional property provided by a given middleware service corresponds to one of the refinements of the ACID properties.

Our specification of transactional properties is based on temporal logic where only the precedence operator among predicates is used in addition to the operators of first order logic. This allows us to keep the notations simple. The following notations are used: $\wedge$, $\vee$, and $\Rightarrow$ denote logical and, or, and implication, respectively; σ (possibly primed or with subscript) denotes a system state; $[\sigma]$ denotes the predicate that holds if the system is in state σ, $[\sigma] \prec [\sigma']$ holds if $[\sigma]$ is verified before $[\sigma']$*. In addition, t (possibly primed or with subscript) denotes a transaction, $pre(t)$ (resp. $post(t)$) denotes the system's state before (resp. after) the execution of transaction t, and $\sigma \rightharpoonup_t \sigma'$ is the specification of t. In that context, a property P *refines* another property P' if $P \Rightarrow P'$.

Let us first examine the specification of the basic ACID properties. A transaction is said to be *atomic* (also known as the *all-or-nothing* property) if it appears to be indivisible. In other words, either the execution of the transaction results in a state transition that goes from the initial state to the final state specified for the transaction or, the system appears as if it had never left the initial state. The following formula captures this property:

$$atomic(t) \quad \equiv \quad ((pre(t) = \sigma) \wedge (\sigma \rightharpoonup_t \sigma')) \Rightarrow ((post(t) = \sigma) \vee (post(t) = \sigma'))$$

The *consistency* property guarantees that given a system in a consistent state and a transaction that executes alone and to completion, the system passes to another consistent state. Hence, for a transaction t and the system states before and after

*Let us also note that we have: $p_1 \prec p_2 \prec \ldots \prec p_n \equiv \bigwedge_{i=1,..,n-1}(p_i \prec p_{i+1})$.

the execution of t, the corresponding system state transition must be dictated by the transaction specification. This property is captured by the following formula:

$$consistent(t) \equiv ((pre(t) = \sigma) \wedge (post(t) = \sigma')) \Rightarrow (\sigma \rightharpoonup_t \sigma')$$

The third basic property is the one that guarantees the *isolated* execution of a transaction, i.e., a transaction t always behaves as if it is the only one executing. Hence, for every transaction t', $t' \neq t$, either t' views a system state that follows the state produced by t or t views a system state that follows the state produced by t'. We have:

$$\begin{aligned} isolated(t) \equiv\ & ((pre(t) = \sigma) \wedge (post(t) = \sigma')) \Rightarrow (\forall\, t', t' \neq t: \\ & ((pre(t') = \sigma'') \wedge (\sigma' \prec \sigma'')) \vee ((post(t') = \sigma''') \wedge (\sigma''' \prec \sigma))) \end{aligned}$$

The final basic transactional property is the one that guarantees *durability* for the results of completed transactions. This means that the system state that results from the execution of transaction t will survive subsequent failures. We get:

$$durable(t) \equiv (post(t) = \sigma) \Rightarrow (\forall \sigma' : [\sigma] \prec [\sigma'] \Rightarrow \sigma \rightharpoonup_S \sigma')$$

where $\rightharpoonup_S$ denotes a system state transition that is correct with respect to the system's specification.

Refining transactional properties

The above transactional properties should be refined to be actually helpful for the synthesis of transactional middleware. Refined properties then serve to characterize the behavior of various transactional models as well as the behavior of available middleware services. Up to now, we managed to refine our basic properties regarding several well-known models (e.g nested, split/join transactions). A detailed description of those refinements is not given here due to the lack of space. In the following, we focus on the refinement of properties that will be used for illustration purpose. These are the transactional properties provided by the CORBA OTS and CCS which respectively provide support for atomicity and isolation. The refinements of basic transactional properties characterize the behaviors of transactional systems, and hence define the behavior of the operations on transactions, i.e., begin, commit, and abort of a transaction. Furthermore, properties are given with respect to the execution of the DPE's operations. Such executions are characterized using the following base predicates in the case of a distributed transactional DPE:

- EXPORT(C_1, C_2, d) holds if component instance C_1 exports data d towards component instance C_2.
- IMPORT(C_1, C_2, d) holds if component instance C_2 imports data d from component instance C_1.
- FAILURE(C, σ) holds if component instance C fails while the system is in state σ.
- BEGIN(C, t) holds if component instance C requires the initiation of transaction t.

- COMMIT(C, t) holds if component instance C requires the commitment of transaction t.
- ABORT(C, t) holds if component instance C requires the abortion of transaction t.

Let us first give a refinement of the *atomic*(t) property under the distributed flat transaction model where we use the notation σ_C to denote the state of component instance C. This refinement consists of refining the value specified for *pre*(t) and *post*(t). We get the following *globalAtomic* property:

$$globalAtomic(t) \quad \equiv \quad ((pre_f(t) = \sigma) \wedge (\sigma \rightharpoonup_t \sigma')) \Rightarrow ((post_f(t) = \sigma) \vee (post_f(t) = \sigma'))$$

with:

$$\begin{array}{lcl} pre_f(t) & = & \bigcup_{C:begin(C,t)} : (pre(C,t) = \sigma_C) \\ pre(C,t) & = & \sigma_C \equiv [\sigma_C] \wedge begin(C,t) \\ post_f(t) & = & \bigcup_{C:begin(C,t)} : post(C,t) = \sigma_C \\ post(C,t) & = & \sigma_C \equiv ([\sigma'_C] \wedge commit(C,t) \wedge ([\sigma_C] \prec [\sigma'_C])) \vee \\ & & (pre(C,t) = \sigma_C \wedge abort(C,t)) \end{array}$$

and where:

$$\begin{array}{lcl} begin(C,t) & \equiv & \text{BEGIN}(C,t) \vee \\ & & (\exists C': (\text{IMPORT}(C',C,d) \wedge (begin(C',t) \prec \text{IMPORT}(C',C,d)) \wedge \\ & & (\nexists\, \text{IMPORT}(C'',C,d'): \\ & & \quad (begin(C'',t) \prec \text{IMPORT}(C'',C,d') \prec \text{IMPORT}(C',C,d)\ )) \wedge \\ & & (\nexists\, abort(C'',t): \\ & & \quad (begin(C''',t) \prec abort(C'',t) \prec \text{IMPORT}(C',C,d)\ )) \wedge \\ & & (\nexists\, commit(C'',t): \\ & & \quad (begin(C''',t) \prec commit(C'',t) \prec \text{IMPORT}(C',C,d)\ ))\ )\ ) \\ commit(C,t) & \equiv & \text{COMMIT}(C,t) \vee \\ & & ((commit(C',t) \wedge (begin(C',t) \prec commit(C',t))) \wedge \\ & & (\nexists\, abort(C'',t): (begin(C'',t) \prec abort(C'',t) \prec commit(C',t)))\ ) \\ abort(C,t) & \equiv & \text{ABORT}(C,t) \vee \\ & & (\text{FAILURE}(C,\sigma_C) \wedge (begin(C,t) \prec [\sigma_C])) \vee \\ & & (abort(C',t) \wedge (begin(C',t) \prec abort(C',t))) \end{array}$$

Let us notice here that providing other refinements for the *atomic* property consists of defining the formulas for *begin*, *commit*, and *abort* according to the behavior of the associated actions. Let us now give a refinement of the *isolated* property, we have:

$$\begin{array}{lcl} globalIsolated(t) & \equiv & \bigwedge_{\forall C:begin(C,t)} IsolatedComponent(C,t) \\ isolatedComponent(C,t) & \equiv & ((\nexists t': begin(C,t) \prec begin(C,t') \prec commit(C,t)) \Rightarrow \\ & & \quad (post(C,t) = \sigma_C)) \Rightarrow \\ & & (\forall t'': begin(C,t) \prec begin(C,t'') \prec commit(C,t)) \Rightarrow \\ & & \quad (post(C,t) = \sigma_C)) \end{array}$$

The above formulas may further be refined to distinguish between the various implementations of mechanisms providing them.

2.2 The Selecting Procedure

Given the proposed description of a configuration and formal specification of transactional properties, selecting middleware services that will be used to enforce the transactional model required for a configuration $\mathcal{C}$, is direct. Let $\{R_i\}_{i=1,\ldots,n}$ be the set of transactional properties characterizing the required transactional model, and $\mathcal{S}$ be the set of available middleware services S_j, $j \leq 1 \leq m$, such that each S_j provides the transactional property P_{S_j}. Then, a transactional middleware can be built for $\mathcal{C}$ if:

$$\forall R_i, 1 \leq i \leq n : \exists \{S_k\}_{k=1,..,m} \subseteq \mathcal{S} | \wedge_{k=1,..,m} P_{S_k} \Rightarrow R_i$$

Selecting middleware services to enforce transactional properties becomes simplified if the developer is provided with a tool that implements systematic retrieval of software according to the above formula. Such a tool can be based on the adequate organization of the database of transactional properties, in a way similar to the work presented in (Mili *et al.* 1994). The database is organized into a lattice structure* that encodes the refinement relation among the formulas defining transactional properties, i.e., any descendant of a property P refines P. Systematic retrieval of middleware services is then based on the following management of the database: *(i)* Upon the availability of a new middleware service, the property it provides is inserted in the database and the service is connected to it; *(ii)* Given the request for a transactional property P, the middleware service that will be returned among those available in the database is –if any– the one that provides a property P' that refines P such that there is no service providing P'' where P' refines P'' refines P. Construction of the database together with the selection of a middleware service with respect to a transactional property requires a tool based on theorem proving technology. There exist various such tools that have been exploited successfully for the retrieval of software components with respect to functional properties expressed in first order logic (Mili *et al.* 1994, Zaremski and Wing 1995, Schumann and Fischer 1997). We further have implemented our own in the ASTER project for the retrieval of software components providing non-functional properties, still expressed in first order logic (Issarny *et al.* 1998). Up to now, we have not yet experimented the use of a tool that deals with transactional properties based on temporal logic. However, we do not see this as a major difficulty since this has already been addressed for richer logics such as real-time temporal logic (Blair *et al.* 1997).

Following the selection of middleware services for a given configuration, a functioning configuration is obtained by composing the configuration's functional components with the selected services. This raises the issue of components and services compatibility with respect to the underlying communication protocol (known as the *architectural matching* problem (Garlan *et al.* 1994)). In the proposed method for transactional middleware synthesis, architectural matching is simplified by request-

*More precisely, there is a lattice structure for each of the basic ACID properties.

ing the developer to specify, for each component, the middleware platform (e.g. CORBA) for which it is targeted.

2.3 The Composing Procedure

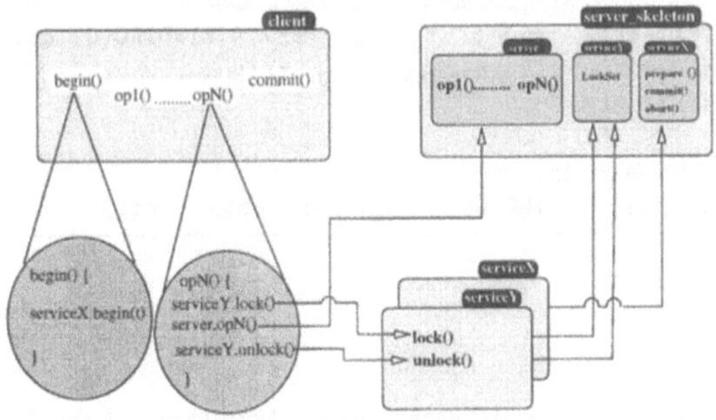

Figure 2 A client/server system configuration and its transactional middleware.

Given a configuration description and the set of selected services for the configuration, the final step of middleware synthesis is the composing procedure. The goal is to generate stub code for both the components that initiate transactions and/or issue requests within a transaction (referred to as client components in the following) and the components that serve requests issued within a transaction (referred to as server components in the following). The produced stub code integrates the configuration's functional components and the underlying middleware services in a full functioning system (see Figure 2). Stub code generation relies on the definition of *integration rules* for each transactional middleware service. The notion of integration rule completes the definition of transactional properties provided by a service. Basically, integration rules specify the code that needs to be added to client and server components. The integration rule for server components amounts to state the piece of code that implements the targeted transactional feature. From the client side, the integration rules subdivide into rules for the following actions: creation (i.e. *begin rule*), validation (i.e. *commit rule*), abortion (i.e. *abort rule*), and operation calls. Rules relating to operation calls subdivide into rules that specify the code to be executed before the call (i.e. *pre_call rule*), when the called is issued (i.e. *op_stub rule*), and after the call returns (i.e. *post_call rule*).

For illustration, the following figure gives the integration rules for a service, called `lock`, providing the isolation property according to the *two-phase locking* algorithm.

```
INTEGRATION lock ::=
 SERVER RULES:
   FORALL(S: SERVER) SKELETON = S ⊎ (lock::LockSet lockSet); END
 CLIENT RULES:
   CONTEXT BEGIN() ::=
     CONTEXT ctx; RETURN ctx;
   COMMIT(CONTEXT ctx) ::=
     FORALL(srv IN ctx) srv.lockSet.unlock(); END
   ABORT(CONTEXT ctx) ::=
     FORALL(srv IN ctx) srv.lockSet.unlock(); END
   PRE_CALL(CONTEXT ctx) ::= SKELETON srv; srv = BINDING(C, op);
     srv.lockSet.lock(); ctx.insert(srv);
   POST_CALL(CONTEXT ctx) ::=
     NULL
   OP_STUB(..., CONTEXT ctx)::=
     SKELETON srv; srv = BINDING(C, op); srv.op(..., ctx);
```

In the figure, words in capital letters denote keywords of the language used for the specification of integration rules. In particular, `SERVER` denotes server components of the configuration, i.e., components that export operations which are bound in the configuration; `SKELETON` denotes the skeleton to be produced for a server component; `CONTEXT` denotes the data structure that characterizes the context of a transaction; and `BINDING(C, op)` returns the instance of the server component that is bound to the imported operation `op` of client component `C`, in the configuration that is processed. The integration rules given for the `lock` service have the following meaning. The one for server components is trivial: components import features of the service using aggregation, which is specified by the symbol ⊎. The rules for client components consist of acquiring a lock on each server that is invoked within a transaction, passing the transaction context on each call to a server, and releasing locks upon the transaction termination.

Given the integration rules provided for middleware services, the stub code for the components of a given configuration is generated by appending, for each type of integration rules, all the corresponding rules of the selected services. In addition, the execution of the stub code generated for client components must preserve possible existing precedence constraints among middleware services (e.g. releasing locks is done after committing the produced results). Hence, the combination of integration rules relevant to client components is accomplished by employing a topological order graph algorithm (Cormen *et al.* 1990). Possible precedence constraints are set upon the insertion of a new service in the service repository. They are defined regarding all possible related services. This last issue gives the impression of an intolerable administration effort. Even so, we must consider that transactional services can be well classified in certain categories and dependencies are only formed between different classes of services providing different transactional properties. For instance, there exist three different classes of concurrency control services providing isolation, namely, serializability graph testing, locking, and timestamp order preserving services. For each one of them, there are different precedence constraints regarding failure recovery services providing atomicity, which can also be categorized in certain classes (e.g. undo, redo, ...).

3 EXEMPLIFYING MIDDLEWARE SYNTHESIS WITH CORBA

This section details the use of the proposed synthesis method through the example of a software system based on CORBA. The example is the same one that goes along with most of the CORBA transactional services implementations. It is a traditional client/server banking system that consists of a number of distributed server components instances (or *objects* using CORBA terminology) associated with a database. Transactional clients issue request operations to the server components for reading and updating the system's state. In order to simplify the example and without loss of generality, we assume that each server component corresponds to a single bank account, which provides operations for withdrawal and deposit. In such a system, it is essential to perform compound operations (e.g. transferring an amount from one account to another is realized as a withdrawal followed by a deposit) within a transaction, in order to preserve the system's consistency. Hence, the traditional ACID properties are required for distributed transactions. The underlying database provides *durability* (i.e. a recovery protocol) and *local atomicity* (i.e. atomic operations) Furthermore guaranteeing *consistency* is system-specific, the remaining requirements are those for *global atomicity* and *isolation*. The following is the ADL description of the system's architecture:

```
COMPONENT BankClient {
  SOURCE: xxx/BANKclient_i.cc; PLATFORM: MIDDLEWARE = CORBA; LANGUAGE = C++;
  EXCEPTIONS: InsufficientFunds {};
  IMPORTS: VOID deposit(IN FLOAT balance);
    VOID withdraw(IN FLOAT balance) RAISES (InsufficientFunds);
  DEFINES TRANSACTIONAL Trans:
    MODEL = BankTrans; BEGIN = t_begin(); COMMIT = t_commit(); ABORT = t_abort(
  REQUIRES: withdraw, deposit : Trans; }
COMPONENT BankServer {
  SOURCE: xxx/BANKserver_i.cc; PLATFORM: MIDDLEWARE = CORBA; LANGUAGE = C++;
  EXCEPTIONS: InsufficientFunds {};
  EXPORTS: VOID deposit(IN FLOAT balance);
    VOID withdraw(IN FLOAT balance) RAISES (InsufficientFunds);
  REQUIRES: NOTHING; }
CONFIGURATION BankSystem {
  USES BankClient, BankServer;
  BINDS BankClient::withdraw: BankServer::withdraw;
     BankClient::deposit: BankServer::deposit; }
TRANSACTION_MODEL BankTrans {PROPERTIES: globalAtomic AND globalIsolated; }
```

Clients import the `deposit()` and `withdraw()` operations which are exported by the server components. In addition, clients require the aforementioned operations to be transactional according to the transaction model defined as the conjunction of the *globalAtomic* and *globalIsolated* properties. Finally, clients specify that the initiation, validation and abortion of a transaction are notified in the client source code through the `t_begin()`, `t_commit()`, and `t_abort()` pseudo-operations, respectively. The source code for these operations is generated during the composing procedure, together with the stub code for the `deposit()` and `withdraw()` operations.

Middleware Synthesis

Two standard CORBA Common Object Services can be used to synthesize a middleware that conforms to the banking system requirements. The OTS service (chapter 10 in (OMG 1995)) provides the *global atomicity* property through a distributed commitment protocol, while the CCS service (chapter 7 in (OMG 1995)) is associated with two-phase and well-formed locking. Given the behavior of two-phase and well-formed locking, it can be formally proved that they imply an isolated execution and hence the *isolatedConfig* property. It follows that the CCS and OTS services can be selected using our method exposed in Subsection 2.2, to meet the banking system's transactional requirements. In order to use these services, including the appropriate extension of the locking functionality provided by the CCS service, the corresponding integration rules must be followed.

The CCS service exports the `LockSet` CORBA IDL interface that provides the `lock()` and the `unlock()` operations. The former operation acquires a lock on the corresponding `LockSet`. If the lock is already held in an incompatible mode by another client, the current operation is blocked until the lock is dropped, using the latter operation. The integration rules that correspond to the CCS service are then the ones given below:

```
INTEGRATION CosConcurrencyControl ::=
  SERVER RULES:
    FORALL(S: SERVER)
       SKELETON = S ⊎ (CosConcurrencyControl::LockSet lockSet); END
  CLIENT RULES:
    CONTEXT BEGIN() ::= CONTEXT ctx; RETURN ctx;
    COMMIT(CONTEXT ctx) ::= FORALL(srv IN ctx) srv.lockSet.unlock(); END
    ABORT(CONTEXT ctx) ::= FORALL(srv IN ctx) src.lockSet.unlock(); END
    PRE_CALL(CONTEXT ctx) ::= SKELETON srv; srv = BINDING(C, op);
      srv.lockSet.lock(); ctx.insert(srv);
    POST_CALL(CONTEXT ctx) ::= NULL;
    OP_STUB(..., CONTEXT ctx) ::=
       SKELETON srv; srv = BINDING(C, op); srv.op(..., ctx);
```

The OTS service provides the `Current` CORBA IDL interface that includes operations allowing a client to initiate (i.e. `begin()`) and complete transactions (i.e. `commit()` and `rollback()`). Moreover, for a server component to be transactional (i.e. the server's ability to retrieve information about the transaction that is associated to an operation being served), it must inherit from the `TransactionalObject` interface, also provided by OTS. The resulting integration rules for OTS are given below:

```
INTEGRATION CosTransactions ::=
  SERVER RULES:
    FORALL(S: SERVER)
       SKELETON = S ◁ CosTransactions::TransactionalObject; END
  CLIENT RULES:
    CONTEXT BEGIN() ::=
       CONTEXT ctx; CosTransactions::Current::begin(); RETURN ctx;
    COMMIT(CONTEXT ctx) ::= CosTransactions::Current::commit();
    ABORT(CONTEXT ctx) ::= CosTransactions::Current::rollback();
    PRE_CALL(CONTEXT ctx) ::= NULL;
    POST_CALL(CONTEXT ctx) ::= NULL;
    OP_STUB(..., CONTEXT ctx) ::=
      SKELETON srv; srv = BINDING(C, op); srv.op(..., ctx);
```

The combination of the integration rules of CCS and OTS given for client components further adheres to the precedence constraint that must be preserved whenever combining a locking service with a service that provides atomicity: locks should be released only after the results produced by a transaction become permanent. After combination of the integration rules, the concluding step of the middleware synthesis is to interpret the rules in stub code, regarding the banking system's architecture. The tool used for achieving interpretation is platform specific and a more detailed description of it can be found in (Zarras and Issarny 1998).

4 CONCLUSION

This paper has presented a method for the systematic synthesis of transactional middleware based on the use of existing standardized services. The main contribution of our work comes from combining the following two points:

(*i*) Synthesis of transactional middleware based on an *open* repository of standard services associated to an *expandable* set of properties.

(*ii*) The whole procedure is *systematic* and *adapts* the primitive properties provided by the standard services.

Let us further point out our contribution through a comparison with related work. The VENARI/ML (Nettles and Wing 1991) environment decomposes the transaction concept in a set of properties realized by object classes offered by the environment. The developer specifies application objects to be atomic, durable etc. However, the limitations existing in such kinds of environments are: the non-expandable property set and the static association between objects implementations and properties (i.e. an object cannot be used both as transactional and non-transactional, because its properties are defined at compile time). Additionally, there is no automation in composing an application that conforms to certain transactional requirements.

In the same spirit of decomposing the transaction concept, we meet the RAVEN system (Finkelstein *et al.* 1994) and the approach proposed in (Ranson 1995) for the TINA architecture. The novelty is that properties are dynamically associated with the objects. In RAVEN, this is done through inheritance and object migration while in the other proposal, the properties are part of the request message issued to a particular object.

An approach that overcomes the closed property set limitation is the combination of ACTA (Chrysanthis and Ramamritham 1994) and ASSET (Biliris *et al.* 1994). ACTA is a formal method for the specification of transaction models and ASSET is a programming library that realizes the features provided by the former (e.g. provides routines to create dependencies between transactions). Nevertheless, implementing a model that is specified in ACTA, through the use of ASSET is up to the developer.

An approach that overcomes the closed property set limitation and also provides automation in building the actual transaction model, is presented in (Georgakopoulos and Hornick 1996). According to that, the developer can require a particular transaction model, expressed in an ACTA-like language. A formal framework is used to verify whether or not a set of application objects support this model. In case the model is not supported, a Transaction Management Mechanism (TMM) can be used to enforce the required constraints. Nevertheless the limitation is the non-expandable set of services. The whole framework is based on the TMM unit. Thus, it lacks the flexibility of using primitive transactional services and exploiting the different features they provide (e.g. optimistic *vs.* pessimistic concurrency control).

The synthesis method presented in this paper aims at overcoming the limitations of the aforementioned approaches. Our goal is the synthesis of transactional middleware based on an open service repository associated to an expandable set of properties, that serves as the basic formal proving theory. Finally let us point out the benefit of our method from the standpoint of software correctness due to the use of formal specification, and from the standpoint of software reuse. In order to better point out the applicability of our framework we plan to examine various case studies including different transaction models and services that come with different distributed programming environments. Finally in the context of our work we wish to provide the specification and implementation of flexible services that can easily adapt to various transaction models.

We are currently working on the integration of the proposed synthesis method in the ASTER development environment based on the software architecture paradigm (Issarny *et al.* 1998). The current version of the ASTER environment supports systematic customization of the ORBIX ORB for enforcing basic non-functional properties, which may be specified using first order logic. Integration of our synthesis method in ASTER requires to address selection of middleware components with respect to properties specified in temporal logic. Another enrichment to be made relates to the automated generation of stub code using integration rules. The current ASTER environment realizes component integration by requiring middleware services to implement a given set of appropriate operations for their combination with other components. On the other hand, the procedure for the combination of services defined by our method provides a way to remove these constraints, and may further be exploited for the synthesis of middleware providing non-functional properties other than transactional. Our final goal would be to provide a uniform approach for building middleware regarding the needs for several kinds of properties. Hence we intend to explore the combination of services that provide different types of properties (e.g transactional, fault tolerance, security) and identify ways to deal with cases where those properties interfere.

REFERENCES

Blair G.S., Blair L. and Stefani J. (1997) A specification architecture for multimedia systems in open distributed processing. *Computer Networks and* ISDN *Systems*, 29.

Biliris A., Dar S., Gehani N., Jagadish H. V. and Ramamritham K. (1994) ASSET: A System Supporting Extended Transactions. *Proceedings of ACM-SIGMOD International Conference on Management of Data*, 44-54.

Cormen T., Leiserson C. and Rivest R. (1990) *Introduction to Algorithms*, MIT Press.

Chrysanthis P.K. and Ramamritham K. (1994) Synthesis of Extended Transaction Models Using ACTA. *ACM Transactions on Database Systems*, 19(3), 450-491.

Finkelstein D., Acton D., Coatta T., Hutchinson N. and Neufeld G. (1994) Object Properties in the RAVEN System. *Proceedings of the 14th International Conference on Distributed Computing Systems*, 502-509.

Garlan D., Allen R. and Ocklerbloom J. (1994) Architectural Mismatch: Why Reuse Is So Hard. *IEEE Software*, 17-26.

Georgakopoulos D. and Hornick M. (1996) Customizing Transaction Models and Mechanisms in a Programmable Environment Supporting Reliable Workflow Automation. *IEEE Transactions on Knowledge and Data Engineering*, 8(4), 630-649.

Gray J. (1981) The Transaction Concept: Virtues and Limitations. *Proceedings of the 7th International Conference in VLDB*, 144-154.

Issarny V., Bidan C. and Saridakis T. (1998) Achieving Middleware Customization in a Configuration-based Development Environment: Experience with the ASTER Prototype. *Proceedings of the International Conference on Configurable Distributed Systems*, 207-214.

ISO/IEC (1994) Reference Model of Open Distributed Processing. ISO/IEC Document 10746.

Mili A., Mili R. and Mittermeir R. (1994) Storing and Retrieving Software Components: A Refinement Based System. *Proceedings of the 16th International Conference on Software Engineering*, 91-100.

Moss E. (1982) Nested Transactions and Reliable Distributed Computing. *Proceedings of the International Conference on Reliability in Distributed Software and Database Systems*, 33-39.

Nettles S. and Wing J.M. (1991) Persistence + Undoability = Transactions, School of Computer Science, Carnegie Mellon University, CMU-CS-91-173.

OMG (1995) CORBAservices : Common Object Services Specification. OMG Document.

Pu C., Kaiser G. and Hutchinson N. (1988) Split-Transactions for Open-Ended Activities. *Proceedings of the 14th International Conference in VLDB*, 26-37.

Ranson R.D. (1995) Less-Than-Transactional Semantics for TINA. *Proceedings of TINA'95*, 2, 243-257.

Schumann J. and Fischer B. (1997) NORA/HAMMR: Making Deduction-based Software Component Retrieval Practical. *Proceedings of the International Conference on Automated Software Engineering*, 246-254.

Shaw M., DeLine R., Klein D., Ross T., Young D. and Zelesnik G. (1995) Abstractions for Software Architecture and Tools to Support Them. *IEEE Transactions on Software Engineering*, 21(4), 314-335.

Zaremski A.M. and Wing J.M. (1995) Specification Matching of Software Components. *Proceedings of the ACM SIGSOFT Symposium on Foundations of Software Engineering*, 6-17.

Zarras A. and Issarny V. (1998) Automated Synthesis of Middleware for Distributed Transactional Applications. *Proceedings of the ACM SIGOPS European Workshop*.

5 BIOGRAPHY

Apostolos Zarras was born at Ioannina, Greece. He received his B.Sc. and M.Sc. degrees from the University of Crete, Hellas in 1994 and 1996 respectively. He is currently working at IRISA/INRIA (ASTER project), while pursuing a Ph.D. at the University of Rennes I. His current research interests include, software architectures, computer aided software engineering and computer architectures.

Valerie Issarny is an INRIA Researcher at IRISA (Rennes, France) since 1993. She obtained her Ph.D. thesis from the University of Rennes I in 1991, on concurrent exception handling. She spent a one-year post-doctoral at the University of Washington in 1992 where she worked on the design of a single address space operating system. She is in charge of the ASTER research project that addresses the construction of distributed systems using the software architecture paradigm.

istributed systems using the software architecture paradigm.

Session 7

Type Safety and Security

Secure Architectures

Simon Gibson, Shelina Gorain, Dean Povey, Peter Clutterbuck
Co-operative Research Centre for Distributed Systems Technology
Level 12, S Block (ITE)
Queensland University of Technology, Brisbane, 4001
{gibson, shelina, povey}@dstc.edu.au, peter@dstc.qut.edu.au
Telephone: +61 7 3864 5120. Fax: +61 7 3864 1282.

Abstract

Hector is a work-in-progress middleware solution for distributed objects. It is modelled on the Reference Model for Open Distributed Processing (RM-ODP) and is designed to sit above a mixture of communication protocols and other middleware environments (such as CORBA and DCE), hence creating a common platform for the interoperability of distributed objects. For a middleware solution to be used in a distributed and heterogeneous environment, in a less than perfect world, it is necessary to consider security implications, and incorporate solutions into the design. The SecArch project attempts to incorporate security into Hector without creating a proprietary solution and by utilising new and developing ideas as well as established and proven security concepts. The project also aims to keep Hector as open and flexible as possible.

Keywords

security, middleware, GSSAPI, python

1 INTRODUCTION

This paper describes research objectives and implementation issues experienced as part of the Distributed Systems Technology Centre's (DSTC's) "SecArch" project. The SecArch project is a collaborative project between the Security and Architecture units of the DSTC. The project was formed to incorporate security into the Hector prototype. Hector is a work-in-progress middleware solution for distributed objects. It is modelled on the Reference Model for Open Distributed Processing (RM-ODP) and is designed to sit above a mixture of communication protocols and other middleware environments (such as CORBA and DCE), hence creating a common platform for the interoperability of distributed objects. For a middleware solution to be used in a distributed and heterogeneous environment, in a less than perfect world, it is necessary to consider security implications, and incorporate solutions into the design. The SecArch project attempts to incorporate security into Hector without creating a proprietary solution and by utilising new and innovative ideas as well as established and proven security concepts. The project also aims to keep Hector as open and flexible as possible.

For clarity the following convention is used: Any objects or classes are shown in *italics* and any attributes or methods of a class are shown in `typed text`.

The layout of the rest of the paper is as follows. The Hector middleware prototype is outlined in the next section. This is followed by a brief introduction to some relevent security concepts. The motivation and design of the SecArch project is then discussed followed by a technical outline of the actual implementation, and then finally some conclusions.

2 HECTOR PROJECT

Hector (Arnold, Bond & Chilvers 1997, Bond, Arnold & Chilvers 1996*b*) is a middleware framework. It provides a consistent environment in which distributed objects may exist. It provides mechanisms for open negotiation and interoperability of communications protocols and includes a rich set of support services. Its design includes the ability to be able to sit above other distributed environments such as DCE and CORBA. By sitting above other platforms Hector will allow interoperability between objects of different types. As an example, Hector could support a CORBA object and allow it to communicate with a DCE server. Hector is modelled on the Reference Model for Open Distributed Processing (RM-ODP), and supports the notion of "bindings". This section only superficially touches on Hector characteristics and outlines some specifics that are pertinent to the integration of security.

Hector supports multiparty bindings, which allow a fabric of distributed objects to be collectively involved in a binding. The binding describes the roles and communication patterns between the roles, to perform some higher level task. This is useful for many tasks that may be difficult to model in a client/server environment. To illustrate by example, imagine the parties involved in a real estate purchase. This could look

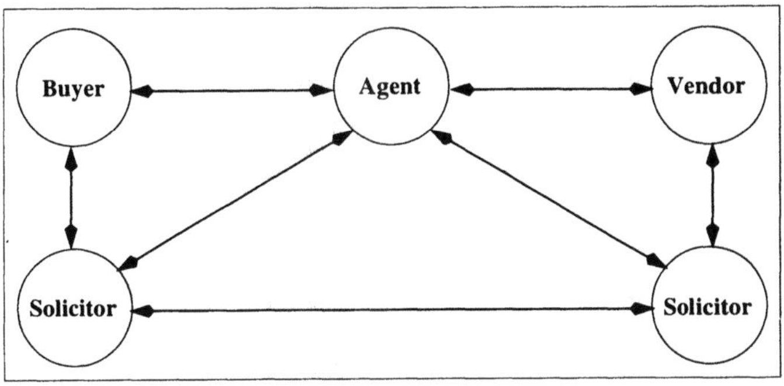

Figure 1 Example Binding

something like the diagram in Figure 1. The diagram depicts 5 objects participating in a binding. In this example the Buyer and Vendor communicate through the Agent and their respective Solicitors. The objects could be in the same process, different processes or different machines, or in any combination thereof.

Hector has been modelled and prototyped by the DSTC's Architecture Unit using Python (van Rossum n.d., Lutz 1996). Python is an interpreted programming language originally developed by Guido van Rosssum. Python was chosen due to its support for Object Oriented (OO) development, its extensibility, its simple, concise (but powerful) syntax and features such as exception handling and automatic garbage collection. These features combine to give a portable code base that is well suited for rapid prototype development.

In the Hector environment objects exist within a *capsule*. The capsule is a threaded process in which application objects can exist. Each object is allocated at least one initial private thread. All communications between objects (both within the capsule and between other capsules) are negotiated and managed by the capsule. In addition, services can be loaded as modules into the capsule to provide services such as Naming, Trading, Event Notification, Type, Policy etc. A conceptual diagram of a capsule is shown in Figure 2. For interaction with a capsule a *CapsuleBrowser* tool can be used. This has a GUI front-end and can be used to load object templates, instantiate objects and interrogate the capsule.

All communications outside of the capsule must be made through the communication layer. The communication layer consists (in part) of *Endpoint* objects that are somewhat analogous to sockets. The *Endpoint* class is an abstract class, designed to be extended to support specific protocols such as TCP and UDP. This hides implementation specifics of transport protocols from the capsule. The methods of *Endpoint* include those for the sending and receiving of messages.

An instantiated application object will have an *Interface* object to explicitly describe and maintain all communications outside of the object. The *Interface* will map the object to a set of *Endpoint*'s that are used in relation to a binding that the object is involved in. Conceptually an object with its external *Interface* and two bound *Endpoints* could be as shown in Figure 3. Figure 4 shows an interface level diagram of

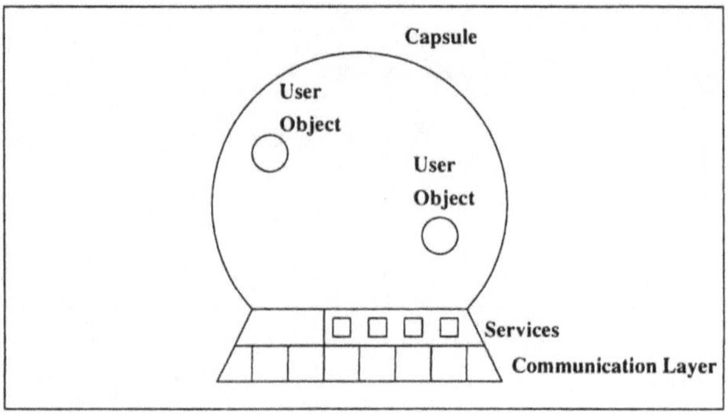

Figure 2 Hector Capsule

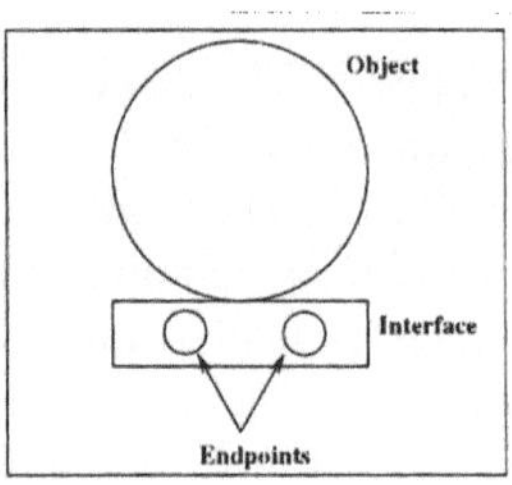

Figure 3 Object with Interface

the earlier real estate example.

The fine grained negotiation of a binding is complicated, so a high level brief description is given here, a more comprehensive description is given in Bond, Arnold & Chilvers (1996*a*). An instantiated object, (call it **ObjectA**), will create an *Offer* object. The *Offer* may contain all supported protocol types and mechanisms along with other information such as security and Quality of Service needs. The *Offer* may be

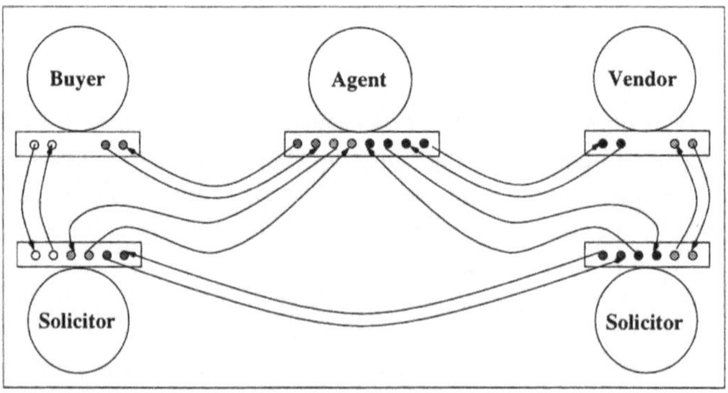

Figure 4 Example Interface Level Binding

exported to a Trader or Name service so that it can be found by other application objects. When another object, (call it **ObjectB**), wishes to connect to the service that **ObjectA** provides, it makes a request. It then receives a *ProxyOffer* from **ObjectA** and compares this with its own *Offer* object to find common protocols and mechanisms. The *Offer* maybe accepted, rejected or a counter offer made. If accepted, all potential participants of the binding are contacted in a similar fashion. **ObjectB** waits for all responses. If any are rejections or counter offers then the process will be repeated.

When unanimous agreement is reached, all participants are notified and instructed to create *Endpoint*s and *Interface*s and return the addresses to the initiator (**ObjectB**). Then all parties are instructed to connect. This creates a binding of objects openly negotiated to agree on communications protocols and mechanisms.

3 SECURITY

In order to provide security for Hector a number of features are required. This section describes some rudimentary security concepts (Oppliger 1997) that are relevant for the implementation of Hector security.

Authentication is the process of verifying that a claim of identity by a peer or entity is correct.

Confidentiality is the process of protecting data from unauthorised disclosure.

Integrity is an assurance that data has not been modified by an unauthorised entity.

Non-Repudiation is the property that prevents an entity from denying that an action or message originated from them. It also prevents the receiver of a message denying that the message was received.

Access Control is the ability for a system to be able to control access to resources. By giving an entity a set of privileges there can be a policy that maps between the privileges and certain allowable actions.

Single Sign On is a mechanism that allows an entity to log on or authenticate itself in multiple domains. The SSO mechanism performs the subsequent logging in to other resources on behalf of the user but only requires the user to log in once.

4 SECURE HECTOR

4.1 Motivation

The motivation for the SecArch project is to secure the Hector environment. For a middleware environment to be deployable it must implement features such as interoperability, scalability and security. This means that the security mechanism (or at least the interface of security) must also be interoperable and able to be utilised in a scalable environment. Since Hector is designed to be able to sit above other middleware environments, the security interface must also be able to co-exist with the security methods of the environments underneath. The communications between objects.must be capable of being secured. This includes authentication of the principals, maintaining the integrity of the messages and also being able to ensure confidentiality of the communications, if so desired. In addition, it would also be desirable to include the ability for access control to be integrated so that access to resources can also be stipulated and controlled.

4.2 Design

This section presents an overview of our design approach (Mohay, Arnold, Gibson, Yung, Gorain, Redhead, Clutterbuck & Rhodes 1997) for the introduction of security into Hector. Our aim was to have security neatly blend into the existing design of Hector. Foremost in the process was the notion of secure bindings. This will secure the communications between the application objects. It was important to the design to use the existing functionality associated with the negotiation, construction and monitoring of the binding process. The *Endpoint* class is closely related to communications and hence the binding, so this is a target point for security integration.

Application objects are instantiated and hence exist within the Hector capsule. They are loaded and created by the user via a *CapsuleBrowser* tool. Since they are effectively owned by the user the identity of the user should be associated with the instantiated object. The design had to consider the security of communications between the CapsuleBrowser tool and the capsule itself and also convey a way to delegate the user's identity to that of the objects themselves. The Generic Security Service Application Programmer Interface (GSSAPI) (Linn 1997) has the ability to deal with the delegation of credentials, which allows the CapsuleBrowser to create contexts on behalf of the user.

The design had to include methods that could co-exist with other mechanisms. To achieve this the *Null_Security* class was designed, this gives a passive interface to security. This is needed where an underlying mechanism provides a secure channel or security is not needed.

In addition to this, the design also covered in high level detail the following points.

Authorisation and Access control The Authorisation service will provide a management interface for users and administrators to view/modify authorisation information about objects and principals. Privileges will be attached to the binding data that will specify allowable events between objects and the use of services by the object. Access control will be able to be enforced during binding time, or an object may use the access control service to implement finer grained access control in a more dynamic manner. The design of the access control system has been influenced somewhat by the Adage authorisation system (Simon & Zurko 1997) and will consist of three major components.

1. Policy service - a repository which stores the policy information so it can be used in later access control decisions. Policy rules are stored as a 5-tuple consisting of:

   - The user/group/role performing an action
   - The object the action is to be performed on
   - The action being performed
   - Time of day this rule is valid
   - A boolean expression describing the rule

2. Naming service - this will associate privilege information with objects and users. Because Hector uses a federated naming service (based on XFN), this privilege information may be derived from a lower level mechanism such as Unix file permissions or DCE access control lists.
3. Access control engine - This determines the appropriate policy rules which apply to this access, and evaluate them using privilege information from the naming service

Audit The Audit service provides secure facilities for storing audit information about the actions of objects. Hector will automatically audit many functions (e.g. bindings, initial authentication), and objects may also access the audit service for their own logging purposes. The audit service will be implemented by a secured server which ensures that the risk of compromise of the auditing information is limited if a particular capsule's security is subverted.

Availability Service availability is an enterprise level Quality of Service (QoS) goal. The Availability Service allows an authenticated user, with legitimate need and intent to access an object based Hector service and receive a rate of mutually agreed progress toward service completion. The Availability Service secures Hector services against denial of service attacks from mischievous or inappropriate service requests.

Initially, Hector service availability will be achieved by the Availability service functioning as a middleware scheduler - receiving and executing service requests whilst descheduling user objects pending service finalisation.

Ultimately however, the goal of service availability will shape Hector services as intelligent containers - receiving user requests, responding with appropriate service-level offers, and subsequently managing the resulting user/service agreement.

Single Sign On The Authentication service will provide SSO facilities so the user does not have to enter passwords every time a different method of security is needed. This will be achieved by means of *credential repository* which stores the credentials required to log on to multiple security mechanisms. As part of the initial boot-up and login, the Hector capsule will obtain a secure connection to the credential repository. When the user logs on to the capsule browser, this authority is then delegated to the capsule. The capsule may obtain credentials for login to subsequent mechanisms by providing a valid credential for the given user to the authentica-

tion service. After it has retrieved the credential for the secondary login, the Hector capsule will load the appropriate SSO module to authenticate the user for the selected mechanism and pass it the retrieved credential.
The Authentication service will also provide a management interface for adding and deleting users, and changing authentication information.

5 IMPLEMENTATION ISSUES

5.1 GSSAPI

The GSSAPI is an API designed by the Common Authenticating Work Group (CAT-WG) (*IETF Common Authenticating Technology Work Group* n.d.) of the Internet Engineering Task Force (IETF) (*Internet Engineering Task Force* n.d.) that allows the integration of security into an application. The API is portable and independent of security mechanism and communication method. The Version 2 GSSAPI (Linn 1997) describes a set of 34 function calls that can be integrated into the application code.

The GSSAPI relies on the notion of secure contexts which are short-term authenticated sessions that can provide integrity and confidentiality to communications between principals. The GSSAPI does not actually provide the security services but provides a standard API for security mechanisms to conform to. The underlying mechanism may be implemented using symmetric or asymmetric techniques but the context establishment will appear the same at the application level.

The following list describes some of the steps needed to create a secure context using GSSAPI calls.

- Import a name converting a string represented identity, such as a user name, into a mechanism specific name using `gss_import_name()`.
- Acquire a credential, which is like acquiring a short-term certificate that authenticates the user, by calling `gss_acquire_cred()`.
- One party initiates the context, using the imported name and acquired credential by calling `gss_init_sec_context()`.
- The other party accepts the context by calling `gss_accept_sec_context()`, after it has also imported a name and acquired a credential.
- The context is negotiated until both parties are satisfied with the level of authentication with respect to each other. This may involve one party not needing to be authenticated to the other or may require mutual authentication.
- Once a context is created, messages can be exchanged using an independent communications method that is applicable to the situation. The message may be encrypted/signed using `gss_wrap()/gss_get_MIC()`* and then decrypted/verified using `gss_unwrap()/gss_verify_MIC()` depending on the context negotiated and the underlying mechanism.

*MIC cryptographic Message Integrity Code

Depending on the context negotiated, it is possible detect to out-of-sequence messages and replays of messages as well as other security services supported by the mechanism.

The above description outlines but a few of the available function calls. The other calls are associated with object identifiers (OID's) for interoperability among mechanisms or are accessor functions for inquiring details of a GSSAPI type, or describe details for delegation of established contexts or are simple management functions.

The needs of the Hector project meant that a generic and flexible method of incorporating security was needed. Due to the distributed and heterogeneous environment that Hector is exposed to, the method had to be independent of any particular security mechanism and had to be independent of any particular communications method. This naturally lead to the GSSAPI being used as an interface for Hector's security service.

5.2 OO Python GSSAPI

The GSSAPI is a standard procedural set of security related function calls that are integrated into the application code, by the programme developer. The GSSAPI standard outlines a semantic description of each function call and also describes a strict binding of data types and the function signatures for a C binding (Wray 1997). The GSSAPI uses a number of "handles" that are pointers to C structs, are opaque to the application programmer and are used as references for passing parameters to the function calls. At this point in time all GSSAPI compliant security mechanisms are written in the C programming language.

Since Hector has been modelled using Python, a Python language binding of the GSSAPI was needed. This was implemented by wrapping the C function calls using the Simplified Wrapper Interface Generator (SWIG) (Beazley 1998, Beazley n.d.) tool. After generating the wrapper code it is compiled and linked with the GSSAPI mechanism code to produce a shared object that can be imported into Python. This gives access to the function calls from Python but did not neatly fit an OO paradigm that was desired for integrating into the existing OO design of Hector. This lead to the development of an object based layer written in Python which grouped function calls with commonality, into method calls of an appropriate class. The logically associated handle is encapsulated as an attribute of the class, giving state to the object and hiding the handle from the application programmer. The five classes created are shown in Figure 5 along with a list of the object methods. The new Python binding (Gibson 1997), outlining the method signatures and return values is not described here as it is beyond the scope of this paper.

The release/delete GSSAPI function calls were embedded into the destructors of each class so that Python's garbage collection facility could be utilised in memory management. This OO Python binding sits above any wrapped GSSAPI compliant mechanism, and has been demonstrated using a local proprietary mechanism as well as Sesame V4 (*SESAME:- Secure European System for Applications in a Multi-vendor Environment* n.d.).

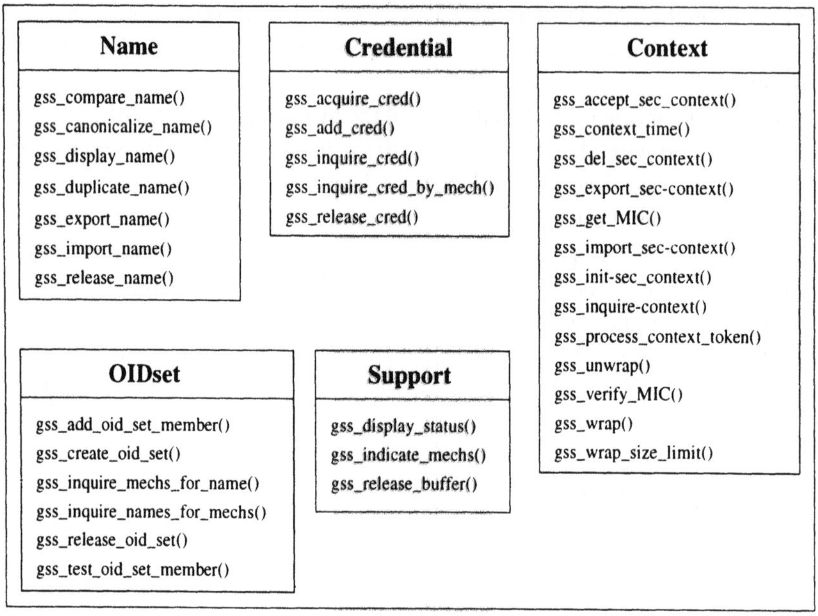

Figure 5 OO GSSAPI Classes

5.3 Securing Communications in Hector

In adding security to Hector it was necessary to consider and utilise as much as possible the facilities that are built in to Hector. This meant that negotiations that occur as a normal part of binding should be utilised to assist in securing the binding. It was also desirable that the security mechanism fitted in with the general style and feel of the existing code structures and hierarchy.

The OO Python binding was imported into the Hector kernel. Each of the GSS-API Python objects were then created as attributes of a *Security* module which may be dynamically loaded by the Hector kernel. This neatly encapsulates the required objects for context creation as shown in Figure 6. For each type of security mechanism supported, a security module is tailored to suit. This means that we could have a *Kerberos_Security* class or a *Sesame_Security* class or a *Null_Security* class etc. This method gives flexibility with regard to the mechanism used and is consistent from a programming point of view. The security mechanism is negotiated as part of the binding process.

The Hector *Endpoint* class is a communication object, described in Section 2. The Endpoint class outlines methods associated with communication including `send()` and `recv()` methods. These methods have functionality added so that the send method will `gss_wrap()` the message before actually sending on the wire and will `gss_unwrap()` the message before passing out of the *Endpoint* object on a receive. If a *Null_Security* object is instantiated then the `gss_wrap()` and `gss_unwrap()` calls are passive and have no effect. If there is a security object instantiated then the mes-

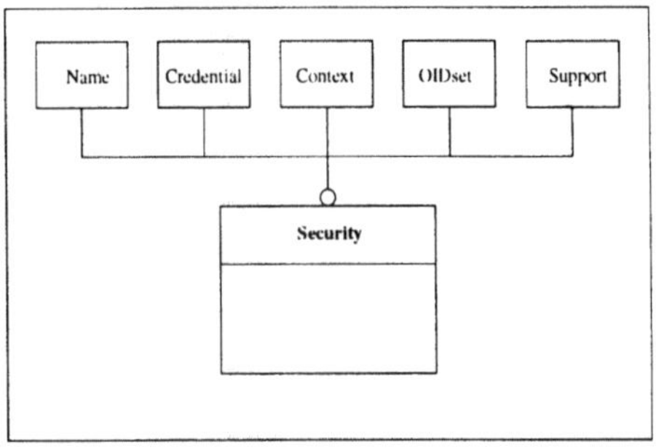

Figure 6 Class Structure

sage can be encrypted/signed depending on requirements and capabilities of the underlying security mechanism and the context that was negotiated.

A small section of the Hector class hierarchy is shown in Figure 7, which shows the *Endpoint* class as an abstract class and that each specialist type *Endpoint* inherits and overrides the abstract class. For implementing security a *SecureEndpoint* class was inserted into the hierarchy inheriting from *Endpoint* and each specialist *Endpoint* inheriting from *SecureEndpoint*. A *Security* object class is encapsulated as an attribute of *SecureEndpoint* called `security`, as shown in Figure 8. A *Null_Security* object is instantiated as the *Security* object by the constructor of a derived *Endpoint*, so by default there is no security. When an *Endpoint* is to become involved in a security context the `security` attribute is replaced by a reference to a *Security* object that is associated with the chosen security mechanism. The *Null_Security* object goes out of scope and is automatically garbage collected. Methods of the *SecureEndpoint* class are called which will begin the secure context negotiation.

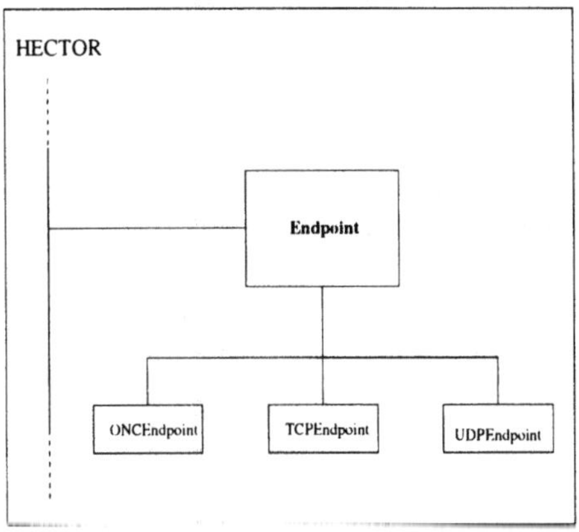

Figure 7 Hector Hierarchy Snippet

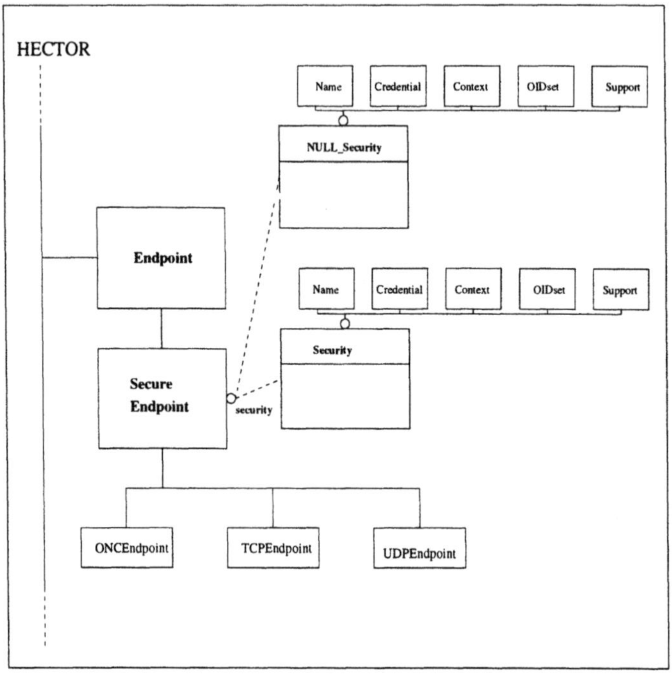

Figure 8 Secure Hector Hierarchy

5.4 Context Negotiation

Securing the Hector environment involves the creation of GSSAPI security contexts between various principals. There are two different types of contexts created. The first occurs between the *CapsuleBrowser* and the *Capsule* and the second type occurs between *Endpoint* objects that are created during the binding process. Essentially these context negotiations are the same with some minor variations.

5.4.1 CapsuleBrowser-Capsule Communications

Security between the *CapsuleBrowser* and *capsule* occurs as a browser connects to a capsule. This is effectively a context between the user and the identity of the account holder under which the capsule process was started. When a browser locates a capsule (either by knowing its address or via a naming or trading service) a context is negotiated, initiated by the browser. The browser must do a `gss_import_name()` on the target's name which it acquires during a handshake prior to context negotiation. The target's imported name is required as a parameter for the `gss_init_sec_context()` call. After each principal is mutually authenticated the browser's credential is delegated to the capsule and stored by the capsule in a table keyed by the browser's Hector_id. This credential can be used later by the capsule on behalf of the browser. The current *Security* object, holding the negotiated *Context* object as an attribute, is also stored, and is keyed using the address of the browser.

The browser can connect to multiple capsules and uses different *Endpoints* for each capsule meaning that each *Endpoint* will have an associated `Security` object containing the negotiated context. The capsule can be connected to multiple browsers via the same *Endpoint* address and must therefore lookup, using the senders address, the appropriate *Security* object before being able to `gss_unwrap()` a received message or `gss_wrap()` a message to be sent to a particular Browser. This effectively provides a secure communications channel between any combination of browser/s and capsule/s.

5.4.2 Object-Object Communications

All *Endpoint*'s have an attribute of a *Null_Security* object when instantiated. When an *Endpoint* becomes part of a binding the capsule will then use the stored delegated credential to create a *Security* object with a secure context negotiated on behalf of the original user. Multiple parties can be involved in a Hector binding emulating real world situations that can be difficult to model with just a client/server paradigm. The binding at a high level appears to be a collection or fabric of objects that can communicate. At a lower level of abstraction there is a collection of pairs of *Endpoint*'s, this collection of *Endpoint* pairs is as illustrated in the earlier example in Figure 4. After the Hector negotiation and the binding is fully established, a context is negotiated between each individual *Endpoint* and its peer, using the appropriate security mechanism, before any object-object communication can occur. Arbitrarily an endpoint is chosen to be an initiator and the peer is the acceptor. A mutually authenticated context is created using the delegated credential that has been stored previously by the capsule. After the context negotiation, there effectively exists a secure binding and messages are wrapped/signed and unwrapped/verified as required.

5.5 Beyond the Current Implementation

Security integration into Hector has resulted in a proof of concept implementation. This has demonstrated secure contexts being created between objects, (including that of multiparty bindings), at the object's low level interface without the object itself being directly aware of security. This has involved coding at the kernel level in Hector and allows the original application code to remain unchanged. It would be desirable to explore and implement functionality beyond that of the existing, as described in Section 4.2, including access control implementing associated policy.

Access control decisions for application objects would be a desirable next step. For implementation, a mechanism capable of decision and enforcement of access control privileges would be required as well as an extension to the Hector *Security* object, for interfacing to this mechanism. This would add extra attribute objects to the *Security* class for the handling of privileges.

Through the SecArch project we hope to continue and expand our research and experiment with integrating security into middleware environments in general. This will entail expanding into other environments including CORBA security. The knowledge gained from milestones reached up until this point, will be used for ongoing R&D into security of distributed objects.

6 DISTRIBUTED OBJECT SECURITY

Security in a distributed object system is a difficult task to achieve because of the desired functionality of such a system. A distributed object system will ideally wish to work over many platforms and potentially invoke and use objects that will reside in different security domains. An application object may or may not wish to even be aware of security. This means that some applications may wish to have more control over its own security demands than that of other applications which will leave security solely up to the underlying architecture. Components of an application system may or may not be fully aware of all objects or components that are utilised throughout the running of an application giving rise to possible security breaches and the vulnerability to "trojan horse" attacks occurring on systems with unknown security levels.

This is of course not an exhaustive list of difficulties of implementing security in a distributed object environment but highlights some areas of potential research. This project has tried to implement a practical method of adding security to a prototype middleware architecture. Through the project we have tried to create a neat and flexible integration of security that is applicable in general to some of the problems that are being encountered with securing distributed object middleware environments.

7 CONCLUSION

Hector, the DSTC's middleware prototype modelled on RM-ODP, is designed to sit above other middleware solutions and provides an environment supporting interoperability amongst distributed objects. For a middleware solution to be deployable in the real world it must in some way address the issue of security. SecArch is a collaborative project seeking to secure the Hector environment. Through the design process some features of Hector have been demonstrated to be secured using an object oriented GSSAPI interface. This has lead to a generic and flexible method of adding security to features, including multiparty bindings, that address authentication, integrity and confidentiality. The interface has blended into the existing hierarchy and utilises some of Hector's existing features. The underlying method of security is not fixed to any particular mechanism but is able to utilise any appropriate GSSAPI compliant solution.

REFERENCES

Arnold, D., Bond, A. & Chilvers, M. (1997), 'Hector distributed objects in python', *Dr. Dobb's Journal* .

Beazley, D. (1998), 'Swig and automated c/c++ scripting extensions', *Dr. Dobb's Journal* **No. 282**, pages 30–36.

Beazley, D. (n.d.), *SWIG:- Simplified Wrapper Interface Generator.* [Web Page], [Accessed Jan 98].

URL: *http://www.cs.utah.edu/beazley/SWIG/swig.html*

Bond, A., Arnold, D. & Chilvers, M. (1996*a*), Binding in hector, Technical report, CRC for Distributed Systems Technology, University of Queensland, Australia.

Bond, A., Arnold, D. & Chilvers, M. (1996*b*), Designing and building an odp environment, Technical report, CRC for Distributed Systems Technology, University of Queensland, Australia.

Gibson, S. (1997), *Object Oriented Python GSSAPI Bindings*. [Web Page], [Accessed Jan 98].
URL: *http://www.dstc.qut.edu.au/MSU/projects/gss-api/V2Python.binding*

IETF Common Authenticating Technology Work Group (n.d.). [Web Page], [Accessed Jan 98].
URL: *http://www.ietf.org/html.charters/cat-charter.html*

Internet Engineering Task Force (n.d.). [Web Page], [Accessed Jan 98].
URL: *http://www.ietf.org/*

Linn, J. (1997), Generic security service api version 2, Internet draft, rfc2078, IETF Common Authenticating Technology WG. [working draft].

Lutz, M. (1996), *Programming Python*, O'Reilly and Associates, Inc.

Mohay, G., Arnold, D., Gibson, S., Yung, D. P. M., Gorain, S., Redhead, T., Clutterbuck, P. & Rhodes, T. (1997), Secarch design document, Technical report, CRC for Distributed Systems Technology, University of Queensland, Australia. [internal draft].

Oppliger, R. (1997), *Authentication Systems for Secure Networks*, ARTECH HOUSE, INC., Norwood, MA 02062.

SESAME:- Secure European System for Applications in a Multi-vendor Environment (n.d.). [Web Page], [Accessed Jan 98].
URL: *http://www.esat.kuleuven.ac.be/cosic/sesame.html*

Simon, R. & Zurko, M. (1997), Adage: An architecture for distributed authorization, Technical report, The Open Group Research Institute. [Web Page], [Accessed Feb 98].
URL: *http://www.osf.org/www/adage/adage-arch-draft/adage-arch-draft.ps*

van Rossum, G. (n.d.), *The Python Programming Language*. [Web Page], [Accessed Jan 98].
URL: *http://python.org*

Wray, J. (1997), Generic security service api version 2: C-bindings, Internet draft, IETF Common Authenticating Technology WG. [working draft].

8 BIOGRAPHY

Simon Gibson gained a BCompSc(Hons) in 1996 from the University of New England, Australia. Since this time he has worked as a research scientist with the security unit of the Distributed Systems Technology Centre, Brisbane, Australia. Prior to this he gained 7 years experience working in the telecommunications industry.

Shelina Gorain graduated with an honours degree in Computer Science from the University of Queensland, Australia in 1995. She has been working as a research scientist for the Distributed Systems Technology Centre (DSTC) since early 1997. Her research interests include web security, ecommerce and human-computer interaction.

Dean Povey gained a BAppSc(Comp) from the Queensland University of Technology in 1993, and a BInfTech(Hons) from the University of Queensland in 1996. He has 6 years of experience in the computing industry as both a researcher in the Security field and a Systems programmer. He is currently employed as a Research Scientist at the CRC for Distributed Systems Technology, where his work includes development of a Public Key Infrastructure, research into trust management and Cryptozilla.

Peter Clutterbuck obtained an MSc in Computing Science in 1996 from Queensland University of Technology. He is currently a PhD candidate at the same university. His research centres upon the contractual availability of distributed, object based resources.

The work reported in this paper has been funded in part by the Co-operative Research Centre Program through the Department of Industry, Science & Tourism of the Commonwealth Government of Australia.

Improving Type-Safety in CORBA

S.C. Crawley (1,2) and K.R. Duddy (1)
1 - CRC for Distributed Systems Technology (DSTC)[1],
2 - Defence Science and Technology Organisation (DSTO)
University. of Queensland, Qld 4072, Australia.
Email: {crawley,dud}@dstc.edu.au

Abstract

CORBA presents a model of distributed computing in which distributed objects communicate using a high-level "information bus" called an Object Request Broker (ORB). In this paper we describe a problem with the current CORBA specification that makes ORB communication non-type-safe in certain situations. We describe a solution to the problem based on the use of unique identifiers, and show how it can be implemented efficiently in both stand-alone and federated CORBA-based systems.

Keywords

CORBA, IDL, interface type, repository id, type safety, type checking, federation

1 INTRODUCTION

One of the main technical selling points of middleware technology such as CORBA (OMG 1997), DCE (Rosenberry 1992) and COM / DCOM (Microsoft 1995) is its ability to exchange data and invoke remote operations or remote procedure calls. In

[1] The work reported in this paper has been funded in part by the Co-operative Research Centre Program through the Department of Industry, Science & Tourism.

general, middleware products try to hide details of distributed computing such as client to server binding and conversion from / to network transmission formats. Instead, they try to present an invocation model that is as close as possible to (local) object invocation and procedure call in non-distributed programming languages.

Type safety is a property that is common to most modern programming languages. In simple terms, a type error occurs when a program gets internally confused about the representation of some value and behaves in an undefined way as a result[2]. A programming language is type-safe if it systematically eliminates the possibility of type errors in programs. For example, standard Pascal makes it impossible to call a procedure with integer argument where a pointer is expected. The advantage of type safety is that it enhances software reliability. A large class of type errors can be detected and corrected at compile time. Any other type errors are guaranteed to be detected at runtime.

Type safety is equally important in distributed computing systems. When a client invokes an operation on a remote object, it supplies arguments of a given type and expect results of a given type. These need to match the object's operation argument and result types for the invocation to work correctly. If there is an interface type mismatch, it should at least be detected reliably at runtime.

Interface type safety in a distributed system is typically maintained by the middleware layer. In CORBA for example, the Object Request Broker (ORB) is responsible for ensuring that invocation parameter passing is type-safe. Unfortunately, the ORB runtime type safety mechanisms defined by the current CORBA specification are not totally reliable.

In the remainder of this paper, we describe the type safety mechanisms defined in the CORBA version 2.1 specifications, and detail the problems that we have identified with them. Then we present a solution based on changes to the CORBA Interface Repository (IFR) specification (OMG 1997a) and discuss implementation issues. Finally we list some other type-related issues with CORBA that need to be addressed.

2 CORBA'S TYPE SAFETY MECHANISMS

The Core Object Model of the Object Management Architecture (OMA) (OMG 1995) defines objects as having identity, state and behaviour. The behaviour of a CORBA object is invoked by sending it operation requests with appropriate arguments and receiving results. These arguments can be references to other objects, or instances of (non-object) data types. An object can typically support (i.e. act on) many kinds of operation request. From the client's viewpoint, these are characterised by operation signatures consisting of the name of the operation, the

---

2 In reality, many programming languages are type-safe if the programmer follows certain rules or avoids using certain unsafe constructs. Type safety should not be confused with static typing. For example, Smalltalk-80 is not a statically type checked language, but its runtime type system ensures that every value has a well defined type, and predictable behaviour.

types of its parameters and results, and the types of any exceptions that it may raise. The type of an interface thus consists of the signatures of the operations that it supports.

An object interface can be defined as a subtype of one or more other interfaces, meaning that it supports all of the operations of the supertype interfaces. Thus, an object reference for an instance of a subtype is guaranteed to be substitutable for a reference to an instance of one of its supertypes. However, a reference to a supertype instance has to be "narrowed" before it can be used for invoking subtype operations.

In the CORBA 2.1 realisation of the Core Object Model, the data type system consists of a number of primitive types (e.g. integers, characters, etc) and constructed types (e.g. enumerations, arrays, structs, etc). Two CORBA primitive data types have particular significance to type safety: Any and TypeCode.

The CORBA Any type is a type-safe universal union type. An arbitrary CORBA object or non-object value can be "inserted" into an Any value and passed or returned through an interface that is not aware of the type. The final recipient of the Any value can then "extract" the original value in a type-safe way.

A CORBA TypeCode value is a non-object representation of a CORBA type. TypeCodes are used primarily to represent the type of a value encapsulated by an Any. A TypeCode consists of a "kind" field that discriminates between the various kinds of CORBA type (e.g. integer, enumeration, etc) and a number of other fields depending on the "kind".

CORBA is defined so that an ORB needs to perform a minimum of runtime type checks. For example, since CORBA ensures that a client always knows the interface type of an object reference, no runtime type checks are required when an operation is invoked. Ignoring the Dynamic Invocation Interface (DII) and Dynamic Skeleton Interface (DSI), runtime type checks are only required in two situations to maintain type safety[3]; i.e. when a client narrows an object reference, and when it extracts a value from an Any.

When a client narrows an object reference to a given interface type, the ORB must ensure that the referenced object's type is substitutable for the interface type; i.e. it must have that type or a subtype of that type. When the referenced object is local to the client, local type information can be used for runtime type checking. Otherwise, the ORB in the client typically[4] invokes the "Object::is_a" operation on the remote object, passing the expected interface type as a RepositoryId string. Currently, this operation must assume that equal RepositoryId strings imply that the corresponding interface types are identical.

When a client extracts a value from an Any, the ORB examines the TypeCode in the Any to check that it matches the type expected by the client. When the embedded value is an object reference, this TypeCode contains the RepositoryId for the reference's interface type. As before, runtime type checking must be

3 As currently specified, the CORBA DII is fundamentally non-type-safe.

4 Some ORBs also make use of type information passed in the vendor-specific part of an object reference. However, this does not work when ORBs from different vendors need to interoperate.

implemented by comparing RepositoryId strings. (TypeCodes for some kinds of non-object type may also contain RepositoryIds. However, type checking cannot rely on these RepositoryIds since the CORBA specification defines them to be optional.)

3 THE PROBLEM WITH CORBA REPOSITORY IDENTIFIERS

As we described in the previous section, the standard method of runtime type checking of CORBA object references is to compare the RepositoryId strings for their interfaces. The CORBA specification *assumes* that for any pair of CORBA interfaces A and B,

$$\text{equiv}(\text{type}(A), \text{type}(B)) \Leftrightarrow (\text{RepositoryId}(A) = \text{RepositoryId}(B)).$$

Unfortunately, the current CORBA specification does not *guarantee* this condition in all cases. Two equivalent (even textually identical) interfaces can have different RepositoryIds. More important, two non-equivalent interfaces can have the same RepositoryIds.

To understand why this is so, we need to explain more about RepositoryIds. The RepositoryId type is defined in the CORBA Interface Repository specification (OMG 1997a). RepositoryIds are CORBA strings which (according to section 7.5.1) "uniquely and globally identify a module, interface, constant, typedef, exception, attribute or operation". In section 7.6, the following three formats for RepositoryIds are defined:

```
"IDL" ":" <identifier> { "/" <identifier> }* ":" <version-no>
"DCE" ":" <uuid-string> ":" <version-no>
"LOCAL" ":" <unspecified>
```

The IDL identifier format is the most commonly used one. The first identifier in the list is optionally a "unique prefix" for the RepositoryId and the remaining identifiers are the names of the modules and interfaces in which the item denoted by a RepositoryId is nested. The version number consists of a major and minor part and defaults to "1.0". The RepositoryId prefix and version number can both be specified using pragmas in the IDL file. For example,

```
#pragma prefix "dstc.edu.au"
module M1 {
     module M2 {
              interface I {
#pragma version I 1.1
              };
     };
};
```

defines the following RepositoryIds

```
Module M1           "IDL:dstc.edu.au/M1:1.0"
Module M2           "IDL:dstc.edu.au/M1/M2:1.0"
Interface I         "IDL:dstc.edu.au/M1/M2/I:1.1"
```

The DCE identifier format uses the string form of DCE's Universal Unique Identifiers (UUIDs). The LOCAL identifier format allows RepositoryIds to contain vendor specific data. However section 7.6.3 of the IFR specification states that LOCAL identifiers "are not intended for use outside of a given repository". An ORB that relies on them for runtime type checking is arguably non-compliant, especially if there might be more than one IFR instance. Both DCE and LOCAL format RepositoryIds can be associated with definitions using the "ID" pragma in IDL.

The CORBA specification clearly assumes that RepositoryIds uniquely identify types. The problem is that it defines no mechanisms for guaranteeing this is the case. Indeed, we can identify three distinct scenarios in which the specification's assumption will be violated:

1. Assume that there are two instances of the CORBA IFR service. We first populate one IFR using an IDL file that defines an interface with a given qualified name, prefix and version, and a given set of operations. Then we create a new IDL file from the first, changing (say) the result type of an operation (*without* changing the interface name, prefix or version!) and use the new file to populate the second IFR. The result is that the two IFRs will use the same RepositoryId to denote incompatible CORBA interfaces.
2. Considering the IDL files from the previous case, suppose that the first file is used to populate the IFR, and the RepositoryId which denotes the interface type is then used within the local ORB and elsewhere. Then after a time, the second file is used to replace the original interface definition with the new one. Now we have parts of the ORB having one meaning for the RepositoryId, and the IFR having a different meaning.
3. Section 7.3.3 of the IFR specification defines an ORB-level API that can be used by any client program to hand-assemble TypeCode values. It is trivial for a client program to create a TypeCode with an arbitrary RepositoryId. The client can then use the unsafe Any constructor to associate the TypeCode with an object reference.

The first two scenarios above can easily arise if the people who administer the ORB or ORBs for an organisation are careless or reckless. In theory, this problem can be addressed by instituting formal configuration control procedures for interfaces within the organisation. The first scenario can also arise when ORBs managed by separate organisations come into contact; e.g. over the Internet. The third scenario entails the programmer deliberately subverting CORBA's type safety mechanisms. We have decided that solving this problem is out of scope.

The problem with RepositoryIds described above can have dire consequences. If a CORBA client thinks that the interface of a remote object is different to what it really is, it may invoke an operation passing the arguments or expecting results of the wrong type. What happens next is undefined. If the unmarshalling code at either end detects the problem (e.g. because the request or reply message has the wrong size) the ORB should raise a System Exception. If unmarshalling fails to detect the problem, garbage arguments and results may be passed. This may lead to incorrect behaviour and crashes in the client or server.

Some CORBA clients need to examine definitions of interfaces at runtime; e.g. so that they can use the DII. The "lookup_id" is typically invoked (by the client or the ORB) on the local IFR to find the interface's InterfaceDef object. If RepositoryIds have multiple meanings, the returned object may describe a different interface to the one supported by the actual object. This may cause the client to invoke operations with incorrectly typed arguments, leading to System Exceptions or worse, as described above. (The problem is that the CORBA specification takes the view that there is a single, "omniscient" IFR. In reality, there may be many IFR instances that are not aware of each other.)

The loophole in the CORBA type system caused by the RepositoryId problem is undesirable, and can clearly be dangerous. CORBA needs an efficient solution that fixes the type system loophole where possible. The solution should also be interoperable with ORBs that implement the current CORBA specification, and should be workable across the range of environments that CORBA aims to support.

There are a couple of "solutions" to the problem which clearly do not work. First, manual configuration management procedures for an organisation's IFRs are only as reliable as the people who perform them, and do not address the problem in an inter-organisation context. Second, some people think that the problem can be solved by using DCE-style UUIDs for CORBA interfaces. Unfortunately, this approach also depends on manual configuration procedures to manage updating of interface version numbers.

4 SOLVING THE REPOSITORY IDENTIFIER PROBLEM

The last section described how a CORBA RepositoryId can denote more than one type, and how this can have disastrous consequences. In this section, we describe a solution to this problem. Our approach is to define a new form of CORBA RepositoryId called a Unique Repository Identifier (URID), whose instances must be created and managed as follows to ensure that one URID denotes one type, and that types associated with unequal URIDs can be compared.

A URID must be generated by the IFR in a way that guarantees that it is globally and temporally unique. The user must be prevented from setting the URID for an interface or other definition via a pragma in the IDL file or any other way. The aim is to ensure that a given URID value can never associated with more than one definition.

Each IFR must ensure that the binding between a URID and its type is immutable. One approach is to forbid all changes to definition objects once they have been assigned a URID. Another approach is to have the IFR automatically generate a new URID whenever it updates a definition object. In the latter case, it would also need to generate new URIDs for all dependent definition objects.

The representation for URIDs needs to have following properties:

- Like other RepositoryIds, URIDs must be represented as CORBA strings for compatibility with existing ORBs.
- URIDs must be guaranteed to be globally and temporally unique. In other words, a given URID value can be generated at most once by at most one IFR.
- A URID must contain enough information to allow a client or the client's local IFR to locate the IFR that generated it.

Note: we do *not* require or assume that equivalent definitions will have the same URID value.

A number of candidate URID representations exist with the above properties, each with its own advantages and disadvantages. Here are some illustrative examples:

a) DCE UUID : "URID" ":" <defn-uuid-string>
This format uses a DCE UUID (OSF 1994) to denote each definition object.

b) DCE UUID + local id : "URID" ":" <ifr-uuid-string> ":" <local-id>
This format uses a DCE UUID to denote the URID's issuing IFR. The <local-id> (here and below) is an identifier that must be temporally unique within the context of the IFR.

c) Domain name + local id : "URID" ":" <name> { "." <name> }* ["/" <port>] ":" <local-id>
This format uses a domain name to denote the IFR.

d) Net address + local id : "URID" ":" <ip-number> ["/" <port>] ":" <local-id>
This format uses the network address (e.g. IP and port numbers) for the IFR.

e) Object reference : "URID" ":" <ior-string>
This format uses the CORBA object reference (e.g. a GIOP IOR) for the definition object in the IFR as a RepositoryId.

Formats (a) and (b) use DCE UUIDs. While DCE UUIDs are guaranteed to be unique, it is not always possible to extract an IFR address from a UUID. Instead, the local IFR would need to support an operation to map URIDs to IFR addresses. Implementing this functionality adds to the complexity of the IFR. In the case of format (a) the number of UUIDs required could present scalability problems.

Format (c) avoids the need for a special UUID mapping service by using the Domain Name Service (DNS) (Mockapetris 1987) or equivalent name service. However, this introduces another dependency that will be burdensome in some environments. Format (d) avoids all dependencies by encoding the IFR's network address in the URID. However, hard-wiring IFR network addresses into URIDs causes problems if an IFR has to be moved to a new location.

Format (e) largely avoids the problems of the other example formats, but suffers from the problem that stringified CORBA object references can be very large. This can be addressed by having the ORB use small object keys for IFR objects, or by using a compact IOR format (Henning 1997) in the URID[5].

At this stage, it is unclear which URID format would be the most suitable one. However, it *is* clear that there are a number of viable alternatives, albeit with a variety of drawbacks. It may be that the best approach is to support multiple URID formats.

If we can assume that IFRs manage URIDs as described above, the following simplistic algorithm can be used to check that two URID format RepositoryIds denote the same interface types:

1. The client compare the two URIDs. If they are equal, then the interfaces are equal.
2. The client locate the IFRs that generated the two URIDs.
3. The client fetches the interface definitions for the URIDs from the respective IFRs.
4. The client compares the interface definitions to determine whether they are equivalent.

As we shall see, the above algorithm can be improved by various forms of caching.

5 TYPECODES AND CORBA TYPE EQUIVALENCE

Since we are proposing that CORBA type safety be based on the equivalence of interface types, we need to understand what type equivalence means in CORBA. Unfortunately, the CORBA specification is rather unclear on this topic. To understand why this is so, we need to explain a bit more about how the specification defines TypeCodes.

As we mentioned earlier, a TypeCode is a description of a CORBA object or non-object type. According to section 7.7 of the IFR specification, a TypeCode consists of a "kind" and a variety of other components depending on the kind. For example, the TypeCode for the type

```
struct X {
     string Y;
     short  Z;
};
```

has a "kind" of "tk_struct", and has components for the struct's tag name and for the names and types of each of its fields. The tag names and field names are encoded as CORBA strings, and the field types as embedded TypeCodes. The problem is that the specification allows many components to be omitted, including tag names, field names, and in some cases repository ids. Indeed, the General Inter-ORB Protocol (GIOP) specification currently allows an ORB to omit these

5 The IOR for the definition object also contains an IOR. However, the cycle can be broken by carefull handling of the IOR for the definition object for CORBA::InterfaceDef.

components when it marshals TypeCodes for network transmission. This means that if an ORB only has TypeCodes, it may only be able to check for "on the wire" structural equivalence of data types. (By contrast, a data type description held in an IFR includes the tag names, field names and so on, and also the definition context for the data type; i.e. the modules and interfaces that contain it.)

The IFR specification defines an "equal" operation on the TypeCode API that can be used to compare two TypeCodes. The semantics of this operation are defined in section 7.7.1 as follows:

> "The equal operation can be invoked on any TypeCode. Equal TypeCodes are interchangeable, and give identical results when TypeCode operations are applied to them."

This semantic is unsatisfactory as a definition of CORBA type equivalence. For example, a pair of TypeCodes for the above "struct" type would be non-equivalent if one had tag names while the other did not. Since any ORB may chose to include or omit tag names when transmitting TypeCodes, type equivalence across ORB boundaries is clearly problematic.

Clearly, CORBA needs a workable specification of type equivalence. In practice, different kinds of equivalence in different situations. The four main type equivalences are as follows, in order of increasing in strength:

- Representational Equivalence requires that types have the same "on the wire" representations. All tag names, field names and so on are ignored, and types are considered equivalent if their component data types are equivalent.
- GIOP Structural Equivalence requires the same "on the wire" representations, and also uses tag names, field names and so on when they are available for both types.
- Structural Equivalence requires that the types have equal declarations. This is like GIOP Structural Equivalence except that tag names, field names and so on, are required and are always taken into account in type checking.
- Name Equivalence requires that the types have the same declaration. This is like Structural Equivalence except that the types must also be declared in equivalent interfaces with identical module scopes.

The above equivalences can be further refined by allowing the client to decide if CORBA typedefs (i.e. tk_alias TypeCodes) should be considered equivalent to the types that they alias. (In the case of name equivalence, this additional criterion is irrelevant.)

Structural and name equivalence checking of TypeCodes can only be performed if the TypeCodes contain the requisite information. Structural equivalence requires tag names, field names and the like. Name equivalence also requires RepositoryIds and a mechanism for comparing their associated declaration scopes. If we want to ensure that an ORB can provide these two equivalences, the IFR (and GIOP) specifications must be changed to make the relevant TypeCode components mandatory. (Note that if the TypeCodes both contain URID format RepositoryIds, a client can always resort to using the IFR to find any type information that is missing.) Alternatively, we need to provide a way for the TypeCode::equal() operation to say that an equivalence is unavailable.

6 TYPE COMPARISON USING EQUIVALENCE SETS

A primary requirement for any runtime type checking scheme is that it should be efficient. In this section, we briefly describe an algorithm for structural type checking that has this property. The algorithm is based on the Equivalence Set algorithm for comparing polymorphic function types described in (Aho 1986). For more details on the variant of the algorithm described here, refer to (Crawley 1996).

The equivalence set algorithm is based on two properties of types and type equivalence in the type systems of interest here:

1. Types are immutable. Thus if two types T1 and T2 can be shown to be equivalent, they will always be equivalent.
2. Type equivalence is transitive; i.e.
   $\text{equiv}(T1, T2) \wedge \text{equiv}(T2, T3) \Rightarrow \text{equiv}(T1, T3)$

The basic algorithm works by building sets of equivalent types which it represents and manipulates in a clever way. Assuming that type nodes are represented as variant records, we add a new "equiv_set" field to the non-variant part of the record type; e.g. in C

```
struct type_node {
     struct type_node *equiv_set;   /* initialised to NULL */
     type_kind kind;
     union variant_part { ... } details;
};
```

Each set of equivalent type nodes is denoted by a type node called the "representative" for the set. If the "equiv_set" field of a type node contains a null pointer, it is a representative. Otherwise, one finds a type node's equivalence set representative by following the "equiv_set" chain. This building block can be coded in C as follows:

```
struct type_node *find_representative (struct type_node *t) {
     while (t -> equiv_set) {
             t = t -> equiv_set;
     }
     return t;
};
```

The second building block is a function that merges a pair of equivalence sets:

```
struct type_node *merge_equiv_sets (struct type_node *rep1, *rep2)
{
     if (rep1 -> equiv_set || rep2 -> equiv_set) abort (...);
     rep1 -> equiv_set = rep2;
     return rep2;
};
```

It is not difficult to see that if we start with a group of singleton equivalence sets (i.e. single type nodes) and merge them in any order, the resulting equivalence set will be a tree of type nodes with the representative at its root.

Assuming acyclic types, the basic equivalence set algorithm looks like the following:

```
int equiv (struct type_node *t1, *t2) {
     struct type_node *rep1, *rep2;
     rep1 = find_representative(t1);
     rep2 = find_representative(t2);
     if (rep1 == rep2) return TRUE;
     if (rep1 -> kind != rep2 -> kind) return FALSE;
     switch (rep1 -> kind) { /* recursively compare
                                  component type */ }
     if (/* components are equivalent */)
             merge_equiv_sets(rep1, rep2);
};
```

When types can be cyclic, the basic equivalence set algorithm above (Aho 1986) must be modified. In the "equiv" function, equivalence sets must be merged *before* making any recursive calls. Thus, when a cycle is encountered, the comparison of the representatives will yield TRUE. If the types then prove to be not equivalent, the equivalence set merges must reversed by setting the "equiv_set" fields back to null. To do this, "equiv" must lock the type nodes and maintain an undo list.

The problem with the basic algorithm is that the worst case cost of "find_representative" is O(N), where N is the number of set members. In the Optimising Equivalence Set variant (Crawley 1996), the average height of the equivalence set tree is reduced by setting "equiv_set" fields to point to the current representative; e.g.

```
if (/* components are equivalent */) {
        merge_equiv_sets(rep1, rep2);
        t1 -> equiv_set = rep2;
        if (t2 != rep2) t2 -> equiv_set = rep2;
};
```

With this optimisation and a closed set of type nodes, the cost of "find_representative", and hence of "equiv" for equivalent types, will converge to a small constant O(1).

Two final points should be noted. First, if multiple type equivalence rules are supported (as described in section 5) a separate equiv_set field is needed for each rule. Second, while the cost of "equiv" should converge to O(1) for equivalent types, it will remain higher for comparing non-equivalent types, depending on how different the types in question are.

7 EFFICIENT RUNTIME TYPE CHECKING FOR CORBA

In the last section we described the basic equivalence set type checking algorithm and a variant that optimises the equivalence sets. These algorithms were designed for type checking within a single address space. In this section, we sketch how they would be applied to CORBA's problem of determining whether two URIDs denote the same type. The key to making this efficient will be to minimise the number of network interactions required.

In cases where clients are mostly accessing objects on the local net, the URIDs they see are most likely to have come from the local IFR. In this case, type checking for equivalent types will typically succeed after a string comparison in the client-side runtime libraries.

When the URID strings are not the same, the client needs to do more work to test for type equivalence. In the simplistic algorithm from section 4, the client fetches the corresponding definitions from the IFRs for the URIDs and then does a structural type comparison. This is too inefficient to be practical, irrespective of the algorithm used for the comparison.

Where possible, a client should make use of local caches of URID equivalences. For example, a client can maintain local equivalence sets for the URIDs that it compares. Negative results (i.e. non-equivalences) should also be cached. If we assume that runtime type checks will nearly always succeed, the (greater) cost of an occasional failure can be absorbed. However, we would like to avoid always having to go off-machine.

When a client's local caches are no help, it must consult an IFR. Rather than fetching the types from their respective IFRs, the client should send both URIDs to one of the IFRs and have it do the equivalence checking. This immediately halves the number of network interactions, since at least one of the type definitions will be local to the IFR doing the comparison. Furthermore, if the IFR has performed the comparison before, the result may already be cached (e.g. in equivalence sets) avoiding the needs for any further network interactions.

The client's best strategy for comparing types is to send a request to compare URIDs to the local IFR, irrespective of their origin. If the local IFR cannot handle the request itself, it can forward it to the IFR for one or other of the URIDs. Using the local IFR as an intermediary allows it to cache results for the benefit of other local clients. This also reduces the load on IFRs that originated the URIDs for common types. Finally, it removes the immediate need for a client to be able to locate the IFR for a given URID.

8 OTHER ISSUES

In previous sections, we have proposed a method for improving the type safety of CORBA object references. We freely acknowledge that the proposal is not yet complete, and that it does not make CORBA fully type-safe. Some of the major outstanding issues are listed below.

- Interoperability -- to allow incremental deployment, it is necessary for the proposed new type checking mechanism to co-exist with the old in a maximally type-safe fashion.
- Other type-safety issues -- a number of other areas have been noted in which CORBA runtime type checking is too "loose". These include the definition of CORBA type equivalence, the potential loss of type information in TypeCode transmission and type safety of operation invocation using the DII.
- Interface Versions -- while the current IFR specification allows multiple versions of an IDL interface to be stored, the IFR's CORBA::Container interface (section 7.5.4) does not allow the client to access more than one of them by name. (In reality, we are not aware of any IFR that supports multiple versions of an interface.)
- IFR and MOF -- in December 1997, OMG adopted the Meta Object Facility (MOF) specification (DSTC 1997). The MOF could be used to build a unified meta-information framework for the OMA. At some point, the IFR will need to be integrated into this framework.

9 CONCLUSIONS

In this paper, we have identified an important "loophole" in the CORBA type system as it is defined in the current CORBA specifications. The root cause of the problem is that CORBA makes unwarranted assumptions about the consistency of repository ids. This loophole is already causing problems for users, and will increasingly do so as CORBA environments get larger and more complex.

We have proposed a solution to this type safety problem based on the use of a new RepositoryId format that an IFR must handle in a particular way. We have presented an algorithm and a set of strategies for efficient runtime type checking of the new RepositoryIds in a federation of CORBA ORBs. We have also briefly noted some consequent and other type-related issues that will be the topic a future paper.

Any complex distributed system that is not type-safe at the point where clients make bindings to servers is likely to suffer from reliability problems. While the algorithms and strategies presented here are described in CORBA-specific terms, we believe that they can easily be adapted for use with other distributed computing platforms. In particular, both DCE and COM / DCOM suffer from interface type safety problems that could be addressed using these techniques.

ACKNOWLEDGEMENTS

The authors would like to thank Michi Henning of DSTC for his support, and for significant technical contributions to this paper.

REFERENCES

Aho, A.V. Sethi, R. and Ullman, J.D. (1986) Compilers: Principles, Techniques and Tools, Addison-Wesley.

BEA Systems, et al. (1997) *ORB Portability Joint Submission (Final)*, part 1, orbos/97-05-15, OMG.

Crawley, S.C. (1996) Type Management using Type Graphs, in *Proceedings of DSTC Symposium '96*. (http://www.dstc.edu.au/symposia/1996/papers)

DSTC (1997) *Meta Object Facility Information*, (web pages). (URL: http://www.dstc.edu.au/MOF/)

Henning, M. and Neville, M. (1997) Waste Not, Want Not -- A Proposal for Shorter IORs, DSTC. (http://www.dstc.edu.au/BDU/staff/ior2/ior_doc.html)

Mockapetris, P.V. (1987) *Domain Names - Concepts and Facilities*, RFC-1034, IETF.

Microsoft Inc (1995) *The Component Object Model Specification.* (http://www.microsoft.com/oledev/olecom/title.htm)

Soley, R.M. and Stone, C.M. (1995) *Object Management Architecture Guide*, 3rd ed, OMG / John Wiley & Sons.

Object Management Group (1997) *The Common Object Request Broker: Architecture and Specification*, Rev 2.1, OMG.

Object Management Group (1997a) *The Interface Repository* - Chapter 7 of (OMG 1997).

Open Systems Foundation (1994) *X/Open DCE: Remote Procedure Call*, Appendix A, X/Open Group.

Rosenberry, W., Kenney, D. and Fisher, G. (1992) *Understanding DCE*, O'Reilly & Associates.

BIOGRAPHIES

Stephen Crawley is a Senior Research Scientist with the Command and Control Information Systems Interoperability Laboratory (CCISIL) of DSTO in Canberra, Australia. He is currently seconded to the DSTC's Architecture Unit where he leads research into distributed type and meta-data management. He is the DSTC's primary architect for the OMG MOF standard. His research interests include C3I systems, distributed object computing, type checking, garbage collection and persistence. Stephen was awarded a PhD in Computer Science by the University of Cambridge in 1986.

Keith Duddy is a Senior Research Scientist with the DSTC's Architecture Unit. His special interest is CORBA. He has been involved in several OMG standards submissions including those for the Trader Service, the Notification Service and the MOF. He is co-author of "Java Programming for CORBA" published by John Wiley & Sons. Keith completed an honours degree in Computer Science at the University of Queensland in 1989. He has also worked in Australian and European computer industries as a UNIX operating systems and network programmer.

Type Checking Stream Flow Endpoints

F. Eliassen, S. Mehus
University of Tromsø
Dept of Computer Science, 9037 Tromsø, Norway
E-mail frank@cs.uit.no, sindrem@stud.cs.uit.no

Abstract

In middleware the notion of interface type is important for supporting type checking of interfaces during bind time. In this paper we present the design of a prototype generic flow type checker founded on a generic type model of stream flows and a general definition of stream flow compatibility ensuring the correctness of binding attempts of stream flow endpoints. The type checker determines compatibility by computing the set of common flow capabilities supported by the two endpoints. We illustrate the application of the type checker through its use as part of a flow binding facility, and as a basis for capability negotiations. The performance of the type checker is critical for its overall usefulness in interactive distributed multimedia applications. We therefore report on the results of some measurements to determine its performance.

Keywords

stream interfaces, flows, type model, compatibility, type checker, performance

1 INTRODUCTION

A basic requirement of today's distributed multimedia applications is the need to communicate multimedia streams of various kinds between source and presentation devices. The majority of today's multimedia applications are closed in the sense that they make assumptions about the kinds of media encodings that can be processed and the assortment of hardware and software required to decode these. Given the lack of accepted standards in the multimedia world, the closed approach to multimedia applications implies that there will be serious drawbacks to future applications in terms of their ability to interoperate.

It is therefore important to have in place middleware capable of flexibly interconnecting stream endpoints despite the fact that they may exhibit various forms of heterogeneity with respect to media stream properties and coding formats. An important foundation on which to build this kind of support is a proper type model for streams - a model allowing stream endpoint conformance and compatibility to be checked and resolved. Informally, compatibility ensures that the properties of a source flow are as expected by the sink.

In this paper we present the design of a generic flow type checker (Mehus, 97) founded on a generic type model for stream flows earlier proposed in (Eliassen & Nicol, 1996). In the type model, a flow type specification is interpreted as a set of potential stream flow properties such as data formats and temporal constraints. This supports the definition of a variety of flow type relationships based on set theory.

The type checker determines compatibility by computing the set of common flow capabilities supported by the two endpoints. We illustrate the application of the type checker in various contexts, including its use as part of a flow binding facility. The performance of the type checker is critical for its overall usefulness in interactive distributed multimedia applications. We therefore report on the results of some measurements to determine its performance.

A particular problem addressed by the type checker implementation, relates to the extentional style of the definitions of flow type and flow type relationships in (Eliassen & Nicol, 1996). We argue that the extensional style is less suitable as a basis for implementation due to performance requirements. We therefore present an intentional style implementation of the type checker as an alternative to the extensional style based on relational algebra.

The remainder of the paper is organized as follows. In section 2, we offer further motivation for our work. Following that, in section 3 we then present the main ideas of a type model for continuous media flows. Section 4 introduces the notion of flow compatibility. Section 5 discusses some design issues of the type checking facility including a flow interface definition language FIDL, while in section 6 we describe the implementation of the type checker. Section 7 reports on the performance of the type checker. Section 8 concludes and discusses some further work.

2 TYPE CHECKING AND BINDING OF STREAM INTERFACES

The notion of stream interface has been proposed as the preferred means to convey media streams (Coulson et al, 1992). A stream interface consists of a collection of source and/or sink media flows. A continuous media flow (such as audio or video) is a time-based value interpreted as a (finite) sequence of temporally constrained data elements. The temporal dimension of the data elements refers to their required time and length of presentation. This is expressed, as a QoS annotation specifying, for example, required sample rate. Stream interfaces have been adopted in the work on Open Distributed Processing (ITU-T Draft Recommendation X.901, 1995) and TINA-DPE (TINA-C, 1995) and more recently by OMG (Object Management Group, 1996).

Bindings are created between compatible stream interfaces for the purpose of exchanging continuous streams as dictated by the type and direction of the flows. During binding, the interfaces to be bound must be type-checked for compatibility. Informally, type-checking means ensuring that the properties of each source flow are as expected by the corresponding sink flow.

Conformance rules for stream interfaces have been deemed outside the scope of the RM-ODP standard (ITU-T Draft Recommendation X.901, 1995); the proposed rationale for which is that the optimum form of subtyping will depend on the application. Although this is a valid observation, the advantages of detecting type errors at compile (or bind) time, rather than at run-time, are no less important for stream interfaces than they are for operational interfaces. In the work of TINA-C, the need for a compatibility relationship for stream flows that is more relaxed than equivalence, is recognized, but no definition is offered (TINA-C, 1995). A recent proposal for audio/video support in CORBA (IONA et al, 1997), also introduces the notion of flow end-point compatibility This determines whether two flow endpoints are connectable. In their proposal two flow endpoints are compatible if they share a common protocol over which they can transport media, and if they share a common format for media encoding/decoding (e.g. MPEG). Hence QoS parameters are not considered.

Microsoft's ActiveMovie framework (Microsoft ActiveMovie, 1996) also includes the notion of "compatibility negotiation" between "pins" (connection points that carry flows between different processing objects). The subject of this negotiation is data compatibility rather than QoS. In contrast, our approach is open-ended and can in principle support any set of flow parameters.

Other works that recognize the need for type checking of continuous media flows during binding but without providing generally applicable definitions, include (Bates & Bacon, 1995) and (Coulson et al, 1992).

3 FLOW TYPE SPECIFICATION

This section offers a brief overview of the type model for stream flows proposed by (Eliassen & Nicol, 1996). Flows are used to model the behaviour of continuous media devices or stored continuous media objects. A flow type declaration provides media descriptor information as additional parameters of the type declaration, i.e.,

$$\texttt{Flow fD } [E_1; E_2; \ldots; E_n] \texttt{ sC}$$

The flow denoted above features multiple element descriptors $E_1, E_2, ..., E_n$. each describing an element type that may occur in an instance of the flow. Each element descriptor includes a declaration of the generic element type such as `Video` or `Audio`, a label that within the flow type specification is a unique name for the element type, and for each generic element type, a specific set of attributes, referred to as a media descriptor, and specifying quality properties of the element type. For images the media descriptor might include attributes such as width, height and depth, color-model, encoding, etc., while for audio could include sample-size, number of channels, and encoding. The media descriptor denoted by `fD` may optionally be used to specify further temporal constraints on the elements of the flow. The symbol `sC` denotes a specification of the structural constraints of the flow. Structural constraints are specified using sequencing expressions similar to regular expression as follows:

`A`	a sequence consisting of single element of the type labeled `A`
`p q`	a sequence satisfying `p` followed by sequence satisfying `q`
`p|q`	the sequence satisfying `p` or the sequence satisfying `q`
`p*`	zero or more occurrences of sequences each satisfying `p`
`p+`	one or more occurrences of sequence each satisfying `p`
`p[n]`	exactly `n` occurrences of sequences each satisfying `p`
`nil`	the empty sequence

The purpose of sequencing expressions is to allow a source or sink to express "indvidual" requirements to the satisfaction of compatibility such as optional types of elements and element dependencies.

The value of a media descriptor is a tuple denoted $[a_1:v_1, ..., a_n:v_n]$ such that the type of v_i is a set of values from some specified domain. The view of an attribute value as a set of "atomic" values, will in general enhance the chances of successful binding. For example when a sink flow type specifies a set of different names on the image encoding attribute, it actually declares that it can accept flows where the images can have any of the indicated formats.

Example 1: The following example is one of a partial specification of an H.261 video flow type featuring several optional playback rates.

```
type VideoPhone = Flow [
      V:Video[encoding:H.261, rate:2..24)];
      A:Audio[encoding:PCM, rate:{8000,16000}] ]
            (V  A+)*| A*
```

This specification states that a VideoPhone flow consists of two different element types labeled `V` and `A` respectively. The structural constraints of the flow is specified as a sequencing expression indicating that an instance of a flow can consist of either video and audio elements, or audio elements only. Hence we may think of the specification as modelling an adaptable flow endpoint.
❑

Interoperability requires standard payload types be defined and uniquely named by appropriate authorities. This is the approach, for example, in the work of the

Internet Engineering Task Force on a real time transport protocol (Schulzrinne et al, 1996) in which specific payload types such as different audio and video encodings, are assigned unique names by an appropriate internet authority. The value of the encoding attribute above could represent such globally unique names.

A media descriptor can be extended with a value constraint that constrains the range of specified values for attributes. This could be used, for example, to capture the aspect ratio property of visual media (in which the width dimension constrains the height dimension).

Definition 1 *(Interpretation of element descriptor)* The interpretation `I(E)` of a element descriptor `E` with media descriptor `e` is a relational algebra restriction of the (extended) cartesian product of the attribute values of the descriptor `e`. ❑

The predicate of the relational restriction is derived from the value constraints of the flow type. Each tuple represents a possible combination of attribute values satisfying the predicate. This means that tuples not satisfying the value constraints of the flow, are removed (see (Eliassen & Nicol, 1996) for details).

Definition 2 *(Quality interpretation of flow type)* The quality interpretation `QI(M)` of a flow type `M` is the (extended) cartesian product of the interpretations of its element descriptors. ❑

Definition 3 *(Structural interpretation of flow type)* The structural interpretation `SI(M)` of a flow type `M` with sequencing expression `p` is the set of element sequences satisfying `p`. ❑

Thus a flow type specification is interpreted as a set of potential flow qualities (QI) and flow structures (SI) that can be produced by a source flow endpoint or is acceptable to a sink flow endpoint. The above interpretation of a flow type allows us to define a variety of flow type relationships based on set theory.

4 FLOW TYPE COMPATIBILTY RELATIONSHIP

The definition of a subtype relationship for flows is based on set inclusion. Hence if a flow declaration modelling a source, is a subtype of a flow declaration modelling a sink, the source-supported set of flow qualities is a subset of the sink-supported set of flow qualities. Due to space limitation, however, we omit the definitions here.

The motivation for introducing the compatibility relationship is based on the observation that it seems too restrictive to require that the source-supported set of flow qualities must be a subset of the sink-supported set of flow qualities to allow attempts to bind. A more appropriate approach would be to allow attempts to bind if they can at least support one common flow quality. This relationship we refer to as *quality compatibility*. If the two flow endpoints can support several common flow qualities, a flow quality negotiation protocol may be employed to choose the actual flow quality to be used.

Definition 4 *(Strict quality compatibility relationship)* Given two flow types M and N with element descriptors $D = \{d_1, d_2, ..., d_m\}$ and $E = \{e_1, e_2, ..., e_n\}$ respectively. Let i and j be indices over (1..m) and (1..n) respectively. Then M is strictly quality compatible with N, denoted $M <>_q N$, if there exists a bijection β between D and E such that d_i and e_j are of the same generic element type, and $I(d_i) \cap I(e_j) \neq \emptyset$ for all $(d_i, e_j) \in \beta$. ❑

It follows from definition 4 that we may for example conclude that $Flow[A;B] <>_q Flow[C;D]$ if $I(A) \cap I(C) \neq \emptyset$ and $I(B) \cap I(D) \neq \emptyset$.

Definition 5 *(Relaxed quality compatibility relationship)* Given two flow types M and N with element descriptors $D = \{d_1, d_2, ..., d_m\}$ and $E = \{e_1, e_2, ..., e_n\}$ respectively. Let i and j be indices over (1..m) and (1..n) respectively. Then M is relaxed quality compatible with N, denoted $M <\sim>_q N$, if there exists a bijection β between non-empty subsets of D and E such that d_i and e_j are of the same generic element type, and $I(d_i) \cap I(e_j) \neq \emptyset$ for all $(d_i, e_j) \in \beta$. ❑

A consequence of definition 5 is that two flow types M and N are relaxed flow quality compatible if a subset of the element descriptors in each of the two flow types, are pair-wise compatible. Thus if $I(A) \cap I(C) \neq \emptyset$, $Flow[A;B] <\sim>_q Flow[C;D]$ even if B and D are incompatible, i.e. $I(B) \cap I(D) = \emptyset$.

Definition 6 *(Structural compatibility)* Two flows of type M and N respectively, are partially structural compatible, denoted $M <>_s N$, if $SI(M) \cap SI(N) \neq \emptyset$, and M is fully structural compatible to N, denoted $M <_s N$, if $SI(M) \subseteq SI(N)$. ❑

Different variants of the compatibility relationship are given by the following definition:

Definition 7 *(Flow compatibility)* A source flow of type M and a sink flow of type N are

i) fully strict compatible, if $M <>_q N$ and $M <_s N$.
ii) partially strict compatible, if $M <>_q N$ and $M <>_s N$.
iii) fully relaxed compatible, if $M <\sim>_q N$ and $M <_s N$.
iv) partially relaxed compatible, if $M <\sim>_q N$ and $M <>_s N$. ❑

In a specific instance of a binding fully relaxed compatibility means that the sink might support element types not supported by the source, and the source may produce flow qualities not required by the sink. However, every flow structure that can be produced by the source is acceptable to the sink. Partially relaxed compatibility means that there might be element types supported by the source that is not supported by the sink and vice versa. Furthermore, partially (strict or relaxed) compatibility means that the source could produce sequences of element types that are not acceptable to the sink. In this case a binding could still be allowed if the flow structures produced by the source can be constrained to the common set of flow structures supported by both the source and the sink flow. This would make the resulting modified source flow type fully compatible with the sink flow type.

5 DESIGN ISSUES OF THE FLOW TYPE CHECKER

In this section we present the semantics of the flow type checker and discuss some design decisions for its implementation.

5.1 Semantics of type checker

The semantics of the type checker can be expressed in terms of the above flow type model as a function

f_{tc} : flowTypeSpec x flowTypeSpec → flowTypeSpec

such that

if f_{tc} `(M,N)` = `P` **then** {
`QI(P) = QI(M)` $\cap$ `QI(N)`
`SI(P) = SI(M)` $\cap$ `SI(N)` }

Hence the type checker computes a flow type specification whose interpretation is equal to the common flow qualities and flow structures supported by both flow endpoints `M` and `N`. If `QI(`f_{tc}`(M,N))` = ∅ or `SI(` f_{tc} `(M,N))` = ∅, we may conclude that `M` and `N` are incompatible. Otherwise they are compatible and the output of f_{tc} specifies their common flow qualities and flow structures.

5.2 Extensional vs intentional style

The semantics of the type checker requires the development of an algorithm that can compute the common flow qualities of two flow specifications. This algorithm can be based on the definitions of sections 3 and 4.

These definitions can be characterized as extensional since they are based on an explicit enumeration of the potential flow qualities of flow endpoints. In fact, as shown in (Eliassen & Nicol, 1996) we may compute the quality interpretation of a flow specification using relational algebra such that the result of the computation is a table where each tuple represents a flow quality supported by the flow end point. The set of common flow qualities supported by two flow endpoints can be computed by a natural join of the two corresponding tables. This provides for fast and easy implementation as well as the ability to rapidly prototype alternative flow type relationships.

However, as a basis for an implementation of the type checker, the extensional style imposes several problems. First of all, it is likely that computing the entire interpretation of media descriptors as tables, and their common qualities using natural join, will consume significant space and time resources. Neither can we expect such an algorithm to scale well. This we also have been able to confirm through some simple experiments. Secondly, the extensional style can not handle ranges of continuous values although it may be argued that this need not be disastrous.

To be able to satisfy typical response time requirements of distributed multimedia applications, therefore, an intentional style implementation where attribute values are represented intentionally (e.g. as range specifications) whenever possible, seems a better choice. However, in general we cannot assume that the domain of every attribute is totally ordered. Hence extensional attribute set values are sometimes needed.

Attribute values are therefore specified as a union of ranges (n..m) and sets $\{x_1,..,x_n\}$. Furthermore, in order to enable the design of faster and less complex algorithms for determining compatibility, we require that the attribute value expressions exhibit a certain normal form. For example, performance wise it is better to replace the expression 1 + (3..5) + {2, 4, 6} with the equivalent expression (1..6).

Definition 8 *(Attribute normal form)* An attribute value expression is in its normal form if it consists of at most one set value and zero or more range values, such that no single value occurs more than once, no ranges overlap, and no ranges represent a singleton. ❑

In (Mehus, 1997) it is shown that all attribute values specified as a union of ranges and sets, can be transformed into attribute normal form.

An algorithm for computing the common qualities of two flow specifications can now be implemented as a series of set intersection operations of attribute normal form expressions. This can be derived from definitions 4 and 5 since the intersection of the qualities of two matching element descriptors can be computed by taking the intersection of their pair wise corresponding attribute value expressions. This is illustrated in the following example. The element types *a* and *b* are compatible. Their "intersection", or set of commonly supported qualities, is given by *c*.

a: Audio [encoding:{ULAW,ALAW}, samplerate:{8000,16000}]
b: Audio [encoding:{ULAW,MPA}, samplerate:{8000}]
c: Audio [encoding:{ULAW}, samplerate:{8000}]

5.3 Simple constraints

The semantics of the type checker requires the development of an algorithm that can solve the following problem: Given two sequencing expression `p` and `q`, compute the sequencing expression `T(p,q)` such that `SI(T(p,q)) = SI(p) ∩ SI(q)`.

The existence of algorithms for determining inclusion and disjointness of sequencing expressions can be resolved by considering the interpretation of a sequencing expression `p` as the language accepted by a corresponding finite automaton `M`, i.e. `I(p) = L(M)`. Let `p`, `q` be sequencing expressions and M_p, M_q finite automata such that $I(p) = L(M_p)$ and $I(q) = L(M_q)$. Then there are algorithms to answer the question whether $L(M_p)$ and $L(M_q)$ are disjoint (i.e. whether p and q are incompatible) (Lewes & Papadimitriou, 1982). However, it seems fair to assume that in the general case the complexity of these algorithms will be far beyond what is required for application in an interactive stream binding facility. It is also obvious that computing the expression $T(p,q)$ is more complex than just determining the presence of compatibility of p and q.

In (Eliassen & Nicol, 1996) it is argued that computing $T(p,q)$ can be done more efficiently by constraining sequencing expressions syntactically. In our current work we are therefore searching for constrained regular languages for specifying structural constraints of flows. In the work represented by this paper we have adopted a syntactically constrained form of sequencing expressions, referred to as *simple constraints* (Mehus, 1997). Simple constraints allow the specification of the types of flow elements that may occur together in a single flow instance. Simple constraints are thus less expressive than sequencing expressions.

A simple constraint is a logical statement containing labels, *and*'s (denoted '&'), *or*'s (denoted '|') and parentheses. For example, $C_1 = (a \mid b)\ \&\ c$ is a simple constraint with label set $\mathrm{lab}(C_1) = \{a,b,c\}$. Both operators are commutative. A simple constraint specifies which constellations of element types are allowed to appear at a flow endpoint. The occurrence of label a specifies that element types labeled a is allowed to appear, but is not required. The operator '|' means *exclusive or*, so C_1 specifies that elements of the types labelled a and b, may not appear together in the same instance of a flow. Finally, the operator '&' is used to specify which element types may appear together in the same flow. Thus C_1 specifies that elements of the types labelled a and c, or b and c, may appear together in the same instance of a flow. It can also be shown that every simple constraint can be rewritten as an equivalent sequencing expression. For example, the simple constraint $(a \mid b)\ \&\ c$ is equivalent to the sequencing expression $(a^*\ \ b^*)^* \mid (b^*\ c^*)^*$. Hence the domain of simple constraints is included in the domain of sequencing expressions. It follows that definition 6 above also applies when using simple constraints instead of sequencing expressions.

If a label set Λ satisfies a simple constraint C, we say that $C(\Lambda)$ is true. For example, $C_1(\{a,b\})$ is false, while $C_1(\{a,c\})$ is true.

Definition 9 *(Interpretation of simple constraint)* Let C denote a simple constraint expression. Then the interpretation of C, $\mathrm{SI}(C)$, is the set of label sets satisfying C, i.e. $\mathrm{SI}(C) = \{\Lambda \mid C(\Lambda)\}$. ❑

It follows from this definition that $\mathrm{SI}(C_1) = \{\varnothing,\{a\},\{b\},\{c\},\{a,c\},\{\{b,c\}\}$.

The above suggests that we may regard a simple constraint as specifying the set of legal presentation alternatives of a media object. However, in contrast to sequencing expressions, a simple constraint has no means for specifying the sequencing or numbering of appearances for the elements of the flow.

Let $\mathrm{con}(F)$ denote the constraint expression of the flow F. By the projection of the interpretation I of a simple constraint expression with respect to a label set Λ, we mean the subset of I containing only those presentation alternatives with labels exclusively from Λ. This we denote $\Pi_\Lambda(I)$. For example, $\Pi_{\{b,c\}}\mathtt{SI}(C_I)$ = $\{\{b\},\{c\},\{b,c\}\}$.

Computing the common presentation alternatives of two flow endpoints is now easy. Let M denote the label set for the commonly supported element types of a source flow S and a sink flow T. The set of common presentation alternatives is then given by $\Pi_M\mathtt{SI}(\mathtt{con}(S)) \cap \Pi_M\mathtt{SI}(\mathtt{con}(T))$.

5.4 The flow interface definition language (FIDL)

The flow interface definition language has been designed for the purpose of supporting our work on a QoS aware flow binding facility. It is used by application programmers to specify properties of (a set of) media flow endpoints. The proposed language bears some resemblance with other IDLs, for example the CORBA IDL (Object Management Group, 1991). However, FIDL has no notion of *methods*.

The syntax of FIDL is illustrated in the example below. The semantics of FIDL is based on the type model described in the previous sections.

Example 2. The following is a simple FIDL specification of a stream interface encompassing a single source flow.

```
stream strExample {
    source flow flwExample {
        video v1 {
            encoding = "MPEG";
            samlerate = (1.0, 10.0) + 20.0; };
        video v2 {
            encoding = "H261";
            samplerate = 29.97;                 };
        audio a {
            channels = {1, 2};
            samplerate = {8000.0, 16000.0};     };
        constraint (v1 | v2 ) & a  //audio with MPEG or H.261
    }; // flow
}; // stream
```

❑

In general, an .fdl file contains information about one stream interface, which is a set of directed flows. Each flow contains a number of element types and an optional simple constraint. Three constructs are available for specifying attribute values: single values, sets, and ranges. Additionally, the '+'-operator allows unions of these to be specified.

For the purpose of our experiments, we also define a hierarchy of generic element types with associated attribute sets (see figure 1). The type model itself does not require a specific media element taxonomy beyond the general requirements described earlier. In order to accommodate encoding specific attributes, a *profile* of eligible attributes and attribute domains are associated to each encoding value.

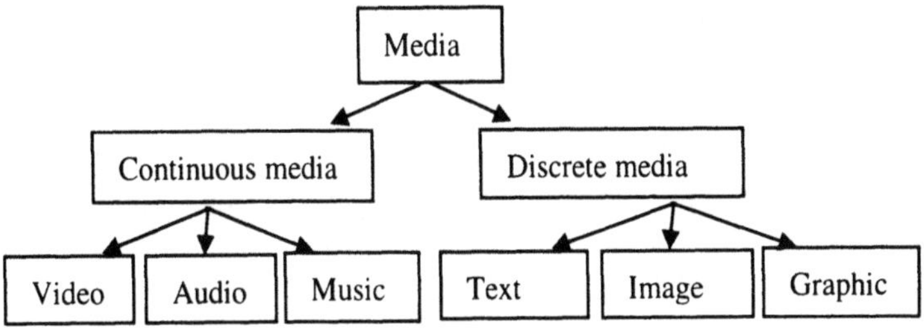

Figure 1: Media element class hierarchy.

In our work we have developed several applications demonstrating the expressiveness of FIDL (Mehus, 1997). One is the use of FIDL in a multi-versioned video server. A multi-versioned video server stores video data in different versions corresponding to different presentation qualities such as encoding, frame rate, and frame size. This allows different clients with different capabilities to view the video data in their preferred quality.

Example 3: The following is an outline FIDL specification of a hypothetical multi-versioned video object:

```
stream strVideo {
    source flow flwExample {
        video high {                    //High-quality MPEG video
            encoding  = "MPEG";         //with sound. Requires 6Mb/s
            subencoding = {"I","P","B","A"};
            ....                    };
        video med {                     //Medium quality DVI video
            encoding = "DVI";           //with sound. Requires 150Kb/s
            subencoding = "rtv";
            ....            };
        video low {                     //Low quality H.261 video
            encoding = "H.261";         //without sound.  Requires 64Kb/s
            ....                    };
        audio au {                      //Audio to be used with H.261
            encoding = "ULAW"               //video version. Available in
            samplerate = {8000,16000}       // two different samplerates.
            ....                    };
        //Three options: MPEG, DVI, or H.261 with ULAW
        constraint          high | med | (low & au)
    }; // flow
}; // stream
```

In this example the same video clip exists in three different qualities; a high-quality MPEG-2 version, a medium-quality DVI version, and a low-quality H.261 version. The latter is video-only and is therefore accompanied by the ULAW audio, as stated in the constraint clause. ❑

6 IMPLEMENTATION OF THE TYPE CHECKER

In this section we describe the implementation of the flow type checker module for compiling and intersecting flow type specifications.

Architecturally, the type checker module consists of four subcomponents as shown in figure 2. The *Parser* and *Compiler* components are responsible for checking the input FIDL specifications syntactically and translating the specifications to equivalent data structures (consisting of C++ objects) that are more suitable for processing than the source code. The *Normalizer* transforms the specification to its normal form, while the *Intersector* is responsible for computing the common flow qualities and flow structures of pairs of source and sink flow types.

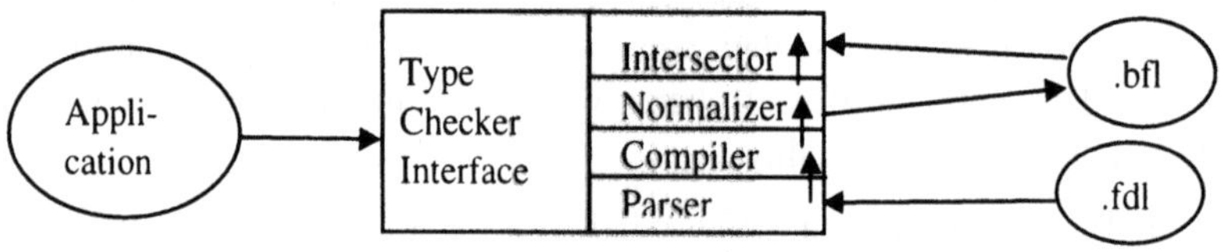

Figure 2: The components and interface of the type checker

The type checker interface consists of a range of methods for operating on flow type specifications. The Normalizer/Intersector also accepts input from other sources than the compiler in the form of binary FIDL specifications (.bfl files).

Example 4. The following program illustrates the functionality of the type checker interface. Two stream type specifications are parsed and intersected. Then a user-defined negotiation is performed for every pair of matching flows.

```
Stream* me   = parseFDL(fileMe.fdl);     // parse .fdl specifications
Stream* you  = parseFDL(fileYou.fdl);
Stream* common = me->intersect(you);  // compute intersection (max match)
Match* match = common->getMatch();
FOR EACH fm IN match {                   // for each match perform
   negotiate(fm.snk, fm.src, fm.com); }  // user-defined negotiation protocol
```
❑

In order to evaluate the expressiveness of the flow type model and the performance of the type checker, a number of demonstrator applications were developed all within the framework of the same generic architecture. This architecture is depicted in figure 3. Each of the multimedia sources in figure 3 has associated quality and structural properties described in FIDL. The helper applications are used as media presenters. The capabilities of these helpers are also given as FIDL specifications.

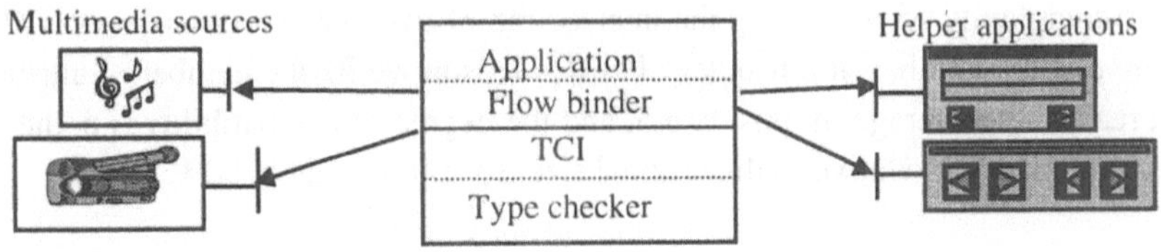

Figure 3: Generic architecture of demonstrator applications

The application in the middle acts as a wrapper for the helper applications, using the type checker to compare the FIDL specifications of endpoints to be bound for compatibility, to negotiate flow qualities and flow structures (i.e. presentation alternatives) , and to set up the necessary stream connections.

7 THE PERFORMANCE OF THE TYPE CHECKER

The intended application of the type checker is as a component of a QoS aware binding facility. Hence its performance might be critical depending on application requirements. In a conference application, binding is done only once prior to a long information exchange phase, and is for that reason not very sensitive to a slow binding protocol, although there are limits.

In contrast, bindings in database applications are typically established and torn down in a more dynamic fashion as a result of querying and browsing the database. This puts stronger requirements on the performance of the binding protocol and associated algorithms.

The type checker has been designed with interactive applications in mind, i.e. applications that frequently request bindings between interfaces. Thus response time is the performance metric we are particularly interested in. We define *response time* to be the period of real time from the service is requested until it is completed.

The load parameters that influence the performance of the type checker, are the number of attributes in a specification, the number of element descriptors, the complexity of simple constraint expressions, and the degree of compatibility between endpoints.

In the experiments we vary the number of element descriptors in a flow specification from 1 to 35 in steps of 5. The complexity of the simple constraint expressions is harder to qualify, but we may use the depth of the corresponding constraint tree as a metric. Thus, the simple constraint expression grows with the number of element descriptors n as follows:

$$a_1 \,\&\, a_2 \mid a_3 \,\&\, a_4 \mid \ldots \mid a_n \quad \text{for } n \text{ odd}$$
$$a_1 \,\&\, a_2 \mid a_3 \,\&\, a_4 \mid \ldots \mid a_{n-1} \,\&\, a_n \quad \text{for } n \text{ even}$$

The complexity of computing the intersection of two element descriptors is $O(a)$, where a is the number of attributes. For this reason we fix the number of attributes to a reasonable average, in this case 5, and the degree of compatibility (i.e. the size of the intersection relative to the original size) to approximately 50%.

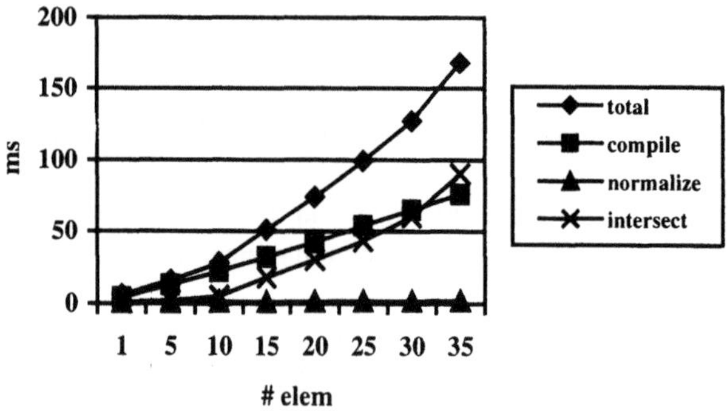

Figure 4: Performance of type checker

The result of the performance evaluation of the type checker is shown in figure 4. The figure suggests that the time needed to type check two interfaces (including computing their intersection) is increasing in a polynomial fashion with the input size. However, both the compile time and the normalization time seem to be linear with respect to the input size. The polynomial contribution therefore must come from the intersection algorithm. For small specifications (less than about 10 element descriptors) the compile time is the absolutely dominating factor. For larger specifications (more than about 30 element descriptors) the intersection phase becomes the major contributor.

A typical size of flow specifications such as specifying the capabilities of a web browser, requires in the order of 10 element descriptors, while a web document specification usually requires less. Furthermore, specifications can normally be compiled and normalized statically (i.e. prior to bind time). Hence the actual performance cost is given by the intersection phase which for smaller specifications is about 5 ms or less, while for larger specifications is about 60 ms or more.

We also evaluated the performance penalty of using the type checker in database applications. This penalty is the time needed to down load a specification from the database server, including the time needed to transform the specification from a table representation into internal format (C++ classes). The database client software, including the type checker and helper applications, are running on a Sun Ultra-1, running Solaris 2.5. The database server (Informix Universal Server) is running on a Sun Ultra-2 workstation, running Solaris 2.5.1. The workstations are connected via a 10 Mb/s Ethernet with normal load, i.e. the Ethernet segment is shared among a few other workstations used for program development.

Our experiments show that the time for down loading specifications grows in a linear fashion, from 5 ms for a one element descriptor flow, to 850 ms for a 30 element descriptor flow. For a typically sized specification (5-10 element descriptors) the time for down loading is 150 – 250 ms. This seems like satisfactory performance for the kind of applications the type checker has been designed for.

8 CONCLUSIONS AND FUTURE WORK

In this paper we reported on the design and performance of a type checker for stream flow endpoints, and the associated Flow Interface Definition Language FIDL. The type checker relies on an earlier proposed type model for stream flows defining various type relationships of stream interfaces, including a compatibility relationship ensuring type correct binding.

The type checker class library includes functionality for parsing, compiling, normalizing, and intersecting flow type specifications. Our experience with the type checker in several applications suggests that the kind of flow type support we propose is both feasible and useful. In particular it constitutes a useful foundation for adaptability and flexibility such as is needed when a database server selects the proper versions of presentation components based on the declared capabilities of a client.

In our current work we focus on various extensions of the flow type model including extensions to support QoS negotiation and configuration of *open bindings* (Blair et al, 1997). QoS negotiation we believe can be supported through specification of a (partial) *order* on flow type interpretations. This enables flow end points to specify preferences and degradation paths among quality alternatives when several flow qualities are supported. Open bindings are explicit bindings represented as a graph of component objects such as filter and protocol objects. Configuration of open bindings we believe can be supported through filter selection by compatibility matching of filter signatures, i.e. when filters are viewed as flow transforming functions.

9 REFERENCES

Bates, J., Bacon, J.(1995) Supporting Interactive Presentations for Distributed Multimedia Applications. *Multimedia Tools and Applications*, Kluwer 1(1), 47-78.

Blair, G. S. et al.(1997) Adaptive Middleware for Mobile Multimedia Applications. *Network and Operating System Support for Digital Audio and Video (NOSSDAV '97),* St Louis, USA, 1997.

Coulson, G., Blair G. S., Stefani, J. B., , Horn, F., Hazard, L.(1992) Supporting the Real-Time Requirements of Continuous Media in Open Distributed Processing. *Technical Report MPG-92-35*, Lancaster University.

Eliassen, F., Nicol, J. R.(1996) Supporting Interoperation of Continuous Media Objects. *Theory and Practice of Object Systems: special issue on Distributed Object Management* (ed. G. Mitchell), Vol.2, No.2, Wiley, 1996, 95-117.

Lewes, H.R., Papadimitriou, C.H., Elements of the Theory of Computation, Prentice Hall, 1982.

Mehus, S. (1997), Type Checking and Binding of Stream Interfaces in a Multimedia Database System, *Thesis for the degree of Cand Scient*, Dept of Computer Science, University of Tromsø, Dec 1997.

Microsoft (1996), Microsoft ActiveMovie: Software Development Kit, Beta Release, June 1996.

ITU-T X.901 | ISO/IEC 10746-1 (1995) ODP Reference Model Part 1: Overview. *Draft International Standard.*

Schulzrinne, H., Casner, R., Frederick, R., Jacobson, V.(1996), RTP: A transport protocol for real-time applications. *IETF*, rfc 1889.

TINA-C (1995) TINA Object-Definition Language, Version 1.3. *TINA-C Deliverable.*

Object Management Group (1996) Control and Management of A/V Streams Request for Proposal. *OMG Document*: telecom/96-08-01.

IONA Technologies, Plc, Lucent Technologies, Inc, Siemens-Nixdorf, AG (1997) Control and Management of A/V Streams Request for Proposal. OMG RFP Submission, *OMG Document*: telecom/97-05-07.

10 BIOGRAPHY

Until recently Frank Eliassen was professor of computer science at the University of Tromsø. He is currently at the University of Oslo. His research interests are generally oriented towards issues of distributed systems and distributed databases caused by requirements of heterogeneity and autonomy. Particular research topics of interest include distributed object management systems, extended transaction models, and interoperability of distributed multimedia systems.

Sindre Mehus graduated as Master of Science (cand scient) at the University of Tromsø in January 1998. He is currently serving is duty in the Norwegian Army. His interests in computer science include distributed systems, multimedia databases, computer networks, scientific visualisation, and object-oriented design and analysis.

Session 8

Mobile Objects

Mobile Java objects

R.J.Hayton, M.H.Bursell, D.I.Donaldson, A.J.Herbert
APM Ltd.
Poseidon House, Castle Park,
Cambridge CB4 3JB
Tel: +44 1223 713111 Fax: +44 1223 359779
Email: apm@ansa.co.uk

Abstract

In this paper we discuss the engineering requirements for adding object mobility to the Java programming language, and give an overview of the design and implementation of our mobile object system. We show that it is helpful to cluster objects for mobility, and that if these clusters represent untrusted pieces of code (for example Agents) then they must be encapsulated both to control their access and to control access to them. We show that managing large numbers of mobile objects in an open environment is a difficult problem, but has its roots in the management of large distributed name spaces. We propose an architecture for relocating moved objects that is both scaleable and tuneable.

The mobile object system we describe has been implemented, and is currently in use as part of an ESPRIT agent project. We are currently evolving the design and implementation to provide additional security and distribution facilities.

Keywords

Java, mobile objects, agents, security, middleware, binding

1 INTRODUCTION

Java is an ideal language for developing distributed applications. It provides both object and interface abstractions, which gives a useful distinction between an object's interface and implementation. It also provides language level introspection, and allows for dynamic code creation. These features make it particularly suited to the design of middleware systems.

With the design of our middleware platform, FlexiNet, we took the approach of extending Java language concepts by adding selectively transparent remote invocation to calls on any interface. We used Java's strong typing support and runtime introspection to allow us to build a strongly typed reflexive binding framework. We further used Java's support for runtime code loading to allow us to create stubs transparently on the fly during program execution. This gives a middleware system which is both extremely flexible and a natural extension of Java's features.

When we turned our attention to mobility, we took the view that this too should be a natural extension of the Java language. We designed a system in which we maintained the FlexiNet view of a "sea of objects" but which allowed objects to move between hosts. Clients of mobile objects need not be aware if a service object is mobile, nor if it has actually moved; they simply continue to use Java references to exported interfaces.

This approach has several advantages. As well as providing a straightforward and familiar programming paradigm, we remain within the well-understood domain of distributed systems. This allows us to leverage existing research when tackling issues of scalability, robustness and security.

2 RELATED WORK

There are an ever increasing number of "agent" systems available, either commercially or as academic projects. Although some provide high level abstractions that might be considered as support for intelligent behaviour, the majority of these systems are basically mobile code platforms. They allow applet-like pieces of code to move through a distributed system, and allow varying degrees of communication between different agents and between agents and hosts or other resources. Examples of these systems include Telescript (GenMagic 1995) and Aglets (Lange 1996).

In general, communications in these systems takes place using messages sent between the various parties. We believe that the advantages of object oriented computing, and in particular distributed object computing, are well accepted, and it is equally advantageous to build mobile systems using objects. Until the advent of the Java programming language, it was difficult to create "deployable" objects so most mobile code systems relied on scripting technology. It is only recently that the possibility of combining mobility and object orientation has emerged.

Existing Java systems that claim some degree of object mobility, do so either by abandoning Java's method invocation abstraction (and taking the message passing route) or by utilising Sun's remote method invocation (Sun 1996). Unfortunately when designing RMI, Sun dictated that each object must be explicitly tagged as a server object or as a data object. Only data objects may be passed by value on a remote invocation. This precludes the possibility of moving server objects, and is a show stopper for most mobile object systems.

Voyager (ObjectSpace 1997), is an exception to this. This is a Java middleware platform that supports mobile services by wrapping them with pre-processor generated classes. However, objects are moved individually and there is no notion of clustering. Although Voyager is closest system to ours, we believe we have a more flexible and scaleable approach. In FlexiNet, an introspection based serialization engine is used, which does not have the limitations of RMI's serializer, and is more portable as it is written using 100% Java.

FlexiNet embraces ODP principles (ODP 1995), and by adding mobile objects to FlexiNet we are providing the ODP relocation and migration transparencies that most other middleware platforms lack.

3 FLEXINET

The FlexiNet Platform is a Java middleware system built as part of a larger project to address some of the issues of configurable middleware and application deployment (APM 1996). Its key feature is a component based 'white-box' approach with strong emphasis placed on reflection and introspection. This allows programmers to tailor the platform for a particular application domain or deployment scenario.

Interfaces on remote objects are represented by **proxies**. Proxies enforce the typing of the remote interface, and perform remote access by utilising **binders**. Each binder is an object capable of creating a *generic* binding between a local proxy object and the remote object it represents. Different binders embody different application requirements or engineering strategies such as choice of protocols and the imposition of security policies or atomicity. Binders may make use of other binders in a recursive way. This keeps individual binders small, and allows application domain-specific binders to be easily created. To manage the flexibility, FlexiNet supports the notion of **multiple name spaces** for interfaces. Names are both strongly typed and structured. Names may be constructed out of other names, or arbitrary data, making the management of aggregate and indirected names straightforward.

3.1 Generic Communications

Rather than using stubs to convert an invocation directly into a byte array representation, we leverage Java's runtime typing support to represent the invocation in a generic (but fully typed) form. This is a reflexive technique central to the design of FlexiNet. The layers of the FlexiNet communication stack may then be viewed as reflexive meta-objects that manipulate the invocation before it is ultimately invoked on the destination object using Java core reflection.

This approach allows middleware (or application) components to examine and modify the parameters and semantics of the invocation using the full Java language typing support. Third part meta-objects can be fully general and are fully type-safe. When designing the Mobile Object Workbench, we decided to implement it as a set of FlexiNet binders, binding protocols and services. In particular the mechanism for communication with a mobile object is essentially communication with a static object together with two reflective layers: a server side layer, which raises an exception if an object has moved, and a client side layer, which relocates and rebinds to the object.

4 REQUIREMENTS FOR MOBILE OBJECTS

4.1 Unbinding

The key feature of a mobile object is that it must be able to move. When we move an object, we effectively copy it to a new location, and then arrange that all references to the old object are replaced with references to the new object. This requires a mechanisms for *unbinding* a previous binding to an object. If objects are referenced directly using language level pointers, unbinding would require changes to the implementation of the Java virtual machine, reducing the advantages of Java as a portable language. Instead we arrange that mobile objects (or more correctly interfaces on mobile objects) are referred to indirectly, using FlexiNet stubs as proxies. This level of indirection allows us to rebind references dynamically whenever objects move.

In addition, to avoid the need to track distributed references, we only perform this rebinding when a reference to a moved object is first de-referenced. The use of stubs and the rebind is transparent to the application programmer, although they may reflect the process, for example to deal with errors.

4.2 Consistency and Threads

At any point in time, an object may be *active* or *passive*. An active object is one that has a thread of control currently executing in it, or passing through it. A passive object is one that is not currently being executed, and hence has no threads active in it. When we move an object we must ensure that the move is *atomic*. To do this the object must be *passivated* - i.e. all processing of the object must be suspended. One approach to this would be to pause any threads running in an object, move the object, and then restart the object and the threads at the new location. This, unfortunately, is impractical, as Java does not allow us to determine the complete state of an active thread at an arbitrary point of execution.

We have chosen to *encapsulate* the object and enforce a locking strategy which ensures that no threads are executing the object at the point of movement. This does not prevent the existence of active mobile objects, or those that contain completely internal threads, but it does require a degree of co-operation with such objects, so that they can be 'shut down' prior to movement, and then 'restarted' at the new location.

The encapsulation mechanism is integrated with the mechanism for transparent re-binding, so that external threads that have blocked pending an object's movement restart and relocate the newly moved object.

4.3 Grouping

In the discussion so far, we have been describing the migration of single Java objects. However there is little utility in moving a single Java object as they are typically very small (for example a linked list will consist of many objects). A more useful unit for mobility is a set of related objects, and we need a mechanism for deciding which parts of a program should move together.

We introduce the notion of a *cluster* as both a grouping and encapsulating construct. References that pass across a cluster boundary are treated differently from those entirely internal or external to it. In particular, when resolving an external reference, the system may have to locate a cluster on a remote machine (possibly after it has moved). References entirely within a cluster can be ordinary Java language references, as no special action needs to be taken when they are de-referenced.

To a programmer, clusters are a straightforward concept. A special function is used to created the initial object populating a cluster, and after this any new object is created in the same cluster as its creator. Generally, clusters are completely transparent to the programmer.

4.4 Failure Modes

When designing distributed systems, there is always the possibility of host or network failure. In particular network partition can result in hosts incorrectly assuming that other hosts have failed. When designing a mobile object system, a key decision is the semantics in the worst case scenario of a network partition during object migration. There are three possibilities. We could allow the possibility of the object existing on both sides of the partition - this was rejected as it introduces an unwanted degree of complexity. The second possibility is to ensure that an object is destroyed if it cannot be uniquely determined which side of a partition it exists in. This is the default semantics chosen in the Mobile Object Workbench. The third possibility is to suspend use of the object until the network is restored. This is being considered in the context of the integration of transactional mechanisms into FlexiNet. Section 6.4 gives a fuller description of the state transitions required to ensure consistent movement.

4.5 Scalability

There are two issues relating to the scalablity of a mobile object system. Firstly, some design choices would require the registration either of all objects, or worse, of all references to all objects. We rejected these approaches as we wish to use the mobile object workbench in an Internet environment, which is both open and has no central administration. The second issue relates to the rebinding to interfaces on an object once it has moved. We would like this to be possible, even if the original host has since failed. This issue is discussed in detail in section 8.

5 REQUIREMENTS FOR MOBILE AGENTS

The mobile object workbench is not a mobile agent system, however it was developed as part of an ESPRIT agent project called FollowMe (FAST 1997), and one of the other partners is developing an agent system on top of it. As mobile agents are an obvious application of mobile objects, it is worthwhile to consider their specific requirements.

5.1 Autonomy

Mobile agents are generally considered to be 'autonomous'. That is to say that it is the agent itself that determines the actions it takes, and in particular controls its movement. In terms of mobile objects and clusters, this gives a requirement for cluster mobility to be initiated only by the cluster itself. The encapsulation mechanism gives provision for this; only threads within a cluster have access to the objects within it, and by giving one of these objects a handle to the infrastructure which controls mobility, this is effectively hidden from the outside world. There are two exceptions to this. Firstly, a malicious implementation of the infrastructure can overcome the FlexiNet encapsulation mechanisms; this is a necessary evil of distributed computing - you have to trust the host. The second exception is that a host may 'legally' destroy an object and reclaim the resources it is using. This is necessary to allow hosts to be manage their own resources. The normal procedure is for a host to inform a cluster that destruction is imminent, in order to allow it to move or shut down cleanly, but a host must always be able to perform a 'dirty' shutdown in order to protect itself from malicious or erroneous agents.

5.2 Security

We have found that the approach of designing and engineering from the point of view of a mobile object system, allowed us build on established security principles, in particular we identify six basic areas of security concern within the Mobile Object Workbench:

1. **Host integrity** - protecting the integrity of a hosting machine and data it contains from possible malicious acts by visiting objects.
2. **Cluster integrity** - it should be possible to determine if a cluster has been tampered with, either in transit or by a host at which it was previously located. We may wish to allow hosts to modify parts of a cluster (e.g. data) but not others (e.g. code).
3. **Cluster confidentiality** - a cluster may wish to carry with it information that should not be readable by other clusters, or by (some) of the hosts which it visits.
4. **Cluster authority** - a cluster should be able to carry authority with it, for example a user's privileges, or credit card details. To provide this we need both cluster integrity and cluster confidentiality.
5. **Access control** - a host should be able to impose different access privileges on different clusters that move to it. Clusters and hosts should also be able to enforce access control on exported methods.
6. **Secure communications** - clusters and hosts should be able to communicate using confidential and/or authenticated communication. Some applications may also require other security communication features, such as non-repudiation.

We believe that unless all of these aspects of security are addressed, any mobile object system will not prove secure enough for real world applications, and we have therefore adopted the principle of including security issues from the outset, rather than as an "add-on", bolted on at a later date. Section 7 discusses our approach to these issues.

5.3 Thread Encapsulation

As clusters representing agents are mutually distrustful pieces of code, it is important that one cluster cannot adversely affect another. In particular one cluster must not be able to invoke a method on a second cluster, and then destroy the thread performing the call, so as to leave the second cluster in an inconsistent state. Equally, if a cluster crashes or intentionally blocks whilst servicing a request, the client must be able to recover, and must not also fail or block indefinitely.

In order to achieve this degree of strong encapsulation, we de-couple all threads that enter or leave a cluster, by spawning and rendezvous, so that the failure of the caller and callee are independent. This thread de-coupling is integrated with the binding system and is transparent to the application programmer.

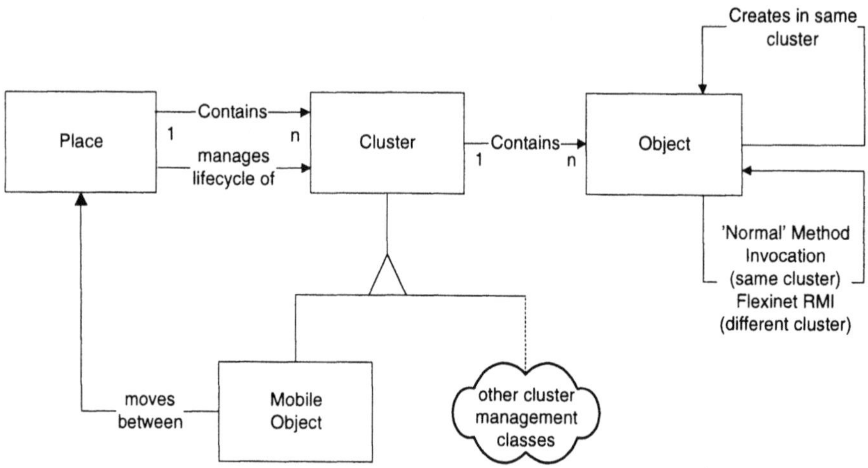

Figure 1 Objects, Clusters and Mobile Objects.

6 THE MOBILE OBJECT WORKBENCH

6.1 Clusters

Figure 1 shows the relationship between (Java) objects, Clusters and Mobile Objects. A Cluster is a Java object containing a grouping of objects which are managed together. A Mobile Object is a specialisation of this which is able to move between Places. Places are themselves objects which abstract execution environments, typically with one Place per JVM. Protection, movement, destruction, charging and other management functions are considered in terms of the lifecycle of Clusters and the interaction between them. It is sometimes useful to consider a Cluster and its contents as a virtual process, and the encapsulation and security concerns around Clusters encourage this view.

An object is the basic building block out of which applications may be built. Objects may contain references to interfaces on other objects anywhere in the system. Objects may directly create other objects, but only within the same Cluster. They may be able to arrange the creation of objects in other Clusters via communication with a Place. Within a Cluster, access to methods/data on objects is determined by standard Java language protection means and takes place using standard Java method invocation. Between Clusters, encapsulation is enforced so that object in one Cluster may only access methods on objects in other Clusters if these methods form part of an interface passed between the clusters.

As communication between mobile (and non mobile) objects takes place using application-level exported interfaces, the Mobile Object Workbench API is entirely concerned with the lifecycle of mobile objects, and is analogous to the Applet or Bean API. The key classes and methods are illustrated in Figure 2.

public class Cluster

`public synchronized void lock()`
`public synchronized void unlock()`
Change the number of locks held on the object. Whilst a lock is held, new calls made on objects in this cluster from other clusters will block.

`public void init()`
Called upon object instantiation. A subclass that requires initialisation arguments, or wishes to return an interface to its creator, should provide an alternative `init(...)` method.

`public void stop()`
A call made by the place if it wishes the cluster to cease processing. The cluster is expected to clean up and then return. When the call returns, the place will destroy the object.

`public void restart(Exception e)`
Called after the cluster is restarted. A subclass which wishes to take action after a restart should override this method.

public class MobileObject extends Cluster

`public void syncMove(Place dest)`
Request a move to the identified place. The current thread will attempt to perform the move. If successful it will exit. The move will not take place until there are no other threads within the cluster.

public interface Place

`public Tagged newCluster(Class cls,Object[] args)`
Create a new cluster at this place. Once created, `init(arg0,arg1,...)` will be called on the new object. The init method may return an interface, which is passed to the creator

Figure 2 Mobile Object Workbench API.

6.2 Binding architecture

Communication between clusters takes place by remote method invocation using a 'standard' FlexiNet binder, together with two additional reflexive layers. On the client side of an invocation is a "cluster location" layer. This examines the internal name used to represent the interface being accessed, and determines the host on which it resides. The procedure adopted is to try the last known location, and only contact the relocation service upon failure.

On the server side of the communication, there is a reflexive "encapsulation layer". This processes incoming calls, checks that they refer to clusters that are (still) located on the host, and performs the synchronisation required to ensure that the cluster is not in the process of moving. Part of the encapsulation process is to de-couple the calling thread, so that client and sever clusters cannot affect each other by killing or otherwise manipulating the thread. This is illustrated in Figure 3.

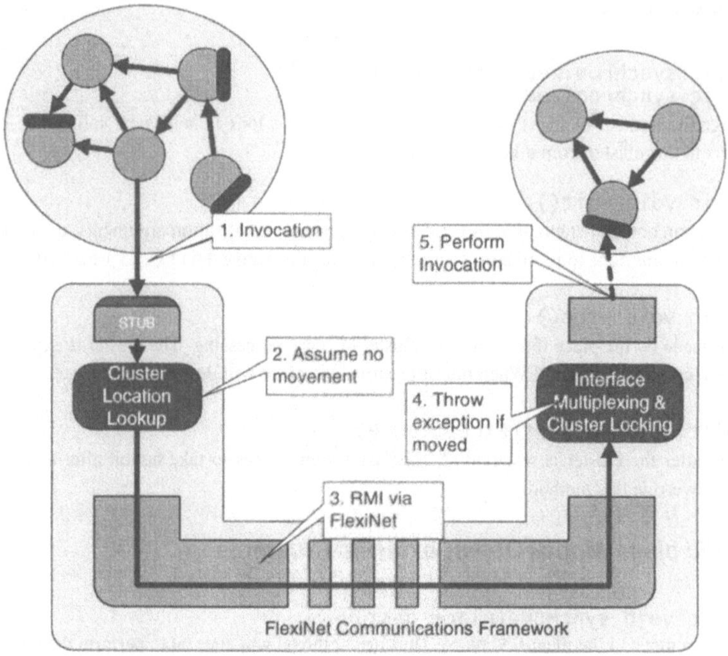

Figure 3 Implementation of inter-cluster calls.

6.3 Orchestrating Mobility

Figure 4 illustrates the states that an instance of a mobile object may be in. The object is initially created in state A_1. This state represents an *active* object that has *one* thread in it (the thread that calls the constructor). When active, the object may create other threads, and methods on its interface may be invoked by objects in other clusters. It will therefore move between active states.

In order to move, a mobile object invokes a `pendMove` or `syncMove` call. Both of these request a move 'as soon as possible', the difference being whether the calling thread returns immediately (`pendMove`) or never returns (`syncMove`). When a move call is invoked, the object enters a pending state. These are identical to active states except that the object will be moved as soon as all executing threads exit (i.e. when it enters state P_0). As a side effect of executing a `pendMove` or `syncMove`, the cluster becomes locked. When locked, calls from other clusters block until the cluster is unlocked.

When a mobile object enters the state P_0 it will undergo a series of transitions that may result in the creation of a new mobile object at a different place. The original mobile object will then be discarded (it enters state X). If an error occurs during this process and it can be safely inferred that the new object has not been created, then this object is returned to state A_1. If the move was initialised by a call

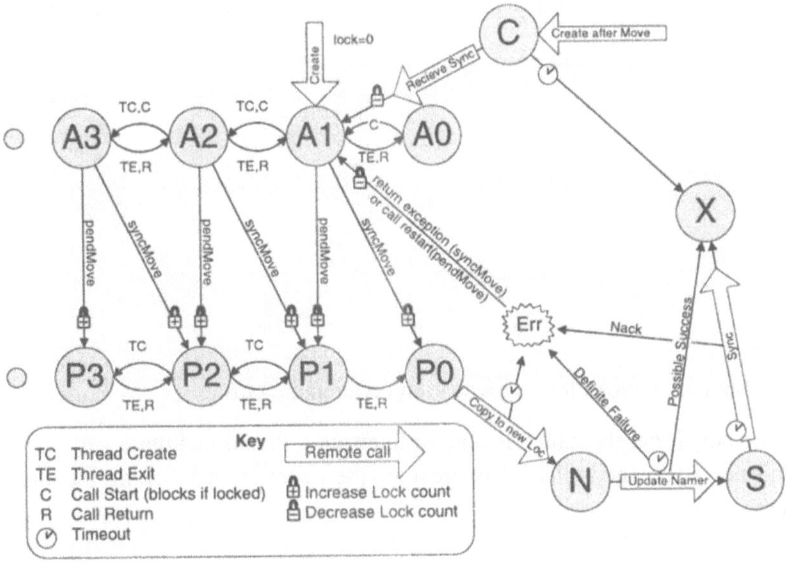

Figure 4 State transitions of a mobile object instance.

to syncMove, then the error status is returned as an exception. If the move was initiated by a call to `pendMove`, the object is restarted by calling the `restart` method, and the exception is passed as a parameter.

The newly moved cluster is an exact replica of the original, and in addition all references to interfaces exported by the original cluster are re-mapped to the new one (effectively the original cluster has moved). It is started in state A_1 by a call to `restart`. The new cluster (or original after failure) will have the same lock status as the original - apart from the lock automatically taken when `pendMove` or `syncMove` was called, which is released. If a cluster wishes to restart in a locked state, then it may obtain an additional lock prior to calling `pendMove` or `syncMove`. This allows newly moved clusters to perform start-up cleanly, before allowing external access.

Copying, rather than moving, a cluster follows exactly the same procedure as `syncMove`. The `copy` operation blocks until there are no other threads and the new cluster has been created, or a failure is detected. After successful synchronisation, or failure, the original object enters state A_1 and the copy operation terminates. The newly created copy commences operation with a call to `copied` in state A_1.

6.4 Method Invocation

When an object in one cluster attempts to invoke a method on an object in another cluster, it must block if the callee cluster is in the process of moving. The state diagram in Figure 5 indicates the process followed by the infrastructure. It

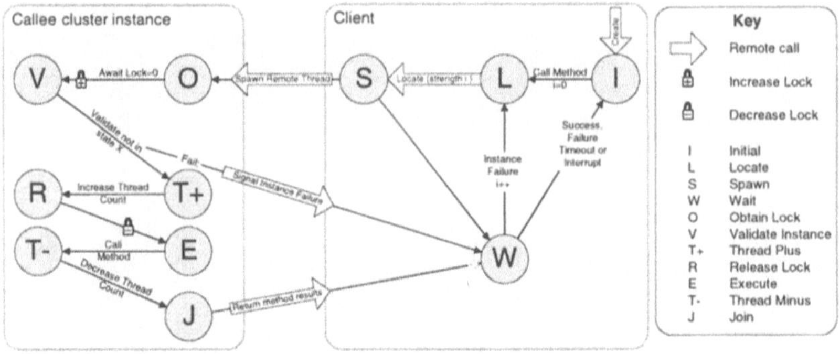

Figure 5 State transitions for an invocation on a remote cluster.

should be noted that the callee is able to interrupt a thread making a call, but that this will not affect the caller. This prevents the caller from blocking the callee's progress.

7 SECURITY

Within a mobile object context, issues of trust take on a different slant to non-mobile systems. In both mobile and non-mobile systems, questions of how much trust is placed in an object must be based on the provenance of that object - where it originated, and its history. In a non-mobile object oriented system, such as the base Java implementation, objects are typically instantiated from class files, having no other state. In Java, these classes may be signed, and a JVM may assign policies to their instantiations based on this signing. In a mobile object context, an object arriving from a remote host has a history that is not captured by the signature on the class file. Class signatures alone do not provide sufficient information on which to assign security policy.

For this reason, we have designed and implemented a Security Manager which extends Java's model by allowing policies to be assigned to instances of objects, rather than just their class. This has been possible because of the strong thread encapsulation we have employed within the Mobile Object Workbench, which gives each cluster its own thread group. As Java allows checking of the thread performing a particular operation, we may determine the cluster from which an invocation originated, and hence enforce the appropriate policies.

This security policy allows hosts to restrict operations allowed by particular clusters, thereby protecting their own integrity. It also provides a good base from which to extend cluster-to-cluster access restrictions.

Cluster integrity and confidentially are enforced by encrypting and/or signing certain objects within a cluster. This prevents a host without sufficient access privileges from examining a cluster's state, and allows one host to detect if a cluster has been modified by a host that it visited earlier. In addition to this, we

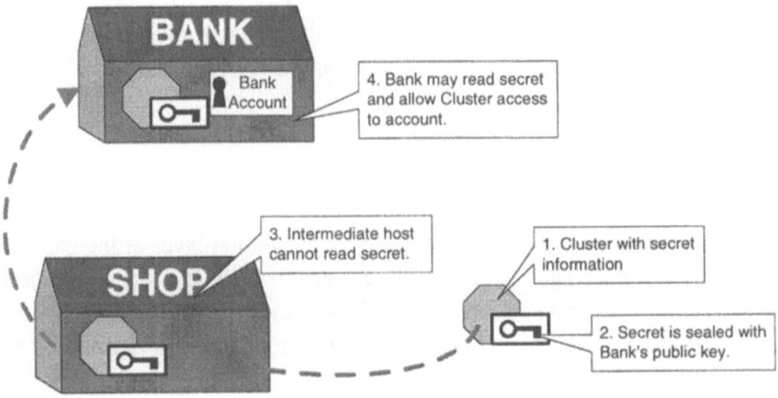

Figure 6 Clusters with Secrets.

must ensure that clusters are not dissected - or a malicious host could 'steal' parts of the cluster that represented encrypted passwords and use them to build its own clusters. To do this, we require a mechanism for specifying, and validating, integrity statements. For example we may annotate a cluster's definition to indicate that a particular field may only be modified by certain hosts. We may then use digital signature techniques to ensure that whenever the field is modified it obtains a signature from the current host, and when other hosts attempt to read this field we can throw an exception if the signature is incorrect.

We are currently developing a system to allow integrity policy statements to be specified. Once specified, the use of secure fields or objects can be made almost transparent to the programmer. All that is required is that they use accessor functions to access the protected fields.

Cluster authority can be implemented using cluster integrity and confidentiality. Together these allow a cluster to carry with it a password or other secret information, without the concern that this secret can be read at any host which is visited. Clearly, once the secret *is* revealed to a host, there is nothing that can be done to prevent the host from misusing it. For this reason we have a model that the mobile object moves into a secure environment before revealing a secret. Figure 6 gives an example; a cluster may move between several hosts before eventually arriving at a 'Bank' host. At this host, it may reveal a password to allow it access to a bank account. However, as the Bank host already knew the password, revealing it has not given the bank any additional privileges, and the security of the password has not been weakened.

Access control and secure communications may be implemented using standard techniques. We use FlexiNet's reflective binding system to allow a cluster to receive notification of an invocation immediately prior to it's execution, so that it may implement its own security policy, and throw an access control exception if appropriate. Secure communication between places may takes place using a FlexiNet binder that support SSL (Netscape 1996). Secure communication between mobile clusters may also take place using SSL, but requires that clusters reveal the information use to prove their identity to the host from which they are communicating. This is reasonable in some circumstances, but should be used with caution.

8 NAME RELOCATION SERVICE

When a call is made on a mobile cluster, the encapsulation layer at the called host will determine whether the cluster (still) exists at this host. If it does not, then the host will raise an exception which is passed back to the callee and caught in the callee's locate layer. This then contacts the name relocation service to determine the new location of the object. The relocation service is a federation of a number of directories. Each directory contains a mapping from old to new cluster addresses. Our naming service was developed with five key properties:

1. We control what entities are able to update the directories - only hosts from which a cluster is moving may update the record for the cluster. This is possible as Cluster names (transparently to the applications programmer) contain information about their current network host. This prevents fraudulent changing of naming records by "spoof" hosts or clusters.
2. We provide a hierarchy of directories, for scale and robustness. This means that an instance of the relocation service may decide to copy the naming record for a cluster up the hierarchy to increase its stability, or to reduce the load placed upon it.
3. We allow naming records to be moved between directories so that an optimal directory location can be chosen for the record (e.g. following the movement of a cluster around the network).
4. We allow caching for performance. A naming record can be kept at a previous host, as well as being passed up the hierarchy, to reduce look-up time.
5. We arrange that a client can locate the appropriate directory for a cluster rapidly, without having to search other directories.

9 IMPLEMENTATION STATUS

The Mobile Object Workbench version 1.1 is currently in use by the members of the ESPRIT FollowMe project. The current implementation supports clusters, mobility and transparent communications as described in this paper. Current work is enhancing the workbench in three ways:

1. We have started work on the construction of a federated network class loader, to allow support for mobile objects that have different views on the Java class name space. Currently a Place cannot support two Clusters that have different interpretations on the mapping between the class named 'A', and the code

implementing this class. These enhancements are important in an Internet environment where there is no global consensus on class names - and to support evolution of classes.

2. We are currently implementing several of the security abstractions outlined in section 7. We have a Security Manager implementation which can enforce different security policies based on the identity of the cluster invoking a call.
3. The current implementation of the Relocation Service does not support the migration of directory entries. We intend to rectify this in the near future.

In addition to specific Mobile Object Workbench issues, work on FlexiNet is continuing. We have recently created added support for secure bindings using SSL and support for CORBA interoperability using IIOP (OMG 1997). Transactional support is underway.

10 SUMMARY

The Mobile Object Workbench was designed primarily to add *mobility transparency* to the distribution transparencies provided by FlexiNet. In this paper we have shown that in order to do this we must add clustering and re-binding mechanisms. If mobile objects are to be used to support autonomous agent systems, then security requirements lead to the need for *encapsulation* mechanisms so that hosts and agents may communicate and co-operate without the need for complete trust. We have approach the design of the Mobile Object Workbench as a distributed system problem, as it has all the traditional issues related to distributed systems; scale, robustness, independent failure modes, distrust, decentralised administration, multiple name spaces and diverging code bases. This approach has lead us to design an architecture, and implementation, that can evolve to meet future needs, and we believe this gives it clear advantages over the ad-hoc approaches of existing mobile agent systems. In addition we have designed the system as a natural extension of the Java language. This makes it straightforward to use, and allows programmers of mobile objects to use the full language facilities.

REFERENCES

APM (1996) FlexiNet - Automating application deployment and Evolution *http://www.ansa.co.uk/Research/FlexiNet.htm*

FAST (1997) FollowMe project overview *http://hyperwav.fast.de/generalprojectinformation*

General Magic (1995) Telescript Language Reference *General Magic Inc.*

Hayton, R.J. and Herbert, A.J. (1998) A flexible component oriented middleware system. *SIGOPS European Workshop'98*

Lange D.B and Change D.T (1996) Aglets Workbench
http://www.ibm.co.jp/trl/aglets
Netscape Inc. (1996) The SSL Protocol
http://home.netscape.com/newsref/std/SSL.html
ObjectSpace (1997) Voyager Core Technology
http://www.objectspace.com/Voyager/
Object Management Group (1997) CORBA/IIOP 2.1 Specification
http://www.omg.org/corba/corbiiop.htm
ODP (1995) ODP Referenec Model
http://www.dstc.edu.au/AU/research_news/odp/ref_model/
Sun Microsystems (1996) Java Remote Method Invocation (RMI)" Specification
http://www.sun.com/products/jdk/1.1/docs/guide/rmi/

BIOGRAPHY

Richard Hayton graduated from Cambridge University in 1996 and joined the department as a research associate investigating LAN multimedia. He was awarded a PhD in 1996 for work on an Open Architecture for Secure Interworking Services (OASIS). He joined APM Ltd in October 1996 and has since been leading work on a flexible Java middleware platform (FlexiNet). His current research interests include support for complex trust relationships in distributed systems.

Douglas Donaldson graduated in Engineering and Computing from Oxford University in 1991. He worked in the Distributed Software Engineering section of the Department of Computing, Imperial College, London from 1992 to 1996, gaining a PhD in object modelling and design of distributed systems. Since 1996, he as worked for the ANSA research group of APM, investigating flexible, object-oriented middleware to support distribution transparencies.

Michael Bursell graduated from Cambridge University in 1994 and spent two years with Cambridge University Press engaged in electronic publishing projects and Internet development. Since joining APM in 1996 he has worked on Java middleware, database integration and FollowMe. Much of his work has focused on issues of mobile code, from Java applets and RMI to push technologies and mobile agents, and he has a particular interest in issues of security around mobile object systems.

Andrew Herbert, Chief Technical Officer of Digitivity Inc and its parent company, APM Ltd. With Digitivity Andrew is developing products for the secure enterprise deployment of Java. With APM, he leads the ANSA industry sponsored programme of research and advanced development into the use of distributed systems technology. The current focus of the ANSA programme includes mobile agents and component-oriented approaches to middleware deployment.

Javanaise: distributed shared objects for Internet cooperative applications

D. Hagimont, D. Louvegnies
INRIA Rhône-Alpes
655, avenue de l'Europe
38330 Montbonnot Saint-Martin, France
Phone: +33 4 76 61 52 62
Fax: +33 4 76 61 52 52
E-mail: Daniel.Hagimont@inrialpes.fr

Abstract

We have implemented a service for the development of distributed cooperative applications on the Internet. This service provides the abstraction of a distributed shared object space. The objects managed by the applications are transparently shared between the client nodes, so that the application developer can program as in a centralized setting.

It consists of a set of system classes and a proxy generator implemented in the Java environment. The service and the applications that use it are dynamically deployed to client nodes at run-time, thanks to Java mobile code. Our system support relies on object replication on the client nodes. Logically related objects are grouped in clusters, the cluster being the unit of sharing, replication and coherence. One of the main advantages of our proposal is that the object clustering policy is tightly coupled with the application code, thus ensuring locality, while keeping clustering transparent to the application programmer.

Keywords

Distributed object-based systems, Internet, Cooperative applications, Java

1 INTRODUCTION

Support for cooperative distributed applications is an important direction of computer systems research, involving developments in operating systems as well as in programming languages. In the 80s, a model that emerged for the support of cooperative distributed applications is that of a distributed shared universe organized as a set of objects. Distributed object-oriented systems such as Emerald (Black, 1987), Clouds (Dasgupta, 1990) or Guide (Hagimont, 1994) belong to this class of systems. More recently, the growth of the Internet, which is now daily used as a cooperation support, logically leads to consider the deployment of distributed cooperative applications over the Internet.

Today, distributing applications on the Internet is closely linked with the Web (essentially URLs) and Java (Arnold, 1996). Therefore, a first attempt to provide distributed shared objects on the Internet was Java-RMI (Wollrath, 1996) which provides remote method invocation between Java objects. Remote objects references may be exchanged and a mechanism called *object serialization* allows distributed programs to exchange copies of objects (as in Sun RPC (rpcgen, 1988)). However, using the RMI facilities, distributed applications are based on the client-server architecture which does not allow objects to be cached and therefore accessed locally. It is possible to manage object replicas using the object serialization facility, but the coherence between the replicas has to be explicitly managed by the application programmer. We believe that object caching is one of the key features required by cooperative applications, especially over the Internet, whose latency and bandwidth are highly variable.

In order to assist the programmer, we propose a new system service called Javanaise which implements the abstraction of a distributed shared Java object space. Objects are brought on demand on the requesting nodes and are cached until invalidated by the coherence protocol. With this system support, the programmer can develop its application as if it were to be executed in a centralized configuration. Then, the application can be configured for a distributed setting without significant modification to the application source code. This configuration is performed by annotating the interfaces of the objects that are distributed, specifying the synchronization and consistency protocols to apply to these objects. A prototype of this service has been implemented on top of Java and consists in a proxy-generator which is used to generate indirection objects (proxies) for the support of dynamic binding, and a few system classes that implement consistency protocols and synchronization functions.

The main advantages of the Javanaise service are:

- Dynamic deployment. Applications are dynamically deployed to the client nodes from the node that hosts the application; thus we don't require applications to be statically installed prior to execution.
- Transparency. A distributed cooperative application can be developed as if it were to be run centralized. Distribution and synchronization are programmed separately from the application code.

- Caching. Our system support allows shared Java objects to be cached on cooperating nodes, thus enabling local invocation on distributed objects and reducing latency.
- Clustering. Grouping objects in clusters is one of the key techniques for achieving good performance by factorizing system costs. We propose to base clustering on the data structures defined in the application. We claim that applications already manage object groups in their internal structure and that clustering should be mapped on this application grouping.

In this paper, we assume that the reader is familiar with object-oriented technologies and especially with Java features (Sun, 1996) such as code mobility, dynamic binding, polymorphism, object serialization and RMI. A longer version of this paper (Hagimont, 1998) includes descriptions of these Java features.

The rest of the paper is structured as follows. We present in section 2 the general motivations for the Javanaise environment. Section 3 presents the overall design choices for this system support. Section 4 describes the implementation principles and the prototype on top of Java is described in section 5. After a discussion of related work in section 6, we conclude in section 7.

2 MOTIVATION

The main motivation for Javanaise is to provide adequate support for developing and executing cooperative applications on the Internet. Cooperative applications aim at assisting the cooperation between a set of users involved in a common task. An example of cooperative application is a structured editor which allows documents to be shared concurrently by remote users. We implemented such a distributed editor in former project (Decouchant, 1993).

These applications are characterized by a large amount of shared data structures which are browsed or edited by cooperating users connected from remote workstations. Since these data structures should be brought to the accessing nodes, at least to be displayed and sometimes to be modified, a caching strategy should be used. Defining the unit of sharing and consistency is the key issue to efficiency.

Another important motivation for Javanaise is to allow remote access to applications without requiring them to be installed on the machine prior to execution. An alternative to installation is to allow these applications to be freely downloaded on a Java virtual machine (just like applets), thus benefiting from a dynamic deployment of the applications with the guarantee that the application cannot corrupt the local host, thanks to Java's type safety. Dynamic deployment of applications also allow users to access the same application (including some persistent data) from any machine connected to the Internet, as long as a Java virtual machine runs on that machine.

Finally, we want to allow programmers to develop application as if they were to be run centralized. Then, a programmer can debug and test its application on a single machine, and then after a simple configuration step, run it distributed using our system support.

The three motivations described above (efficiency, easy administration, easy development) constitute the guideline which leads us to the design of Javanaise.

3 BASIC DESIGN CHOICES

This section presents our design choices for the Javanaise system support. Their translation to implementation principles is presented in the section that follows.

3.1 Managing clusters

The main problem we have to solve is to efficiently manage distributed replicas of Java objects while keeping distribution transparent to the application programmer:

- Managing object replicas requires mechanisms for faulting on objects, invalidating and updating objects in order to ensure consistency. These mechanisms should be hidden to the application programmer, who should only manipulate Java references as if every object were local.
- Previous experiments with the management of distributed fine grained objects have shown that efficiency is closely linked with object clustering (Hagimont, 1994). A cluster of objects is a group of objects which is supposed to be coarser grain (than a single object). Therefore, since system mechanisms are generally applied to coarse grained resources (e.g. IOs), they are applied to clusters, thus factorizing the costs of these mechanisms for all the objects within a cluster. However, clustering works well only if objects co-located within the same cluster are effectively closely related.

The mechanisms we want to factorize are naming, binding and consistency mechanisms. In order to be able to dynamically bind a reference to a remote object, we need to associate a unique name with each object, thus allowing the object to be located and brought to the requesting node. In order to implement object binding*, we need to manage indirection objects that allow object faults to be triggered if the reference is not yet bound. In order to manage objects consistency, we need to exchange messages between cooperating nodes to invalidate and update copies according to a consistency model.

Managing clusters of objects is a means for amortizing these costs (indirection objects, messages) over a group of objects that are inter-dependent. Inter-dependence means here that if one object of the group is accessed, most of the objects included in the group are likely to be used in the near future.

* without modification to the Java virtual machine.

3.2 Application dependent clustering

Our previous experiments with object clustering (in the Guide system (Hagimont, 1994)) relied on a system support that allows any object to be stored in any cluster. The system exports to applications a cluster management interface allowing objects to be stored in or migrated to any cluster. From the programmer's point of view, managing clustering is complex and most of the time leads to a default policy which is inefficient and doesn't actually use the flexibility of the clustering interface.

In Javanaise, we propose to implement what we call *application dependent clustering*. This approach is inspired by the observation that cooperative applications tend to manage logical graphs of objects in their data structures. For example, a cooperative structured editor manages chapters that are composed of sections, themselves composed of subsections and paragraphs. We claim that some of these graphs should be managed as clusters by the system since they correspond to closely related objects according to the application semantics.

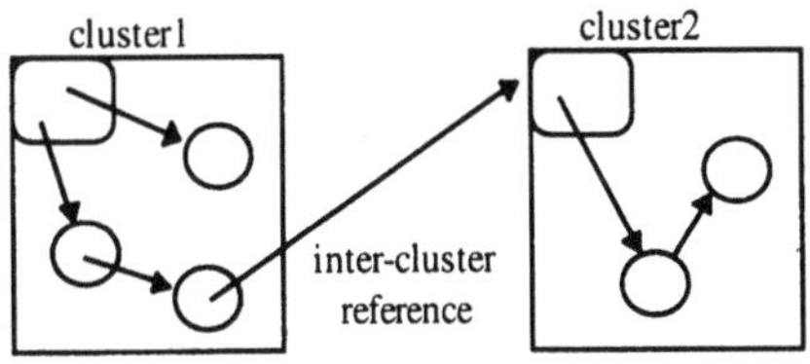

Figure 1. Management of clusters

In Javanaise, a cluster is an application-defined graph of Java objects. A cluster is identified by a Java reference to a first object (called a *cluster object*) and the graph that defines the cluster is composed of all the Java objects that are accessible from the cluster object (the transitive closure). The boundaries of this graph are defined by the leaves of the graph and by the references to other cluster objects. A reference to another cluster object is called an *inter-cluster reference* (Figure 1). The Java objects within a cluster are called *local objects*.

A cluster object is an instance of a class (defined by the programmer) which has been defined (when the application is configured to be run distributed) as being a cluster class. Only interfaces of cluster objects are exported to other cluster objects, which means that the interface of a cluster object may only include methods whose reference parameters are references to cluster objects. Therefore, local objects in one cluster are only accessible from objects within the cluster.

At this step, it is important to notice that RMI implicitly enforces application dependent clustering. Indeed, since RMI imposes that any reference parameter in the interface of a Remote class is a reference to a Remote object, a Remote object is completely equivalent to a cluster object. A Remote object can create many local (non-remote) objects but cannot export references to these local objects.

With RMI, as for Javanaise, configuring the application for distribution consists in specifying which classes are Remote (resp. Cluster). Then, only Remote objects are globally visible and the applications only pay for objects declared Remote.

The basic difference between Javanaise and RMI is that Javanaise provides cluster caching. This means that a cluster is loaded on the client node the first time it is used, and then accessed locally. Furthermore, Javanaise enforces objects consistency whenever objects are cached on different machines, as will be shown in the next sections.

3.3 Application programming

The programmer develops applications using the Java language without any language extension nor system support classes (libraries). An application can be debugged and tested locally (on one machine).

Configuring the application for distribution first consists in specifying which classes are cluster classes. The configurator should take into account the data structures managed in the application, i.e. the links between the classes that compose the application. However, this separation between the configuration and the application code makes it possible to experiment with different configurations for the same application without any modification to the application. However, we claim that logical groupings already exist in most cooperative applications.

Since an application is developed centralized, it does not deals with synchronization and consistency problems. A second step in the configuration is to associate a synchronization and a consistency protocol with each cluster. This is done at the level of the interfaces of the cluster classes. The interfaces of the cluster classes are annotated with keywords that define the consistency and synchronization protocols associated with the clusters.

At the moment, we have only implemented a single reader / multiple writers protocol. In the interface of a cluster, it is possible to associate a mode (reader or writer) with each method. When the method is invoked on a cluster instance, a lock in that mode is taken and a consistent copy of the cluster is brought to the local host. However, we will experiment with different consistency/synchronization protocols in the near future.

4 IMPLEMENTATION PRINCIPLES

Here, we describe the implementation principles used to manage distributed shared clusters of Java objects.

4.1 Managing cluster binding

Since a cluster is a graph of Java objects, clusters may be brought dynamically on a requesting node using the Java serialization mechanism (Riggs, 1996).

The problem is to manage dynamic binding of references to objects that may be brought dynamically from remote nodes. Since the unit of naming and caching is the cluster, we have to provide a mechanism for dynamic binding of inter-cluster references.

Our implementation relies on intermediate objects called *proxies* (Shapiro, 1986) which are transparently inserted between the referenced cluster and the cluster which contains the reference. A proxy contains a Java reference that points to the referenced cluster object if it is already there and null if not. It also contains a unique name associated with the cluster, allowing the cluster to be located and a copy to be brought on the local host.

The class of the proxy object is generated from the interface of the cluster class to which it points. This proxy implements the same interface as the cluster object. Each method invocation is forwarded to the actual cluster object if the reference is already bound, i.e. if the Java reference in the proxy is not null. If this Java reference is null, then a function of the runtime system is invoked in order to check whether the cluster is already cached (subsequently to the binding of another inter-cluster reference). A copy of the cluster is fetched if required and the Java reference in the proxy object is updated.

In the following, we call this proxy a *proxy-out object*. Proxy-out objects are stored in the cluster which contains the reference to the cluster (Figure 2).

4.2 Managing cluster consistency and synchronization

First, the problem is to manage invalidates and updates of clusters according to a consistency protocol. In this section, we only describe the mechanism that we used, independently from the consistency protocol which is applied.

A cluster can be invalidated on one node (Java virtual machine) simply by assigning to null the Java references in the proxy-out objects that reference the cluster. All the Java objects included in the invalidated cluster are then automatically garbage collected by the Java runtime. However, instead of dynamically looking for all the proxy-out objects that point to the invalidated cluster (which would be complex and inefficient), we decided to manage another type of proxy called *proxy-in object*, which is inserted between the proxy-out object and the cluster it points to (Figure 2). A proxy-in object is stored in the cluster which is referenced. Similarly to proxy-out objects, a proxy-in object forwards method invocations to the referenced cluster if its internal Java reference is not null. If this Java reference is null, then a function of the runtime system is invoked in order to fetch a consistent copy of the cluster and the Java reference in the proxy-in object is updated.

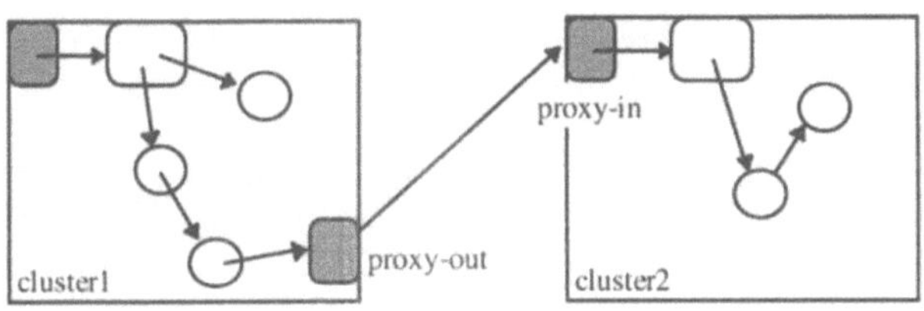

Figure 2. proxy-in and proxy-out objects

Then, a cluster invalidation on one node simply consists in assigning to null the Java reference in its associated proxy-in object.

Therefore, we deal with two kinds of cluster faults:

- proxy-out faults. When the Java reference in a proxy-out object is null, a copy of the referenced cluster is fetched. This copy of the cluster includes a proxy-in object pointing to the cluster object.
- proxy-in faults. When the Java reference in a proxy-in object is null, a copy of the referenced cluster is fetched. This copy of the cluster does not include a copy of the proxy-in object which is already there.

In both cases, the consistency protocol may require the cluster to be invalidated on some other nodes, using its proxy-in object on that node.

At this point, we are able to invalidate and update clusters for consistency management. With the mechanisms described above, we can manage strong consistency for a cluster, ensuring that only one copy of the cluster is accessible on one node.

However, in most cases, a synchronization scheme is associated with the consistency protocol. For example, this is the case for the entry *consistency protocol* (Bershad, 1993) which allows applications to lock objects and guarantees objects coherence only when a lock is taken. Such a synchronization scheme can be implemented in the proxy-in object.

In our prototype, we allow an access mode (reader or writer) to be associated with each method in a cluster interface, which means that a lock on the cluster must be taken before entering the method. This locking strategy in managed in the proxy-in object which knows which lock is being held on the current node. An invalidation on one node is in this case a lock request to the proxy-in object, that may block until all locks are released on that object.

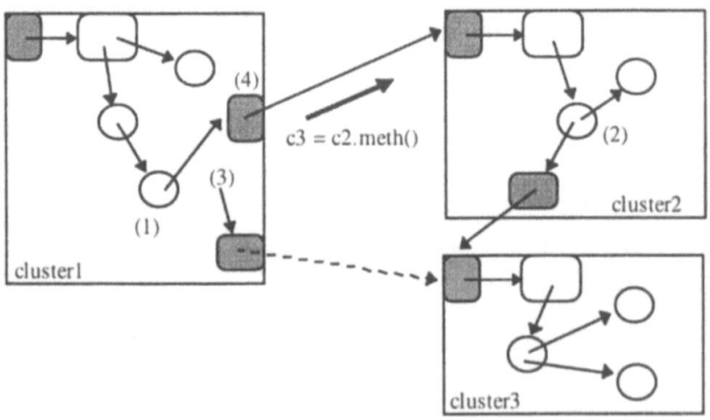

Figure 3. Parameter passing

4.3 Managing reference parameter passing

In the interface of a cluster object, methods may only have reference parameters that are references to cluster objects. When such a reference is passed at execution time, the system must ensure that a reference which enters a cluster will point to a proxy-out object. This is ensured by the proxy-out objects for onward parameters and the proxy-in objects for backward parameters (Figure 3).

In Figure 3, a local object in *cluster1* (1) performs an invocation (*c3 = c2.meth()*) on *cluster2*. The invoked method returns a Java reference stored in *cluster2* (2), which is a reference to *cluster3*. In order to be able to store a reference to *cluster3* in *cluster1*, the system must create a proxy-out which points to *cluster3* (3). This proxy-out object is created by the proxy-out in *cluster1* which is associated with the reference to *cluster2* (4).

An onward reference parameter would be managed similarly by the proxy-in object in *cluster2*.

When managing proxy-out objects for entering parameters in a cluster, we need to guarantee that all the references to a cluster *C* within the cluster point to the same proxy-out object. This is especially important when comparing two variables that contain cluster references (within one cluster). To do this, we manage in each cluster a table which registers the proxy-out objects which already exist in the cluster. When a reference enters the cluster and if an associated proxy-out object already exists in the cluster, then this proxy-out object is used and no additional proxy-out object is created. Therefore, we avoid having two proxy-out objects associated with the same external reference in one cluster.

5 PROTOTYPE ON JAVA

We have implemented a prototype of this system support and we describe it in this section.

5.1 Overall architecture

The overall architecture is illustrated on figure 4.

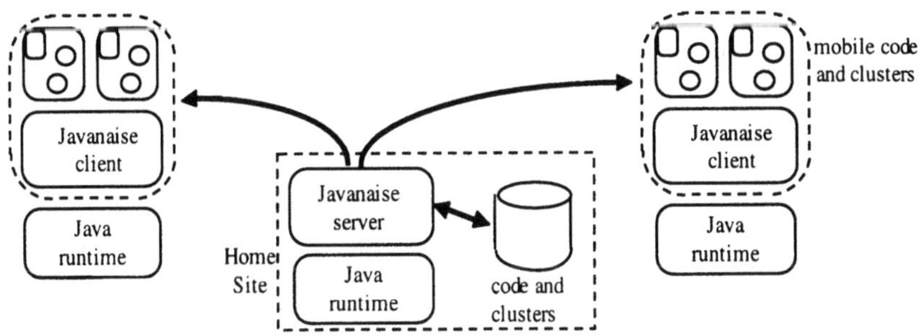

Figure 4. Architecture

In our prototype, we assume that the code of Javanaise, the code of the application and the persistent clusters are stored on a node called the Home Site of the application. The code of Javanaise and the code of the application are dynamically deployed to the client nodes when the application is invoked. An application is made available on the Home Site through a Web server and identified and located with a URL. The application is launched using an Applet viewer, the code of the application and of Javanaise being downloaded on client nodes just like an Applet. Clusters are then fetched on demand by the requesting nodes and shared following the consistency protocol.

The Javanaise system support consists of:

- the proxy generator which generates proxy-out and proxy-in classes from the interface of a cluster. Proxy-out and proxy-in classes provide mechanisms for reference binding and consistency management.
- some system primitives (*Javanaise client*) that are available on the client nodes and used by the proxies on these nodes. *Javanaise client* maintains a table of the clusters (proxy-in objects) that are already present on the local host.
- some system code (*Javanaise server*) that participates in the binding and consistency protocols on the home site. The Javanaise server maintains a table which registers the locations and locks held for all the clusters.

5.2 Generation of proxies

Proxies are generated from the interface of a cluster class using a proxy generator. Let's see the Java code skeleton of the proxy-out and proxy-in classes generated from the cluster interface below.

```
public class Cluster1 implements Cluster1_itf {
    public void method1 (Cluster2_itf obj);    : read
    public Cluster3_itf method2 (); : write
}
```

This definition describes the interface of the cluster class *Cluster1* which implements the *Cluster1_itf* interface. Two methods are defined, the first one taking a onward reference parameter and the second returning a reference parameter. The first method requires a read lock before execution and the second a write lock.

Below is the proxy-out class generated from the above interface definition. The name of this class is actually *Cluster1*, because when a program manipulate a reference to a *Cluster1* instance, it is in fact a reference to a proxy-out object which implements the same interface.

```
public class Cluster1
  implements Cluster1_itf {
  int oid;
  Pin_Cluster1 p_in;
public Cluster1 () {
  p_in = new P_in_Cluster1();
  oid = p_in.my_id();
}
public void method1 (Cluster2 obj) {
  if (p_in == null)
    p_in = (P_in_Cluster1)
      jvn_client.get_p_in(oid, read);
  p_in.method1(obj);
}
public Cluster3 method2 () {
  if (p_in == null)
    p_in = (P_in_Cluster1)
      jvn_client.get_p_in(oid, write);
  Cluster1 p = p_in.method2();
  // clone proxy-out
  // for backward parameter
  p = clone_p_out(p);
  return p;
}
}
```

This class defines two instance variables, *oid* which is the unique identifier of the object the proxy-out refers to, and *p_in* which points to the proxy-in object. The identifier is unique in the context of the application; our prototype currently manages distributed shared objects for applications stored on a single Home Site, but it can be extended to manage different Home Sites simply by using URLs.

The first method is the constructor. When a user program invokes the creation of a *Cluster1* object, it actually creates a proxy-out object which in turns creates a proxy-in object which creates the real instance of *Cluster1* (see below in the proxy-in class). If a constructor with parameters is defined, a constructor is generated accordingly in the proxy-out and proxy-in classes and implements the same interface.

The two other methods check the binding of the reference to the cluster. If the reference has not already been bound, *Javanaise client* is invoked is order to get a copy of the cluster (including the proxy-in object) with a lock in the corresponding mode*. Then the invocation is forwarded to the proxy-in object.

Notice that the *method2* method returns a reference to a *Cluster3* instance. The reference returned by this method is a reference to a proxy-out object in the invoked cluster. Then, we must create a clone of this proxy-out object, which will be stored in the cluster receiving the reference. This clone gets created only if a proxy-out object for the received reference doesn't yet exist in the receiving cluster. The table which registers the existing proxy-out objects in the cluster is stored in the cluster itself. In this code skeleton, we omitted the code related to the management of this table (to keep it readable).

Below is the generated proxy-in class. The proxy-in class also defines a variable *oid* for the unique identifier of the object and a variable *obj* which points to the real cluster instance. It also contains a variable *lock* which indicates the lock that is held on the local host on this cluster (read, write or none).

* The locking mode is specified here in order to get both the copy of the cluster and the lock on that cluster in a single request.

```
public class P_in_Cluster1
  implements Cluster1_itf {
  int oid;
  Real_Cluster1 obj;
  int lock;
  int nreaders;
public P_in_Cluster1 () {
  obj = new Real_Cluster1();
  oid = jvn_client.register_id(this);
  nreaders = 0;
}
public void method1 (Cluster2 obj) {
  if ((obj == null) || (lock == none)) {
    obj = (Real_Cluster1)
        jvn_client.get_obj(oid, read);
    lock = read;
  }
  // clone proxy-out
  // for onward parameter
  Cluster2 p = clone_p_out(obj);
  nreaders ++;
  // effective call
  obj.method1(p);
  nreaders --;
  if ((lock == read) && (nreaders == 0)) {
    jvn_client.release_lock(oid, read);
    lock = none;
  }
}
public Cluster3 method2 () {
  if ((obj == null) || (lock != write)) {
    obj = (Real_Cluster1)
        jvn_client.get_obj(oid, write);
    lock = write;
  }
  // effective call
  obj.method1(obj);
  jvn_client.release_lock(oid, write);
}
}
```

The constructor of the proxy-in class creates the real instance of *Cluster1* which has been renamed in *Real_Cluster1* (by the proxy generator) since the proxy-out class has been renamed in *Cluster1*. Then, *Javanaise client* is invoked in order to allocate a unique object identifier*. A reference to the proxy-in object is passed in order to initialize Javanaise internal tables (detailed below).

The two methods checks whether a copy of the cluster with the requested lock is present. If not, a copy and/or a lock are requested to *Javanaise client*. The locking policy currently implemented allows multiple readers and one writer at a time.

A lock held on a cluster is managed in the proxy-in object of the cluster. The proxy-in object invokes *Javanaise client* in order to request the lock. The proxy-in object also includes primitives (upcalls not present in the above skeleton) that may be invoked by Javanaise client in order to check the status of the lock on the cluster and block a lock request from a remote node until the lock is explicitly released. The methods in the proxy-in object which manipulate the lock variable are synchronized.

5.3 Management of consistency and synchronization

In order to manage consistency and synchronization, two tables are maintained, one in *Javanaise client* and one in *Javanaise server*.

First, in *Javanaise server*, we need to be able to locate any cluster and any lock. *ServerTable* is a table which keeps track of all the clusters that have an image in

---

* In the current prototype, this allocation is forwarded to Javanaise server which ensure the identifier uniqueness..

memory (see next section for clusters stored on disk). This table associates with each cluster (known by its *oid*) the locations (node addresses) of all the images of the cluster in memory. If the cluster is in read mode, the table gives a list of the nodes that obtained a read lock on the cluster. If the cluster is in write mode, the table gives the address of the node which hosts the unique copy.

This table is used in order to locate one copy (in read mode) or the last copy of the cluster. When a collision on a lock occurs (the cluster is locked in write mode), the request is sent to the writer node and *Javanaise client* responds only when the lock is released.

The second table (*ClientTable*) is managed in *Javanaise client*. This table records the clusters that are cached on the local host. This table associates with each cluster (*oid*) the Java reference to the proxy-in object which represents the cluster. Using the *ClientTable*, *Javanaise client* can check the status of the cluster on this node and wait for a lock to be released by the proxy-in object (with the *release_lock* primitive).

All the interactions between Javanaise clients and Javanaise server are based on message passing using the socket interface. A message always includes a header object which describes the message type. This header may be followed by (i.e. point to) a cluster object which is a graph of Java objects. These objects, the header and the cluster, are serialized in order to obtain a flat string of bytes which is sent on the socket. In order to be serializable, each object of the application must implement the *Serializable* Java interface, which means that it inherits default methods that are invoked to serialize the object. The default serialization behavior is to flatten the object state and to do it recursively following every Java reference in the object state. To stop this recursion, we redefined these serialization methods for the proxy-out objects : we only save the *oid* field of the object and reset to null the Java reference when the object is deserialized.

5.4 Management of persistence

In Javanaise, clusters are persistent, which means they survive the application that created them. Clusters are stored on disk on the Home Site of the application, one file per cluster. Recall that each cluster is identified with an *object_id* (an integer) which is a unique identifier.

In Javanaise server, the *ServerTable* keeps track of all the clusters that have an image in memory on one of the client hosts. When a cluster is requested and the cluster is not represented in memory, the cluster is read from its storage file. The byte stream read from the file is deserialized and sent to the requesting client (and the *ServerTable* updated). When an application terminates on a client node and if some modified clusters are no longer used (cached on any node), they are serialized and copied back to their storage files on the Home Site.

5.5 Deployment of an application

Applications in Javanaise are deployed dynamically to the client nodes just like Applets. A Javanaise application is made available as an Applet through a Web server and a client typically starts the application using an Applet viewer. This Applet contains the *main* entry point of the program.

An initialization primitive is provided, which initializes the Javanaise environment, but also returns a Java reference to a name server object. This name server allows symbolic names to be associated with Cluster objects' references. The *register* method registers a cluster reference with a given symbolic name and the *lookup* method returns the cluster reference associated with a symbolic name. In the implementation, passing a cluster reference to the *register* method is actually passing a proxy-out object reference to the name server (which registers a copy of the proxy-out object). Getting a cluster reference from the name server is actually getting a proxy-out object.

We have described the prototype of the Javanaise runtime we have implemented on top of Java. In the rest of the paper, we relate our work to previous experiments and conclude with our continuation perspectives.

6 RELATED WORK

In this section, we briefly relate our contribution to other projects which address the same issue.

As stated in the introduction, a first attempt to provide distributed shared objects on the Internet is Java-RMI (Wollrath, 1996) which provides remote method invocation between Java objects. However, using the RMI facilities, distributed applications are based on the client-server architecture which does not allow objects to be cached and therefore accessed locally. It is possible to manage object replicas using the object serialization facility, but the coherence between the replicas has to be explicitly managed by the application programmer.

Another approach for sharing Java objects on the Internet is the management of distributed shared tuple spaces. Several projects (JavaSpaces (Sun, 1997), Jada (Ciancarini, 1997)) proposed Java toolkits that implement this abstraction, inspired by the Linda language. Cooperation between distributed applications is achieved via tuple spaces. By exchanging tuples through tuple spaces, applications can exchange data or synchronize. The drawback of this approach is that every cooperation with any remote application must be explicitely implemented using the set of tuple management primitives. We believe that application level objects should be implicitely shared between applications, as in the Corba (or RMI) philisophy.

Most of the work described in this paper was influenced by the ideas developed in several projects from the 80's ((Dasgupta, 1990), (Hagimont, 1994)), addressing the issue of the design and implementation of distributed object-based operating systems. Javanaise can be seen as a grant child of these systems. Its main contribution is to study the application of a similar paradigm (a distributed shared object space) to cooperative applications on the Internet. This paradigm has been integrated into the Java world in order to allow dynamic deployment of shared applications to the client hosts.

7 CONCLUSION AND PERSPECTIVES

In this paper, we presented our experience with providing a runtime environment for the development of cooperative application on the Internet. In our environment, applications are developed using the Java language, and made available on the Internet through a Web server just like an Applet. Applications are dynamically deployed to client nodes, thanks to Java mobile code, and the Java objects managed by the applications are transparently shared between application instances.

In order to allow for efficient object caching on client nodes, our runtime manages clusters of Java objects, the cluster being the unit of sharing, caching and consistency. Clusters are brought on demand on the client nodes and shared following a specified consistency and synchronization protocol. Our claim is that object grouping in clusters can be derived from the application structure by specifying which classes correspond to clusters, other classes defining local objects within clusters.

We have implemented a prototype of the Javanaise runtime, composed of a preprocessor which generates required proxy classes from the interfaces of cluster classes, and of system classes which manage consistency of cluster replicas cached on client nodes.

The continuation of this work is to validate and evaluate this system support through full scale cooperative applications.

BIBLIOGRAPHY

Arnold K. and Gosling J. (1996) The Java Programming Language, *Addison-Wesley*.

Bershad B. N., Zekauskas M. J., and Sawdon W. A. (1993) The Midway Distributed Shared Memory System, *Proceedings of the 38th IEEE Computer Society International Conference (COMPCON'93)*, pp. 528—537.

Black A., Hutchinson N., Jul E., Levy H. and Carter L. (1987) Distribution and abstract types in Emerald, *IEEE Transactions on Software Engineering*, 13(1).

Ciancarini P. and Rossi D. (1997) Jada: A Coordination Toolkit for Java, *Technical Report C, Department of Computer Science, University of Bologna, Italy*.

Dasgupta P., Chen R., Menon S., Pearson M., Ananthanarayanan R., Ramachandran U., Ahamad M., LeBlanc R., Appelbe W., Bernabeu-Auban J., Hutto P., Khalidi M. and Wilkenloh C. (1990) The Design and Implementation of the Clouds Distributed Operating System, *Computing Systems*, 3(1), pp. 11—45.

Decouchant D., Quint V., Riveill M. and Vatton I. (1993) Griffon: A Cooperative, Structured, Distributed Document Editor, *Technical Report 93-20, Bull-IMAG.* http://sirac.imag.fr/~hagimont/papers/93-20-griffon-RT.ps.gz

Hagimont D., Chevalier P.Y., Freyssinet A., Krakowiak S., Lacourte S., Mossière J. and Rousset de Pina X. (1994) Persistent Shared Object Support in the Guide System: Evaluation & Related Work, Proceedings of the *9th Conference on Object-Oriented Programming, Systems, Languages and Applications (OOPSLA).*

Hagimont D. and Louvegnies D.(1998) Javanaise: distributed shared objects for Internet cooperative application, *Long version of this paper.* http://sirac.inrialpes.fr/~hagimont/papers/98-middleware-long.ps.gz

Riggs R., Waldo J., Wollrath A. and Bharat K. (1996) Pickling State in the Java System, *Computing Systems*, 9(4), pp. 313—329.

rpcgen (1988) An RPC Protocol Compiler, Sun Microsystem, Inc.

Shapiro M. (1986) Structure and Encapsulation in Distributed Systems: The Proxy Principle, *Proceedings of the 6th International Conference on Distributed Computing Systems*, pp. 198—204.

Sun (1996) JDK 1.1 Documentation, *Sun Microsystems.* http://www.javasoft.com/products/jdk/1.1/docs/index.html

Sun (1997) JavaSpace Specification, *Sun Microsystems.* http://chatsubo.javasoft.com/javaspaces/index.html

Wollrath A., Riggs R. and Waldo J. (1996) A Distributed Object Model for the Java System, *Computing Systems*, 9(4), pp. 291—312.

BIOGRAPHY

Daniel Hagimont is "Chargé de Recherche" (research scientist) at INRIA Rhône-Alpes (Grenoble, France). He received his Phd from Institut National Polytechnique de Grenoble in 1993. In 1993-94, he held a post-doctoral position at the University of British Columbia (Vancouver, Canada). He is currently a member of the Sirac project at INRIA, Grenoble, where he leads a group working on distributed operating systems.

Denis Louvegnies graduated from the Université Joseph Fourier (Grenoble, France) in 1997. He is currently a Master student at the same university. The results presented in this paper corresponds to his Master's work.

Mole 3.0: A Middleware for Java-Based Mobile Software Agents

J. Baumann, F. Hohl, K. Rothermel, M. Schwehm, M.Straßer
Institute of Parallel and Distributed High-Performance Systems
University of Stuttgart
Breitwiesenstraße 20-22
D-70565 Stuttgart, Germany
Phone: +49/711/7816-275, Fax: +49/711/7816-424
baumann|hohlfz|rothermel|schwehms@informatik.uni-stuttgart.de

Abstract

Mole is one of the first Java-based mobile agent systems. It runs on an unmodified Java virtual machine on PCs under Windows 95/NT and on workstations under several UNIX dialects. Earlier versions of Mole have provided a basic infrastructure for communication and migration of mobile agents. Version 3.0 of Mole has been strongly revised and several requests and proposals from users of the earlier versions of Mole were integrated into the new release. In particular Mole supports communication between agent groups and the concept of sessions. The infrastructure of Mole includes a resource manager, a directory service and a global naming scheme for agents. In order to support the design of agents, a graphical agent monitor allows to visualize the system behavior as a whole or of a single agent in particular. Mole further provides a thread management unit to overcome some shortcomings of the Java virtual machine. Mole provides a simple means for installation and configuration of the system. This paper describes the architecture and infrastructure of Mole 3.0.

Keywords

Middleware, Java, mobile agent system, agent migration, agent communication

1 INTRODUCTION

Mobile agents are a new programming model for distributed systems. Generally a mobile agent is a process that can act within a distributed system on behalf of its user. In particular such processes must be able to move freely from node to node in a distributed system and to continue processing asynchronously even if its user is (temporarily) not connected with the system any more. To allow this functionality, each computing node of the distributed system must provide a suitable infrastructure. Such a platform for mobile agents consists basically of a virtual machine (engine) that must run on each participating node of the distributed system. The engine manages two types of objects: places and agents. A place is an object that provides an infrastructure for executing agents. An agent is a process that can reside on a place and that can communicate with other agents. Stationary agents can provide services and system resources to other agents. A mobile agent can actively move from one place to another (agent migration) and can access or provide services by communication with other agents. Applications of mobile agents can be found among others in the areas of network management, electronic commerce and mobile computing.

The idea to send machine independent executable messages via a network can be traced back to the very beginning of the Internet, where the Decode-Encode-Language (DEL) was considered to run interactive programs on remote consoles of a networked system (Rulifson 1969). Later the idea emerged independently in the area of radio network communication, where the SOFTNET project used Forth-messages to transmit data as well as to reprogram the underlying network (Zander 1981). Another early approach was the Network Command Language by Falcone (1987). In the early nineties the term `messengers' was used by Tschudin (1993) to denote active messages programmed in his Postscript-like language M0. The term `mobile agent' was coined in a white paper by General Magic Inc. (1994, republished by White 1997a, 1997b). General Magic's Telescript language was specifically designed for mobile agent programming and already included most of the concepts of later mobile agent systems, but it was dropped when it became clear that it could not compete with Java as a commercial product. In the sequel several mobile agent systems have been developed in the research community. The research systems were based on such diverse programming languages like untyped scripting languages, e.g. Agent Tcl, an extension of Tcl by Gray (1995, 1996), or strongly typed functional languages like MAP based on Scheme by Perret and Duda (1996), but the mainstream of the systems today are based on Java. Examples are Mole by Straßer, Baumann and Hohl (1996) or Aglets by the IBM Aglets Workbench Team (1997). Other approaches use a language independent approach like TACOMA by Johansen, van Renesse and Schneider (1994, 1995) or Ara by Peine and Stolpmann (1997). Recently, several companies and research groups have presented MASIF, a proposal for the standardization of mobile agent systems (Milojicic *et al.* (1998)).

This paper presents Version 3.0 of Mole, one of the first Java-based mobile agent systems. The paper proceeds with an overview of the Mole system in Section 2. Then basic concepts of the Mole system like agent migration in Section 3 and agent communication in Section 4 are presented. Section 5 continues with a description of the agent infrastructure provided by Mole and Section 6 introduces the graphical agent monitor of the system. Implementational issues are discussed in Section 7 and the installation procedure is sketched in Section 8.

2 MOLE SYSTEM OVERVIEW

Our model of an agent-based system – as various other models – is mainly based on the concepts of agents and places. Places provide the environment for safely executing local as well as visiting agents. An agent system consists of a number of (abstract) places, being the home of various services. Agents are active entities, which may move from place to place to meet other agents and access the places' services. Note though, that communication between agents is not restricted to local communication. Global communication is explicitly supported as well. In our model (see Figure 1), agents may be multi-threaded entities, whose state and code is transferred to the new place when agent migration takes place. Each agent is identified by a globally unique agent identifier. An agent's identifier is generated by the system at agent creation time. The creating place can be derived from this name. It is independent of the agent's current place, i.e. it does not change when the agent moves to a new place. In other words, the applied identifier scheme provides location transparency. A place is entirely located at a single node of the underlying network, but multiple places may be running on a given node. For example, a node may provide a number of places, each one assigned to a certain agent community, allowing access to a certain set of services or implementing a certain prizing policy. Places are divided into two types, depending on the connectivity of the underlying system. If a system is connected to the network all the time (except for network failures and system crashes), a place on this system is called "connected". If a system is only temporarily connected to the network, e.g. a user's PDA (Personal Digital Assistant), the place is called "associated".

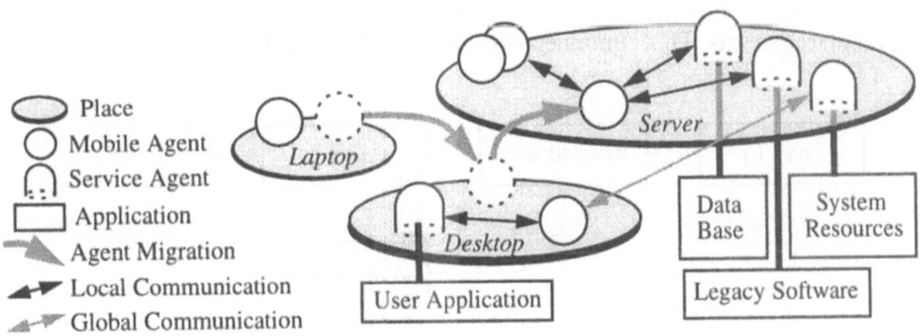

Figure 1 Mole System Overview

3 AGENT LIFE-CYCLE AND AGENT MOBILITY

3.1 Life-cycle of an Agent

After an agent is created, its initialization routine `init()` is processed (see Figure 2). The arguments given to the agent at creation time are passed to this routine. The programmer can set up the internal state and initialize the agent attributes. At this time the agent is still outside any place. Now the agent system injects the agent into the system as if it had just arrived after a migration. First the agent is made known to the place, but other agents are not yet allowed to communicate with it. The `prepare()`-method is called, allowing the agent to do its place-specific setup, e.g. identifying local services. Finally the agent is started by calling the `start()`-method. Now normal processing takes place. The agent can start its own threads, use local services, and can communicate locally or remotely. The agent stays on the place until it decides to either migrate or to terminate.

If the agent wants to migrate it calls the method `migrateTo()` (described in more detail in the next section). The system suspends the agent's threads, serializes the agent and sends it to the target place. If the target place accepts the agent, the agent is injected into the system and started again via the methods `prepare()` and `start()`. Now the target place sends an acknowledgment back to the source place which removes the suspended agent from the system. If the target place does not accept the agent, an error message is sent back and the agent resumes its work on the original place. It receives an exception as the result of the failed migration, and can react e.g. by trying to migrate to another place. If the agent has reached the end of its life, it calls the method `die()`. The system now stops all threads of the agent, removes it from the place, and deletes the agent.

Additionally the system supports periodic operation. This provides a simple mechanism for the programmer to implement recurring tasks, e.g. checking a database for changes if no trigger mechanism exists. If an agent implements the interface `Periodical`, then the system, in addition to calling the `init()`-method, executes the method `heartbeatInit()`. Now as soon as the `start()`-method has been called for the first time, the system begins executing a method called `heartbeat()` in regular intervals. This continues until the `die()`-method is called.

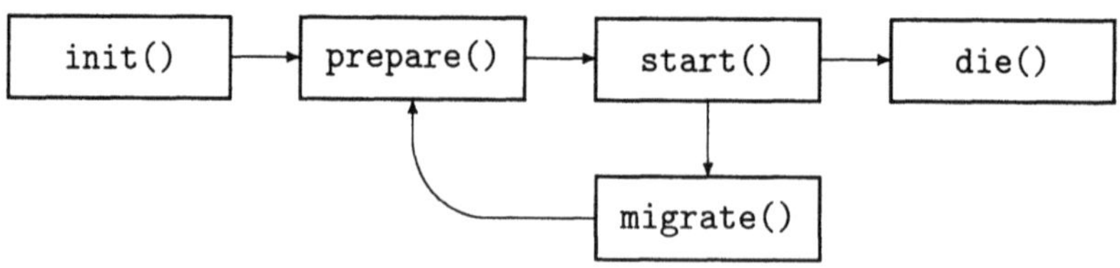

Figure 2 Life-cycle of a Mobile Agent

3.2 Agent Migration

The concept of a mobile agent supports process mobility, i.e. program executions may migrate from node to node of a computer network. Obviously, for migrating agents not only code but also the state information of the agent has to be transferred to the destination. An agent's state is subdivided into data state and execution state. While the first includes the agent's global and instance variables, the latter comprises the local variables and the active threads. According to Ghezzi and Vigna (1997) two types of agent migration can be distinguished: weak migration and strong migration. With strong migration, the underlying system captures the entire agent state (consisting of data *and* execution state) and transfers it together with the code to the next location. Once the agent is received at its new location, its state is automatically restored. From a programmer's perspective, this scheme is very attractive since capturing, transfer and restoration of the complete agent state is done transparently by the underlying system. On the other hand, providing this degree of transparency in heterogeneous environments at least requires a global model of the agent state as well as a transfer syntax for this information. Moreover, an agent system must provide functions to externalize and internalize agent state. Since the complete agent state (including data and execution state) can be large – in particular for multi-threaded agents – strong migration might be a very time-consuming and expensive operation. These difficulties have led to the development of the *weak migration scheme*, where only data state information is transferred. The size of the transferred state information can be limited even more by letting the programmer select the variables making up the agent state. As a consequence, the programmer is responsible for encoding the agent's relevant execution states in the program variables. Moreover, the programmer must specify a start method that decides on the basis of the encoded state information where to continue execution after migration. While this method may substantially reduce the amount of state to be communicated, it puts an additional burden on the programmer and makes agent programs more complex.

The difference between weak and strong migration is a change in semantics, but not in expressive power. One of the design goals of Mole is the ability to run on every Java Virtual Machine (VM). A normal Java VM does not support capturing the state of a thread, which would be a prerequisite for capturing the execution state. Thus our decision was to choose the changed semantics of weak migration and gain the ability to run Mole on unchanged Java interpreters. This includes that, while agents in Mole can be multi-threaded, after a migration only one thread is started. If more threads are necessary the agent has to start them explicitly.

Weak migration in Mole is implemented by using a part of the Remote Method Invocation package RMI, the object serialization provided as part of Java 1.1. After an agent thread calls the `migrateTo()`-method, all threads belonging to the agent are suspended (not stopped). No new messages and calls (RPC) to the agent are accepted. After all pending messages to the agent have been delivered, the agent is removed from the list of active agents. Now the agent is serialized using the object serialization. The object serialization computes the transitive closure of all objects belonging to the agent (ignoring transient objects and threads), and creates a system-independent representation of the agent. This serialized version of the agent is sent to the target place that re-instantiates the agent. If any of the Java classes needed are not available locally, the target place requests these classes either from a code server (Hohl, Klar and Baumann 1997), or from the source place of the migration. Now the agent is re-instantiated. One new agent thread is started. First the `prepare()`-method is called to initialize the place-specific attributes. Then this thread begins its work at the `start()`-method. As soon as the thread takes control of the agent, a success message is sent back to the source place. The source place now terminates all threads pertaining to the agent and removes it from the system. If at any stage of the migration an error occurs, the migration is stopped and the agent threads at the source place are resumed. The control flow continues after the `migrateTo()` statement, where error handling can be implemented (an exception is thrown in the case of failure).

4 AGENT COMMUNICATION AND THE SESSION CONCEPT

As will be seen below, a session between agents can be established only if the agents can identify each other. In our model, there are basically two ways how agents can be identified, the unique agent identifiers – comparable to object identifiers – and the badges. Agent identifiers are well-suited for identifying service agents, as long as there exists a directory system that maps user-defined service names to service agent identifiers. Note, however, that the directory service is not part of our base system, i.e. we clearly separate the mechanism for identifying services from the one for finding services. As a consequence, different naming schemes and directory systems can be used on top of this system. The directory service provided by Mole is described in Section 5.2.

4.1 Badges

In the case of mobile agents the concept of agent identifiers is not always sufficient. Assume for example, that an agent wants to meet some other agent participating in the same task at a given place. If only agent identifiers were available, both agents would have to know each other's identifiers. Actually, for identification it would be sufficient to say "I want to meet at place XYZ an agent participating in task ABC". This type of identification is supported by the concept of badges. A badge is an application-generated identifier, such as "task ABC", which agents can *pin on* and *pin off*. This badge does not necessarily have to be unique, it simply represents a role of an agent at a given time. As long as the agent provides the functionality associated with this role, it wears the badge. An agent may have several badges pinned on at the same time. Badges may be copied and passed on from agent to agent, and hence multiple agents can wear the same badge. For example, all agents participating in a subtask may wear a badge for the subtask and another one for the overall task. The agent that carries the result of the subtask may have an additional badge saying "Carry-Result". Using badges, an agent is identified by a *(place identifier, badge predicate)*-tuple, which identifies all agents fulfilling the badge predicate at the place identified by the place identifier. A badge predicate is a logical expression, such as ("task ABC" AND ("Carry-Result" OR "Coordinator")). Obviously, this is a very flexible naming scheme, which allows to assign any number of application-specific names to agents. To change the name assignments two functions are provided, `pinOnBadge(badge)` and `pinOffBadge(badge)`.

4.2 Sessions

A session defines a communication relationship between a pair of agents. Agents that want to communicate with each other, must establish a session before the actual communication can be started. After session setup, the agents can interact by remote method invocation or by message passing. When all information has been communicated, the session is terminated. Sessions have the following characteristics: Sessions may be intra-place as well as inter-place communication relationships, i.e. two agents participating in a session are not required to reside at the same place. In order to preserve the autonomy of agents, each session peer must explicitly agree to participate in the session. Furthermore, an agent may unilaterally terminate the sessions it is involved in at any point in time. Consequently, agents cannot be trapped in sessions. While an agent is involved in a session, it is not supposed to move to another place. However, if it decides to move anyway, the session is terminated implicitly. The main reason for this property of sessions is to simplify the underlying communication mechanism, e.g. to avoid the need for message forwarding.

The question may arise why sessions are needed at all. There are basically two reasons: firstly, the concept of a session can be used to synchronize agents that want to meet for cooperation. Note that the first property stated above allows agents to meet even if they stay on different places. The concept of a session is introduced to allow agents to specify which other agents they are interested to meet at which places. Furthermore, it allows agents to wait until the desired cooperation partner arrives at the place and indicates its willingness to participate. Secondly, we want to support both *stateless* and *stateful* interactions. In contrast to the first, the latter maintain state information for a sequence of requests. Obviously, if they encapsulate stateful servers, service agents have to be stateful also. A prerequisite for building stateful entities are explicit communication relationships, such as sessions.

In order to establish sessions, two methods are provided, `PassiveSetUp()` and `ActiveSetUp()`. The first operation is non-blocking and is used by agents to express that they are willing to participate in a session. In contrast, `ActiveSetUp()` is used to issue a synchronous setup request, i.e. the caller is blocked until either the session is successfully established or a timeout occurs. If `ActiveSetUp()` succeeds, it returns the reference of the newly created session object to the caller. Input parameter `PlaceId` identifies the place, where the desired session peer is expected, and `PeerQualifier` qualifies the peer at the specified place. A `PeerQualifier` is either an agent identifier or a badge predicate. Note that at most one agent qualifies in the case of a single agent identifier, while several agents may qualify if a single badge predicate is specified. In that case a randomly picked agent is chosen. To avoid infinite blocking, the parameter `TimeOut` can be used to specify a timeout interval. The operation blocks until the session is established or a timeout occurs, whatever happens first. The parameters `PeerQualifier` and `PlaceId` of the operation `PassiveSetUp()` are optional. If neither of both parameters is specified, the caller expresses its willingness to establish a session with any agent residing at any place. By specifying `PlaceId` and/or `PeerQualifier` the calling agent may limit the group of potential peers. For example, a group may be limited to all agents wearing the badge "Stuttgart University" and/or that are located at the caller's place. As pointed out above, before a session is established both participants must agree explicitly. An agreement for session setup is achieved if both agents issue matching setup requests. Two setup requests, say R_A and R_B of agents A respectively B, match if `PlaceId` in R_A and R_B identifies the current place of B and A, respectively, and `PeerQualifier` in R_A and R_B qualifies B and A, respectively.

If a setup request issued by an agent matches more than one setup request, one request is chosen randomly and a session is established with the corresponding agent. A combination of calls to the `PassiveSetUp()` and `ActiveSetup()` method allows a client/server style of communication. The agent playing the server role once issues `PassiveSetUp()` when it is ready to receive requests. When an agent playing the client role invokes `ActiveSetup()`, this causes the `SetUp()` method of the server side to be invoked implicitly. `SetUp()` implicitly establishes a session with the caller and assigns a thread for handling this session. Therefore, once the server agent has called `PassiveSetup()`, any number of sessions can be established in parallel, where session establishment is purely client driven. If both agents issue (matching) `ActiveSetUp()` requests this corresponds to a rendezvous. Both requesters are blocked until the session is established or a timeout occurs. This type of session establishment is suited for agents that want to establish peer-to-peer communication relationships with other agents. Communication between agents is peer-to-peer if both have their own "agenda" in terms of communication, i.e., both decide – depending on their individual goals – when they want to interact with whom in which way.

At any time, a session can be terminated unilaterally by each of the both session participants, either explicitly or implicitly. A session is terminated explicitly by calling `SessionObject.Terminate()`, and implicitly when a session participant moves to another place. When a session is terminated, this is indicated by calling the `SessionTerminated()`-method exported by agents. Moreover, all resources associated with the terminated session are released. We want to mention, that for easier programming, we still allow the programmer to use "traditional" Mole-RPC based communication or messages without the need of a session overhead, giving them the opportunity to issue single communication acts.

5 AGENT INFRASTRUCTURE

5.1 Resource Manager

Resource management is necessary for two purposes. One is accounting, the other is resource control. Accounting is a prerequisite for commercial applications with agents, and resource control is necessary to prevent e.g. denial-of-service attacks. In Mole the following resources are managed: CPU time, local network communication, communication with remote networks, number of created children, and total time at the local place. The CPU time used is calculated by counting the time slices given to threads of an agent. Mole has a central scheduler, the MCP (Master Control Process), that schedules all threads in the Mole system. We decided to implement our own scheduler, when problems with Java 1.0 led to the conclusion that the Java scheduler of the Solaris implementation had problems with concurrent execution of more than four threads of the same priority. This results from the Java specification being imprecise in this respect. The network communication is an important cost factor. Thus it is important for both accounting and resource control. Because all agent communication has to use the mechanisms provided by the agent system, control is done here. When an agent arrives at one place the arrival time is logged. This way the total time at the local place can be computed without problems. One other resource is not managed, the memory consumption of an agent. While in principle extremely important, it can not be implemented with acceptable costs without modifying the Java virtual machine.

5.2 Directory Service

A directory service is an electronic database that contains information on entities. An example for a full-fledged directory service is X.500 (see e.g. Chadwick (1994)). In our Mole system we simply provide a local directory service. It supplies information on agents providing a service denoted by a string. This local directory service exists on every place. An agent can register itself locally if it provides a service by submitting a string identifying the service to the directory service. Another agent wanting to use this service first asks the directory service. The directory service returns a list containing all agents providing the service. This list is either empty, or contains one or more agent identifiers. The agent now chooses one of the agent identifiers and contacts the agent.

5.3 Code Server

The efficient migration of code is clearly one of the most important performance aspects in the design and implementation of a mobile agent system. In Mole a specific mechanism optimizes the code transfer as much as possible. This *Code Server* caches the implementation (i.e. classes) of the agents and distributes it as efficient as possible. Moreover it provides fault tolerance by assigning more than one server for the code. But even in the case that the code server functionality is lost temporarily (e.g. in case of network partitions) a fall-back mechanism transferring the code from the source site of the arriving agent provides the guarantee that no additional fault sensitivity is introduced into the system. For details about the code server concepts in Mole Version 3.0 please refer to Hohl, Klar and Baumann (1997).

5.4 Orphan Detection and Termination

Orphan detection in an agent system is very important both from the user's and from the system side, because a running agent uses resources which are valuable to both user and system. The user has to pay for resources, and the system has only a limited amount of them. So if the user does not need the results of a distributed computation in progress anymore he wants to be able to terminate the computation to minimize the resulting cost. With an orphan detection mechanism the user simply declares those agents as orphans that should be terminated. Orphan detection guarantees that the now useless agents can be determined by the system and removed, thus freeing the resources they have bound. In Mole, a generic mechanism (TOD – Termination and Orphan Detection) has been implemented that allows a flexible use of different orphan detection and termination mechanisms according to the specifications of the agent owner and the owner of a place. The TOD mechanism allows the transparent introduction of new mechanisms without administrational overhead. Orphan detection mechanisms that already have been implemented are the energy concept (Baumann 1997) and the shadow concept (Baumann and Rothermel 1998). While the energy concept constrains the resources an agent can use by defining an amount of energy needed for every use of a resource, the shadow concept defines a distributed structure allowing to find and control an agent regardless of its location.

5.5 Security Model

In Mole, the *Sandbox* security model is enforced by implementing a simple concept. In Section 2 we presented our agent model, and with it mobile and service agents. Mobile agents are the normal user agents, programmed and employed by the user. They have absolutely no access to the underlying system. Service agents are agents with access to system resources, providing controlled, secure abstractions of these resources inside the agent system. Furthermore, service agents may offer access to legacy software, using the native code interface offered by Java. This does not cause any security problems, because the service agents are immobile and may be started only by the administrator of the place. User agents may only communicate with other agents and have no direct access to system resources. Additionally it can be decided on a per-place basis which types of agents to allow on a place. Only agents that are derived from a specific type can migrate to a place. This mechanism can be used to implement access restrictions. Take e.g. a place that allows only agents of a very specific type. These can only be created at one other, open place. Then every agent wanting to access a service on the first, closed place has to migrate to the open place and request a service. This service then creates one of the specific agents that migrate to the closed place.

6 GRAPHICAL AGENT MONITOR

In Mole the graphical agent monitor `Moleview` is used to examine places, agents, and messages sent between the agents (see Figure 3). The snapshot has been made while running part of the test suite at installation time. Every `Moleview` window contains the information for one of the places that are inspected. In this example the place `testlocation2` has been examined. We can see three agents on the place with their descriptions. In the lower left corner of the window the services provided by agents are printed (in the example none). In the lower right corner of the window the local and remote communication in which the agents on this place participate is logged. RPCs as well as messages are logged with their message id, sender and receiver. Additional information about the agents, the provided services, the messages, and the RPCs can be acquired by using an inspector window.

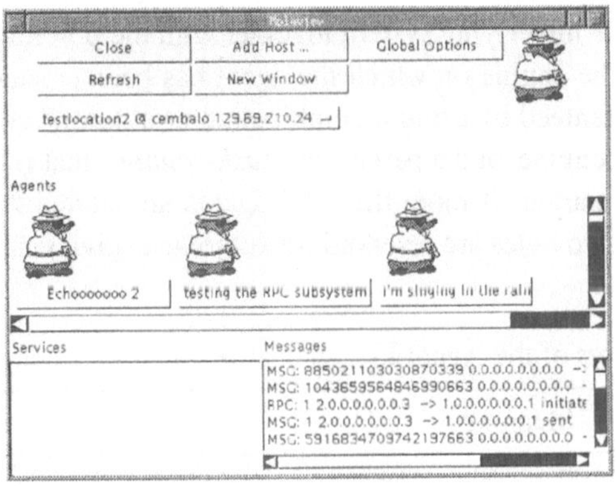

Figure 3 The Graphical Agent Monitor

7 IMPLEMENTATIONAL ISSUES

7.1 Agent Identifiers and Name Resolution

In Mole, an agent is seen as a unique entity. This view is supported by using a globally unique name for every agent. This name is immutable, i.e. it does not change when the agent migrates. The uniqueness can only be guaranteed if the system creates the names used. If the system creates the agent identifiers, then these identifiers should be devisable without global knowledge. Additionally it is of advantage to be able to derive the site where the agent has been created from the agent identifier. Why do we place such constraints on the agent identifier? First, to be able to identify an agent (this is needed for communication, termination etc.), its name must be locally unique. Second, to be able to do the same after an agent has migrated, the name has to be immutable. From this follows that the agent identifier has to be globally unique. This can only be guaranteed if the system itself provides a service to create agent identifiers conforming to these requirements. If global knowledge is needed to create this agent name, then either an expensive mechanism has to be implemented to obtain the global knowledge, or a single point of failure is introduced if e.g. an identifier server is included into the system (see e.g. the Amoeba sequencer proposed by (Tanenbaum 1995)). The ability to derive the site where the agent has been created is of advantage e.g for localization algorithms utilizing the home location registry approach. This approach is used in GSM (*Global System for Mobile Communications*, see e.g. (Mauly and Paulet, 1992)), where the identifier of the user (his telephone number) leads to a designated place (the home location registry) that contains the information how this user can be reached.

The agent identifier in Mole is created from information that can be obtained locally. Table 1 lists the components of the agent identifier. The Internet Protocol Version 6 address of the underlying system together with the port number of the engine allows to identify the engine on which the agent has been created. The uniqueness of the name is guaranteed by using a combination of a normal counter that is set to 0 at the start of the engine, and a persistent *crash counter*, that is incremented every time the engine is started. If more than 2^{32} agents are started the crash counter is incremented, too. Two bytes are reserved for future use, giving a total of 24 bytes.

Table 1 Components of the Agent Id

Number of Bytes	Meaning
4	Dynamic counter, incremented for each new agent identifier.
4	Crash counter, incremented every time the system is started, also incremented if dynamic counter overflows.
12	IP Version 6 address of the system on which the engine runs.
2	The port number of the engine.
2	Reserved for future use (set to 0).

7.2 Thread Management Unit

One disadvantage of the Java language is that in some respects it is underspecified. One of the underspecified areas is the thread management. For instance if two threads of the same priority run in a virtual machine, nothing is said about the scheduling used. It might even happen that only one of the threads is executed, and only when it has terminated the other threads are performed. This led to many problems in the platform-independent development of Mole, and we decided to implement our own thread scheduler. One of the few guarantees that Java gives is that a thread with higher priority is executed in preference to threads with lower priority. Our scheduler was implemented using this property of Java as follows: One designated thread called Master Control Process (MCP) is started when the Mole engine is started, and controls all Mole threads (including all threads running in agents) at runtime. This MCP-thread gets the highest possible priority (apart from system threads). All other threads are on the lowest possible priority. The MCP-thread has a list of these threads and grants them their time slices by way of changing their priorities. In regular intervals (time slices) the MCP-thread wakes up, lowers the priority of the running Mole thread, takes the next thread from its list and changes its priority to its own. Now it sleeps for the length of the time slice, after which the next thread is scheduled. This way the Mole system guarantees that threads are executed "concurrently" in time slices. A feature of the MCP is that the computing resources can be managed as well.

7.3 Web Integration

One of the key arguments against the introduction of new technologies is the cost for installation and maintenance. Mole provides a modified version of the system that runs, as an applet, in every browser able to interpret Java programs. A browser environment is very restrictive regarding access to the underlying computer system. Thus a relay component running on a computer with a normal installation of Mole provides the functionality that cannot be supported directly on a system without access to the underlying computer. This allows a user to start agents from within a browser, to let them migrate to and from the own computer system by simply clicking on a URL. This dramatically increases the potential number of users, who can, without having to install Mole, use the agent system.

8 INSTALLATION

Mole is a research development designed to experiment with new concepts arising in the context of mobile agents. It is available for free on the World Wide Web. The Java source code, documentation and sample agents can be downloaded from: `http://www.informatik.uni-stuttgart.de/ipvr/vs/projekte/mole.html`

8.1 System Requirements

Mole is undemanding regarding hardware and software requirements, especially compared to Telescript (White, 1997b). This is due to the design focusing on the use of an unmodified Java Virtual Machine and existing hardware. While this does not allow e.g. strong migration or the control of the memory consumption of agents, it allows Mole to run on every hardware platform that runs a Java Virtual Machine version 1.1 or higher. We have tested the system on various computer types and operating systems. PC's with a Intel Pentium (we have not tested systems with Intel 486) or compatible CPU with main memory ranging from 16 to 128 MBytes under Windows 95, Windows NT V3.51 or V4.0, OS/2 or Linux runs the system as well as Sun Sparc with Solaris, IBM RS/6000 with AIX, or HP workstations with HPUX.

8.2 Configuration Files

Two main configuration files exist for Mole, the global resource file `globalmolerc`, and the user-specific resource file `~/.molerc` (under Windows 95/NT: `C:\.molerc`). These contain global as well as user specific definitions for variables that can be read by system agents at runtime. This way a simple method of configuring arbitrarily complex system agents is provided. The following three variables are predefined:

`$(HOME)` is the absolute path to the user's home directory.
`$(USER)` is the login name of the user.
`$(CWD)` is the working directory.

Furthermore, many of the settings of the Mole system itself are defined in the resource files. Examples are the debug level and the location of the global Mole installation. Moreover, a user can define user-specific values depending on global values set by the system administrator in the global resource file.

9 CONCLUSIONS AND FUTURE WORK

We have presented a platform for Java-based mobile agents, a research development that implements many new concepts of mobile agent systems. Besides a basic infrastructure like weak migration of agents and local/global communication between agents and agent groups, the emphasis of the Mole system lies on providing a comfortable infrastructure for the agents. In particular, Mole implements a resource manager for accounting and resource control, a directory service, a thread management unit and a global naming scheme for agents. The usage of Mole is supported by simple means for installation and configuration and by a graphical agent monitor.

Earlier Versions of Mole have been used e.g as the prototypical infrastructure for an electronic document system by Konstantas, Morin and Vitek (1996), as a simulation environment for distributed network management by Siemens in the project Swarms and as an execution environment for Tandem server classes by Straßer *et al.* (1997). In order to make mobile agents usable in a commercial setting, our current research investigates further extensions to the system infrastructure. In particular, methods for orphan detection and agent termination have been investigated by Baumann and Rothermel (1997), coordination of agent groups has been investigated by Baumann and Radouniklis (1997), an approach for securing agents against malicious hosts has been investigated by Hohl (1997) and a protocol for preserving the exactly-once-property of mobile agents by Rothermel and Straßer (1997).

REFERENCES

Baumann, J. (1997) *A Protocol for Orphan Detection and Termination in Mobile Agent Systems*. Bericht Nr. 1997/09 der Fakultät Informatik, University of Stuttgart, Germany.

Baumann, J. and Radouniklis, N. (1997) Agent Groups in Mobile Agent Systems, in *Distributed Applications and Interoperable Systems* (eds. König, H.; Geihs, K. and Preuß, T.), Chapman & Hall, London, pp. 74–85.

Baumann, J. and Rothermel, K. (1998): The Shadow Approach: An Orphan Detection Protocol for Mobile Agents, in *2nd Int. Workshop Mobile Agents '98*, Springer Verlag, to appear.

Chadwick, D. (1994) *Understanding the X.500 Directory*. Chapman & Hall, London.

Falcone, J. R. (1987) A Programmable Interface Language for Heterogeneous Distributed Systems. *ACM Trans. Computer Systems*, **5**(4):330–51.

Ghezzi, C. and Vigna, G. (1997) Mobile Code Paradigms and Technologies: A Case Study, in *1st Int. Workshop on Mobile Agents* (eds. Rothermel, K. and Popescu-Zeletin, R.), LNCS 1219, Springer-Verlag, Berlin pp. 39–49

Gray, R. S. (1995) *Agent Tcl: Alpha Release 1.1*. Technical Report, Department of Computer Science, Dartmouth College, Hanover, NH.

Gray, R. S. (1996) Agent Tcl: A flexible and secure mobile agent system, in *Proc. 4th Annual Tcl/Tk Workshop*, pp. 9–23.

Hohl, F. (1997) *An approach to solve the problem of malicious hosts*. Bericht Nr. 1997/03 der Fakultät Informatik, University of Stuttgart, Germany.

Hohl, F.; Klar, P.; and Baumann, J. (1997) Efficient Code Migration for Modular Mobile Agents, in *Proc. 3rd ECOOP Workshop on Mobile Object Systems*, dpunkt-Verlag, Heidelberg, Germany. (to appear)

IBM Aglets Workbench Team (1997) Aglets Workbench, in *Mobile Agents* (eds. Cockayne, W. R. and Zyda, M.), Manning Publ., Greenwich, pp. 165–83.

Johansen, D.; van Renesse, R. and Schneider, F. B. (1994) Operating System support for mobile agents, in *Proc. 5th Workshop on Hot Topics in Operating Systems*, IEEE Comp. Soc. Press, pp. 42–5.

Johansen, D.; van Renesse, R. and Schneider, F. B. (1995) *An Introduction to the TACOMA Distributed System*. Technical Report 95–23, Department of Computer Science, University of Tromso, Finland.

Konstantas, D.; Morin, J. H. and Vitek, J. (1996) MEDIA: A Platform for the Commercialization of Electronic Documents, in *Object Applications* (ed. D. Tschiritzis), University of Geneva, pp. 7–18.

Milojicic, D.; Breugst, M.; Busse, I.; Campbell, J.; Covaci, S.; Friedman, B.; Kosaka, K.; Lange, D.; Ono, K.; Oshima, M.; Tham, C.; Virdhagriswaran, S. and White, J. (1998) MASIF: The OMG Mobile Agent System Interoperability Facility, in *2nd Int. Workshop Mobile Agents '98*, Springer Verlag, to appear.

Mauly, M. and Paulet, M. (1992) *The GSM System for mobile Communication*. Europe Media Publications S. A., ETSI, Palaiseau, France.

Peine, H. and Stolpmann, T. (1997) The Architecture of the Ara Platform for Mobile Agents, in *1st Int. Workshop on Mobile Agents* (eds. Rothermel, K. and Popescu-Zeletin, R.), LNCS 1219, Springer-Verlag, Berlin, pp. 50–61.

Perret, S. and Duda, A. (1996) Implementation of MAP: A system for mobile assistant programming, in *Proc. IEEE Int. Conf. Parallel & Distributed Systems.*

Rothermel, K. and Straßer, M. (1997) *A Protocol for Preserving the Exactly-Once Property of Mobile Agents.* Bericht Nr. 1997/18 der Fakultät Informatik, University of Stuttgart, Germany.

Rulifson, J. (1969) DEL, in *Internet Engineering Task Force*, Network Working Group, Request for Comments 5, ftp://ds.internic.net/rdc/rfc5.txt

Straßer, M.; Baumann, J. and Hohl, F. (1996) Mole: A Java Based Mobile Agent System, in *Special Issues in Object-Oriented Programming* (ed. Mühlhäuser, M.), dpunkt-Verlag, Heidelberg, Germany. pp. 327–334.

Straßer, M.; Baumann, J.; Hohl, F.; Radouniklis, N.; Rothermel, K. and Schwehm, M. (1997) *ATOMAS: A Transaction-oriented Open Multi Agent-System. Annual Report.* Bericht Nr. 1997/14 der Fakultät Informatik, University of Stuttgart, Germany

Tanenbaum, A. (1995) *Distributed Operating Systems.* Prentice Hall.

Tschudin, C. F. (1993) *On the Structuring of Computer Communications.* Ph.D. Thesis, University of Geneva, Suisse.

White, J. E. (1997a): Mobile Agents, in *Software Agents* (ed. Bradshaw, J. M.) AAAI/MIT Press, Menlo Park, CA, pp. 437–72.

White, J. E. (1997b) Telescript, in *Mobile Agents* (eds. Cockayne, W. R. and Zyda, M.), Manning Publ., Greenwich, pp. 37–57.

Zander, J. 1981: SOFTNET – Packet Radio in Sweden, in *ARRL Amateur Radio Computer Networking Conferences 1–4*, The American Radio Relay League, Newington, CT, reprinted 1985, pp. 1.7–1.10.

Joachim Baumann has studied computer science at the University of Stuttgart. Since 1994 he is research assistant at the IPVR and from 1996-1997 additionally member of the Object Systems Group at the University of Geneva. He currently works on agent termination and orphan detection.

Fritz Hohl has studied computer science at the University of Stuttgart. Since 1995 he is a research assistant at the IPVR working on mobile agent security.

Kurt Rothermel received his doctoral degree in computer science from Stuttgart University in 1985. He then worked at IBM Almaden Research Center and IBM European Networking Center. Since 1990 he is full professor at the University of Stuttgart and head of the `distributed systems' research group at the IPVR.

Markus Schwehm has studied mathematics at the Universities of Karlsruhe and Munich. He received his doctoral degree in computer science from the University of Erlangen in 1996. In 1997 he joined Tandem Research Labs working on active data bases. Since 1997 he is project leader of the Mole project at the IPVR.

Markus Straßer has studied computer science at the University of Stuttgart. Since 1995 he is research assistant at the IPVR working on fault tolerant and transactional execution of agents.

Session 9

Web Services

Active Cache: Caching Dynamic Contents on the Web

Pei Cao, Jin Zhang and Kevin Beach
Computer Sciences Department
University of Wisconsin-Madison
1210 West Dayton Street
Madison, WI 53705, USA
{cao,zj,kbeach}@cs.wisc.edu

Abstract

Dynamic documents constitute an increasing percentage of contents on the Web, and caching dynamic documents becomes an increasingly important issue that affects the scalability of the Web. In this paper, we propose the Active Cache scheme to support caching of dynamic contents at Web proxies. The scheme allows servers to supply cache applets to be attached with documents, and requires proxies to invoke cache applets upon cache hits to furnish the necessary processing without contacting the server. We describe the protocol, interface and security mechanisms of the Active Cache scheme, and illustrate its use via several examples. Through prototype implementation and performance measurements, we show that Active Cache is a feasible scheme that can result in significant network bandwidth savings at the expense of moderate CPU costs.

Keywords

World-Wide Web, caching, scalability, Java applets, network security

1 INTRODUCTION

The growth of the Internet and the World Wide Web has significantly increased the amount of online information and services available to the general population of the society. However, the client/server architecture employed by the current Web-based services is inherently un-scalable. Caching at proxies that are located at network access points has been proposed as a solution to the scalability problem. Unfortunately, caching in the Web today has been seriously limited by the inability to cache dynamic documents, including documents that change upon every access, documents that are results of queries, and documents that embody client-specific information (for example, cookies). Furthermore, lack of server control on accesses to cached documents results in the "caching busting" practice from the servers, severely undermining the scope of cacheable documents.

To solve these problems, we propose a scheme called Active Cache, which migrates parts of server processing on each user request to the caching proxy in a flexible, on-demand fashion via "cache applets." A cache applet is a server-supplied code that is attached with a Universal Resource Locator (URL) or a collection of URLs. The code is typically written in a platform-independent programming language such as Java When caching a document, the proxy also fetches the corresponding cache applet. When a user request hits on the cached copy and the proxy would like to service the request, the proxy must invoke the cache applet with the user request and other information as arguments. The cache applet then decides what the proxy will send back to the user, either giving the proxy a new document to send back to the user, or allowing the proxy to use the cached copy, or instructing the proxy to send the request to the Web server. Furthermore, the applet can deposit information in a log object, which is sent back to the server periodically and when the applet or the document is purged from the cache.

Cache applets allow servers to obtain the benefit of proxy caching without losing the capability to track user accesses and tailor the content presentation. They can perform a variety of functions, for example, logging user accesses, rotating advertising banners, checking access permissions, constructing client-specific Web pages, etc. They also enable proxies to be more than just caches of static information, but rather caches of objects, i.e., data with a method that is invoked when the data are supplied from caches. In essence, they turn Web documents from *datagram* to *objects*.

The proxy, when caching a document with cache applets, has the full freedom to not invoke the applet but send the user request directly to the server. *The proxy promises to not send back a cached copy of a document without invoking the corresponding cache applet.* On the other hand, if a document is cached but the corresponding applet consumes too much resource, the proxy can simply send the request to the Web server. Furthermore, just as the proxy is not obligated to cache any document, it is not obligated to cache any applet. The proxy agrees to not service a cache hit if the corresponding applet is not in cache.

The proxy's freedom of managing its own resource and the association between cache applets and URLs allow an on-demand migration of server functionalities. The proxy only fetches and executes the applet when there are user requests to the associated URL. Controlling its own resource allocation, the proxy can devote resources to the applets associated with the hottest or the most important URLs to its users. Since the proxy that receives the user request is typically the closest proxy to the user, the scheme automatically migrates the server processing to nodes that are close to users, significantly increasing the scalability of Web-based services.

In this paper, we describe the protocol and interface between the server-supplied cache applets and the proxies in the Active Cache paradigm, and the security mechanisms to guard the applets' execution and protect the proxy. We then give examples of cache applets to illustrate the Active Cache paradigm, and discuss proxy's resource management policies. Finally, we report our experience with an early Active Cache prototype, focusing on the overhead incurred by cache applets.

2 THE ACTIVE CACHE PROTOCOL

In Active Cache, the Web server specifies the association between a cache applet and a URL-named document by sending a new entity header, "CacheApplet," with the document:

- CacheApplet: code = "code.class", archive = "code.jar", codebase = "codebase_url"

The header follows the convention for applet specification in HTML documents. It specifies that the applet "code.class" at code base "codebase_url" is the cache applet for the document, and associated classes are grouped in an archive (4). Codebase and archive directives are optional. Since HTTP/1.1 allows the introduction of new entity headers, and requires that if a proxy does not recognize an entity header, it should forward the header, the server can be assured that Active-Cache enabled proxies will receive the header even if they have parent proxies.

For security concerns, we require that the codebase of the applet, if present, has the same server URL as the document. That is, only the Web server who provides the document can supply the applet for it.

An Active-Cache enabled proxy agrees to fulfill the following obligations:

- if the document is cached and a user request hits on the document, it will either invoke the cache applet, or send the request directly to the server.
- if the applet's execution fails due to any reason, the request is sent to the server;
- if the applet's execution succeeds, the proxy will take the appropriate action based on the return value of the FromCache method (see below);
- each applet can deposit information in a special log object (whose name is the name of the applet appended by ".log"), and the proxy will send the log object back to the server periodically. If the proxy evicts the log object from the cache, it will first send the object to the server.

In other words, the proxy will not return a cached reply to the user unless the cache applet has been executed successfully, and the applet can deposit information in the log object which will eventually be reflected back to the server.

However, the proxy decides whether it wants to cache the document, when it fetches the applet and the archive, and whether it wants to invoke the applet. Furthermore, the proxy can evict any document or any applet from its cache at any time. The only constraint on the proxy is the above agreement.

The proxy's freedom means that the cache applet may not process every request to the document, and some requests might instead go to the original server. The applet does not capture every request to the document, but captures every "cache hit" to the document.

2.1 Active Cache Interface

The cache applet must implement an interface called "ActiveCacheInterface." Currently, we require that the applet be written in Java. The interface defines a function called FromCache. The function is called when an access hits in the document, and the arguments of the function call include the user request, the IP address of the client machine, the name of the client machine, the document in cache, and a new file descriptor for the applet to write when constructing a new Web page. The prototype of the function is listed below:

- public abstract int FromCache(String User_HTTP_Request, String Client_IP_Address, String Client_Name, int Cache_File, int New_File);

The arguments are included based on the principle that any information that the server can gather if the request goes to the server can be seen by the cache applet. The function can only return three values:

- 1: the content placed in New_File is to be returned to the user as the reply to the HTTP request;
- 0: the content in Cache_File can be returned to the user as the reply;
- -1: the request must be forwarded to the server.

All other return values are treated as -1.

The cache applet can only call the ActiveProxy class to perform its functions. The ActiveProxy class provides the native methods for file access , cache query, locking and unlocking as well as sending requests to servers. Currently, the methods include:

- public native static boolean is_in_cache(String URL);
- public native static int open(String URL, int mode);
- public native static int close(int fd);
- public native static int create(String URL, int mode);

- public native static int read(int fd, byte[] buf, int size);
- public native static int write(int fd, byte[] buf, int size);
- public native static long lseek(int fd, long off, int where);
- public native static int send_request_to_server(String HTTP_Request);
- public native static int lock(int fd);
- public native static int unlock(int fd);
- public native static String curtime();

As we gain more experience with the Active Cache paradigm, other necessary methods might be added to the ActiveProxy class.

An applet's execution can be aborted at any time. All changes to files and objects are voided if the execution is aborted. In other words, file changes are not committed until the applet finishes its execution.

The restrictions on the use of the proxy calls are the following:

- is_in_cache, open for read, lseek, read and close can only be called on URL-named documents that are from the same server. In other words, the proxy verifies that the server URL of the document is the same as the server URL of the cache applet;
- open for write, create, write, lock and unlock can only be applied to URL-named objects that the applet has created; the create call automatically appends the applet's URL to the object's name;
- send_request_to_server can only send HTTP requests to the Web server; the method automatically connects to the server where the cache applet comes from.
- curtime provides a timing granularity of one second.

Furthermore, all exceptions are caught and result in a return value of -1 for the FromCache method.

Objects created by an applet (including the log object) are invisible to the outside world except to the original server that sends the applet. A server can gather the log objects of its applets through the Internet Cache Protocol (ICP) (3). ICP is originally designed for cache sharing and serves as a convenient channel for servers to gather log objects.

In addition to the ActiveProxy methods, the only other packages present in the Java run-time environments are java.util, java.text, java.math, java.security and java.sql. All other packages, including java.io, java.lang, and java.systems, are simply not loaded. The proxy can do so because the cache applet has only one purpose, that is, performing per-request processing of the document, and thus needs a very simple security interface.

2.2 Cache Applet Examples

The Active Cache protocol allows a rich variety of processing to be accomplished at the proxy system. Below, we describe the applets we have implemented.

2.2.1 *Logging User Accesses*

One of main reasons many Web servers disable caching is to collect information on who access their documents. Both server and proxy suffer from such practice, as the former has to buy a lot of resources to handle the volume of incoming requests, and the latter has to pay for the Internet traffic. Active cache solves the dilemma by using a log applet.

We have implemented a log applet, whose FromCache method simply writes the client IP address, the date of the access, and the HTTP request to the log object. The applet is assured that the log object will be sent back to the server eventually. The Java code looks like the following:

```
  public static int FromCache(
String User_HTTP_Request,
String Client_IP_Address,
String Client_Name,
int Cache_File,
int New_File) {

int fd = open("logapplet.log", APPEND_ONLY);
int status = lock(fd);
String date = new curtime();
log_to_file(fd, date, Client_Name,
User_HTTP_Request, Client_IP_Address);
status = unlock(fd);
close(fd);

return(0); // 0 means use the cached file
}
```

2.2.2 *Advertising Banner Rotation*

Another reason that servers disable caching is to change the presentation of the document upon every request, for example, putting on different advertising banners. This again conflicts with proxy caching. Active Cache solves the problem by attaching an ad-banner-rotation applet with each document.

The applet, when invoked, first checks for the object that specifies the banners, their positions in the document, and their frequencies of appearance. If the object is not in cache, it sends a request to the Web server to fetch the object. The applet then goes through the cached document, and for every image that is specially marked to be an advertisement banner, decides which banner should be put there according to the specifications, and changes the image URL. It then puts the new document in the New_File and returns 1.

The applet implements a simple frequency-based rotation. Other algorithms can be implemented. The applet can record the state needed by the algorithms in the object. It can further record in the log object the banner choices that it has made.

2.2.3 *Access Permission Checking*

Existing cache systems for the Internet typically provide very limited support to access control of server contents: for example, only allowing the same user to access the document again. Using cache applets, the server can gain the benefits of proxy caching without sacrificing the access control.

The cache applet, upon receiving a request from the user, checks whether the user request is accompanied with an access authorization. An access authorization is a cookie that contains a signed statement from the server. If not, the request is sent to the server (whose response would include a cookie for future requests if the user is allowed to access the contents). Otherwise, using the server's public key, the applet verifies whether the server has signed the certificate. If so, the applet grants access to the document. If not, the applet merely returns -1 and the request is redirected to the server, who will send the appropriate access violation messages.

2.2.4 *Client-Specific Information Distribution*

Today, many information providers allow users to specify preferences of the categories of information that they would like to receive. A typical example is `my.yahoo.com`, which is among the busiest sites on the Internet. The client-specific pages currently cannot be cached at the Web proxies, increasing the load at the Web server and the traffic on the Internet. Active cache solves the problem again by using a cache applet that constructs client-specific pages based on a database of base documents.

We have implemented a simply cache applet for this purpose. Upon receiving the client request, the applet first probes a database object to see if it stores the mapping between the client ID (extracted from the cookie) and its preference. If not, it fetches the preference from the server. After obtaining the preference, the applet composes the Web page. For each individual information item, it first tries to read the item from the cache, and if the item is not cached, fetch it from the server and cache it. It then composes the page and returns it to the user.

Thus, the cache applet filters out the redundancy in the information transmitted by the server for the client-specific pages, and allows individual information items to be cached and reused by the proxy. For a proxy with a large client population, the savings in network bandwidth can be significant. It also allows schemes such as Pointcast to avoid having to write its own proxy servers, and support broadcasting schemes such as SkyCache.

2.2.5 *Server-Side Include Expansion*

Similar to the ad-banner-rotation applet, the SSI applet allows expansion of Server-Side Include (SSI) (5) variables at the proxy site, thus allowing the correct caching of SSI-based dynamic documents. The applet scans the cached document, and for each specially marked SSI variable, update the value of the variable in the document, and put the new document in New_File. The proxy can correctly expand variables DATE_GMT, DATE_LOCAL, REMOTE_ADDRESS, and REMOTE_HOST. Other

SSI variables are typically related to the server and do not change from request to request.

2.2.6 *Delta Compression*

Studies (8) have shown that transmitting the changes (deltas) between the new and old versions of dynamic information can reduce network traffic significantly. Delta compression can be easily implemented with cache applets.

We have implemented an applet that upon receiving a client request, sends a request to the original server, including the current request and the last-modified-time of the document. After the server responds with the difference between the new document and the cached version, the applet constructs the reply to the client request using the diff and the cached version.

A similar cache applet can support delta compression of query responses. For example, a query of a particular company's stock quote can be handled by the applet, which simply asks the server for the number and then composes the Web page based on a cached response.

3 SECURITY MECHANISMS

In the Active Cache environment, the proxy system is particularly vulnerable to two types of security attacks: an applet's illegal access to information belonging to other Web servers, and denial-of-service attacks. To guard against the first type of attacks, we rely on a type-safe language with built-in security mechanisms, a well-defined security interface, and static examination of the code. To guard against the second type of attacks, we rely on user-request triggered execution of cache applets, run-time accounting of resource consumptions, and limiting the resource consumptions.

3.1 Language-based Protection

For the language of the cache applet, we choose Java because of the large amount of research efforts invested on Java security. Its platform-independence and built-in security mechanisms contribute to our decision. In the Active Cache environment, the Java security problem is simplified by the fact that the applet is used for only one purpose: processing a user request at the proxy site and constructing a response. Thus, the java.io libraries, the process/thread management libraries and other system-related libraries are simply absent from the cache applet's run-time environment to prevent the security problems associated with their use.

The security interface of the cache applets is quite simple: all an applet can do is to ask whether some objects exist in the cache, read and write the objects, and communicate with the server where the applet comes from. Furthermore, accesses to objects are restricted as described in Section 2.

The restrictions are designed with the assumption that each server is a security entity, applets from the same server trust each other, and applets from different servers do not cooperate. Thus, an applet has read access to all information in documents and objects from the same server. However, each applet can only manipulate the objects that it creates or is attached to. We impose this constraint for simplicity and safety. The flexibility of the scheme is not compromised, because one applet can always be attached to many documents.

The restrictions are enforced by two mechanisms. The ActiveProxy class implements the constraints. Java's type safety and run-time mechanisms prevent applets from bypassing the ActiveProxy class and gaining raw access to information and resources. Recent research results have significantly improved the robustness of Java's run-time environments (10). Thus, we rely on the existing mechanisms to force the applet to use the ActiveProxy class to access its objects as well as the computation and networking resources. The ActiveProxy class is also the place where we keep track of resources consumed by each applet.

In addition, we use static examination of the classes and functions called in the cache applet code to prevent manipulations of Java "class" methods to circumvent our restrictions. When the cache applet is first loaded, the proxy examines the symbol table to check for "class" method calls and calls to unloaded packages. If the applet cannot pass the inspection, the proxy will not cache the reply.

3.2 Resource Accounting

The proxy keeps track of an applet's resource consumption in the following five aspects:

- storage size, that is, the sum of sizes of objects created and written to by the applet;
- disk bandwidth consumption, that is, the amount of file bytes read and written by the applet;
- network bandwidth consumption, including all the bytes sent and received in the Send_HTTP_Request function;
- CPU usage, including user time and system time;
- virtual memory size (an applet can exhaust kernel page table resources by allocating a large amount of virtual memory; thus, the size of the virtual address space needs to be constrained);

Mutexes and locks are not included because each applet can only lock objects created by it, and all locks are automatically relinquished upon termination of the applet execution. We also do not track process-related operations because the applet cannot spawn new threads or processes. Rather, each applet is executed in a new process when a user request for the active object arrives.

The storage size, disk bandwidth and network bandwidth consumptions are kept track of by the ActiveProxy class methods, since they must be called in order for the applet to gain access to those resources. The process running the applet also sets a one-second alarm and record the CPU time and virtual memory sizes in the alarm handler. Limiting the CPU and virtual memory sizes is implemented by the setrlimit system call before branching to the applet's execution.

To prevent denial of service attacks, the proxy imposes upper-limits on all five resources. By default, the upper limit for CPU time is proportional to the latency of sending the request to the server and receiving the response. The virtual memory size is proportional to the length of the response to the client request. The storage size and disk bandwidth limit are also proportional to the response size. Finally, the network bandwidth consumption cannot exceed the response size. The limits are designed with the assumption that the goal of caching the documents is to reduce network traffic. If the goal of caching is for reliability or other reasons, the limits can be raised by the proxy. In our initial prototype, we simply use fixed constants for these limits for ease of implementation.

4 RESOURCE MANAGEMENT POLICIES

An important design question for Active-Cache enabled proxies is the resource management policy. Essentially, the policy must make three decisions:

- should a document (with or without a cache applet) be cached?
- when a user request arrives, should the proxy invoke the applet or send the request to the server?
- what are the upper resource limits for each applet?

The decisions are made depending on the reason for the cache applet.

There are typically two reasons why a proxy wants to cache a document or object: to reduce outgoing network traffic, and to improve the availability of a distributed service. When the proxy's goal is to reduce network traffic, the proxy is willing to cache the most-frequently requested documents or objects, even if they are from untrusted servers. When the proxy's goal is to improve service availability, the proxy often knows about the service's importance to its users, trusts the server, and is willing to invest more resource to host it.

Thus, we have two categories of applet-attached documents (in other words, objects): un-negotiated ones and negotiated ones. Un-negotiated objects are from untrusted servers; their primary purpose is to perform processing at the proxy site to avoid network traffic to the server. Negotiated objects are from servers that go through a negotiation protocol with the proxy. They receive more resources and are cached at the proxy for as long as necessary.

Un-negotiated objects Resource management for un-negotiated objects is relatively straightforward. To decide whether an object should be cached, the proxy estimates the benefit and the cost of caching, and passes the information to the cache replacement module. A cost-aware cache replacement algorithm can be used to decide whether an active object is cached, for example, the GreedyDual-Size algorithm (2

). The benefit of caching is calculated in terms of saved network bandwidth, estimated by the size of the response to each client request. The cost of caching includes the storage cost of the active object, the CPU cost of the applet, and the network communication incurred by the applet in the send_request_to_server calls. When an active object is first loaded, all costs are assigned a default value. The cost estimates are then adjusted every time the applet is invoked.

The proxy always attempts to invoke the cache applet if the object is cached. However, if the CPU or the disk arm is overloaded during the execution of the applet, the proxy terminates the execution of the applet, voids all file changes made by the applet, relinquishes all its locks, and directs the user request to the server.

In general, the upper resource limits for un-negotiated applets should be kept proportional to the size of the responses to client requests, that is, the savings in the network bandwidth. The exact scaling factors still need investigation. As we build more applets on top of Active Cache, we expect to gain more insight into the issue.

Negotiated objects To establish a negotiated object, a server and a proxy should enter a protocol in which the server identifies the service, specifies the estimated storage, networking and CPU needs of the applet, and specifies the desired duration of caching. The proxy examines the amount of interests in the distributed service from its users, the importance of the service and the credential of the server, in order to decide whether to host the service. If the proxy hosts the service, it caches the object and the applet for the specified duration, always invokes the applet upon user requests, and imposes the resource upper limits as specified by the server.

We have not yet designed the negotiation protocol because we need more experience with applications that need it. In particular, it is not clear whether the proxy should provide support for real-time constraints, and to what degree. Full-fledged real-time support complicates the design of the proxy. It is possible that for most Active cache applications that need latency guarantees (for example, distributed collaboration and multimedia streaming), the proxy needs only guarantee prompt execution of the cache applet upon client requests and periodic execution of the applet (via an alarm service). We plan to evaluate various design choices as we develop those applications.

Currently, resource management policies in Active Cache are still research topics. In our current prototype, all documents are un-negotiated objects. We use the simple LRU policy in deciding which document to cache, regardless of whether the document has associated cache applet or not. We also impose fixed constants on the resource consumption of all cache applets. These choices are purely for the ease of implementation, and we plan to refine them soon.

5 PROTOTYPE IMPLEMENTATION AND PERFORMANCE

We have implemented a prototype Active Cache as an extension of the the CERN httpd proxy (6). The original CERN httpd software offers traditional caching of Web documents and HTTP protocol support. We have modified the daemon to recognize the CacheApplet header, and to invoke the appropriate applet upon cache hit.

A cache-applet attached document is stored as a regular document in the CERN proxy. The CacheApplet header is stored as part of the document. The header identifies the associated applet and archive. The CERN httpd proxy handles each user request in a separate process. (Despite its process-forking overhead, CERN httpd performs amazingly well compared to other sophisticated proxies (7).) The process model significantly simplifies our implementation, because we can limit the resource consumption of applets by using setrlimit calls prior to calling the applet. Sending the log object back to the server is implemented via a HTTP "POST" request to the server. If the server is unreachable, the proxy retries the transmission periodically up to a configurable time period, after which an alert message is sent to the proxy administrator and human intervention is required.

The prototype implements the active cache protocol and the security mechanisms described before. If an applet does not pass the static examination, both the document and the applet are deleted from the cache. All objects created by the applet are stored in a special directory whose name is the applet's URL. The implementation of the write and lock methods limits the operations to the objects in the special directory only. The implementation of the read method verifies that the object has the same URL as the server URL of the applet. The Java run-time environment is set up with the appropriate security manager.

5.1 Applet Overhead

To measure the overhead incurred by the cache applets, we use the WebStone 2.0 standard Web server benchmark (9) and compare the response times of the original CERN httpd proxy and the Active Cache proxy with various cache applets. In each of our Active Cache tests, we assume that all the documents are associated with the same applet. We test the "null" applet, the user access logging applet "log," the advertising banner rotation applet "ads," the access permission checking applet "apc," the server-side include expansion applet "ssi," and the client-specific information distribution applet "csid."

Though WebStone is a Web server benchmark, it can be used to test the performance of the proxy upon cache hits of different sizes. We use the filelist.standard in the WebStone 2.0 benchmark and create five files of size 500B, 5KB, 50KB, 500KB and 5MB. The clients request the files with the specified frequency in filelist.standard. The proxy machine is installed between the clients and the server. Since there are only five files involved, once the proxy cache is warmed up, all requests are cache hits and the test stresses the proxy system, instead of the server system. We run experiments with 1, 10 and 20 WebStone clients. The experiments all last over 10 minutes to obtain stable results. Our test platform includes SPARC 20 workstations running Solaris 2.4 as the client and the server machines. Our proxy machine for the "null," "apc," "log," and "ssi" applets is a 99MHz Intel x86 workstation running Solaris 2.5. Our proxy machine for the "ads" and "csid" applets is a SPARC20 running Solaris

Proxy	1 client	10 clients	20 clients
null	1.47	1.75	1.73
log	2.16	2.31	2.24
ads	1.40	2.44	3.23
apc	2.50	2.73	2.72
ssi	3.81	4.00	3.80
csid	1.06	2.04	2.23

Table 1 Ratio between the response time when the cache applet is used and the response time under the original CERN httpd proxy.

2.6; due to a bug in the Java thread library on the Intel platform, these two applets hang on the Intel platform. We are working on resolving the problem.

Table 1 lists the response time degradation of each applet, that is, the ratio between the client response time when invoking the applet and the client response time under the original CERN httpd. The "null" applet result shows that the mechanics of establishing a Java virtual machine and invoking the applet costs 47% to 75% degradation in response time. There are a number of reasons for it, including the increase in the process image and the corresponding increase in the forking cost, and the CPU overhead for finding the class, finding the method, and invoking the method. The other applets increase the client latency by a factor of 1.5 to 4.

Monitoring the proxy system using "vmstat" shows that the performance degradation is mostly caused by CPU overheads. In particular, the "ads" applet and the "ssi" applet incur CPU overhead that is proportional to the document size because they scan the cached document. The CPU overhead appears to heavily depend on the coding of the applet and the efficiency of Java implementations, particularly string operations. As the speed of Java improves and as we fine-tune our applet implementation, the CPU overhead will be reduced.

The measurements show that for a proxy system to support the Active Cache protocol and yet maintain the same throughput, its CPU resource needs to be increased. Fortunately, the workload is easily parallelizable and multi-processor systems or clusters of workstations can improve the throughput significantly. In most proxy systems today, disk arms and network connections are typically the bottlenecks, not the CPU resources. Whether the Active Cache paradigm will change the situation remains to be seen.

To summarize, our prototype implementation shows that Active Cache is a practical and feasible scheme to implement in proxies. It increases the CPU demands, and in a sense, trades local CPU resources for network bandwidth savings. Given that in today's technology, microprocessors are typically the cheap resources, the tradeoff is well worthwhile. We believe that the benefits of Active Cache greatly outweigh its implementation cost, and every proxy should support the Active Cache protocol.

5.2 Internet Traffic Reduction through Active Cache

In today's bandwidth-hungry Internet, Active Cache's trading CPU for Internet traffic reduction is well worthwhile. Companies typically spend $6,000 to $10,000 *per month* for a T1 line to the Internet; a PC workstation that can function as a proxy costs less than $2,000 today.

Compared with traditional caching, Active Cache can increase cache hit ratios significantly. One source of the increase is the widespread use of cookies. Studies of HTTP traces from the AT&T WorldNet Internet Service Provider (1) have revealed that 30% of all user requests carry cookies. Traditional proxies cannot cache replies to these requests because doing so would violate the semantics of the HTTP/1.0 protocol. As a result, they can only achieve object hit ratios around 35% and byte hit ratios around 30%. Active Cache proxies, on the other hand, can cache replies to requests carrying cookies with the help of server-supplied cache applets, and can achieve object hit ratios around 55% and byte hit ratios around 41%, according to the AT&T trace study.

Another source of the increase is the popularity of user-tailored information providers, such as "my.yahoo.com." These information providers allow a user to choose among a collection of news and information items to be included in a customized Web page. The number of items is typically less than 1000, and each item is typically less than 1KB. Active cache proxies, at the help of applets from these Web sites, can cache the individual information items and provide the customized pages from the cache. Since each customized page is typically over 20KB, as long as the proxy has over 100 users, the cache applets will cut more than half of the traffic to these Web sites.

Though it is difficult to perform trace-driven studies of Active Cache since most proxy traces anonymize the URLs, existing studies do demonstrate the need and the potential benefits of Active Cache. Given the sharp contrast in the cost of computing versus the cost of wide-area communication, Active Cache will be an integral component of future Web caching technologies.

6 RELATED WORK

Many prior research projects influence the design of the Active Cache scheme, in particular, mobile objects and agents. The evolution of Java as a mature language for mobile code makes the scheme possible.

Cache applets are similar to regular browser applets and servlets[4]. Compared with regular browser applets, cache applets have a simple, uniform security interface, which greatly simplifies the security problem. Compared with servalets, cache applets run at proxy sites as "guests" and face many resource constraints.

There are many studies on Web proxy caching. However, few have addressed the caching of dynamic contents. Robinovich et al have proposed macro-encoded HTML documents that are expanded at the browser site[1]. The work is similar to ours in the sense that both try to move the work away from the server. Indeed, a cache applet can easily implement the processing for macro-encoded documents. Compared with macro-ended HTML, cache applets are more flexible and powerful, and can support functions such as access control.

Finally, the principle of Active Cache is very similar to Active Networks, in that both treat packets as objects instead of datagrams. The difference is that Active Cache focuses on Web caching and proxies, while Active Networks focus on Internet evolution and routers. Proxies typically have full-fledged operating systems and less stringent performance requirements than routers, making Active Cache a somewhat easier research problem.

7 CONCLUSION AND FUTURE WORK

We propose the Active Cache protocol to support caching of dynamic documents on the Web. We have described the motivation behind the protocol, its design, interface, security mechanisms and resource management strategies. Using examples, we illustrate the flexibility and the potential of the scheme. Using prototype implementation and WebStone-based performance measurement, we show that cache applets typically increase the client latency by a factor of 1.5 to 4, and the degradation is mainly due to CPU overhead.

Much future work remains. We are currently extending Active Cache to support caching continuous media in the proxies. In particular, we are investigating cache applet implementations of RTSP, a protocol for transmitting continuous media on the Web. We are also extending Active Cache to support the notification protocol NTSP and its applications. Another important area that we are currently working on is resource management policies in Active Cache proxies. We are investigating appropriate resource limits and negotiation protocols, and the performance of cost-aware cache replacement algorithms. Finally, we are investigating ways to optimize Active Cache implementations and cache applets.

REFERENCES

[1] Ramon Caceres, Fred Douglis, Anja Feldmann, Gideon Glass, and Michael Rabinovich. Web proxy caching: The devil is in the details. In *Proceedings of 1998 SIGMETRICS Internet Server Performance Workshop*, June 1998. http://www.research.att.com/ misha/.

[2] Pei Cao and Sandy Irani. Cost-aware WWW proxy caching algorithms. In *Proceedings of the 1997 USENIX Symposium on Internet Technology and Systems*, December 1997.

[3] National Lab for Applied Network Research. Icp working group.

http://ircache.nlanr.net/Cache/ICP/, 1998.

[4] Javasoft Inc. Java applets, servlets and the jar guide. *http://www.javasoft.com/products/*, 1997.

[5] Netscape Inc. Generating dynamic html documents. *http://www.netscapeworld.com/nw-05-1997/nw-05-clue.html*, 1997.

[6] A. Luotonen, H. Frystyk, and T. Berners-Lee. CERN HTTPD public domain full-featured hypertext/proxy server with caching. Technical report, Available from http://www.w3.org/hypertext/WWW/ Daemon/Status.html, 1994.

[7] Carlos Maltzahn, Kathy Richardson, and Dirk Grunwald. Performance issues of enterprise level web proxies. In *Proceedings of the 1997 ACM SIGMETRICS International Conference on Measurement and Modelling of Computer Systems*, pages 13–23, June 1997.

[8] Jeffrey C. Mogul, Fred Douglis, Anja Feldmann, and Balachander Krishnamurthy. Potential benefits of delta encoding and data compression for http. In *Proceedings of ACM SIGCOMM'97*, August 1997. Available from http://www.research.att.com/ douglis/.

[9] Gene Trent and Mark Sake. WebSTONE: The first generation in HTTP server benchmarking. Technical report, MTS, Silicon Graphics Inc., February 1995. available from http://www-europe.sgi.com/TEXT/ Products/WebFORCE/WebStone/paper.html.

[10] Dan S. Wallach, Dirk Balfanz, Drew Dean, and Edward W Felten. Extensible security architecture for java. In *The 16th Symposium on Operating System Principles*, May 1997.

8 BIOGRAPHY

Jin Zhang received his bachelor degree of Computer Science in 1992 from Tianjin University, PRC. He received his Master's degree of Computer Science in 1995 from Tsinghua University, PRC. Currently he is a graduate student of Computer Science Department of University of Wisconsin-Madison. He joined the WisWeb group and worked with Professor Pei Cao since Sept. 1997. His main project is ActiveCache.

Pei Cao received her Ph.D. degree from Princeton University in 1995 and is currently Assistant Professor of Computer Science at University of Wisconsin-Madison. Her research interests are in World-Wide Web, operating systems and computer architecture. She currently leads the WisWeb research project which focuses on various aspects of Web caching. She is a member of the IEEE Computer Society Task Force on Internetworking.

Kevin Beach received his bachelor degree of Mechanical Engineering in 1997 from Rutgers University, USA. He is now a graduate student at Computer Science Department of University of Wisconsin-Madison. He joined the WisWeb research group in January 1998. His current project is Multimedia over Active Cache.

Saperlipopette!: a Distributed Web Caching Systems Evaluation Tool

Guillaume Pierre and Mesaac Makpangou
INRIA SOR group
78153 Le Chesnay Cedex - France
Tel: +33 1 39 63 57 55 — Fax: +33 1 39 63 53 72
Guillaume.Pierre@inria.fr — Mesaac.Makpangou@inria.fr
http://www-sor.inria.fr/

Abstract

Designing a distributed cache infrastructure to improve the Web performance for the users of a large-scale organization is a difficult task. To guide the decisions of system administrators, we propose Saperlipopette!, a tool that can be used to evaluate, *a-priori*, the quality of the service offered by each potential configuration of the distributed cache infrastructure. Saperlipopette! is based on trace-driven simulations. Our methodology is two-fold. First, we monitor the targeted organizations' Web related activity. Second, we replay the organization's access pattern while simulating the distributed Web support infrastructure.

This paper presents the information gathering as well as the design of the tool. We show that beyond a certain cache's size, the performance stays constant whereas the consistency continues to decrease. We also evaluated a number of distributed configurations, among which peer-to-peer Relais cooperation proved to be the best one.

Keywords

Web caches, configuration, performance evaluation, Relais.

1 INTRODUCTION

The performance of the World-Wide Web is getting worse and worse because the number of users grows faster than the network infrastructure capacity. To improve the Web performance for their members, many organizations cache documents that are likely to be requested in the near future. For a small-scale organization, that is an organization of a few dozen members located in the same local area network, a single shared proxy cache is often enough to make the performance acceptable. For large-scale organizations (i.e. thousands of members, possibly located at geographically separated sites), the use of a single proxy cache by all members will certainly not achieve the best possible system performance, at least for the members located far away from the cache.

1.1 Background on Distributed Caching System for the Web

There are mainly three kinds of Web caches: client caches are integrated in the browsers for improving a user's perceived performance; server caches are placed in front of Web servers for speeding up their response time; and proxy caches are placed at an intermediate location and shared by a group of related users (e.g. members of the same intranet or extranet, users located in the same region or country). Our work targets groups of proxy caches.

Proxy caches can run in isolation from each other or cooperate with one another. Four main cooperation strategies have been defined. The first strategy is hierarchical cooperation (Chankhunthod *et al.* 1996): it consists of building a tree-structure where nodes are caches. When a cache misses a document, it delegates the resolution of the request to its parent. Eventually, the requested document is returned to the cache that initiated the request; it then returns this document to the requesting client. On its way back, the response can be cached at each node it traverses.

The second strategy is the inter-cache protocol as implemented by Harvest and Squid (Chankhunthod *et al.* 1996, ICP 1994). When a cache misses a document, it broadcasts lookup messages to its siblings. If none of its siblings can serve this request, the cache retains the control of how to obtain the document.

The two remaining cooperation protocols are represented by CRISP (Gadde *et al.* 1997a) and Relais (Makpangou & Bérenguier 1997). Both systems allow a group of cooperative caches to share a common directory that lists documents cached by the entire group. The main difference between these systems is the representation of this directory. CRISP favors a centralized management whereas Relais replicates this directory at each cache location. For both systems, when a cache misses a document, it looks at the common directory. If a partner owns the requested document in its cache, the request is forwarded to it. If not, the request is sent to the original server (possibly through a parent cache).

The above cooperation strategies don't require the same investment and don't impose the same constraints. For instance, a parent cache will probably need more storage and more CPU than its children; it would be better placed nearer to the backbone than its children. On the other hand, cooperative caches need good network connections between each other and with the source servers.

1.2 Configuration Issues

The benefits of using one particular distributed cache depends on the users' access patterns, the cooperation strategy used by the group, the placement of caches and the sizing of the group of caches. We call any particular set of choices a *distributed cache configuration* (or simply a *configuration*). We also include in the distributed cache configuration the selection of a particular set of internal cache policies: replacement strategy, cache consistency management, deciding which documents to cache, and storage management.

What makes configuring a distributed Web caching system difficult is the lack of information about the performance of candidate configurations. With the current state of the art, a system administrator must choose and setup one particular configuration, evaluate it *a-posteriori*, and probably refine that configuration a number of times before reaching an acceptable result. This approach has a number of drawbacks: (i) it is necessary to invest in the hardware and the software with no guarantee of the resulting performance; (ii) it is impossible to evaluate a large number of configurations, so administrators may miss the optimum solution; (iii) it is difficult to compare the performance of different configurations because the users' access patterns and the network quality of service change as well as the Web cache configuration; (iv) during the configuration's refinement process, users can become discouraged and decide to bypass the caches.

1.3 Saperlipopette!

We present Saperlipopette!, a tool for evaluating *a-priori* the performance of distributed Web cache configurations. It allows a system administrator to capture the characteristics of its users' access patterns as well as his network quality of service. Then it allows the captured traffic to be replayed in differently-configured systems, and to analyze the resulting performance. Given the quality of service and cost information produced by Saperlipopette!, administrators can objectively decide on the appropriate configuration to use.

The rest of the paper is organized as follows. Section 2 presents some related work. Section 3 describes the methodology that we use, and Section 4 presents the design of the the simulation tool that constitutes the heart of Saperlipopette!. Section 5 discusses two case studies that we achieved with Saperlipopette!. Section 6 outlines some perspectives for this work and Section 7 draws some conclusions.

2 RELATED WORK

A lot of work has been done during the last few years on evaluating and improving the performance of Web caches. They can be classified into three groups: statistical analysis on collected traces, evaluations of elementary protocols, and general configuration recommendations.

Studies of the first group try to characterize users' access patterns, and draw some general cache design recommendations. For example, Bestavros et al. showed that Web traces exhibit a high locality, but that most redundant requests concern small documents (Bestavros *et al.* 1995). This result suggests the use of main memory caching (Markatos 1996). They also showed that LAN-level cache sharing can much improve performance. Another interesting study models "perfect" caching algorithms (i.e. algorithms that always take correct decisions based on knowledge of future requests). Such algorithms cannot improve latency more than 26% without prefetching, or 57% with prefetching (Kroeger *et al.* 1997). The main drawback of such studies is that they only give hints on the efficiency of algorithms; they cannot predict the user-perceived performance for a given configuration.

The second group encompasses studies that evaluate the benefits of particular caching policies. Many of them have evaluated the cost and performance of caches for particular replacement policies (Arlitt & Williamson 1996, Cao & Irani 1997, Kim *et al.* 1998, Williams *et al.* 1996), particular consistency protocols (Gwertzman & Seltzer 1996, Worrell 1994), particular cooperation protocols (Gadde *et al.* 1997b) or prefetching techniques (Padmanabhan & Mogul 1996). These studies often rely on trace-driven simulation tools. However, they run the protocols inside rough models of their environment. Such techniques bring out useful comparisons, but they ignore the side effects of the overall caching configuration on the resulting performance. Moreover, they are not designed for predicting the resulting performance in the particular case of a given user's traffic.

A number of experienced system administrators have published information about large-scale experiments, for national caches (Neal 1996, Smith 1996) and for distributed cooperative caching infrastructures (Melve *et al.* 1997, Wessels 1996). Unfortunately, these reports don't help a lot for building a distributed caching system designed for a particular user population. Only a few studies on personalized configuration that we know of address the sizing of isolated caches (Duska *et al.* 1997): *"Small client populations need 1-GB of cache per 35,000 requests/day and larger populations 1-GB per 70,000 to 100,000 requests/day"*. Saperlipopette! proposes a solution for personalizing such recommendations to a particular user's traffic, and for extending its scope to all aspects of configurations: internal caching protocols, distributed architecture and sizing.

3 THE METHODOLOGY

We are interested in evaluating the gain and the costs of using a distributed cache system (i.e. a group of caches) for accessing Web documents. We are mainly concerned by the users' perceived quality of service. To achieve this, we rely on simulations. This choice allows one to replay the same sequence of requests while simulating different numbers of caches, cache locations, cooperation strategies, and so on.

As it is difficult to forge realistic users' access patterns, we decided to run trace-driven simulations. We capture the actual Web traffic of the target organization (intranet or extranet) and replay the same sequence of requests in the simulation. By varying the system configuration, we can determine its impact on the resulting performance.

3.1 The Metrics

A caching system has three main effects on its environment: reducing user-level latency, reducing the load of the worldwide network, and reducing the load of the Web servers. Conversely, it introduces inconsistency problems: the delivered documents are not always up-to-date. The metrics we want to provide are the ones that characterize the user-perceived quality of the the Web system. They include the performance gain and the delivered documents' inconsistency.

The performance of the Web (with or without caches) can be expressed either by the average request latency or the average document retrieval time. The former measures the average amount of time between the beginning of the request and the instant at which the first byte of the response is received; the latter gives the average total duration of requests. The performance gain due to the use of a cache can be obtained by calculating the ratio of the latency (or retrieve time) when the cache system is used, by the one of a configuration with no cache.

The delivered documents' consistency metric is defined as the percentage of outdated documents retrieved from the system. To determine if a delivered document is outdated, we compare its "`Last-modified`" field with the one of the document in the server at the time of the request. If the two timestamps agree (either because the document was retrieved from the server or because the document on the server was not updated since it was previously downloaded by the cache), the document is considered up-to-date. If not, it is considered out-of-date.

3.2 Information Gathering

The information gathering consists of capturing all the Web traffic characteristics needed for the simulation. For that, we exploit the logs of one or several Web proxies carrying the traffic. As the information contained in the logs is insufficient, we collect additional data with a separate tool which directly contacts the Web servers. We also monitor the network's quality of service.

3.2.1 *Collecting Information about Document Consistency*

To evaluate the cache consistency metric for a given cache system, one expects Saperlipopette! to compare, for each request, both the timestamp of the copy actually delivered to the client and the timestamp of the document that *should have been* delivered. These timestamps are the values of the `Last-modified` fields of those copies. We call the former timestamp the *delivered timestamp* and the latter the *ideal timestamp*.

To generate such information, Saperlipopette! needs only one input datum: the ideal timestamp of each request. When the simulated system performs a cache miss, it assumes that the timestamp delivered by the server is the "ideal" timestamp. It then caches this document together with the ideal timestamp. Then, it logs a record in which the delivered and the ideal timestamps of the document are identical. When the simulated system performs a cache hit, it considers the timestamp attached to the cached document as the delivered timestamp. Hence, it logs a record containing the cached timestamps and the ideal timestamp.

If the proxy used for the monitoring of the traffic is not acting as a cache, it is straightforward to obtain the ideal timestamps (the delivered timestamp is equal to ideal timestamp). That's what Digital have done for collecting their Web proxy traces (Kroeger *et al.* 1996). However, if we monitor an extranet that already has caches, things get complicated. The proxy logs, when caches are used, can only indicate the timestamp of the documents that were delivered during one execution of a particular system configuration, not the timestamp of the document that *should have been* delivered if there were no cache. To address both cases, we separate the traffic monitoring and the gathering of document consistency related information.

Every night, we run a robot which replays the requests of the day. It sends HTTP `HEAD` requests to the Web servers, and looks at the `Last-modified` field of the response. If we call T_{req} the actual timestamp of the request and $T_{lastmod}$ the timestamp of the `Last-modified` response of the server, we can distinguish two cases:

- If $T_{lastmod} \leqslant T_{req}$, then we know that the `Last-modified` field of the document didn't change since the time of the request. We can then use $T_{lastmod}$ as the "ideal" timestamp.
- If $T_{req} < T_{lastmod}$, then the document has been updated between the time of the request and the time of the robot request. We then have no information on the "ideal" timestamp of this request. To reflect this uncertainty, Saperlipopette! calculates the consistency metric both in the worst and best case (i.e. when all uncertain requests are assumed to return out-of-date documents, or when they are assumed to return up-to-date documents).

3.2.2 *Collecting Information about Network Performance*

For simplicity reasons, the simulation assumes the absence of communication failures, network partitions, disconnections or crashes. It also ignores the delays due to computation or disk accesses. For building the performance metrics, it only needs data about the elapsed network transfer times. To determine the user-perceived performance, the simulator relies on knowledge of the actual document size as well as the characteristics of connections with document providers (both proxy caches and source servers). Once those are known, Saperlipopette! can determine the performance gain metric.

To obtain the actual sizes of documents, we face the same problem as for the document consistency related information: the cache logs cannot indicate the size of the documents that should have been delivered. To gather the actual sizes of documents, we used the same solution, i.e. to make our robot look at document sizes as well as timestamps.

To determine the connection characteristics, we took a very simplistic approach: for each Web server involved in our traces, we estimate the average latency and bandwidth observed for typical Web requests to that server. We built another small monitoring tool dedicated to network performance measurements: periodically, during daytime, it sends one HTTP GET request to each of the Web servers involved in our traces. We decided to request the root document of each server (i.e. its home page). This guarantees that documents retrieved this way are of approximately of the same size (a few kilobytes), and are representative of typical Web requests. In addition, the tool also monitors the internal connections (between clients and caches, and between the caches).

4 SIMULATION TOOL DESIGN

The heart of Saperlipopette! is a trace-driven distributed cache simulation tool built on top of a generic discrete event scheduler.

4.1 The Distributed Cache Simulation

To ease the evaluation task, we designed a highly modular and parameterizable distributed cache simulation which conforms to the design of Oléron (Baggio & Pierre 1997). Roughly, a Web cache is decomposed into several independent modules which implement elementary features: consistency control, replacement, inter-cache cooperation, and so on. To define a new policy, one only needs to inherit from the corresponding abstract class and code the specificities of the algorithm.

To setup one particular configuration, the evaluator instantiates (i) a simulated server for responding to all missed requests; (ii) a number of caches with their internal policies, their dimensioning and their cooperation scheme; (iii) and a number of clients (one per cache), each with the scenario it is to execute. All clients and caches are also given the network connections characteristics as perceived from their location.

4.2 The Scheduler

Although we consider a distributed Web infrastructure (with multiple clients, caches and servers), we run a mono-process simulation. Hence, the simulation relies on an event scheduler to trigger all the actions of the distributed system: these include issuing requests, arrivals of requests or responses, documents' time-to-live expirations, etc.

The scheduler manages an event handler queue. An event handler is an object of any C++ class that inherits from the `EventHandler` base class. It must implement a `go()` method which defines the behavior of the handler. Each event handler to be executed by the simulation must be registered with the scheduler, together with its wake up time. The scheduler is in charge of sorting the event handlers, and triggering them at the right time. It also manages the simulated time: when no event is running, it can safely bring forward the simulated time, and triggers the next event handler immediately.

For simplicity reasons, the scheduler doesn't allow concurrent execution of events. This imposes an important constraint: each event must be instantaneous in terms of the simulated time. In our model, an instantaneous operation (e.g. a local cache lookup) is implemented as a single event. Conversely, an operation which takes some simulated time (e.g. a document request) has to be divided into two events: the first event starts the computation, calculates the duration of the operation, creates a new event handler, registers it with the scheduler at the calculated termination time, and returns control to the scheduler. At the requested time, the scheduler will trigger the second handler, which can then finish the operation.

For example, the simulation of a cache request is done via two event handlers. The `BeginOfRequest` handler implements the beginning of the request: it makes a lookup for the URL in the cache. If it finds it, then it returns the document immediately. If it doesn't find it, it initiates a request to the Web server. For that, it first computes the timestamp at which this request will arrive; it creates a `ServerRequest` handler, and registers it to the scheduler (Figure 1). Later on, the scheduler will trigger the `ServerRequest`, allowing it to deliver the request to the server (Figure 2).

5 APPLICATIONS

We present here two example studies realized with Saperlipopette!: the first one shows the impact of a cache's size on the resulting performance and consistency; the second studies the impact of different distributed caching architectures on the resulting performance.

5.1 Collected Traces Analysis

The example we chose to work on is an extranet, namely the INRIA network. INRIA comprises five research units, located in different parts of France. The system

```
void BeginOfRequest::go() {
  if (cache.lookup(request.url())) {
    /* Cache HIT  */
    request.client().deliver_document();
  }
  else {
    /* Cache MISS */
    Timestamp     t = scheduler.now() + request.duration();
    EventHandler *e = new ServerRequest(request);
    scheduler.register(e,t);
  }
}
```

Figure 1 Simple pseudo-code BeginOfRequest handler

```
void ServerRequest::go() {
  request.get_server()->receive_request(request);
}
```

Figure 2 Simple pseudo-code ServerRequest handler

we studied is the overall caching system, intended for enabling INRIA personnel to browse the Web. We actually collected the two main research units' cache traces (Rocquencourt and Sophia) from the 13th September 1997 to the 9th February 1998. Table 1 shows some of its characteristics. We also measured the network QoS, which we summarize in Table 2.

A quick statistical analysis of the trace shows interesting results. By comparing the number of requests and the number of unique requests, we can see that the theoretical maximum Hit rate of Rocquencourt is $(1021417 - 674212)/1021417 = 34.0\%$, Sophia's one is 34.2%, and the whole group's one is 37.3%.

These figures also show the potential of resource sharing between Rocquencourt and Sophia. If we compare the number of unique requests for Rocquencourt, Sophia, and all together, we see that there are $392262 + 674212 - 1014390 = 52084$ unique documents requested by both Rocquencourt and Sophia. This represents 5.1% of the total number of unique documents.

Table 1 Requests trace characterictics

	Nb reqs	*Nb unique reqs*	*Nb Clients*	*Avg doc size*
Rocq	1021417	674212	726	13.4 kb
Soph	596499	392262	364	11.4 kb
All	1617916	1014390	1089	12.1 kb

Table 2 Network quality of service

	Local connection	*Rocq-Soph*	*INRIA-external servers*
Avg. latency	5 ms	100 ms	7569 ms
Avg. bandwidth	300 kb/s	45 kb/s	1.3 kb/s

5.2 Scope of the Simulation

As previously pointed out, the simulator can be configured in many ways. One can easily change the internal policies (replacement, consistency control, inter-cache co-operation), the dimensioning, the number and placement of the caches. Of course, if we vary all of these parameters at the same time, an exponential number of configurations must be simulated. We decided to limit this number by fixing the following parameters:

- The replacement policy we use in the following studies is LRU.
- The consistency control policy we use is Alex(Gwertzman & Seltzer 1996) (often called TTL): it allocates a Time-To-Live to incoming documents proportional to the document's age. When a document's TTL expires, it is ejected from the cache. In our studies, we use a fixed proportion of 30% for all documents, which is representative of typical cache configurations.

The variable parameters are the cache size, the placement of the caches and the cooperation scheme between them: no cooperation at all, hierarchical relations and Relais-like cooperation. This latter protocol is a simplified version of Relais (Makpangou & Bérenguier 1997): it assumes no propagation delay for the replicated shared directory; and all the consistency control parts of Relais have been ignored.

5.3 Impact of Cache Size

The experiment presented here is simple: whereas INRIA users are actually located in two different places, we assume they are all present in a single location. Every user accesses a single shared cache. We change the cache's size, and watch the variations of documents' inconsistency and retrieve time reduction (Figure 3). The reductions are given by comparing the observed performance with the one of a configuration with no cache at all.

We can see that performance increases when the cache size increases. The performance reaches an asymptote near 1.5 Gb: adding cache storage space doesn't improve significantly the performance. One can't get more than a 22% reduction in retrieve time from this cache.

The inconsistency also increases when cache size increases. A large storage space

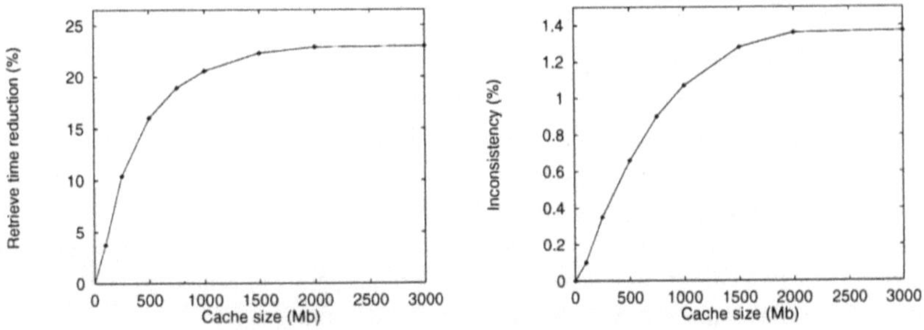

(a) Retrieve time reduction (b) Inconsistency

Figure 3 Performance and consistency of a single Web cache

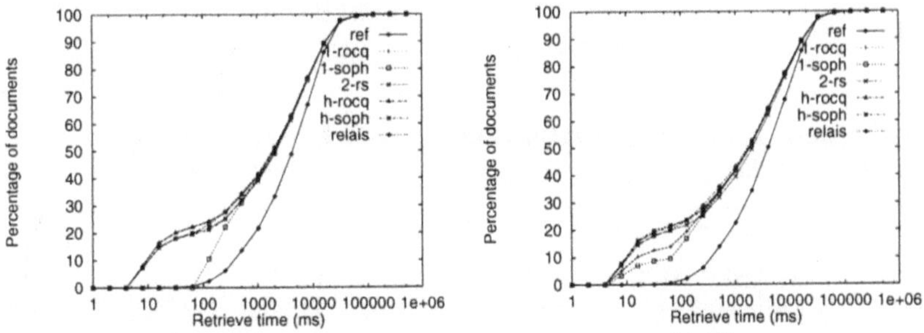

(a) Rocquencourt (b) All

Figure 4 Infinite size caches

allows documents to stay longer in the cache, increasing their probability of becoming out-of-date. As for the retrieve time, inconsistency reaches an asymptote; but it does so at a higher cache size (near 2 Gb). After a certain size, adding extra storage space hardly increases performance, but significantly increases inconsistency: most of the extra cache hits actually deliver out-of-date documents.

5.4 Impact of the Distributed Architectures

We show here the impact of several distributed caching architectures on the resulting performance. The architectures we simulated are presented in Table 3. They include a reference configuration with no cache at all, two configurations with one single cache located at Rocquencourt or at Sophia, and three cooperative configurations. The cooperation scheme can be hierarchical relationship (with the parent cache at Rocquencourt or Sophia), or peer-to-peer Relais-like cooperation.

5.4.1 Infinite Cache Size

We study here caches with an infinite storage size. To analyze the results in detail, we show the cumulative retrieve time both as graphs and tables. They show the percentage of documents retrieved in less than a given duration.

Figure 4 and Table 4 show the cumulative retrieve time for infinite size caches,

Table 3 Configurations

Config	*Description*
Ref	No cache at all: the clients access directly the servers.
1-rocq	One single cache, located at Rocquencourt.
1-soph	One single cache, located at Sophia.
2-rs	Two caches at Rocquencourt and Sophia, with no cooperation between them.
h-rocq	Two caches; Rocquencourt's cache is the parent of Sophia's cache.
h-soph	The same as h-rocq, but the parent is at Sophia.
relais	Two caches cooperating with a Relais-like protocol.

Table 4 Cumulative retrieve time (infinite size caches — All users)

Config	*Ref*	*1-soph*	*1-rocq*	*2-rs*	*h-soph*	*h-rocq*	*relais*
128 ms	2.26%	16.90%	19.45%	21.79%	23.48%	23.63%	23.48%
1024 ms	22.52%	41.71%	41.99%	39.47%	41.97%	42.18%	43.14%
8192 ms	67.76%	77.11%	77.19%	75.92%	77.16%	77.24%	77.59%

from the point of view of Rocquencourt users and all users. We don't show the point of view of Sophia users, as their profile is very similar to the one of Rocquencourt.

We can observe the "no-cache" reference curve, which has a well-known shape: almost no document is retrieved within 100 ms, then most documents are retrieved between 1 second and 100 seconds. The curves for configurations including caches have a different shape: about 20% of the documents are retrieved within 100 ms; the curve remains significantly higher than the reference until 20 seconds retrieve time.

The graphs show that caches widely improve document retrieval time. For example, 22.52% of the documents are retrieved within 1024 ms without any cache, whereas the caching configurations increase this proportion to 43.14%. This corresponds to the user-level experience of Web caches: many more documents are retrieved "instantaneously".

The Figure 4(a) shows the perceived improvement for Rocquencourt users only. We can see three different shapes: the reference one, the one of "good" caching strategies (1-rocq, 2-rs, h-rocq, h-soph, relais), and a single one staying between them (1-soph). This curve corresponds to an obviously sub-optimal configuration: one single cache, placed in Sophia. Of course, the high latency between Rocquencourt and Sophia degrades the documents' retrieve time, even in the case of cache hits. Nevertheless, as Rocquencourt-Sophia bandwidth is quite good, this curve joins the others when latency becomes a negligible part of the total retrieve time. This

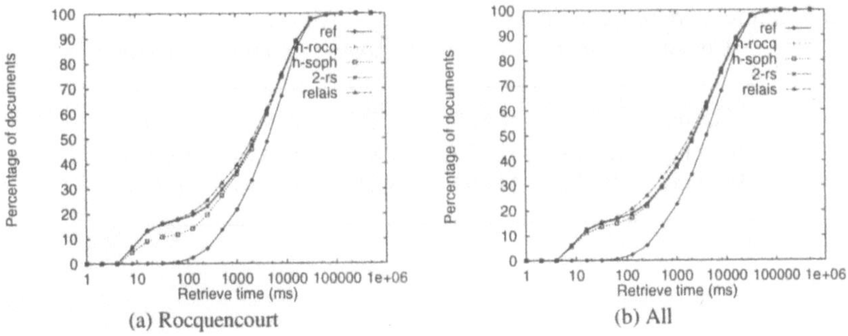

Figure 5 1 Go total size caches

effect is identical from Sophia's point of view, with a single cache located at Rocquencourt.

From the overall user group's point of view, we can distinguish three groups of configurations: the reference, the configurations with a single cache, and the distributed configurations. The performance of all distributed configurations are very close, except the 2-rs configuration, which has significantly lower performance (Table 4). This shows that inter-cache cooperation increases performance. The documents downloaded at high cost by one cache can be later obtained at low cost by a partner cache.

If we try to distinguish the cooperative configurations, we see that hierarchical configurations are slightly better than peer-to-peer ones for very small retrieval times whereas peer-to-peer configurations are better for higher retrieval times. But no real difference distinguishes the two cooperation schemes.

5.4.2 Limited Cache Size

We then wondered if the distributed configurations would have very different performance for smaller caches: inter-cache cooperation (either via hierarchical or via peer-to-peer relations) should be much more useful when sharing limited resources. We studied the previous distributed configurations, in the case of a total of 1 gigabyte being distributed among two caches (we ignore the single-cache configurations, as they proved to be sub-optimal). For all configurations, Rocquencourt had 700 Mb of storage space and Sophia had 300 Mb (because Rocquencourt has much more traffic than Sophia), except for the h-soph configuration where Sophia had 700 Mb and Rocquencourt had 300 Mb. The cumulative retrieval times are shown in Figure 5 and in Table 5.

This time, we clearly see that cooperative caches lead to better performance than non-cooperative ones; among cooperative relations, peer-to-peer caches are better than hierarchical ones.

We next decided to retain the peer-to-peer configuration only, and search for the optimal storage size distribution between the two caches. Figure 6 shows the average retrieval time improvement when varying the storage space distribution.

If we observe the shape for Sophia, we can see that the optimal configuration for

Table 5 Cumulative retrieve time (1 Gb cache — All users)

Config	*Ref*	*2-rs*	*h-soph*	*h-rocq*	*relais*
128 ms	2.26%	18.88%	17.21%	18.91%	20.61%
1024 ms	22.52%	37.15%	37.82%	38.33%	40.70%
8192 ms	67.76%	74.89%	75.33%	75.54%	76.53%

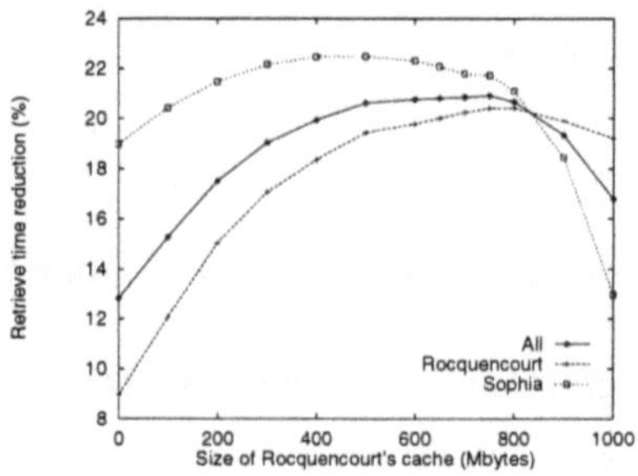

Figure 6 Retrieve time reduction of peer-to-peer cooperating caches

their users is not to take all the storage space. The optimal distribution, from their point of view, is to take 500 Mb, and leave the remaining 500 Mb for Rocquencourt. We explain this as follows: in the case of having all the storage for themselves, they don't benefit from Rocquencourt's users retrievals. In the other hand, if they give some storage space to Rocquencourt, they lose some local hits due to the fact that their local cache is smaller, but benefit from Rocquencourt's retrievals. Of course, if Sophia's cache gets too small, then they will start to have a lot of "neighbor hits", but will see increased retrieval time because the latency between Rocquencourt and Sophia is higher than the local one.

Similarly, from the point of view of Rocquencourt, the optimal placement is 800 Mb at Rocquencourt and 200 Mb at Sophia. The conflicting interests of both sites are balanced when allocating 750 Mb to Rocquencourt and 250 Mb for Sophia: no site gets the best possible performance, but this balance optimizes the overall performance.

This application study shows how we can use Saperlipopette! for evaluating and comparing distributed architectures. We showed that, in the particular case of INRIA, peer-to-peer cooperation leads to better performance than hierarchical cooperation; and any cooperation is better than no cooperation at all. We also showed how Saperlipopette! helps the sizing and placement of caches: if Rocquencourt and Sophia decided to invest in a total 1 Gb of storage space, the optimal placement would be 750 Mb at Rocquencourt and 250 Mb at Sophia.

6 FUTURE WORK

The current prototype presents a number of limitations. They can be classified in two categories: some are due to human factors, others are introduced by simplifications we made (both in the gathering and simulation processes).

The caches' quality of service has an impact on the users' behavior. For example, if a Web caching system suddenly becomes much faster, users will probably start to browse more. Similarly, if users notice that caches always deliver up-to-date documents, they will stop using the "reload" button of their browser. Our evaluation tool doesn't anticipate such possible changes on users' behavior and assumes that the users will conform to their past behavior.

The data collection process ignores a number of requests issued by users of the target system. (i) It takes into account only the HTTP requests; our simulator doesn't include FTP or Gopher protocols. (ii) It selects only the GET requests because documents obtained via POST or other HTTP methods are generally not cached. It also ignores the requests to CGI scripts for the same reason. (iii) Some requests lack reliable information (e.g. the ideal timestamp).

The wide-area network simulation needs to be improved: it is currently based on simple measurements, and doesn't simulate the network failures or performance fluctuations. Another simplification we made on the simulator is that it only takes into account the network costs, whereas under high load the disk performance has proved to be crucial (Smith 1996). Similarly, a number of protocols have been simplified in the simulator's implementation.

We also plan to develop additional policy modules for the simulator: caching policies (e.g. invalidation consistency control protocols), cooperation (e.g. ICP), prefetching and automatic mirroring. These protocols will allow us to continue the case study of INRIA traffic. We also plan to use Saperlipopette! for studying other target environments.

Saperlipopette! can also be used for fast evaluation of newly designed caching algorithms. Instead of integrating the new algorithm in a real caching system (which can be a long and painful process), it is easy to build a rough version in the simulator. After an evaluation, and possibly a refinement process, one can decide if actually deploying the new algorithm is worth the implementation cost or not.

7 CONCLUSION

We presented Saperlipopette!, a distributed Web cache evaluation tool. This tool can help large-scale organizations to make the decisions that suit their needs: the quality of the service offered to its members as well the costs to the organization. It can help to optimize the use of resources of large organizations. Finally it can help save money by identifying sub-optimal configurations.

We discussed the utilization of Saperlipopette! to evaluate various configurations of a distributed cache shared by the personnel of INRIA-Rocquencourt and INRIA-

Sophia. Though this study is still in its preliminary phase, we reported some initial results. Beyond a certain cache's size, the performance stays constant whereas the consistency continues to decrease. We also evaluated a number of distributed configurations, among which peer-to-peer Relais cooperation proved to be the best one.

Our future plans are to complete this study as well as to use our tool to evaluate potential benefits of different configurations. We also consider using Saperlipopette! to guide the refinement of some existing cache policies.

REFERENCES

Arlitt, M. F. & Williamson, C. L., (1996) Trace-driven simulation of document caching strategies for Internet Web servers. `http://www.cs.usask.ca/faculty/carey/papers/webcaching.ps`.

Baggio, A. & Pierre, G., (1997) Oléron: supporting information sharing in large-scale mobile environments. In *Proceedings of the ERSADS '97 seminar*. Zinal, Switzerland.

Bestavros, A. *et al.*, (1995) Application-level document caching in the Internet. In *Proceedings of the 2nd International Workshop in Distributed and Networked Environments (IEEE SDNE '95)*. Whistler, British Columbia.

Cao, P. & Irani, S., (1997) Cost-aware WWW proxy caching algorithms. In *Proceedings of the 1997 Usenix Symposium on Internet Technologies and Systems (USITS-97)*. Monterey, CA.

Chankhunthod, A. *et al.*, (1996) A hierarchical Internet object cache. In *Proceedings of the 1996 Usenix Technical Conference*. San Diego, CA.

Duska, B. M. *et al.*, (1997) The measured access characteristics of World-Wide-Web client proxy caches. In *Proceedings of the 1997 Usenix Symposium on Internet Technologies and Systems (USITS-97)*. Monterey, CA.

Gadde, S. *et al.*, (1997a) Reduce, reuse, recycle: An approach to building large Internet caches. In *Proceedings of the HotOS '97 Workshop*.

Gadde, S. *et al.*, (1997b) Directory structures for scalable Internet caches. Technical Report CS-1997-18, Duke university.

Gwertzman, J. & Seltzer, M., (1996) World-Wide Web cache consistency. In *Proceedings of the 1996 Usenix Technical Conference*. San Diego, CA.

ICP, (1994) Internet cache protocol specification 1.4. `http://excalibur.usc.edu/icpdoc/icp.html`.

Kim, I. *et al.*, (1998) Analysis of buffer management policies for WWW proxy. In *Proceedings of the International Conference on Information Networking (ICOIN-12)*. Tokyo, Japan.

Kroeger, T. M. *et al.*, (1996) Digital's Web proxy traces. `ftp://ftp.digital.com/pub/DEC/traces/proxy/webtraces.v1.2.html`.

Kroeger, T. M. *et al.*, (1997) Exploring the bounds of Web latency reduction from caching and prefetching. In *Proceedings of the 1997 Usenix Symposium on Internet Technologies and Systems*. Monterey, CA.

Makpangou, M. & Bérenguier, E., (1997) Relais : un protocole de maintien de cohérence de caches Web coopérants. In *Proceedings of the NoTeRe '97 symposium*. Pau, France.

Markatos, E. P., (1996) Main memory caching of Web documents. In *Proceedings of the 5th International WWW Conference*. Paris, France.

Melve, I. *et al.*, (1997) Building a Web caching system - architectural considerations. In *Proceedings of the 8th Joint European Networking Conference*. Edinburgh, Scotland.

Neal, D., (1996) The Harvest object cache in New Zeland. In *Proceedings of the 5th International WWW Conference*. Paris, France.

Padmanabhan, V. N. & Mogul, J. C., (1996) Using predictive prefetching to improve World-Wide Web latency. In *Proceedings of the ACM SIGCOMM '96 Conference*. Stanford University, CA.

Smith, N. G., (1996) The UK national Web cache - the state of the art. In *Proceedings of the 5th International WWW Conference*. Paris, France.

Wessels, D., (1996) Evolution of the NLANR cache hierarchy: Global configuration challenges. `http://www.nlanr.net/Papers/Cache96/`.

Williams, S. *et al.*, (1996) Removal policies in network caches for World-Wide Web documents. In *Procedings of the ACM SIGCOMM '96 Conference*. Stanford University, CA.

Worrell, K. J., (1994) *Invalidation in large scale network objects caches*. Master's thesis, Faculty of the graduate school of the University of Colorado.

8 BIOGRAPHY

Guillaume Pierre is a PhD student at University of Evry val d'Essonne and at INRIA SOR group. His main interests are flexible systems and Internet performance optimization. His thesis focuses on performance studies and optimization for distributed Web caching systems.

Mesaac Makpangou received a Ph.D. from University Pierre et Marie Curie of Paris (France), in february 1989. He then spent a one-year post-doctoral at Cornell, in the ISIS group with Professor Kenneth Birman, where he developped the Isis' longhaul stuff. Since 1990, he holds a "Chargé de Recherche" position at INRIA, within the SOR Group. His current research interest concerns efficient support of large-scale cooperative applications.

Experience With Top Gun Wingman: A Proxy-Based Graphical Web Browser for the 3Com PalmPilot

Armando Fox, Ian Goldberg, Steven D. Gribble, David C. Lee,
Anthony Polito, and Eric A. Brewer
445 Soda Hall
University of California at Berkeley
Berkeley, CA, USA 94720-1776
1-510-643-9475, 1-510-642-5775 (fax)
{fox,iang,gribble,lcddave,aspolito,brewer}@cs.berkeley.edu

After an inauspicious debut, communication-enabled personal digital assistants (or PDA's) and handheld PC's are being "rediscovered" as mobile information access terminals. In response, developers have attempted to bring complex applications such as Web browsers to such devices. However, the limited resources available on thin client platforms make them unsuitable for hosting such applications. In this paper, we advocate moving application complexity from thin clients to an *adaptive middleware proxy* (AMWP), an infrastructural application server platform designed to support large populations and diverse applications. We describe one such application, Top Gun Wingman, a graphical, split Web browser for the Palm Pilot PDA that is currently in use by more than 11,000 users around the world. Our discussion focuses on the design philosophy, implementation, performance, and lessons learned from our experience with the Wingman client and the middleware proxy that supports it.

Keywords
middleware, adaptive, proxy, Palm Pilot, topgun wingman

1 MOTIVATION

We would like to connect "thin clients" to the Internet, especially convergent mobile devices such as *smart phones*, while allowing them to leverage at least some of the installed infrastructure of Web content and services. However, the limited capabilities of these devices—smaller displays, more limited user interfaces, lower bandwidth, and limited processing power and memory—complicate direct porting of desktop applications such as Web browsers. In the past (Fox, Gribble, Chawathe & Brewer 1996, Fox, Gribble, Brewer & Amir 1996) we have argued for the use of *transformational proxies*, which perform on-the-fly, datatype-specific lossy compression, as a mechanism for application-level content adaptation that circumvents the limitations of thin clients. We have generalized this approach into a full set of building blocks and programming interfaces for constructing proxy-based applications that adapt to network and client variability. In this paper we describe our *adaptive middleware proxy* (AMWP) approach in the context of Top Gun Wingman, the world's first graphical Web browser for the 3Com PalmPilot.

Existing commercial products such as Microsoft Pocket Internet Explorer for Windows CE and HandWeb for the 3Com PalmPilot attempt to directly port the largest reasonable subset of features from desktop browsers onto thin clients. In contrast, Wingman is not a port, but a true *split application* in which a substantial amount of the application complexity has been pushed to a back end proxy server. The proxy server implements a simple building-block programming model called TACC (Fox 1997), which supports application modules that perform Transformation, Aggregation, Caching, and Customization of Internet content.

We discuss the implementation in detail in Section 2.

1.1 Claims and Contributions

Because we exploit infrastructure computing, Wingman's performance and feature set compare very favorably not only with its direct competitors, but with many desktop browsers as well. In particular, we make the following claims for the AMWP-based implementation of the Wingman browser, which we support with specific examples and later generalize to other thin-client Internet services:

1. The AMWP approach results in **better performance** than a reduced port or least-common-denominator, standards-compliant implementation that runs entirely on the client. We provide evidence for this in Section 2.6.
2. AMWP enables **new features and behaviors** for the client, many of which would be awkward or impossible without proxy support. By hosting the complex parts of the application on the TACC proxy, complex applications can be robustly supported on very simple clients. For example, the AMWP approach has been used to bring the MBONE mediaboard application to the Palm Pilot (Chawathe, Fink, McCanne & Brewer 1998).

3. AMWP **transparently leverages more of the existing infrastructure** of content and services, since on-the-fly transparent translation and compression are effective techniques for delivering acceptable performance between existing servers and thin or legacy clients. Such thin clients might not otherwise be capable of handling content and services designed for modern, "common case" clients.
4. AMWP-based services are **cost effective to operate and expand** because of the simplicity of the client software, the generality of our building-block approach for the middleware proxy, and our proven commodity-PC cluster server implementation (Fox, Gribble, Chawathe, Brewer & Gauthier 1997). Cost efficiency makes widespread deployment of AMWP-based applications feasible even for very large (hundreds of thousands of users) communities.

1.2 Map of Paper

In Section 2 we motivate the three-tier client-proxy-server model as a platform for deploying middleware-based services for mobile and thin clients. We describe our general approach, give quantitative experience from work leading up to Wingman, and introduce the TACC programming model that supports Wingman and other applications. We also give details of the implementation and performance of both the Wingman client and its cluster-based TACC server back-end (discussed previously in (Fox, Gribble, Chawathe, Brewer & Gauthier 1997)), and describe how the AMWP approach enables specific features that make Wingman competitive with both desktop browsers and other thin-client browsers. In Section 3, we attempt to draw some lessons based on our experience in both implementing Wingman (and AMWP applications in general) and serving a worldwide community of over 11,000 users. We discuss related and future work in Section 4.

2 ARCHITECTURE AND IMPLEMENTATION

We argue for a *proxy-based approach* for middleware applications, in which proxy agents placed between clients and servers perform computation- and storage-intensive tasks, such as datatype-specific lossy compression, on behalf of clients. Properly applied, this approach reduces the bandwidth demands on the infrastructure through lossy compression (Fox & Brewer 1996, Fox, Gribble, Chawathe, Brewer & Gauthier 1997), and allows legacy and other nonstandard (including thin) clients to interoperate with existing servers.

Furthermore, by performing client adaptation at a shared infrastructural proxy, we avoid inserting adaptation machinery at each origin server. Application partitioning arguments have long been used to keep clients simple (as in (Watson 1994*a*)); we simply split the application between client and proxy, rather than between client and server. From the client's perspective, the proxy is simply a server that gets the data from someplace else.

2.1 TACC: A Programming Model for AMWP Applications

We have evolved a programming model for proxy-based applications called TACC (Fox 1997, Fox, Gribble, Chawathe, Brewer & Gauthier 1997): *transformation* (distillation (Fox, Gribble, Brewer & Amir 1996), filtering, format conversion, etc.), *aggregation* (collecting and collating data from various sources, either offline or on-the-fly), *caching* (both original and transformed content), and *customization* (persistent store of user profiles, allowing the service to tailor its output to each user's needs or device characteristics). Each *TACC worker* specializes in a particular task, for example, scaling/dithering of images in a particular format, conversion between specific data formats, extracting "landmark" information from specific Web pages, etc. Complete applications are built by *composing* workers, by *chaining* them (in the Unix pipeline sense), or allowing one worker to *call* another as a subroutine or (parallel, asynchronous) coroutine. The *dispatch rules* that determine which workers are invoked to satisfy a particular user request can either be hardcoded for each application, or controlled dynamically by the workers themselves. A runtime platform called a *TACC server* is expected to provide mechanisms for hosting workers, instantiating dispatch rules, providing high availability, and recovering from errors such as dispatch loops, infinite mutual recursion, or worker instability; we describe our prototype TACC server in the next section.

Workers serially process tasks from a task queue; each task corresponds to some component of satisfying a user request, e.g. scaling and transforming an inline image on a Web page. Each worker is expected to be *atomic and restartable*, in order that the TACC server (a prototype implementation of which we describe below) be able to exploit a repertoire of availability and scaling mechanisms. There are several ways in which a worker can achieve this goal, including being completely stateless (as in Wingman), performing only idempotent operations, or sharing reconstructable group state via mechanisms such as Scalable Reliable Multicast (SRM) (Floyd, Jacobson, Liu & McCanne 1995).

Customization is central to TACC: the TACC server is expected to manage persistent *user profiles* (lists of key/value pairs) that allow workers to provide user-customized service. The TACC server identifies a user via incoming IP address, cookies, or some other client-specific identifier, and automatically routes the appropriate profile information to the worker(s) that will be used to satisfy the request. API's are provided for workers to modify or access profile data directly, and to generate HTML forms that allow users to edit their profiles without requiring direct worker involvement.

TACC provides a very general programming model that subsumes transformation proxies (Fox, Gribble, Chawathe & Brewer 1997), proxy filters (Zenel 1996), customized information aggregators, and search engines. The TACC programming environment, which currently consists of Unix-hosted interface files and build/test harnesses, provides the inter-worker and intra-worker API's, composition rule API's, and glue that allows workers to be authored in a variety of languages (currently C/C++, Perl 5, Java, and Tcl).

2.2 Scalable Cluster-Based TACC Server

A *TACC server* is a platform that instantiates TACC workers and the dispatch rules for routing network data traffic to and from them, and provides support for the inter-worker calling and chaining API's. Roughly, a TACC server is to TACC workers as the Unix shell and runtime are to Unix programs. Our decision to use a cluster of commodity PC's as the basis for our TACC server implementation, as well as the design goals for the cluster runtime software, were motivated by several straightforward observations:

- The inherent hardware redundancy of clusters can be harnessed to provide high system availability.
- For "embarrassingly parallel" workloads with favorable computation to communication ratios, fast and inexpensive system-area networks such as switched 100 Mb/s Ethernet or Myrinet (Myricom 1995) allow a cluster to be treated as a single large computing resource.
- Using commodity PC's as the unit of scaling allows the service to ride the leading edge of the cost/performance curve as it is incrementally expanded.

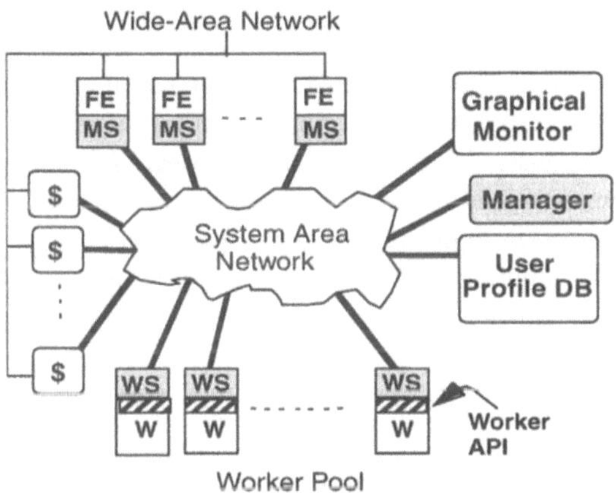

Figure 1 Components of a cluster-based TACC server include front ends (FE), TACC workers (W) and caches ($), a user profile database, a graphical monitor/administration interface, and a fault-tolerant load manager whose functionality logically extends into the manager stubs (MS) and worker stubs (WS).

We describe our system architecture at a high level; a detailed description can be found in (Fox, Gribble, Chawathe, Brewer & Gauthier 1997). The software-component block diagram of our scalable TACC server is shown in Figure 1. *Front ends* receive client requests from the outside world and "shepherd" them through the system, by fetching Internet content via the *caches*, matching the request with the appropriate user profile from the *customization database*, and queueing the request for service by one or more *TACC workers* that will process the data according to the user preferences. Front ends maximize system throughput by maintaining state for many simultaneous outstanding requests, and can be replicated for both scalability and availability. The *Load Balancing/Fault Tolerance manager* is responsible for internal reactive load balancing (including exploiting an *overflow pool* of general-use machines), autostarting and reaping TACC workers, and detecting and recovering from various system failures, including crashed components and network partitions, via multicast heartbeat and process-peer fault tolerance. The entire system is administered through a *Graphical Monitor*, which supports asynchronous error notification via email or pager, temporary disabling of system components for hot upgrades, and visualization of the system's behavior using Tcl/Tk (Ousterhout 1994).

Our working prototype of the cluster runtime provides a set of mechanisms (described in (Fox, Gribble, Chawathe, Brewer & Gauthier 1997)) to support incremental scaling, internal load balancing, and high availability for TACC applications. Hiding this machinery behind the TACC API's keeps TACC applications easy to write even though they will be deployed to large user communities who will expect continuous availability (so-called "24 × 7 operation"). Our cluster has been hosting Wingman on the Berkeley NOW (Network of Workstations) since October 1997, using four dedicated SPARCstation-10's and an overflow pool of up to 100 SPARC Ultra-1 Enterprise servers, about five of which are in use at any given time.

The availability mechanisms in the cluster runtime have kept the system running virtually continuously* despite a variety of observed failures (worker crashes, temporary interconnect partitions, and unexpected node reboots, among others), in addition to the aggressive fault-injection experiments described in (Fox, Gribble, Chawathe, Brewer & Gauthier 1997). Although (as described in that paper) the cluster's availability mechanisms cannot completely mask front-end failures, Wingman masks them using a client-side front-end failover mechanism, similar to Netscape proxy auto-configuration (Netscape Communications Corporation 1998).

2.3 Wingman as a TACC Application

The 3Com PalmPilot's austere graphics library supports a single native bitmap format, and text objects are not automatically word-wrapped and must consist entirely of text in a single visual style (bold, etc.). The principle of client competence (that the client should only perform tasks for which it is competent) therefore suggests that HTML parsing and tag-to-font mapping, page layout with client-specific font metrics, and image scaling with conversion to native bitmap format all be left to the TACC proxy. The proxy side of the Wingman browser uses four TACC workers: the

*During February 1998, we experienced frequent sporadic downtime, which was ultimately traced to a configuration change on the cluster that caused remote execution to sometimes break.

image processor, the HTML processor, the zip processor, and the *aggregator request service.* The TACC model and API's allow parallelism to be exploited in various ways; for example, all inline images are prefetched in parallel with HTML parsing, and whenever possible multiple images are converted in parallel by calling multiple workers.

2.3.1 Image and HTML Processors

The **image processor** reads GIF and JPEG images (the two most common Web formats (Gribble & Brewer 1997)), converts them to an intermediate bitmap form, optionally scales, color-quantizes and dithers, and finally outputs the result in either the PalmPilot's native image format (Tbmp) or our enhanced 2-bit-per-pixel format.

The **HTML processor** parses HTML markup, maps HTML tags to supported font attributes, and generates an intermediate-form page layout. Because the HTML processor knows the client's font metrics and display properties, it can wrap text, flow text around inline images, etc. (A client identification token in the initial client-to-proxy handshake is used to select the correct client profile. The layout code and intermediate layout form are client-independent.)

When inline image tags are encountered, the HTML processor fetches the image, determines how much it should be scaled down using a simple set of heuristics we developed, * and dispatches the original image to an image processor to do the actual scaling and format conversion. Image processing is done asynchronously and in parallel for all images; the HTML parser continues laying out the page in the meantime, and arranges to rendezvous with the image data before returning to the client a simple display list of images and text, using a tokenized markup we have developed that allows the complete page (including all inline images) to be sent as a single object.

2.3.2 Aggregators

An *aggregator* queries one or more Web sites for specific content and collates and formats the results for presentation to the client. (The Metacrawler (go2net, Inc. 1997) service on the Web is a recent example of a Web-based aggregator.) Although Wingman's aggregator mechanism was originally designed as a substitute for HTML forms support, aggregators have become our general mechanism for retrieving information from multiple content sources and filtering that information to best suit the needs of the PalmPilot user. The **aggregator request service** allows access to proxy-based content-aggregation applications.

In Wingman, an aggregator consists of a very simple PalmPilot-native UI that allows the user to write some text describing what is being requested (e.g. the query terms for a Web search, the ticker symbol for a stock quote, etc.). When the "OK" button is tapped, the contents of the form are transmitted to the Wingman TACC proxy's aggregation worker. The worker uses the content of the first box to determine which service the user is requesting (search engine, stock quote, etc.) and the

*Roughly speaking, larger images are shrunk more aggressively, imagemaps are shrunk less aggressively to preserve embedded text, and images are pinned to the screen size of the PalmPilot.

content of the second box as parameters to the aggregator. A site-specific aggregator handler then converts this data to an HTML form submission on the proxy side, and the results from the origin server are formatted by the HTML processor. We have deployed aggregators for Yahoo, HotBot, AltaVista, DejaNews, Yahoo's stock quotes service, and TripQuest.

2.3.3 Zip, PalmOS, and Doc Support

If the client fetches a Zip file (a popular format for PalmPilot software archives), the **zip processor** formats a listing of the archive contents in HTML, such that following the link for a particular archive member will cause the zip processor to return the selected member. The HTML created by the zip processor is then parsed by the HTML processor for conversion to our binary markup, just as for normal Web pages. This mechanism exploits TACC's ability to easily *compose* different workers to quickly create new client abilities.

The proxy passes PalmOS *databases* (persistent object stores on the PalmPilot) unmodified, which allows users to use Wingman to install new data and applications onto their PalmPilots; for example, a proxy-side AportisDoc (Aportis Inc. 1998) converter module allows users to immediately save the text of a Web page in this popular e-book format.

2.4 Client Implementation and User Experience

The "look and feel" of the Wingman browser intentionally resembles desktop browsers, but with specific additions and modifications motivated by the nature of the PalmPilot platform and small device UI's in general. Like desktop browsers, Wingman has a hotlist (bookmark) feature, a local user-controllable cache, and an automatic history cache. Aggregators (described above) are handled by a special aggregator request window containing a popup menu of all available aggregators and a text area for entering aggregation specific data, such as a search string.

The *refinement interface* allows users to zoom in on scaled-down images (Figure 2). Clicking on an image brings up a popup menu that allows the user to view the original image or follow the link (if applicable). Even for images that have no link to follow, we chose to have the popup menu appear anyway (with the "follow link" item disabled) to avoid disorienting the user with different click behaviors for different image types. We originally proposed a mechanism of this kind for regular Web surfing in (Fox & Brewer 1996), but Wingman completely integrates the refinement interface into the user experience.

2.5 Noteworthy Implementation Details

Following the long-standing recommendations of (Clark & Tennenhouse 1990), complete, ready-to-render pages are delivered as application data units (ADU's). This simplifies the client logic considerably: when the network layer delivers a network event, it means that an entire, self-describing ADU is waiting in a buffer ready to

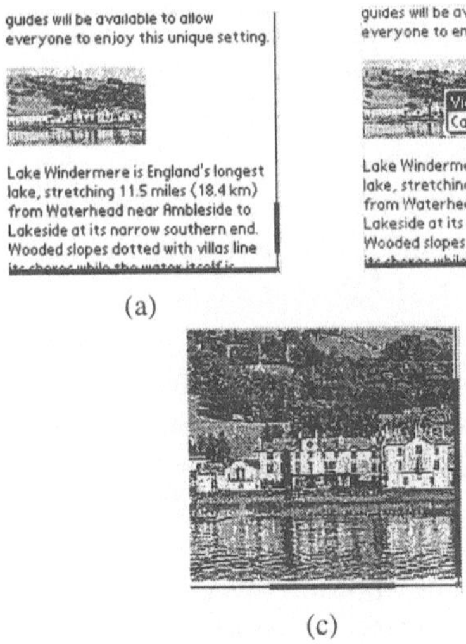

Figure 2 Top Gun Wingman screenshots: (a) the Middleware '98 conference Web page, (b) the refinement popup menu, and (c) the refined image.

be rendered. Contrast this with traditional HTTP: in that protocol, a network event merely indicates that some number of bytes has arrived, but framing is left entirely to the application. Furthermore, in HTTP, inline images are generally fetched using independent transactions (perhaps in parallel), requiring a nontrivial amount of connection management overhead on the client. Application-level framing eliminates these concerns, makes the client simpler, and enables a "push-friendly" model of asynchrony that even allows out-of-order ADU delivery. Although Wingman was not explicitly designed to support disconnected operation, the ADU-based network layer has no notion of underlying "connection state", so it is possible for a page to be split into ADU's whose arrival is separated by complete (but temporary) network disconnection. This behavior makes it possible to retarget a Wingman-like application for connectionless datagram networks, such as the paging network. We return to these ideas in Section 3.

2.6 Performance

We measured the relative performance of Top Gun Wingman and its competitors over the same bandwidth connection: Netscape Navigator for Windows 95, and two PalmPilot-specific Web browsers, HandWeb and Palmscape. Note that of the three PalmPilot browsers tested, only Wingman supports display of images. As we show below, even with this significant additional functionality, Wingman's performance is still often superior because of its split design.

We measured the average end-to-end latency (elapsed time between clicking on a link and completion of loading the page) for each of a collection of 15 different Web pages chosen to represent the various types of pages on the Web today; we selected pages with varying but representative page sizes, quantity of inline images, content, and location. The pages were initially fetched into the proxy's local cache, to eliminate the highly-variable Internet latencies from the measurements.

Our Internet gateway is a Pentium 133/64MB running Red Hat Linux 5.0 and connected to the Internet via a 128Kb/s ISDN connection to UC Berkeley. To simulate a variety of connection speeds, the PalmPilot browsers were connected to the gateway machine via PPP over an RS-232 serial link. By varying the serial port speed between 57600 and 19200, we simulated low speed connections with slightly lower latency than a typical modem (120ms). 19200 bps is representative of current wide-area and metropolitan-area wireless networks, including Metricom Ricochet (Metricom Corp. 1998), CDPD, and PCS. We believe that such technologies are of particular interest to the mobile professionals who currently comprise a large market segment for devices such as the PalmPilot. 57600 was chosen to represent fast wireline (56K) modems as well as a variety of emerging metropolitan-area picocell wireless data services.

2.6.1 Comparison to Other PalmPilot Browsers

Despite the fact that Wingman is a graphical browser while Palmscape is a text only browser, Wingman was still faster than Palmscape in 93% of the sites tested, not including those sites that caused Palmscape to crash (see below). At 19200 bps, Wingman was at least twice as fast as Palmscape 43% of the time. At 57600 bps, as the time to display a page becomes more CPU bound, this number rises to 54%. The PalmPilot's slow 16 MHz Motorola DragonBall 68328 CPU and limited memory make HTML parsing and layout painfully slow; Wingman relies on the cluster-based proxy for HTML parsing and layout.

In 10% of the test cases, Palmscape crashed while loading the page. We suspect the crashes occur because of the intricate HTML constructs often found on commercial sites; stably capturing all HTML corner cases is difficult, and unlike our TACC server, the PalmPilot client cannot gracefully shield the user from such failures. In this sense, our proxy makes Wingman a more stable and reliable application than its peers.

2.6.2 Comparison to Desktop Browsers

Compared to Netscape running on a Pentium II 300/128MB, Wingman was still faster at downloading and displaying pages in 77% of the test cases. In this situation the latency savings come from the image processor reducing images' resolution and color depth of image before transmission over a slow link (we demonstrated this savings originally in (Fox & Brewer 1996)). Although Netscape receives and displays more data, that excess data is useless to a device with limited display resolution and depth, such as the PalmPilot. At 57600 bps Wingman is at least two times faster than Netscape 33% of the time, and at 19200 bps this number increases to 73%. This re-

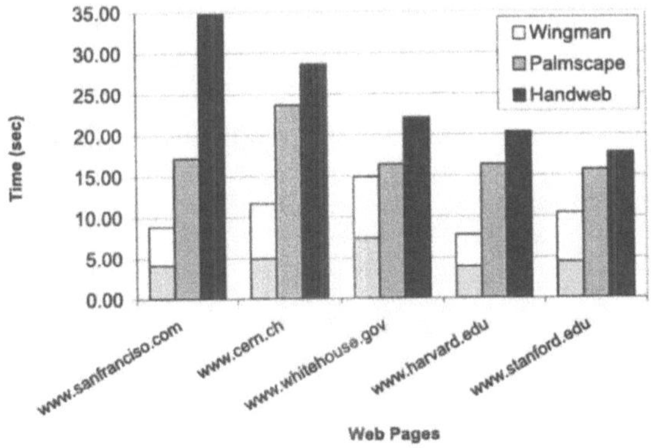

Figure 3 Comparison of end-to-end latency among Wingman, Palmscape, and HandWeb at 57600 bps.

sult reinforces our original hypothesis that a proxy system for thin clients is useful even when the client CPU's are fast enough to display and parse complex pages.

Figure 4 compares Wingman and Netscape Navigator at 19200 and 57600 bps for a number of different Web pages. The top number above each pair of bars is the total number of bytes transferred from the TACC proxy to the Wingman client, i.e. the size of the Wingman ADU corresponding to the delivered page with all inline images. The bottom number is the number of bytes transferred from the origin server to the Netscape client, i.e. the total size of the HTML, all inline images, and HTTP header overhead. The relatively small differences in Wingman's performance at 19200 and 57600 bps suggest that back-end processing dominates latency, whereas with Netscape the network bandwidth dominates latency.

Wingman's HTML processor was written in Perl for fast prototyping and to exploit Perl's superior regular-expression and string manipulation facilities. We conservatively estimate that a factor of five to ten in performance would result from rewriting the HTML processor in a faster language (C/C++); this estimate is compatible with past work comparing the performance of interpreted, compiled, and byte-compiled languages (Romer, Lee, Voelker, Wolman, Wong, Baer, Bershad & Levy 1996). This would make Wingman the fastest browser in virtually all the test cases, even considering image processing latency, leaving only the link bandwidth as the limiting factor in performance.

3 LESSONS AND EXPERIENCE

Top Gun Wingman has been deployed and in use by the general Internet population since October of 1997. Since then, we have processed tens of millions of requests

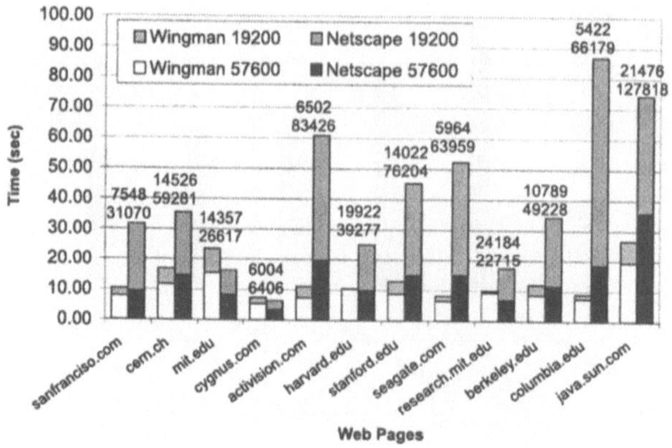

Figure 4 End-to-end latency: Wingman vs. Netscape Navigator at 19200 and 57600 bps for a selection Web pages.

from over 11,000 users.* In this section we share the insights into design, implementation, and operational issues that we have gained from running such a well-used middleware service.

3.1 Moving Complexity to the Proxy

A graphical Web browser is a complex application. The Web consists of many intricate and verbose data formats, hastily designed protocols, and pervasive malformed HTML and image formats that the browser must robustly handle. Even page layout is difficult, given the complex elements such as nested tables, frames, and forms that exist in modern HTML. Implementing a browser is daunting even on a desktop platform with strong operating system support and abundant computation and storage; porting one to a device such as the PalmPilot is difficult to imagine. With only 1-2MB of SRAM, such a device can't even hold all the code. The small heap size (32KB), limited code segment size (32KB relative jump maximum), and lack of native OS support for shared libraries further complicate development.

However, all that the PalmPilot really needs to do is render primitive data types such as images, formatted text, and links. By offloading all of the complex Web browsing functionality (such as HTML parsing, GIF decompression, JPEG rendering, HTTP processing, etc.) to our middleware proxy, we have successfully avoided dealing with all of the PDA resource limitations. Our resulting implementation ef-

*At its peak, the service was processing several requests per second, and was seeing requests from more than a thousand unique IP addresses per day. We estimate that there have been more than 11,000 downloads of the Wingman client software to date.

forts were concentrated on the Unix TACC server implementation, which was rapid and robust because of the rich and mature Unix development environment.

The partitioning of complexity away from the client has had a number of powerful benefits:

- **Client independent back end:** The implementation of the Wingman back end is structured as a pipeline of transformations, only the last of which makes any assumptions about client-specific data formats. This means that porting Wingman to a new PDA platform requires two development efforts: writing the rendering shell on the PDA itself, and creating a new final back end pipeline stage corresponding to that shell. We have made the job of application porting simpler through a well designed application partitioning.
- **Transparent functionality upgrades:** Because most of the complex components of the Wingman implementation reside in the proxy back end rather than the client, it became possible for us to extend the browser's functionality without changing any of the code running at the client. The first example of this was when we improved the graphics transformer (Haeberli 1997) that converts GIF and JPEG images into PalmPilot images (and which also performs lossy compression through resolution and color depth reduction). The improved converter performs edge enhancement, giving users the impression of greater contrast and better image clarity. By simply dropping the new transformer into our proxy, every Wingman user instantly began seeing improved quality images. The zip archive processor and AportisDoc processor are further examples of this mechanism: we have been able to extend the browser to understand new data types without modifying the client implementation. We can extend this strategy in the future to support new technologies such as XML, again without browser changes.
- **Backward compatibility:** During our initial deployment, we rapidly released new versions of the client-side implementation containing bug fixes, UI enhancements, and new features such as a client-side cache and imagemap support. The proxy uses the client version number (embedded in the initial handshake from the client) to determine what objects the client can handle. For example, this mechanism ensures that image maps are only sent to clients whose version number indicates they are capable of handling this feature. The mechanism is similar in spirit to HTTP feature negotiation, but the version-to-feature binding is done late (at the proxy) and can be easily changed. By putting this capability in our middleware, we shielded end servers from having to deal with this additional client heterogeneity.

3.2 Middleware Availablility

As any designer of highly available services will attest, the devil is often in the implementation details. In our AMWP architecture, it is the responsibility of the TACC server to provide availability and robustness mechanisms that are independent of any worker; the mechanisms employed in our cluster-based TACC server give rise to the requirement that each TACC worker be restartable and atomic (alluded to in section 2.1). We have found that despite this programming restriction, the orthogonal separation of availability/robustness from worker code has made the overall system simpler to engineer and more robust, and allows new workers to be prototyped more quickly since they inherit these behaviors for free.

The 11,000 real users stressing our proxy implementation revealed a number of interesting corner cases in the TACC server design and Wingman implementation that caused service delays and even interruptions. For example, our initial design of the Wingman transformation pipeline included a "dispatch" worker that would route data to subordinates based on the type of the data it receives (HTML, Zip files, etc.), and then block until the subordinate(s) finished. The long blocking latency made it appear to the TACC server that the dispatcher worker was overloaded, causing more of them to be spawned until there was almost one dispatcher per outstanding outstanding user request. This resulted in hundreds of processes being spawned across our cluster, filling the cluster nodes' process tables and causing the service to become unavailable.

Except for failures due to such rare but interesting cases, all Wingman outages have been due to factors beyond our control, such as disrupted service from our campus ISP and power failures that weren't caught by the departmental UPS.

4 RELATED AND FUTURE WORK

Middleware services such as filtering and on-the-fly compression have become particularly popular for HTTP (Internet Engineering Task Force 1997), whose proxy mechanism was originally intended for users behind security firewalls. The mechanism has been used to shield clients from the effects of poor (especially wireless) networks (Fox & Brewer 1996, Liljeberg, M., et al. 1996), perform filtering (Zenel 1996) and anonymization, and perform value-added transformations on content, including Kanji transcoding (Sato 1994), Kanji-to-GIF conversion (Yee 1995), application-level stream transducers (Brooks, Mazer, Meeks & Miller 1995), and personalized agent services for Web browsing (Barrett, Maglio & Kellem 1995). Infrastructure proxies have also been used as a mechanism for application partitioning, as in the Wit project (Watson 1994*a*, Watson 1994*b*) which focuses on partitioning between the mobile and fixed infrastructure. The Video Gateway (Amir, McCanne & Zhang 1995) is an example of an infrastructure proxy that performs application-level adaptation and serves as a multicast to unicast protocol gateway.

Application design and implementation on PDA or smartphone class devices has recently generated significant research effort. In (Fox, Gribble, Chawathe, Polito, Ling, Huang & Brewer 1997, Fox & Brewer 1996, Shimada, Iwami & Tomokane 1997), the user interface issues associated with introducing proxy controls as an orthogonal extension to a Web browser interface are explored. (Schilit & Bickmore 1997) describes an intelligent proxy that attempts to classify HTML pages into a fixed number of bins, and performs semantic compression and layout modification based on the chosen bin to repurpose the page for a PDA.

Our TACC middleware has actually been used to implement a variety of distinct applications besides Wingman. TranSend (Fox, Gribble, Chawathe & Brewer 1997) is a Web acceleration proxy that performs on-the-fly, datatype-specific compression, in particular on GIF and JPEG images; it has been available to the public since April 1997 and some of its main ideas have been instantiated commercially as Intel QuickWeb.* Top Gun Mediaboard is an electronic shared whiteboard (a derivation of the desktop *mediaboard* (Chawathe et al. 1998) application) for the PalmPilot, in which TACC workers perform protocol adaptation as well as data transformation; it is in prealpha use at UC Berkeley, and performs satisfactorily even over slow links such as the Metricom Ricochet wireless packet radio modem (Metricom Corp. 1998). Top Gun Mediaboard extends Wingman's markup and protocol to accommodate the draw operations and user interactions required by a shared whiteboard.

The commercial ProxiWeb client (ProxiNet, Inc. 1998) adds proxy-based implementations of features missing from Wingman, including secure connections, cookies, and HTML forms. Future research includes merging Top Gun Wingman and Top Gun Mediaboard, resulting in a "generic thin client" application that acts as the drawing, rendering, and interaction shell for proxied applications such as MBONE access, Web access, or an environment-aware interaction device (Hodes, Katz, Servan-Schreiber & Rowe 1997). We will also further explore the security and privacy implications of middleware in general (in comparison to end-to-end security) and Wingman in particular, attempting to apply some ideas from our earlier work on security protocol adaptation for thin clients (Fox & Gribble 1996).

5 CONCLUSIONS

This paper described the proxy-based architecture and implementation of Top Gun Wingman, the first graphical Web browser for the PalmPilot PDA. We described our middleware philosophy, which we refer to as the Adaptive Middleware Proxy (AMWP) approach: let the client do only what it does well (client competence), and push all other functions to a transparent infrastructure proxy. The proxy side of Wingman was described in terms of our TACC (transformation, aggregation, customization, caching) programming model for interactive Internet services, and discussed our experience with a publicly-available cluster-based TACC server that has been operational since late 1997 with virtually no unscheduled downtime.

Our experience with Wingman, as well as with the other TACC applications we briefly described, supports our claims for the Adaptive Middleware Proxy (AMWP) approach. Wingman has better performance than a reduced client-only port, has new features and behaviors (such as browsing software archives and saving e-books, in the case of Wingman), and has the ability to almost completely leverage the entire

* There is no formal connection between QuickWeb and TranSend.

existing Web-based content and services infrastructure. Our proxy implementation has low administration cost (due to our commodity-PC cluster design and graphical administration interface) that makes it realistic to operate services on a 24×7 basis for large user communities, and the ability to add features at the proxy largely eliminates the client software distribution problem and preserves backward compatibility when client upgrades do occur.

In addition, our experience with a user community of over 11,000 suggests that users will have no problem accepting middleware as a pervasive element of Internet services. For these reasons, and because Wingman demonstrates key technologies needed to rapidly deploy specialized information-delivery services for thin clients, we believe that the principles successfully demonstrated by Top Gun Wingman will play a prominent role in the coming wave of applications for convergent thin client devices.

5.1 Acknowledgments

We extend our appreciation to the many students, staff, and faculty at UC Berkeley who have helped us support our proxy cluster, debug our applications, suggest feature enhancements, and act as reviewers for this paper. Special thanks go to Tim Kimball for all of his support efforts and Paul Haeberli for allowing us to use his high quality graphics transformation code. Finally, we would like to thank the PalmPilot user community for their tireless support and encouragement.

REFERENCES

Amir, E., McCanne, S. & Zhang, H. (1995), An Application Level Video Gateway, *in* 'Proceedings ACM Multimedia 1995'. Available at `http://http.cs.berkeley.edu/~elan/articles/pub/vgw.ps`.

Aportis Inc. (1998), 'AportisDoc Overview'. `http://www.aportis.com/products/AportisDoc/benefits.html`.

Barrett, R., Maglio, P. P. & Kellem, D. C. (1995), How To Personalize the Web, *in* 'Conference on Human Factors in Computing Systems (CHI 95)', Denver, CO. WBI, developed at IBM Almaden; see `http://www.raleigh.ibm.com/wbi/wbisoft.htm`.

Brooks, C., Mazer, M. S., Meeks, S. & Miller, J. (1995), Application-Specific Proxy Servers as HTTP Stream Transducers, *in* 'Proceedings of the Fourth International World Wide Web Conference'.

Chawathe, Y., Fink, S., McCanne, S. & Brewer, E. A. (1998), A Proxy Architecture for Reliable Multicast in Heterogeneous Environments. Currently under review.

Clark, D. & Tennenhouse, D. (1990), 'Architectural Considerations for a New Generation of Protocols', *Computer Communication Review* **20**(4), 200–208.

Floyd, S., Jacobson, V., Liu, C. & McCanne, S. (1995), A Reliable Multicast Framework for Light-Weight Sessions and Application Level Framing, *in* 'ACM SIGCOMM '95', Boston, MA, pp. 342–356.

Fox, A. (1997), The Case for TACC: Scalable Servers for Transformation, Aggregation, Caching and Customization. Qualifying Exam Proposal, UC Berkeley Computer Science Division. http://www.cs.berkeley.edu/~fox/papers/quals.ps.

Fox, A. & Brewer, E. A. (1996), Reducing WWW Latency and Bandwidth Requirements via Real-Time Distillation, *in* 'Proceedings of the Fifth International World Wide Web Conference', World Wide Web Consortium, Paris, France.

Fox, A. & Gribble, S. D. (1996), Security On the Move: Indirect Authentication Using Kerberos, *in* 'Proc. Second International Conference on Wireless Networking and Mobile Computing (MobiCom '96)', Rye, NY.

Fox, A., Gribble, S. D., Brewer, E. A. & Amir, E. (1996), Adapting to Network and Client Variability via On-Demand Dynamic Distillation, *in* 'Seventh International Conference on Architectural Support for Programming Languages and Operating Systems (ASPLOS-VII)', Cambridge MA.

Fox, A., Gribble, S. D., Chawathe, Y. & Brewer, E. (1997), TranSend Web Accelerator Proxy. Free service deployed by UC Berkeley. See http://transend.cs.berkeley.edu.

Fox, A., Gribble, S. D., Chawathe, Y. & Brewer, E. A. (1996), 'Adapting to Network and Client Variation Using Active Proxies: Lessons and Perspectives', *IEEE Personal Communications*. Special issue on adapting to network and client variability.

Fox, A., Gribble, S. D., Chawathe, Y., Brewer, E. A. & Gauthier, P. (1997), Cluster-Based Scalable Network Services, *in* 'Proceedings of the 16th ACM Symposium on Operating Systems Principles', St.-Malo, France.

Fox, A., Gribble, S. D., Chawathe, Y., Polito, A., Ling, B., Huang, A. C. & Brewer, E. A. (1997), Orthogonal Extensions to the WWW User Interface Using Client-Side Technologies, *in* 'User Interface Software and Technology (UIST) 97', Banff, Canada.

go2net, Inc. (1997), 'Metacrawler search service'. http://www.metacrawler.com.

Gribble, S. D. & Brewer, E. A. (1997), System Design Issues for Internet Middleware Services: Deductions from a Large Client Trace, *in* 'Proceedings of the 1997 USENIX Symposium on Internet Technologies and Systems', Monterey, California, USA.

Haeberli, P. (1997), 'Personal communication'.

Hodes, T. D., Katz, R. H., Servan-Schreiber, E. & Rowe, L. (1997), Composable Ad-hoc Mobile Services for Universal Interaction, *in* 'Proc. Third International Conference on Mobile Computing and Wireless Networking (MobiCom '97)', Budapest, Hungary.

Internet Engineering Task Force (1997), 'Hypertext transfer protocol - http 1.1', RFC 2068.

Liljeberg, M., et al. (1996), Enhanced Services for World Wide Web in Mobile WAN Environment, Technical Report C-1996-28, University of Helsinki CS Department.

Metricom Corp. (1998), 'Ricochet Wireless Modem'. http://www.ricochet.net.

Myricom (1995), Myrinet: A Gigabit Per Second Local Area Network, *in* 'IEEE Micro'.

Netscape Communications Corporation (1998), 'Netscape Proxy Automatic Configuration', http://home.netscape.com/eng/mozilla/2.02/relnotes/unix-2.02.html#Proxi%es.

Ousterhout, J. K. (1994), *Tcl and the Tk Toolkit*, Addison-Wesley.

ProxiNet, Inc. (1998), 'ProxiWeb Thin Client Web Browser', http://www.proxinet.com.

Romer, T. H., Lee, D., Voelker, G., Wolman, A., Wong, W. A., Baer, J.-L., Bershad, B. N. & Levy, H. (1996), The Structure and Performance of Interpreters, *in* 'Seventh International Conference on Architectural Support for Programming Languages and Operating Systems (ASPLOS-VII)', Cambridge, MA.

Sato, Y. (1994), 'DeleGate Server'. http://wall.etl.go.jp/delegate/.

Schilit, B. & Bickmore, T. (1997), Digestor: Device-Independent Access to the World Wide Web, *in* 'Proc. Sixth International World Wide Web Conference (WWW-6)', Santa Clara, CA.

Shimada, T., Iwami, N. & Tomokane, T. (1997), Interactive Scaling Control Mechanism for World Wide Web Systems, *in* 'Sixth International World Wide Web Conference (WWW-6)', World Wide Web Consortium, Santa Clara, CA.

Watson, T. (1994*a*), Application Design for Wireless Computing, *in* 'Mobile Computing Systems and Applications Workshop'.

Watson, T. (1994*b*), Wit: An Infrastructure for Wireless Palmtop Computing, Technical Report CSE-94-11-08, University of Washington. `http://snapple.cs.washington.edu:600/papers/wit.ps`.

Yee, K.-P. (1995), 'Shoduoka Mediator Service'. `http://www.shoduoka.com`.

Zenel, B. (1996), A Proxy Based Filtering Mechanism for the Mobile Environment. Thesis Proposal.

6 BIOGRAPHY

Armando Fox received a BSEE from M.I.T. and an MSEE from the University of Illinois, has worked as a CPU architect at Intel Corp., and is currently completing his Ph.D. at the University of California, Berkeley, as a researcher in the Daedalus/BARWAN and InfoPad projects. He will be an assistant professor at Stanford University starting in January 1999. His primary interests are application-level support for adaptive mobile computing, design of reliable distributed systems to support infrastructural applications, and user interface issues related to mobile computing.

Ian Goldberg is a Graduate Student Researcher and founding member of the Internet Security, Applications, Authentication and Cryptography (ISAAC) research group at UC Berkeley. His research areas include cryptography, security, privacy systems, and digital cash. He holds a B.Math. from the University of Waterloo, Canada, and a M.Sc. from UC Berkeley, USA.

Steven Gribble received a combined Computer Science and Physics B.Sc. from the University of British Columbia in 1995, and a Computer Science M.Sc. from the University of California, Berkeley in 1997. He is currently pursuing his Ph.D. at Berkeley, and expects to graduate in May of 2000. His interests include application-level support for adaptive mobile computing, and system and compiler support for scalable, highly-available infrastructure services.

David C. Lee received a Bachelor of Science in Electrical Engineering Computer Science from the University of California, Berkeley, in May 1998. Though currently working in industry, he plans to go to graduate school within a few years.

Anthony Polito received a Bachelor of Arts in Computer Science from the University of California, Berkeley in 1998. He plans to go to graduate school in 1999.

Eric A. Brewer is an Assistant Professor of Computer Science at U.C. Berkeley, and received his Ph.D. in CS from MIT in 1994. Interests include mobile and wireless computing (the InfoPad and Daedalus projects); scalable servers (the NOW, Inktomi, and TranSend projects); and application- and system-level security (the ISAAC project). Previous work includes multiprocessor-network software and topologies, and high-performance multiprocessor simulation.

Session 10

Events

Event-based Distributed Workflow Execution with EVE

Andreas Geppert, Dimitrios Tombros
Department of Computer Science, University of Zurich
Email: {geppert || tombros}@ifi.unizh.ch

Abstract

In event-driven workflow execution, events and event-condition-action rules are the fundamental metaphors for defining and enforcing workflow logic. Processing entities enact workflows by reacting to and generating new events. The foundation on events facilitates the integration of processing entities into coherent systems. In this paper, we present an event engine, called EVE, implementing event-driven execution of distributed workflows. Its functionality includes event registration, detection and management, as well as event notification to distributed, autonomous, reactive software components which represent workflow processing entities. We describe the distributed, multi-server, multi-client architecture of EVE and its use for workflow execution.

Keywords

event-based systems, workflow management, distributed workflow execution

1 OVERVIEW

Workflow management (Georgakopoulos et al. 1995) has recently found great attention in the information systems field, as it allows to capture knowledge about business processes and to define and enact workflows. **Workflow management systems** (WFMS) are software systems providing workflow definition and execution functionality. **Workflow types** consist of subworkflows and atomic work steps, data flows between them, execution order constraints, as well as assignment of tasks to **processing entities** (PE). The productive use of WFMS requires that they effectively support the integration of heterogeneous information resources, people and applications. The resulting integrated system is called a **workflow system** (WS).

Current commercial WFMS do not effectively support the representation, control, and coordination of PE that operate in distributed environments, that are heterogeneous with respect to their automation degree and programmatic interfaces, that evolve over time, and that operate both independently and as part of a WS. Several research efforts address some of these problems (see section 2), especially those pertaining to distribution and heterogeneity. The proposed solutions, however, do not effectively support flexible representation/integration of PE and runtime evolution of the WS architecture; they also propose a strongly coupled integration framework and rigid task structure.

We propose a **layered event-based** approach providing for a domain-specific architecture model in which PE are represented as autonomous reactive components communicating through parameterized events. The behavior of these components is expressed by **event-condition-action rules** (ECA rules) as provided by active database management systems (ACT-NET 1996). The lowest layer is formed by an event-based middleware layer and execution platform–called EVE–able to integrate these components and make the WS schema executable. Although event-based systems are recognized as the architectural style of choice for loosely coupled systems (Barrett et al. 1996), to the best of our knowledge, no other approach so far uses events as the **only** integration and coordination mechanism for distributed, heterogeneous, and dynamically configurable WS. Event-based WS-architectures and workflow execution have various advantages:

- The event-based coordination model allows complete process specification without imposing limitations on the concrete process architecture. Complex process situations are expressed by composite events, and coordination is accomplished by defining the appropriate reactive behavior for PE.
- The architecture of the WS can be changed during workflow execution (subject to process restrictions).
- A powerful and uniform mechanism to express component behavior is provided; its use for failure and exception handling is straightforward.
- The correct execution and the monitoring of the workflows is guaranteed based on formal semantics (Tombros et al. 1997*b*).

The remainder of this paper is organized as follows. In section 2 we position EVE and survey related work. The WS-architecture model is briefly presented in section 3. We describe the architecture of EVE in section 4 and the realization of distributed event detection and workflow execution in section 5.

2 RELATED WORK

ECA rules have been proposed by several authors for workflow execution, (e.g., Barbara et al. 1994, Casati et al. 1996, Dayal et al. 1990, Kappel et al. 1995). Some of these systems (Barbara et al. 1994, Dayal et al. 1990) use composite events to detect complex workflow situations. EVE, however, is the first system using ECA-rules for workflow management addressing the problem of distributed event-based workflow execution.

Current commercial WFMS are typically built around a centralized process engine and relational database server. Two event-based coordination systems, Yeast (Krishnamurthy & Rosenblum 1995) and CoopWARE (Mylopoulos et al. 1996), have a purpose similar to EVE; both have, however, a centralized event-detection and rule execution architecture. Additionally, Yeast supports only event-action rules.

A number of research systems consider distributed workflow execution. ObjectFlow (Hsu & Kleissner 1996) uses a graph-based workflow definition model. Steps are executed by agents coordinated by a–potentially–distributed workflow engine which however accesses a centralized DBMS to store workflow states. WIDE (Ceri et al. 1997) proposes a distributed hierarchical workflow engine which stores process states in a centralized relational DBMS. In $METEOR_2$ (Sheth et al. 1996), process scheduling is distributed among various task managers. The distribution of the task managers is implemented through CORBA (OMG 1995). In Mentor (Wodtke et al. 1995), workflows are modeled using state-charts which are partitioned to each involved PE. Each PE-specific state-chart is executed locally on the PE workstation.

Various aspects of the implementation of EVE, such as naming services, can be facilitated by the functionality of CORBA (OMG 1995) or other distributed object technologies. The emphasis of our research in EVE however, is to complement these efforts by concentrating on a reactive event-based coordination and integration architecture–with its accompanying advantages for heterogeneous system integration–instead of a message-based approach. Event-specification functionality in EVE is richer than in CORBA Event Services (OMG 1997) Also, EVE fully supports ECA rule services, the standardization of which is still only under consideration by OMG.

3 A MODEL FOR WORKFLOW SYSTEM ARCHITECTURES

In this section, we briefly introduce the model we propose for the description of workflow system architectures. In general, workflow types can be specified in a more abstract way, for example using a graph-based formalism, and mapped onto the architecture model level. Here we simply assume that the basic elements of a workflow can be specified in some way, i.e., workflow structure in terms of atomic activities and subworkflows, dependencies between the steps of a workflow, etc. This specification is subsequently mapped to the behavior of processing entities which compose a WS architecture. Note however, that the event-based coordination layer we propose

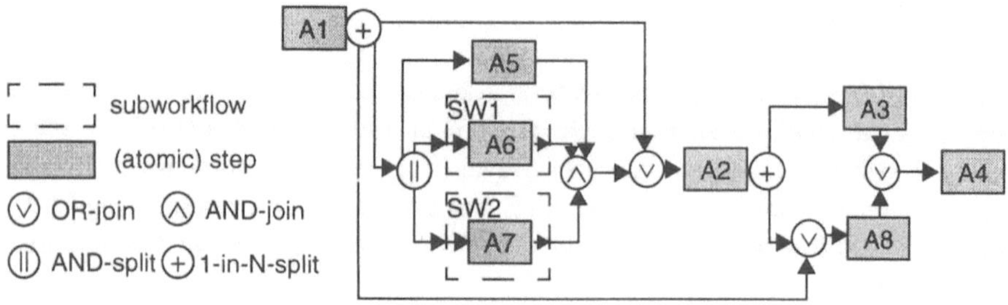

Figure 1 Structure of the example workflow type

is independent from the modeling formalism used. This section serves to illustrate the purpose of an abstract-level specification layer in the overall event-based architecture.

3.1 A Workflow Example

We use as an example the processing of a health insurance claim (HIC) (Fig. 1). The workflow is initiated once a HIC arrives at the insurance agency. An insurance agent creates a file containing the diagnosis, treatments, claimed amount, and the insurance number (step *A1:HandleHIC*). If the policy has expired, a rejection letter is prepared (*A8:PrepReject*). If the claimed amount does not exceed 300 CHF the claim is directly accepted, a corresponding entry is made in the customer database (*A2:LogClaim*), and a check is prepared (*A3:PrepAccept*) and printed (*A4:Print*). Otherwise, various controls have to be made: a control in the local database whether the prescribed treatment is covered by the patient's insurance (*A5:CntrlCoverage*). A request to a central clearing house to control whether equivalent but less expensive medication is available. This is done in subworkflow *SW1*, consisting of the step *A6:CntrlMedication*. On the other hand, in subworkflow *SW2* executed at the insurance company headquarter, a medical expert controls whether the treatment actually suits the diagnosis (*A7:CntrlTreatment*). When all controls are completed, a corresponding entry is made in the customer database (*A2:LogClaim*), and either a rejection letter (*A8:PrepReject*) or a payment check (*A3:PrepAccept*) is printed (*A4:Print*).

3.2 Brokers and Services

The Broker/Services model (B/SM (Tombros et al. 1997*a*)) is used to define a schema of the software and process architecture of workflow systems. Workflow type specifications are mapped to elements of the B/SM. In general, each atomic step corresponds to the execution of a service. ECA rules define when and how services are executed in the context of workflows. From the perspective of B/SM, a WS consists of reactive components called **brokers** representing PE. Broker behavior is defined by ECA rules describing their reaction to simple events (e.g., service requests) or composite events (e.g., a request within a specific time interval) in the action-part of the rules. Different types of brokers represent human user interfaces, organizational groups, external applications, and WFMS-components.

Primitive event types represent atomic happenings. Two kinds of primitive event types are distinguished: broker interaction events (requests (*REQ*), replies (*RPL*), and exceptions (*EXC*) for services and workflows) and time event types. Time events can be absolute, relative, or periodical. Composite event types represent complex, process-specific situations by combining primitive or further composite events. They are constructed using event type constructors. For instance, a conjunction (*CON*) occurs when both component events occur, regardless of their relative order.

An event definition can be restricted by a time interval, defined by two events; events are considered as relevant only if they occur within the interval. Further restrictions can be specified for composite events, e.g., it can be required that the components have to occur within the same workflow. Distributed composite events are formalized in Tombros et al. (1997*b*).

Broker functionality is described by **services** specified by a signature, i.e., the service name, its request parameters, and possible replies or exceptions. Broker interaction is based on broadcasting parameterized events. Service execution is started by a request event from the client broker and is terminated when a reply or one of the exceptions defined for the service is generated by its server broker. The server is dynamically determined based on service parameters, organizational relationships, or the workflow execution history in ways not further specified here. A workflow instance starts executing when its initiation request event occurs. Workflows are thus executed by the provision of the services requested. Services and their providers are associated by m:n relationships (**capabilities**) implying a predefined behavior for a broker whenever the service is requested, i.e., ECA rules of the form:

```
ON  service-request-event (service parameters)
[IF conditions on parameters and broker state are true]
DO  execute service provision actions;
    generate reply event;
```

Workflow production data which is manipulated by PE in workflow steps is generally stored in external systems which might not be accessible to the WFMS. Brokers may, however, provide access to some of the production data to the WFMS-engine by providing interfaces as part of their state. The broker state can be manipulated in the action parts of their ECA rules.

The main advantages of using the B/S model to describe workflow system architectures consist in the simplification of the system integration task and in the provision of powerful general purpose definition mechanisms for functional, informational, and behavioral aspects of workflow systems. Various aspects of workflow specifications as well as heterogeneous processing entities can be mapped to a relatively simple and homogeneous representation layer, which can then be directly transformed into an executable form.

In the example, the broker *MEDICHECK* is located at the company clearing house; it offers the service *CntrlMedication.* The broker *Medical Expert* represents a person and is located at the headquarter. Finally, the broker *DBCL*, located at the insurance agency, represents an Oracle client and provides the service *LogClaim*.

4 EVE: A EVENT-DRIVEN WORKFLOW EXECUTION ENGINE

From a point of view of the software architecture model, a runtime system and workflow engine is needed to transform a B/SM schema into an operational WS. This runtime system forms the middleware allowing brokers to execute workflows. A straightforward mapping between the event-based B/SM and the execution engine is achieved by providing an **event-based middleware layer**. In other words, workflows are executed by brokers reacting to and generating events. This approach requires the following functionality:

Distribution. Since processing entities typically are distributed over a network and workflows should be executable in a distributed manner, EVE must support distribution. This requires distributed event detection and communication facilities between EVE-servers and their clients.

Runtime repository. In order to maintain the necessary meta information to operate a workflow system, naming, persistence, and retrieval services are needed. These are provided by the runtime repository which stores the instantiated workflow system schema and the populated database. The instantiated schema can be altered at runtime and evolution of a WS is thus possible without shutting down and recompiling the whole system.

Workflow execution. In order to execute workflows in an event-driven style, event detection, event notification, and task assignment services are needed. These services should also allow to execute workflows on remote sites. These tasks are accomplished by leveraging event-based systems and services to workflow execution.

Event history management. In order to facilitate maintenance of workflow systems, logging, monitoring, and analysis services have to be provided. These services rely on event histories maintained by EVE. The event history is made persistent and recoverable by using the corresponding services of the underlying object manager, Shore (Carey et al. 1994).

Failure handling. In general, two types of failures can be distinguished: system failures and failure at the workflow execution level. EVE provides exception event notification mechanisms which combined with ECA rules are used in the definition of reactions to workflow execution errors as proposed for example, in Dayal et al. (1990). Finally, by communicating with brokers via special adapters and persistent event queues, EVE is able to handle temporary unavailability and failures in the connectivity of brokers.

The execution of a workflow starts (or proceeds) as soon as some event is generated by a broker. The local EVE-server then performs event detection and rule execution. Within the execution of each rule, task assignment determines responsible brokers, which are then notified and react as defined by their ECA rules. Particularly, brokers can generate new events, which again are handled by EVE-servers, and so on transitively (Fig. 2). The advantage of this approach is that due to the event-driven interaction, brokers do not have to know the providers of the requested services. Furthermore, once events are forwarded to responsible PE, they can be handled asynchronously by the PE.

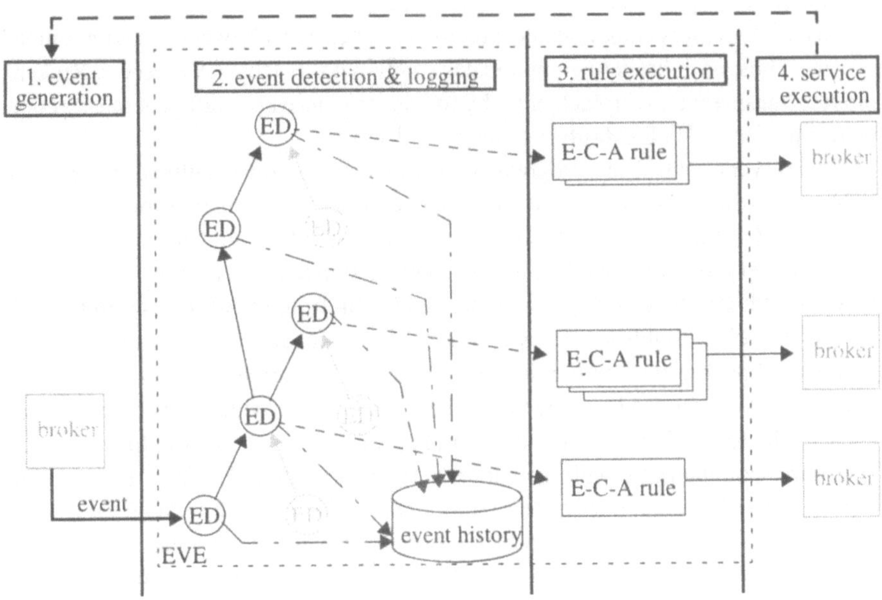

Figure 2 The workflow execution process in EVE

Brokers can also request the execution of (sub-)workflows by generating workflow request events in one of their ECA rules. Such subworkflows can be executed at the same or a remote server. We however require that all the atomic steps directly contained in the same workflow are executed on the same site, i.e., on any machine of the LAN managed by a particular EVE-server. This site is called the **home site** of the workflow. Subworkflows can be executed at sites other than the home site of their parent workflows, and different instances of the same workflow type can also have different home sites. This is not a limitation as the required distribution can be achieved by appropriately specifying subworkflows, whereas it significantly eases synchronization of servers and leads to better synchronization performance (see section 5.2).

4.1 Multi-Server Architecture and Communication

Brokers involved in workflows typically reside on different machines, which results in WS that are physically distributed to a varying degree, e.g., on different machines within the same domain/LAN, or on different organizational subnets. EVE supports the distributed execution of workflows through a **multi-server/multi-client** architecture. The provided middleware services make distribution transparent for brokers and the PE they represent.

Workflow systems consist of multiple **EVE-servers** which provide the aforementioned services. The most important ones of these are described in more detail below; we first however, present EVE's client/server architecture and communication mechanisms. EVE-servers communicate directly with their local brokers and with remote servers. Thus, each broker communicates solely with its local EVE-server. Brokers interact transparently with each other by forwarding the events they generate through platform-specific **EVE-adapters** to their local server.

EVE-servers control the progress of workflows. Control is defined in terms of ECA rules, which determine what has to happen when a particular primitive or composite event occurs; the rule actions normally involve task assignment and broker notification. Servers accept and handle client connection requests over a "well-known" network address. Brokers may log in into and logout from the system, whereby each logged-in broker establishes its own communication channel with its server. EVE-servers exchange administration information about the current location and connectivity of brokers using a lazy-update strategy. They also provide persistent queues of events to be forwarded to disconnected brokers once these are back online.

Brokers communicate with their local servers through EVE-adapters. These are libraries linked to the broker code which represent the interface of the EVE-system to brokers. They provide communication transparency for server login as well as for event generation and notification. Adapters handle temporary server unavailability by keeping persistent queues of client-generated events. Brokers are informed of the occurrence of interesting events by callbacks by their adapter which provides a listening port to the EVE-server.

An EVE-server forwards over the network event occurrences to the adapters of brokers that are registered in the runtime repository as interested in these events. During the execution of broker actions, new events may be generated by the broker. The broker then informs through its EVE-adapter the local EVE-server about the occurrence of these events. The EVE-server in turn performs event detection, logs these events as well as eventual resulting composite events in the event history, and forwards the occurrences to other interested local brokers and to the servers of interested remote brokers. An overview of the architecture of EVE and the example workflow system is presented in Fig. 3. EVE-servers reside at the insurance agency, at the company headquarter, and the clearing house.

The communication infrastructure is implemented using the Adaptive Communication Environment (Schmidt 1994). EVE-servers are implemented on Solaris 2.5 through extensions to the acceptor pattern of ACE that dispatches a handler for each

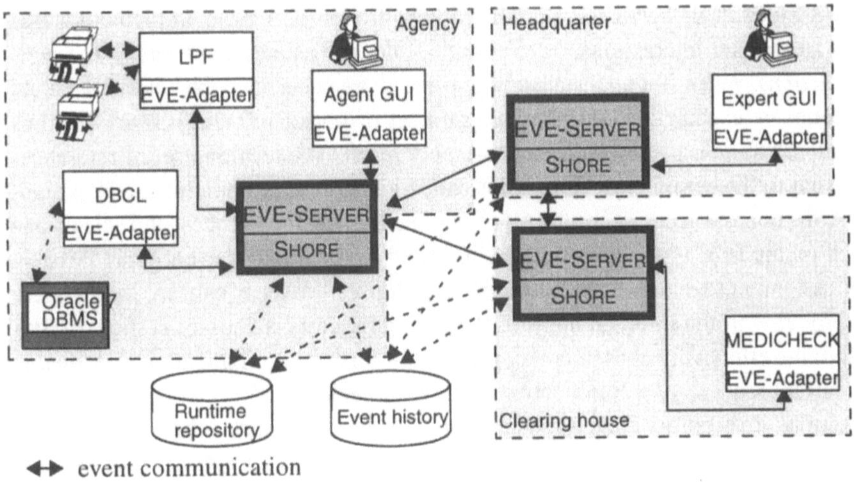

Figure 3 Architecture of EVE and the example workflow system

connecting broker. This handler is responsible for incoming events and initiates the appropriate actions in the workflow engine, i.e., triggers the event detection cycle. The adapter implementation is client-language specific. Currently, Java and C++ versions are operational.

4.2 The EVE Runtime Repository

The runtime repository implements naming, persistence, and query services and thus contains information needed to execute workflow instances. The explicit representation of this meta-information in the runtime repository leads to a higher degree of flexibility, compared to approaches that use hard-wired, interpretive techniques for workflow execution, and better maintainability of WS, compared to compilation-based approaches. The repository is managed by EVE-servers on top of the object-oriented database system Shore (Carey et al. 1994). The runtime repository contains the following information:

- workflow types: name, initiation and termination events, active and terminated instances;
- specification of the participating brokers including their context-specific behavior and responsibilities;
- organizational relationships among brokers and between brokers and groups;
- event types corresponding to those defined in the event part of broker ECA rules; and
- ECA rules defining the structure of workflows.

ECA rules in EVE–not to be confused with broker ECA rules–implement workflows and broker interactions. An EVE-rule is defined as a triple *(event type, condition, action)*. Whenever an instance of the event type occurs and the condition holds, the action is executed. Conditions return a set of object references, they are thus considered to hold if they return a non-empty result. The resulting set of references is passed to the action part. Conditions can, e.g., be used to implement task assignment: the condition computes the set of eligible brokers for a request and selects one based on the task assignment strategy specified for the request event type. Possible task assignment strategies are **random**: any eligible broker is chosen; **load-based**: the broker with the minimal number of pending requests is chosen; **responsibility-based**: the effectively chosen broker must fulfill further requirements as specified in the current request; or a combination of these strategies.

Actions are arbitrary code fragments, typically including task assignment and subsequent broker notification of a service request. EVE-rules reside on EVE-servers; they are compiled to dunamic link libraries together with the workflow system schema and loaded upon execution time whenever the corresponding rule fires.

The execution of the service *LogClaim* for example, can start when the execution of the subworkflows *SW1*, *SW2*, and the service *CntrlCoverage* is completed. This is expressed by two rules residing at the agency server:

```
ON CON(RPL(CntrlCoverage.OK, HIC),
   CON(RPL(SW1.Done, Result),RPL(SW2.Done, Result)))
DO raise(REQ, LogClaim, HIC, SW1.Done.Result, SW2.Done.Result)

ON REQ(LogClaim,HIC, HIC, SW1.Done.Result, SW2.Done.Result))
IF br = assign(LogClaim)    // filter: returns assigned broker
DO br->notify(REQ, LogClaim, HIC, SW1.Done.Result, SW2.Done.Result)
```

5 WORKFLOW EXECUTION

In order to allow event-driven workflow execution, EVE has to implement detection and signaling of events to interested brokers. Composite event detection is an issue extensively considered in centralized ADBMS (Chakravarthy et al. 1994). However, the semantics of composite events are different in a distributed system. Thus the concepts and techniques used in centralized ADBMS are inadequate for distributed environments and need to be extended.

5.1 Event Occurrences and Event Detection

Event occurrences are the actual happenings of interest at some point in time and are instances of event types. Each occurrence has several attributes:

- the event type of the occurrence

- the occurrence site
- a unique site-specific occurrence identifier
- the timestamp when the event occurred
- the name of the requested service or its reply
- a workflow identifier within which the event has occurred
- the identifier of the broker which raised the event
- a list of component occurrences in case of composite events
- a list of typed parameters (i.e., production data).

Events are detected by persistent event detector (ED) objects residing in EVE-servers. In order to generate a new primitive event, a broker notifies its server about the occurrence via its adapter. The server then forwards the occurrence to the appropriate ED. Time events are detected based on the system clock. After primitive event detection, composite event detection takes place. For that matter, we adapted the approach originally proposed for the centralized ADBMS Sentinel (Chakravarthy et al. 1994). A composite ED is a graph, where nodes are event types and edges represent event composition. Nodes are marked with references to not-yet-consumed component occurrences. When an event is detected, parent nodes are informed and check whether the new event together with already obtained component events can form a new event composition. This check is performed in an event type-dependent way. If multiple instances of a component event type exist, the oldest adequate one is chosen; this is the chronicle consumption mode (Chakravarthy et al. 1994), which is the appropriate one for workflow management. In case the new event cannot be consumed, the ED stores a reference to it until a composition is possible, i.e., until new sibling component occurrences have been received. Event detection is recursive; whenever a parent node can compose a new occurrence, it in turn informs its parents, a.s.o. in a bottom-up manner.

In addition to event composition edges, event nodes reference rule objects. If a (primitive or composite) event occurrence is detected which has a rule attached to it, then the rule is added to the list of rules to be fired. This firing actually takes place as soon as the event detection cycle has been terminated.

5.2 Distributed Event Detection and Synchronization

Timestamps play a crucial role in defining semantics of composite events and define the ordering of event occurrences. In centralized environments a global time can be assumed for this ordering, whereas it does not exist in distributed environments. In EVE we thus adopt the approach of Schwiderski (1996) to deal with distributed event ordering. We assume that each site has a local clock. Local clocks are synchronized with a precision p. Event occurrences can be globally ordered, provided that the granularity g_g of the global time-base is larger than p. In the $2g_g$-precedence model (Verissimo 1993), two events occurring at different sites are ordered whenever the timestamp of one event is at least $2g_g$ larger than that of the other one. If the difference of the timestamps is less than $2g_g$, then the events are considered to occur concurrently. If two events occur at the same site, then they can be ordered whenever they are at least one clock tick apart. For details on timestamp computation with the $2g_g$-precedence model, see (Schwiderski 1996).

In the chronicle consumption mode (Chakravarthy et al. 1994), the correct event composition relies on the ordering of component occurrences using timestamps. New events can only be composed if no older adequate component event has occurred at some site. This poses a special problem in distributed environments, since the signaling of events from remote sites typically takes different amounts of time or may even be temporarily impossible due to a detector site crash, and the order of arrival of events from different remote sites may not be the same as their order of occurrence. Thus, an ED can correctly compose new events out of components originating from multiple sites only if it is synchronized with the detectors of its components and so on recursively. Furthermore, efficiency considerations dictate that the effort to synchronize servers and their event detectors should not overly burden the workflow execution process, i.e., the number of affected detectors and of messages needed to exchange synchronization information should be kept minimal. Only servers co-operating within some specific workflow instance need to be synchronized, because events generated within instances of unrelated workflow types are neither temporally nor causally related. Thus, synchronization is needed for event detectors that detect workflow termination events or directly or indirectly contain such events as components.

The detector synchronization works as follows (see Fig. 4): whenever a broker attached to a server S_1 requests a (sub) workflow and S_1 forwards this request to another server S_2, then the affected detectors are informed that they need to synchronize with S_2. Thus, each detector maintains the information on which servers it needs to synchronize (the **synchronization set**) with. For each server S_i in the set, a reference counter records the number of workflow instances requested by S_1 at S_i. S_1 also records for each server in a synchronization set when the last event was received. From this set, the global time can be derived until which the local server is synchronized with the involved remote servers: the **synchronization point**, which is the minimum of the events' timestamps least recently received from the remote servers. The server which has signalled this event is called the **most recently synchronized site**, MRS. Since it is guaranteed that all events with timestamps earlier than the synchronization point have been received, it is safe for an ED to consume these events for composite event detection.

Whenever one of the affected detectors at S_1 receives an event or a component event, the timestamp of this event will be larger than the synchronization point. In case the event was **not** sent by the MRS, the received event is queued and not further processed. Otherwise, the new MRS is determined (which then also determines the new synchronization point), and all queued events that occurred prior to the new synchronization point are flushed, i.e., processed as in centralized event detection.

Two kinds of events exchanged between servers are relevant for synchronization: synchronization events and workflow termination events. Synchronization events do not bear any specific meaning, but only indicate that the sending server is still alive.

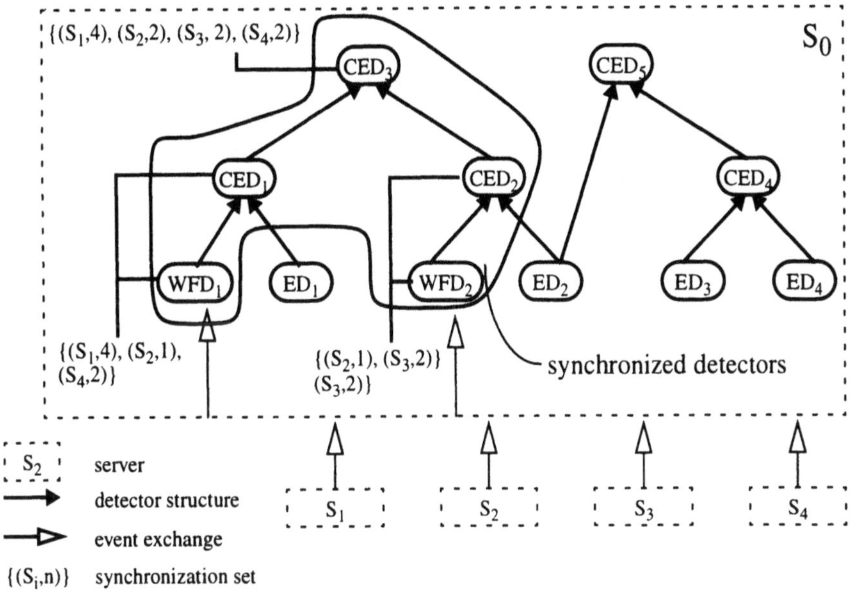

Figure 4 Synchronization of Servers and Event Detectors

They are sent out at predefined intervals to all servers from which request events for still executing (sub)workflow instances have been received. In case a server receives such an event, it knows that it has received all previous workflow termination events from the remote server and can exploit this information for synchronization of its detectors.

Workflow termination events indicate the completion of a workflow instance; they are processed by ED. In case such an event is received, the reference counter of the respective server in the corresponding synchronization set is decremented. If the new counter value is 0, then no more instances of the corresponding workflow type are active at the remote server. This server can thus be deleted from the synchronization set of the respective detectors and their ancestors. This procedure allows to minimize for each server and workflow type the number of remote servers it has to be synchronized with. Consequently, detectors at S_1 are only then synchronized with S_i if S_i in fact currently executes on behalf of S_1 one or more instances of the workflow type. In our example, the detector of the event *CON(RPL(CntrlCoverage.OK, HIC), CON(RPL(SW1.Done, Result), RPL(SW2.Done, Result)))* has to be synchronized with the ED for its component events.

5.3 Summary

EVE is the middleware for distributed workflow execution by reactive components. The event-based style of EVE eases the integration and coordination of these reactive components and the maintenance and evolution of workflow systems. EVE's multi-server architecture along with distributed event detection and detector synchronization avoids a centralized architecture; it is therefore potentially more efficient and less vulnerable to functionality degradation in case of site crashes, depending of course on the workflow specifications currently executing. Special-purpose services in EVE (such as task assignment) enable reactive components to execute workflows in an event-driven style; B/S schemas of workflow systems can thus be made executable in a seamless way.

6 CONCLUSIONS

A proper software architecture of workflow systems is crucial in order to adequately structure the entire environment and to fulfill further requirements such as flexible integration of PE or reusability of PE-definitions. We use a layered event-based architecture for workflow systems. Specifically, we have introduced the distributed event engine EVE serving as the underlying execution platform for workflows. An event-based approach to workflow execution combines runtime efficiency with flexibility. The contributions of this paper can be summarized as follows:

- a novel architecture for a distributed WS is presented providing the functionality for event-driven workflow execution; and
- an integrated framework addresses problems relevant to the distributed execution of workflows, e.g., event-detection, global event history.

Further work remains to be done on how to specify and implement semantic recovery mechanisms in EVE based on ECA rules. We will also address workflow type evolution, particularly with respect to long running workflows and organizational change.

REFERENCES

ACT-NET Consortium (1996), 'The Active Database Management System Manifesto: A Rulebase of ADBMS Features', *ACM SIGMOD Record* **25**(3).

Barbara, D., S. Mehrota & M. Rusinkiewicz (1994), INCAS: A Computation Model for Dynamic Workflows in Autonomous Distributed Environments, Technical report, Dep't of Computer Science, University of Houston.

Barrett, D.J., L.A. Clarke, P.L. Tarr & A.E. Wise (1996), 'A framework for event-based software integration', *ACM Trans. on Software Engineering and Methodology* **5**(4).

Carey, M.J., D:J. DeWitt, M.J. Franklin, N.E. Hall, M.L. McAuliffe, J.F. Naughton, D.T. Schuh, M.H. Solomon, C.K. Tan, O.G. Tsatalos, S.J. White & M.J. Zwilling (1994), Shoring up Persistent Applications, *in* 'Proc. ACM-SIGMOD', Minneapolis.

Casati, F., S. Ceri, B. Pernici & G. Pozzi (1996), Deriving Active Rules for Workflow Management, *in* 'Proc. 7th DEXA', Zurich, Switzerland.

Ceri, S., P. Grefen & G. Sanchez (1997), Wide - a distributed architecture for workflow management, *in* 'RIDE'.

Chakravarthy, S., V. Krishnaprasad, E. Anwar & S.-K. Kim (1994), Composite Events for Active Databases: Semantics, Contexts and Detection, *in* 'Proc. 20th VLDB', Santiago, Chile.

Dayal, U., M. Hsu & R. Ladin (1990), Organizing Long-running Activities with Triggers and Transactions, *in* 'Proc. ACM-SIGMOD', Atlantic City, NJ.

Georgakopoulos, D., M. Hornick & A. Sheth (1995), 'An Overview of Workflow Management: From Process Modeling to Workflow Automation Infrastructure', *Distributed and Parallel Databases* **3**(2).

Hsu, M. & C. Kleissner (1996), 'ObjectFlow: Towards a Process Management Infrastructure', *Distributed and Parallel Databases* **4**(2).

Kappel, G., P. Lang, S. Rausch-Schott & W. Retschitzegger (1995), 'Workflow Management Based on Objects, Rules, and Roles.', *Bulletin of the IEEE Technical Committee on Data Engineering* **18**(1).

Krishnamurthy, R. & D.S. Rosenblum (1995), 'Yeast: A General Purpose Event-Action System', *IEEE Trans. on Software Engineering* **21**(10).

Mylopoulos, J., A. Gal & K. Kontogiannis (1996), A Generic Integration Architecture for Cooperative Information Systems, *in* 'Proc. 1st CoopIS', Brussels, Belgium.

OMG (1995), 'The Common Object Request Broker: Architecture and Specification. Revision 2.0', Object Management Group.

OMG (1997), 'CORBAServices: Common Object Services Specification', Object Management Group.

Schmidt, D.C. (1994), ACE: an Object-oriented Framework for Developing Distributed Applications, *in* 'Proc. 6th USENIX', Cambridge, MA.

Schwiderski, S. (1996), Monitoring the Behavior of Distributed Systems, PhD thesis, University of Cambridge.

Sheth, A., K. Kochut, J. Miller, D. Worah, S. Das, C. Lin, D. Palaniswami, J. Lynch & I. Shevchenko (1996), Supporting State-wide Immunization Tracking using Multi-paradigm Workflow Technology, *in* 'Proc. 22nd VLDB', Bombay, India.

Tombros, D., A. Geppert & K.R. Dittrich (1997*a*), The Broker/Services Model for the Design of Cooperative Process Oriented Environments, Technical Report 97.06, Dep't of Computer Science, University of Zurich.

Tombros, D., A. Geppert & K.R. Dittrich (1997*b*), Semantics of reactive components in event-driven workflow execution, *in* 'Proc. 9th CAiSE', Barcelona, Spain.

Verissimo, P. (1993), Real-time Communication, *in* S.Mullender, ed., 'Distributed Systems', 2nd edn, Addison-Wesley, chapter 17.

Wodtke, D., J. Weissenfels, G. Weikum & A. Kotz-Dittrich (1995), The Mentor Project: Steps Towards Enterprise-wide Workflow Management, *in* 'Proc. 12th ICDE', New Orleans.

7 BIOGRAPHY

Andreas Geppert is a senior research associate at the Department of Computer Science at the University of Zurich. He received his diploma in Computer Science from the University of Karlsruhe in 1989 and a PhD in Computer Science from the University of Zurich in 1994. His current research interests include object-oriented and active database systems, workflow management, and construction of database management systems and information systems.

Dimitrios Tombros is a research associate at the Department of Computer Science at the University of Zurich. He received his diploma in Business Information Science from the University of Zurich in 1991 and a MSc in Computer Science from Stanford University in 1994. His current research interests include workflow management, workflow system composition, and event-based software architectures.

An architecture to support storage and retrieval of events

M.D. Spiteri and J. Bates
University of Cambridge Computer Laboratory,
New Museums Site, Pembroke Street, Cambridge, U. K.
Telephone: +44-1223-334600 Fax: +44-1223-334678
Email: {Mark.Spiteri, John.Bates}@cl.cam.ac.uk

Abstract

This paper describes the architecture we designed and constructed to support the storage and retrieval of *events*. We define an event as an asynchronous occurrence containing parameterised details of an activity that has occurred within a distributed component. Our past experience has demonstrated how using events as the glue to build distributed *active* systems simplifies the construction of complex applications, and enables legacy stand-alone components to be rapidly integrated within a larger collaborative environment. Examples of such active systems are interactive multimedia applications, distributed debugging environments, co-operative working applications, agent architectures, and active. Our motivation for storing events is that events represent indexing points into application sessions. Our *event repository* architecture can capture and store events, as well as *inject* them back into distributed application components to simulate replay of sequences of activity, or for re-building lost state. The architecture co-exists and inter-operates with other event-based active systems, as well as with middleware event services like traders and brokers. Using a generic object-oriented model for events, the repository architecture provides powerful search and retrieval facilities, enabling extraction of behaviour patterns, searching for simple and composite occurrences, and replay of stored sequences. We illustrate how the repository can be a viable alternative to past system-specific solutions in areas like capture of collaboration and memory prosthesis, and visualisation of user mobility.

Keywords

Distributed event programming, capture, storage, retrieval, replay

1 INTRODUCTION

This paper describes the architecture we designed and constructed to allow the storage and retrieval of events. This architecture, sometimes also referred to in this document as an *event repository*, co-exists with other middleware event services like traders and brokers, and can capture and store events, as well as *inject* them back into applications to simulate replay of sequences of activity, or for re-building lost state. Section 1.1 describes our motivations for carrying out this novel work. Section 1.2 describes some related work which has addressed aspects of these issues, while Section 1.3 outlines applications we have built as case studies of how the architectural services developed can be used. A brief discussion of our event paradigm and its use in building distributed applications using event-based components is found in Section 2. Section 3 details the architecture we designed to meet our requirements, and which we used successfully in support of the applications illustrated. In particular, Section 3.4 discusses our replay and retrieval interface. Section 4 concludes and presents a summary of our work.

The underlying framework to our system is our distributed event-based programming paradigm developed in previous work of the OPERA group (Bacon, 1995 and Bates, 1996/1). This is designed to support the construction of large-scale *active* systems, that is those in which run-time notification of events can cause further actions to be initiated. Examples of such potentially active systems are interactive multimedia applications, co-operative working applications, agent architectures, active databases and mobility aware applications that can respond to changes in users' physical locations. Events are asynchronous messages of different types with type-specific parameters, and can represent widely different activities like shared drawing strokes, logging on, launching an application, modification of a document, a application state change, taking books out of the library, a phone call, detecting a new location sighting (i.e. changing office), etc.

1.1 Motivation

Previous research (Bacon, 1995 and Bates, 1996/1) has demonstrated that in an environment of ubiquitous computer deployment, constructing distributed applications from reusable active components leads to efficient and dynamically re-configurable systems. Using these results as the basis of this work, we have identified a new requirement to support emerging scenarios; that the events used to *glue* together these applications can be stored, used for querying and replay, and as a basis for higher-level services.

For example, when used in conjunction with multimedia storage servers, captured event instances permit replay and support complex queries on historical records of multi-party computer-supported collaborative sessions. This enables the conference participants or other users to review and browse the conference recording, and replay all or segments of it. Another scenario in which storage of generic events is particularly useful is a memory recollection environment like a memory prosthesis (Lamming, 1994). This requires storage of various active information relating to user activities like document creation, media annotation, application usage, and location information, such as Active Badge sightings

(Harter, 1994). Temporal index and querying facilities are then required to be able to locate and review the activities carried out during any time period. Other application areas we have identified as beneficiaries of our architecture are systems monitoring for distributed debugging, logging of phone and workstation usage for automatic diary generation, tracking of phone data for telecommunications fraud detection, and acquisition and analysis of marketing information for Internet commerce. Within some scenarios it is desirable to be able to use information from all these different sources together, hence creating a better and more fine-grained virtual picture of the human and computer activities monitored.

We propose that a generic service architecture that can store and retrieve 'event instances' is a novel and desirable approach to handling these and other situations with similar requirements. Our event store is general purpose and can be used for a wide range of applications previously only catered for by bespoke solutions.

1.2 Related work

Storage of event instances or 'messages', 'notifications', 'actions' or 'traces' has been carried out in a number of application domains, but it has not been the focus of the research, and has been side-lined as secondary to issues like system optimisation and efficiency. Consequently no generic multiple-purpose event detection and storage architecture has been proposed. Of relevance to this investigation are projects undertaken in specific environments where some of the issues have been investigated, primarily:

- Ford (1991) and other authors (Lee, 1991) have examined event detection and capture for storage purposes in the context of fault-tolerant computing and distributed debugging. Logs are maintained of event 'traces', where these traces represent low-level system activities like processor communication. This work has largely assumed integration with a debugging environment and is tailored for specific classes of events. Mansouri-Samani (1995) has attempted extending query support to be more generic.
- Usability studies, as in Badre (1993). Such systems tend to focus on capturing local user interface events and do not consider distributed environments.
- Temporal databases and their query languages. These tend to be more concerned with how the data changes over time. The focus of this research has been mainly on the semantics and optimisation of temporal query algebras. The theory behind these languages and algebras is quite advanced, but only a few experimental implementations have been carried out (Goralwalla, 1995). While some aspects of this research are relevant to the proposed investigation, such as expressing of temporal intervals for querying, the emphasis on database states and their variance in time is not as relevant.
- Memory assisting tools like the memory prosthesis (Lamming, 1994). Video records of a user's activities are maintained and accessed by indexing through a listing of activities the user undertook (like typing, using the phone, opening documents, changing office). The Coral suite of tools (Minneman, 1995) support real-time capture and subsequent access to informal collaborative activities. While inspiring our work, we differ in having taken the approach of using more generic support in the form of our event store. Tools like these can

be built more easily by employing our architecture, and would benefit from our powerful retrieval mechanism.

In summary, other projects have investigated aspects of this proposed research in differing and specific contexts. Our research distinguishes itself by focusing on providing a generic platform for event modelling, storing and retrieval. This avoids bespoke services, allowing any event classes in an open environment to be stored.

1.3 Case-study applications

In this section we describe two applications employing the event repository's functionality; monitoring and review of user activities, and tracking of user movements to be able to replay them in a virtual reality environment.

1.3.1 Distributed activity monitoring

We have used the event store to capture, and then be able to browse and replay online collaboration and user activity. Using the event paradigm we have authored a collaborative platform which includes video/audio conferencing, text channels and shared drawing. Simultaneously, we monitor workstation activities like logging-on and file operations, web browsing, as well as tracking of the physical location of users through Active Badges, monitoring usage of phones, printers and borrowing of library books. These activities generate events, which are propagated through the network to various components. Our applications are built by gluing together existing components and specifying what actions to take in response to event notification. This is also the mechanism for tailoring existing applications. Our applications can dynamically use any activity as a trigger to perform some actions, for example, if two users are seen together in the same real-world location, then play them a video message on the nearest workstation briefing them on the progress of a project.

Events from these external sources, together with events relating to synchronisation of the collaborative environment components, are automatically indexed by the event repository, thus allowing later replay and/or querying of a session. We have used this to generate high level minutes of meetings and for automatic generation of diaries. Media streams associated with a collaborative session are also stored (of at least the person who is speaking). These stored sessions can be replayed at normal, slower or faster speeds, and the replaying positions can be specified in temporal terms relative to the beginning of the session or with respect to *any other event or sequence of events* within the session. On the assumption that the human mind often forgets specific details but remembers relationships to other activities which occurred before or after, we can perform queries corresponding to expressions like 'show me the URL of the slide that John showed after Giles joined the meeting', and 'show me the name of the book I took out of the library last month, just before I met Pawel in the corridor'.

Our collaborative working environment takes into account users' physical location by detecting their Active Badge. If a user moves to a new location, the application is notified, and his/her portion of the application follows them to the nearest, or a selected computer (Bates, 1996/2). This enables users to keep in touch with one another whilst on the move. When the user's components complete a

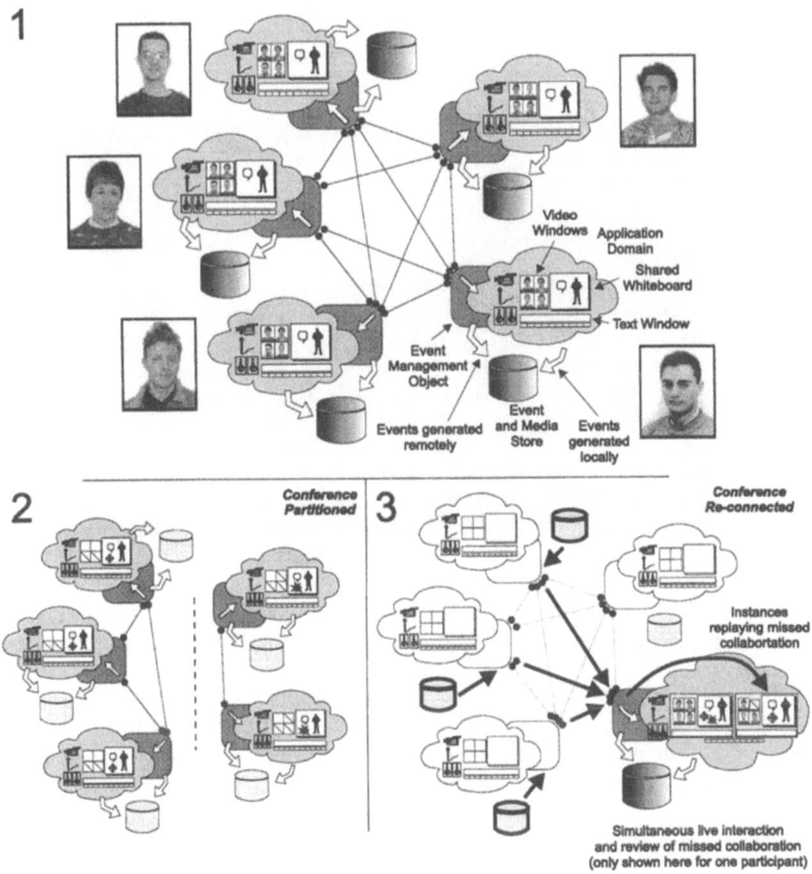

Figure 1. Use of event repository in support of disconnected operation

move to a new workstation, the components can once again communicate with the other users' conference components and network services.

At this point, to build their state to a level consistent with that of other users, the components require all the events missed from the period of disconnection. The situation is complicated by the fact that while one user was disconnected, other users may also have been disconnected and thus no user has a consistent view of the application. A solution to this problem is for each user to store events from the session so that each has a consistent view of at least the events generated locally. After re-connection, users can request that each user send them only the events generated by each user locally. We used this problem as another application of our event store.

A similar problem can result if the network fails temporarily, resulting in the conference being partitioned into two or more segments. An enhancement, to show a user what happened whilst he/she was disconnected, is to create exact copies of all local objects and to use the replayed events to update the copies. The user can then decide whether or not to add these updates to his/her session. If the disconnection was due to network partitioning and not mobility, then this approach

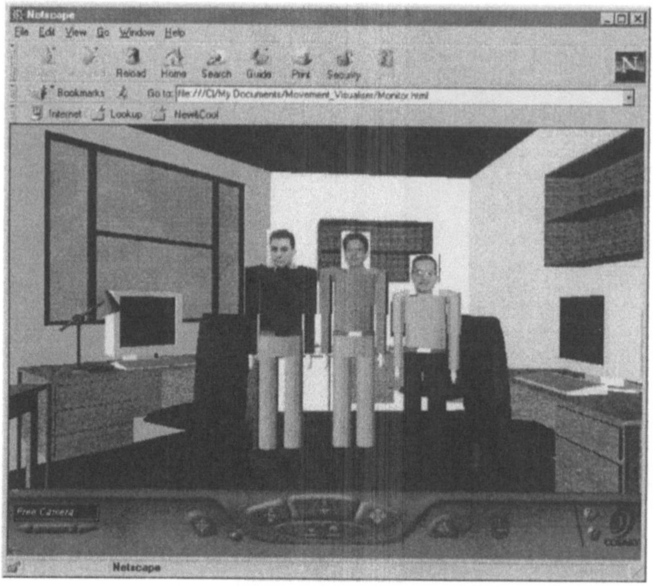

Figure 2. Reflecting the real-world, the authors and a colleague are portrayed in real-time in a virtual representation of office T11 by the VR mobility 'visualiser'.

applies to all users since disconnected working in one or more partitions may have occurred. In this case, all users can discuss what happened within the conference partitions, and decide which of the event sequences they wish to be added to the session. Figure 1 illustrates this process.

1.3.2 Virtual reality (VR) - distributed virtual world system

In our multi-user virtual world, a user steers a course through a 3D graphical environment, interacting with objects populating the world. Making each user's VR world event-based means that multiple users' instances of the same world can be interfaced, without the need for explicit interoperation. If a user moves location in the virtual world, events are notified, specifying the new location. This is analogous to tracking a mobile user in the real world. Events are also notified if a user interacts with an object in the virtual world, e.g. a virtual whiteboard. This is analogous to interacting with the user interface of a traditional application.

To test this out we used VRML97 (ISO/IEC, 1997) to build a representation of our Computer Laboratory's main building. Dynamically generated *avatars* representing various members of the department, as well as objects to interact with, are also implemented. In response to injected actions, avatars and objects can be added to the world dynamically; the VRML97 to realise an object is spliced into a world instance at run-time by a controlling Java management applet. The Java component is also responsible for forwarding events from each user's world to interested clients. Using our event storage and retrieval architecture we have also used these components, unmodified, to *replay* past activity like users' movements. We have employed this to monitor emergency evacuations of a building, since one can move around the VR model and observe how people negotiated the exits and where potentially dangerous bottlenecks occurred. See Figure 2.

2 PRINCIPLES OF EVENT-BASED SYSTEMS

This section introduces distributed systems development using asynchronous events as background to storage and retrieval. By using events as a uniform activity metric, systems/applications can be built around a generic event-response paradigm. Single or ordered combinations of events can be used to trigger further actions within the system/application. Using events as the uniform interchange of activity between the possibly distributed components simplifies the construction of a complex system/application. We developed our event system initially using a locally developed distributed object system, and later re-designed it as a layer above CORBA, using the latter as a distributed programming platform but remaining conceptually separate from it. Our event paradigm goes beyond other event systems like the CORBA Event Service (OMG, 1997) in that it provides support for higher level services like trading, brokerage, composition of new events through specification of event sequences and provision for secure interworking services. Multiple interested clients on the same channels are also allowed.

2.1 Components and glue

Event-based programming relies on two main concepts:

- Existing event-based components are used as the building blocks of applications. These may be distributed around the local network or Internet. They can inform interested users of pertinent events, such as a change in the location of a mobile user. The power of event-based system building is that no component has to be designed to work specifically with any other component.
- To compose many event-based components into an active system, a federator component must be written. This is the bespoke part of the system, composed of event-based rules that describe actions to take in response to the receipt of certain events from the components within the system. Rules act as distributed systems integration glue, using any class of event from any components to drive any other components by injecting any actions.

In a multi-user application, for example a multimedia conference, each user owns a set of components, but the overall system is composed of the interacting set of all users' components. In such a situation, it is likely that each user will have a separate federator component to take care of his/her own components.

2.2 Event classification and brokerage

One event source can generate events of one or more event classes. An event class has typed attributes, instances of which uniquely identify a captured activity. For example, an event source that provides information about the locations of users can offer monitoring facilities for the following class of event: `LocationEvent(Domain, Name, Type, Location)` which identifies that an entity has changed location in a specific domain. Distributed event-based objects advertise the event classes they can monitor for by exporting them to an event broker. Clients can query the event broker, to search for appropriate event sources. Inheritance can be used to create sub-classes of events. For example, a new event class `FineGrainedLocation` can provide a 3D fix on a user, rather than just a named location. This can be built on top of a GPS system or a fine-grained office-based system (Ward, 1997), thus providing latitude, longitude and altitude information. In our design, the event broker is the custodian of the class hierarchy for its local event domain. Querying the event broker for a particular class of event returns all event sources that can monitor for the class and all its sub-classes.

2.3 Registration for filtering

To reduce network traffic and avoid clients of event sources having to perform filtering to decide whether a particular event is of interest, our event system allows interested parties to *register interest* in events with certain characteristics. Only events that match the registered patterns are dispatched to the interested parties, thus reducing network traffic and filtering requirements.

To register interest with an event source, clients provide an *event template*. This is an event instance, with fields for exact match filled in and those for wildcard match expressed as variables. Examples for class `LocationEvent` are as follows:

- `LocationEvent('cl.cam.ac.uk', 'John.Bates', 'Person', L)` - Report wherever John is seen in the Computer Lab.
- `LocationEvent('cl.cam.ac.uk', P, 'Person', 'Meeting Room')` - Report when anyone is seen in the Computer Lab meeting room.

When event instances are notified to clients, values for all class attributes are given, e.g. the instance `LocationEvent('cl.cam.ac.uk', 'John.Bates', 'Person', 'Meeting Room')` means John has been seen in the meeting room.

2.4 Federation using rules

Event-based components also have an interface for action injection. This allows a client of a component to invoke methods that inject actions into the component. The action injection interface methods for a component are often the same as the classes of event that the object can notify.

Federating the operation of event-based components involves authoring a glue component, known as a federator. This component contains event-based rules. Each rule specifies one or a combination of events that, if detected, trigger a set of actions on components. As an illustration, consider how several drawing boards can be used to create a shared drawing application. Each board owner can author a federator; the federator registers interest in drawing events with all of the involved drawing boards (each of which may differ from the rest in implementation). When the federator is notified that a line has been drawn, it can inject an action into the local board to draw a corresponding line. The other users' federators register with the non-local boards; each board notifies events whenever it is drawn on. This approach is more flexible than hard-coding a shared-drawing application; the stand-alone drawing boards can be used in many more contexts than if it was part of a hard-coded system.

3 STORAGE AND RETRIEVAL OF EVENTS

As illustrated in Section 1.1, there are various motivating reasons to provide real-time storage of events coupled with powerful and useful paradigms for retrieval and replay. Events in different environments differ considerably in parameters, frequency and security requirements, and we have striven to provide a generic platform to support different event classes, while at the same time providing the functionality differing scenarios are likely to require.

Classification of stored events

As briefly mentioned in Section 2.2, events are represented as instances of event classes inheriting from the base class 'event'. This base class encapsulates the basic properties of an event as an instance of an action, or phase of an activity, occurring at a point in time, having a unique timestamp, scope, originating source, version (if applicable) and ownership tag if desired. Since events can be categorised through inheritance relationships, it becomes possible to execute generic query operations on abstract classes, which then automatically include the sibling class instances. The class hierarchy can be appended-to dynamically, and it is possible to have multiple class hierarchies defined simultaneously by tagging their member classes with different interface versions.

Storing events in sessions

A session provides a context to associate related event instances, this being particularly useful for limiting the scope of retrieval and replay. A session is set up by an application; the application sends events that it wants to be stored in the session to the event store. An example is a person's diary containing all events pertinent to his activities, or a chronicle of every individual's movements while exiting the building in an emergency drill. Any class of event can be stored in a session. An event instance can appear in multiple sessions.

3.1 Repository architecture

We designed and built our own database sub-system tailored for capture of high volumes of multiple streams of relatively small data objects (events) which need not be modified as they are to constitute a historical record. Every instance of the event repository consists of various components working concurrently and co-operatively, primarily a number of repository clients, and a repository server. While we have striven to keep the server component of the architecture as generic as possible to be of use in different scenarios with diverging requirements, the repository clients can be tailored to be highly specific to the application. Our aim in designing this architecture was to provide a core set of generic services coupled with highly and easily tailored components, so that the whole can provide the required facilities without compromising on speed and efficiency. The architecture of the event repository is illustrated in Figure 3.

A specialised repository client registers interest with one or more event sources for the particular event type to be stored. Security is managed by passing a certificate on registration, which is presented to the client on notification. It interfaces with the event sources and passes the events notified to the repository

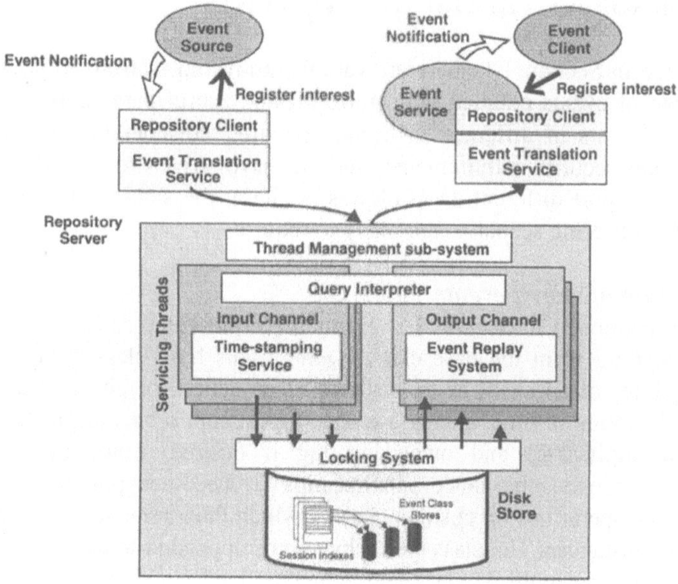

Figure 3. Event store architecture

server, which timestamps the events and stores them. The client also acts as a command parser for instructions sent to the repository by a user, a user application or intelligent agent. While these commands are mostly to do with subsequent retrieval of the information stored, some operations are related to storage, like definitions of new event types, and creation and definition of sessions. The client also functions as the base for building value added services during output operations.

The repository server receives the command queries and event streams through the repository clients, and can handle multiple input and output streams concurrently. Depending on the distributed application in support of which the repository is being used, there may be one centralised instance of the repository server capturing the activity information, or there may be multiple distributed instances; for example, one per domain or even one per user, as discussed in Section 3.2.

While any previous timestamp the event instances would have been tagged with, from the source or some intermediate broker, is retained, the repository considers the time of storage as the main timestamp. Consequently it structures and orders data according to this. While there are considerations for and against this, we decided to make this distinction because in this case the repository is acting as a distinct view of the application, in much the same way as the user it is associated with in a collaborative session has a specific view of the collaboration. In loosely coupled distributed environments where large distances and consequently large latencies are involved, the user cannot receive messages like, for example, video or shared drawing board actions, in 'correct' order. While technically this view does not depict the way actions really happened, nevertheless it does reflect the way the user saw the interaction, and if the storage tool is to be of assistance in review and recollection of ideas, then it is important also to retain the 'incorrect' viewpoint, which then becomes correct from the user's perspective. This scenario also implies separate instances of the event store for every user.

If desired, it is still possible to override the default ordering by storage timestamp, and order the event instances according to the source timestamp, through buffering in the repository client. If an existing event type is suddenly to be indexed according to a new timestamp, then the repository tags this event type as a newer different version of the previous one, so as not to mix up the historical records and cause conflict upon retrieval.

To optimise storage and retrieval, events of different types are stored in different files, on the same or on different file systems. This reduces the processing and streamlines the procedure for storage while making use of the resources available in the current computing domain by capitalising on the available disk parallelism. It is possible for multiple clients to start supplying events of the same types, in which case the separate handling threads co-operate so as to timestamp and store the instances correctly. Events are added to a particular class file by appending. This being historical data, it cannot be modified and is strictly ordered.

3.2 Repository Configurations

Depending on the service one wishes to provide to higher-level applications, an event repository can be used in different configurations:

- as a *system wide resource*, monitoring all event instances from one or more sources. An example is a centralised repository instance that captures all movement sightings from all Active Badges in a domain. Application components can then interface with it to request a replay or analysis of these movements. The event repository then injects these active components with the movement events as if they were happening in real time. In this configuration the repository is instantiated with system rights and allows users to request replay from it according to individual access lists on the event classes. One example case study using this configuration is visualisation of mobility in virtual reality for review of emergency procedures. In this scenario the event repository injects events into the mobility visualising component.
- as a *user-centred service*. A user can instantiate an event repository service and configure it to monitor all event types of interest to him. The repository is given the same security rights as the user has, and thus it can request to be notified of all events the user (or any of his applications) is entitled to receive. It is up to the user (or his agents) to configure the repository to organise events into sessions of relevance useful for subsequent retrieval. Such a configuration can be used to monitor all activities the user or his agents engage in, an example being for automated diary generation. The repository could monitor all workstation activities in the background, receive notifications from system-wide services like the user's movement sightings and use of library facilities, and monitor his engagement in online collaborative activity.
- as an *application-specific service*. An active application can instantiate an event repository and use it for its own requirements. A debugging application can thus use the repository to monitor system execution, allow analysis and review of the resulting trace and then destroy it once it terminates execution.

In collaborative scenarios, it might be desired not to keep a permanent record of the interaction, but nevertheless use the event repository to support disconnected operation. One way of achieving this is to have the conference management objects instantiate their own event repositories, use them to provide replay for participants after network partitioning, but then destroy them and all their records once the collaboration terminates.

3.4 Event query and replay

We provide a language to manipulate stored event classes and instances, as well as event sessions. Queries can be composed through a query interface provided by the repository client, either interactively, in advance, or dynamically by application components. Initially we used a subset of OQL (Cattell, 1996) as interface to the stored data, with additional keywords to support replay. However we found using OQL to express contextual-temporal relationships, as well as enable notions of temporal intervals in which one or more sequences of events might have occurred, as unwieldy. We thus added a number of new constructs, to facilitate expressing of temporal queries as well as make better use of the specialised storage for events. Note that we define an event as an atomic activity metric denoting an occurrence happening at a fixed single-valued point in time. We then define an interval as being bounded at both ends by a specified time value or an event. A composite event, on the other-hand, can consist of a sequence of atomic events or other composite events, but is also tagged with a fixed point in time, this being the end of the sequence, or when the 'composite event finally occurred'.

The event repository supports various retrieval operations. An application can request:

- Replay of events within a time interval. Straightforward replay of events of a specific type can be requested from the beginning of the 'recording' to the current time 'now', or for any interval in between. Once the interval to be replayed is evaluated, the repository server starts sending out the stored events as they occurred, with the same temporal separation. The client then translates them if and as required by the application, injecting events into its components as if they were occurring in real time. If the replay is from a session, different event types may be involved. Replay can also occur at multiples or fractions of the original recording speed. E.g. *'Replay at twice the original speed from the video conference records from when John displayed an image of a motorcycle but before Mark relayed the promotional video'*.
- Replay of events within a time interval matching specific characteristics. A filter can be applied to replay operations as the above, but *'replay only events with a parameter called 'Name' containing 'Mark''*.
- Retrieval of events as per the above categories but returned right away. It can be useful to receive a log of the events that occurred within a certain period, maybe for visualisation or data mining purposes where a replay is not explicitly required.
- Retrieve information relating to the number and nature of specified patterns of occurrences or *composite events*. It is possible to define a composite event and then request information as to how many times and when did it occur. E.g.

'Retrieve all instances of the sequence when Alarm A was followed by Alarm B and Alarm C did not go off in the meantime.'

All operators take a 'set of possibilities' and return a set of possible results based on using the cross-product of the operand sets or some other specific consumption model as specified through the query syntax. Base or abstract classes can be specified during queries, in which case the query will encompass all event classes that inherit from that class. The limited space available in this paper does not allow for a complete treatment of the event query syntax but we will provide the basic syntactic operators below and then give some examples. Our replay/retrieval syntax provides for a number of classes of operators, the main ones being:

Content comparison and equivalence

- `=, <, >, !=, <=, =>`
  These operators can be used to compare events of the same class, or compare specific event fields against specified values.
- (a.<field1> <operator> x `and` a.<field2> <operator> y)
  returns a set of events (of type a) whose <field1> and <field2> both compare to the respective values x and y as specified.
- (a.<field1> <operator> x `or` b.<field2> <operator> y)
  returns a set of events (or mixed type a and b) whose either <field1> or <field2> (as applicable) compare to the respective parameters as specified. a and b do not have to denote the same event class, nor to have the same set of attribute fields.

Temporal context

- ((<event>|<interval>) `before` (<event>|<interval>) [`without` <event>] [`within` <timevalue>])
  (a `before` b) returns the set of all a which are followed at some point by a b, where a and b can be either events or intervals. (a `before` b `within` <timevalue>) returns the set of all a that are followed by a b within the specified time period denoted by <timevalue>. (a `before` b `without` c) returns the set of all a that are followed by a b and no c occurred in between.
- ((<event>|<interval>) `after` (<event>|<interval>) [`without` <event>] [`within` <timevalue>])
  like the previous construct but in this case the a that were preceded at some point by a b are considered.
- (<event> `equal` <event>)
  (a `equal` b) returns the set of all a that occurred at the same time as a b.

Interval operators

An interval is defined as having a start time and an end time, and can encapsulate any number of events occurring within those inclusive boundaries. When an interval is defined within a query, a new object instance of the interval class type is constructed, and this provides the following methods that can be employed within the query itself.

Some maintenance functions are provided like; `start()`, which returns the time value denoting the start of the interval, `end()`, the end boundary, `events()`, the number of events within it, and `eventAt(x)`, the event at position `x`.

An interval is specified as follows:

- `(:` (<timevalue> | <event>) (((`until` | `to`) (<timevalue> | <event>)) | `for` <timeamount>) `:)`

  `(:` and `:)` denote that an interval is being specified. `until` and `to` differentiate between excluding or including the second time value itself. These operators default to a 'start-point' consumption model. A start time is matched with the closest end point and then not used again in any further matches. If `for` is used the second parameter must be a relative amount of time, which is then added to the starting boundary to compute the ending boundary of the interval.

There are a number of relationships between intervals, all of which can be specified in terms of the `start()` and `end()` operators of the interval object class. `before` and `after` have already been discussed in the context of event operators. The other operators we have provided reflect the ways in which an ordered pair of intervals can be related. These are `equal`, `meets`, `overlaps`, `during`, `starts`, `finishes`, `contains` and their inverses. `intersect` and `join` are interval operators that create new intervals on which queries can be applied.

Composite/sequence pattern operators

A composite event is denoted as an event defined in term of a sequence of other basic or composite events. It exists only within the context of the current query and is defined by specifying a path template, also equivalent in meaning to a sequence or pattern. Operations on paths are carried out by enclosing the template in `[: :]`, as in `[:` A `followedby` (B `or` C) `without` E `:]`

A composite 'path' does not return single event instances, but rather constructs a set of new composite event objects (if successful) which each contain pointers to all the basic events they were made up from within the session timeline. Functions are provided which can extract relevant information from the resulting construct.

Syntax Examples

We will illustrate the use of the syntax through the following simple examples;

- '*Replay from the group's diary from when Mark entered room T12 and John was there.*' One way of expressing this is to find the period when John was in T12 and then see if Mark was seen within that period in the same room. If this is successful, then replay from that instance onwards.

```
replay fromsession OperaDiary
fromwhere (badge.Name='Mark.Spiteri' and badge.location='T12')
during (: (badge.Name='John.Bates' and badge.Location='T12')
until (badge.Name='John.Bates' and badge.Location!='T12') :)
```

- '*Retrieve when Jean walked from the tea-room to her office (T15) and started editing a document sometime last week.*' Instead of replaying this will return all event sequences which match the specification provided. A simple way of specifying this is:

```
retrieve fromsession JeanDiary
eventsOf( [:(badge.Name='Jean.Bacon' and badge.Location='Tea-
Room')
followedby (badge.Name='Jean.Bacon' and badge.Location='T15')
followedby (workstation.documentedit.user='Jean.Bacon'):]
during (: 10/02/1998 to 17/02/1998 :) )
```

To summarise, it is possible to find events relative to other events that have occurred before or after them, as well as with respect to specified bounded intervals. Intervals can be operated on to determine overlapping periods, and if desired, output can be filtered so that only specific event types, or events with specific parameters, are returned.

4 SUMMARY

In previous publications we demonstrated that in an environment of ubiquitous computer deployment, constructing distributed applications from reusable active objects (i.e. capable of responding to externally generated events they have registered interest in) leads to efficient and dynamically re-configurable systems. Using these results as the basis of this work, we then identified a new requirement to emerging scenarios; that the events used to glue together these applications can be stored, used for querying and replay, and as a basis for higher-level services.

In this paper we have illustrated our design for an architecture providing storage and retrieval of generic events representing human and computer-based activities. We have achieved this by modelling activities uniformly as events and providing a model for representing event classes and instances, an architecture for distributed event detection, a specialised database storage sub-system, and a model for querying and retrieving event-based information. Although we are still working on various aspects of the event storage architecture, early results with our prototype applications indicate we have mostly been successful in addressing our motivating factors. In particular we provide a solid alternative to various bespoke solutions, as well as offering functionality that those alternatives did not provide.

One test application we have built and discussed is storing conference sessions in conjunction with real-world monitoring, for review or as a memory aid. The replay facilities support recreating all of, or sections of, a conference as it happened using events as temporal indices to other media. We have used replay from our event store as a useful tool for re-building application state following disconnection or mobility, as well as allowing instant review of missed interaction. In our second illustrated case study we have captured mobility events and then injected them into a 3D virtual representation of the building the events were taken from. Amongst other things, this has enabled us to visualise and review emergency evacuation procedures. Both case-studies emphasise the feasibility of the event store as a valid resource in distributed environments; in particular with regards to quick and painless interfacing with applications, efficient event capture and storage, and provision of powerful retrieve and replay facilities.

5 REFERENCES

Bacon J., Bates J., Hayton R., and Moody K. (1995) Using Events to build distributed applications, in *2nd International Workshop on Services for Distributed and Networked Environments*, IEEE.

Badre A. N., Hudson S. E., and Santos P. J. (1993) An Environment to Support User Interface Evaluation Using Synchronized Video and Event Trace Recording, Technical

Report, Graphics, Visualization and Usability Center, Georgia Institute of Technology, USA.

Bates J. (1996/1) A Framework to support Large-scale Active Applications, in *SIGOPS European Workshop*, ACM.

Bates J., Halls D., and Bacon J. (1996/2) A Framework to support mobile users of multimedia applications, *ACM Mobile Networks and Nomadic Applications*, 1.

Cattell R. G. G., Barry D. K. (1996) *The Object Database Standard: ODMG 2.0*, San Francisco, CA: Morgan Kaufmann Publishers.

Ford R. (1991) Non-Intrusive Real Time Event Capture, in *Proceedings of the ACM/ONR Workshop on Parallel and Distributed Debugging*, pages 225–227, Santa Cruz, CA, USA.

Goralwalla I. A., Tansel A. U., and Tamer Ozsu M. (1995) Experimenting with Temporal Relational Databases, Technical Report, Department of Computer Science, University of Alberta.

Harter A. and Hopper A. (1994) A distributed location system for the active office, *IEEE Networking*, 8(1).

ISO/IEC, The VRML Consortium Incorporated (1997). *VRML97 - The Virtual Reality Modelling Language Specification*, International Standard ISO/IEC 14772-1:1997

Lamming M., Brown P., Carter K., Eldridge M., Flynn M., Louie G., Robinson P., and Sellen A. (1994) The Design of a Human Memory Prosthesis, *The Computer Journal*, pages 153–163.

Lee I., Iyer R.K., and Tang D. (1991) Error/failure analysis using event logs from fault tolerant systems, in *21st Int. Symp. on Fault-Tolerant Computing (FTCS-21)*, pages 10–17, IEEE Computer Society Press, Montreal, Que., Canada.

Mansouri-Samani M. and Sloman M. (1995) GEM: A Generalised Event Monitoring Language for Distributed Systems, Technical Report, Imperial College Department of Computing, United Kingdom.

Minneman S., Harrison S., Janssen B., Kurtenback G., Moran T., Smith B., and van Melle B. (1995) A Confederation of Tools for Capturing and Accessing Collaborative Activity, in *Proceedings of the 3rd ACM International Conference on Multimedia*, pages 523–534, San Francisco, CA USA.

Object Management Group (OMG) (1997) Event Service Specification, ftp://www.omg.org

Ward A., Jones A., and Hopper A. (1997) A New Location Technique for the Active office, *IEEE Personal Communications*, 4.

6 BIOGRAPHIES

Mark D. Spiteri graduated in Computing and Physics from the University of Malta in 1994, and later that year joined the Department of Computer Science and A.I. as a research assistant. As a Commonwealth Scholar, he moved to the University of Cambridge in 1995 where he is currently a PhD candidate. He is carrying out research in distributed multimedia environments, collaborative systems, and paradigms for storage and retrieval of active information.

John Bates holds the Heller Senior Research Fellowship in Object-Oriented Computing, at St. Catherine's College Cambridge. John's research is based at the University of Cambridge Computer Laboratory. The main thrust of his work is in applying object and event technologies, to support end-user requirements of distributed computer systems. Areas of application to date include multimedia, computer-supported collaborative work, and support for mobility.

Run-time Monitoring of Distributed Applications

Xavier Logean, Falk Dietrich, Hayk Karamyan, Shawn Koppenhöfer

Institute for computer Communications and Applications (ICA)
Swiss Federal Institute of Technology Lausanne (EPFL)
CH-1015 Lausanne
url: http://icawww.epfl.ch, email: xavier.logean@epfl.ch
Phone: +41 21 693 5257, Fax: +41 21 693 6610

Abstract

In this paper we present a method to perform run-time monitoring of distributed applications built on top of a distributed object oriented processing environment. For this, we instrument the code at the compilation time in order to send notifications to an Observer when relevant events occur in the system; the instrumentation is done in an automated manner, requiring a minimum of programmer interactions. One advantage of our run-time monitoring approach is that it does not hinder the development process already adopted. In our proposal, the choice of the information to select for observation is made simple by the definition of events which are generic and useful for all distributed applications; the user does not need to specify them. We apply our run-time monitoring method to a telecommunication service implemented on top of the distributed processing environment CORBA Orbix^{TM} from IONA.

Keywords

Distributed systems, monitoring, observation, CORBA, events.

1 INTRODUCTION

Distributed systems are widely used today. Despite the large community of users of these systems, the unpredictability of the physical environment and the failure to satisfy design assumptions can cause unexpected conditions or violations of system constraints at run-time. It is highly desirable, that under these error conditions, total system failure does not occur and critical system functions of the system are maintained. In other words, constraint violation must be detected and appropriate actions taken. Run-time monitoring is a means by which problems can be detected on-line.

Run-time monitoring is aimed particularly at dealing with security and safety-critical problems that may occur in systems even when they are produced using the most rigorous development process and/or formal methods. It is possible for such systems to display incorrect behavior, due to failures in the underlying hardware, the compilation, operating systems, system design, communication protocol, etc. It is important in such cases to control the extent to which a program may execute after reaching an inconsistent state. Previous research demonstrated the feasibility of run-time monitoring during the testing and debugging phase of the software life-cycle (Bates 1995), (Brutch, Karmarkar, S., Walzel, Marti & U.W. 1996). Monitoring of distributed systems is also used for the management of such systems (Perrow 1994). More recently, Queiroz and Madeira developed a run-time monitoring approach used for management purpose for CORBA multiware applications (Queiroz de & Madeira 1997).

In this work, we propose a run-time monitoring approach for distributed applications built on top of an object-oriented distributed processing environment such as CORBA. In our approach, the user of our system does not need to deal with implementation issues. Indeed, all the needed code can be generated automatically and added to the system with little human interaction. Furthermore, the information that can be monitored is made selectable via a set of predefined observable events which capture the behavior of the distributed application.

The main component of our monitoring method is the *Observer*. The Observer receives all the information that are monitored from the different instrumented part of the application. The Observer proposes powerful functionality via a simple user interface. In the case of large scale systems, the introduction of a central Observer can constitute an important bottleneck. Therefore, with our approach it might not be possible to monitor all the objects of a huge system. In some cases, we can circumvent the problem by applying a selective monitoring only on the interesting objects. In order to solve the scalability issue we plan to study methods to distributed the central Observer.

In Section 2, we explain the framework and present the necessary notions to understand our run-time monitoring proposal. In Section 3, the run-time observation mechanism is presented. The complete scenario of run-time monitoring is detailed in Section 4. In Section 5, we apply the different concepts to a prototype of a telecommunication service. Finally, Section 6 concludes by indicating the directions we will explore in the future.

2 DESCRIPTION OF THE APPROACH

2.1 Framework and Terminology

Today, distributed application are built with the help of Distributed Processing Environment (DPE). With such environment, the specifier of the service does not need to deal with distribution issues when specifying the distributed application. The RPC mechanism or sophisticated socket mechanisms that ensures distributed features of the application are completely hidden from the programmer. Thus, the design of the distributed application consist of: (1) identifying the objects required for the application (2) defining the interfaces to those objects (3) implementing the different interfaces (4) writing a server program that creates instances of the implementation classes (5) writing a client program that accesses the server objects.

For the design purpose different languages are available to choose from: IDL (Interface Definition Language) (OMG 1998) which is specific the Common Object Request Broker Architecture (CORBA) and ODL (Object Description Language) which is specific to the Telecommunication Information Networking Architecture (TINA) (Kitson, Leydekkers, Mercouroff & Ruano 1995). ODL can be considered as a super set of IDL.

These different languages of specification make no assumptions about the implementation details. The application can be implemented in C++, JAVA, smalltalk, etc. But thanks to the IDL/ODL specification, all the operations will be present (implemented) in either implementation language. This interesting property allows us to propose a method independent of the implementation language.

In an application built on top of a DPE an operation can be either a "function" like operation or a one-way operation. A "function" like operation returns a result value and the object invoking this operation is blocked until the result of the operation is produced. A one-way operation or a *notification* is an operation without a result value. A notification can be considered as the sending of message without any acknowledgement.

Taking the abstraction level given by the specification (ODL/IDL) the applications are seen as a set of objects having one or many interfaces and capable of invoking operations on other objects. The objects of the system have no shared memory nor shared variable and communicate only by message passing. In Figure 1, the objects are depicted with boxes. The interfaces are represented by the black rectangles attached to the boxes. The operations are represented as lines connecting the different objects. The notation used in this paper to denote that an object o_1 invokes the operation *op*() on object o_2 is: $o_1!o_2.op()$.

We can divide the events happening in the system into three types:

- **internal events** are events characteristic of the behavior of the individual objects. An internal events affects only the object at which it occurs. No communications between objects is involved in such events. For example, internal events are the set of internal steps implied by the execution of an operation defined in the interface. Internal events are not visible from the DPE.

- **external events** are invocation, acceptance and termination of operations from one object to another one. External events are all the events that are visible at the interface of the objects, all events that are involved in the communication inter-objects.
- **environmental events** are events managed by the DPE environment (e.g., the 'bind' of a client object to a server object or the creation and deletion of an object). These events encompass the actions that the DPE has to accomplish in order to ensure the distribution issues.

Since the DPE hides the distribution issues, looking at the environmental events would mean that we are scrutinizing the behavior of the DPE; this is not within the scope of our work (the monitoring of a distributed applications). It is also not our purpose to examine the internal behavior of the objects; excellent debugging tools already exist. These tools can be used to test the internal functionality and behavior of each object. We are only interested in the abstraction level provided by the ODL/IDL specification.

We only consider ***observable events***. The set of observable events encompasses the external events and the environmental events *creation* and *deletion*. The observable

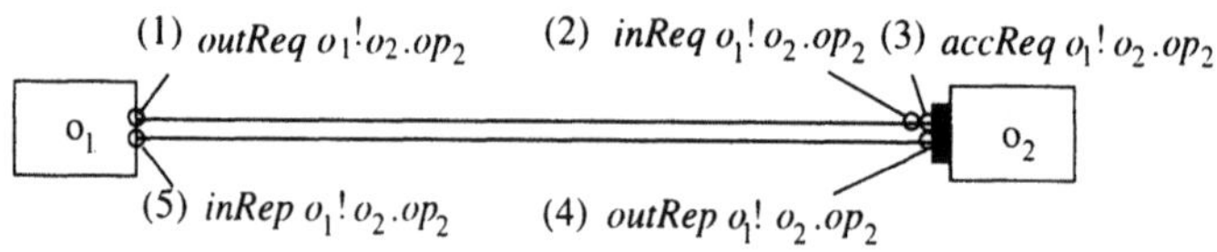

Figure 1 Observable events

behavior model of our system is therefore defined as the succession of observable events which are defined as follows (see Figure 1):

1. **out request:** An object (or the environment) requests the invocation of an operation on an object (target object).
2. **in request:** The request arrives at the target object. Only a single request can be processed by an object at any time. If an operation request arrives while an object is already processing another request, the newly arriving request will be queued and, in a multi-threaded DPE, a new thread will be allocated.
3. **accept request:** The target object accepts the request and starts executing the operation. The 'in request' event falls together with the 'accept request' event if the receiving object starts executing the operation without queuing the request.
4. **out reply:** The operation request has been processed and the target object is ready to transfer the result back to the source object. In the time between 'accept request' and 'out reply' it may be necessary for the target object to call operations on other objects in order to successfully complete the operation.

5. **in reply:** The source object (or the environment) receives the results of the operation. The source object has been blocked during the time between the 'out request' and 'in reply'.
6. **creation:** The creation of an object.
7. **deletion:** The deletion of an object.

Obviously, the two events *out reply* and *in reply* are not defined for the notifications. The detailed definition of these events can be found in (Dietrich, Logean, Koppenhoefer & Hubaux 1998). In that work, we defined a complete set of events for OO distributed system (processes, objects, threads and system events).

2.2 Run-time monitoring development process

Consider Figure 2 for an overview of the development process of distributed applications in the CORBA framework. The white boxes depict the normal development process of distributed applications; the gray boxes describe the extensions we propose in order to allow the automatic instrumentation for run-time monitoring. Rounded boxes denote tools.

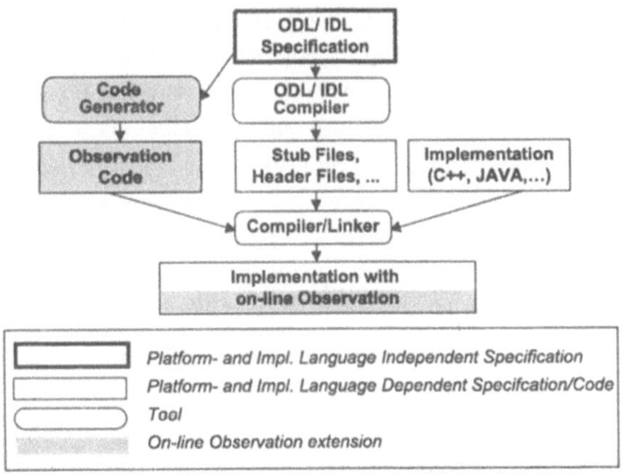

Figure 2 Global framework

The IDL/ODL specification of the interfaces is passed to an IDL/ODL compiler associated with the DPE which generates stub code and header files which are then linked to the actual implementation code thereby shielding the developer of the distributed application from the difficult task of handling the distribution issues.

In addition to passing the IDL specifications to the IDL compiler, the *code generator* is fed with the IDL specifications. This code generator tool generates some generic observation code which also needs to be linked to the actual implementation and forms the on-line observer part of the implementation. This process of introducing features that facilitate the testing process is frequently referred as part of a Design

For Testability (DFT) process (Dssouli, Karoui, Petrenko & Rafiq 1996). In (Chechik & Gannon 1994), Chechik and Gannon propose annotating C code in order to check whether the code satisfies the requirements. The monitoring of applications based on the manual instrumentation of the code can be very efficient for the developer of the application but rather inappropriate for a tester who does not have a deep understanding of the implementation. This tester would have to understand all (at least part of) the code to figure out how and where to instrument it. Manual instrumentation is therefore currently an ad. hoc solution for specific cases, but is not systematic and methodical enough to be applied in the general cases. In our proposal, the system of trace generation is automatically added by the code generator without the need for understanding or manually instrumenting the code of the distributed application.

The traces are collected by an ***Observer.*** The interface of the Observer is specified and normalized, and then the Observer is implemented once and for all. By using its interface, and the standardized protocol GIOP (General Inter-ORB Protocol) (OMG 1998) it is irrelevant if the implementation of the Observer is in the same implementation language as the distributed application or not. The Observer can be used in every system so long as the object of the system use its interface. This means that the code generator introducing the trace generation mechanism which is used to send *notifications* to the Observer via its interface, is the only piece that depends on the implementation language used for developing the application.

The observable information (list of objects, operations and attributes) that the user can select from is provided to the Observer by parsing the IDL/ODL specification with an appropriate tool. The only thing that the user has to do is to select what to observe, and the remaining work, including the instrumentation, is done automatically. Unlike other approaches (e.g., (Al-Shaer, Abdel-Wahad & Maly 1997) (Sankar & Mandal 1990)) the definition of the different monitorable information is automatically done by the compilation process by analyzing the IDL/ODL specification. Each operation and attributes* in the specification will be associated with five observable events (out Request, in Request , accept Request, out Reply, in Reply) each object implies two events (creation and deletion).

The Observer is notified of each creation and deletion of objects active in the system and assigns an Id to each objects. The Observer maintains a table with the list of objects currently existing in the system and their respective Id. This table is used to perform selective monitoring, according to the selections of the user.

3 MONITORING

Sections 3.1-3.2-3.3, give the different details of the instrumentation. In Section 3.4, we present the methods to automatically add the instrumentation for monitoring.

---

*Two operations are automatically defined to act on the attributes defined in the specification: the *set* and *get* operations.

3.1 Instrumentation of the code

Among the object-oriented distributed platforms based on CORBA, many offer support for run-time observation. For example, Orbix^{TM} from IONA (IONA 1997) provides the *filtering* mechanism. A filter allows a programmer to specify that an additional code is to be executed before or after the normal code of an operation. The CHORUS Cool distributed platform offers a mechanism similar to Orbix^{TM} filters, termed *interceptors*. In our work we make the assumption that a run time observation mechanism, that we term with the generic word '*Filter*', is provided by the distributed platform. This assumption is not restrictive. In the case where such a mechanism is not offered by the distributed platform, a proxy object that plays the role of the Filter can be added for each object within the system. Such work is performed in the IRI project (Al-Shaer et al. 1997). Notice that The Object Management Group has now standardized the notion of *Filter* in the CORBA 2.2 specification under the name *Interceptors* (OMG 1998).

We use the "breakpoints" provided by the Filters to send notifications to the observer. The Filters are put everywhere but activated and parameterized only as needed. This would allow to select specific information to observe without requiring the program be recompiled. However, in the case that we want to remove the Filters completely, we still need to recompile the code. With the help of the specification, the code generator adds observation code to the system in order to build parameterized filters. This generic code encompasses:

- the *notification mechanism*. This mechanism allows the monitored information to be sent to the Observer. This code is exactly the same for each object of the system. Details on the notification are given in Section 3.2
- a *selection mechanism*. This mechanism allows the user to select specific data to be monitored per the object. This selection mechanism is based on: (1) an operation *select* that is offered to the user in order to select the information, (2) a database (table) containing all the data that can be monitored on the object, a special field is reserved for marking if a data has to be monitored. This field is updated by the *select* operation.
- some *specific* code to guarantee the causal dependences (order) of notifications (this is detailed in Section 3.3)

3.2 Notifications

Our monitoring approach is based on a notification mechanism that carries the monitored data to the Observer. A notification is an operation invoked on the Observer. A notification is sent each time an *observable event* occurs in the system. We identify three types of notifications. The first one that we term as *Notification* is sent at each external event (see Section 2.1) and depicted in Table 1. The second and third are termed, respectively, as *Creation* and *Deletion* and denote the creation and deletion of objects. The creation and deletion of an object can be observed by adding (via the code generator) an instruction for notification in the constructor and destructor of the objects, or by spying on the messages given by the DPE. *Creation* contains the name and type of the object created and returns its Id given by the Observer. *Deletion* encompasses the Id of the object deleted. This Id is the one that the Observer assigned to the object earlier, just after its creation.

Parameters	Information
`ObjId`	Identification of the object sending the notification
`OpName`	Name of the operation invoked
`OpParameters`	All parameters of the operation
`OrigObjId`	Identification of the object invoking the operation that is the event source
`TargetObjId`	Identification of the object on which the operation is invoked
`EventId`	Event identification (e.g., out request)
`Timestamp`	Time-stamp of the process when the notification was sent

Table 1 Parameters of the Notifications

The method used for the *Notifications* and *Deletions* is *asynchronous* reporting whereas *Creations* uses *synchronous* reporting. The use of *synchronous* reporting might also be possible for the three types of notifications. Such a reporting mechanism blocks each object till the result of the notification is received. Thus, the delay introduced depends also on the processing rapidity of the Observer. This means that synchronous reporting can accentuate the impact of monitoring on the system by slowing down the entire system.

3.3 Monitoring management

In general, we cannot assume that the DPE will guarantee that the Observer will receive the notifications in the same order in which they have been sent. Therefore, the establishment of the "true" order of the events is mandatory in order to be able to follow what happened in the system. Let us consider a system of two objects o_1 and o_2, assumed to be already created, in which o_1 invokes the operation *op*() on o_2. According to the definition of the causal precedence or *happened before* relation (noted $\rightarrow$) given by Lamport (Lamport 1978), thea ble 2 gives the causal dependencies of our observable events. The order of the events as seen by the Observer (via the notifications) must reflect the order of events as defined by the happened before relation.

In order to catch causal dependencies, we could try to synchronize the different clocks of each process involved in the distributed computation. However, the different distributed objects of our system do not share a global memory and communicate only by operations (two-way or one-way). Distributed systems may not have built-in physical time and can only approximate it. The Network Time Protocol (NTP) proposed within the Internet community (Mills 1990) allows clocks to be synchronized to a few tens of milliseconds. Taking into account that observing the system will have some impact on it and that we can not assume that the notifications inter-arrival delay will always be less than tens of milliseconds, such a synchronization is not adequate for distributed system.

outReq $o_1!o_2.op()$	$\rightarrow$	inReq $o_1!o_2.op()$
inReq $o_1!o_2.op()$	$\rightarrow$	accReq $o_1!o_2.op()$
accReq $o_1!o_2.op()$	$\rightarrow$	outRep $o_1!o_2.op()$
outRep $o_1!o_2.op()$	$\rightarrow$	inRep $o_1!o_2.op()$

Table 2 Causal dependencies of observable events

Another method to preserve causal dependencies is the use of *logical clocks*. Logical clocks are implemented for each object by assigning a *timestamp* to events. This timestamp represents the logical clock and is advanced according to certain rules. The implementation of the timestamp mechanism requires deciding what data structure to use and then determining the set of rules to update the data structure.

The system of logical clocks is used to preserve the causal ordering of our notifications. In simple words, causal ordering is the natural extension of FIFO ordering in the case of more then one sender and receiver. A system respecting the *causal ordering* (Raynal, Schiper & Toueng 1991)requires that the messages are delivered respecting the 'happened before' relation: an object receiving a request op_2 can know, thanks to the logical clock, if a request op_1, which has been sent before, has not been received. In this case, it delivers request op_2 only after op_1 has been received and proceeded.

Raynal, Schiper and Toueg present in (Raynal et al. 1991) a simple way, called the *RST* algorithm, to implement a system respecting the causal ordering. For this, they use matrix timestamps associated with a vector at each object.

The algorithm we are using to maintain the causal ordering of notifications is based on RST. Our algorithm is only used to ensure that the causal ordering can be reconstructed at the Observer site. Each object obj_i of the system is associated with a vector timestamp. Each element of the timestamp is a pair $(obj_{Id}, \#events)$, where obj_{Id} is the Id of one object of the system and $\#events$ is the number of notifications sent by object obj_{ID} to the Observer as known by obj_i.

The number of notifications sent by each object is propagated through the system by piggybacking the timestamp with the requests. The size of the timestamp is equivalent to the number of objects in the system. As the number of object in the system evolutes (depending on the creation and deletion of objects) our algorithm is capable of maintaining a dynamically sized timestamp.

3.4 Automatization of the instrumentation

Instrumenting code is made up of installing a notification mechanism, a causal ordering mechanism and a selection mechanism. Since the notification mechanism and the causal ordering mechanism are completely generic, it is easy to automatically add each of them in each Filter. The introduction of a selection mechanism is more complex. The database for the selection is different for each object. As mentioned in Section 3.2, the data that must be monitored includes the operations with their parameters, and the attributes of the objects. This information can be obtained from the IDL/ODL specification. In Figure 3, an example of an ODL specification is given. The name of the object can be obtained from the `Object` field. By looking

```
Interface Interface_1                     Object Object_name
  {Behavior "..."                          {Behavior "..."
   Usage "used to..."                       attributes
    op_1(in int a, out int b);               int attr_1;
    op_2(in bool c, out int d);             support
   };                                        Interface_1; };
```

Figure 3 Example of ODL specification

at the `supports` field, the different interfaces that the object `Object_name` supports can be retrieved; this allows the different operations of the object to be obtained. In the example, `Object_name` has two operations `op_1` and `op_2` from the interface `Interface_1`.

By parsing the ODL specification, the name of the operation, the parameters and the attributes can be obtained and can therefore be used to construct the database that has to be introduced in each Filter in the system. In the example, the database for the `Object_name` contains the two operations `op_1` and `op_2` and the attribute `attr_1`. The Observer also has a copy of all the databases of the objects and offers a menu to the user allowing him to select special items of an object to monitor.

The *select* operation offered by each object has two arguments: the type of the data to monitor and the name of the argument to monitor. An example is, if the `op_1` has to be monitored, the *select* operation invoked by the Observer on the object `Object_name`, after the user has selected the data to monitor thanks to a menu, would be: `select(type operation, name op_1);`

A big advantage of the *select* operation is that the configuration of the monitoring can change at run-time. The user can select a new data to monitor at run-time without the need to recompile the code or to add new instrumentations in the code. Our monitoring instrumentation is *parameterizable at run-time*. Similarly to the *select* operation, an *unselect* operation is implemented.

3.5 Impact of the monitoring mechanism on the ordering of events

When monitoring a system, it is crucial to know if the observation is the one of the system or a new one introduced by the monitoring mechanism. The delay introduced by the monitoring mechanism (Filters) can affects the order of occurrence of events. In other words, the introduction of the monitoring mechanism might effect an order that is not present in an unmonitored execution.

The impact of the monitoring mechanism can be reduced by decreasing the processing introduced by the Filters. This can be performed by optimizing the number of notifications sent to the observer by concatenating the two notifications sent at the outReq and inReq points and the one sent at the outRep and inRep. This notifications can later be interpreted by the observer and split into two different events. The processing is moved from the Filters to the Observer.

We are currently working on the evaluation of the intrusive effect of our monitoring method from a theoretical point of view, by formalizing the problem, and by an experimental approach, by proceeding to statistical measurement of the delays introduced by the monitoring mechanism in our prototype.

4 COMPLETE RUN-TIME MONITORING SCENARIO

Let us consider that the generic observation code has been added into the implementation of the distributed application and that all objects are equipped with Filters able to send notifications to the Observer. The scenario of run-time monitoring is sketched in the Figure 4. The Filters are first activated and parameterized according to the wishes and selections of the user. Then, at run-time the notifications are sent to the Observer whenever an observable event (i.e., an event that has been selected for monitoring) occurs in the computation. At run-time the user can change the configuration of the Monitoring system by selecting other objects/operations to monitor. Figure 4 also illustrates the global design of the Observer. The Observer is made up of four modules:

- The **Graphical User Interface** provides the user with a list of objects and operations of the system. Through the GUI the user selects what to observe and the GUI hands the selection to the Filtering Manager. The GUI also displays all the notifications received.
- The **Filtering Manager** is in charge of activating and parameterizing the filters involved by the selection of the user. This is done by invoking an operation on all the objects involved in the selection. Notice that for this purpose the code generator adds two operations to each object: *Attach()* for activating the Filters and *Detach()* for desactivating the Filters.
- The **Observation Manager** receives all the notifications sent by the filters. Based on the timestamp parameter of the notifications, it reorders the notifications and gives them to the GUI and The Observation recorder.

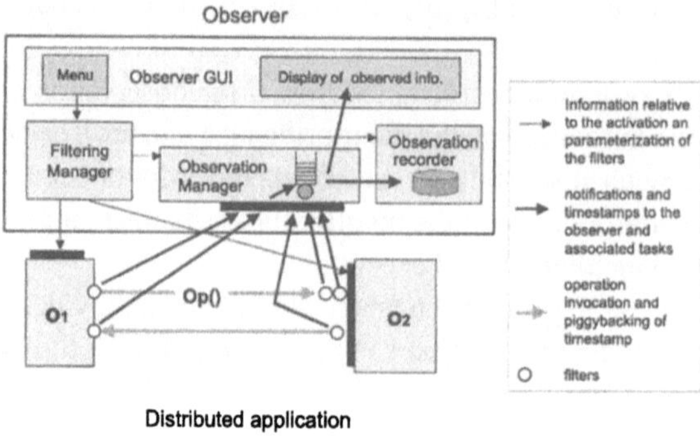

Figure 4 Scenario of run-time monitoring

- The **Observation recorder** provides the functionality of storing notifications in a database. This database could then be used to analyze a crash, a special behavior or to replay an execution trace.

5 CASE STUDY

The Telecommunication Information Networking Architecture (TINA) consortium (Chapman & Montesi 1995) proposes an architecture for telecommunication services. The proposed architecture defines a set of components to implement. The collaboration of these different objects, plus a set of service specific objects, implements the logic of the desired service. The monitoring method proposed in this paper is currently applied in the framework of the SPOT(Service Pilot On TINA) project (Mercouroff, Bengtsson, Hellemans & Lehmann 1997) in collaboration with Swisscom. The main focus of the SPOT project is on service integration and service platform interworking. The different partners of the UNISOURCE consortium and a number of Telecommunications companies (Alcatel Telecom, Ericsson) deploy different high performance multimedia TINA services over the European ATM network and ensure their interoperability. In this framework Swisscom provides a Desktop Video Conferencing Service (DVC) on which our monitoring methodology is applied.

In order to facilitate the integration of our work in the SPOT platform, we have developed a prototype that implements the logic of a basic TINA service (a chat service). Our implementation uses the Object Request Broker (ORB) from Orbix^{TM} IONA (IONA 1997) as DPE.

In order to spy on the distributed system, we use the *Filtering* mechanism provided by Orbix^{TM}, which is of two forms: *per-process* and *per-object* filtering. Per-process filters monitor all incoming and out-going operations to and from an address space; per-process filtering is applied when an invocation leaves or arrives at an address space. Per-object filters apply to individual objects. The observation is based on four forms of per-process filters *out request, in request, out reply, in reply* and two forms of per-object filtering *pre, post.* The filtering mechanism offers the possibility of piggy-backing information with the requests. For example, at the 'out request filter' extra data can be added to the request as far as the 'in request filter' removes it afterwards.

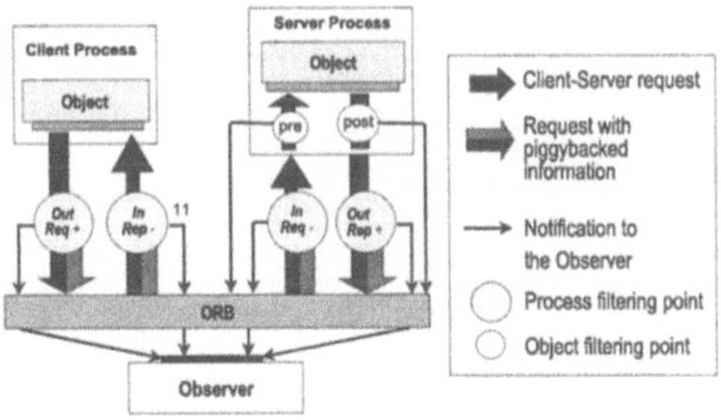

Figure 5 Observation mechanism based on process filters

In Figure 5, the different filters are illustrated in the case of an object in a client process invoking an operation on an object within a server process. When the request exists the object, the first filter point (out request) is reached. At that point, a notification is sent to the observer, the timestamp algorithm is executed, and then the timestamp and useful information are piggybacked to the other object. The request is then proceeded by the ORB and reaches the server process. When the 'inRequest' filtering point is reached, the piggybacked information is extracted and removed from the request and a notification is issued. The server will then handle the piggybacked timestamp, update its current one and forward the request to the right object. When the request reaches the object the Object filtering point 'pre' is reached and a notification is sent. The same scenario is applied for the reply phase of the request in the case of an operation request (the chain of filters being in that case: post, out-Reply and in-Reply). In the case of a one-way operation, no return is sent.

In Figure 6, the GUI of our tool, which is called MOTEL (MOnitoring and TEsting tooL), is depicted. A GUI (*New Information to Monitor*) allows to select from a menu or enter by hand the objects and operations to monitor. The result of the run-time monitoring can be displayed either in a *Table* and/or *Timeline*. In the *Table* (*Observer Message* part of the main window of MOTEL), all the content of the (reordered) notifications is displayed. The *Timeline* display option (bottom window in Figure 6) allows to have a complete and intuitive understanding of the evolution of the running application.

6 CONCLUSION

In this paper, we propose an integrated approach for performing run-time monitoring of distributed application built on top of a DPE implementing CORBA. The proposal

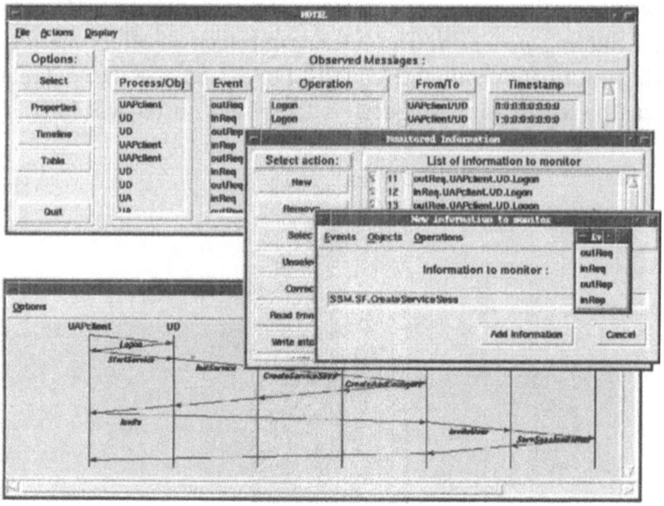

Figure 6 GUI of our Prototype

is integrated in the sense that it fits very well with the development process of distributed applications. The users of such a system need not to be aware of the details of the implementation in order to monitor the system. Based on the IDL specification of the system, they select what to observe. All the underlying monitoring operations are automatically performed, and in particular the code is instrumented in an automated manner.

Our work is based on the introduction of an Observer which receives notifications sent by each distributed objects at some breakpoints defined by a Filtering mechanism. A timestamp mechanism dealing with the dynamic number of objects in the system is used to reorder the notifications. An advantage of our approach is its granularity: the focus can be put on a single event, on an operation, on all operations of an objects, on a group of objects, on a set of operations on different objects,etc.

All the concepts have been successfully applied onto a prototype.

6.1 Current and Future Work

We are currently investigating the impact of our monitoring approach on the system. This will help us in deciding how to introduce hierarchical observation as well as how to distribute the Observer. Our ultimate goal is to use the observation information to be able to test at run-time that a set of predefined properties on the system are not violated (Logean, Dietrich & Hubaux 1998) (Dietrich, Logean & Hubaux 1998). The properties are then translated into automata which are fed with our observed information. When a property is violated an error is discovered.

7 ACKNOWLEDGEMENTS

This work presented in this paper is part of the ErnesTINA project funded by Swisscom. The authors would like to thank our partners of Swisscom and Alcatel Alsthom Research Marcoussis for very useful discussions on the topic of this paper. The authors are also grateful to Prof. Jean-Pierre Hubaux for numerous comments and discussions.

REFERENCES

Al-Shaer, E., Abdel-Wahad, H. & Maly, K. (1997), A scalable monitoring architecture for managing large-scale distributed multimedia systems, *in* 'Proc of Management of Multimedia Network and Services (MMNS)'.

Bates, P. (1995), 'Debugging heterogeneous distributed systems using event-based model of behavior', *ACM Transactions on Computer Systems* **13**(1), 1–31.

Brutch, P., Karmarkar, A., S., G., Walzel, K., Marti, W. & U.W., P. . (1996), SMT: A system monitoring tool for DCE, *in* A. Schill, C. Mittasch, O. Spaniol & C. Popien, eds, 'Distributed Platforms', Chapman & Hall, pp. 245–257.

Chapman, M. & Montesi, S. (1995), *Overall Concepts and Principles of TINA, Version 1.0, TINA-C Deliverable*, TINA-C.

Chechik, M. & Gannon, J. (1994), Automatic verification of requirements implementation, *in* 'ISSTA'94', Seattle, Washington.

Dietrich, F., Logean, X. & Hubaux, J.-P. (1998), Testing temporal logic properties in distributed systems, *in* 'IFIP International Workshop on Testing of Communicating Systems (IWTCS)', Tomsk, Russia.

Dietrich, F., Logean, X., Koppenhoefer, S. & Hubaux, J. (1998), A temporal logic based approach to the deeign of object-oriented distributed systems, Technical Report /SSC/1998/011, Swiss Federal Institute of Tchnology, Lausanne, Communications System Division,.

Dssouli, R., Karoui, K., Petrenko, A. & Rafiq, O. (1996), Towards testable communication software, *in* A. Cavalli & S. Budkowski, eds, 'Protocol Test Systems VIII', Chapman & Hall, pp. 237–251.

IONA (1997), *Orbix 2: Programming guide, Version 2.2*, IONA Technologies PLC.

Kitson, B., Leydekkers, P., Mercouroff, N. & Ruano, F. (1995), *TINA Object Definition Language (TINA-ODL) Manual 1.3*, TINA-C.

Lamport, L. (1978), 'Time, clocks and ordering of events in a distributed system', *Communications of the ACM* **21**(7), 558–565.

Logean, X., Dietrich, F. & Hubaux, J.-P. (1998), TINA service validation: The ErnesTINA project, *in* 'IEEE ICC Conference (also Tech. Report. Swiss Federal Institute of Technology, Communication Systems Division, SSC/1997/028)', Atlanta.

Mercouroff, N., Bengtsson, J., Hellemans, P. & Lehmann, L. (1997), Implementation of services for computer supported cooperative work on TINA : the SPOT project, *in* 'Proc of ISS'97'.

Mills, D. (1990), 'On the accuracy and stability of clocks synchronized by network time protocol in the internet system', *ACM Computer Communications* **20**(1), 65–75.

OMG (1998), *The Common Object Request Broker Architecture and Specification (CORBA),version 2.2*, Object Management Group (OMG).

Perrow, G. (1994), Monitoring techniques in distributed systems management, Technical Report 421, Computer Science Department, University of Western Ontario.

Queiroz de, J. & Madeira, E. (1997), Management of corba object monitoring for multiware platform, *in* 'Open Distributed Processing and Distributed Platforms', Chapman & Hall, pp. 122–133.

Raynal, M., Schiper, A. & Toueng, S. (1991), 'The causal ordering abstraction and a simple way to implement it', *Information Processing Letters* **39**, 343–350.

Sankar, S. & Mandal, M. (1990), Concurrent run-time monitoring of formally specified programs, Technical Report CSL-TR-90-425, Computer Systems Laboratory, Stanford University.

8 BIOGRAPHY

X. Logean graduated in 1995 from the Swiss Federal Institute of Technology (EPFL) with a degree in Electrical Engineering. He is currently a Ph.D. student in Institute for computer Communications and Applications (ICA) at the EPFL. His main research interests are in testing and monitoring of distributed systems.

F. Dietrich studied computer science at the Technische Universität Dresden, Germany, and at Rensselaer Polytechnic Institute, Troy, NY, USA. He is currently working towards a Ph.D. at the Institute for computer Communications and Applications (ICA) at the EPFL in Switzerland.

H. Karamyan received the Diploma degree in mathematics from Yerevan State University, Armenia, in 1997. He spent half year in the Telecommunications Laboratory at the Swiss Federal Institute of Technology in Lausanne, contributing to the ErnesTINA project. His research interests include distributed systems and fault tolerance.

S. Koppenhoefer successfully completed a double honours program at the Faculty of Mathematics of the University of Waterloo in 1990. In 1996 he completed his PhD. Dissertation describing a formal models for synchronous time-critical control systems. He was invited to join the telecommunications Laboratory (TCOM) where he assumed teaching responsibilities with his course entitled "Introduction to Networks and Protocols". Currently, he works at the ICA in the area of security protocols and formal logics of trust and belief.

INDEX OF CONTRIBUTORS

SPONSORS

The organising committee would like to thank the following organisations, which have all made financial contributions towards Middleware'98.

EPSRC

KPN Research

HP Laboratories, Bristol

Lancaster University
Distributed Multimedia
Research Group

ICL

The Olivetti & Oracle
Research Lab

IONA Technologies

Sun Microsystems

MIX
Papier aus verantwortungsvollen Quellen
Paper from responsible sources
FSC® C105338

If you have any concerns about our products,
you can contact us on
ProductSafety@springernature.com

In case Publisher is established outside the EU,
the EU authorized representative is:
Springer Nature Customer Service Center GmbH
Europaplatz 3, 69115 Heidelberg, Germany

Printed by Libri Plureos GmbH
in Hamburg, Germany